THE ATLANTIC ALCIDAE

The Evolution, Distribution and Biology of the Auks Inhabiting the Atlantic Ocean and Adjacent Water Areas

Contributors

Jean Bédard

Tim R. Birkhead

Michael S. W. Bradstreet

Richard G. B. Brown

Peter G. H. Evans

Anthony J. Gaston

Michael P. Harris

Peter J. Hudson

David N. Nettleship

THE ATLANTIC ALCIDAE

The Evolution, Distribution and Biology
of the Auks Inhabiting the Atlantic
Ocean and Adjacent Water Areas

Edited by

David N. Nettleship

Seabird Research Unit
Canadian Wildlife Service
Bedford Institute of Oceanography
Dartmouth, Nova Scotia, Canada

Tim R. Birkhead

Department of Zoology
University of Sheffield
Sheffield, England

1985

ACADEMIC PRESS
Harcourt Brace Jovanovich, Publishers

**London   Orlando   San Diego   New York
Austin   Montreal   Sydney   Tokyo   Toronto**

ACADEMIC PRESS INC. (LONDON) LTD.
24–28 Oval Road
LONDON NW1 7DX

United States Edition published by
ACADEMIC PRESS, INC.
Orlando, Florida 32887

British Library Cataloguing in Publication Data

The Atlantic Alcidae : the evolution, distribution
    and biology of the auks inhabiting the Atlantic
    Ocean and adjacent water areas.
    1. Auks   2. Seabirds—Atlantic Ocean
    I. Nettleship, David N.   II. Birkhead, T. R.
    598'.33'09163   QL696.A3

Library of Congress Cataloging in Publication Data
Main entry under title:

The Atlantic Alcidae.

    Bibliography: p.
    Includes indexes.
    1. Auks.   2. Birds—Atlantic Ocean.   I. Nettleship,
David N.   II. Birkhead, Tim R.
QL696.C42A84   1985   598'.33   85-6196
ISBN 0–12–515670–7 (alk. paper)
ISBN 0–12–515671–5 (paperback)

PRINTED IN THE UNITED STATES OF AMERICA

85 86 87 88   9 8 7 6 5 4 3 2 1

This volume is dedicated to the memory of

FINN SALOMONSEN
(1909–1983)

*whose outstanding contributions to knowledge of the
Atlantic alcids during six decades of study has greatly
stimulated all students of auks and other seabirds, and
whose classic monograph entitled* The Atlantic Alcidae *(1944)
provided the foundation for this book*

Contents

2 Distribution and Status of the Atlantic Alcidae

DAVID N. NETTLESHIP AND PETER G. H. EVANS

3 Breeding Ecology of the Atlantic Alcidae

MICHAEL P. HARRIS AND TIM R. BIRKHEAD

4 Ecological Adaptations for Breeding in the Atlantic Alcidae

TIM R. BIRKHEAD AND MICHAEL P. HARRIS

5   Population Parameters for the Atlantic Alcidae

PETER J. HUDSON

6   Feeding Ecology of the Atlantic Alcidae

MICHAEL S. W. BRADSTREET AND RICHARD G. B. BROWN

7   Development of the Young in the Atlantic Alcidae

ANTHONY J. GASTON

8   Coloniality and Social Behaviour in the Atlantic Alcidae

TIM R. BIRKHEAD

9   The Atlantic Alcidae at Sea

RICHARD G. B. BROWN

Contributors

Numbers in parentheses indicate the pages on which the authors' contributions begin.

Jean Bédard (1), Département de Biologie, Université Laval, Québec, Québec, Canada G1K 7P4

Tim R. Birkhead (155, 205, 355), Department of Zoology, University of Sheffield, Sheffield, England S10 2TN

Michael S. W. Bradstreet (263), LGL Limited, environmental research associates, King City, Ontario, Canada L0G 1K0

Richard G. B. Brown (263, 383), Seabird Research Unit, Canadian Wildlife Service, Bedford Institute of Oceanography, Dartmouth, Nova Scotia, Canada B2Y 4A2

Peter G. H. Evans (53, 427), Edward Grey Institute of Field Ornithology, Department of Zoology, University of Oxford, Oxford, England OX1 3PS

Anthony J. Gaston (319), Canadian Wildlife Service, Ottawa, Ontario, Canada K1A 0E7

Michael P. Harris (155, 205), Institute of Terrestrial Ecology, Banchory Research Station, Banchory, Kincardineshire, Scotland AB3 4BY

Peter J. Hudson (233), The Game Conservancy, Leyburn, North Yorkshire, England DL8 3HG

David N. Nettleship (53, 427), Seabird Research Unit, Canadian Wildlife Service, Bedford Institute of Oceanography, Dartmouth, Nova Scotia, Canada B2Y 4A2

Preface

This book is the first comprehensive overview of the biology and ecology of the Atlantic Alcidae and it aims to provide a summary and synoptic view of current knowledge of the subject. The contributors are among the most active researchers and teachers in the field of seabird ecology and behaviour; their chapters attempt to bring together the most significant information available on the Atlantic auks, and also to present new research findings, particularly those derived from the intensive and integrated studies performed during the last 10–15 years. The book, then, is a first attempt to see where we stand. The chapters both summarize what is known of fundamental aspects of the birds' biology and identify the gaps in our information, thus providing an idea of what work is required in the future. Its contents should satisfy the needs of a wide variety of readers, from those requiring specific details of an individual species to those concerned with broad biological concepts or theoretical ideas derived from the comparison of species' life histories, or of direct environmental management application.

The contents of the volume separate clearly into two parts: broad introductory overviews of basic features of the Atlantic Alcidae (Chapters 1–4), and reviews which synthesize, with different degrees of detail, quite specific subject areas (Chapters 5–10). Chapter 1 examines the evolution, adaptive radiation and systematics of the group as a whole, in an attempt to provide a succinct perspective of its evolutionary history. Chapter 2 provides a general description of the patterns of distribution and abundance of the birds throughout the study area of the North Atlantic and the adjacent seas, a brief summary of the principal oceanographic characteristics of the region which influence those patterns, and an attempt to draw some conclusions on present status of and recent changes in populations of each species. Chapters 3 and 4 are concerned with the reproductive ecology of the group, first by highlighting details of fundamental breeding characteristics species by species (Chapter 3) followed by syntheses of what these indicate as adaptations for breeding (Chapter 4). Chapters 5–7 deal with relatively narrow subject areas including survival rates and the factors influencing other primary population parameters (Chapter 5), feeding ecology both inside and outside the breeding season (Chapter 6) and developmental patterns of the young (Chapter 7). Chapter 8 discusses some aspects of the reproductive behaviour and sociality of species, and how these relate to food, predation, competition and structures of breeding regimes. Chapter 9 reviews what is known of the distributions and movements of populations at sea, particularly *outside* the breeding season, and what these patterns reveal of the birds' pelagic ecology. The final chapter attempts to translate some of the information given earlier on the principal characteristics and ecological requirements of the Atlantic auks into a form which highlights the biological significance of recent population changes, their possible causes and what actions can be taken to implement a rational and meaningful conservation policy.

In the end, we must make clear certain limitations of this book. First and foremost is the fact that it does not claim to cover all aspects of the biology of the Atlantic Alcidae. Instead, it aims to provide an up-to-date review of those subject areas considered by us to be most instructive in permitting a comprehensive insight into our species group, one from which a start can be made to understand better its role in the marine ecosystem both locally and over the entire North Atlantic. Secondly, we must admit that our attempt to integrate chapters and restrict "themes" has only been partially successful. The need to allow authors some freedom to show certain interrelationships important to individual topics has resulted in some overlap between chapters. This is particularly true, for example, of sections dealing with recent changes in population size and status, and problems associated with methodologies used to measure key population parameters: Chapters 2, 5 and 10. Overall, the benefits of such repetition seem to outweigh any drawbacks and, indeed, do serve to reemphasize important subjects, some of which are high-priority items for further attention and study.

Altogether, we hope that this book will serve as a valuable information source and as a guide to help direct future studies of the Atlantic auks and their marine environment. Alcids, and the ecosystems of which they are a part, present us with an exciting challenge to better understand the complexities of their composition and ecological roles. This is a fascinating group of marine birds, highly sensitive to changes in the marine environment and most worthy of our best efforts to understand and preserve them.

As editors, we are particularly appreciative of the efforts made by the authors to produce their contribution within the framework of the original chapter synopses and for meeting our rather rigid deadlines. We owe them our apologies for the delays that prevented the publication of the book by its originally scheduled date. We are pleased, however, that the volume itself has remained virtually unchanged from what was originally conceived and planned.

We and all other contributors are very grateful to our colleagues who found the time to read and criticise drafts of certain chapters, and in several instances, provide preprints, manuscripts of works in progress, and other unpublished data and materials: R. Bailey (Chapter 10), H. J. Boyd (Chapter 2), R. G. B. Brown (Chapter 2), D. K. Cairns (Chapter 7), R. A. Davis (Chapter 6), E. K. Dunn (Chapter 10), G. M. Dunnet (Chapter 10), C. Edelstam (Chapter 1), A. J. Erskine (Chapter 2), J. Fjeldsa (Chapter 1), J. A. van Franeker (Chapter 2), G. Friske (Chapter 1), A. J. Gaston (Chapters 2–4, 8, 9), U. N. von Blotzheim Glutz (Chapter 1), I. M. Goudie (Chapter 9), M. P. Harris (Chapters 2, 8), J. Hislop (Chapter 10), H. Howard (Chapter 1), K. Kampp (Chapter 2), J. de Korte (Chapter 2), J. R. Krebs (Chapter 8), G. LaPointe (Chapter 1), A. R. Lock (Chapter 9), P. Lyngs (Chapter 2), F. Mehlum (Chapter 2), H. Meltofte (Chapters 1, 2), J.-Y. Monnat (Chapter 2), R. J. O'Connor (Chapter 7), B. Olsen (Chapter 2), S. L. Olson (Chapter 1), D. B. Peakall (Chapter 10), C. M. Perrins (Chapter 10), A. Peterson (Chapters 1, 2, 9), J. F. Piatt (Chapter 9), W. J. Richardson (Chapter 6), F. Salomonsen (Chapters 1, 9), S. G. Sealy (Chapter 1), T. J. Stowe (Chapter 2), J. G. Strauch, Jr. (Chapter 1), and J. F. Wittenberger (Chapter 8). Their criticism and assistance improved the volume greatly, though any errors that remain are the sole responsibility of the authors and editors.

We are also very grateful to numerous other individuals who have provided invaluable assistance in the preparation of this book. First and foremost was the effort made by Andrew Macfarlane in helping to prepare the Localities Index, as well as in proofreading the entire manuscript of the book for inconsistencies in place-name usage and errors of omission and commission made by contributors in preparing their reference lists. Joyce Dagnall, Angela Nettleship, Jim Paton and Michelle Smith bravely endured innumerable drafts, editorial changes and corrections to manuscripts; only through their great patience and understanding was the final book manuscript achieved. Susan Johnson, Georgina Macfarlane have been very helpful in responding to calls for help with proofreading drafts of certain chapters, as have Arthur Cosgrove in redrawing contributors' figures where necessary, often on very short notice, Susan Hoyt, Betty Sutherland and Elaine Toms in searching out, verifying and correcting certain bibliographical information and Susan Greaves in helping to track down geographical place-names. Angela Nettleship and Jayne Pellatt were invaluable in helping correct the page proofs of the entire book; we owe additional thanks to Angela Nettleship for processing, typing and proofreading both the Localities and Subject Indexes. We also wish to thank our friends at Academic Press for providing encouragement and guidance during the lengthy process in the volume's development. And finally, we must express our grateful thanks to the Canadian Wildlife Service—Environment Canada (the employer of one of us (D.N.N.)), for allowing us to undertake the editing and production of the book at the Bedford Institute of Oceanography and supplementing the cost of its publication.

August 1985   *David N. Nettleship*
                                                                   Tim R. Birkhead

THE
ATLANTIC
ALCIDAE

*The Evolution, Distribution and Biology
of the Auks Inhabiting the Atlantic
Ocean and Adjacent Water Areas*

CHAPTER 1

Evolution and Characteristics of the Atlantic Alcidae

JEAN BÉDARD

Département de Biologie, Université Laval, Québec, Québec, Canada

I. INTRODUCTION

Extravagant colours and structures do not surprise us when they are encountered in organisms of the balmy tropics. But when they are found in birds occupying some of the most inhospitable boreal and arctic seas,

1

they seem somewhat out of place. With their eccentric crests, brightly pigmented feet and mouth cavities, vastly inflated beaks and often strikingly coloured plumages, the 23 living species of Alcidae have truly an extraordinary appearance. They occur in an almost uninterrupted arc from the eastern Canadian Arctic right through the North Atlantic and the eastern shores of the Arctic Ocean to the Bering Sea and the North Pacific.

Compared to the austral penguins, the northern alcids are much smaller animals. In fact, the largest living alcid, the Common Murre (*Uria aalge*), is, at 1000 g, barely the size of the smallest member of the penguin family, the diminutive Fairy Penguin (Stonehouse 1975). In many ways, the alcids are less profoundly modified in structure than the penquins for their marine existence. While the latter have lost the power of aerial flight, the alcids retain a dual-purpose wing which enables them to fly both in the air and in the water. But with respect to this remarkable underwater proficiency, the penguins and the alcids are convergent and both have undergone extensive morphological and ethological radiation. All are highly susceptible to land predators and are compelled to congregate on nesting sites inaccessible to these animals; there, they will sometimes form colonies numbering millions of individuals. Finally, all species tend to be long-lived and have low reproductive rates. With their antipodal distribution, the alcids and the penguins are truly ecological counterparts separated from each other by a 5000-km-wide belt of tropical waters.

The family Alcidae deserves study for its own sake. But recent conflicts with human activities in the northern seas have given a more pragmatic impetus to such an interest: massive reproductive failure in some species deprived of their over-harvested food base or large-scale die-offs in pelagic fisheries have awakened a new and pressing concern for this highly specialized group of birds. Although the primary aim of this volume is to review our current knowledge of the population biology of the North Atlantic representatives of the family, more than passing reference will be made to topics susceptible to interest marine biologists and environmental managers.

This first chapter will introduce the family Alcidae, outline the major morphological and ethological characteristics of its living representatives and then review the evolutionary history and major patterns of adaptive radiation of the family as a whole. The chapter will also review the various classification schemes that have been proposed for the family and will present an assessment of the geographic variation in the six living species that inhabit the North Atlantic Ocean. Finally, in a rather unorthodox sequence, the chapter will describe the patterns of moult and interpret their significance in this group of seabirds.

II. CHARACTERISTICS

A short synopsis of the family Alcidae will be presented: much more detailed information can be found in Ridgway (1919), Storer (1945), Kaftanovskii (1951), Kuroda (1954, 1955), Kozlova (1957), Verheyen (1958), Stettenheim (1959), Judin (1965), Spring (1968, 1971) and Hudson et al. (1969), upon whose work the present summary is based. The aim here is to identify the major traits of the overall morphology, plumage, bone and muscle systems and behaviour which characterize the family. None of these traits is diagnostic of the group when taken singly. Yet, the alcid type is quite homogeneous and easy to recognize in the field.

A. Overall Morphology

The volant forms are small to medium-sized (*Alle* at 140 to 170 g, *Cepphus* about 400 to 450 g, *Fratercula* about 375 to 550 g, *Alca* about 625 to 750 g and *Uria* about 800 to 1000 g), while the only non-volant form recently encountered in the Atlantic, the Great Auk (*Pinguinus*), probably weighed in the neighbourhood of 5500 to 8000 g (Stonehouse 1968; Bédard 1969a). Because the wing is considerably shortened (see below) and reduced in area so as to improve underwater propulsion, aerial flight is direct and rapid but not maneuverable. Wing-loading is high and take-off is difficult, especially in *Uria*. There is no obvious sexual dimorphism although the females in most species tend to be slightly lighter and smaller than the males, but there are exceptions, apparently brought about (in the case of weight) by the stage of the breeding cycle. Bianki (1967) has summarized data from early Russian workers showing the existence of a size differential favouring the females in *Alca torda* but unfortunately, the data are incomplete and cannot be analysed statistically. One surprising exception in the family is that of *Endomychura craveri* in which the female is larger than the male in wing length (Jehl and Bond 1975), but the equivalent difference in the congeneric *hypoleuca* does not reach statistical significance. The hind limbs are short and shifted backwards but, despite some lateral compression, are not so deeply modified as in the foot-propelled diving grebes and loons. Ability to move on land among North Atlantic representatives increases in the following order: *Uria lomvia*, *U. aalge*, *Alca*, *Fratercula*, *Cepphus*, *Alle*. The mouth cavity is coloured during the breeding season in *Alca*, *Fratercula* and *Cepphus*. The caeca are undeveloped in all except *Cepphus*. The syrinx is tracheo-bronchial and bears two pairs of syringeal muscles. All species are vocal, some much more so (*Uria*, *Aethia*) than others (*Fratercula*). The anterior toes are always fully webbed and the uropygial gland is surmounted with feathers. All Atlantic forms have a simple horny covering on the bill with the exception of *Fratercula* which has nine distinct plates, all of which are shed during the moult.

B. Plumage

The feather covering is extremely heavy and although no data are known to me, the relative weight of this tissue is probably very high. The contour feathers have an aftershaft. The apteria are small and down-covered. There are 16 rectrices in *Fratercula*, 12 and sometimes 14 in *Cepphus* (Asbirk 1979a) and normally 12 in all other Atlantic genera. The eleventh primary is not functional while the tenth is the longest. There are 15–19 secondaries. The birds have one complete moult and at least one partial moult per year (see below). The nostrils are concealed by feathers in all Atlantic auks with the exception of *Fratercula*, where these open-ings are exposed. *Alle, Uria, Alca* and *Pinguinus* possess white-tipped secondaries, the exact function of which is unknown.

C. Osteological and Myological Characteristics

The alcids do not possess anatomical structures which are exclusive adaptations for wing-propelled swimming, such as a wedge-shaped bone at the elbow in the Sphenisciformes (Stettenheim 1959). But the wing nevertheless displays several modifications connected with underwater flight. There is considerable shortening of the forearm (antebrachium) and the latter is always shorter than the carpals. The forearm is always shorter than the humerus in the Alcidae while this is not always true in the related Laridae. This general reduction of the wing is clearly advantageous in a dense medium. There is a remarkable strengthening of all the wing ele-ments (enlargement of ligaments, thickening of connective tissue binding the remiges, hardening of the rachis of the coverts, etc.). The first finger of the hand (manus) is missing. The crest for the attachment of the *m. supracoracoideus* extends over almost the entire length of the sternum, underlining the relative importance of that muscle in raising the wing in a heavy medium like water. The triosseal canal whereby the *m. supracora-coideus* connects to the wing is correspondingly enlarged.

The ribs are attached to the sternum. The thoracic vertebrae are all free and have well-developed hypapophyses. According to Ridgway (1919), this latter trait can be used as a key character for the family. The general flexibility of the vertebral column is viewed as a prerequisite in allowing the flexions and torsions of a diving bird (Stettenheim 1959). The hallux is absent in all species but some of the associated structures such as the vestigial extensor muscle and foramen are preserved in some species (Hudson *et al.* 1969). The tarso-metatarsus is not as laterally compressed as in most foot-propelled diving birds. By comparison to the closely allied gulls, the tarsus is considerably shortened.

The interorbital septum is incomplete. The vomer is free, blade-like and cleft posteriorly. The maxillo-palatine is laminate in *Alle, Uria, Alca* and *Cepphus* but is conch-shaped in *Fratercula*. The nasal bones are schizorhinal, the nostrils are porous and interconnected. The lateral processes of the basisphenoids which are present in gulls appear also in certain alcid types (*Fratercula* and most Pacific genera) but not in others (*Uria, Alca, Alle, Cepphus*). The upper mandible is strongly hinged with the cranium. The bones are generally not pneumatic, except for the coracoids and scapulars of some genera. Two skeletal character states, a twisted coracoid and the absence of synsacral strut, were considered by Strauch (1978) to be diagnostic of the Alcidae (within the Charadriiformes). But more extensive investigation failed to confirm the universality of the latter character among the family (J. G. Strauch, personal communication).

No exclusive muscle structure is encountered in the Alcidae. But, in connection with the underwater flight habit, there has been a profound change in the *m. pectoralis/m. supracoracoideus* ratio normally found in closely related aerial forms such as gulls. This ratio runs between 3.0 and 4.0 in most Atlantic genera as opposed to 11.7 in a typical gull (*Larus argentatus:* Kaftanovskii 1951).

The muscles responsible for the compression of the breast feathers to reduce buoyancy when diving, *m. cucullaris,* are exceptionally enlarged in the Alcidae when compared to other Charadriiformes (Stettenheim 1959) and this may constitute a fairly typical trait.

D. Ethological Characteristics

Most alcids are gregarious (some extremely so) at all times of the year (see Chapter 8, this volume). All Recent species are marine and all share the ability for underwater flight to varying degrees: this ability seems most developed in *Pinguinus, Uria* and *Alca* and less developed in *Fratercula* and *Alle*. In the latter, buoyancy problems must be considerable. Diving depth can be considerable and extreme values of 70 fathoms (130 m) are given for *U. lomvia* (Holgersen 1961).

The mating system is simple with monogamy and long-lasting pair stability apparently prevalent. Both sexes share nearly equally the incubation of the one egg laid (two in the amphioceanic *Cepphus* and in *Endomychura* and *Synthliboramphus* of the Pacific) and the feeding of the young.

The egg is heavily pigmented in *Alca, Uria, Pinguinus* and *Cepphus* and has pale but visible blotches in *Fratercula* and *Alle*. The young are semi-precocial in *Cepphus, Fratercula* and *Alle* and were probably semi-precocial in *Pinguinus* while in *Uria* and *Alca* the development of the young follows a pattern intermediate between precocial and semi-precocial (Sealy 1973a). Food is carried to young *Alle* in a sublingual pouch and transferred to the nestling in a mucus-bound mass; in other genera food is carried length-wise (*Uria*) or cross-wise in the bill. In *Cepphus* and *Uria*, only one fish is carried at a time while in *Alca* and *Fratercula*, several fish may be ferried in a single load. The food is dropped to the ground in front of the young or is presented to them. The nest is non-existent in *Uria* or primitive in *Alca* and *Cepphus* and complex (excavated) in *Fratercula*. All species handle nest material and this is sometimes highly ritualized.

III. ORIGIN AND EVOLUTIONARY HISTORY

The claim for the antiquity of the auk family has been a leitmotiv of alcid literature (Storer 1945, 1960; Howard 1950; Kozlova 1957). But such a claim is not actually founded upon a clear phylogeny with very ancient forms. At any rate, it is not so clear a lineage as is available for instance in the loons (Gaviiformes) in which undoubted representatives (e.g., *Colymboides*) have been described from the Early Eocene some 50 million years ago (m.y.a.) (Feduccia 1980) or the Sphenisciformes, which are known by clearly identified genera from the Late Eocene and Early Oligocene (Simpson 1975).

The earliest report of an auk, that of *Uria antiquua* by Marsh (1870) in Mid-Miocene deposits of North Carolina (12–17 m.y.a.), lent some respectable age to this most important genus of the alcid family. But these deposits are currently designated as Lower Pliocene in age (5–7 m.y.a.: Olson and Gillette 1978; Olson 1985; see also below). *Cerorhinca dubia*, initially described from Mid-Miocene diatomite deposits by Miller (1925), has also been reclassified as Late Miocene in origin (Howard 1981). In fact, the alcid fossil record interrupts rather abruptly in the Upper Miocene of the Pacific and in the Mid-Miocene of the Atlantic (Table 1.1). What happened between the Mid-Miocene and the Eocene or the Upper Paleocene, some 30–40 million years further back in time, is wholly undocumented. Kozlova's (1957) contention that the auks can be traced back to the Lower Paleocene (some 60 m.y.a.) is apparently based on an earlier contribution by Lambrecht (1933), who suggested that the extinct subfamily Nautilornithinae (Wetmore 1926) of the fresh-water lake beds of Wyoming were indeed precursors of the Mid-Miocene (now known to be Late Miocene) auks. Storer (1960), however, considered the Nautilornithinae as a "collateral" group of unspecialized aquatic birds that disappeared near the end of the Eocene without leaving a trace. Wetmore (1926) also indicated that the wing of the Nautilornithinae was proportionately longer than that of modern auks, which made it unlikely that they had developed by then the underwater flight capability so typical of the Alcidae. Furthermore, *Nautilornis* was certainly not marine as its occurrence in the fresh-water continental seas near the present state of Utah (Wetmore 1926) makes it difficult to link this genus with the now wholly marine auks. More important still, Feduccia and McGrew (1974) established clearly that *Nautilornis* should rather have been referred to as *Presbyornis*, a Charadriiforme near the ancestry of the Anseriformes (Olson and Feduccia 1980). The only other genus that has been described from this epoch, *Hydrotherikornis,* also viewed as a Nautilornithinae (Brodkorb 1967), was associated with marine sediments of the Upper Eocene in Oregon, United States.

But the fact that broad diversification of the family had taken place by Late Miocene nevertheless indicates that the family was already of considerable age. The absence of earlier fossils greatly hampers our understanding of the evolution of the group but a consideration of the major changes in the shapes and interconnections of the oceanic basins in which these birds must have evolved and a consideration of the gradual and important climatic changes that occurred during the Cenozoic and the evolution of the alcids should enable us to make at least a few educated guesses as to how, when and where this remarkable diversification took place.

At the turn of the Tertiary, some 60 m.y.a., the North Atlantic was a juvenile ocean, a mere diverticulum of the broad South Atlantic Ocean. The land masses of Europe and North America were connected by the Greenland mass which effectively blocked all marine connections between the Pacific Ocean and the incipient North Atlantic (the "Caribbean Atlantic") via the northern route (Dietz and Holden 1970; Hallam 1973). This situation began to change during the Paleocene with the rifting of the continents, the expansion of the already formed but smaller Arctic Ocean and the scattering of the arctic islands (the Canadian Arctic Archipelago, the Novaya Zemlya group, Spitsbergen, etc.) at the same time that the presumed alcid ancestor began to swim in the coastal waters of the northern hemisphere. Meanwhile, the Pacific Ocean was of the approximate size and shape that it is now (Adams 1981). It is not surprising, therefore, that the Pacific Ocean is viewed by most bird students as the center of origin for most (Storer 1960) or all (Kozlova 1957; Udvardy 1963) modern Alcidae.

TABLE 1.1

The Cenozoic and Recent Geological Periods and the Major Fossil Finds of Alcidae[a]

Era	Age	Millions of years before present	North Atlantic finds	Geographic interconnection (Bering Strait)	North Pacific finds
Quaternary	Pleistocene		*Pinguinus impennis, Uria affinis* and several neo-species		*Uria aalge, Synthliboramphus antiquus* and several neo-species
Tertiary	Pliocene	3	*Pinguinus alfrednewtoni, Australca grandis, Uria ausonia* (?), *Uria antiquua* (?), *Alle, Fratercula, Lunda* (?)	Closed	*Mancalla diegensis, M. californiensis, M. cedrosensis, Alcodes* sp., *Brachyramphus pliocenum, Ptychoramphus tenuis, Cerorhinca minor, Cerorhinca* sp.
	Miocene Upper	5		Open	*Praemancalla lagunensis, P. wetmorei, Uria brodkorbi, U. paleospheris, Cepphus olsoni,*

			Brachyramphus pliocenum, Endomychura sp., Aethia rossmoori, Aethia sp., Cerorhinca dubia
Middle	11		
		Closed	
Lower	17	Miocepphus mclungi	
Oligocene	23		
Eocene	38		(Hydrotherikornis oregonus)
Paleocene	53		
	63		

a The approximate time scale (from Frakes 1979) and the presence or absence of a northerly connection between the Atlantic and the Pacific via the Bering Strait are also shown. Based on summaries in Brodkorp (1967), Hopkins (1967), Nelson *et al.* (1974), Olson (1985) and detailed reports by Miller (1925), Miller and Bowman (1958), Howard (1949, 1966, 1968, 1971, 1976, 1978, 1982), and Barnes *et al.* (1981). The genus *Hydrotherikornis*, a presumptive ancestor of the Alcidae (Olson 1985), is included to better fix one's mind upon the gap in the fossil record.

As mentioned above, the Pacific and the Atlantic oceans were not connected by way of the Arctic Ocean until the end of the Cenozoic. But of course, interconnection between the two water bodies was possible via the broad subtropical or equatorial corridor between the drifting North and South Americas, the Thetys Sea. Many marine animals presumably used this corridor during the Upper Miocene and the Pliocene, and Ekman (1953) accounted for many faunal exchanges between the two oceans through this southern route.

The geography and climatic conditions that prevailed during the period of alcid evolution differed considerably from the Present. Throughout the Eocene–Oligocene–Lower Pliocene span of 35 to 40 million years, the ocean-surface waters were much warmer than they are now (Savin 1977) and the presumed high rates of evaporation caused high surface salinities (Lisitzin 1972); these factors were probably not conducive to high biological productivity. Equator-to-pole gradients in surface temperatures during the period of presumed early alcid history were only of the order of 4 to 6°C. In Early Eocene, polar surface temperatures were estimated to be about 10°C and even the cooling of the Oligocene made it such that the polar regions remained under a very much warmer regime than at present.

Thus, the contemporary image of alcids in frigid waters nesting along inhospitable and icy ocean margins and avoiding, except under the most extraordinary circumstances, the temperate or sub-tropical waters of the northern hemisphere is broadly different from the image that we must form after examining the geographic and climatological evidence. The very early auks had evolved as birds of tropical or subtropical seas. We can speculate then that the radiation and broad expansion of types and ecological forms that we know today could not have developed under these tropical or near-tropical conditions. Durham (1952), Addicott (1970) and Frakes (1979) have assembled evidence indicating that to a warm Paleocene–Eocene period succeeded a much cooler Oligocene, followed by a warm Miocene. But they point out that the cooling in the Oligocene did not create cold or frigid conditions but rather temperate ones throughout the northern hemisphere. Periglacial conditions in the ocean waters of the northern hemisphere did not occur until very late in the Tertiary. Prior to that, the equator-to-pole temperature gradient in the surface waters was merely 15°C as compared to 25 to 30°C at present (Savin 1977). According to Frakes (1979), the large accumulation of ice in the northern continents and the consequent effects upon neighbouring water bodies (ice reaching sea level) did not supervene until a mere 3.2 m.y.a. Thus, the most likely period when radiation in the Alcidae occurred is in the Mid- to Late Oligocene. At that time, the North Atlantic Ocean exhibited its present shape and thus offered sufficient ecological opportunities. A sharp cooling of the surface temperatures [Wolfe 1971; see also Briggs (1970), Savin (1977) and Frakes (1979) for more general summaries] by as much as 7°C (average annual mean) also took place. Thus ecological conditions in the oceans presumably improved (through increases in biological productivity), setting the stage for ecological radiation. The ancestor of the alcid which had presumably acquired the ability to move efficiently under water by the use of its partly opened wings, whereby opening up the possibility of pursuing pelagic prey and no longer only more sluggish and benthic inshore forms, seized this opportunity to radiate and invade a whole new ecological realm. There is evidence that this radiation occurred simultaneously in the North Atlantic and in the North Pacific, a fact to which we will return below. But according to evidence summarized by Stanley (1979) for a vast numer of vertebrate groups, the radiation followed the acquisition of the key characteristic (underwater 'flight') and the development of favourable ecological conditions must have been sudden. Once again, I suggest that this took place during the Late Oligocene. The major alcid ecological types we know today would have arisen then and persisted until now. The fact that genera, first encountered virtually unchanged from their Recent counterparts, first appeared 5–7 m.y.a. makes it easy to assume that they had come straight and unchanged from the Mid- to Late Oligocene ecological radiation, a further 20 million years back in time. This is an admittedly speculative view of what happened, but for lack of better evidence, I hope it will be considered sufficiently coherent to serve until such evidence is found.

A more cloudy aspect of this depiction centers on the simultaneous radiation giving rise by convergence to at least three major 'types': a flightless 'great auk' type (*Praemancalla* and *Mancalla* in the Pacific, *Pinguinus* in the Atlantic), one 'auklet' type (*Aethia*, *Ptycoramphus* and *Cyclorrhynchus* in the Pacific and *Alle* in the Atlantic) and one 'murre' type (*Uria* in the Pacific and in the Atlantic (?), *Alca* in the Atlantic). It has been generally recognized that this radiation has led to a much greater diversity in the North Pacific than in the Atlantic. Undoubted exclusive Recent and fossil genera amount to 10 in the former basin (*Praemancalla*, *Mancalla*, *Brachyramphus*, *Endomychura*, *Synthliboramphus*, *Aethia*, *Ptychoramphus*, *Lunda*, *Cyclorrhynchus* and *Cerorhinca*) while we can list only three exclusive North Atlantic genera (*Pinguinus*, *Alca* and *Alle*) and a fourth, *Australca*, of questionable identity (Olson 1977). Even adding *Miocepphus* to the Atlantic repertoire would not nearly balance out the situation. Finally, three genera, *Fratercula*, *Cepphus* and *Uria*, have a Present amphioceanic distribution. Both Storer (1952) and Udvardy (1963) considered that *Uria* evolved in the North Atlantic and moved to the North Pacific only recently. The presence of *Uria* remains in Mid-

Miocene deposits of North Carolina and the finding of Mid-Pliocene remains (*U. ausonia*) in Italy, together with the failure to locate the bird in
fossil form on the margins of the Pacific Ocean supported this interpretation. But the recent discovery of *Uria* in Late Miocene deposits of California (Barnes *et al.* 1981; Howard 1981, 1982) profoundly alters these
views. Furthermore, it now seems evident that the Atlantic finds of *Uria*
were wrongly assigned to that genus: according to Olson (1985), both *Uria*
antiquua and *U. ausonia* should rather be regarded as belonging to *Australca*. It now seems likely that *Uria* developed in the Pacific basin and
later moved to the North Atlantic. The finding of a form closely allied to
Uria in Mid-Miocene deposits of Maryland (*Miocepphus*) supported, albeit indirectly, Storer's and Udvardy's views but according to S. L. Olson
(personal communication), *Miocepphus* is closer to *Alca* than to *Cepphus*
and has been unfortunately named. What is even more shattering to these
early views is the recent finding in the Lee Creek phosphate mine of
North Carolina (Upper Miocene–Lower Pliocene, about 5 m.y.a.) of remains showing the existence of a complex alcid community containing
perhaps as many as a dozen distinct species among which are two puffins
(one most certainly belongs to *Fratercula,* the first-ever fossil of that
genus), one dovekie (most certainly *Alle,* also the first-ever find of a fossil
dovekie), one *Pinguinus* and one *Alca*-like type (Olson 1985). But preliminary examination reveals no *Uria* or *Cepphus* at a time when both are
present in the Pacific (Barnes *et al.* 1981; Howard 1981, 1982).

Unfortunately, many of the remains from the North Carolina deposits
are represented by hard-to-identify bone shafts (S. L. Olson, personal
communication) and it may be some time before a detailed analysis of this
unique material can be completed.

How then are we to reconcile the presence of a rich and diversified auk
assemblage in the ancient North Atlantic biota with the hitherto entrenched views of relative faunistic poverty in this basin (Briggs 1970)? It
is generally well established and accepted that even though the opening of
the Norwegian Sea connected the North Atlantic and the Arctic oceans,
there still remained a major barrier preventing contact with the North
Pacific: the Bering Land Bridge which existed during most of the Tertiary.
This supports views expressed earlier according to which separate boreal
and temperate faunas could develop in complete isolation in the North
Atlantic and the North Pacific for as long as 40 to 50 million years (Briggs
1970, 1974). But, during a brief episode towards the end of the Miocene,
some 5 m.y.a., the land bridge collapsed (Hopkins 1959, 1967; Briggs
1970; Nelson *et al.* 1974), thereby permitting faunistic exchanges via the
arctic basin (Ekman 1953; Briggs 1970). It is known that some faunistic
groups, rich and diversified in the Pacific, seized this opportunity to reach

the North Atlantic and exerted considerable influence on the local communities. Briggs (1970) summarized evidence from many groups of marine organisms according to which the Pacific forms displayed competitive superiority while the less diversified and less aggressive North Atlantic forms did not. If the North Pacific Alcidae seized this opportunity, the wave of immigrants could have brought to the Atlantic almost every single Pacific auk type, including at least one murre (actually two, see below), at least one puffin and several of the auklets and murrelets; the latter two groups later disappeared, however, perhaps in view of the more rigorous conditions (Briggs 1970) in the North Atlantic and now figure in the Lee Creek deposits. Some indigenous North Atlantic types may have disappeared following this invasion but at least *Pinguinus, Alle* and *Alca* survived through the competition and the climatic changes.

The revised history outlined above is probably more compatible with the ecological theory than earlier views (summarized in Udvardy 1963) whereby the impoverished North Atlantic alcid fauna was aggressively sending new invading forms into the richer and more stable North Pacific one (Storer 1952; Fisher and Lockley 1954; Kozlova 1957; Johansen 1958; Udvardy 1963). Of course, plausibility remains a frail substitute for hitherto incomplete evidence.

Two other groups of birds were also at least temporarily successful in this new adaptive zone (Bédard 1969a) represented by the subsurface oceanic waters: the Giant Pelecaniformes of the family Plotopteridae radiated quite broadly in the North Pacific before becoming extinct by the Mid-Miocene (Olson and Hasegawa 1979; Feduccia 1980) and the Giant Sphenisciformes in the southern hemisphere (Simpson 1976). Their disappearance (concurrent?) was, according to Simpson (1976), somehow related to the intensive radiation of seals and porpoises. It is not known how the large flightless auks of the northern hemisphere were spared this presumed competitive exclusion and how they ever managed to radiate and diversify. Also, it is noteworthy that seals, porpoises and Alcidae have today a universally and apparently benign, stable and even harmonious sympatric distribution. [See Udvardy (1963) for several examples.]

If we accept for the time being (1) the theory of two independent lineages for ancestral auks, one richer in the Pacific and one impoverished in the Atlantic, (2) the suggestion of a broad injection of Pacific forms in the North Atlantic via the Bering Strait towards the Upper Miocene, (3) the subsequent interruption of faunal exchange afterwards until the Quaternary reopening of the Bering Strait and (4) the unexplained disappearance of many North Atlantic forms towards the end (?) of the Pliocene, we may now attempt to interpret briefly the presumed history of the amphioceanic *Uria, Cepphus* and *Fratercula*. The splitting of *Fratercula* into a large

North Pacific *corniculata* and a smaller and darker North Atlantic *arctica* would trace back to the Upper Miocene instead of the Pliocene as suggested by Udvardy (1963). That the two species never subsequently reinvaded each other's range is matter for speculation. *Uria* could have differentiated into a cold-water-adapted Arctic Ocean and North Atlantic *lomvia* and a warmer-water *aalge* in the North Pacific, a differentiation beginning sometime around the same period. Reinvasion of the North Pacific by *lomvia* via the frigid shores of the Arctic Ocean is easy to imagine during the Upper Pliocene (or, less likely during one of the interglacials of the Quaternary), for the range of this species is presently continuous in the hemisphere. Invasion of the North Atlantic by the more pelagic *aalge* requires, however, warmer conditions than presently prevailing, for the species keeps away from arctic waters and a gap of about 2000 km now separates the closest North Atlantic and North Pacific breeding stations (see Tuck 1961, Fig. 3). Finally, *Cepphus* may have followed *Uria,* giving rise to a darker (but this time smaller) North Atlantic *grylle* with a predilection for cold low-arctic and high-arctic waters and a browner, slightly larger, temperate–boreal *columba–snowi–carbo* complex. Not surprisingly, the now well-differentiated *grylle* could very well be reinvading the North Pacific, for its *mandtii* population of the Chukchi Peninsula and northern Alaska most certainly winters in the Bering Sea and even nests in the northern part of this basin (Bédard 1966; Divoky *et al.* 1974; Sowls *et al.* 1978).

The Alcidae have certainly benefited greatly from the gradual cooling of the northern oceans through their evolutionary history. The consequent increase in productivity that coincides with the increase in oxygen of the upper layers of the ocean made it remotely possible that a southern, tropical or sub-tropical faunal connection could have remained between the two auk lineages. Most likely, the presence of faunal exchanges centering around the Arctic Ocean and the Bering Strait is an ecologically meaningful phenomenon, though probably a fairly recent one. According to Frakes (1979), it was a mere 3.2 m.y.a. that a more or less important ice cover developed in this ocean as the deteriorating climate on the surrounding land masses brought continental ice sheets to sea level. This trend in faunal exchanges is likely to continue and from now on, the evolutionary history of the family will continue to be centered in this area.

IV. ADAPTIVE RADIATION

As hinted at above, we know little of the circumstances under which the adaptive radiation that led to the present remarkable degree of diversification in the Alcidae took place. We may presume that it was triggered by the development of underwater flight on the one hand and that it was sudden, which in geological terms may mean several hundreds of thousands of years, on the other. But the stage was presumably set for this event, as argued above, as the ecological opportunities increased in the boreo-temperate zones of the northern hemisphere with the pronounced cooling of the Mid-Oligocene. A marked pole-to-equator temperature gradient in surface waters of the oceans and a corresponding zonation in marine faunas were developing; in the Pacific Ocean, the sheer size of the basin, along with the presence of numerous peripheric seas that were already in existence (the Bering, Japan, Okhotsk Seas) created a mosaic of conditions rather optimal for diversification. Similarly on the Atlantic side, the connection between the Arctic Ocean and the North Atlantic was rapidly completed and since the North Atlantic had nearly reached its current size and shape, it was also offering numerous similar opportunities: an arctic diverticulum, a Mediterranean basin, and, on either side of the Greenland land mass, two large and independent seas. This model of simultaneous radiation occurring in the Pacific and in the Atlantic requires that the key adaptation referred to above had occurred sometime previously in a proto-alcid stock common to both seas, or, less likely, that it appeared independently in two distinct alcid stocks.

As discussed elsewhere by a number of bird students (Kozlova 1957; Kartaschew 1960; Storer 1960; Bédard 1969a; Feduccia 1980), the shift to the subsurface waters of the oceans could not occur at a better time: this vast and rich ecological realm was virtually unoccupied by small to medium-sized warm-blooded vertebrates. Even forms like *Phalacrocorax,* or Anseriformes like the eiders (*Somateria*), the scoters (*Melanitta*) or the Labrador Duck (*Camptorynchus*) which, whether they existed at the time or came later could not be seen as competitors for they were limited to the inshore feeding domain or were, at any rate, much less efficient at pursuing prey. Certainly, foot propulsion should not be viewed as a lowly and inept mode of underwater locomotion. Species such as the Ruddy Duck or the Oldsquaw are extremely efficient divers that can reach great depths (Feduccia 1980) and whose propulsive mode entailed none of the major and irreversible structural modifications required of the newly forming auks of the Oligocene. But, contrary to these few birds, the early alcids were suddenly able to reach almost any soft-bodied oceanic prey, be it pelagic or benthic, and whatever its size (within limits) and whatever its swimming mode. Only the hard-shelled, mainly inshore benthic prey like the echinoderms and gastropods appear to have been almost wholly ignored in this broadening of the food base. Kaftanovskii (1951) has suggested on the basis of close relationships between larids and alcids that the underwater flying habit evolved from a prolongation of a dive made by a flying bird, much like living gulls perform today. But Stettenheim (1959), in an interesting discussion, proposed rather that a larid-like ancestor would possess, in view of its morphology highly adapted for gliding and buoyant flight, fewer preadaptations for developing underwater flight than a less differentiated or less specialized wader-like ancestor. He therefore traces back the evolution of alcids 'from birds which walked and flew along shores to those which dived while wading or while swimming on the surface of the water' (Stettenheim 1959, p. 201).

Although the swimming behaviour of the Alcidae underwater has been studied in tanks (Stettenheim 1959; Spring 1968; J. Bédard, unpublished observations), in order to understand the mechanics of locomotion in such a dense medium, no one to my knowledge has attempted to measure the swimming speed attained. Kooyman (1975), while discussing the question of speed in underwater locomotion of the Sphenisciformes, remarked that it is easily over-estimated when based on subjective impressions, probably in view of the apparently effortless and remarkably fluid movement that the bird displays. Kooyman (1975) gives two estimates of maximum speed in trained Adélies ranging between 7.2 and 9.6 km/hour. To those who have watched Black Guillemots fishing or social diving from the top of cliffs, such estimates may appear deceptively low. Yet, swimming speeds attained in the Alcidae are probably lower because of additional drag caused by the larger wing and by the lack of a highly specialized body covering and finally, in view of the much smaller size and less efficient volume-to-mass ratio. Uspenski (1956) has published estimates of swimming speed of 5.4 to 7.2 km/hour in the Black Guillemot but most likely, small forms like plankton-feeding *Alle* or *Aethia* attain an underwater speed that is substantially lower still, yet remaining amply sufficient to gather drifting or slow-swimming zooplanktonic crustaceans. Speed is but one aspect of underwater propulsion and even if the latter is not as considerable as one might intuitively have expected, it seems likely that the overall characteristics, such as greater manoeuverability, greater instantaneous power and perhaps, bioenergetically more efficient propulsion, probably meant that underwater 'flight', as it is, constituted by comparison to foot propulsion, a genuine breakthrough.

Modern views on the development of similar groups of vertebrates in terrestrial environments, whenever placed in similar circumstances, indicate that competition plays a vital role in accelerating the differentiation or the radiation (Stanley 1979). How this factor did intervene in early alcid communities is of course impossible to reconstruct. I have made the case elsewhere (Bédard 1969a) that this competition concerned mainly the acquisition of food. Adaptations for taking different prey types and sizes are thus reflected in the bill morphology and concern mainly its length and width as well as the pattern of tongue cornification and the arrangement of palatal structures. The major trends identified (Bédard 1969a) were as follows: in the plankton-feeders, a widening of the beak and of the palate, an increase in the number of palatal denticles and the development of a fleshy soft and agile tongue together with a sublingual diverticulum that enables the bird to transport loads of small, virtually formless prey. Only the Dovekie (*Alle alle*) in the North Atlantic possesses these traits. In the North Pacific, several species developed along this model (*Aethia, Ptychoramphus, Cyclorrhynchus, Synthliboramphus;* for the latter, see Sealy 1975a).

The opposite trend towards exclusive fish-feeding is accompanied by a narrowing of the beak and tongue cornification (the latter to be used as a lever to immobilize the prey against the rows of regularly arranged palatal denticles). This trend is clearly exemplified by *Alca* in the Atlantic, *Endomychura* and *Brachyramphus* in the Pacific and by the amphioceanic *Uria aalge* and *Cepphus* spp.

Not surprisingly, some species maintained a degree of plasticity and retained somewhat intermediate characteristics of beak and accordingly have rather eclectic tastes. These are the amphioceanic *Fratercula* and *Uria lomvia* as well as the North Pacific *Cyclorrhynchus* and a few other endemics such as *Cerorhinca* and *Lunda*. Roughly similar trends, a broadening of the beak in a plankton-feeding set, a narrowing of the beak in a fish-feeding set and intermediate generalists, have been described in Recent penguins by Zusi (1975). Trends in body size parallel to those described by this author for the alcids (Bédard 1969a) were not, however, found in the penguins by Zusi. But a detailed comparison is not always possible for the food habits, though well known in Alcidae (Pearson 1968; Bédard 1969b; Golovkin *et al.* 1972a; Ogi and Tsujita 1973, 1977; Sealy 1975a; Wehle 1976; Hunt *et al.* 1981; see also Chapter 6, this volume) are very incompletely known in penguins (Stonehouse 1968; Kooyman 1975), which prevents the identification of parallels.

Not merely restricting his examination to the superficial structures of the penguin mouth cavity, Zusi also examined the body support for the food-getting structure, the articulation of the jaw and the associated musculature. Unfortunately, no such study has been undertaken in the Alcidae. Spring (1968, 1971) suggested that it would probably be instructive to attempt such detailed morphological comparisons especially within the genus *Uria* where somewhat divergent trends (*aalge* is an exclusive fish-feeder while *lomvia* is adding much macro-zooplankton to its diet) that seem straightforward (Bédard 1969a) are rendered much more complex due to variations in beak dimensions.

Though differing in the number of elements they contain, the alcid sets of the North Atlantic and of the North Pacific oceans are remarkably convergent. In the Atlantic–Pacific, we had a flightless (at least one, but more likely a few well-differentiated species in either case) tall fish-feeder, very susceptible to land predators (*Pinguinus–Mancalla*); a fish-feeding volant form near the upper body size limit compatible with aerial flight (*Alca, Uria–Uria*); a plankton-feeding type (*Alle–Aethia, Ptychoramphus*); a medium-sized generalist (*Fratercula arctica–F. corniculata, Lunda, Cyclorrhynchus*); a small-bodied inshore fish-feeder (*Cepphus–Cepphus, Endomychura, Brachyramphus*).

All other characteristics of this bird family that relate to breeding (Sergeant 1951; Bédard 1969c; Tschanz and Hirsbrunner-Scharf 1975), to social behaviour, post-hatching development (Sealy 1973a) or to other aspects of the biology have left imprints that have merely been superimposed upon the basic adaptations that relate to feeding. In general, these adaptations do not invoke profound structural modifications. However, the burrow-digging habit in *Fratercula* has led to a marked enlargement of the inner toe. The deepening and lateral compression of the beak, which is sometimes also attributed to the development of digging behaviour (Kozlova 1957), can, however, be seen to play a very different role: the extravagant beak of *Fratercula* (and for that matter, that of *Lunda, Aethia* and *Cyclorrhynchus*) is enlarged and strikingly coloured simply to enhance its function in communication during courtship (Bédard 1969a). As indirect evidence, we can point out that a host of burrow-digging Procellariiformes and Passeriformes have frail and unmodified beaks that perform this function well. As to the rear claw, it is difficult to see how it could be applied to digging.

Radiation has also affected overall appearance of the birds of the family. But in the Atlantic, six of the seven Recent species are strikingly similar: black above and white below, both in summer and in winter. The seventh, the Black Guillemot, has a nearly all black summer plumage but a predominantly white winter one. But, in the Pacific, representatives of the family display a wealth of pigmentation types: jet black *Lunda* and *Cepphus,* deep grey *Aethia cristatella, Cerorhinca monocerata* and *Ptychoramphus aleuticus,* mottled black summer plumage of *Aethia pusilla,* mottled brown summer plumage of *Brachyramphus marmoratus* and *B. brevirostris,* year-round grey and white plumage of *Endomychura* and *Synthliboramphus.* The diversity of pigmentation types encountered in this family of cold environments diminishes the applicability of the intuitively simple model of black upperparts (to siphon the solar heat) and white underparts (to exclude the cold or to block heat losses to the cold waters). But the plumage of northern auks is so thick and so remarkably insulating that it is doubtful if significant heat losses can occur through it in the first place. Furthermore, trying to balance heat gain by wearing black upperparts in latitudes where the winter night considerably outlasts the daylight period seems also a perplexing way of controlling energy losses. Phillips' (1962, 1964) suggestion that the predominantly white underparts in fish-eating species would enable these predators to get closer to their aquatic prey before being detected is not really pertinent for, as we have seen, several fish-eating auks have dark underparts. But furthermore, the diving auks approach their prey tangentially or from the side and not from above as do gulls and their allies. Until someone has modelled the physics of pigmentation in this group of birds, it is perhaps just as well to view their overall colouration patterns as adjustments to social, rather than physical, factors.

V. CLASSIFICATION

The position of the Alcidae Vigors 1825 within the class Aves as well as the deciphering of the relationships among the various elements constituting the group proper have been the object of a heavy outpouring of thoughts for the past hundred years. Sibley and Alquist (1972) gave a thorough summary of these attempts, and by the use of judicious quotes, gave us an aperçu of the fierceness of the debates that surrounded them. Some of the classification attempts were based on egg shape and colouration (Dawson 1920), intestinal convolutions (Gadow 1889; Mitchell 1896, 1901), osteological comparisons (Shufeldt 1903; Wetmore 1940), feather structure (Chandler 1916), overall anatomical characters (Verheyen 1958), electrophoretic patterns of lenticular and muscle proteins (Gysels and Rabaey 1964) and egg-white proteins (Sibley and Alquist 1972). The sometimes widely diverging views that came out of such studies cannot easily be reconciled. But a few overall resonances seem to predominate. The auks make a 'closcly knit' group (Sibley and Alquist 1972), and attempts to split it into a number of components, some of which should be closer to Spheneisciformes, others closer to the Charadriiformes, are ill-founded and often based on questionable investigation techniques (Sibley and Alquist 1972).

The auks should be placed close to the gulls and shorebirds. The many attempts at linking the auks with the loons, grebes or Procellariiformes (in particular the Pelecanoididae) or with any combination of these generally turned out to be untenable on one or sometimes many scores. Nevertheless, most of these attempts converged on two points: (1) the auks are members of or, at any rate, are very close to the Charadriiformes; (2)

within the limits of this nearly unanimously recognized association, their distinctiveness should be underlined by an ordinal status next to the Charadriiformes, or a subordinal status within the latter, or a superfamily or at the very least a family status within that order.

Organization of the 23 neo-species has also given rise to stunningly different results. Although there is little disagreement on the generic status of most alcids, except for recurring and sporadic debates over the status of *Endomychura* and *Brachyramphus,* the way in which these are assorted in infra-familial groupings is quite diverse. Thus, Coues (1868) proposed one family Alcidae and three subfamilies. Beddard (1898) proposed one family but five subfamilies. Dawson (1920) proposed five distinct families within a single order, the Alciformes. Peters (1934) proposed a single family. Storer (1945) suggested organizing the living representatives into two families and seven tribes. But later (Storer 1964), he revised his position and recommended a single family subdivided into seven tribes. His classification seems the most coherent and this is the one I have retained in Table 1.2.

Underlying these debates over ordering the living alcids into an acceptable system is the desire to respect a presumed order of antiquity. By convention, the first-listed elements (tribe, genera or species) of a classification are also the most 'primitive'. Thus, the Alcini of Storer (Table 1.2) would group 'primitive' *Alca, Uria* and *Pinguinus* while his proposed Aethiini would assemble 'younger' elements. One could submit, however, that according to the inferred pattern of more or less simultaneous and rapid radiation that likely occurred in early alcid history, one can hardly be taken as 'older' or more 'primitive' than the other. At any rate, decisions on the primitiveness of any given character cannot be better than purely subjective and even a sophisticated statistical treatment of subjective decisions of this sort (Hudson *et al.* 1969) cannot render them objective. These authors recommend that the Aethiini should rather come first in a classification of the family while the Razorbill and the murres with the most developed proficiency at diving should be viewed as the most specialized Alcidae. My opinion is that the Alcidae evolved along two independent lineages (a Pacific and an Atlantic one) more or less at the same time and each surviving type has maintained its baggage of adaptations until the Present. A lesser proficiency at diving in the Aethiini may actually represent a trade-off against maintaining higher proficiency on land and in the air which in turn permits a wider choice of nesting situations. Avoiding the dead-end of ultra-specialization by the puffins and the auklets may indeed represent an advanced trait. Quite clearly, such arguments can rapidly become wholly mundane.

All the morphological characteristics reviewed earlier are very gener-

TABLE 1.2

Classification of the Recent Alcidae[a]

General grouping	Genus and species
Order: Charadriiformes	
Family: Alcidae	
Tribe:	
Alcini	*Pinguinus impennis*
	Alca torda
	Uria aalge
	Uria lomvia
Allini	*Alle alle*
Cepphini	*Cepphus grylle*
	Cepphus columba
	Cepphus carbo
Brachyramphini	*Brachyramphus marmoratus*
	Brachyramphus brevirostris
Synthliboramphini	*Endomychura hypoleuca*
	Endomychura craveri
	Synthliboramphus antiquus
	Synthliboramphus wumizusume
Aethiini	*Aethia pygmaea*
	Aethia pusilla
	Aethia cristatella
	Ptychoramphus aleuticus
	Cyclorrhynchus psittacula
Fraterculini	*Fratercula arctica*
	Fratercula corniculata
	Lunda cirrhata
	Cerorhinca monocerata

[a] After American Ornithologists' Union (1957) and Storer (1964).

ally shared by all representatives of the family in the Atlantic with one notable exception, that of *Fratercula*. The position of the nostrils, the bill plates, the unusual moult pattern, the nest-digging behaviour and the lamination of the maxillo-palatine bone remove this genus from the set. *Alca, Alle, Pinguinus, Uria* and *Cepphus* share more similarities among themselves than they do with any other Pacific representatives.

VI. GEOGRAPHIC VARIATION

When Pontoppidan, Brehm, Pallas, Mandt, Nilsson and others began to appreciate the existence and the extent of geographic variation within the various species of Alcidae, more than 150 years ago, they had access to very limited museum material and supporting ecological knowledge. Even later workers who had the opportunity either to introduce and describe new patterns of geographic variation or to revise and evaluate the forms described to that date (Witherby, Lönnberg, Salomonsen) still had limited resources. Although the museum series upon which they reached taxonomic decisions seemed fairly large in some cases, they were strongly biased by age and/or seasonal factors. Salomonsen (1944), whose major revision of the North Atlantic auks has been used as a baseline study by all alcid students for nearly four decades, carried out his study under particularly pressing circumstances. Salomonsen worked in exile, had access to very limited collections, and was unable to obtain essential loans from non-Swedish institutions in view of the war conditions. Some of the series he had at his disposal were therefore extremely short and/or extremely biased towards one locality, one age group or one seasonal condition. Reaching decisions on the validity of many forms under such circumstances was truly a tour de force and his 1944 monograph remains to this day as an example of thoroughness and perspicacity.

But over the past decades, continuous addition of new material together with a growing body of knowledge of oceanographic factors, bird densities and relative abundance, along with an unravelling of the hitherto unsuspected movements revealed by banding recoveries, have led to a new appraisal of a number of the previously described forms. In reviewing the situation, I have proceeded as follows: I review first the situation, species by species, as described by Salomonsen (1944); then I introduce the varied views of subsequent students, in particular, those of Storer (1952), Pethon (1967), Asbirk (1979a), and Glutz von Blotzheim et al. (1982). Afterwards, I examine overall trends and put forward a tentative summary of the current views on the geographic variation in this family along with a broader discussion of clinal tendencies encountered in several of the North Atlantic species. The order followed is that of Salomonsen (1944).

A. Razorbill, *Alca torda* (Fig. 1.1)

Salomonsen (1944) named three forms of this species. A small-winged and small-billed *islandica* with a variable number of furrows on the bill, distributed along the coasts of Iceland, the Faeroes, the British Isles, the Channel Islands and the coast of western France. Two larger forms (longer-billed, deeper-billed and longer-winged) were also recognized: one, *torda,* restricted to the brackish waters of the Baltic and the fresh waters of Lake Ladoga; the other, *pica,* covering the remainder of the range not included in the two previously mentioned forms, that is, eastern

Fig. 1.1.   Razorbill (*Alca torda*). (Photo by E. Verspoor.)

America, Greenland [for distribution there, see Bédard (1969d) and Lloyd (1976a,b)], the entire Norwegian coast, Bjørnøya, the White Sea and Murmansk. The diagnostic difference between *torda* and *pica* was said to rest upon the number of distal (in front of the white-coloured) furrows in the beak, the former being more strongly corrugated. But all subsequent workers have rejected this Baltic entity. Thus, Kozlova (1957) and Kartaschew (1960) retain only *islandica* and *torda* (agglomerating *torda* and *pica*). Similar views are also expressed in the most recent revisions (Glutz von Blotzheim *et al.* 1982). There is compelling evidence to indicate that the number of furrows in the beak of this species varies with (among other things), the age of the bird (Lloyd 1976a). Such a relationship has been described in *Fratercula* by Petersen (1976b) using known-age birds from the Vestmannaeyjar. The existence of such variability is of course not questioned by Salomonsen, but I contend that it is impossible to describe

Fig. 1.2.   Great Auk (*Pinguinus impennis*). (Courtesy of the University Museum of Zoology, Cambridge, England.)

taxonomic entities without an appropriate and rigorous control of age factors in the series of specimens compared.

If we use wing length as an indicator of size, the smallest Razorbills are to be found in Iceland, the Faeroes, the British Isles and Brittany. But within the range of the proposed *pica* race, size is not uniform: the Canadian birds are the smallest, the Swedish ones intermediate in size and the Greenland ones largest. The size variability does not follow a clear ecological or even geographic gradient.

B. Great Auk, *Pinguinus impennis* (Fig. 1.2)

The Great Auk was an apparently undifferentiated species occupying boreal latitudes across the North Atlantic.

C. Dovekie, *Alle alle* (Fig. 1.3)

Salomonsen (1944) examined only the southernmost typical *alle*. Specimens from widely distributed localities such as northwest Greenland,

Fig. 1.3.   Dovekie (*Alle alle*). (Photo by D. Roby.)

eastern Greenland, Jan Mayen, northern Iceland, Bjørnøya and Spitsbergen are said to be similar in size and colouration. This is not surprising, considering the extensive trans-Atlantic movements that are being revealed now by banding recoveries, which show that birds from Spitsbergen spend the winter in west Greenland and most likely mix with some local birds at least (see Salomonsen 1967, for a summary).

But Salomonsen (1944) also recognized the larger *polaris* (wing length 130 to 136 mm as opposed to 113 to 129 mm for *alle*) earlier described by Stenhouse (1930) on the basis of 10 specimens from Franz Josef Land. Birds nesting in the New Siberian Islands are also presumed to belong to this larger race. The splitting of *Alle* has been accepted by all as being a solid example of geographic differentiation in the family. However, I have measured in the Zoological Museum of the University of Copenhagen, a July-breeding bird (No. 53,182) from Spitsbergen with a wing length of 134 mm, well within the range of *polaris*. Several other birds from the same area also in this collection had wing lengths measuring between 120 and 130 mm and should therefore be assigned to *alle*. But it seems to me that the original description of *polaris* was based on a very small sample and that a more extensive examination might reveal the existence of a less abrupt size difference than so far proposed. Until someone examines the series of Dovekies from Franz Josef Land in the Leningrad and Moscow museums, we will have to accept the existence of two separate races on either side of a line between Spitsbergen and Franz Josef. But these two land masses are both in the same high-arctic zone (*sensu* Salomonsen 1972a) and no sharp discontinuity in oceanographic conditions is known to occur in this area that might parallel this morphological differentiation. Of course, the latter may also be maintained or strengthened by divergent migratory habits and in this connection, it is worth noting, as did Norderhaug (1966), that if the entire Spitsbergen population is present in southwestern Greenland in winter, then all or some of the Dovekies that winter along the Norwegian coast may come from Franz Josef and the Soviet Arctic. But differentiation between these two forms may be related to recent glacial history. It is conceivable that the larger of the two forms developed in a refugium along the arctic coast basin while the smaller one was restricted to the glaciated coasts of the North Atlantic. The use of distinct wintering areas as well as distance may have reinforced the differentiation; there is evidence that such differences in migratory habits between the two forms persist to this day (see below).

The discovery of several Dovekies in the Bering Sea, along with evidence that some of these belong to an established population (Bédard 1966; Breckenridge 1966; Holmes 1968), and the fact that these specimens have been assigned to both *alle* and *polaris* (Sealy *et al.* 1971) does not help to clarify the situation.

D. Common Murre, *Uria aalge* (Fig. 1.4)

When Salomonsen described two new North Atlantic forms in 1932, he made of this species the second-most differentiated auk with five forms. One, *albionis,* is a brownish-backed murre with inconspicuous stripes on the sides and a small body size (relative to typical *aalge*) occupying the southernmost parts of the range in the eastern Atlantic (i.e., the southern parts of the British Isles, the Farne Islands, Helgoland, Brittany and south). A form restricted to the Iberian Peninsula (*ibericus*) was not retained by Salomonsen. Second, a Baltic *intermedia* with upperparts somewhat darker than those of *albionis* and somewhat paler than typical *aalge,* was also described. As to *aalge,* the third type, it was said to have a more blackish, slate-coloured back and more conspicuous dark streaks on the sides than either *albionis* or *intermedia.* The type locality of *aalge* is Iceland but its distribution extends to the western Atlantic, to all of the Canadian seaboard, the Greenland coasts and, in the eastern Atlantic, to the northernmost parts of the British Isles (Outer Hebrides, Orkneys and the Shetlands), Scotland and western Norway to some vaguely defined

Fig. 1.4. Common Murre (*Uria aalge*). (Photos by E. Verspoor, upper, and A. Macfarlane, lower).

point along this shore where it is said to change to a very dark *hyperborea,* the fourth type. The latter has heavy streaking on the flanks, much larger size (wing) but a shorter bill than the typical *aalge* which it now replaces northwards to Bjørnøya, Murmansk and Novaya Zemlya. Finally, Salomonsen recognizes a darker subset of *aalge,* a fifth type, which he treats as a different subspecies restricted to the Faeroe Islands, *spiloptera.*

Ecologically oriented monographs of North Atlantic auks by Kozlova (1957) and Kartaschew (1960) retained these five subspecies although Kozlova repeated the doubts raised by Witherby *et al.* (1941) regarding the validity of *intermedia* and *spiloptera*. Storer (1952), who made a thorough review of the genus in the northern hemisphere, also retained the five forms catalogued by Salomonsen. However, on the basis of 10 specimens, he thought that *intermedia* was weakly differentiated. He also examined 13 specimens of *spiloptera* in North American collections and judging from measurements and other traits such as the degree of spotting in the underwing, found himself unable to distinguish the Faeroe birds from the Scottish *aalge*. Yet, he maintained the identity of the subspecies which Salomonsen himself (1944, p. 39) agreed was perhaps not worth keeping after all. As to *hyperborea,* Storer had access to insufficient material and he provisionally maintained the form. Pethon (1967) found that none of the specimens collected along the Norwegian coastline (83 were examined) could be assigned with any degree of certainty to either *aalge* or *hyperborea:* at least, the level of success in separating the forms was far below that expected according to established taxonomic procedure. The eastern Atlantic situation was examined by Glutz von Blotzheim *et al.* (1982), who considered that *U. aalge* varied in this broad geographic expanse between only two clearly recognizable forms: a northernmost very dark, heavily streaked, long-winged, deep- and short-billed murre bearing rough white spots under the wing (*hyperborea*); a southernmost brownish-topped, longer-billed murre with light streaking on the sides and smaller and fewer spots under the wing (*albionis*). All intermediate populations, that is including the races *aalge, spiloptera* and *intermedia,* were impossible to tell apart from each other and from the two extremes of the cline. The authors nevertheless recommended that the three forms be regrouped under *aalge.* Wijs (1978) reached more pronounced conclusions and stated that none of the Atlantic forms could be safely distinguished. He felt, however, that 'in most cases', the brownish-backed *albionis* with unspotted underwings should be properly distinguishable from the others which should be referred to the *aalge* race.

Although Glutz von Blotzheim *et al.* (1982) found a general gradient in the darkening of the back in the Common Murre going northwards, Storer (1952) did not find that this trait could be related, when the entire North Atlantic stock was considered, to gradients in the temperature of the surface waters of the ocean. Latitudinal trends in size in the western Atlantic are not very important, but a weak tendency for an increase in wing length is apparent in Storer's data for birds of the Gulf of St. Lawrence and those of southwestern Greenland.

E. Thick-billed Murre, *Uria lomvia* (Fig. 1.5)

Throughout its immense North Atlantic range, a single morph is recognized and labelled *lomvia.* Salomonsen and a few others have noted,

Fig. 1.5.   Thick-billed Murre (*Uria lomvia*). (Photo by D. N. Nettleship.)

however, that the Icelandic birds are smaller. The remarkable aspect of the distribution of this Atlantic auk is that it is the only one which has a continuous span through to the Pacific Ocean. The links between the Atlantic and Pacific stocks include two weakly differentiated subspecies: *eleonorae* which occupies Severnaya Zemlya and the New Siberian Islands, and *heckeri* which has a very restricted distribution centered on Wrangel Island, just north of the Chukchi Peninsula. From the Bering Strait south to the Aleutian Islands, the *arra* subspecies takes over. The habits of *eleonorae* and *heckeri* are hardly known and I suspect that these have much closer relationships with the Pacific *arra* than with the North Atlantic nominate form.

A pronounced size gradient in this undifferentiated form is nevertheless observed in the western Atlantic. Contrary to what has just been described in *U. aalge,* the wing length of this bird decreases northwards

from 222 to 224 mm in the Gulf of St. Lawrence to 213.8 mm in Baffin Bay
(Storer 1952, p. 179). The bill length decreases similarly from 38.5 to 35.7
mm while the bill depth follows an analogous trend (14.88 to 13.82 mm).
Actually, the size differences between populations at both ends of the
cline are larger in this undifferentiated species than they are between
several of the racial entities proposed for several of the other North
Atlantic auks.

F. Black Guillemot, *Cepphus grylle* (Fig. 1.6)

This is the most plastic of the North Atlantic auks and Salomonsen
(1944) recognized and/or described seven different races in this inshore
species. The nominate form, *grylle,* according to Salomonsen (1944, p.

Fig. 1.6.   Black Guillemot (*Cepphus grylle*). (Photo by Evie Weinstein.)

43), is 'larger than any other Atlantic form'. The bill is said to be longer and heavier and the wing is also decidedly longer. The bird is restricted to the Baltic Sea and is a late-spring (pre-alternate) moulter which has apparently little contact with the neighbouring populations of western Sweden, which are said to belong to *atlantis*. The latter apparently differs quite substantially in the timing of its moult (see data in Asbirk 1979a) and is also much smaller than *grylle* (wing length ranges from 155 to 168 mm in the latter and from 169 to 182 mm in the former). It also has a smaller and slenderer bill than the Baltic endemic and is said to occupy the following shores: western Sweden, eastern Denmark, British Isles (especially Ireland and Scotland), Shetland, Orkney and the Inner and Outer Hebrides as well as the entire Norwegian coastline north as far as the Murmansk Coast and the shores of the White Sea, eastern America from the northern Maine coast to some vaguely determined point in southern Labrador where the form merges into a transitional *arcticus*. The latter does not differ at all from *atlantis* (see data in Salomonsen), at least as far as body dimensions are concerned. However, *arcticus* is reputed to have considerably more white in its winter plumage than its more boreal counterpart. Yet, only two specimens in winter plumage were examined by Salomonsen.

The form *atlantis* would also include the Icelandic Black Guillemot population, as the birds from there are quite similar to the widely distributed form. However, a slight increase in the amount of black in the white wing mirror is caused by the extension of the black pigmentation along the outer margin of the greater wing coverts. These project onto the white speculum causing a streaked appearance which is said to characterize quite well the Icelandic birds. Hørring (1937) therefore described a local variant under the name *islandicus*, a form which Salomonsen recognized readily.

Three more subspecies have been described. *Cepphus g. faeroensis*, said to be sedentary around the Faeroe Islands, would be a smaller, darker, shorter-winged version of *atlantis*. *C. g. ultimus* would be a northern form of Black Guillemot with a distinctly shorter bill than neighbouring *atlantis* and would occupy the range just north of the latter in northern Labrador, in Hudson Bay, throughout the Canadian Arctic and along the entire coast of western Greenland north to the limit of the range near the Arctic Ocean shores of northernmost Greenland.

Finally, a very distinctive *mandtii* occupies the high-arctic (*sensu* Salomonsen 1972a) breeding locations of Jan Mayen, Bjørnøya, Spitsbergen, probably all of the eastern Greenland coast, Franz Josef Land and Novaya Zemlya together with the same breeding outposts occupied by *Uria lomvia* along the eastern shores of the Arctic Ocean, namely Severnaya

Zemlya and the New Siberian Islands, Wrangel Island and the northern Alaskan coast. *Cepphus,* like *Uria lomvia,* has a continuous distribution between the Atlantic and the Pacific. The *mandtii* race has much more white in the wing than any other form with the possible exception of *ultimus.* But it can easily be separated from the latter by the size of the bill. In *mandtii,* the greater wing coverts are 'constantly white almost or right to the base' (Salomonsen 1944, p. 101). The overall winter dress of *mandtii* is also much whiter than that of any other form.

The views of subsequent alcid students on the identity of these seven races have been quite contradictory and diverse. In a thorough review of the genus, Storer (1952) retained *grylle, islandicus, faeroensis, ultimus* and *mandtii* but rejected *atlantis.* He therefore amalgamated all the North American birds as well as those from southern and western Greenland, Norway and the British Isles to *arcticus.* Storer (1952) examined 11 adult Black Guillemots from Iceland. Although these cannot be distinguished from the now all-inclusive and broadly distributed *arcticus* on the basis of measurements, Storer maintained that its unique wing pattern was distinctive. He examined a single specimen of the weakly differentiated *faeroensis* and was unable to propose any action other than maintaining the race typical of this island group. Storer also recognized that *ultimus* must intergrade with *arcticus* along the western Greenland coast and the Labrador shores. Contact of this *ultimus–arcticus* complex with *mandtii* is not recognized on the previously mentioned shores, but might exist along the eastern coast of Greenland. Specimens from the latter area cannot be safely assigned to one or the other.

Kozlova (1957) and Kartaschew (1960) accepted entirely Salomonsen's scheme with the following exception: Kartaschew rejected *arcticus* which he assimilated into *ultimus.* Vaurie (1965), who dealt with the entire set of forms for the Atlantic, suggested a rather profound revision. In his view, *grylle, atlantis, faeroensis* and *arcticus* should form a single subspecies (*grylle*), while *ultimus* and *mandtii,* despite the aforementioned difference in measurements (especially of the bill), should be regrouped under *mandtii.* Only *islandicus* was spared in view of its unique wing pattern.

Ingolfsson (1961), who was privileged to examine 69 specimens, noted that *faeroensis* could not be distinguished from the British Isles *atlantis* and he proposed to abolish the former race. The *islandicus* material, however, appeared strongly differentiated to him and he proposed to maintain this subspecies. Asbirk (1979a) examined in depth a fair sample of birds from the Kattegat area of Denmark and indicated that the birds from this area differed sharply from those of the inner Baltic. There is thus a sharp discontinuity between the population of the Baltic and that of the North Sea and, more generally, that of the Atlantic. The Danish population with short-winged (average around 161 mm), short-billed (average around 31 mm) and early-spring-moulting individuals would be easy to tell apart from the long-winged (174 mm), long-billed (32.9 mm) and late-moulting Baltic ones. Thus, Asbirk (1979a) proposed to retain the race *grylle,* which had been discarded entirely by Vaurie (1965), and suggested that the Kattegat birds be considered to belong to *atlantis* (of Salomonsen) or *arcticus* (of Storer).

Finally, the most recent revision of the species (Glutz von Blotzheim *et al.* 1982) makes a rather stunning suggestion: *ultimus* is abandoned and the birds from the Eurasian Arctic, Alaska, northwestern Greenland are included under *mandtii* while *arcticus* is restricted to birds from the southwestern part of Greenland (from Disko Bay, south) and northern Labrador. This *arcticus* form is seen as intermediate between *mandtii* and the boreal *atlantis,* which occupies the entire eastern American seaboard south of mid-Labrador, the British Isles, western Scandinavia and the White Sea shores. Finally, *islandicus* is retained as a strongly marked, short-winged form while *faeroensis* is also retained on the diagnosis of a thicker bill (than *islandicus*); *grylle* is also retained as a distinctive endemic.

If we now examine the mosaic of forms and races in an attempt to identify clinal tendencies in morphology that could be related to latitude or to ecological variables, one finds that the situation becomes still more complex. In the eastern Atlantic, there is a pronounced northward decrease in wing length and overall size from the Baltic (presumed *grylle*) to the Norwegian coast and then to Murmansk (presumed *atlantis*). But Bianki (1967) pointed out that the birds from Murmansk and the White Sea, in general, were as different from the typical *atlantis* stock (by being much smaller with a wing length of 152 mm, on the average), to which they were arbitrarily assigned than the *atlantis* race itself (wing length: 162 mm) from the Baltic *grylle* (wing length: 174 mm). Bianki even insisted that the White Sea Black Guillemots should be considered racially different from *atlantis.*

On the west side of the Atlantic, the situation is not as clear and the wing length of this species has apparently not responded to changes in latitudes. Storer (1952, Table 17) examined 463 individuals and found less than 3 mm difference in the value of this character in boreal Bay of Fundy and south (165.1 mm) across the Gulf of St. Lawrence, the Labrador coast, the Baffin Island coast and all the way to high-arctic Ellesmere (167.8 mm). Furthermore, this small change in wing length followed an irregular trend. Culmen length over the same broad latitudinal gradient decreased slightly (Storer 1952, Table 19) from about 31.5 to 28.0 mm. Such relative morphological stability is remarkable when one remembers that this latitudinal range encloses entirely the range of two subspecies recognized by Salomonsen: *atlantis* and *ultimus*. Of course, *ultimus* was mainly characterized by the amount of white in the winter plumage, but this was not considered as a very convincing diagnostic characteristic.

The race *islandicus* essentially resembles *atlantis* on the basis of size and its identity is based on wing pattern only. However, while comparing birds from Newfoundland and Iceland in the U.S. National Museum, I was unable to distinguish them on the basis of this character alone: actually, some Newfoundland individuals were found to display the diagnostic *islandicus* trait to a greater extent than some genuine *islandicus* specimens.

The two high-arctic Black Guillemots constitute a very complex subspecies pair. If one follows the slow but discrete decrease in size between birds nesting along the Norwegian coast and northwards to east Murmansk and birds from Novaya Zemlya, there occurs an abrupt gap as one goes from (presumed) *atlantis* to *mandtii*. The difference in body weight between the two forms in the summer amounts to nearly 100 g or about 25%. Corresponding differences in wing length and other body dimensions cannot easily be compared for lack of published accounts and lack of Soviet specimens in western museums, but they ought to be considerable.

This clear gap in size between low-arctic and high-arctic Black Guillemots in the eastern Atlantic has no equivalent in the western part of this ocean where the boreal form intergrades into a low-arctic one and then into a high-arctic (presumed *ultimus*) one in a smooth and very shallow gradient. In fact, the *ultimus* of Ellesmere Island and extreme northwestern Greenland is exposed to conditions just as severe as those that prevail in Spitsbergen, Franz Josef Land and the Soviet Arctic (*mandtii*), but there is no equivalent response in overall size.

Admittedly, the relations between the two high-arctic Black Guillemots *mandtii* and *ultimus* are not clear and Vaurie's (1965) suggestion, reformulated by Glutz von Blotzheim *et al.* (1982), does little to clarify them.

The rather unequivocal differentiation between the high-arctic *mandtii* and the boreal low-arctic *grylle* is most likely related to the recent glacial history and to the existence of a high-arctic refugium (or refugia) (Salomonsen 1972a).

G. Atlantic Puffin, *Fratercula arctica* (Fig. 1.7)

Three races of *Fratercula arctica* have been described. First, *grabae* is a small boreal puffin of the southeastern Atlantic occupying the islands of Brittany, the British Isles, the Faeroes, western Sweden and southern

Fig. 1.7.   Atlantic Puffin (*Fratercula arctica*). (Photo by D. N. Nettleship.)

Norway. But within this realm, one finds considerable variation in body mass, in dimensions of the wing and beak, a trend that is perceived by Salomonsen as having a northerly slant. The second race (*arctica*) regroups the populations from the 'low-arctic' North Atlantic (Salomonsen 1972a), that is, Iceland, Norway (north of Bergen), western Greenland (to Melville Bay) and the entire North American coast. Finally, *naumanni* would be a large and exclusively high-arctic puffin, typical of Spitsbergen, Novaya Zemlya and eastern Greenland.

Some workers have either agreed with this overall appraisal (Kartaschew 1960) or argued with some aspects of the assigned boundaries of the range of the various races. Thus, Kozlova (1957) has assigned the birds from the western shores of the South Island of Novaya Zemlya to *arctica* instead of to *naumanni* as done by Salomonsen. Belopol'skii (1957) recognized only two races, namely *naumanni* and *arctica* (including *grabae*). Pethon (1967), after failing to locate the postulated Norwegian boundary between *arctica* and *grabae* because of extensive overlap between the two and in view of a diffuse set of complex trends affecting not only the wing length but also the bill length and the bill height, proposed in accordance with Myrberget (1963) to treat the *arctica–grabae* complex rather as a clinally varying stock, not as distinct recognizable races. However, *naumanni* is seen as a distinctly larger northern form, easily distinguished from any of the *arctica–grabae* complex. Only the case of the Bjørnøya birds, with much shorter wing length than the closest Fenno-Scandian *arctica–grabae*, poses a problem so far unresolved.

Petersen (1976a) compared material from the southern and northern coasts of Iceland: the size difference he found (affecting especially the beak dimensions as well as the tarsus and the wing length) between these two populations, presumed to belong to the same race (*arctica*), were more important than the size differences between birds from southern Iceland and birds from the Faeroe Islands, the latter supposedly representatives of the smaller *grabae*.

In their review, Glutz von Blotzheim *et al.* (1982) took the following stand: the large *naumanni* form can be distinguished without any difficulty (one exception, the Jan Mayen birds). Just as was the case for *Alle* and *Cepphus,* the existence of a large, high-arctic form and of a smaller Atlantic one could perhaps be traced back to Pleistocene events and in particular to the existence of one or several refugia north of the glaciation belt in which the *naumanni* form would have acquired the particularities of size that it maintains to this day. However, the birds from the remainder of the Atlantic basin are pooled under the form *arctica* (including *grabae*); Glutz von Blotzheim *et al.* (1982) note that the incoherence of clinal variation (despite repeated claims to the contrary by Salomonsen 1944, 1972a) makes it difficult to recognize safely these presumed subspecies. Thus the birds from St. Kilda (western Scotland) have shorter wings than those from Skomer (South Wales), while these have shorter wings still than those from the Isle of May in eastern Scotland (Glutz von Blotzheim *et al.* 1982).

Clinal variation within the subspecies *arctica* has been examined by Myrberget (1963) and Pethon (1967) in the eastern Atlantic. Pethon documented a change in wing length from about 163 mm in southern Norway to about 174 mm in Finnmark. Bill length and bill height follow the same trends. But even the largest birds along this shore are substantially smaller than the average *naumanni* representative from Spitsbergen.

In the western Atlantic, the available data are insufficient to detect clinal tendencies, if any, in *arctica* of the eastern American seaboard. But according to Salomonsen (1967), the wing length of this form would vary between extreme values of 161 and 176 mm, a range close to that (161–182 mm) determined by Nettleship (1972) for birds breeding on Great Island in Newfoundland. Up in Thule district, the large *naumanni* would measure between 175 and 193 mm. But the split range of this admittedly much larger race, Thule District and eastern Greenland on the one hand, and Spitsbergen and northern Novaya Zemlya on the other, is very perplexing.

H. General Discussion of Variation

Geographic variation among the North Atlantic Alcidae is complex and confusing. Although much of the complexity is admittedly intrinsic and reflects the operation of real biological forces, much of it stems from methodological inadequacies and we must appreciate the importance of these before attempting to make any conclusions.

Several of the subspecies of North Atlantic auks were described by ornithologists who freely compared their own measurements with values published by colleagues without, in several instances, the assurance that these were obtained in similar ways. Two very respected ornithologists, for instance, have produced quite dissimilar sets of measurements for the supposedly same races as a result of divergent methods: there is a full 2-mm difference on the average between the bill depth values of the murre specimens measured by Salomonsen and those measured by Storer, a difference that cannot be attributed to geographic variation (Storer 1952, Table 29). The classical divergence in the wing measurement technique between North American (chord or unstretched) and European (stretched) workers may also cause discrepancies of 2 to 5% in the figures obtained, a difference that often exceeds reported size differences between described subspecies. [See Asbirk (1979a) for further discussion of this subject.]

Another cause for the current confusion in our understanding of geographic variation can be imputed to the inadequacy of museum collections. Many, if not most, of the specimen series upon which the original descriptions were based were strongly biased as to origin (often, one locality only for a race ranging over hundreds of thousands of square kilometres), as to age or as to season. A few examples will suffice to illustrate this point. Thus, the existence of a double gap along the Norwegian coastline in *Uria aalge* (*aalge* to Vesteralen and *hyperborea* north of that point) and in *Fratercula arctica* (*grabae* off Stavanger and *arctica* north and west along the coast) was judged from the examination of 28 murre specimens and 38 puffins (Salomonsen 1944); many if not most of these birds were in winter plumage and could then originate from Bjørnøya, the White Sea or elsewhere in the eastern Atlantic and should not have been used in the circumstance. [See Pethon (1967) for a discussion of this situation.] The need for further examination and comparison of Dovekies from Spitsbergen and especially the Soviet Arctic before concluding to the validity of *alle–polaris* has been made clear in the body of the text. Finally, the case of *Fratercula* studied by Petersen (1976a) is also revealing: the presence in the museums of continental Europe of puffins collected mainly in northern Iceland led workers to think that all Icelandic puffins belonged to the small *arctica* set until Petersen showed that the body measurements of puffins from the southern and northern coasts of this country were very different. In fact, it looks as though a zoogeographic barrier or discontinuity of some importance runs across Iceland separating the warm, Gulf-stream-influenced Southwest and the cold, arctic-waters-influenced North and Northeast, a fact which early students failed to appreciate in view of insufficient material. Besides *Fratercula, Uria aalge* might well illustrate this point: the proportion of bridled birds is generally lower than 10% on the north coasts of Iceland, ranges between 7.3 and 22.3% on the west coast and between 22.3 and 52.8% on the south coast (Fisher and Lockley 1954; Southern 1962; Einarsson 1979). This proportion is a very stable trait within a population (Southern 1966) and such extreme differences between colonies a few hundred kilometres apart could be an indication of the existence of such a discontinuity. Similar trends in other species (A. Petersen, personal communication) lead to the same conclusions. It should not be concluded that only the Icelandic birds are poorly represented in museum collections: so are those from eastern Greenland, Jan Mayen, Bjørnøya, Spitsbergen and the Canadian Arctic.

Furthermore, several of the characteristics selected to diagnose races were, in my opinion, of dubious value. Some varied in the most erratic fashion, such as the 'white on the wing' character used for the Black Guillemot [introduced by Salomonsen (1944) and later used by Storer (1952) and Asbirk (1979a)]. The degree of streaking on the sides and the number and size of spots on the underwing of the murres are also very poor and erratically variable characters [see Pethon (1967) for convincing evidence on that matter] that cannot easily be measured for they are impossible to examine on museum specimens. Finally, several descriptions of North Atlantic races include appreciation of subtle clines in hue or shade (especially the darkness of the back in murres and the degree of whiteness of the winter plumage in the Black Guillemot). Some of these trends may be real, but I argue that it is imperative that birds in comparable plumage condition be used for such comparisons and that the birds borrowed from appropriate institutions be brought to one location in order to reduce the subjective overtones of statements referring to this set of characters. No reviewer of the geographic variation in the North Atlantic Alcidae has deemed necessary to do so and most have generally been content with examining specimens from their own corner of the Atlantic basin. Thus, Storer (1952) reviewed birds from North American collections while Glutz von Blotzheim *et al.* (1982) revised the group on the basis of specimens in European (non-Soviet) institutions. What is really needed is an intensive review by a single investigator of specimens borrowed from all parts of the range.

As fresh ecological data accumulate, we are also compelled to revise many of our old and cherished views. Thus, the Black Guillemot was supposed to be a rather sedentary form and as a consequence, has differentiated more broadly (Salomonsen 1944; Kaftanovskii 1951; Storer 1952). But there is no *a priori* reason this species should be any more sedentary than any other of the inshore ducks, cormorants and gulls that share the same habitat. Actually, one might even turn this old argument around and suggest that its predilection for inshore waters might even force it (despite its ability to content itself with leads in the ice for several winter months: Uspenski 1956) to migrate more than other alcid species (at least *mandtii*) because in the northern part of its range, at least, the winter ice conditions must deprive it of much of its foraging domain. In fact, Renaud and Bradstreet (1980) claim that the percentage of the Black Guillemot population that winters in the high arctic is very small. Petersen (1977) has also reported *C. g. mandtii* in Iceland in winter while Mead (1974) has reported a Swedish juvenile in the British Isles as has Myrberget (1973a), clear evidence of important southerly movements by *Cepphus* during the winter in Scandinavia. Finally, recent banding recoveries reveal that some birds from western Iceland winter along the southwestern and eastern Greenland coasts (Petersen 1977, 1981: five recoveries so far), a rather perplexing find since the west Greenland birds themselves are seen as sedentary (Salomonsen 1967).

What of clinal variation among North Atlantic auks? Are there general patterns that can be extracted? Do the auks that present such clinal tendencies in size respond to the same environmental factors and in the same fashion? Salomonsen (1965, 1967) has been a fervent proponent of the existence of a narrow relationship between latitude on the one hand and size and colouration in several seabirds on the other. He applied this concept to *Fulmarus glacialis* (Salomonsen 1965) and concluded that there existed a very 'zonal' relationship in that species between such morphological attributes and latitude: small-bodied, dark fulmars in the high-arctic belt and large-billed light ones in the boreal province with intermediate forms in the low-arctic belt. Another of Salomonsen's examples (1944, 1972a) was the Atlantic Puffin, which has a very short wing (165 mm) in the Channel Islands, at the extreme southeast of its North Atlantic range, and a very long one (195 mm) in Spitsbergen and in northwestern Greenland. Measurements from nearly a dozen localities in between are seen to fall along a very regular size gradient from boreal through the low-arctic to the high-arctic province. Without wishing to falsify this interesting relationship, I want to mention nevertheless that it contains perhaps more 'noise' than initially thought. Thus, the Icelandic situation described above as well as that depicted for size variation between British colonies increase considerably the confidence limits of the relationship.

This general model, however, of an increase in size in a northerly direction is not universal, at least among the alcids: just as a reminder, the wing length of the puffin increases northwards along the Norwegian coast while that of the Black Guillemot decreases. The wing length of the Thick-billed Murre decreases substantially northwards in the western Atlantic while it increases in the related Common Murre along the same shores. Thus, every single case must be carefully examined and new material will often be needed before we come to an understanding of these clinal relationships in the northern auks. In a careful and exhaustive study, Jehl and Bond (1975) found a weak cline in the *Synthliboramphus–Endomychura* evolutionary unit of the North Pacific between a large (long-winged and long-legged) but short- and deep-billed murrelet in the north (*S.*) to a small but longer- and thinner-billed one in the south.

One trend that seems fairly consistent is for northern populations of Black Guillemots to increase the proportion of white in their winter plumage. One pattern that also seems to be general is the existence of a gap in the auk populations of Norway and Fenno-Scandia on the one hand and those of Spitsbergen and Novaya Zemlya on the other (well shown in *Cepphus* and *Fratercula* at least). A gap between the North Sea and the Baltic exists in the case of *Cepphus* but had to be abandoned in the case of *Uria* (*a. aalge*) and *Alca* (*t. torda*) for lack of sufficient differentiation and despite a very propitious Quaternary history. Another pattern seems to be that birds from Franz Josef Land, the New Siberian Islands and the Soviet Arctic (*Alle, U. lomvia*) differ apparently quite substantially from their closest Atlantic relatives. Perhaps these birds and their local races (*polaris, eleonorae* and *heckeri*) are truly typical of the Arctic Ocean and

relate more to the Pacific basin than to the Atlantic. The center of differentiation of the Faeroe Islands (*U.a. spiloptera* and *C.g. faeroensis*) also
had to be abandoned for lack of sufficiently clear diagnostic characteristics among its alcid inhabitants.

In conclusion, very few of the 20 subspecies of North Atlantic auks can
be recognized from each other with a reasonable degree of accuracy, let
alone with compliance with the generally accepted rules of taxonomic
procedure (the '75% rule', Mayr 1969). If I were to produce a list of those
forms which I feel can be safely recognized, I would be propagating the
same weakness which I condemn, for I would have to base my own
assessment on published accounts or inadequate museum material and
diagnoses which I feel are genuinely biased and/or incomplete. One fundamental contradiction seems to underlie this whole attempt at ordering
variation among Atlantic auks. Every single alcid student has recognized
the existence of important and, in some cases, very pronounced clinal
tendencies in several of the measured characters, yet have attempted to
superimpose upon such clinally varying groups, some artifical *a priori*
envelopes or sets. Actually, it serves no useful purpose in my opinion to
assign the name *islandicus* to the Black Guillemot of Iceland, for instance.
Besides being unjustified in this particular case (the character is neither
quantifiable nor exclusive), this manner of doing can also become a binding concept and it may even hamper our recognition of the fact that this
population is evolving and exchanging with neighbouring ones in a series
of processes (migration, etc.) that can become the object of exciting
studies.

As a reaction to over-splitting tendencies of past workers, Myrberget
(1963) and Pethon (1967) have suggested that most alcids should be recognized when the identity of a given population is in doubt, by the nomen-
clatural technique (B.O.U., 1956) of giving to it the name that includes the
assigned subspecific names for the two extreme ends of the cline. For
instance, Pethon recommends that the puffin from the Norwegian coast
be designated *Fratercula arctica* cl. *grabae/naumanni*. But giving such a
cumbersome name to a population does not increase our understanding
either. As we have seen, within the alcid family, the clinal tendencies
operate in every possible direction and these directions within a given
species may often diverge for two different structures while a third one
may remain unaffected by geographic position.

I contend therefore that for the next several years, or until such a time
when museum collections have vastly improved and until ecologically
meaningful data on movements, moult, breeding season, pair formation,
and so on, have been assembled and until bird taxonomists are in a position to standardize and expand their comparisons, the North Atlantic

auks, without exception, are better identified by reference to their colony of origin, without reference whatsoever to artificial and really misleading categories.

VII. MOULT

Several students have written about the moult in Alcidae (Verwey 1922, 1924; Salomonsen 1944; Stresemann and Stresemann 1966; Birkhead and Taylor 1977; Bédard and Sealy 1985); but none of these contributions can be considered to be definitive. The great scarcity of good museum material may be only one cause for our present ignorance in this area of alcid biology. Intrinsic complexity of the moult pattern in this family in which all species have a huge geographic range and where all exhibit long-deferred sexual maturity may be another. In the discussion that follows, I have adopted Humphrey and Parkes' (1959) system of classifying moults and plumages.

A. Plumage Succession

The overall appearance of the North Atlantic Alcidae does not change markedly from summer to winter, with the exception of *Cepphus* in which the jet black summer colouration disappears under a whitish, salt-and-pepper winter dress. In *Alle, Alca, Uria* (and *Pinguinus*), the lower sides of the face and the underside of the neck are the only areas that turn from black to white between summer and winter. Finally, in *Fratercula*, the winter plumage is darker than the summer plumage, as a dark brown or greyish facial patch develops around the eye just at the close of the breeding season that persists for the duration of the winter along with the broad black neck collar.

Facial ornaments disappear in *Fratercula* following a spectacular moult of the bill plates (Coues 1868; Bureau 1877, 1879) and of the horny, vermilion eye ring and a fading and shrinking of the lemon-yellow rictus. In *Uria lomvia*, the white 'gape marks' fade more-or-less completely (Tuck 1961) while in *Alca*, an important thinning of the bill occurs in early fall, following the shedding of the bill covering; the elegant white furrow remains, however. In *Fratercula*, the legs turn from brilliant orange to dull yellow while in *Cepphus*, they turn from scarlet red to pale reddish.

Four of the living species (*Alca torda, Uria aalge, U. lomvia, Alle alle*) have partial pre-alternate (pre-nuptial) moult in the spring which involves the face and throat areas and a complete pre-basic (post-nuptial) moult in the fall involving all the contour and flight feathers. A fifth species, *Cep-*

phus grylle, has a more extensive feather growth in the spring which brings it from a predominantly white winter dress to an almost black summer one. But there is evidence that only a part of the body covering is involved despite the very pronounced change in appearance that results. Following the breeding season, this species also undergoes a total pre-basic moult involving both flight and contour feathers. The last living North Atlantic auk, *Fratercula arctica,* apparently conforms to no established scheme and its rather unusual moult pattern will be reviewed below.

All living auks of the North Atlantic go through a period of flightlessness because during the moult, the flight feathers are dropped and replaced simultaneously. The case of *Pinguinus* with its progressive moult of the primaries (Salomonsen 1945) remains a perplexing case, but, unfortunately, we will never be able to do more than speculate on the biological reasons for this situation. The duration of the flightless period has been estimated at 45 to 50 days (Birkhead and Taylor 1977) in captive *Uria aalge,* but is presumably shorter in wild individuals. As a rule, one might expect that there will be compelling reasons for shortening the duration of flightlessness: the daily need to move to shifting feeding grounds, in some cases the need to undertake fairly extensive 'migratory' movements—although Gaston (1980) has shown that flightless birds may move over considerable distances—and in some cases, the need to steer away from shores and assorted dangers could represent real biological pressures. The momentary loss of flight feathers probably does not hamper at all the underwater 'flight' efficiency, as has been convincingly argued by Storer (1960), at least in larger auks.

1. DOVEKIE, *ALLE ALLE*

The fledgling leaves land at about 75% of adult weight (Norderhaug 1980) dressed like a diminutive adult Dovekie, complete with superciliary white spot, white-tipped secondaries and white spots in the tertiaries. These contrasting markings may have a social function. Stempniewicz (1981) believes that the similarity between the juvenal and adult plumages has a role in lowering predation pressure by gulls on land. This juvenal plumage is changed almost immediately (Kozlova 1957) to a first basic plumage through a partial, first pre-basic moult involving the lower face and throat areas. During the first winter, it is certainly still possible to distinguish such individuals from older ones by bill dimensions and presumably also by the fluffy character of the plumage and by the down mark at the tip of individual feathers.

Although this has not been confirmed by banding recoveries, the bulk of yearling Dovekies probably stay away from the breeding colonies during the first summer following hatching. Those few that are collected on the breeding sites or at sea have a first-alternate plumage which they must have acquired sometime in April and May and is characterized by extremely worn and faded flight feathers and upper wing coverts. This wear is in fact diagnostic but its causes are obscure. These feathers, parts of the juvenal plumage, have been worn for only 4–8 weeks longer than the similar feathers in adult birds and the latter do not exhibit such wear. These yearlings presumably undergo a complete definitive pre-basic moult sometime in late July and early August, probably a bit earlier than the adults from which they will no longer be distinguishable.

The adults, following the departure of the semi-independent young, will undergo an apparently very rapid moult: flightlessness occurs in the neighbourhood of the breeding sites and the definitive basic plumage is probably complete by early October. An adult female collected in Scoresby Sound on the west coast of Greenland (No. 53,024 in the Zoological Museum of the University of Copenhagen) has a new wing and is turning to winter plumage by 15 September. Another, an adult male, collected near Godhavn on 30 October (No. 55,190 in the Zoological Museum of the University of Copenhagen), has not quite completed its pre-basic moult. Uspenski (1956) quotes early observations on Novaya Zemlya according to which the pre-basic moult was completed by 12 September while his own observations indicated a somewhat later date.

2. RAZORBILL, *ALCA TORDA*

The young of the Razorbill leaves the breeding site at about 20% of the adult weight (Plumb 1965; Bédard 1969d) and dressed in a temporary juvenal feather coat without remiges and rectrices which will immediately intergrade into a first basic plumage. In this first winter dress, the 3- to 8-month-old Razorbill is still recognizable by its shorter wing, the texture of its plumage and its overall size.

What follows afterwards has been aptly described by Verwey (1922), Salomonsen (1944) and Kozlova (1957) and resembles closely what I have described in *Alle*: briefly, the first alternate plumage is acquired 1–2 months later (May) than in the adults (March and April) and the complete definitive pre-basic moult leading to the definitive basic plumage supervenes earlier than in adults. Thereafter, the maturing bird will adopt a moult schedule that comes to resemble more and more that of its breeding adult congeners and this adjustment will spread over the following 2–4 years (Chapter 5, this volume).

3. THICK-BILLED MURRE, *URIA LOMVIA*

The shift from juvenal to first basic to first alternate to definitive basic is similar in this species to that already described in *Alca* and the mentioned delays between breeding adults and subadults also apply. The partial definitive pre-alternate moult involving the throat and face feathers in birds in their second year after hatching and in older individuals occurs sometimes during April (Salomonsen 1944). An intriguing reference in Uspenski (1956) suggests that the bulk of first-year birds remain at sea and retain the white winter pattern on the cheeks. Thus, contrary to evidence obtained by Verwey (1922) and others, there would be no first alternate plumage but rather a direct transition from first basic to definitive basic plumage, sometime during June and July.

4. COMMON MURRE, *URIA AALGE*

The situation here resembles in every respect that just described in *U. lomvia* with, however, one major distinction: in the most southerly populations, the adult birds undertake the partial pre-alternate moult immediately following completion of the total pre-basic moult in the fall. Thus, birds in alternate plumage may be found visiting British colonies as early as October and November (Birkhead 1976a). But available evidence indicates that a gap, whose duration probably increases as one moves towards the north, exists between these two moulting episodes. Thus, the Common Murres of Novaya Zemlya probably do not undertake their pre-alternate moult until late winter or early spring, since arrival at these arctic colonies does not occur until early May (Uspenski 1956; Belopol'skii 1957). According to Salomonsen (1944), the body moult takes place before the wing and tail moult, but this is not well documented. Actually, several reports indicate rather that the birds become flightless almost immediately after leaving the colonies, at which time the body moult cannot have progressed very far. The situation may further differ among the sexes, since the males are known to accompany the fledgling at sea and females may indulge in an earlier moult.

5. BLACK GUILLEMOT, *CEPPHUS GRYLLE*

Near-adult size is attained on the breeding site by the young of this species. But the juvenal plumage worn upon departure (Asbirk 1979a) begins to grade almost immediately into a paler first basic plumage. In fact, we may even wonder whether the slight change in aspect between these two successive feather coats is not the result of a continuing, uninterrupted moult. In the following spring—late April to June, according to Petersen (1981)—the yearling bird will adopt a very adult-like black first alternate plumage whose diagnostic trait will be the presence of brownish spots in the otherwise white wing mirror (Asbirk 1979a; Petersen 1981). But the persistence of some brown juvenile feathers in the mirror in known-age adults militates against the use of this sole trait to identify 2-year-old individuals as has been done by Asbirk (1979a). Some yearlings may also retain a sprinkling of white feathers in the breast and throat areas, but this is not exclusive to this age category for known-age breeding adults may also exhibit such a trait (Asbirk 1979a; Petersen 1981). Another trait will also tell apart yearling *Cepphus* from adult birds at a glance, namely the extreme wear and discolouration of the flight feathers and of the upper part of the wing. This trait was beautifully displayed in a sizable collection of marked year-old individuals assembled by Aevar Petersen in Iceland and now in the drawers of the Museum of Natural History at Reykjavík. Thus, the moult in late summer of the first year following hatching will lead to a definitive basic plumage that will be changed to a definitive alternate in the period March to May (depending on location) of the second year following hatching. According to Petersen (1981), most Black Guillemots start breeding when 4 years old, although some may start when 3 or even 2. When at the breeding station during their first complete summer, yearlings sometimes defend a breeding site, but do not attempt to reproduce.

In late summer and fall, body moult begins before the flight feathers are shed (Salomonsen 1944; Petersen 1981); the reasons for this are not clear. The whole process seems to be completed by the beginning of December (Salomonsen 1944).

6. ATLANTIC PUFFIN, *FRATERCULA ARCTICA*

The moult pattern in this species is truly unusual, not only by comparison to other members of the family, but by comparison to other birds as well. Important contradictions and outright confusion still exists on the question of the moult in this species, despite the contributions and comments of Salomonsen (1944), Lockley (1953a), Myrberget (1963), Stresemann and Stresemann (1966) and especially Harris and Yule (1977).

The fledgling retains its juvenal plumage throughout the first winter (Salomonsen 1944; Lockley 1953a). These birds will then undertake a partial moult involving the flight feathers between March and May of the year following hatching, for birds of the British Isles (Harris and Yule 1977), and somewhat later for individuals of more northerly populations and of the western Atlantic. Stresemann and Stresemann (1966) also obtained evidence that the flight feathers are replaced as early as 8 months following their acquisition (sometimes in March or April). According to these workers, these same individuals undergoing the spring moult of the flight feathers would moult again later in the same year, in November–December, and from then on, remain in step with the moult schedule of adult birds. But the evidence for such a pattern is not complete. In this connection, Swennen (1977) noted that four of five 'young' captive puffins moulted their primaries in January–March (hence, when about 7 to 9 months old) and then again in the following fall (August–October). The data are fragmentary, but it appears that the pattern was repeated during the second year of captive life while in the third year, and presumably thereafter, only the fall moult of the primaries and secondaries subsisted. Thus, the conflicting evidence put forward by some workers showing that most of the flight feathers moult takes place between November and January (Lockley 1953a; Myrberget 1963; Stresemann and Stresemann 1966) or October through April (Salomonsen 1944; Harris and Yule 1977) could stem from the existence of this very peculiar age-related moult pattern.

The only observation upon which all workers agree is that very soon after completion of breeding, the beak plates and facial ornaments are shed or lost (Bureau 1877, 1879; Myrberget 1963; Harris and Yule 1977) and the face darkens, especially around the eyes. Harris and Yule (1977) claim that body moult (apparently partial pre-alternate) occurs in late winter and throughout the spring, sometimes continuing into the breeding season. Lockley (1953a), apparently basing his summary on data in Salomonsen (1944), suggests that body moult in adult birds takes place during the fall, a fact not clearly stated in Salomonsen's original writings. Harris and Yule remark that some degree of body moult can be observed in the Atlantic Puffin on specimens collected in almost any month of the year. It is possible that the long-deferred [third to sixth year after hatching—see Harris (1981)] sexual maturity contributes to this great variability in timing of the moult and to the apparent lack of a clear seasonal pattern. After the fourth year, subadults become nearly indistinguishable from breeding adults, but until breeding age, each yearly cohort probably follows its own internal schedule. Since subadults may in fact outnumber the breeding adults and since moulting birds used in the aforementioned studies were, by necessity, obtained in the winter and likely belonged to different populations with distinctive moulting schedules of their own, the complexity of the overall situation is greatly increased. A clear indication of the latter influence is given in Harris and Yule (1977), who interpret that dead beached birds (in moulting condition) found in late March in northeastern British Isles were probably northern birds, for at such a late date, most local (breeding) birds should have been back at their nesting colonies, or should be about to do so, and therefore should not be moulting.

B. Timing of Moult

Profound differences in the timing of the breeding season between localities will be accompanied by appropriate adjustments in the timing of the moult. In some cases, the relationship is fairly clear and direct: thus, early pre-alternate moult in October in the Common Murre of the British Isles is related to a year-round availability of breeding ledges and to a strong social pressure to defend a breeding site. No pressure of this sort is to be expected in the Common Murre of the Vestmannaeyjar, which return to the colonies in February (A. Petersen, personal communication), or in the birds of Novaya Zemlya, which because of ice conditions can get to the neighbourhood of the breeding grounds only 3–4 weeks before laying. Similar instances have been described in *Uria lomvia* by Belopol'skii (1957): the duration of the pre-laying period in that species is about 5 days in the colonies of the Kara Strait, while it extends to nearly 3 months in those of the eastern Murmansk Coast. Though not documented, concurrent adjustments in the timing of the pre-alternate moult in the spring must occur in every one of these populations.

In some instances, the divergence in moult pattern is not due to gross environmental differences in ice cover or general weather. Thus, in *Cepphus,* the endemic Baltic population seems to undergo the spring partial pre-alternate moult a full 2 months later than the nearby populations from southern Sweden, Denmark and Norway. This trait has been underlined by Asbirk (1979a) and is generally taken as one further sign of limited gene exchange between these populations. Salomonsen's suggestion that this difference is a response to lower water temperatures in the Baltic is a possible explanation. One might remark though, that if this is so, an earlier pre-basic moult in the warmer waters of this enclosed basin might be expected in the late summer–early fall, if at all compatible with the local breeding schedule. There is no evidence that such a response is occurring.

C. Moult and Breeding

Bédard and Sealy (1985) have observed that some overlap between breeding and moulting occurred in the small *Aethia* of the Bering Sea. In *A. cristatella,* breeding adults without any sign of body moult were obtained only during a short period of about 4 weeks in June and early July (courtship and laying). Otherwise, moult activity was considerable and by mid-August (middle of the nestling stage), more than half of the birds displayed sometimes intensive body moult and always appreciable degrees of (descendant) wing moult. A less pronounced overlap was found in *A. pusilla*. A similar situation has been described in *Ptychoramphus aleuticus* by Payne (1965), who also discussed at length (Payne 1972) the implications of this biological phenomenon.

In the North Atlantic, no such overlap during the terrestrial part of the breeding cycle has been found, except in *Fratercula*. Birds of that species handled on the breeding grounds almost always display some degree of body moult and sometimes completion of flight feather replacement as well (Harris and Yule 1977). But in this species, the bioenergetic implications of such minor overlap between these two energy-demanding activities are probably slight, or at least they do not appear to be as important as they seem to be in *Aethia cristatella*, for instance. But studies in northerly populations of that species may turn out to be very instructive in that respect.

D. Moult and Migration

Few North Atlantic alcids perform extensive, tightly scheduled migrations of the type encountered in shorebirds or terns [but see Mead (1974) and also Lloyd (1976a) and Chapter 9, this volume] and little evidence of critical adjustments between these two life-cycle processes has been forthcoming. In *Uria* spp. of Newfoundland, both the fledgling and the flightless adults leave the surroundings of the breeding colonies and swim northwards along the Labrador coast for some weeks at least. A similar northerly movement has been described in the Razorbill of the North Shore of the Gulf of St. Lawrence (Bédard 1969d). But the ecological significance of such local, small-amplitude geographic shifts has not yet been demonstrated.

It seems to be otherwise in *Uria lomvia* and *Alle alle* though, especially in populations from Spitsbergen, Murmansk and Novaya Zemlya which undergo, soon after breeding, a trans-Atlantic crossing of some regularity and significance (well depicted in Salomonsen 1967, Figs. 11 and 12). Not surprisingly, the Dovekie seems literally to 'rush' into the pre-basic moult. The flightlessness that may last most of August and part of September certainly precedes the movement, be the latter a slow drift or a concentrated and highly directional movement that will bring these birds to the west coast of Greenland (Norderhaug 1967). There is possibly an adaptation there but the interpretation is subjective. In the same two species of the west Greenland coast, the flightless birds apparently drift across the Davis Strait and then southwards towards northern Newfoundland and the Grand Banks wintering areas (Evans 1981a). The case of the Dovekie is probably the only one among the Atlantic auks which might reveal a real connection between the timing of the moult and migration. In most other species, the connection is probably loose and not particularly stressful for the bird.

It is worth noting that, contrary to earlier beliefs according to which the Thick-billed Murres of Novaya Zemlya and the Barents Sea colonies did not perform more than short-range migrations (Uspenski 1956), recent banding recoveries suggest rather the existence of impressive trans-Atlantic movements similar to those described in *Alle*. Analogous pressure on the moulting schedule may therefore exist also in the Thick-billed Murre, although Uspenski (1956) mentions that the heavy pre-basic moult seems to take place in October, at a time when *Alle* has apparently moved out of the Barents Sea. Salomonsen mentions that these European *lomvia* reach Greenland by November. The spring pre-alternate moult also seems to be relatively precocious (February) even in the northerly populations studied by Uspenski.

E. Discussion

Stresemann and Stresemann (1966) have proposed that throughout its evolutionary history, the family Alcidae was at first characterized by small forms that retained the power of flight during the moult of the flight feathers. Thus, the development of synchronous wing moult, together with its consequent flightlessness, appeared as larger forms evolved (that this is an unlikely possibility is borne out by the fact that the small *Alle*, *Brachyramphus* and *Synthliboramphus* all have simultaneous wing moult!: in the latter, where critical wing-loading intervenes, a protracted wing moult with even a slight reduction in aerial flight capabilities would be worse than a condensed and greatly abridged synchronous moult with flightlessness. The loss of most of the wing area is not a handicap for underwater swimming, as has been summarized by Storer (1960) and as can be deduced from the writings of Stettenheim (1959), for the loss of wing area means improved underwater efficiency. There remain a number of obscure points, however: the presence of progressive wing moult in the large extinct *Pinguinus* is difficult to account for as is the synchronous wing moult in the small *Alle*. The failure of *Alle* to conform to the general pattern of progressive wing moult encountered in its small-body-size North Pacific counterparts (*Ptychoramphus* and *Aethia*) is not easily accounted for either. One may note, however, that *Alle*, with its high-arctic distribution has been under considerable pressure to shorten its breeding cycle as much as possible. I have discussed this question elsewhere (Bédard 1976) and have shown that a shortening of the nestling stage was apparent in that species. Nothing of the sort is certainly apparent in *Ptychoramphus*, where the protracted breeding season may extend over 4 months and where double-brooding even occurs (Manuwal 1972). In *Aethia cristatella*, nesting in the northern part of its range, there is some evidence for the need of rather tight adjustments between the moult cycle and the breeding cycle (Bédard and Sealy 1984). But the solution adopted seems to be to tolerate some overlap between the two cycles while maintaining flight capability throughout.

The complex moult cycle of *Fratercula* is far from being adequately described, let alone understood. It offers, however, an interesting challenge and if approached in a comparative frame of mind, simultaneous investigations of *Fratercula corniculata* and *Lunda cirrhata* of the North Pacific with puffins of the North Atlantic might turn out to be most instructive.

The presence of a distinctive juvenal plumage in *Cepphus*, *Alca*, *Uria* and *Alle*, a situation which may appear puzzling from a bioenergetics viewpoint, may very well be a non-problem. Perhaps we want to find two distinct moulting episodes bearing two different names while in practice, only one may exist. It may very well be that the juvenile leaving the nest never stops growing feathers in a continuous process until it reaches its first complete winter dress (first basic). In *Alca* and *Uria*, where the body mass changes markedly over the few weeks that immediately follow nest departure (from about 150 g to 700–1000 g in 4 to 6 weeks), appropriate and constant adjustments in the extent and character of the feather coat is mandatory. But in *Cepphus*, the presumed or inferred existence of a true juvenal plumage may constitute merely a phase of continuous plumage development and our difficulty in understanding it be more semantic than bioenergetic. A situation similar to that in *Alca* and *Uria* may prevail in *Alle alle*, where the body mass also requires considerable adjustments. But the speed at which the change from juvenal to 'winter' plumage takes place is not known at this time. Collection of known-age birds at sea to elucidate many of these questions would be needed as would be the rearing in captivity of juveniles of all North Atlantic species.

CHAPTER 2

Distribution and Status of the Atlantic Alcidae[1]

DAVID N. NETTLESHIP

Seabird Research Unit, Canadian Wildlife Service, Bedford Institute of Oceanography, Dartmouth, Nova Scotia, Canada

PETER G. H. EVANS

Edward Grey Institute of Field Ornithology, Department of Zoology, University of Oxford, Oxford, England

[1] This chapter was prepared in association with the program "Studies on Northern Seabirds", Seabird Research Unit, Canadian Wildlife Service, Environment Canada (Report No. 162).

53

I. INTRODUCTION

This chapter describes the distribution and numbers of the seven alcid species (six living, one recently extinct) in the North Atlantic, by examining what is known of the sizes and geographic ranges of breeding populations and their present status in relation to recent changes. Of the alcids occupying the Atlantic, only the Common Murre and the Thick-billed Murre also breed in the Pacific Ocean. The Razorbill, Dovekie, Black Guillemot, Atlantic Puffin and the now extinct Great Auk are confined to the Atlantic and parts of the Arctic Ocean. The earliest detailed review of the family Alcidae was by Coues (1868), but that authoritative work was largely taxonomic. A number of multi- or single-species studies followed (Bureau 1879; Grieve 1885), but the first thorough account of the Atlantic Alcidae was that by Salomonsen (1944), who reviewed their geographic variation and seasonal distributions. That classic study formed the basis of knowledge of the distribution of the whole group occupying the Atlantic and adjacent waters. Other studies soon followed, including more detailed examinations of individual alcid species or genera (Storer 1945, 1952), as well as general reviews of their biology (Lockley 1953a; Fisher and Lockley 1954; Belopol'skii 1957; Tuck 1961). Those studies and additional data from regional avifaunal surveys and geographic summaries (Salomonsen 1935, 1950; Witherby *et al.* 1941; Baxter and Rintoul 1953; Uspenski 1956; Kozlova 1957; Kartaschew 1960; Bannerman 1963; Løvenskiold 1964) formed a reasonably complete picture of the breeding distribution of species in the North Atlantic, but information on the abundance of species was far from complete and mainly limited to orders of magnitude. The pioneering efforts to generate estimates of total world population sizes by Lockley (1953a) for Atlantic Puffin and by Tuck (1961) for both murre species were important first steps in assessing bird numbers and possible relationships with certain marine regions. However, data on colony sizes were very incomplete even in areas now easily accessible, and many concentrations of breeding birds in more distant and remote regions, such as the Arctic, were still not known to science.

Recently, interest in seabirds, especially the auks, increased, largely owing to their relative vulnerability to man-made disturbances in marine waters and the general decrease in population sizes (Bourne 1972, 1976; Nettleship 1977a), and opportunities to investigate patterns of distribution and abundance of alcids have become far more numerous. Several intensive surveys of seabirds have been made since the mid-1960s, culminating in detailed regional reviews covering major geographic areas (Cramp *et al.* 1974; Brown *et al.* 1975; Nettleship and Smith 1975; Yeatman 1976, Norderhaug *et al.* 1977; Salomonsen 1979a; Guermeur and Monnat 1980; Nettleship 1980; Henry and Monnat 1981) and general accounts for individual species (Harris 1976a; Lloyd 1976b). Information on distribution is still incomplete for most northern areas (e.g., Greenland, Iceland, Jan Mayen, Svalbard, Franz Josef Land), and estimates of the sizes of populations in many other areas are not completely satisfactory because of limitations of census techniques, but present data on species populations and numbers are vastly improved over 20 years ago. Further refinement of census methodologies and more complete surveys will follow, but a summary of the existing literature and collected records on the distribution and abundance of the Atlantic Alcidae should reveal what research and development still is needed. Furthermore, this chapter should also put into perspective the magnitude of recent changes in status of species occupying certain marine areas and allow an assessment of possible causal relationships and limiting factors. Although the preliminary hypotheses may prove incorrect or inconclusive, they should direct effort towards more thorough research on the ecology and interrelationships of species. That in turn should lead to a better understanding of population characteristics and to more careful analysis of the biological significance of population changes that have already taken place and that are now occurring.

The description of the present distribution, abundance and status of species is dictated largely by anticipated uses of the information. Each species is identified by its recognized vernacular and scientific names (using the nomenclature of the 1957 American Ornithologists' Union Checklist and more recent supplements), followed by a short summary of the world distribution and faunal classification (see below for terminology). The full details of distribution, abundance and status are then presented in two sections which form the major part of each species review.

A. Breeding Distribution and Abundance

This section gives the distribution and estimated size of the total breeding population in the Atlantic and adjacent waters (includes Baffin Bay and adjacent channels, Greenland and Barents Seas north to Svalbard and Franz Josef Land, east to Novaya Zemlya, and south to the Mediterranean Sea and the Gulf of Maine), including the relative abundance in the geographic areas that make up the breeding range within the Atlantic, and the numerical distribution in relation to marine zones.

B. Regional Populations and Status

This section summarizes the breeding distribution, numbers and status in each geographic region.

The information is summarized in the species tables, where the most recent population data on distribution and bird numbers are summarized by geographic region, with survey dates and sources of the estimates for each area. The tables are supplemented by the species maps which show the breeding distribution in the North Atlantic and how it relates to the zonation of the marine environment.

Several difficulties were encountered in the preparation of the species reviews. First was the disparity of information available. Details on the relatively well-studied murres, Razorbills and Atlantic Puffins were relatively adequate, but the information on Dovekies and Black Guillemots was very sketchy and incomplete, so that the population estimates are no more than informed guesses. In the case of the Great Auk, much of the meagre historical information is necessarily speculative except at specific sites where that bird was known to have bred. Although provisional estimates must be used with caution, they provide a fair reflection of each species' relative abundance in different geographic areas.

Even where survey information was complete, it was essential to standardize the units (individuals or pairs) used by investigators to report their census results. Most estimates were given in 'numbers of breeding pairs' following conventional census methodologies (Nettleship 1976a; Birkhead and Nettleship 1980); values presented as 'numbers of birds or individuals' were converted to pairs by applying correction factors (Nettleship 1976a; Birkhead and Nettleship 1980) appropriate for the species, date, and geographic area involved, which ranged from 0.60 for Razorbills (Lloyd 1976b) and 0.67 for Common Murres (Stowe and Harris 1984; P. G. H. Evans, unpublished observations) in the British Isles, to 0.75 for Thick-billed Murres in arctic Canada (Gaston and Nettleship 1981). Details of procedures used to make rough estimates of the birds present in areas where census information was limited or non-existent are given directly in the regional accounts. The population figures given have been rounded off and orders of magnitude have been used where complete survey data are not yet available: order 1, 1–10 pairs; order 2, 11–100 pairs; order 3, 101–1000 pairs; order 4, 1001–10,000 pairs; order 5, 10,001–100,000 pairs; order 6, 100,001–1 million pairs; and order 7, >1 million pairs.

A major difficulty in a work such as this is to review changes in population status where much of the historical information is qualitative or fragmentary. However, no review of the Atlantic Alcidae would be complete without some outline of the dramatic numerical and geographic changes in species populations known to have taken place in this century and during the 1800s. Some of the historic information is complete and straightforward, but much is not. In the present chapter, the widely scattered literature has been brought together to form a preliminary base of information on population status. In some cases this has led to descriptive reviews which may seem excessively lengthy, but it was determined not only by the amount of information available but also by the need to qualify old population information in the light of subsequent works. Although the status summaries have sometimes led to incomplete and unsatisfactory conclusions, for example, in the identification of possible causes of the changes in bird numbers, they do provide starting points from which to work towards fuller and more complete histories of species populations in the North Atlantic.

The meanings of certain terms used in the species summaries are defined as follows: *breeding range* covers the geographic range within which a species is known to breed regularly; *breeding area* describes an island or length of coast where alcids breed; and a *breeding station* is a colony or location where birds are known to reproduce. The term *colony* is used quite loosely for a group or aggregation of breeding conspecifics, ranging in size from only a few pairs to hundreds of thousands. Small and large aggregations are differentiated by referring to the former as breeding groups and the latter as colonies.

II. MARINE ENVIRONMENT OF THE NORTH ATLANTIC

The physical properties (notably, sea-surface temperature, salinity, ice cover) of the upper water layers (less than ca. 25 m depth) of the sea affect the distribution of seabirds as discussed by numerous researchers, particularly Murphy (1936), Fisher and Lockley (1954), Serventy (1960), Bourne (1963), Salomonsen (1965, 1972a) and Ashmole (1971). The breeding distributions of alcids in the North Atlantic are closely correlated with the occurrence and interactions of two water masses: *Polar* water from the Arctic Ocean and *Atlantic* water from the central North Atlantic. Areas of greatest marine productivity appear to occur close to convergences of these water masses and associated with upwellings and convection currents along the coasts and around islands. The greatest concentrations of birds are found both at colonies during summer and at sea outside the breeding season, in these areas. The following summary of the principal circulation patterns in the North Atlantic is based on Sverdrup *et al.* (1942), Bailey *et al.* (1954), Mosby (1960), Sømme (1960), Hachey (1961), Collin and Dunbar (1964), Cushing (1971), Meserve (1974), and Norderhaug *et al.* (1977).

The oceanographic zonation of the North Atlantic Ocean is determined

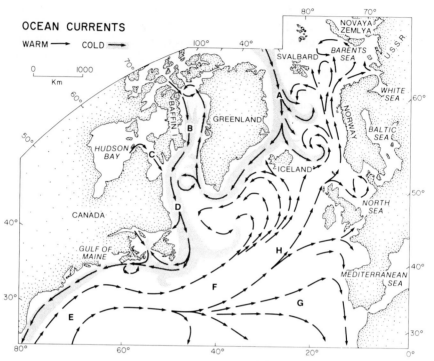

Fig. 2.1. Oceanographic zonation as determined by ocean currents (see text) in the North Atlantic and adjacent waters (after Salomonsen 1965, 1972a; Dunbar 1968; Ashmole 1971).

by two major patterns of circulation (Fig. 2.1). The *East Greenland Current* (A), the principal outflow from the Arctic Ocean, brings cold *Polar* water of low salinity into the Greenland Sea and along the whole length of the east coast of Greenland. A lesser outflow through *Baffin Bay* (B) and *Hudson Strait* (C) passes down the east coast of Canada as the *Labrador Current* (D). Farther south, the dominant feature between ca. 15°N and 45°N is a clockwise gyre of warm water which circulates around the Sargasso Sea. The western side of this gyre, the *Gulf Stream* (E), takes warm, highly saline water up the east coast of North America past the southern Grand Banks and continues east, as the *North Atlantic Current* (F), towards Europe. Then, one branch, the *Canary Current* (G), runs south past the coasts of Portugal and northwestern Africa and turns west again towards America at ca. 15°N. A wind-induced upwelling along these coasts at certain seasons brings cool, nutrient-rich water to the surface, which in turn stimulates a very large local coastal production of phytoplankton and zooplankton. The Canary Current is a classic 'eastern boundary upwelling', comparable to, if weaker than, those in the Peru,

California and Benguela Currents. The northern branch of the *North Atlantic Current* (H) flows northeastwards past the west coasts of the British Isles and Norway. Its influence is felt as far north as the west coast of Svalbard, and as far east as the Murmansk Coast and western Novaya Zemlya. A subsidiary branch reaches the south coast of Iceland where it is deflected southwestward by the *East Greenland Current* (A) and then travels as far north as ca. 70°N along the west coast of Greenland. It is the interactions between cold *Polar* water from the Arctic Ocean and the warm water from the tropics that are the primary influence on the distribution of alcids in the North Atlantic.

Ice cover is strongly influenced by those two major current systems (Fig. 2.2). The water masses associated with the North Atlantic Current are warm and free of ice throughout the year. Even such northerly regions as the south half of the west Greenland coast, the Irminger Sea, Iceland, and northeast to west Spitsbergen and east to the Murmansk Coast are ice-free in winter because those waters remain relatively warm. On the

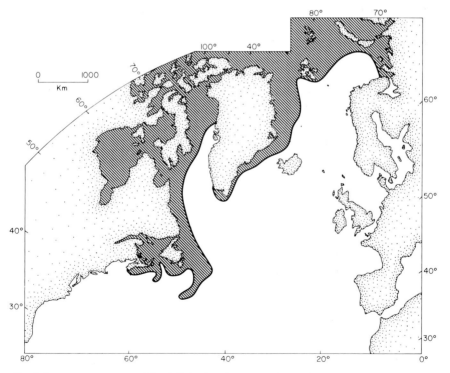

Fig. 2.2.   Average extent of the drift-ice border (hatched areas) in April–May in the North Atlantic.

other hand, in *Polar* water areas such as east Greenland, central Baffin Island and among the Canadian Arctic islands, ice persists through much of the summer. Winter pack-ice occurs as far south as eastern Newfoundland, often extending even farther south in spring (see Fig. 2.2 for limits of drift-ice). The occurrence of ice best contrasts the two sides of the North Atlantic; in the west the cold Arctic Ocean outflow produces a maximum pack-ice limit which extends as far south as Cape Breton (47°N), whereas in the east the warm North Atlantic Current limits ice cover to areas north of ca. 75°N.

Where ice persists into the summer months (in *Polar* water areas such as the central Canadian Arctic islands, central Baffin Island, most of east Greenland, northern Svalbard and Franz Josef Land) there are no large colonies of alcids. With few exceptions, breeding stations are located where the waters become ice-free predictably early enough each year for the birds to be able to fit in their breeding cycle (a minimum of 8 weeks for murres, longer for other species) before environmental conditions required for reproduction deteriorate and winter begins. Thus ice, either directly or indirectly, is one of the more important physical factors determining the northern limits of distribution of auks and other seabirds. [For details see Salomonsen (1950, 1979a), Norderhaug *et al.* (1977) and Brown and Nettleship (1981).]

Salomonsen (1965, 1972a), Dunbar (1968) and Ashmole (1971) have combined temperature–salinity relationships with data on the distribution of marine invertebrates to define four major water zones in the North Atlantic (Fig. 2.3; terminology after Salomonsen 1965):

1. High arctic (Dunbar's 'arctic')—unmixed water of polar origin, with surface layers close to freezing (0–3°C) even in August, the warmest month, and salinity usually below 31‰
2. Low arctic (Dunbar's 'subarctic')—comprising a mixture of high-arctic and boreal water, where the upper water temperatures in August are 4–10°C with salinities 31–34‰
3. Boreal—a broad band formed by the North Atlantic Current, with August surface temperatures 10–19°C, and salinities of 31 to 35‰ (which overlap with those of the low-arctic zone)
4. Cool subtropical (Ashmole's 'subtropical')—the waters immediately south of the boreal zone (south of the North Atlantic Current) where August surface temperatures are usually 19–23°C and salinity is >35‰

The boundaries of the marine zones appear on all the species breeding distribution maps to simplify interpretation of distributions relative to water types. However, although the boundaries are well defined by

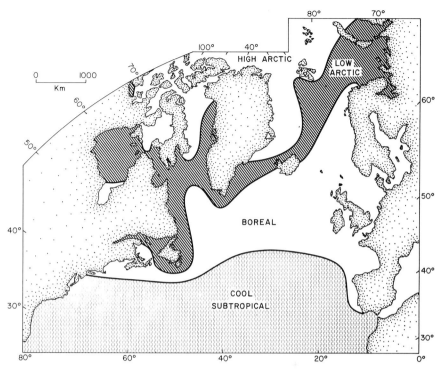

Fig. 2.3.   Oceanographic zonation in the North Atlantic and adjacent waters (after Salomonsen 1965, 1972a; Dunbar 1968; Ashmole 1971).

oceanographic factors, they are not fixed; they fluctuate both seasonally and between years, and are restricted to the surface water (less than ca. 25 m depth).

The Atlantic Alcidae breed only in boreal, low- and high-arctic water areas. Species distributed in all three zones are called *boreo-panarctic,* whereas those occurring only in two zones are referred to as *panarctic* (low and high arctic) or as *boreo-low arctic* (boreal and low arctic).

III. GREAT AUK, *Pinguinus impennis*

Summary: North Atlantic monotypic boreo-low arctic species, extinct since about 1844. Formerly bred on islands in the Gulf of St. Lawrence, east Newfoundland, Iceland, northern Scotland and probably in the Faeroe Islands and a few other sites in both the eastern and western North Atlantic. Wintered offshore, mostly in boreal waters with some penetration south into the cool subtropical zone.

A. Breeding Distribution and Abundance

The Great Auk was exclusively an Atlantic species and was the largest and only recent flightless member of the Alcidae. All the auks are expert divers using their wings to swim underwater, but only the Great Auk had flipper-like wings too short for flight. It was the original 'penguin', but that name later was transferred to the unrelated penguins of the Southern Hemisphere which independently had developed similar adaptations. The last authentic record of Great Auks seen alive was in 1844 off the south-west coast of Iceland (see below), and now it is not possible to determine the role this unique flightless alcid played in the natural ecosystem of the North Atlantic.

1. DISTRIBUTION

Great Auks apparently bred in large colonies at a small number of offshore islands in low-arctic and boreal waters of the North Atlantic, from Bird Rocks in the Gulf of St. Lawrence and Funk Island off New-foundland, east to Iceland, northern Britain (Orkney Islands, St. Kilda), and probably the Faeroe Islands. In winter, the birds remained offshore and ranged from southern Greenland south to southern Spain and Florida.

A comparison of the known and putative Great Auk colonies (Fig. 2.4, Table 2.1) with the range of the Razorbill (Fig. 2.5, Table 2.2) suggests that the southern limit of the Great Auk's range coincided with that of the Razorbill, but that the Great Auk did not go as far north. The centre of the Razorbill's breeding range in North America, for example, is in southeast Labrador, whereas the Great Auk was seldom seen in waters off Labra-dor or northern Newfoundland (Cartwright 1792). The absence of known Great Auk colonies in the southern part of the Razorbill's range in Europe probable reflects a longer history of persecution by humans in the eastern Atlantic where its original breeding range may have been wider.

The exception to this generalization is the putative colony on "Gunnb-jorn's Skerries", supposedly located on the southeast coast of Greenland (Fig. 2.4, site 11). No Razorbills breed along the east coast of Greenland today (Salomonsen 1967, 1979b), and it is unlikely that the Great Auk could have done so more recently than about 1600, possibly 1200, when that coast became more or less permanently ice-bound (see below). Salo-monsen (1950) and Fisher and Lockley (1954) believed that Great Auks bred on "Gunnbjorn's Skerries" on the basis of stories that birds were taken there in about 1220 and 1590. These skerries are identified nowa-days as Leif's Ø and Erik den Rødes Ø near Angmagssalik (Holm 1918), but the mediaeval accounts do not place them precisely and agree only in that they lay somewhere west of Iceland (Nansen 1911). It has recently

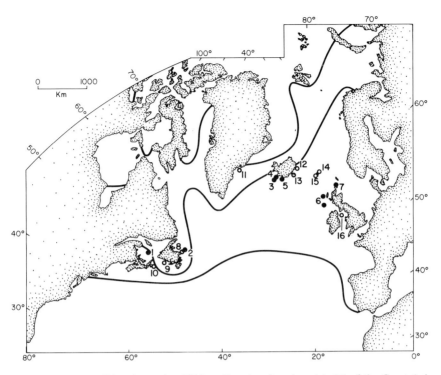

Fig. 2.4.   Known (●) and putative (○) breeding sites (numbered 1–16) of the Great Auk (*Pinguinus impennis*). See Table 2.1 for names and locations of numbered sites.

been suggested that the "skerries" were actually mirages of the Greenland mountains farther west (Lehn and Schroeder 1979). By the 1590s heavy pack-ice persisted along the east coast of Greenland as far south as Angmagssalik for most of the year, and ships bound for west Greenland maintained an offshore course to stay clear of it (Nansen 1911); it is unlikely that one could have reached the coast near Angmagssalik either deliberately or by accident. By the same token it is improbable that Great Auks could have bred on ice-bound islands close to the coast and thus vulnerable to predation by arctic fox and polar bears. Fox have reached Jan Mayen, about 300 km across the ice from Greenland, and are a serious menace to the seabirds breeding there (Marshall 1952). It seems more likely that the account of the visit 1590 is a garbled version of a visit to one of the then extant Great Auk colonies off south or southwest Iceland. However, ice conditions were less severe around 1220 (Nansen 1911; Lamb 1972), and so it is possible that Great Auks did breed in east Greenland in an earlier era.

TABLE 2.1

Distribution of Known and Putative Breeding Sites of the Great Auk (*Pinguinus impennis*)[a]

Site number[b]	Colony location	Position	
	Known colonies		
1	Bird Rocks, Magdalen Is., Gulf of St. Lawrence	47°50'N,	61°09'W
2	Funk Island, E. Newfoundland	49 46	53 11
3	Geirfuglasker, Fuglasker, S.W. Iceland	63 41	23 16
4	Eldey, Fuglasker, S.W. Iceland	63 44	22 56
5	Geirfuglasker, Vestmannaeyjar, S. Iceland	63 19	20 30
6	St. Kilda, W. Scotland	57 49	08 34
7	Papa Westray, Orkney Is., N. Scotland	59 21	02 54
	Putative colonies[c]		
8	Penguin Is., N.E. Newfoundland[d]	49°27'N,	53°48'W
9	Penguin Is., S. Newfoundland[d]	47 23	57 00
10	Cape Breton Is., Nova Scotia	46 10	60 45
11	'Gunnbjorn's Skerries', S.E. Greenland[e]	?65 50	36 25
12	Hvalbakur, S.E. Iceland	64 36	13 14
13	Tvísker, S.E. Iceland	63 56	16 12
14	Fugloy, N.E. Faeroe Islands	62 20	06 17
15	Streymoy, W. Faeroe Islands	62 08	07 00
16	Calf of Man, Irish Sea	54 03	04 50

[a] From Grieve (1885) and Fisher and Lockley (1954).

[b] Corresponds with site numbers shown in Fig. 2-4.

[c] Fisher and Lockley (1954) list the Tusket Islands (misidentification—should be the Mud Islands; see Grieve, 1885), off southern Nova Scotia, and George's Islands, Maine, as putative colonies, but we follow C. W. Townsend in Bent (1919), Godfrey (1959, 1966) and Tufts (1961) in rejecting these: bones found in Indian shell middens is not evidence of breeding (George's Islands) and the observations made by S. Champlain in 1604 (Mud Islands) refer to Northern Gannets, *not* Great Auks.

[d] The two 'Penguin' Islands are included only because of their names. The late L. M. Tuck (personal communication) believed that Newfoundland place names such as these were often assigned or reassigned at random, and that there was no evidence that Great Auks had ever bred at either site. Peters and Burleigh (1951) considered the habitat of both to be unsuitable.

[e] Salomonsen (1950, 1967) accepted 'Gunnbjorn's Skerries' as a known colony. The site, recorded in the sagas, is now believed to be Leif's Ø and Erik den Rodes Ø in Angmagssalik District, S.E. Greenland. However, Lehn and Schroeder (1979) suggest that they were merely mirages of the Greenland mountains seen from well offshore (for further discussion see the text).

To summarize, it seems that the Great Auk can best be described as a bird of low-arctic and boreal waters, concentrating in summer for breeding mainly at locations along areas of mixing of these two water types (based on known and suspected breeding sites, historical and archaeological information). Its winter range was likely much wider, though still probably largely confined to southern portions of boreal or boreal-low arctic waters with some penetration into the cool subtropical zone.

2. ABUNDANCE

There are no numerical data on Great Auks at known breeding places. By the beginning of the seventeenth century, when written records begin, Funk Island seems to have been the largest surviving Great Auk colony—perhaps the only one, and the bird occurred elsewhere only in small numbers at a few inaccessible sites around Iceland and Scotland (Grieve 1885). Whatever the actual size of the total Atlantic population at that time, the species was well known by sailors and fishermen, especially those involved in the fishery on the Newfoundland Grand Banks. So conspicuous was the Great Auk in Newfoundland waters that its habits and movements were well documented by the mid-1600s as evidenced by Nicolas Denys' rather full account in his classic review *The Description and Natural History of the Coasts of North America* (Acadia), first published in 1672 and based upon his observations recorded between 1632 and 1669:

> The Great Auk (*Pennegoin*) is another bird, variegated in white and black. It does not fly. It has only two stumps of wings, with which it beats upon the water to aid in fleeing or diving. It is claimed that it dives even to the bottom to seek its prey upon the Bank. It is found more than a hundred leagues from land, where nevertheless, it comes to lay its eggs, like the others. When they have had their young, they plunge into the water; and their young place themselves upon their backs, and are carried like this as far as the Bank. There one sees some no larger than chickens, although they grow as large as geese. All those birds are (considered) good to eat by the fishermen. As for myself I do not find them agreeable. They taste of oil because of the quantity of fish and of livers they eat; and they serve to make fish oil. The fishermen collect them for this purpose. There are vessels which have made as much as ten to twelve puncheons of it. This is nearly everything which is practised in the fishery for green Cod upon the Grand Bank.

Moreover, Great Auks were so common and numerous on the Grand Banks that they became incorporated into late seventeenth- and eighteenth-century editions of the *English Pilot* (from 1671 until 1803) for sailors to use them as navigation markers in locating the Banks (see, e.g., Lysaght 1971, p. 168; see also Chapter 9, this volume, for details).

At a very rough guess, something of the order of 100,000 pairs of Great Auks may have bred on Funk Island (D. N. Nettleship, unpublished observations; see also Chapter 3, this volume). That population was evidently large enough to have survived raids on it for food, bait and oil from soon after its discovery about 1520 through to the middle of the eighteenth century. Only a short time later, probably between 1770 and 1780, the form of exploitation changed from one of procuring fresh meat to obtaining feathers for a commercial mattress industry (see below). That change in use marked the doom of the remaining Great Auks at Funk Island: they were slaughtered systematically each summer for their feathers, and the colony became extinct by about 1800 (Grieve 1885; Lucas 1890; Bent 1919). Thus in less than 100 years, the Great Auk went from being sufficiently numerous and widespread on the Newfoundland Grand Banks to be used by sailors as an "indicator of position" to not being seen again by anyone. Although numbers were most certainly reduced considerably earlier than the 1790s, Bonnycastle (1842) was quite correct in stating that the day of the Great Auk as a "sure sea-mark" on the banks was over, as was the existence of the species in Newfoundland waters and elsewhere.

B. Status and Recent History

The Great Auk is extinct. The last authentic record was from Eldey, a volcanic island about 16 km off Cape Reykjanes, southwest Iceland, where two adult Great Auks were caught and killed, and their single egg broken, on 3 June 1844, by collectors (Newton 1861; Grieve 1885). Grieve rejected reports of a sighting of a Great Auk on the Grand Banks in 1852 and of one found dead in Trinity Bay, Newfoundland, in 1853 because of the absence of adequate supporting information. Given that Razorbills and other large auks can live for 20 years or more (Tuck 1961; Lloyd 1974; see also Chapter 5, this volume), a few Great Auks could have survived into the 1850s and beyond. Hayes' (1872) report of a Great Auk killed in Disko Bay, west Greenland, in 1870, seems a bit too late to be believable, although a chick hatched in 1843 might have survived for that long.

The precise date of the discovery of Funk Island and its birds is unknown. It was not named on the earliest known chart of east Newfoundland (from Strait of Belle Isle to Placentia Bay), Gaspar Corte Real's "Cantino Mappemonde" of 1502. Funk Island first appeared on a map by Pedro Reinal, provisionally dated 1504–1505, where it was called "y dos aves", meaning "island of birds". However, the Reinal map included some discoveries made later by Joao Alvares Fagundes. It seems quite likely that Fagundes, a Portuguese shipowner from Viano do Castelo, discovered and named Funk Island "Isla de Pitigoen" ("island of penguins") around 1520, which would mean that the Reinal map was no earlier than 1521 (Morison 1971). By the late 1520s European fishing vessels were a common occurrence in east Newfoundland (Lounsbury 1934; Innis 1940). For example, on 3 August 1527 John Rut, an English sailor and explorer, reported at least 14 European ships in the St. John's harbour, and some were already utilizing Great Auks on Funk Island, either regularly or sporadically, for food. (Note: the change of the calendar in 1752 necessitates adding 14 days to earlier dates cited here and below for comparison with modern dates.) By the time Jacques Cartier made his first voyage to the New World in 1534, most sailing masters were probably aware of Funk Island. Cartier's own description of his trip on 21 May 1534 to Funk Island clearly indicates that he too was already aware of the rich food supply awaiting his arrival (Bigger 1924: 6–7; Hakluyt 1904, p. 184).

And the significance of Funk Island was not forgotten, as Cartier made it his first stop after sailing from France on 26 May 1535 to begin his second voyage (Biggar 1924; Hakluyt 1904, pp. 210–211). His vivid description of the place ensured that others would soon follow, in addition to those already knowledgeable of the bird wealth at the Funks. By 1536 Newfoundland's great fishery and rich wildlife resources, including Funk Island, were so well known that Richard Hore, a London leather merchant, chartered two vessels (*Trinity* and *William*) to transport 30 gentlemen tourists to Newfoundland to view its wonders. In early June 1536 they landed on the "Island of Penguins" to enjoy a feast of Great Auks (Hakluyt 1904, p. 4).

The Grand Banks fishery continued to grow, and by the early 1580s the French fishing fleets brought very little fresh stores with them, relying instead on the Great Auks at Funk Island and other fresh food available at sea (e.g., fish, other seabirds, marine mammals) (Anthonie Parkhurst, in Hakluyt 1904, p. 14; Sir Humphrey Gilbert, in Hakluyt 1904, p. 49). Parkhurst's records of the fishing fleets present in 1578 (Hakluyt 1904, pp. 10–11) gave an impressive record of the potential impact of fisheries on the Great Auk population at Funk Island:

English: 50 vessels (increased from 30 to 50 between 1574 and 1578)
Spanish: more than 100 vessels fishing cod and an additional 20–30 whalers
Portuguese: about 50 vessels
French: about 150 vessels

It is unlikely that every fishing boat sailing for the Newfoundland fishery routinely put in to the Funks for fresh meat. The vessels that did were probably those fishing off the east coast (perhaps even on the Funk Island Bank), and particularly those with local staging areas or those which depended on curing their fish ashore. The presence of even a sporadic exploitation of birds each year over an extended period could have accomplished the reduction of the population of Great Auks at Funk Island. The combined impact of the actual removal of breeding birds and the destruction of eggs and young associated with their capture must have reduced the annual production of young considerably. Furthermore, the exploitation of the birds was not limited to the colony, but continued at sea outside the breeding period (Grieve 1885; see also Denys 1672). The wonder is that it took another 150 years to reduce the population to a level from which it could not recover!

The exploitation of Great Auks continued and grew as the fishery expanded, but no concern was expressed about the birds' welfare. In 1622 Richard Whitbourne praised the Great Auk in his *A Discourse and Discovery of Newfoundland* as "God made the innocencie of so poor a creature to become such an admirable instrument for the sustenation of man". This attitude persisted to the middle of the eighteenth century, by which time the Great Auk was probably already greatly reduced in numbers and in imminent danger of local extinction. George Cartwright, a gentleman adventurer-trapper who lived in Labrador for most of the period 1770–1786, noted the problem and predicted its outcome. On 5 July 1785, while moored in Shoal Cove, Fogo Island, he recorded in his journal (Cartwright 1792, Volume III, p. 55):

> A boat came in from Funk Island laden with birds, chiefly penguins. . . . . *But it has been customary of late years, for several crews of men to live all the summer on that island, for the sole purpose of killing birds for the sake of their feathers, the destruction which they have made is incredible. If a stop is not soon put to that practice, the whole breed will be diminished to almost nothing, particularly the penguins* (emphasis added).

By about 1800 this prediction was a reality. No longer was the Great Auk a conspicuous feature delimiting "the edge and inside the banks" (Bonnycastle 1842), but instead an extreme rarity for a few years prior to its final extermination sometime between 1844 and 1853.

The record of the Great Auks inhabiting European areas is poor (Table 2.1, Fig. 2.4), as are details and dates of its disappearance. Numbers were small when historic records begin, but it seems likely that sizeable populations formerly occurred at St. Kilda, the Faeroe Islands and southern Iceland. The histories and last dates considered to be authentic by Grieve (1885) and Fisher and Lockley (1954) for the major Great Auk breeding sites in Europe are as follows:

1. *Britain*: Last authentic record was the sighting of a single bird at the entrance to Waterford Harbour, Ireland in 1834.
   A. *St. Kilda*: Present and breeding in small numbers during the first half of the seventeenth century, an irregular visitant by the early

1700s; the last Great Auk was seen and captured in early summer 1821 on Hirta.

B. *Orkney Islands and Shetland Isles*: Rare and irregular breeder through the seventeenth and eighteenth centuries; a pair was discovered breeding on Papa Westray (Orkney) in 1812 and the female collected; the male escaped but was killed in 1813 when it returned to the same site (the male is in the British Museum).

2. *Faeroe Islands*: Rare as a breeding bird by the late 1700s; the last record believed to be plausible for the Faeroes is 1 July 1808 at Stóra Dímun where a single bird was claimed to have been killed.

3. *Iceland*: A regular breeder at three locations off the south coast through the eighteenth century, but rare by 1800.

A. *Geirfuglasker, Vestmannaeyjar* (site 5, Fig. 2.4): Last known breeding about 1800.

B. *Geirfuglasker, Fuglasker* (site 3, Fig. 2.4): Breeding until 1830 when the islet sank owing to volcanic disturbance.

C. *Eldey, Fuglasker* (site 4, Fig. 2.4): Breeding established in 1830 after neighbouring Geirfuglasker was destroyed (see B, above); the last site known to be inhabited by breeding Great Auks and quickly eradicated by collectors: 1830—two boats took 20 or 21 birds; 1831—24 birds taken; 1834—at least 9 birds and several eggs; 1840—one egg collected; 1841—3 birds and one egg taken; 1844—2 Great Auks caught and killed, and their egg broken, on 3 June. Eldey was revisited in 1846 and 1860, but no sightings were made of Great Auks on land or at sea; in fact, the two birds killed in June 1844 were the last Great Auks to be seen alive with certainty by anyone anywhere.

IV. RAZORBILL, *Alca torda*

Summary: North Atlantic polytypic boreo-low arctic species. Breeds between 73°N and 43°N from Hudson Strait and west Greenland south to Gulf of Maine, and from Iceland, Jan Mayen, Bjørnøya and northwest Russia (White Sea) south to Brittany and the Baltic Sea. Winters mostly offshore in northern boreal waters south to Long Island (New York), Azores and western Mediterranean.

A. Breeding Distribution and Abundance

The Razorbill is a boreo-low arctic species confined to the North Atlantic, breeding in the east from northwest France, Britain, Denmark, Swe-

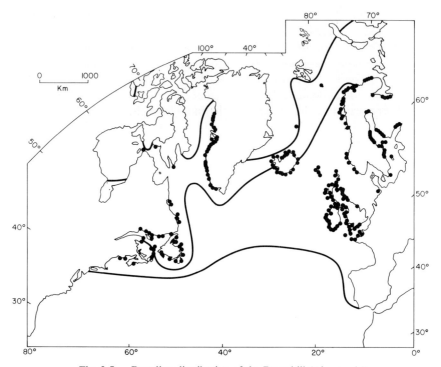

Fig. 2.5.   Breeding distribution of the Razorbill (*Alca torda*).

den, and northwest Russia north to Bjørnøya, Jan Mayen and Iceland,
and in the west from west Greenland and south through Atlantic Canada
to Maine (Fig. 2.5). The total world breeding population is estimated to be
around 700,000 (range: 0.3–1.2 million) pairs (Table 2.2), one of the smallest breeding populations of any of the Atlantic auks (Black Guillemot
appears to be smaller) and very few compared to the relatively enormous
numbers of Dovekies, murres and Atlantic Puffins (see below). Of this
total, 70% breed in Iceland with another 20% in the British Isles; the
remaining 10% is divided between the western and eastern Atlantic, with
about 15,000 pairs in Atlantic Canada and 30,000 pairs in Norway. The
bulk of the world population breeds in northwest Iceland on the edge of
the boreal and low-arctic water zones.

B. Regional Populations and Status

1. CANADA AND MAINE

The Razorbill breeds mainly in small colonies scattered widely through
Atlantic Canada, with the bulk of the North American population centred

in southern Labrador. There are at least 59 colonies in eastern Canada (57) and Maine (2) with a total population of about 15,000 breeding pairs, of which 10,000 (68%) breed in Labrador, 3500 (24%) in the Estuary and the Gulf of St. Lawrence, 800 (5%) in eastern Newfoundland, 300 (2%) in the Scotian Shelf–Bay of Fundy–Gulf of Maine areas, and about 100 pairs (<1%) in the Hudson Strait region (Nettleship 1980 and unpublished observations; Gaston and Malone 1980; Chapdelaine and Laporte 1982). The largest breeding groups are at the Gannet Islands (5500 pairs) and the Bird Islands (1530 pairs) in southern Labrador (Nettleship 1980 and unpublished observations).

The North American population was persecuted by humans (egging and hunting) up to the early 1900s, by which time its numbers were substantially reduced throughout its range and it was locally close to extinction (Bent 1919). Numbers remained low or continued to decrease up to the 1950s. In the Gulf of St. Lawrence Razorbills have decreased over both the long and short terms. Numbers at Bird Rocks, Magdalen Islands, the last stronghold of the species at the turn of this century, declined from about 1800 birds in 1904 (Bent 1919) to 300 birds in 1961 (Bagg and Emery 1961). In contrast to this, regular surveys at seven sites along the north shore of the Gulf between 1960 and 1982 showed a decline from 16,200 individuals in 1960 (Moisan 1962) to 14,950 in 1965 (Moisan and Fyfe 1967), to 4300 in 1972 (Nettleship and Lock 1973), to 3060 in 1977 (Chapdelaine 1980), and to only 2380 in 1982 (Chapdelaine and Brousseau 1984), an overall decrease of 85% in 22 years. The surveys conducted in 1972, 1977 and 1982 used virtually identical techniques (Nettleship 1973a, 1976a; Nettleship and Lock 1973) and suggest a decrease of 45% between 1972 and 1982. Elsewhere, since the mid-1950s numbers have remained relatively stable or increased slightly. Small gains have occurred at many sites in eastern Newfoundland. A comparison of nine Labrador colonies examined in 1952 and 1953 (Tuck 1953), and again between 1978 and 1981 (Elliot et al. 1978; Lock 1979; Birkhead and Nettleship 1982a; D. N. Nettleship, unpublished observations) shows decreases at four sites, increases at four, and one unchanged; there was an overall increase of about 20%. Given the small total North American population and the large decreases occurring in the Gulf of St. Lawrence, the Razorbill requires immediate attention and detailed study in Canadian waters.

2. GREENLAND

Razorbills breed in small numbers widely scattered along the west Greenland coast in the low-arctic zone as far north as Melville Bay and south to Julianehåb District; it is absent from the southernmost tip and the east coast of Greenland (Salomonsen 1950, 1967, 1981). Details of loca-

TABLE 2.2

Distribution and Estimates of Breeding Population Sizes (Pairs) of the Razorbill (*Alca torda*)

Region	Regional totals		Census date	References
	Pairs	%		
Canada and New England				
E. arctic	100	<0.1	1979	Brown et al. (1975); Gaston and Malone (1980)
Labrador	10,000	1.4	1972–1983	Nettleship (1980 and unpublished)
E. Newfoundland	800	0.1	1967–1980	Nettleship (1980)
Gulf of St. Lawrence	3,500	0.5	1972–1982	Nettleship (1980 and unpublished); Chapdelaine and Laporte (1982); Chapdelaine and Brousseau (1984)
Scotian Shelf–Bay of Fundy–Gulf of Maine	300	<0.1	1971–1980	Nettleship (1980); Lock (1971); Drury (1973–1974 and personal communication)
TOTALS	ca. 15,000 (1,500–5,500)	2.1		
W. Greenland	3,500	0.5	1965, 1971, 1974, 1983	Joensen and Preuss (1972); Evans (1974a, 1984); Salomonsen (1979c); K. Kampp (personal communication)
Iceland	500,000[a] (100,000–1 million)	70.7	—	Gardarsson (1982); Petersen (1982 and personal communication)
Jan Mayen	100	<0.1	1983	van Franeker and Camphuijsen (1984)
Faeroe Islands	3,000[b] (1,000–5,000)	0.4	1974	B. Olsen (personal communication)
British Isles				
Scotland	86,000	12.1	—	Cramp et al. (1974); Lloyd (1976b); Stowe and Harris (1984)
England	4,000	0.6	—	Cramp et al. (1974); Lloyd (1976b); Stowe and Harris (1984)

Location	Pairs	%	Year(s)	References
Wales	5,000	0.7	—	Cramp et al. (1974); Lloyd (1976b); Stowe and Harris (1984)
Ireland	50,000	7.0	—	Cramp et al. (1974); Lloyd (1976b); Stowe and Harris (1984)
Channel Islands	<100	<0.1	—	Cramp et al. (1974); Lloyd (1976b); Stowe and Harris (1984)
TOTALS	145,000[c]	20.5	—	Cramp et al. (1974); Lloyd (1976b); Stowe and Harris (1984)
Brittany, France	<50	<0.1	1980–81	Henry and Monnat (1981)
Helgoland, Germany	5[d]	<0.1	1981	Vauk (1982)
Denmark	250 (200–250)	<0.1	1983	Joensen (1982); P. Lyngs (personal communication)
Sweden	4,300	0.6	1977–1983	Nord (1977); S. O. F. (1978); Andersson (1979); Grenmyr and Sundin (1981); Gustafsson and Hogstrom (1981); P. E. Jonsson (personal communication)
Finland	4,000	0.5	1970–1983	Lippens and Willie (1972); Hilden (1978); M. Kilpi (personal communication)
Norway	30,000	4.2	1966–1982	Brun (1979); Barrett and Vader (1984)
Bjørnøya	<50[e]	<0.1	1980, 1982	van Franeker and Luttik (1981); M. P. Harris and S. Wanless (personal communication)
Kola Peninsula and White Sea (U.S.S.R.)	2,000	0.3	—	Bianki (1967)
TOTALS	707,000 (300,000–1.2 million)	100.0		

[a] This is in order 5 and guessed to be around 500,000 pairs (Gardarsson 1982), mainly in the low-arctic zone concentrated toward the boundary with boreal waters; A. Petersen (personal communication) places total numbers at a lower level, probably between 200,000 to 300,000 pairs.

[b] Rough estimate only—see text.

[c] This estimate may be high by about 18,000 pairs owing to an apparent decrease in Razorbill numbers at Horn Head, Ireland, from 45,000 birds, ca. 26,000 pairs in Cramp et al. (1974) in 1969–1970 to 13,000 birds (ca. 7800 pairs) in 1980 (Stowe 1982a; Watson and Radford 1982).

[d] Breeds sporadically: one pair in 1975, three in 1980 and five in 1981 (Rheinwald 1982; Vauk 1982).

[e] A total of 14 birds recorded in 1980 at four locations and breeding status described as 'may breed in very small numbers' (van Franeker and Luttik 1981).

tions and bird numbers are known only for the northernmost colonies (Joensen and Preuss 1972; Evans 1974a, 1984) and for some in the Frederikshåb District in the south (Salomonsen 1979a). Using these incomplete data, the total population has been estimated at 1500 to 5500 pairs (Evans 1984) and is provisionally placed at about 3500 pairs. Declines were noted at all four colonies surveyed between 1965 and 1974 (Evans 1974a, 1984); otherwise there is no information on status of this small population.

3. ICELAND

Razorbills breed on sea-cliffs around most of the coast of Iceland, usually in association with murres, and numbers are highest at the large murre colonies at Látrabjarg, Haelavíkurbjarg and Hornbjarg on the northwest peninsula (Reinsch 1976; Petersen 1982). The population is smaller than those of the Common and Thick-billed Murres (see below), in the order of 100,000 to 1 million breeding pairs (Gardarsson 1982; Petersen 1982). The population is tentatively placed at 500,000 pairs (Gardarsson 1982, and personal communication), mainly in low-arctic waters close to the boundary of the boreal zone. Population status is uncertain.

4. JAN MAYEN

Razorbills breed in very small numbers in crevices on cliffs among the murres at Splittodden-Skrinnodden, and possibly at a few other locations where murres occur (e.g., Kvalrossen). They were first found breeding in 1983 by van Franeker and Camphuijsen (1984), who estimated the size of the population to be low in order 3, probably not many more than 100 pairs. Although earlier observers at Jan Mayen did not report Razorbills, van Franeker and Camphuijsen feel that the birds were probably present but went undetected. That small group is the only Razorbill population known to breed in the high-arctic zone.

5. FAEROE ISLANDS

Razorbills usually occur in small breeding groups, most commonly on sea-cliffs along the west coast of Streymoy and the Mykines (Nørrevang 1960; Joensen 1966). There has been no survey of Razorbills in the Faeroes, although B. Olsen in Lloyd (1976b) estimated the breeding population at 5000 pairs in 1974 (based on a ratio between murres and Razorbills). That estimate was later considered too high, and the population estimate has been revised at between 1000 and 5000 pairs, probably around 3000 pairs (B. Olsen, personal communication). It is possible that the population declined 60–75% during the last 25 years as recorded for murres (Dyck and Meltofte 1975; B. Olsen, personal communication; see also Common Murre, Section VI).

6. BRITAIN AND IRELAND

About 20% of the world population of Razorbills breeds in the British Isles (Table 2.2). Colonies are normally small and distributed widely along most coastlines in Scotland and western Ireland. In southeast England it is absent, and in northwest and northeast England and the east coast of Ireland it occurs very locally and in small numbers. The population is estimated to be about 145,000 pairs (Cramp *et al.* 1974; Lloyd 1976b; Stowe and Harris 1984), of which roughly 59% breed in Scotland, 34% in Ireland, and 3% each in England and Wales with very small numbers in the Channel Islands (Cramp *et al.* 1974). They are concentrated in the north, particularly in Shetland (notable Foula and Fair Isle) and Orkney (notably Westray), northwest and north mainland Scotland (Handa Island, Clò Mór, and Caithness coast) and along the west coast of Ireland (notably Horn Head, which together with Clò Mór, are the largest colonies in Britain and Ireland). Other substantial Razorbill colonies in Ireland exist on Rathlin Island, Lambay Island, Great Saltee and Clare Island.

Historical data are sketchy, but it seems likely that Razorbill numbers declined through the eighteeth and nineteenth centuries owing to destruction caused by an expanding and more mobile human population (Parslow 1973a). Descriptions of a number of large Razorbill colonies in the last century and beginning of this century suggest some major declines. For example, the islands of Mull and Skye (Inner Hebrides, Scotland), and Papa Stour (Shetland) all held 'immense' numbers during the 1850s through the 1880s, but now have only small numbers or none at all (Graham 1890; Harvie-Brown and Macpherson 1904; Baxter and Rintoul 1953; Cramp *et al.* 1974). 'Hundreds if not thousands' were described as breeding on the Scilly Isles until 1914 and 1915, and this declined to a low of 75 birds in 1961 (Penhallurich 1969). The breeding range has remained almost unchanged since 1900, although declines have occurred through this century at colonies in southwest and southern England (e.g., Lundy and Isle of Wight), south Wales and southern Ireland (notably Great Saltee) (Paludan 1947; Merikallio 1958; Snow 1971; Parslow 1973a; Cramp *et al.* 1974; see also Chapter 10, this volume). Results of surveys since 1971 indicate that Razorbill numbers continue to decline in parts of southern England (e.g., Isle of Wight), southwest Wales (Skokholm) and west Ireland (Horn

Head), but elsewhere are currently stable, or increasing slightly (e.g., South Stack, North Wales; Cliffs of Moher, west Ireland; Fair Isle, Shetland; Orkney and eastern England) (Harris 1976b; Lloyd 1976b; Evans 1978; Furness 1981; Stowe 1982a; Wanless *et al.* 1982; Watson and Radford 1982; Stowe and Harris 1984).

7. BRITTANY, FRANCE

The small breeding population, estimated to be about 40 to 50 pairs in 1980–1981 (Henry and Monnat 1981), was distributed over four areas on the north and west coasts of Brittany: Cap Fréhel (15–18 pairs), Les Sept Iles (20–30 individuals), Roches de Camaret (4 pairs) and Cap Sizun (1 pair). In 1965 the population at Les Sept Iles alone was 450 pairs, but it was reduced to only 50 pairs following the *Torrey Canyon* oil disaster in 1967 (Yeatman 1976; Guermeur and Monnat 1980). Overall, the Brittany population decreased from 500 to 520 pairs in 1965–1966 to its present (1980–1981) known size of 40 to 50 pairs (Henry and Monnat 1981).

8. HELGOLAND, GERMANY

Formerly Razorbills bred on Helgoland in small numbers among a large colony of Common Murres; the colony had declined to only 12 pairs by 1939 (R. Drost, in Schultz 1947) and to a single pair by 1956 (Lloyd 1976b). Apparently they still breed sporadically at Helgoland, with one pair recorded in 1975, three in 1980, and five in 1981 (Rheinwald 1982; Vauk 1982).

9. DENMARK

About 200 to 250 pairs of Razorbills breed on Graesholm, a small islet northeast of Bornholm in the southern part of the Baltic Sea (Franzmann 1974; Salomonsen 1979c; Joensen 1982; P. Lyngs, personal communication). Numbers have declined at this and other Baltic colonies (see below), probably as a result of the severe ice-winters in the early 1940s and by hunting in combination with chronic chemical pollution in the Kattegat and Baltic Seas (Salomonsen 1979c). Hunting (with no bag limit) of Razorbills in Denmark was allowed from 1 October to the end of February each winter until 1978 (Salomonsen 1979c; H. Meltofte, personal communication). Since hunting was prohibited, Razorbill numbers have become relatively stable, or even slightly increased (P. Lyngs and H. Meltofte, personal communication).

10. SWEDEN AND FINLAND

Small colonies of Razorbills are widely scattered from Stora Karlsö (Gotland) in the Baltic north along the west coast of the Gulf of Bothnia, and in southwest Finland along the Gulf of Finland. The size of the Baltic population of Razorbills in earlier times is unclear. It most likely declined through the nineteenth century owing to human persecution (egging and hunting), but later increased into the early part of this century once the colonies were protected, as did the Common Murre (Hedgren 1975). Numbers of birds in the Baltic are also influenced by prolonged and cold winters. A decrease at Stora Karlsö from 10,000 to 15,000 pairs in 1939 to 2000 to 3000 pairs in 1942 following three severe winters, as well as the reduction and extinction of colonies on islands along parts of the Finnish coast (von Haartman 1947, 1971), has been attributed to severe ice conditions in the Baltic (Voous 1960). The Baltic population (excluding Denmark) is now estimated to be about 8300 breeding pairs, with 4300 in Sweden (Nord 1977; S.O.F. 1978; Andersson 1979; Grenmyr and Sundin 1981; Gustafsson and Hogstrom 1981; P. E. Jonsson, personal communication) of which 1500 breed on Stora Karlsö (Gustafsson and Hogstrom 1981), and at least 4000 pairs in Finland (Lippens and Willie 1972; Hilden 1978; M. Kilpi, personal communication).

11. NORWAY

Razorbills breed in small groups in rocky cliffs along the west coast from Rogaland District in the south through eastern Finnmark to the Kola Peninsula, though absent from the Nord- and Sør-Trøndelag Districts. The current breeding population is estimated to be about 30,000 pairs (Brun 1979; Barret and Vader 1984) at 27 sites (Brun 1979), with over 68% (20,000 pairs) of the total population in the Troms–western Finnmark region concentrated mainly on Nord-Fugløy (10,000 pairs), Hjelmsøya (7000 pairs) and Gjesvaer (2500 pairs). Røst in the Lofoten Islands south of Troms accounts for another 13% (3900 pairs) and Rundøy, the only large colony in the southern sector, comprises 9.5% (2800 pairs).

Significant declines in population size, estimated to be in the order of 10 to 20%, between 1964 and 1976 have been attributed to a number of factors including oil pollution, hunting, commercial fisheries and drowning in fishing nets (Brun 1979). The present status of the population is uncertain, although recent surveys indicate that numbers may have stabilized or even increased slightly.

12. BJØRNØYA

Razorbills breed in very small numbers at Bjørnøya. Van Franeker and Luttik (1981) recorded a total of 14 birds near Sørhamna, Evjebukta, Fugleodden and Lundenaeringane. They estimated the number of breeding pairs to be midway in order 2 (Table 2.2), although many more may have gone undetected in the large southern murre colonies (J. A. van Franeker, personal communication). Breeding was not confirmed until 1982 when an egg was found (M. P. Harris and S. Wanless, personal communication).

13. KOLA PENINSULA AND WHITE SEA (RUSSIA)

Razorbills breed in small colonies at a few locations along the Murmansk Coast (Kola Peninsula), and in the White Sea in both Kandalakshskaya Guba and Onega Bay. The precise locations and sizes of the colonies are lacking. Bianki (1967) [summarizing Gerasimova (1962) and Kokhanov and Skokova (1967)] reported only 320 pairs on the Murmansk Coast, with 250 pairs on Ostrova Sem'ostrovov, 35 pairs on Ostrova Aynovskiye and another 35 pairs scattered along the coast. Counts made earlier by Gerasimova (1962) and Skokova (1962) identified five colonies comprising 285 pairs (Norderhaug et al. 1977, p. 78), but this total did not include Ostrova Sem'ostrovov or Ostrova Aynovskiye. Bianki (1967) estimated higher numbers in the White Sea with at least 1600 pairs breeding in Onega Bay and about 75 pairs at two sites in Kandalakshskaya Guba: Sredniye Ludy opposite Ostrov Velikiy (ca. 25 pairs) and on Zaych'i Ludy (ca. 50 pairs) between Guba Knyazhaya and Kovda. Thus the size of the breeding population in northern Russia 20 years ago was of the order of 2000 pairs. No recent information on status is available.

V. DOVEKIE, *Alle alle*

Summary: North Atlantic polytypic high-arctic species. Breeds between 82°N and 60°N on coasts from east Baffin Island (Home Bay area) and northwest Greenland (Thule region) east to Severnaya Zemlya, and south to southwest Greenland (Julianehåb District), northern Iceland (Grímsey) and Novaya Zemlya. Winters offshore mainly in low-arctic waters from the Newfoundland Grand Banks to northern Norway, but also regularly in the boreal zone south over the Scotian Shelf and Gulf of Maine east to northern Scotland and the North Sea; rarely farther south.

A. Breeding Distribution and Abundance

The Dovekie is a high-arctic species with a breeding range restricted almost entirely to the high-arctic marine zone (Fig. 2.6). Its principal colonies are in the Thule region of northwest Greenland (north of 75°N), Scoresby Sound and Liverpool Land in east Greenland, Jan Mayen, western Spitsbergen, Franz Josef Land, and the northwest tip of Novaya Zemlya (Salomonsen 1950, 1967, 1979a, c; Fisher and Lockley 1954; Freuchen and Salomonsen 1958; Kartaschew 1960; Dement'ev et al. 1951; Norderhaug et al. 1977; van Franeker and Camphuijsen 1984). There are also small populations in east Baffin Island (Home Bay area), west Greenland (mainly in the Upernavik District, between 69°N and 75°N), Bjørnøya, Severnaya Zemlya, a very small one on Grímsey on the north coast of Iceland, and the possibility of other smaller ones on Ostrov Bennetta in the New Siberian Islands and Little Diomede Island in the Bering Strait (Salomonsen 1950, 1967, 1979a; Kartaschew 1960; Belopoloskii 1957; Breckenridge 1966; Norderhaug et al. 1977; van Franeker and Luttik 1981; Petersen 1982; Finley and Evans 1984).

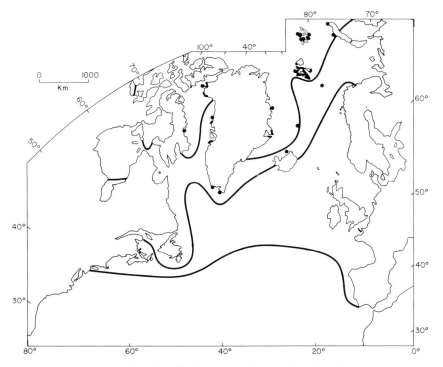

Fig. 2.6.   Breeding distribution of the Dovekie (*Alle alle*).

It has been suggested that the Dovekie is the most numerous seabird in the North Atlantic, and possibly the most abundant alcid in the world (Salomonsen 1944, 1950; Fisher and Lockley 1954; Norderhaug 1970). The only previous attempt to estimate the world population of the Dovekie was by Salomonsen (1950); he estimated the greatest concentration of the species to be in Greenland with at least 30 million birds in the Thule region (northwest Greenland) and populations of about 10 million birds each in the Scoresby Sound area (east Greenland), Jan Mayen, Spitsbergen, Franz Josef Land and Novaya Zemlya (Salomonsen 1950; Freuchen and Salomonsen 1958, p. 196). Although the total breeding population is undoubtedly very large, that first guess of about 80 million birds is now believed to be high, particularly for areas other than northwest Greenland. However, detailed counts of the various colonies are still lacking and such estimates of Dovekie numbers as have been made are only rough guesses. When existing population data are brought together and arranged by orders of magnitude (see below for regional population reviews), the total population may be placed around 12 million (range: 8–18 million) pairs (Table 2.3). Using the regional values as an index of relative abundance, they show that the bulk of the population breeds in northwest Greenland with the remainder concentrated at only four other regions: Spitsbergen, Franz Josef Land, Jan Mayen and east Greenland. The Dovekie is a true high-arctic breeder in the North Atlantic, with almost the entire population breeding in the high-arctic zone.

B. Regional Populations and Status

1. CANADA

Dovekies breed in very small numbers in east Baffin Island. The size of the total population is unknown, but small numbers do breed on at least one island in northern Home Bay (Fig. 2.6). In 1983 Finley and Evans (1984) found two eggs and two chicks at Abbajalik (ca. 69°N), the first and only documented breeding record of the Dovekie in Canada. This suggests that small groups (orders 1 and 2) may occur at a few locations along the east coast of Baffin Island and adjacent areas. However, total Dovekie numbers must be small because no other breeding stations have been recorded even though numerous surveys have been made. The population is tentatively placed in order 3 (Table 2.3), and is considered to be marginal with a restricted distribution.

2. GREENLAND

The Dovekie breeds in immense colonies, each perhaps comprising several millions of birds in the Thule region of northwest Greenland, from Etah south to Melville Bay, and in small numbers (6000 pairs) in the

TABLE 2.3

Distribution and Estimates of Breeding Population Sizes (Pairs) of the Dovekie (*Alle alle*)

Region	Regional totals Pairs	%	Census date	References
Canada	<1,000	<1	1983	Finley and Evans (1984)
Greenland				
Thule region (N. of 75°N)	10 million[a] (7–15 million)	80	1940–1978	Salomonsen (1950, 1967, 1979a); Freuchen and Salomonsen (1958); Renaud *et al.* (1982)
Upernavik, Disko Bay, Frederikshåb and Julianehåb	6,500	<1	1936–1965	Salomonsen (1950, 1967, 1979a); Joensen and Preuss (1972); Evans (1974a, 1981a, 1984)
E. Greenland Scoresby Sound	500,000[b]	4	1974	Meltofte (1976); K. de Korte (personal communication)
Iceland (Grímsey)	<10[c]	+	1981–1983	Petersen (1982); P. G. H. Evans (unpublished observations)
Jan Mayen	50,000[d]	<1	1983	van Franeker and Camphuijsen (1984)
Bjørnøya	10,000[e]	<1	1980	van Franeker and Luttik (1981); J. A. van Franeker (personal communication)
Spitsbergen	1 million[f] (0.4–1.6 million)	7	—	F. Mehlum (personal communication); Norderhaug *et al.* (1977); Norderhaug (1980)
Franz Josef Land	250,000[g]	7	—	Golovkin (1984)
Novaya Zemlya	50,000[g]	<1	1948–1967	Uspenski (1956); Zelickman and Golovkin (1972); Golovkin (1984)
Severnaya Zemlya and New Siberian Islands	75,000	—	1958–1959	Uspenski (1959); Golovkin (1984)
TOTALS	ca. 12,000,000 (8–18 million)	100		

[a] Rough guess only; guesses range from 14 to 30 million birds, or 7–15 million pairs.

[b] Rough guess only; probably high in order 6 or low order 7, but certainly well below the guess of 5 million pairs made by Pedersen (1930).

[c] Only five birds seen in 1981 and seven in 1983, interpreted as two to three breeding pairs (Petersen 1982; P. G. H. Evans, unpublished observations), or order 1.

[d] Rough estimate only; van Franeker and Camphuijsen (1984) place it in order 5, probably around 50,000 pairs.

[e] Rough estimate only; van Franeker and Luttik (1981) place it low in order 5, close to 10,000 pairs—see text.

[f] Rough estimate only, probably high in order 6 or low order 7; value used based on most recent estimate of 400,000 to 1.6 million pairs (F. Mehlum, Norwegian Polar Research Institute).

[g] Rough estimate only; see text.

Upernavik District (with virtually all at one colony, Horse Head), on small skerries in Disko Bay (200–300 pairs) and possibly as scattered pairs (10–20) farther south in Frederikshåb and Julianehåb Districts (Table 2.3); there are also large colonies (at least 1 million birds or 500,000 pairs) in east Greenland on the south side of Scoresby Sound and north along Liverpool Land (Salomonsen 1950, 1967, 1979a,c; Joensen and Preuss 1972; Evans 1974a, 1981a; Meltofte 1976). Salomonsen (1950, 1967) included Shannon Ø as another east Greenland colony on the basis that Dovekies had been seen in summer in the pack-ice offshore, but Meltofte *et al.* (1981) found no evidence of breeding Dovekies, or of any recent colony there, in 1976.

Estimates of numbers at the major colonies are at best indications of an order of magnitude, but overall the population must be very large (Table 2.3). Freuchen and Salomonsen (1958) put the Thule population at 30 million birds, and an independent estimate indicated at least 14 million individuals in that region (Renaud *et al.* 1982). Those figures represent 7–15 million pairs, which are averaged as roughly 10 million pairs for this chapter. The Scoresby Sound population was originally guessed at around 10 million birds (Pedersen 1930; Freuchen and Salomonsen 1958). A detailed census has yet to be made, but recent surveys showed that although 10 million was probably an overestimate, the population was certainly over 1 million birds (Meltofte 1976; K. de Korte, personal communication), or 500,000 pairs. The status of those large populations is unknown, although smaller colonies south of Upernavik District and along the west coast have decreased or disappeared since the late 1930s, possibly due to climate amelioration (Salomonsen 1967, 1979a; Joensen and Preuss 1972).

3. ICELAND

Iceland is the southern limit of the Dovekie's breeding range (Fig. 2.6). It formerly bred on the mainland (e.g., Langanes, Melrakkaslétta and Skjálfandi), but now the total population is two or three pairs on Grímsey (Petersen 1982). The decline over the last century was attributed to the climatic amelioration that was most marked in the first half of the twentieth century (Gudmundsson 1951; Petersen 1982).

4. JAN MAYEN

Dovekies are widely distributed around the island, breeding almost everywhere in small groups of less than 1000 pairs (van Franeker and Camphuijsen 1984). Freuchen and Salomonsen (1958) guessed the population to be not much less than that in the Scoresby Sound area of east Greenland (*ca.* 500,000 pairs). But the survey by van Franeker and Camphuijsen (1984) in 1983 indicated numbers to be much lower, definitely in order 5 and probably around 50,000 pairs (Table 2.3).

5. BJØRNØYA

Dovekies breed in small numbers all along the coast, with only four large colonies known (van Franeker and Luttik 1981 and personal communication): Vesalstranda ('thousands of pairs') and Brettingsdalen (at most 3000 pairs); eastern slope of Miseryfjellet; Alfredfjellet above lake Ellasjøen (at least 3000 pairs), and scattered groups near Tunheim (totalling several hundreds of pairs). Van Franeker and Luttik (1981) concluded that the total Bjørnøya population was probably low in order 5, or slightly exceeding 10,000 pairs (Table 2.3). The status of that small population is not known.

6. SPITSBERGEN

The main part of the population breeds in boulder scree on mountain slopes close to the sea, with smaller numbers in crevices on steep rocky cliffs and in talus at the cliff base; the largest colonies are in Vestspitsbergen, in the region of Magdelenefjorden and Hornsund (Stempniewicz 1981). Norderhaug et al. (1977) reviewed existing information and listed 34 colonies (excluding those on Bjørnøya) comprising 21 in order 4, 9 in order 5, and 4 in order 6. The population probably is not more than 3.2 million birds (Norderhaug 1980), and is estimated to be between 400,000 and 1.6 million breeding pairs and likely more than 1 million pairs (F. Mehlum, personal communication). The Spitsbergen population is undoubtedly very large, second only to that found in northwest Greenland (Table 2.3), but its status is unknown.

7. FRANZ JOSEF LAND

Information on the size and status of this population is lacking. The nineteenth-century explorers (Nansen 1897) and Gorbunov (1932) indicated a very large population with some colonies probably exceeding 100,000 birds (Kartaschew 1960). Norderhaug et al. (1977) showed the colonies to be concentrated in the southwestern part of the archipelago, with only a few scattered through the remaining area, and extending to the northernmost island at almost 82°N. They listed 34 colonies, which by orders of magnitude (based on the qualitative descriptions presented) were 10 in order 3, 9 in order 4, 13 in order 5, and 2 in order 6, giving a population estimate of 1.7 million pairs. However, Dovekie numbers must be limited because so little of Franz Josef Land is ice-free or suitable for nesting (Norderhaug *et al.* 1977), and the population has been tentatively placed at 250,000 pairs (Golovkin 1984; see also Table 2.3).

8. NOVAYA ZEMLYA

The Dovekie breeds at only three locations in Novaya Zemlya, all on the west coast towards the northern tip: Ostrova Oranskiye, Bol'shoy Ledyanoy Zaliv and Guba Arkhangel'skaya (Uspenski 1956; Norderhaug *et al.* 1977). Only the population at Guba Arkhangel'skaya was considered to be fairly large (Belopol'skii 1957), and it was later estimated to have only 11,000 birds (Zelickman and Golovkin 1972) or about 5500 pairs (Golovkin 1984). This suggests that the population is relatively small, certainly well below the 'millions of birds' reported earlier (Freuchen and Salomonsen 1958). It most likely falls in order 5 and is tentatively placed at 50,000 pairs until additional information is obtained (Table 2.3). The status of the Novaya Zemlya population is poorly known; workers in the area (Uspenski 1956; Belopol'skii 1957; Zelickman and Golovkin 1972) did not mention any change, but Golovkin (1984) suggests that populations may have increased since 1950.

9. SEVERNAYA ZEMLYA AND NEW SIBERIAN ISLANDS

Details of these populations are very scanty. Severnaya Zemlya was not included in the list of large colonies given by Belopol'skii (1957), and neither area was identified as being particularly important for Dovekies by Kartaschew (1960). Kartaschew (1960) placed most of the Severnaya Zemlya birds on the north coast of Ostrov Oktyabr'skoy Revolyutsii; it is believed that there are also some birds breeding at Mys Chelyuskin on the Taymyr coast opposite Ostrov Bol'shevik (the southernmost major island of the Severnaya Zemlya group) and on Ostrov Bennetta in the New Siberian Islands (Kartaschew 1960). Uspenski (1959) estimated that there were at least 75,000 breeding pairs in 10 colonies on the Severnaya Zemlya archipelago. Overall, those populations represent the eastern limit of the Dovekie's breeding range and most likely comprise only a small number of birds. There is an obvious need to obtain more details on the population size and status of Dovekies at these two locations.

VI. COMMON MURRE, *Uria aalge*

Summary: Circumpolar polytypic boreo-low arctic species. Breeds colonially between 76°N and 40°N on islands and coastal cliffs mainly in the northern part of the boreal zone and low-arctic waters, with small numbers in the southern region of the boreal zone. Colonies occur in the

North Atlantic from southern Labrador and Greenland south to Bay of
Fundy and from Iceland, Jan Mayen, Bjørnøya and northwest Russia
south to Portugal; in the North Pacific from Bering Strait south to central
California and northern Japan. Winters mainly offshore with most birds in
boreal waters, but some in cool subtropical zone south to Georges Bank
and western Mediterranean (Atlantic) and southern California and southern Japan (Pacific).

A. Breeding Distribution and Abundance

The Common Murre is a boreo-low arctic species breeding in the western Atlantic from the Bay of Fundy, Gulf of St. Lawrence, east Newfoundland, Labrador and west Greenland east to Iceland, Jan Mayen, the
Faeroe Islands, British Isles (Shetland Isles, Orkney Islands, mainland
Scotland, Ireland, England, Wales, Channel Islands), and Brittany south
to Spain and Portugal, and northeast to Helgoland, Baltic Sea, west Norway, Murmansk Coast of the Kola Peninsula, Bjørnøya, Spitsbergen and
Novaya Zemlya (Fig. 2.7). The size of the breeding population in the
North Atlantic is estimated to be about 4 million (range: 3.0–4.5 million)

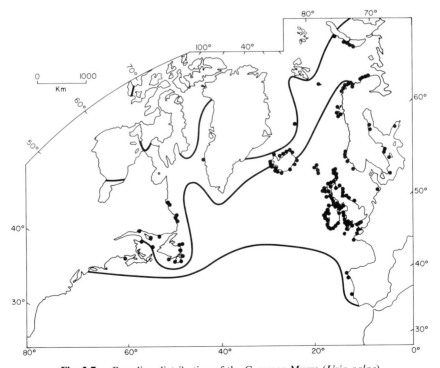

Fig. 2.7.   Breeding distribution of the Common Murre (*Uria aalge*).

TABLE 2.4

Distribution and Estimates of Breeding Population Sizes (Pairs) of the Common Murre (*Uria aalge*)

Region	Regional totals Pairs	%	Census date	References
Canada				
Labrador	72,000	1.7	1978–1983	Nettleship (1980 and unpublished)
E. Newfoundland	500,000	12.0	1972–1980	Nettleship (1980 and unpublished)
Gulf of St. Lawrence	29,000	0.7	1974–1982	Nettleship (1980); Chapdelaine and Brousseau (1984)
Bay of Fundy	50[a]	<0.1	1981	W. H. Drury (personal communication)
TOTALS	600,000	14.4		
W. Greenland	400[b] (300–500)	<0.1	1980, 1983	Salomonsen (1950, 1967, 1981); Evans (1984); K. Kampp (personal communication)
Iceland	1.6 million (0.8–1.6 million)[c]	38.4	1954–1965	Einarsson (1979); Gardarsson (1982); Petersen (1982)
Jan Mayen	500[b]	<0.1	1983	van Franeker and Camphuijsen (1984)
Faeroe Islands	300,000	7.2	1983	Olsen (1982 and personal communication); H. Meltofte (personal communication)
British Isles				
Scotland	656,000[d]	14.7	1969–1979	Stowe and Harris (1984)
England	23,500	0.6	1969–1980	Stowe and Harris (1984)
Wales	16,000	0.3	1969–1980	Stowe and Harris (1984)
Ireland	86,000	2.1	1969–1981	Stowe and Harris (1984)
Channel Islands	<100	<0.1	1969–1980	Stowe and Harris (1984)
TOTALS	781,600	18.7		
Brittany, France	290	<0.1	1980–1981	Henry and Monnat (1981)
Spain and Portugal (Iberian Peninsula)	100	<0.1	1981–1982	Bárcena *et al.* (1984)
Helgoland, Germany	2,000	<0.1	1981	Vauk (1982)
Denmark, Sweden and Finland (Baltic Sea)	9,400	0.2	1971–1983	Hedgren (1975); Nord (1977); Hilden (1978); S. O. F. (1978); Andersson (1979); Grenmyr and Sundin (1981); Gustafsson and Hogstrom (1981); Joensen (1982);

TABLE 2.4 (*Continued*)

Region	Regional totals		Census date	References
	Pairs	%		
Denmark, Sweden and Finland (Baltic Sea) (*Continued*)				P. Jonsson (personal communication); M. Kilpi (personal communication); P. Lyngs (personal communication)
Norway	110,000	2.6	1974–1981	Brun (1979); Barrett and Vader (1984)
Kola Peninsula	17,000	0.4	1960–1976	Gerasimova (1962); Skokova (1962); Shkliarewicz (1977); Golovkin (1984)
Bjørnøya	750,000 (0.4–1.0 million)	18.0	1980	van Franeker and Luttik (1981)
Spitsbergen	150[e] (100–200)	<0.1	—	F. Mehlum (personal communication); Norderhaug et al. (1977)
Novaya Zemlya	750	<0.1	1950	Uspenski (1956)
TOTALS	4,170,000 (3.0–4.5 million)	100.0		

[a] Discovered breeding on Yellow Murr Ledge in June 1981 by W. H. Drury at which time 25 eggs and 50 birds were counted. Murres became locally extinct at this site in the 1800s and had not recolonized the area by 1973; adults with young were seen at sea between Grand Manan Island and Machias Seal Island in 1973 (Squires 1976) and in 1980 by Gunnlaugsson (W. H. Drury, personal communication).
[b] Rough estimate only—see text.
[c] Estimate reduced by 50% to account for possible reductions in populations—see text.
[d] British Isle totals are 1983 populations derived from census counts in the years shown.
[e] Rough estimate only, thought to be between 100 and 200 pairs (F. Mehlum, personal communication).

pairs, with 15% in the western Atlantic and 85% in the eastern Atlantic (Table 2.4). About 70% of the total population breeds in the southern part of the low-arctic zone (Fig. 2.7), which includes particularly large numbers concentrated at a very few colonies in east Newfoundland (12%), Iceland (38%) and Bjørnøya (18%). Most birds breeding in boreal waters occur in the Faeroe Islands (7%) and Scotland (ca. 15%), with smaller and more widely dispersed colonies elsewhere through Britain, Ireland, Scandinavia, and northwest Russia. Only small relict breeding groups remain in Germany, France, Spain and Portugal (Table 2.4).

B. Regional Populations and Status

1. EASTERN CANADA

Common Murres have an extremely limited breeding range in eastern North America, with 95% of the population in east Newfoundland and southern Labrador (Table 2.4). The most recent surveys (1972–1983) give a population estimate of about 600,000 breeding pairs, of which 83% (500,000 pairs) breed in east Newfoundland with most at Funk Island (396,000 pairs), Green Island (74,000 pairs) and southern Labrador (72,000 pairs, mostly at the Gannet Islands: 46,600 pairs). There are only eight other colonies, seven in the Gulf of St. Lawrence (29,000 pairs) and Yellow Murr Ledge in the Bay of Fundy (< 50 pairs), which together comprise only 5% of the population in eastern Canada. This highly aggregated pattern of breeding distribution exposes the eastern North American Common Murre population to considerable risk, particularly from offshore oil and fisheries developments underway in Newfoundland and Labrador.

The Common Murre was once exceedingly numerous and widespread in temperate waters of northeastern North America (Tuck 1961). It is now very much reduced, with many former colonies in the Gulf of St. Lawrence and farther south extirpated during the nineteenth century. Details of these historical breeding sites and the reasons for their demise are well documented (Knight 1908; Bent 1919; Johnson 1940; Palmer 1949; Tuck 1961; Drury 1973–1974). The large reduction in numbers since the mid-1800s was mainly owing to severe and lengthy human persecution by egging and shooting at the colonies; such destruction continued well into the 1900s and continues on a more limited scale in certain remote areas.

After the *Migratory Bird Treaty* of 1916 between Canada and the United States, federal bird sanctuaries were established along the North Shore of the Gulf of St. Lawrence in an attempt to safeguard the surviving small populations. Counts at these colonies since 1925 showed a very slight increase up to 1940 (Lewis 1931, 1937, 1942), followed by an irregular decline, reaching in 1972 a level lower than in 1925 when protection began (Moisan and Fyfe 1967; Nettleship and Lock 1973). Surveys from 1972 onwards using well-standardized census procedures showed murre numbers increasing from 5635 birds in 1972, to 9235 in 1977, and 11,905 in 1982, a level similar to that in the period 1935–1960 (Chapdelaine 1980; Chapdelaine and Brousseau 1984). This small increase is encouraging, but murre populations, once removed or significantly reduced, seem unlikely to reappear and show rapid sustained recovery unless conditions are optimal (i.e., source of original disturbance removed and very favourable breeding conditions—see below). The failure to recover fully is striking when it is remembered that the North Shore population was once large enough to allow an estimated harvest of 750,000 eggs annually in the late 1800s (Coues 1861; Frazer 1887; Johnson 1940; Tuck 1961).

In Newfoundland and Labrador, where persecution was equally severe, populations were also reduced or destroyed (Townsend and Allen 1907; Bent 1919; Todd 1963). Murre colonies in Newfoundland were probably eradicated relatively early, much as described for Great Auks at Funk Island (see above) by French, Spanish, Portuguese and English fishermen using them as a source of fresh food, fish bait and oil from the 1600s onwards. Heavy exploitation of seabirds in Labrador probably took place later, particularly in the second half of the nineteenth century when the inshore cod fishery developed and coastal settlements were established (Gosling 1910; Innis 1940). With heavy small-boat fishing in nearshore waters, the bird colonies were undoubtedly discovered and exploited by collection of eggs and shooting of adults. By the late 1800s the eastern North American Common Murre population was at an all-time low, with only very small groups surviving.

Numbers of Common Murres remained low in both Newfoundland and Labrador from the turn of this century for three or four decades. At Green Island, Witless Bay, Common Murres were found breeding about 1936, the first time within the memory of the oldest fishermen in the area (Tuck 1961), as the Newfoundland population began to expand and recolonize old breeding areas. Once established, the population at Green Island increased dramatically, from at least 3000 pairs in 1941 (Peters and Burleigh 1951) to roughly 10,000 in 1951, and 50,000 pairs in 1959 (Tuck 1961). Small colonies of murres were established on nearby Gull Island and Great Island in the early 1960s or slightly earlier (Peters and Burleigh 1951), and the Green Island population was about 74,000 breeding pairs in 1979–1980 (Nettleship 1980).

The Common Murre population at Funk Island also increased enormously during this period, though population data during the period of rapid increase (1945–1959) are difficult to interpret. In the 1500s, when Jacques Cartier (in 1534 and 1535), Sir Humphrey Gilbert (in 1583) and others stopped at Funk Island to take on supplies of Great Auks, murres, and other seabirds for food (Hakluyt 1904, pp. 4, 10–11, 14, 49; Biggar 1924; Tuck 1961), murres were limited in space owing to the presence of Great Auks. The Common Murre population was doubtless smaller than today, as it would be difficult to have 100,000 pairs of Great Auks as well as 400,000 pairs of Common Murres breeding on a rock with an area of only about 0.2 km^2. Numbers no doubt were significantly reduced through the 1700s, particularly late in the century when both Great Auks and murres were commercially exploited for their feathers and oil (Cartwright 1792) as well as for food and bait. In 1874 Milne (1875) suggested the presence of reasonably large numbers of murres, but by 1887 Lucas (1890) recorded 'comparatively insignificant' numbers. No details exist after this until the 1930s. V. C. Wynne-Edwards circled Funk Island by boat on 29 June 1934, confirming the presence of breeding murres, but could not land owing to rough seas; the 10,000 individuals or pairs attributed to him by Johnson (1940) and included by Tuck (1961) represented only a 'wild guess based on birds on the sea and flying overhead and should not be used as an estimate of population size' (V. C. Wynne-Edwards, personal communication). In 1936 Gilliard (1937) esimated 10,000 breeding pairs restricted to the southwestern part of the island, and Peters and Burleigh (1951) estimated 15,000 pairs in 1945. Tuck's (1961) first estimate of 40,000 pairs in 1951 suggested a substantial increase since 1945, but differences in census techniques do not permit an exact comparison. The counts made by Tuck (1961, Table 5) between 1951 and 1959 show that the population underwent an enormous and rapid increase in size, although by how much and at what rate are uncertain. According to L. M. Tuck (personal communication), once the estimates of numbers moved from tens of thousands into hundreds of thousands it became extremely difficult to place a satisfactory figure on population size. Estimates from 1956 onwards were made by adding a percentage to the previous figure, knowing that the population had increased but without being able to measure it in a quantitative manner. The figure of 500,000 pairs in 1959 represented a 25% increase compared to 1958, but cannot be compared with later, systematic estimates. To differentiate between 300,000 and 500,000 pairs on the ground was, and remains, impossible. In 1972 a systematic aerial–ground quadrat method of estimating the Common Murre population at Funk Island produced a figure of 396,000 pairs (see Birkhead and Nettleship 1980, Table 3, for details). If we assume that this aerial–ground technique provided a reliable estimate (additional tests in 1975 and 1980 suggest that this is the case) and that murres on Funk Island have continued to increase since 1959 (which is confirmed by ground photographic records), the population size in 1959 was probably somewhere between 250,000 and 300,000 pairs. The Funk Island population has increased in certain areas since 1972 and now probably exceeds 400,000 pairs (D. N. Nettleship, unpublished observations).

Events in Labrador were similar, though less dramatic because of the smaller numbers of birds. Several ornithologists visited colonies along the Labrador coast in the early 1900s (Austin 1932; Tuck 1961; Todd 1963), but no thorough estimates of murre numbers were obtained. L. M. Tuck's surveys in 1952–1953 showed slight increases at sites examined in 1926–

1927 by Austin (1932), and the apparent reestablishment of birds at two or three others in southern Labrador (Tuck 1961). The most dramatic increases occurred between 1954 and 1978, with increases at all seven previously surveyed locations for an overall increase from about 12,600 to 55,000 breeding pairs (Tuck 1961; Brown et al. 1975; Elliot et al. 1978; Lock 1979; Nettleship 1980). Despite possible differences in census techniques, the magnitude of the change suggests a substantial increase in numbers over the 25-year interval.

Reasons for the increases in the Newfoundland and Labrador populations are obscure. One possibility is that over-exploitation of Atlantic cod, the baleen whales and seals over the last 30–40 years may have resulted in an unusually high availability of capelin for murres and other capelin feeders. When the other capelin predators are removed or markedly reduced in numbers, a surplus of capelin theoretically becomes available to the birds. This might increase annual productivity and adult survival, reduce pre-breeding mortality, and result in rapid growth of the murre population. Allowance for this 'harvestable surplus' of capelin was identified in the Canada Department of Fisheries and Oceans modelling exercise in the early 1970s in deriving their total allowable catch (TAC) figures for the now ongoing commercial capelin fishery. Emigration of murres from areas under heavy persecution by humans (e.g., North Shore of the Gulf of St. Lawrence) may have occurred, but its contribution to the observed increases must have been small as populations on the North Shore were severely reduced several decades before the Newfoundland–Labrador increases began. Emigration from the eastern North Atlantic, as suggested by Southern et al. (1965), also seems unlikely on the basis of patterns of dispersion (see Chapter 9, this volume) and high fidelity to the natal colony. Once the original overestimates have been corrected the increases can be explained by the productivity of the birds themselves, given the presence of a food-rich environment throughout the year due to the reduction of cod, seals and whales. The test of this hypothesis is now under way: as commercial exploitation of capelin off east Newfoundland continues (since 1972), capelin stocks will diminish, to be followed by declines in capelin-associated species, such as murres and other alcids (Nettleship 1977a). The capelin fishery collapsed, and the offshore fishery was closed by regulation from 1978 to 1981. Time will reveal what impact such reduction in capelin availability will have on recruitment and size of the murre population breeding in Newfoundland waters.

In summary, the Common Murre in eastern America is now much reduced in numbers and restricted in distribution compared to earlier times, with 90% of the population breeding at two sites in eastern Newfoundland and one in southern Labrador. The marked decline in numbers over the last 200 years was caused mainly by egging and shooting at colonies. No substantial recovery has occurred in southern parts of its range; elsewhere populations have either maintained their numbers at reduced levels, or have increased substantially from the late 1940s to the early 1970s, particularly in east Newfoundland and southern Labrador. The species may still be increasing slightly in Newfoundland and Labrador, but the impact of the recent commercial capelin fishery is not yet known.

2. WEST GREENLAND

Common Murres breed in very small numbers at Sermilinguaq, Sukkertoppen District, and at Ydre Kitsigsut, Frederikshåb District. At Sermilinguaq, the repeated collection during summer of adult Common Murres (since the late 1800s) in summer plumage, and with developed ovaries and incubation patches, suggested that they did breed there among the large numbers of Thick-billed Murres (Salomonsen 1950, 1967), but this was confirmed only recently by N. Andersen, who placed numbers at no more than a couple of hundred pairs (K. Kampp, personal communication). Another small breeding group was discovered at Ydre Kitsigsut in the late 1970s by F. Jensen, and estimated to be about 200 pairs in 1983 (K. Kampp, personal communication).

3. ICELAND

The Common Murre breeds around the entire island on coastal cliffs, headlands and skerries, with most birds concentrated at three sites on the northwest peninsula (Fig. 2.7). The large colonies at Látrabjarg (620,000 pairs), Haelavíkurbjarg (400,000 pairs), and Hornbjarg (360,000 pairs) together comprise more than 90% of the total Icelandic Common Murre population of about 1.6 million breeding pairs (Table 2.4; Einarsson 1979; Gardarsson 1982; Petersen 1982). All 19 colonies listed by Einarsson (1979) include both Common and Thick-billed Murres, with numbers of the two species roughly similar at the three largest sites located in low-arctic waters, but with mostly Common Murres at the eight smaller colonies along the south coast. Only about 110,000 pairs of Common Murres (7%) breed at colonies associated with boreal waters; all the rest occur in the low-arctic zone. Einarsson (1979) emphasized that those estimates were made mainly between 1954 and 1965, but some as long ago as 1938, so they can only be taken as a rough index of abundance. Furthermore, one colony (Grímsey) in the past (1934 and 1949) was thought to have three times as many Thick-billed Murres as Common Murres (Foster *et al.* 1951), whereas a survey in 1983 indicated that Common Murres exceeded Thick-billed Murres by nearly 10 to 1 (P. G. H. Evans, unpublished observations). A detailed census of the major colonies is urgently required, both to provide an assessment of present numbers and to clarify the major differences between those census figures from the 1950s and those reported from 1979 (see below).

The status of the Icelandic population, thought to be perhaps the largest concentration (38%) of breeding Common Murres in the Atlantic (Table 2.4), is poorly known. No obvious changes in numbers were noted since 1955 (F. Gudmundsson, in Reinert 1976; Petersen 1982 and personal communication). However, counts by Sharp (1980) in 1979 at two of the largest colonies were much smaller than those reported by Einarsson (1979): 61,000 pairs (81,250 birds $\times$ 0.75) instead of 400,000 pairs at Haelavíkurbjarg and 9400 pairs (12,500 birds $\times$ 0.75) instead of 360,000 pairs at Hornbjarg, differences of -85 and -97%, respectively. It seems improbable that changes of that magnitude could have gone unnoticed over a 20- to 25-year period, particularly since both colonies are visited irregularly to collect eggs. However, it is quite likely that small annual changes in numbers would go undetected. So even though part of the difference is probably due to differences in census techniques, we cannot be certain that no decrease in population size at both Haelavíkurbjarg and Hornbjarg has taken place. Moreover, the fact that substantial oceanographic changes have also occurred in the last half century (G. Olafsson, personal communication; see also Chapter 10, this volume) lends further evidence in support of a reduction. For the moment, we can only tentatively conclude that some decline in bird numbers may have taken place, possibly due to climatic amelioration, but that the differences between methods used to estimate bird numbers during the surveys prevents any realistic estimate of the extent of the decrease to be made. Thus, there are important questions concerning population size and status, which are fundamental to understanding the global significance of the Iceland *Uria* population as well as the local situations.

Such information on population size and status is also needed to assess the effects of natural and human-induced disturbances on seabirds and their marine environment. For example, what impact are international commercial fishery ventures having on Icelandic alcid populations, including the Common Murre? What effect might a widely fluctuating fish biomass (e.g., collapse, closure and reopening of the Icelandic-Norwegian capelin fishery between 1981 and 1984) have over the long term on murres and other seabirds in Iceland and neighbouring areas? Clearly, the need to establish a monitoring system for alcid populations in Iceland, comparable with those now in place in eastern North America and northwest Europe, must be considered of the highest priority for seabird work in Iceland.

4. JAN MAYEN

Common Murres breed in small numbers at one or two locations in Jan Mayen. In 1983, van Franeker and Camphuijsen (1984) found about 200 to 300 birds breeding at Splittodden-Skrinnodden on cliffs among 1000 pairs of Thick-billed Murres, the first Common Murres to be seen by observers at Jan Mayen. Three birds were also recorded near the Thick-billed Murre colony at Branderpynten, but none occurred elsewhere when checks were made including the large murre colonies at Storfjellet and Kvalrossen; no surveys of the murre colonies between Kapp Wien and Sørvestkapp were made. Van Franeker and Camphuijsen (1984) have concluded that the total Jan Mayen population is small, probably midway in order 3. The incomplete ornithological record of Jan Mayen precludes any assessment of status change of the population.

5. FAEROE ISLANDS

The Common Murre is an abundant breeding bird in the Faeroes. A census in 1972 of the 18 colonies produced a total of 590,000 birds, or about 390,000 pairs (Dyck and Meltofte 1975). The colonies are scattered on the north and west coasts, with 83% of the birds at seven sites on the southern islands, which include the large populations on Skúvoy (142,000 pairs), Sandoy (68,000 pairs) and Stóra Dímun (46,000 pairs) (Dyck and Meltofte 1975). However, annual counts since 1972 of a portion of the Skúvoy colony (9000 pairs in 1972) show a steady decline to only about 60% of that total in 1983 (Olsen 1982 and personal communication). Furthermore, the overall reduction of 20% between the late 1950s and early 1970s, based on estimates from Skúvoy (Dyck and Meltofte 1975), may more likely have amounted to about 60%. This means that the total decline of the Faeroese murre population may have been as high as 75% during the last 25 years and that it now totals about 300,000 pairs (B. Olsen, personal communication; Table 2.4).

The suspected declines in the Common Murre populations are difficult to assess. Dyck and Meltofte (1975) concluded that shooting and snaring of birds during the breeding season combined with other mortality factors (e.g., oil fouling, drowning in fishnets) may be responsible. They also pointed out the possibility of other contributing factors such as climatic change (Reinert 1976) or food shortages due to over-fishing, and even competition for breeding sites with the expanding Northern Fulmar population (B. Olsen, personal communication). Direct utilization of murres for food by egging and capturing adults at the colony is an age-old custom in the Faeroes, and the fowling practiced over the centuries did not appear to cause reduction in any of the seabird populations involved (Salomonsen 1935, 1979c). In the 1940s Salomonsen estimated the annual kill at 60,000 birds 'but it is certainly very much higher than that' (Williamson 1948). Since the mid-1940s, the shooting and snaring of murres at sea has increased, and the annual toll in the 1970s was estimated to have been about 100,000 to 150,000 birds (Dyck and Meltofte 1973; Salomonsen 1979c). Shooting was permitted year-round until 1979, except within 3 nautical miles of any colony in the breeding season, and there were no bag limits (Dyck and Meltofte 1975; H. Meltofte, personal communication). Thus the combined pressure from shooting and snaring together with drowning in fishnets may account for much of the reduction in murre numbers. Due to that steady and marked decline, murres (and Razorbills) were given full protection against any persecution, including the removal of eggs, from 1 April to 15 August each year between 1980 and 1985 (H. Meltofte and B. Olsen, personal communication).

6. BRITAIN AND IRELAND

The Common Murre breeds colonially on sea-cliffs, rock stacks and coastal islands around most of the British Isles. It is absent in southeast England and scarce and local in northwest England and the east coast of Ireland (Fig. 2.7). Its breeding distribution resembles that of the Razorbill (Fig. 2.5), but where they coexist the numbers of murres are nearly always much larger (Cramp et al. 1974). In the most recent analysis of colony counts Stowe and Harris (1984) calculated the average annual rate of increase for 104 colonies examined to be about 5% since 1969. If this rate of increase is applicable to all colonies, the total British and Irish murre population has risen from 577,000 birds [interpreted directly as pairs in Cramp et al. (1974), i.e., $k = 1.0$, even though Seafarer counts were virtually always counts of individuals] in 1969–1970, to 1.1 million birds in 1983 (Stowe and Harris 1984). However, there have been regional differences in rates of increase. If these are taken into account, the total breeding population is about 781,600 pairs (Table 2.4), nearly 19% of the Atlantic population in 1983, with about 656,000 pairs (84%) located in Scotland, 86,000 pairs (11%) in Ireland, 23,500 pairs (3%) in England, 15,000 pairs (2%) in Wales and only about 100 pairs in the Channel Islands (Stowe and Harris 1984).

The largest colonies in Britain and Ireland are in the Shetland Isles at the Isle of Noss (42,800 pairs) and Foula (40,200 pairs), which together with smaller colonies at Sumburgh Head, Hermaness, and Fair Isle make up about 142,500 pairs, or about 18% of murres in the British Isles. Elsewhere in Scotland there are 88,500 pairs in the Orkney Islands, which includes large colonies at Westray (36,700 pairs), Copinsay (16,000 pairs), and Marwick Head (12,000 pairs). The remainder (386,000 pairs) are scattered along the mainland coast, with a concentration in the northeast adjacent to the Orkneys. Numbers are particularly high along the Caithness coast where eight colonies total almost 95,500 pairs, the largest of which are at Wick-Lybster (25,100 pairs) and Duncansby-Skirza Head (12,500 pairs). Numbers are less high in the northwest, but some large colonies occur at Clò Mór (3400 pairs) near Cape Wrath, Handa (25,000 pairs), Shiant Islands (5300 pairs), North Rona (6000 pairs) and St. Kilda (14,500 pairs) (Stowe and Harris 1984). In England, the major colonies are in the northeast at the Farne Islands (7100 pairs) in Northumberland and around Flamborough Head and Bempton Cliffs (ca. 10,000 pairs) in Humberside, with scattered small colonies on the west coast from St. Bees Head (ca. 1700 pairs) in Cumberland and the Isle of Man (900 pairs) south to Lundy and the north Devon coast (1700 pairs), and only very small breeding groups elsewhere. Most birds in Wales are on coastal islands and headlands in Pembrokeshire (5000 pairs), Caernarvonshire (4400 pairs) and Anglesey (1500 pairs). In Ireland most colonies are along the north and west coasts with the largest on Rathlin, County Antrim (19,000 pairs) and the Cliffs of Moher, County Clare (8700 pairs); colonies are less numerous on the south and east coasts, but significant numbers do occur on Lambay Island, County Dublin (7700 pairs) and the Saltee Islands, County Wexford (8600 pairs). Together, the colonies in Wales and southeast Ireland make the southern Irish Sea an important region for breeding murres (Stowe and Harris 1984).

Status changes of the Common Murre mirror in many ways those of the Razorbill. Although virtually no quantitative data exist from 1900 or before, descriptions of colonies indicate that many were considerably larger than they are now. On the island of Mull, Inner Hebrides, there were 'myriads' in the 1860s where now there are none (Graham 1890; Cramp et al. 1974). Likewise neighbouring Tiree had an estimated 400 pairs in 1891 but none now (Boyd 1958; Cramp et al. 1974). At Ailsa Craig in southwest Scotland, there were said to be 50,000 pairs in 1910, but there are now fewer than 5000 pairs (Gibson 1951 and personal communication). On the northeast coast of England, at Bempton Cliffs, 130,000 eggs were apparently taken at least in 1 year where now there are about 13,000 birds (Nelson 1907; Stowe and Harris 1984). On Bardsey Island, North Wales, 'some hundreds' in 1905 have been reduced to less than 100 birds through the last 20 years (Norris 1953; Bardsey Bird Observatory Reports, 1965–1983). On the Scilly Isles, off southwest Cornwall, there have been a number of colonies in the past, the largest of which was said to have 'hundreds if not thousands' until 1914 to 1915, whereas the entire island group is now considered to have less than 40 pairs (Penhallurich 1969; R. W. Allen, in Stowe and Harris 1984). On the other hand, the colony on the Isle of May in eastern Scotland has increased from 300 pairs in 1888 to between 11,000 and 12,000 pairs in 1981 (Baxter and Rintoul 1953; Harris and Galbraith 1983).

Unfortunately, there is too little information to determine what status changes may have taken place between 1900 and 1930, although Baxter and Rintoul (1953) considered that the colony on the Isle of May had changed very little between 1907 and 1924. A colony on the south coast of England, between Dover and St. Margaret's Bay, was described as large from the mid-1800s until the end of the century. By 1895 it had declined to 60 pairs, and then to 36 pairs in 1908, becoming extinct by about 1910, although this was attributed to rock falls (Tuck 1961). Marked declines also occurred at many colonies from around 1930, mainly in southwest and southern Britain, particularly on Lundy, the Welsh islands, Dorset, Devon and Cornwall coasts, and the Isle of Wight, Hampshire, and Great Saltee, Ireland (Cramp et al. 1974). These persisted to around 1970, although declines are still apparently occurring in some colonies (Stowe 1982a; Stowe and Harris 1984; see also below).

Counts of murres since 1970 at a selection of colonies throughout Britain and Ireland indicated that numbers have increased at most locations (Stowe 1982a; Wanless et al. 1982). Increases appeared to be widespread in north and east Britain (Scotland and east England) with mean annual rates of increase ranging from 5 to 14%. Elsewhere in Britain, 13 of 15 colonies examined showed no change during the period of study (1972–1979), the exceptions being declines at two colonies in southwest Wales, although single counts indicate a number of decreases at small colonies along the Cornish coasts. In Ireland, numbers remained stable or increased on the north coast, but 6 of 15 study plots at four colonies along the west coast showed decreases ranging from 2 to 5% (Stowe 1982a). In summary, murres appear to be increasing in north and east Britain, and remaining fairly stable elsewhere, though with some declines in southwest Britain and Ireland (Harris 1976b; Stowe 1982a; Stowe and Harris 1984).

7. BRITTANY, FRANCE

The breeding population was estimated to be about 250 pairs in 1977–1978 (Henry and Monnat 1981), with 178 pairs at colonies in Côtes-du-Nord (Cap Fréhel and Les Sept Iles) and 70–75 pairs in Finistère (near Ile de Crozon). Information from the past suggests that numbers were considerably reduced by 1900. They increased to several thousand birds in the period 1930–1940, after which the population declined more or less continuously to the 1970s (Yeatman 1976; Guermeur and Monnat 1980). In the late 1960s the population was of the order of 300 pairs, but between 1971 and 1978 it reached its lowest recorded level of not more than 230 pairs. The 1980–1981 population is tentatively placed at 290 pairs; Henry and Monnat (1981) suggest that numbers are being maintained only by immigration, probably from southern Britain or Ireland.

8. SPAIN AND PORTUGAL

Very small breeding groups along the west coast of the Iberian Peninsula totalling a little over 100 pairs in 1981–1982 (Table 2.4): west Galicia in Spain – Islas Sisargas (6 pairs), Cabo Villano (30 pairs), Islas Cíes (2 pairs); and the Ilhas Berlengas (75 pairs) in Portugal (Bárcena et al. 1984). The Iberian Common Murre population has decreased dramatically over the last 20–25 years, from about 20,000 birds in the 1950s to roughly 300 birds at present. At the Ilhas Berlengas there were 6000 pairs in 1939 and 1948, at Islas Cíes there were 500 pairs around 1960, and at Capelada (Rias Altas region, Spain) numbers decreased from 1200 pairs in about 1960 to none by 1981 to 1982. Oil pollution is believed to be the major cause of these declines, but human disturbance at the colonies during the breeding season (egg collecting, shooting of adults), hunting, and commercial fisheries (both competition for fish food and drowning in fishing nets) are also thought to be important (Bárcena et al. 1984; Teixeira 1983). The population is considered to be in danger of extinction.

9. HELGOLAND, GERMANY

Schultz (1947) reported 6000 birds seen in 1947 and suggested that the breeding population was perhaps 2000 pairs. The population was estimated to be only 1000 pairs from 1960 to 1969, after which numbers decreased to 775 pairs in 1973 and 1974 (Vauk 1982). In recent years the population has steadily increased, from 825 pairs in 1975 to 2000 pairs in 1981 (Rheinwald 1982; Vauk 1982).

10. DENMARK, SWEDEN AND FINLAND (BALTIC SEA)

The Common Murre breeding population in the Baltic Sea between 1971 and 1974 was from about 8800 to 11,000 pairs (Hedgren 1975). It is restricted to nine colonies (one each in Denmark and Finland, seven in Sweden), with the bulk of the population at two sites near Gotland off the east coast of Sweden: Stora Karlsö (6400 pairs) and Lilla Karlsö (1200 pairs). The only other significant colony is at Graesholm (1000–1500 pairs: Salomonsen 1979c; Joensen 1982; P. Lyngs, personal communication), about 17 km northeast of Bornholm (Denmark). The remaining six colonies are very small (< 50 pairs each) and situated along the coast south of Stockholm (Källskären, Bodskär), in the Gulf of Bothnia (Gnäggen, Bonden), and in the Gulf of Finland (Aspskär). The total breeding population at present is estimated at about 9400 pairs (Table 2.4), with about 7800 pairs in Sweden, 1500 pairs in Denmark, and around 50 pairs in Finland.

Common Murres were almost exterminated in the Baltic Sea during the nineteenth century, probably because of persistent disturbance at the colonies (egging and killing of adults) and hunting outside the breeding season. By 1880, the only breeding population known was some 20 birds at Stora Karlsö (Voous 1960; Hedgren 1975). Stringent protective measures were imposed, and this small breeding group increased in size and expanded geographically until by 1942 numbers were estimated to be 15,000 birds (Tuck 1961). Higher population figures for the Baltic as a whole (e.g., 50,000 pairs by 1936; Voous 1960) and for individual colonies (e.g., 35,000–40,000 pairs on Stora Karlsö in the 1950s: Hedgren 1975) must have been overestimates, as according to Hedgren (1975) numbers have probably not changed markedly since the 1950s, although in Denmark and Finland (former recolonized in 1930) the populations are apparently increasing (Grenmyr and Sundin 1981; Gustafsson and Hogstrom 1981; Hirschfeld *et al.* 1982; Joensen 1982; M. Kilpi, personal communication; P. Lynys, personal communication).

11. NORWAY

The Common Murre breeds colonially at 25 locations along the west coast with the population (1974–1981) estimated to be 110,000 pairs (Brun 1979; Barrett and Vader 1984). A northern group of 18 colonies extends from Røst in Nordland District north to Kobbholmfjorden, Sør-Varanger District adjacent to the Kola Peninsula and includes about 92% of the population, and a smaller group of 7 colonies in the south is centred around Rundøy in Møre og Romsdal District. About 70% of the Norwegian population breeds in the Troms–western Finnmark region at Hjelmsøya (70,000 pairs) and Nord-Fugløy (9000 pairs). Other large colonies in the northern sector are Syltefjorden (9000 pairs) and Hornøya (4000 pairs) in eastern Finnmark District, and Røst (6800 pairs) and Vaerøy (1750 pairs) in Nordland District. The only significant colony in the southern group is on Rundøy (9000 pairs). The population breeds mainly in the northern part of the boreal zone (Fig. 2.7).

The Common Murre has decreased markedly in many parts of Norway since the 1940s, as have most alcids (Brun 1969, 1971, 1979). Between 1964 and 1974 the population declined from approximately 161,000 to 99,500 breeding pairs, a decrease of 38% over 10 years (Brun 1979). Information is more limited prior to 1964, but the Sør-Fugløy colony decreased from 10,000 pairs in 1940 to 4000 in 1961, and to only 10 breeding pairs by 1974 (Brun 1979); that population is now extinct (Barrett and Vader 1984). At eight colonies resurveyed since 1974 (most in 1981), two remained the same, four increased and two decreased (Barrett and Vader 1984). The total increase amounted to about 9500 pairs, but much of that was offset by decreases elsewhere. Moreover, several small colonies present in 1974 have disappeared, and the magnitude of the suspected decline at Røst (Tschanz and Barth 1978) is still uncertain (Barrett and Vader 1984). By using the 1981 results for seven colonies and 1974 data for the other colonies, the Norwegian population can be estimated to exceed 100,000 pairs (Barrett and Vader 1984), perhaps as high as 112,000 pairs (Table 2.4). However, until the decline at Røst is assessed and other colonies have been resurveyed, the present size and status of the Common Murre population in Norway cannot be determined accurately. The tentative conclusion is that the population is still declining though perhaps at a reduced rate, and that its total size is no larger and perhaps less than in 1974. The declines since the 1940s are believed to result from human activity, mainly excessive hunting, drowning in fishing nets near colonies, alteration of the summer food supply through commercial fisheries, and disturbance at the colonies by increased visitation during the breeding season and introduced predators, especially feral mink (Brun 1979; Folkestad 1982; Barrett and Vader 1984).

12. KOLA PENINSULA (MURMANSK COAST)

Common and Thick-billed Murres breed together at about 10 small colonies along the Murmansk Coast of the Kola Peninsula (Fig. 2.7). Information on the positions and sizes of the colonies [mainly from work by Gerasimova (1962) and Skokova (1962)] has been summarized by Norderhaug et al. (1977), while Golovkin (1984) gives a review of more recent counts in the region. The colonies extend from Mys Maynavolok south-east to Guba Dvorovaya. The most important of the mainland colonies are Mys Maynavolok (1500 pairs in 1960), Mys Gorodetskiy (2600 pairs), Guba Podpakhta (320 pairs), and Gavrilovskiy (850 pairs). Five hundred pairs of *Uria* spp. have also been recorded breeding on Ostrov Bolshoy Gusinets (Golovkin 1984). There are also important colonies in the Ostrova Sem'ostrovov section of the Kandalaksha State Zaporedrisk (a nature reserve), where on Ostrov Kharlov, Common Murres declined from 3700 pairs in 1938, during the mid-1950s and mid-1960s, but then recovered to reach a maximum of 4200 pairs in 1976 (Shkliarewicz 1977). The number of breeding *Uria* spp. on neighbouring Ostrov Kuvshin increased from 2500 pairs in 1938 to 10,000 in 1976 (Shkliarewicz 1977). The remainder of the Murmansk Coast comprises only small colonies, totalling about 100 pairs of *Uria* spp. in 1960 (Gerasimova 1962; Golovkin 1984). The combined *Uria* populations have been estimated to comprise, on average, 80% Common Murres at all sites except at Ostrov Kuvshin and Guba Dvorovaya (70% Common Murres) and Guba Sel'pinskaya (Thick-billed Murres absent). Those proportions lead to an estimate of about 17,000 pairs of Common Murres breeding along the Murmansk Coast, with 7000 (41%) at Ostrov Kuvshin and 3000 (18%) at Guba Dvorovaya. All colonies are in the low-arctic marine zone.

13. BJØRNØYA

The murre population of Bjørnøya is very large (Jourdain 1922; Bertram and Lack 1933; Duffey and Sergeant 1950; Lütken 1969; Williams 1971, 1974; van Franeker and Luttik 1981). The present sizes of the two *Uria* populations and changes that may have occurred since 1921 are virtually unknown. Murres breed in mixed colonies around the entire island with very large colonies on the southern cliffs (from Glupen to Sørhamna) and smaller colonies elsewhere. No precise estimates of the murre populations were made by the early investigators, but the immense numbers were summarized by Fisher and Lockley (1954) as 'an unknown number of millions of Brunnich's and Common Guillemots'. Both species are breeding in low-arctic waters.

The survey on Bjørnøya by van Franeker and Luttik (1981) in 1980 showed a similar pattern of distribution to earlier descriptions: the bulk of the population at the south end of the island with smaller breeding groups on the west, north and east cliffs. The two *Uria* species were about equal at the huge colonies in the south, but Thick-billed Murres predominated (60–90%) at most other locations examined. Franeker and Luttik concluded that the combined *Uria* population totals approximately 2 million birds with numbers of the two species roughly the same: 1 million birds, which might be interpreted as 750,000 breeding pairs (Table 2.4). Van Franeker and Luttik (1981) emphasized that 2 million murres is a rough estimate only, but they were confident that the murres at Bjørnøya 'must be counted in millions and not in thousands' and are doubtless somewhere low in order 7.

The status of the Bjørnøya population is not known. In 1970 Williams (1971) estimated the total murre population to be about 310,000 birds. However, van Franeker and Luttik (1981) viewed that count as an underestimate caused by differences in survey techniques, partly because their 1980 estimate of 2 million birds was similar to one in 1965 by Lütken (1969). The ratio of Common to Thick-billed Murres at the large southern colonies was reported to be 2:1 in 1948 (Duffey and Sergeant 1950) but 1:1 in 1980 (van Franeker and Luttik 1981). That suggests a marked change in either or both of the *Uria* species during the past 30 years. (See Section VII on Thick-billed Murres for additional details.)

14. SPITSBERGEN

The Common Murre breeds in very small numbers at one location in Spitsbergen; about 100 to 200 pairs breed at Fuglehuken, northern Prins Karls Forland, on the cliffs among 24,000 pairs of Thick-billed Murres, and smaller numbers of Northern Fulmars, Black-legged Kittiwakes and Atlantic Puffins (Norderhaug 1974; Norderhaug et al. 1977; F. Mehlum, personal communication). Breeding has long been suspected in the region as birds were collected in summer (Jourdain 1922; Tuck 1961; Løvenskiold 1964), but firm evidence of breeding and of the size of the population are recent (Norderhaug 1974).

15. NOVAYA ZEMLYA

Common Murres breed in very small numbers along with Thick-billed Murres at eight locations along the west coast from Guba Arkhangel'skaya near the northern end south to Ostrov Kuvshin, exclusively in low-arctic waters (Fig. 2.7). In 1950, Uspenski (1956) estimated the total number of Common Murres in Novaya Zemlya to be no more than 1000 birds, or about 750 pairs (Table 2.4), with the largest colony (300–400 birds) on the south shore of Guba Bezymyannaya. Nothing is known of the present status of the Common Murre population, but declines in Thick-billed Murres between 1942 and 1967 (see below for details) suggest that few Common Murres remain in Novaya Zemlya today.

VII. THICK-BILLED MURRE, *Uria lomvia*

Summary: Circumpolar polytypic panarctic species. Breeds between 82°N and 46°N on islands and sea-cliffs of the North Atlantic from northern Baffin Bay south to Gulf of St. Lawrence and southeast Newfoundland, and from Iceland, Jan Mayen, Bjørnøya, northern Norway, Taymyr Peninsula through eastern Siberia to Cape Parry in Amundsen Gulf and south in the North Pacific to the Aleutian Islands and northern Japan. Most numerous north of *U. aalge* during breeding season, with only a small fraction of the population overlapping with it in southern regions. Winters offshore mainly in low-arctic waters, but some in the northern part of the boreal zone south to the North Sea, Gulf of Maine, Gulf of Alaska and Sea of Japan.

A. Breeding Distribution and Abundance

The Thick-billed Murre is a panarctic species (Fig. 2.8). It is, with the Dovekie, numerically the dominant arctic seabird in the Atlantic region,

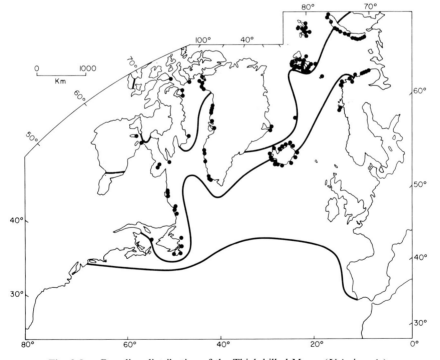

Fig. 2.8.   Breeding distribution of the Thick-billed Murre (*Uria lomvia*).

TABLE 2.5

Distribution and Estimates of Breeding Population Sizes (Pairs) of the Thick-billed Murre (*Uria lomvia*)

Region	Regional totals		Census date	References
	Pairs	%		
Canada				
Lancaster–Jones Sounds	406,000	5.9	1972–1979	Nettleship (1980)
E. Baffin I.	250,000	3.7	1973–1981	Nettleship (1980 and unpublished)
Hudson Strait	785,000	11.5	1972–1983	Nettleship (1980); D. N. Nettleship and A. J. Gaston (unpublished); G. Chapdelaine (personal communication)
Labrador–Newfoundland	12,000	0.2	1972–1983	Nettleship (1980 and unpublished)
Gulf of St. Lawrence	<1,000	<0.1	1973–1984	Nettleship (1980 and unpublished)
TOTALS	1,454,000	21.4		
W. Greenland				
Thule region (north of 75°N)	130,000[a]	1.9	1936	Salomonsen (1950)
Upernavik District	200,000[b] (200,000–400,000)	2.9	1965–1974	Joensen and Preuss (1972); Evans and Waterston (1976); Evans (1984); K. Kampp (personal communication)
Umanak and Jakobshavn Districts	100,000[a]	1.5	1946–1949	Salomonsen (1950)
Sukkertoppen, Godthab and Frederikshåb Districts	5,000[c]	<0.1	1946, 1949, 1971, 1974, 1981, 1983	Salomonsen (1950, 1979a); Boertmann (1979); K. Kampp (personal communication)
TOTALS	435,000	6.4		
E. Greenland Scoresby Sound area	35,000 (30,000–40,000)	0.5	1973–1974	de Korte (1973); Meltofte (1976)

Iceland	2 million[d] (0.8–2.0 million)[e]	29.4	1954–1965	Einarsson (1979); Peterson (1982)
Jan Mayen	75,000	1.1	1983	van Franeker and Camphuijsen (1984)
Bjørnøya	750,000 (0.4–1.0 million)	11.0	1980	van Franeker and Luttik (1981)
Spitsbergen	1 million[d]	14.7	—	F. Mehlum (personal communication); Norderhaug et al. (1977)
Franz Josef Land	100,000[d]	1.5	—	Uspenski (1959); Golovkin (1984)
Novaya Zemlya	945,000	13.9	1967	Uspenski (1956); Zelickman and Golovkin (1972)
Norway	1,200	<0.1	1974–1981	Brun (1979); Barrett and Vader (1984)
Kola Peninsula (Murmansk Coast)	6,000	<0.1	—	Gerasimova (1962); Skokova (1962); Norderhaug et al. (1977)
Severnaya Zemlya, Taymyr Peninsula and New Siberian Is.	?[f]	—	—	See text
TOTALS	6,800,000 (4.9–7.5 million)	100.0		

[a] Salomonsen's estimates from the 1930s and 1940s have been reduced by 50% to account for reductions in populations noted elsewhere since that time (Salomonsen 1970, 1974, 1979a,c; Joensen and Preuss 1972; Evans and Waterston 1976; Kampp 1982) and converted to pairs by using a factor (k) of 0.75. [Figures given in Salomonsen (1950) and expressed as pairs are estimates from counts of individuals which were converted directly into pairs using k = 1.0.]

[b] Figures given as individual birds by Joensen and Preuss (1972) and Evans and Waterston (1976) have been converted to pairs using a factor (k) of 0.75. The Kap Shackleton colony is thought to have undergone a considerable decrease since 1965 (40–80%), and a detailed survey in 1983 by K. Kampp (personal communication) places the population at 100,000 to 150,000 pairs—see text.

[c] The nine colonies comprising Ydre Kitsigsut, Frederikshåb District, and estimated at 56,000 pairs in 1971 (Salomonsen 1979a) are believed to be now (1983) much smaller, probably around 4000 pairs and no more than 10,000 pairs (K. Kampp, personal communication).

[d] Very rough estimate only—see text.

[e] Estimate reduced to account for possible reductions in populations—see text.

[f] Uspenski (1959) gives nearly 20,000 pairs of Uria spp. on Ostrov Preobrazheniya.

with especially large populations in Hudson Strait, Lancaster Sound, Jones Sound, northwest Greenland, Iceland, Bjørnøya, Spitsbergen, Franz Josef Land, and Novaya Zemlya (Table 2.5), although many populations have been seriously depleted within the last 40 years or more by collection of eggs and killing of birds at the colonies, excessive hunting outside the breeding season, and massive mortality through drowning in fishing nets (Salomonsen 1967, 1970, 1979c; Tull et al. 1972; Nettleship 1977a, 1980; Norderhaug et al. 1977; King et al. 1979; Kampp 1982 and personal communication; Petersen 1982). Smaller populations occur in Scoresby Sound (east Greenland) and at Jan Mayen, with only very small groups scattered elsewhere including northern Norway, along the Murmansk Coast of the Kola Peninsula, Severnaya Zemlya east through the New Siberian Islands to the Chukshi Peninsula, Wrangel Island and the Bering Sea and into the North Pacific (Table 2.5).

The North Atlantic breeding population is estimated to be about 6.8 million (range: 4.9–7.5 million) pairs, with about 24% in the western Atlantic and 76% in the eastern Atlantic (Table 2.5). About 75% of the population breeds in the northern part of the low-arctic zone, with many of the largest colonies close to the interface between high-arctic and low-arctic waters (i.e., in northwest Greenland, Iceland, Jan Mayen, Spitsbergen, Novaya Zemlya). The remainder breed in the high-arctic zone, with only a very few (0.1%) in the northern part of the boreal zone (southern Iceland and Norway).

B. Regional Populations and Status

1. EASTERN CANADA

The Thick-billed Murre breeds in colonies, often immense, almost entirely in the cold polar waters north of 57°N, where more than 95% of the eastern North American population occurs at only 11 sites (Nettleship 1980; Gaston and Nettleship 1981). Surveys between 1972 and 1983 indicate a breeding population of about 1,454,000 pairs, of which 406,000 (28%) breed in the Lancaster–Jones Sound region (four colonies), 250,000 (17%) in southeast Baffin Island (two colonies), 785,000 (54%) in Hudson Strait (five colonies), with only small numbers farther south, 12,000 pairs (<1%) in Labrador and eastern Newfoundland (10 colonies) and fewer than 1000 pairs (<0.1%) at Bird Rocks in the Gulf of St. Lawrence (Nettleship 1980 and unpublished observations). The largest colonies in the high arctic are at Coburg Island (160,000 pairs), Cape Hay, Bylot Island (140,000 pairs), and Prince Leopold Island (86,000 pairs). Farther south there are large colonies near Reid Bay, southeast Baffin Island (100,000–

200,000 pairs), at Akpatok Island (north: ca. 350,000 pairs; south: ca. 120,000 pairs) in Ungava Bay, and at eastern Digges Island (180,000 pairs) and Cape Wolstenholme (114,000 pairs) in Digges Sound. Altogether those 1.4 million pairs represented 75% of the Thick-billed Murres breeding in the western Atlantic.

Surveys of Thick-billed Murres in the eastern Canadian Arctic only began in the mid-1950s, and several colonies were little known until the early 1970s (Nettleship 1973b). Insufficient information exists to determine what change in populations have taken place over the long term. Change since the mid-1950s are also difficult to assess, as the population figures from the 1950s (Tuck 1961) were only coarse first estimates generated to provide an index of the relative sizes of the colonies surveyed. Nevertheless, data gathered between 1972 and 1983 indicate a substantial reduction at several colonies in the eastern Arctic since the mid-1950s. A comparison of photographs of sections of the colony at Cape Hay taken in 1957 (Tuck 1961) and in 1976–1979, suggested a decline of 20 to 40% during that interval (Nettleship 1977a and unpublished observations). Furthermore, surveys (1981–1983) of the south and north colonies on Akpatok Island also suggested decreases of 20 to 30% since the first survey by Tuck (1961) in 1954 (G. Chapdelaine, personal communication); it seems quite likely that similar decreases have occurred at the colonies in Digges Sound (D. N. Nettleship, unpublished observations). All of this is consistent with first impressions reported following preliminary surveys of all known arctic colonies in 1972 (Brown *et al.* 1975; Nettleship 1977a).

The declines at high-arctic colonies can probably be attributed to events in west Greenland, where the Lancaster–Jones Sound population goes after the breeding season to spend part of the winter (Tuck 1961; Salomonsen 1967; Gaston 1980). In the years 1969–1971 an estimated 200,000–300,000 murres, many from the Lancaster–Jones Sound region (Salomonsen 1967, 1970), were drowned each fall (September–November) in salmon gill-nets (Tull *et al.* 1972; Christensen and Lear 1977) as they migrated south along the west coast of Greenland. The offshore salmon fishery began in 1968 and continued until 1976 when restrictions to reduce it were imposed (Salomonsen 1979b). That mortality, combined with about 20,000 Lancaster–Jones Sound birds (one-tenth of the total) shot annually in west Greenland [Kampp 1982: reanalysis of hunting mortality in west Greenland indicates that earlier assessment of the kill toll (Salomonsen 1970, 1979c, 1981) were overestimates] and other human-related and natural factors, probably exceeded the annual production of young (474,000 young produced annually by a breeding population of 677,000 pairs—the estimated size of the Lancaster–Jones Sound population in

1957). The evidence points to a drastic decline in the Cape Hay colony since 1957, and several colonies in Greenland have declined as well (Salomonsen 1970, 1979c; Joensen and Preuss 1972; Evans and Waterston 1976; Kampp 1982). The 'unnatural' mortality of murres breeding at low-arctic sites (e.g., Akpatok Island, Digges Island, Cape Wolstenholme) includes the legal hunt of murres off Labrador and Newfoundland in winter. There are no bag limits, and recent surveys in the hunting seasons of 1977–1978, 1978–1979 and 1979–1980 put the average annual murre kill at 450,000 birds, mostly Thick-billed Murres (Wendt and Cooch 1984). This hunting pressure, combined with mortality from oil pollution, net-drowning, commercial fisheries, and natural sources, may well account for the declines suspected at Akpatok Island and elsewhere. Numbers at Prince Leopold Island and Digges Island remained stable from 1975 to 1979 and from 1980 to 1982, respectively, albeit at levels probably much reduced from earlier times (D. N. Nettleship and A. J. Gaston, unpublished observations). Numbers of Thick-billed Murres in southern regions are lower than they once were (Bent 1919; Johnson 1940; Tuck 1961), but they have probably always been relatively small; increases have occurred at several small colonies in southern Labrador (e.g., Gannet Islands) since the early 1950s. To summarize, major declines in numbers (probably 20–40%) have occurred in the eastern Canadian Arctic since the mid-1950s; populations at certain colonies may now be stable (since 1973–1975) but at significantly reduced levels.

2. GREENLAND

Thick-billed Murres breed in large colonies along the west coast from Hakluyt Ø (77°N) in the Thule region south to Umanaq District, with the population concentrated at Kap Shackleton (or Agparssuit) in Upernavik District, the largest Thick-billed Murre colony (*ca.* 100,000 pairs; K. Kampp, personal communication) in Greenland (Salomonsen 1950, 1967; see also Table 2.5). Other large colonies (order 5) are at Saunder Ø and Agpat in the Thule region, Sanderson's Hope in Upernavik District, Sagdleq in Umanak District, and Ivnaq (or Ritenbenk) in Jakobshavn District. Farther south there are only small colonies, although a total of 56,000 pairs bred on six islands at Ydre Kitsigsut (Frederikshåb District) in 1971 (Salomonsen 1979a; note: total of 61,200 pairs given in Salomonsen's Table 1 includes counts of individuals, which when converted using $k = 0.75$ gives 56,000 pairs, *not* 61,200) but numbers have since declined (see below). The population on the east coast is restricted to three colonies near Scoresby Sound: about 3000 pairs (1973) at Raffles Ø off Liverpool Land (de Korte 1973), roughly 30,000 pairs (1974) near Kap Brewster and a small colony (1974) on the east point of Steward Ø (Meltofte 1976). About 60% of the west Greenland birds breed towards the northern boundary of the low-arctic zone, with those in the Thule region and in east Greenland in high-arctic waters.

Major reductions in population have taken place in west Greenland over the last 50 years, with many colonies either decreasing dramatically or disappearing altogether, mainly owing to over-exploitation by humans and associated disturbance at breeding colonies (Salomonsen 1970, 1974a, 1979a, c; Evans and Waterston 1976; K. Kampp, personal communication). The absence of detailed survey information from the 1930s and 1940s makes it difficult to determine precisely how large the declines have been. However, in Upernavik District, where reliable colony counts have been recorded since the mid-1960s, a survey in 1983 suggested that the northern colonies (Kap Shackleton, Kípako) declined by no less than 20–40% since 1965 while those in the south (Sanderson's Hope, Kingigtoq) decreased by at least 50% (K. Kampp, pers. comm.). Furthermore, a comparison of figures given in Evans and Waterston (1976) for counts made at four colonies (Sanderson's Hope, Kípako, Agpatsiait and Kingig-tuarssuak II) in 1965 and 1974 indicate declines of 34, 67, 39, and 86% respectively. In Umanak and Jakobshavn Districts (Disko Bay region), census information is less precise (within orders of magnitude), but major declines are known to have occurred. For example, the Sagdleq colony (Umanak District) may have declined from 500,000 birds in 1921 to 125,000–250,000 in 1949 [Salomonsen (1950); note: figures given in Salomonsen (1950) and expressed as pairs are estimates from counts of individuals which were converted directly into pairs by using a factor $k = 1.0$] and to far fewer than that at present (K. Kampp, personal communication). The Ivnaq colony (Jakobshavn District) was put at 50,000 birds in 1946 (Salomonsen 1950), but in 1980 it was no more than 10,000 birds and possibly as low as 5000–6000 (N. Andersen, in K. Kampp, personal communication). Although those populations have declined alarmingly and continue to do so, the magnitude of the change is difficult to assess owing to the unknown reliability of the early figures which may have been over-estimates of colony size (K. Kampp, personal communication). South of Disko Bay, declines have also taken place. The Sermilinguaq colony (Sukkertoppen District) was more than 100,000 birds in 1925, but in 1946 it had diminished to only 5000 birds (Salomonsen 1950). In Frederikshåb District, the majority of colonies still exist albeit smaller in size. The colony established at Arsuk Fjord in 1972, which increased from 100 pairs in 1973 to 5000 to 10,000 birds in 1976, probably came about through immigration from neighbouring colonies at Ydre Kitsigsut where distur-bance (egging and shooting) was high (Salomonsen 1979a). The Ydre

Kitsigsut colonies were estimated at about 56,000 pairs in 1971 (Salomonsen 1979a), but they totalled only around 4000 pairs in 1983; the magnitude of the decrease is uncertain as the 1971 estimate was probably high (K. Kampp, personal communication). Populations in east Greenland are probably similar in size to when they were first examined by Pedersen (1930) in the 1920s (Salomonsen 1950), although mortality in fishing nets off southwest Greenland may have caused population declines.

Salomonsen (1970, 1974a, 1979a,c) described the factors responsible for the massive declines in murre populations in west Greenland— namely, uncontrolled hunting and egging at colonies, shooting outside the breeding season, and drowning of birds in salmon gill-nets during their southward swimming migration along the west coast. The major problem was, and continues to be, that most of the 100,000 Greenland murres shot each year in Upernavik and Umanak districts were adults taken at the colonies during the breeding season; those shot farther south were largely juveniles, which had far less consequences on population sizes than the removal of breeders (Kampp 1982). Furthermore, the associated disturbance by hunters and eggers at colonies certainly has an important adverse effect on annual productivity (Evans and Waterston 1976). Murres can still legally be shot during summer in northwest Greenland, and the hope that the game laws prepared by Salomonsen (1974a) for the Greenland Provincial Council and enacted 1 January 1978 would at least slow the decline in Thick-billed Murres, is poor (K. Kampp, personal communication). New, more effective legislative measures are needed to reduce disturbance and shooting at colonies in summer. The international Greenland salmon fishery (1968–1976) also contributed to the decline of Greenland murres (see Section VII, B, 1 on eastern Canada for additional details), probably to the same extent as summer hunting (Kampp 1982). Since the closure of that fishery in 1976, the impact of the limited domestic salmon fishery is thought to have been minimal (Kampp 1982), although recent changes in fishing practices (net type, distribution and timing) may have resulted in a renewal of significant net mortality of murres in west Greenland (Piatt and Reddin 1984).

3. ICELAND

Thick-billed Murres are known to breed at 19 sites distributed around the coast of Iceland (Fig. 2.8), normally among Common Murres, with over 95% of the total population (estimated to be 1,950,000 pairs) at only three colonies on the northwest coast: Látrabjarg (420,000 pairs), Haelavíkurbjarg (800,000 pairs) and Hornbjarg (640,000 pairs). The only other large colonies are on Drangey (50,000 pairs) and Grímsey (30,000 pairs), the other 14 colonies ranging in size from 10 to 650 pairs with the 8 colonies on the south coast in boreal waters totalling 1900 pairs (Einarsson 1979). Einarsson (1979) emphasized that the estimates of murre numbers were made over a lengthy period of time (most between 1954 and 1965, but some as long ago as 1938), and may be out of date. They nevertheless indicate a very large population, almost wholly restricted to immense breeding groups at a few locations.

Quantitative information from earlier times does not exist (Petersen 1982). Surveys at two major colonies in 1979 (Sharp 1980) suggest problems, as estimates at both Haelavíkurbjarg and Hornbjarg were much lower in 1979 (Sharp 1980) than in the late 1950s (Einarsson 1979): 61,000 pairs (81,250 birds × 0.75) instead of 800,000 pairs at Haelavíkurbjarg, and 82,500 pairs (110,000 birds × 0.75) instead of 640,000 pairs at Hornbjarg, differences of −92 and −87%, respectively. Furthermore, counts of birds at Látrabjarg in 1981 and Grímsey in 1983 indicate reductions of around 25% (A. Gardarsson, personal communication) and 75% (P. G. H. Evans, unpublished observations), respectively. Most if not all of these differences could reflect differences in survey procedures. However, as with Common Murres in Iceland (see Section VI, B, 3 above), it seems very possible that marked changes in bird numbers have taken place since Einarsson (1979) made his counts. If this is the case, differences between census techniques used prevent an accurate assessment of the declines to be made. Thus, the only estimate that can be assigned to the Icelandic Thick-billed Murre population is a range from high order 6 to low order 7. There is a real need to determine accurately the current size and status of that population, which may comprise as much as 29% of the Atlantic total.

4. JAN MAYEN

The population of Thick-billed Murres breeding at Jan Mayen is known to be large, but only recently has an attempt been made to determine its size. Fisher and Lockley (1954) stated that the island's seabird population probably exceeded 1 million birds and that the Thick-billed Murre colony was vast. Tuck (1961) suggested that Thick-billed Murres may be the most abundant seabird there, although Dovekies are also numerous. In 1983 van Franeker and Camphuijsen (1984) performed an extensive survey of seabirds on Jan Mayen. In the north on cliffs around Beerenberg they found a large colony (*ca.* 60,000 birds) at Storfjellet and only small ones elsewhere: Splittodden-Skrinnoden (1500 birds), Fulmarfloget (low in order 4), and Fugleberget (1000 birds). South of that were colonies at Kvalrossen (3400 birds), on the eastern cliffs (mainly at Sørvestkapp) of

Sørbukta (10,000 birds), and at least two concentrations between Kapp Wien and Sørvestkapp (both low in order 5), where bad weather hampered observations. Van Franeker and Camphuijsen (1984) estimated the size of the total population at 100,000 individuals, or about 75,000 breeding pairs (Table 2.5). There is no information on population status.

5. BJØRNØYA

Thick-billed Murres breed around the entire island, along with Common Murres, concentrated in very large colonies at the southern end (from Glupen on the west coast south to Fuglefjellet and east to Sørhamna) with only smaller colonies elsewhere. In 1980 van Franeker and Luttik (1981) found those smaller groups to consist mainly of Thick-billed Murres (60–90%), whereas at the huge colonies in the south the two species were almost equal (i.e., 50% Thick-billed Murre). They estimated the combined *Uria* population to be about 2 million birds, and concluded that Thick-billed Murres made up about one-half, equivalent to about 750,000 pairs, all in low-arctic waters.

The murres at Bjørnøya have been viewed by ornithologists over several decades (Jourdain 1922; Bertram and Lack 1933; Duffey and Sergeant 1950; Lütken 1969; Williams 1971, 1974) and the number of murres has remained large, but whether the populations are stable or not is unknown. The ratios of Common Murres to Thick-billed Murres reported in 1948 (Duffey and Sergeant 1950) and 1980 (van Franeker and Luttik 1981) were similar for the smaller colonies (predominance of Thick-billed Murres), but altered at the large southern colonies from about 33% Thick-billed Murres in 1948 to roughly 50% in 1980. What this may mean to both *Uria* populations is unclear. Various possibilities exist, but only a thorough examination of the data gathered in 1948 and 1980 may allow meaningful conclusions.

6. SPITSBERGEN

There is a very large population in Spitsbergen, chiefly on headlands in the Hopen region (Lyngefjellet, Kollerfjellet) in the southeast, Bellsund region (Ingeborgfjellet) in the southwest, and Hinlopen region (Alkefjellet) in the northeast (Løvenskiold 1964; Norderhaug et al. 1977). In a review (excluding Bjørnøya), Norderhaug et al. (1977) listed 48 colonies with more than 1000 pairs: 30 in order 4, 14 in order 5, and 4 in order 6. The colonies tended to be clustered towards the boundary between the high-arctic and low-arctic marine zones (Fig. 2.8), with roughly 25% high-arctic and 75% low-arctic sites. The most recent estimate (1982) of the Spitsbergen population by the Norwegian Polar Research Institute was about 1 million pairs, as a very rough estimate (F. Mehlum, personal communication). The status of that large and important population is not known.

7. FRANZ JOSEF LAND

Thick-billed Murres are known to breed at 13 colonies, mainly on cliffs and capes in the southwest part of the archipelago, but with at least two small colonies along the north coast including Mys Fishera, the northern-most (*ca.* 81°N) murre colony known (Norderhaug *et al.* 1977). The populations have been described as vast (Salomonsen 1950; Fisher and Lockley 1954; Tuck 1961), but few quantitative estimates exist. Norderhaug *et al.* (1977) reviewed available information (based largely on Gorbunov 1932); those mostly qualitative colony descriptions (following methods outlined for Dovekies at Franz Josef Land in Section V, B, 6 above) produced an estimate of roughly 450,000 pairs constituting one large colony at Mys Flora on Ostrov Nortbruk (*ca.* 100,000 pairs), six colonies in order 5, five in order 4 and one in order 3; this rough estimate indicates a population somewhere in order 6 (>100,000 pairs). Golovkin (1984) gives the total population size as 100,000 pairs (Table 2.5), on the basis of surveys by Uspenski (1959), with the most important colony (*ca.* 50,000 pairs) at Ostrov Nortbruk. It seems unlikely that any of the Franz Josef Land seabird populations (Dovekie, Thick-billed Murre, Black Guillemot) can be very large, because the archipelago is small, about 90% covered in ice, and surrounded by dense pack-ice on all but the southwest edge. Nothing is known of the status of this high arctic population.

8. NOVAYA ZEMLYA

The Thick-billed Murre breeds in very large numbers at 42 Colonies along the west coast from Ostrov Gemskerk and Ostrova Oranskiye south to Guba Sakhanikha. Uspenski (1956) estimated a total of 1,880,000 birds (*ca.* 1,410,000 pairs), using census data from 1942 and 1950. However, two of the largest colonies (Guba Arkhangel'skaya and Zaliv Vil'kitskogo) apparently declined from 700,000 birds in 1942 (Uspenski 1956) to 391,000 birds in 1967 (Zelickman and Golovkin 1972), a decrease of about 44% (unfortunately these two colonies were not censused by

Uspenski in 1950). If the 1942 estimate of 2,250,000 birds (Uspenski 1956) was reduced by 44%, the total population in 1967 might be 1,260,000 birds, or 945,000 pairs. Of that total, 58% bred at only three colonies: Guba Arkhangel'skaya (22%), Zaliv Vil'kitskogo (9%) and Guba Bezymyannaya (27%). About 10% of the population breeds in high-arctic waters with the remainder in the northern part of the low-arctic zone (Fig. 2.8).

The history of the Novaya Zemlya population is one of excessive exploitation of murre eggs and killing of birds by humans (Uspenski 1956; Belopol'skii 1957; Tuck 1961; Norderhaug et al. 1977). Before the commercial exploitation began, the largest colony, in Guba Bezymyannaya (comprising three parts: North Bezymyannaya, South Bezymyannaya, Ostrov Kutov), was estimated to be 1,640,000 birds in the years 1933–1934 (Krasovski 1937). Under exploitation, the population quickly declined to 600,000 birds by 1942 and to only 290,000 birds in 1948, a decrease of 82% in 14 years (Uspenski 1956). In 1947 the murre 'harvest' was halted and the colony made a bird sanctuary; by 1950 bird numbers had increased to 371,000 individuals (Uspenski 1956). If the 1942 estimate of 600,000 birds was reduced by 44% (the decline recorded between 1942 and 1967 at Guba Arkhangel'skaya and Zaliv Vil'kitskogo), the 1967 estimate for Bezymyannaya would be 336,000 birds. That suggests that the initial recovery may have been short-lived, with return to the original size either unlikely or occurring at an extremely slow rate.

Events at Guba Bezymyannaya are representative of Novaya Zemlya, although timing of the onset of exploitation differed between regions (Uspenski 1956). At Mys Chernetskogo, for example, the population exceeded 200,000 birds in 1942, but in 1950 only 55,000 birds remained. At Mys Lil'ye, numbers declined from about 200,000 in 1925 to only 1000 in 1950 (Uspenski 1956). The catastrophic results of exploitation are a quick and massive reduction in bird numbers followed by permanently reduced populations or local extinctions.

In summary, Thick-billed Murre colonies in Novaya Zemlya have been reduced considerably (40–50%) by excessive exploitation, particularly between 1930 and 1947, and evidence from two of the largest colonies (Zelickman and Golovkin 1972) suggested that populations had not recovered by 1967. Increases reported during the early period of protection (1947–1950) were of short duration and the colonies are *very far* from having been 'completely restored' (Uspenski 1956; Tuck 1961). The use of northern Novaya Zemlya as a site to test nuclear weapons since 1950 will have done nothing to enhance the birds' chances for recovery. Only additional data will permit an assessment of the present status of the population.

9. NORWAY

Thick-billed Murres were first discovered breeding in Norway in 1964; they may have always been present along with Common Murres, but went undetected because of their very small numbers (Brun 1979). The population is estimated to be about 1200 breeding pairs, of which 850 (71%) breed at Hjelmsøya, 200 (17%) at Hornøya, and the rest distributed at six other sites from Vedøya (Røst) in the south to Kjøfjorden in the northeast (Brun 1979; Barrett and Vader 1984). That small northern boreal breeding population is thought to be stable (Barrett and Vader 1984).

10. KOLA PENINSULA (MURMANSK COAST)

The Thick-billed Murre breeds in small colonies at about nine sites, along with Common Murres, on the Murmansk Coast, from Mys May-navolok in the north, south to Guba Dvorovaya (Norderhaug et al. 1977). Gerasimova (1962) and Skokova (1962) estimated the combined Uria population to be 20,000 pairs. Gerasimova (1962) placed the proportion to Thick-billed Murres at 20% for seven of the nine colonies, and 30–35% at the other two locations, which gave a total of about 5400 pairs of Thick-billed Murres on the Kola Peninsula, all in low-arctic waters. Golovkin (1984) suggests that the population has increased since Gerasimova's estimates.

11. SEVERNAYA ZEMLYA, TAYMYR PENINSULA AND NEW SIBERIAN ISLANDS

Information on populations breeding east of Novaya Zemlya in the Kara and Laptev Seas is very limited. The colonies are scattered and small relative to those on Novaya Zemlya (Belopol'skii 1957). In the Kara Sea, there are breeding groups at Ostrov Uyedineniya (off Mys Che-lyuskin, northern tip of Taymyr Peninsula) and at two locations on Ostrov Oktyabr'skoy Revolyutsii (Mys Arkticheskiy and Fiord Matusevicha) in Severnaya Zemlya (Dement'ev et al. 1951; Belopol'skii 1957; Tuck 1961). In the Laptev Sea, only Ostrov Preobrazheniya, situated at the entrance to Khatangskiy Zaliv, and the New Siberian Islands (Stolbovoy, Be-l'koyskiy, Bennetta, Henrietta) are reported as having colonies of Thick-billed Murres (Belopol'skii 1957; Kartaschew 1960; Tuck 1961)—all relatively small breeding populations (e.g., 20,000 pairs of Uria spp. combined on Ostrov Preobrazheniya: Uspenski 1959). There are no colonies of significance farther east until Chaunskaya Guba and Wrangel and the Herald Islands (Kartaschew 1960; Tuck 1961; Portenko 1972).

VIII. BLACK GUILLEMOT, *Cepphus grylle*

Summary: Circumpolar polytypic boreo-panarctic species in the Atlantic and Arctic oceans. Breeds between 82°N and 43°N, from the eastern Canadian Arctic and west Greenland south to Gulf of Maine, east to northern British Isles, Scandinavia and the Baltic Sea and east along northern Russia to the Chukchi and Beaufort seas. Replaced by the sibling Pigeon Guillemot *C. columba* in the Bering Sea and northeast Pacific and by the related Spectacled Guillemot *C. carbo* in the northwest Pacific. Mainly sedentary, wintering close to the breeding area except where the waters are severely ice-bound or completely frozen over.

A. Breeding Distribution and Abundance

The Black Guillemot is a boreo-panarctic species breeding in all marine waters north of the cool subtropical zone (Fig. 2.9). It is less colonial than other Atlantic auks, usually breeding in small groups (5–100 pairs) or as single pairs scattered along the coast except in the northern part of its range where relatively large breeding concentrations also occur. The species' wide dispersion makes it seem almost ubiquitous albeit in small numbers. However, details of the breeding distribution are very sketchy or totally lacking, and even in boreal water areas records from systematic coastal surveys are at best only partially complete. Even less is known of the sizes of the various populations, and attempts to generate such figures will likely produce an underestimate of the Black Guillemots present. What follows is a very coarse first effort to provide some indication of the breeding distribution and numbers in the Atlantic and adjacent arctic seas.

Black Guillemots are especially numerous in the eastern Canadian high Arctic (Lancaster Sound and Jones Sound area), west and southeast Greenland, Iceland, Norway, Spitsbergen and probably Franz Josef Land (Table 2.6). In southwest Greenland and the rest of eastern North America from southeast Baffin Island and the Hudson Bay–Hudson Strait region south through Labrador, the Gulf of St. Lawrence, Newfoundland to the Bay of Fundy, and Maine and Massachusetts, numbers are relatively small and the birds widely scattered. Elsewhere in the eastern Arctic and Atlantic they breed only in small groups in Jan Mayen, Faeroe Islands, northern parts of Britain and Ireland, Baltic Sea (Sweden, northern Denmark, Finland, Estonia, Latvia), along the Murmansk and Terskiy coasts

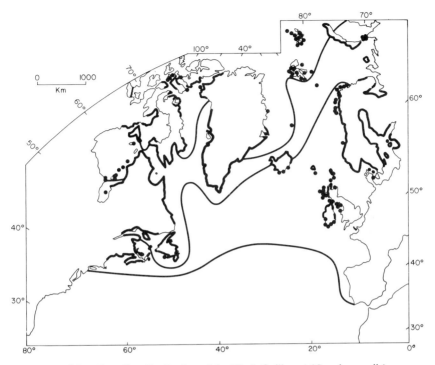

Fig. 2.9.   Breeding distribution of the Black Guillemot (*Cepphus grylle*).

of the Kola Peninsula and the White Sea, Bjørnøya, and Novaya Zemlya. Farther east they occur on many islands through Severnaya Zemlya, New Siberian Islands to Wrangel Island, Chukchi Peninsula, Cape Thompson (Alaska) in the Chukchi Sea east to Herschel Island and Cape Parry on the southern coast of the Beaufort Sea.

The number of Black Guillemots breeding in the North Atlantic and adjacent Arctic seas in tentatively placed at around 270,000 (range: 200,000–350,000) pairs (Table 2.6). About 53% of the total is concentrated in three areas: 55,000 pairs (20%) around northern Baffin Bay (40,000 in Canadian high arctic and 15,000 in northwest Greenland), 50,000 pairs (18%) in Iceland and 22,000 pairs (8%) in Norway. The largest aggregation appears in Iceland, mainly in low-arctic waters but near the convergence of both boreal and high-arctic waters (Fig. 2.9). However, the largest colonies known are in high-arctic waters, in the Lancaster and Jones Sounds region (2000–10,000 pairs) and Scoresby Sound (2000 pairs). Elsewhere, they are scattered in small groups, especially in areas where marine zones overlap (e.g., southeast Greenland, northern Norway, Spits-

TABLE 2.6

Distribution and Estimates of Breeding Population Sizes (Pairs) of the Black Guillemot (*Cepphus grylle*)

Region	Regional totals		Census date	References
	Pairs	%		
E. Canada and New England				
E. high arctic	40,000	15	1972–1979	Nettleship (1974, 1977b, 1980)
E. low arctic (S.E. Baffin, Hudson Strait–Bay area)	10,000[a]	4	—	Sutton (1932); Manning (1946, 1949, 1981); D. N. Nettleship (unpublished)
Labrador	5,000	2	1972–1982	Brown et al. (1975); Lock (1979); Nettleship (1980 and unpublished)
Newfoundland	10,000[a]	4	1967–1980	Nettleship (1980 and unpublished)
Gulf of St. Lawrence	5,000	2	1972–1982	Nettleship (1980 and unpublished); Chapdelaine and Brousseau (1984)
Scotian Shelf–Bay of Fundy–Gulf of Maine	1,500	<1	1970–1971	Lock (1971); Drury (1973–1974)
New England	5,000[b]	2	1970–1972	Drury (1973–1974)
TOTALS	76,500 (50,000–100,000)	29		
W. Greenland	25,000[a] (15,000–40,000)	9	—	Salomonsen (1950, 1967, 1979a); Joensen and Preuss (1972); Evans (1974a, 1984); see also text
E. Greenland	15,000[a] (8,000–22,000)	6	—	Salomonsen (1950); Meltofte et al. (1981 and personal communication); K. de Korte (personal communication)
Iceland	50,000[a]	19	1974–1980	Petersen (1981, 1982)
Jan Mayen	500	<1	1983	van Franeker and Camphuijsen (1984)
Faeroe Islands	2,000[a] (1,000–2,000)	<1	—	Nørrevang (1960); Joensen (1966); B. Olsen (personal communication)

TABLE 2.6 (*Continued*)

Region	Regional totals		Census date	References
	Pairs	%		
British Isles				
Scotland	7,600	3	1969–1970	Cramp *et al.* (1974)
England	40	<1	1969–1970	Cramp *et al.* (1974)
Wales	10	<1	1969–1970	Cramp *et al.* (1974)
Ireland	740	<1	1969–1970	Cramp *et al.* (1974)
TOTALS	8,400[c]	3		
Denmark, Sweden, Finland and Estonia–Latvia S.S.R. (Baltic Sea)	20,000[a] (16,000–23,000)	7	—	Nord (1977); Asbirk (1978); Hilden (1978); S. O. F. (1978); Andersson (1979); Rodebrand (1979); Gustaffsson and Hogstrom (1981); Ahren (1982); Hirschfeld *et al.* (1982); Joensen (1982); P. Jonsson (personal communication); M. Kilpi (personal communication)
Norway	15,000 (11,000–19,000)	5	1970–1983	Brun (1979); Barrett and Vader (1984); R. Barrett (personal communication)
Kola Peninsula and White Sea area	3,700	1	1953–1964	Bianki (1967); see also text
Bjørnøya	300	<1	1980	van Franeker and Luttik (1981)
Spitsbergen	15,000[a] (10,000–20,000)	5	—	F. Mehlum (personal communication)
Franz Josef Land	15,000	5	—	Uspenski (1959); Norderhaug *et al.* (1977); see also text
Novaya Zemlya	5,000	2	1950–1955	Uspenski (1956, 1959)
Severnaya Zemlya, Taymyr Peninsula, east to Chukchi Sea	15,000	5	—	Uspenski (1959); Golovkin (1984)
TOTALS	266,000 (0.20–0.35 million)	100		

[a] Very rough estimate only—see text for details.

[b] Drury (1973–1974) reports a total of 3425 pairs breeding at 114 locations in New England; this total was increased as Drury felt the estimate was probably low due to weather conditions during the survey.

[c] Recent studies in Shetland suggest that the total population may have been underestimated during Operation Seafarer (P. J. Ewins, personal communication), although this may be compensated for to some extent by the fact that counts in 1969–1970 included many non-breeders in its population estimate.

bergen). Unlike the other Atlantic alcids, Black Guillemots are distributed rather evenly over the major marine zones with about 40% of the population breeding in high-arctic waters, and 30% each in low-arctic and boreal waters.

B. Regional Populations and Status

1. EASTERN CANADA AND NEW ENGLAND

Black Guillemots are relatively ubiquitous throughout that vast geographic area, breeding mainly in small groups scattered along rocky coasts where waters are ice-free during summer (Fig. 2.9). The population is probably in the order of 50,000 to 100,000 breeding pairs, with the largest concentrations in the high-arctic region (Table 2.6).

The estimate of population size is a rough one. No complete estimate of the numbers of Black Guillemots exists for any major region, except perhaps for the area around Lancaster and Jones Sounds. However, the results of local surveys at several locations within a region provide a reasonable estimate of average density which can be extrapolated to adjacent coasts. Those figures can then be combined with data from site-specific studies to produce a total estimate of the birds in the region (Table 2.6). About 52% of the total is in the high arctic, where in addition to many small aggregations, large colonies exist at North Kent Island (*ca.* 3000 pairs), Calf Island (*ca.* 5000 pairs) and near Skruis Point (*ca.* 10,000 pairs) in western Jones Sound and at Prince Leopold Island (4000 pairs) in western Lancaster Sound (Nettleship 1974, 1977b, 1980, and unpublished observations; Nettleship and Smith 1975; Nettleship and Gaston 1978; Renaud and Bradstreet 1980; Burton 1982). The remainder are distributed fairly evenly along rocky coastlines from southeast Baffin Island west through Hudson Strait to Foxe Basin and Hudson Bay (13%), south through coastal Labrador (6%) to the Gulf of St. Lawrence (6%), Newfoundland (13%), Scotian Shelf–Bay of Fundy area (2%) and Gulf of Maine and adjacent areas (6%) (Sutton 1932; Manning 1946, 1949, 1952, 1981; Templeman 1945; Manning and Coates 1952; Manning and Macpherson 1952; Macpherson and McLaren 1959; Ellis and Evans 1960; Todd 1963; L. M. Tuck 1967; Freeman 1970; Peck 1972; Drury 1973–1974; Brown *et al.* 1975; Lock 1979; Nettleship 1977b, 1980 and unpublished observations). Those regional estimates probably reflect the relative proportions of the population breeding in the various regions. They are likely underestimates, but only a very demanding survey effort would permit an accurate assessment of populations.

The eastern North American Black Guillemot population was persecuted by humans (by egging and shooting of adults) through the 1800s,

particularly in southern Labrador and the Gulf of St. Lawrence (Townsend and Allen 1907; Bent 1919; Lewis 1925) and to a lesser extent in the
Bay of Fundy and New England (Knight 1908; Pettingill 1939; Drury
1973–1974). For example, on a survey in Labrador in 1912, Bent (1919)
found the Black Guillemot one of the commonest seabirds, but underlined
that 'Their eggs are persistently collected for food all summer and it is a
wonder that they are not entirely exterminated.' Because the species is so
widespread and occurs everywhere in only small numbers, few attempts
have been made to measure changes in population. The exception is the
North Shore of the Gulf of St. Lawrence where counts of seabirds have
been made regularly at 10 locations. Black Guillemot numbers were very
low (300 birds) on the first survey in 1925 (Lewis 1925). Once protection
was established under the Migratory Bird Convention Act, they rapidly
increased to 1500 birds by 1945 (Hewitt 1950) at which level the population remained relatively constant until 1965 (Moisan and Fyfe 1967). Since
then, numbers declined steadily to only 450 in 1982 (Nettleship and Lock
1973; Chapdelaine 1980; Chapdelaine and Brousseau 1984). Causes of the
decline are obscure, but disturbance at the breeding sites, commercial
fisheries and chemical pollution have all increased along the North Shore
of the Gulf of St. Lawrence over the last 25 years. In the Bay of Fundy–
Gulf of Maine area the guillemot population increased from about 600
pairs at 24 sites in 1931 to about 3800 pairs at 123 sites in the years 1970–
1972 (Drury 1973-74); numbers have remained relatively stable at the
traditional breeding locations. There is virtually no information on the
status of populations breeding in Newfoundland, Labrador and the Arctic
(Nettleship 1977a).

2. GREENLAND

The Black Guillemot breeds nearly continuously along the west coast
north to Washington Land (80°N–81°N), except for parts of Melville Bay
where heavy pack-ice persists through the breeding season (Fig. 2.9).
Numbers are highest between Disko Bay and Inglefield Land; south of
Disko small numbers occur regularly to Qagssimiut, and are less numerous south of there (Salomonsen 1950, 1967, 1974b, 1979a, 1981; Joensen
and Preuss 1972; Evans 1974a, 1985; K. Kampp, personal communication). On the east coast, the species breeds regularly from Cape Farewell
north to Scoresby Sound. Salomonsen (1950) described it as common
along the Kong Frederik VI Kyst, relatively abundant ('nests in great
numbers') in Angmagssalik District north to Kap Dalton. It is a common
breeding bird north of there to Kap Brewster, where about 2000 pairs
breed (Pedersen 1930), and all along the outer coast of Liverpool Land
and on the islands off that coast with total numbers between 5000 and

20,000 birds (K. de Korte, personal communication); farther north, the only known breeding site is Hvalros Ø (40 pairs in 1932: Pedersen 1934; at least 50 birds in 1976: Meltofte *et al.* 1981), although a few pairs may occur on Clavering Ø (Salomonsen 1967). Breeding may also take place sporadically north of Hvalros Ø when ice conditions permit; at Maroussia, Manniche (1910) found five or six birds breeding in 1908, but no signs of breeding were observed in 1969 or 1970 (Meltofte 1975). About 60 to 70% of the Greenland Black Guillemot population breeds in the high-arctic zone, with the remainder associated with low-arctic waters.

The population estimates were generated as described for eastern Canada (see above), using data given by Salomonsen (1950, 1967, 1979a), Joensen and Preuss (1972), Evans (1974a, 1984), K. Kampp (personal communication), K. de Korte (personal communication), and H. Meltofte (personal communication). The accuracy of the procedure is unknown, but it provides a rough indication of relative abundance along the various coasts, suggesting that there may be around 25,000 (range: 15,000–40,000) pairs in west Greenland and 15,000 (range: 8000–22,000) pairs on the east coast (Table 2.6).

It is impossible to draw firm conclusions about status simply because earlier data are too meagre. Even in Frederikshåb District (southwest Greenland), one does not know if the 304 breeding pairs recorded in 1971 represents a substantial decrease in population or if numbers were always small (Salomonsen 1979a). However, human persecution of seabirds has increased considerably in the last 50 years all along the west coast, and has resulted in the reduction or extirpation of many colonies of other species (Salomonsen 1970, 1974a, 1979a,c); most colonies surveyed in 1965 and 1974 showed substantial declines in Upernavik District (Joensen and Preuss 1972; Evans 1974a, 1984). Hunting of Black Guillemots is intensive, especially in September and October, when the young are dispersing; the annual kill is believed to be significant relative to the size of the population (Salomonsen 1967), but an analysis of the band recoveries is needed to confirm this (K. Kampp, personal communication). The available evidence indicates a general reduction owing to excessive hunting. Reports from investigators working in and north of Scoresby Sound (east Greenland) between 1973 and 1976 suggest no major change in Black Guillemot numbers (de Korte 1974; de Korte and Bosman 1975; Meltofte 1975, 1976; Meltofte *et al.* 1981).

3. ICELAND

The Black Guillemot breeds in small groups along most coasts except in the south where rocky habitat suitable for nesting (mainly boulder scree) is limited (Fig. 2.9). Details are lacking, but the breeding population appears to be centred in the northwest region, a pattern shared by Razorbills and murres (Petersen 1981). Most breeding assemblages known are small (<100 pairs); the largest groups known occur on coastal islands in Breidhafjördhur (Petersen 1981), where on Flatey alone 417 pairs (in about 15 small groups) bred in 1977 (Petersen 1979). The total population in Iceland is between 10,000 and 100,000 breeding pairs (Petersen 1982), and the species' widespread distribution and locally high densities (Gudmundsson 1953a; Petersen 1981) suggest that the breeding population may be high in order 5, perhaps close to 50,000 pairs (Table 2.6). The birds seem to be concentrated near the boundary of the low-arctic and boreal marine zones, with roughly 60 and 40% in each zone, respectively. Black Guillemots are common in coastal waters of Iceland all year-round (Gudmundsson 1953a).

Information is insufficient to determine population status. The establishment and rapid spread of feral mink in Iceland over the years since 1940–1950 may pose a serious threat to the Black Guillemot population. Declines have already occurred at several locations, and the previously large breeding areas at Ögur and Ennishöfdhi are now almost deserted (Petersen 1981). Those decreases along the coast (where mink are numerous) may reflect a shift in breeding distribution to islands offshore (e.g., Flatey) where there are no mink (Petersen 1981, 1982). The increases in Black Guillemots (on Flatey and elsewhere) largely coincide with the extermination there of brown rats, another introduced predator which is known to have caused drastic reduction in Black Guillemot numbers throughout Flateyjarhreppur in the 1930s (Petersen 1981). Any attempt to interpret local changes in Black Guillemot numbers will also have to assess the importance of other disturbances, particularly the collection of eggs and young at the colony (presently much reduced), hunting outside the breeding season, and, more recently, drowning in fishing gear (Petersen 1982 and personal communication). The Black Guillemot requires attention and additional study to determine more precisely the actual size of the population (it could be the largest concentration of Black Guillemots in the Atlantic—see Table 2.6), and to assess the relationship between expanding populations of feral mink and decreases in Black Guillemots.

4. JAN MAYEN

Black Guillemots breed regularly on Jan Mayen, but only in very small groups or pairs scattered along the sea-cliffs. The size of the population is difficult to estimate. Von Fischer and Polzeln (1886) found them breeding in small numbers in 1882–1883, as did Musters (1930) in 1921, but Bird and Bird (1935) in 1934 and Seligman and Willcox (1940) in 1938 reported no evidence of breeding. Part of the difficulty is related to the summer weather; extremely thick fog, reducing visibility to less than 40 m, is normal daily from June to August, and is a major obstacle to survey work (Bird and Bird 1935; Seligman and Willcox 1940). However, in 1983 van Franeker and Camphuijsen (1984) surveyed the coastline around the island and estimated the population to be in order 3, probably around 500 breeding pairs (Table 2.6). There is no information on population status.

5. FAEROE ISLANDS

The Black Guillemot breeds on all the Faeroe Islands, usually in small groups (3–10 pairs) among boulders along the seacoasts. The largest groups (up to several hundred pairs) occur in rock scree slopes under steep sea-cliffs; a few pairs breed in crevices on the cliffs (Nørrevang 1960; Joensen 1966). No complete census has been made, but B. Olsen (personal communication) estimates the total population at around 2000 pairs.

The status of this boreal population is not known. Black Guillemots had be͏ꞏꞏꞏ reduced to small numbers in the early 1900s by excessive harvesting of young prior to fledging (Joensen 1966). With game acts in 1897 and 1928 to protect all birdlife, the Black Guillemot population slowly increased to its present size (Joensen 1966; Salomonsen 1979c), and with local protection for several decades, the population is stable or increasing (B. Olsen and H. Meltofte, personal communication).

6. BRITAIN AND IRELAND

The Black Guillemot breeds in small groups and scattered pairs along rocky coasts, mainly in the north and west of Scotland and Ireland (Fig. 2.9). The species is virtually absent along the entire east, south and southwest coasts of Britain. The total number of pairs attending breeding areas was estimated to be about 8400 in 1969 to 1970, of which 90% bred in Scotland, 9% in Ireland, and the remainder in England and Wales (Cramp et al. 1974); the largest single group (340 pairs) recorded was on Auskerry in the Orkney Islands, but since then sizeable populations have also been identified on Fetlar (1200 breeding birds) and Mousa (320 breeding birds) in Shetland (P. J. Ewins, personal communication). The population in the British Isles is boreal, and represents approximately 3% of the total Atlantic population (Table 2.6).

In Britain and Ireland, the only reasonably complete survey was made in 1969 to 1970, and censusing the species in the past, even on a local scale, has been minimal (Cramp *et al.* 1974). The Black Guillemot appears to have decreased in some areas through the nineteenth century, becoming extinct in former breeding areas in eastern Scotland, Yorkshire and north Wales (Alexander and Lack 1944; Parslow 1973a). Causes of these declines are unknown (Alexander and Lack 1944), but egging and killing of adults and young have almost certainly contributed to the decline. There is no evidence of major change this century, although there is a southward expansion of range, most noticeable on the east coast of Ireland where populations are increasing and several new breeding groups have been established, although this may simply be the recolonization of former breeding areas (Cramp *et al.* 1974; see also Parslow 1973a). The 'ESSO *Bernica*' oiling incident in Sullam Voe, Shetland, during winter 1978–1979 caused heavy mortality among Black Guillemots leading to a temporary decline in winter numbers, although numbers have since recovered (Heubeck and Richardson 1980 and personal communication). There is a need for detailed census work.

7. DENMARK, SWEDEN, FINLAND, ESTONIA AND LATVIA

The Black Guillemot breeds in small numbers from eastern Denmark and western Sweden south to northern Holland, along the eastern coast of Sweden from southern Blekinge to the head of the Gulf of Bothnia, and along the west and south coasts of Finland to Estonia and Latvia in the Gulf of Riga area (Fig. 2.9). Black Guillemots are fairly regular in the Kattegat, though always in very small numbers, more abundant in Sweden and Finland, and rare in the Gulf of Finland southwards to Latvia. The total number of Black Guillemots in that entire area is estimated at about 20,000 breeding pairs (Table 2.6), with 11,000 to 12,000 pairs in Sweden (Nord 1977; S.O.F. 1978; Andersson 1979; Rodebrand 1979; Grenmyr and Sundin 1981; Gustafsson and Hogstrom 1981; Ahren 1982; Hirschfeld *et al.* 1982; P. Jonsson, personal communication) and 5000 to 10,000 pairs in Finland (Hilden 1978; M. Kilpi, personal communication). In Denmark, numbers were 400–450 pairs in 1977, with roughly 50% at Norde Rønner, and Hirsholmene in the northern part of Kattegat, and the remainder scattered on other small islands including Tunø, Vejrø, Hesselø, and Sejerø (Asbirk 1978; Joensen 1982 and personal communication). In western Sweden guillemot numbers are small, restricted to skerries and islets south to Hallands Väderö. Within the Baltic and the Gulf of Bothnia, the species is much more numerous, scattered on coastal islands from southern Blekinge around the entire coastline to the Gulf of Finland where breeding groups are mainly 10–30 pairs in size, with the main part of the population east of Helsinki. Black Guillemots do not breed on the south Baltic coast from Latvia south and west to Denmark (Salomonsen 1944; Voous 1960; Løppenthin 1963a; Bergman 1971; Olsson 1974; Asbirk 1978). The entire population breeds in the boreal marine zone.

The size of the Black Guillemot populations in the Kattegat and Baltic Sea area are below the levels they were at the turn of this century. In the Kattegat as a whole, many locations where guillemots formerly bred are now deserted and numbers are drastically reduced (Salomonsen 1944; Andersson and Rosenlund 1973). In the Danish islands, however, numbers have increased from a low of 100 pairs in the 1920s (Asbirk 1978). The reasons may be immigration from Swedish colonies along the east coast of the Kattegat owing to increased predation by feral mink in that region in the early 1960s and protection against shooting and egging since 1967. The temporary decreases observed from 1965 to 1972 were probably associated with the seven major oil spills during that interval (Asbirk 1978; H. Meltofte, personal communication). In the Baltic, populations are continuing to decline (Salomonsen 1944, 1979c; Nordberg 1950; Grenquist 1965; Hilden 1966; Bang 1968; Andersson and Rosenlund 1973; Olsson 1974; Asbirk 1978).

8. NORWAY

Black Guillemots are distributed along the entire coast of Norway, breeding either as single pairs or in small groups. They are much more numerous in the northern regions (particularly Nord- and Sør-Trøndelag, Troms and Finnmark districts) than in the south (Barrett and Vader 1984; R. Barrett, personal communication). Based on a complete survey of the coast in 1970–1974, the breeding population was estimated to be 22,000 breeding pairs (Brun 1979). However, more recent surveys indicate a total population of between 11,000 and 19,000 pairs, which, if taken as roughly 15,000 pairs, comprises about 5% of the Atlantic population (Table 2.6). Most of the population breeds in boreal waters, but the birds increase towards the boundary with the low-arctic zone.

In 1974, the Black Guillemot was considered to be the only auk in Norway that had not decreased since detailed censuses began in 1961 (Brun 1979). Since then, the population has decreased sharply, particularly in Troms District where numbers have fallen by half since the 1930s (Barrett and Vader 1984). The decline is widespread, including populations breeding south of Troms in the districts of Nordland, Trøndelag and Møre og Romsdal. That marked decrease in numbers since the mid 1970s is not restricted to Black Guillemots, as declines have also been recorded in Shags, Great Cormorants, murres and puffins. The decrease in the Black Guillemot population appears to be related to the recent spread of feral mink, especially in Nordland and Nord- and Sør-Trøndelag, and Møre og Romsdal districts, and to significant increases in hunting outside the breeding season (Folkestad 1982; Barrett and Vader 1984).

9. KOLA PENINSULA AND WHITE SEA

The Black Guillemot breeds in small groups along the coasts of the Kola Peninsula, and in the western White Sea; it is absent from the east shore of the White Sea (Bianki 1967). The total population is about 3700 pairs (Table 2.6), of which 2100 pairs (57%) breed on the Murmansk Coast, fewer than 100 (3%) along the Terskiy Coast, about 300 (8%) in Kandalakshkaya Guba, and 1200 (32%) in Onega Bay (Bianki 1967). Norderhaug et al. (1977) reported only 1200 pairs breeding at nine colonies along Murmansk instead of 2100 pairs. Their total was based on work by Gerasimova (1962) and Skokova (1962), whereas Bianki's value comes from Gerasimova (1961); we have used Bianki's (1967) higher figure in the absence of additional information. About 57% of this population occurs in the low-arctic marine zone (Murmansk Coast), with the White Sea birds breeding in boreal waters.

The status of the population is unknown, as quantitative information on marine birds prior to the early 1950s is virtually non-existent. Banding studies of Black Guillemots in Kandalakshkaya Guba between 1948 and 1964 (totals banded: 1036 fledglings, 56 adults) indicated that many birds were shot in the White Sea during the fall hunting season, and about 22% of both pulli and yearlings drowned in fishing nets annually (Bianki 1967). The influence of those sources of mortality on guillemot numbers is unknown.

10. BJØRNØYA

Black Guillemots breed in small numbers widely scattered along the coast. The total population was estimated to be at least 300 breeding pairs in 1980 (van Franeker and Luttik 1981); it is located in low-arctic waters. There is no information on population status.

11. SPITSBERGEN

Black Guillemots appear to be concentrated along the west coast where they breed in rock crevices on sea-cliffs, almost always in association with other colonially breeding seabirds (Norderhaug *et al.* 1977). They have been reported breeding at 24 of the 75 seabird colonies examined where the total number of all species present exceeds 1000 pairs (Norderhaug *et al.* 1977). The most recent estimate by the Norwegian Polar Research Institute is 10,000–20,000 breeding pairs (F. Mehlum, personal communication). The population is provisionally placed at about 15,000 pairs (Table 2.6), with all birds breeding in the high-arctic marine zone at its southern boundary (Fig. 2.9).

12. FRANZ JOSEF LAND

The Black Guillemot is known to breed through the archipelago, as single pairs, in small groups or in large colonies either on cliffs or in rocky boulder fields and scree slopes. Of the 38 major seabird colonies known in Franz Josef Land, 28 have Black Guillemots (Norderhaug *et al.* 1977), and large colonies are reported from the southwest part of Zemlya Georga to the extreme northeast, and including Skala Rubini where an unusually large colony is estimated at about 1000 pairs (Norderhaug *et al.* 1977). The total population of Black Guillemots was estimated at 15,000 pairs (Table 2.6) by Uspenski (1959) and there have been no surveys since then (Golovkin 1984). The population breeds in high-arctic waters and there is no information on its status.

13. NOVAYA ZEMLYA

In Novaya Zemlya Black Guillemots breed in small groups along the entire west coast from Mys Men'shikova north to Mys Zhelaniya; they are less abundant on the east coast, restricted to a few places between Mys Zhelaniya and Guba Litke in the south (Uspenski 1956). They sometimes occur in separate colonies, but most often are found scattered through colonies of other species or as solitary breeding pairs. Uspenski (1959) carried out a census and estimated 5000 pairs for the whole region (Table 2.6). The population breeds in both the high- and low-arctic marine zones, but the proportion in each cannot be determined at present. Nothing is known of the status of the population. In 1950 N.N. Kartaschew recommended the exploitation of Black Guillemots (harvesting eggs and young) for commercial development, but their general inaccessibility apparently disqualified them from becoming a major target of the seabird industry (Uspenski 1956). There is no doubt that large numbers are killed by shooting and drowning in fishnets in the area. The influence of these and other mortality factors on the population is unknown.

14. SEVERNAYA ZEMLYA EAST TO CHUKCHI SEA

Details on the Black Guillemots east of Novaya Zemlya are very limited. In the Kara Sea, they breed in small numbers on Ostrov Vaygach and on at least two of the major islands comprising Severnaya Zemlya. Uspenski (1959) estimated a total of about 15,000 pairs for 10 colonies in that archipelago. In the Laptev Sea there are breeding groups on Ostrov Malyy Taymyr, around Mys Chelyuskin (northern Taymyr Peninsula), on Ostrov Preobrazheniya and Ostrov Bol'shoy Begichev at the mouth of Khatangskiy Zaliv, and the New Siberian Islands (including Ostrov Bennetta). East of this, small breeding groups occur at suitable locations along the coast from Chaunskaya Guba to the Chukchi Peninsula and on Wrangel Island (Belopol'skii 1957; Kartaschew 1960; Uspenski *et al.* 1963). Most of those populations breed in high-arctic waters. There is no information on population status.

IX. ATLANTIC PUFFIN, *Fratercula arctica*

Summary: North Atlantic polytypic boreo-panarctic species. Breeds between 79°N and 44°N in the North Atlantic and adjacent arctic seas from the high Arctic in eastern Canada and west Greenland south to Gulf of Maine and from Iceland, Spitsbergen, Novaya Zemlya and northwest Russia (White Sea) south to northern France. Widely dispersed offshore in winter, mostly in boreal waters south to Massachusetts, the Azores, Canary Islands and the western Mediterranean.

A. Breeding Distribution and Abundance

The Atlantic Puffin is a boreo-panarctic species restricted to the North Atlantic. It breeds in northwest France, Britain, Ireland, Norway and the Murmansk Coast (Kola Peninsula), Novaya Zemlya, Bjørnøya, Spitsbergen, Jan Mayen, Faeroes, Iceland, east and west Greenland, eastern Canada and Maine (Fig. 2.10). The total breeding population is around 5.8 million (range: 3.8–8.2 million) pairs with the main concentration in Iceland where at least 3 million pairs (51%) breed (Table 2.7). Most of the remainder is divided between Norway (1.2 million pairs, 21%), the Faeroe Islands (500,000 pairs, 8%), British Isles (730,000 pairs, 12%), and eastern Canada (348,000 pairs, 6%); elsewhere, numbers are very small. Close to 60% of the population breeds in the boreal zone (mainly southern Iceland, Faeroes, Britain and Ireland, Norway), 40% in low-arctic waters (most of eastern Canada and west Greenland, northern Iceland, Kola Peninsula,

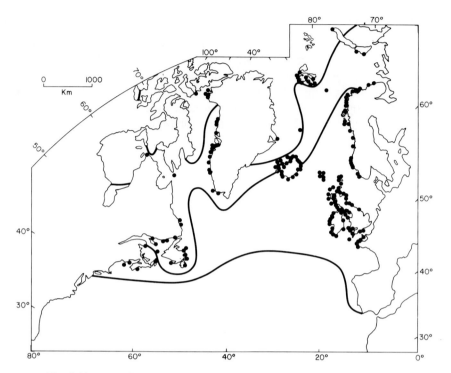

Fig. 2.10.   Breeding distribution of the Atlantic Puffin (*Fratercula arctica*).

Bjørnøya and southern Novaya Zemlya), and less than 1% in the high-arctic marine zone (high-arctic Canada, northwest and east Greenland, Jan Mayen, Spitsbergen and northern Novaya Zemlya).

B. Regional Populations and Status

1. EASTERN CANADA AND NEW ENGLAND

The majority of Atlantic Puffin's population in North America breed on a small number of islands along the coasts of southeast Newfoundland and Labrador. The total of 365,000 breeding pairs is spread over about 55 colonies with 270,000 pairs (74%) at 18 colonies in east Newfoundland, 87,000 (24%) at 17 colonies in Labrador, 7500 (2%) at 13 sites in the Gulf of St. Lawrence, 1100 (<1%) at 4 sites from Nova Scotia to Maine, and very small numbers (<0.1%) at 3 locations in the eastern Canadian Arctic (Table 2.7). The largest concentration is in Witless Bay, Newfoundland, where 225,000 pairs nest mainly in grass-hummocked maritime slopes on

TABLE 2.7

Distribution and Estimates of Breeding Population Sizes (Pairs) of the Atlantic Puffin (*Fratercula arctica*)

Region	Regional totals Pairs	%	Census date	References
Canada and New England				
E. arctic	200	<0.1	1973–1982	Nettleship (1980 and unpublished); Gaston and Malone (1980)
Labrador	87,000	1.5	1978–1983	Nettleship (1980 and unpublished)
E. Newfoundland	270,000	4.6	1973–1984	Nettleship (1980 and unpublished)
Gulf of St. Lawrence	7,500	<0.1	1977–1982	Chapdelaine (1980); Nettleship (1980); Chapdelaine and Brousseau (1984)
Scotian Shelf–Bay of Fundy–Gulf of Maine	1,100	<0.1	1971–1983	Drury (1973–1974 and personal communication); Brown *et al.* (1975); Korschgen (1979); Nettleship (1980 and unpublished)
TOTALS	365,000	6.2		
W. Greenland	4,000[a] (2,500–5,500)	<0.1	1900–1965	Salomonsen (1950); Joensen and Preuss (1972); Evans (1974a, 1984)
E. Greenland	100[b]	<0.1	—	Salomonsen (1950, 1967, 1974a, 1981)
Iceland	3 million[a] (1–5 million)	51.0	—	Petersen (1982 and personal communication)
Jan Mayen	5,000[a]	<0.1	1934, 1947	Bird and Bird (1935); Seligman and Willcox (1940); Marshall (1952)
Faeroe Islands	500,000[a] (0.5–0.75 million)	8.5	1979	E. Mortensen and B. Olsen (personal communication)
British Isles				
Scotland	645,000	11.0	1969–1980	Brooke (1972); Harris (1976a,b, and personal communication); Evans (1978); Furness (1978a); Harris and Murray (1978)
England	20,000	0.3	1974–1980	Harris (1976a and personal communication)

132   David N. Nettleship and Peter G. H. Evans

TABLE 2.7 (*Continued*)

Region	Regional totals		Census date	References
	Pairs	%		
Wales	10,000	0.2	1976–1979	Harris (1976a and personal communication)
Ireland	45,000	0.6	1969–1979	Harris (1976a and personal communication); Evans and Lovegrove (1974); Lloyd (1982)
Channel Islands	300	<0.1	1977–1980	M. P. Harris (personal communication)
TOTALS	720,000	12.2		
Brittany, France	<200	<0.1	1980–1981	Henry and Monnat (1981)
Norway	1,258,000	21.4	1964–1982	Brun (1979); Barrett and Vader (1984); A. O. Folkestad (unpublished observations)
Kola Peninsula (Murmansk Coast)	16,300 (16,000–17,000)	0.3	1959–1961	Gerasimova (1962); Skokova (1962); Norderhaug et al. (1977); Golovkin (1984)
Bjørnøya	600	<0.1	1980	van Franeker and Luttik (1981)
Spitsbergen	<10,000[a]	0.2	—	F. Mehlum (personal communication)
Novaya Zemlya	300	<0.1	1950	Uspenski (1956, 1959)
TOTALS	5,880,000 (3.8–8.2 million)	100.0		

[a] Rough estimate only—see text for details.
[b] Single colony on Raffles Ø possibly now extinct; a few pairs were reported breeding by A. Pederson and C. Cottam in the 1920s–1930s (Salomonsen 1950), but no evidence of nesting has been found during recent surveys of the Scoresby Sound area (de Korte 1973; Meltofte 1976).

three islands (Gull Island, 60,000; Green Island, 17,000; Great Island, 148,000) within 8 km of each other. The only other North American colonies of note are Baccalieu Island (order 5, probably ca. 30,000 pairs: D. N. Nettleship, unpublished observations), and Small Island (ca. 10,000 pairs) along the east Newfoundland coast, and the Gannet Islands (41,000 pairs), Outer Gannet Island (8000 pairs) and Herring Islands (17,000 pairs) in southern Labrador. Other colonies are small and scattered, from the

Kidlit Islands (2200 pairs) and Nunaksuk Island (3400 pairs) southeast of Nain, Labrador, south to Machias Seal Island (900 pairs), Bay of Fundy, and Matinicus Rock (125 pairs) and Eastern Egg Rock (10 pairs) off Maine (Brown *et al.* 1975; Korschgen 1979; Nettleship 1980 and unpublished observations). Four very small colonies (< 100 pairs) are known or suspected in the eastern Canadian Arctic, three in the low Arctic (two islets off Western Digges Island: Gaston and Malone 1980; southeast Resolution Island: J. Brownlie, personal communication) and one far north in the high Arctic (Princess Charlotte Monument at the entrance to Jones Sound: D. Orienti, personal communication) where there may be a few other undiscovered breeding groups. Breeding has been confirmed at the two islands in Digges Sound, whereas those off the east coast of Resolution Island and at Princess Charlotte Monument are putative breeding stations based on sight records of birds on the cliffs and birds carrying food, respectively.

Populations in Labrador, Gulf of St. Lawrence, Nova Scotia, New Brunswick and Maine have declined considerably since the 1880s. Much of the reduction resulted from excessive egging, shooting and destruction of nesting habitat and by the introduction of domestic animals. This persecution began early in the south. In the Gulf of Maine and Bay of Fundy, populations had been severely reduced by 1833 when J. J. Audubon visited the region and wrote that numbers were 'one [bird] perhaps now for a hundred that bred there 20 years ago' (Bent 1919). By the 1880s most populations were on the verge of extinction, and those that nested on Matinicus Seal, Large Green (Matinicus Island), and Western Egg Rock were soon eliminated. By the turn of the century, only very small numbers remained, but those on Matinicus Rock and Machias Seal persisted and are the only colonies left today, except for the small breeding group that recolonized Eastern Egg Rock in 1981 (five pairs) through an intensive CWS–NAS reintroduction project at that site (S. W. Kress and D. N. Nettleship, unpublished observations). Numbers have increased slowly, from 1 or 2 pairs at Matinicus Rock in 1900 to about 125 pairs in 1976–1977, and from 300 birds at Machias Seal in 1902 to 900 pairs in 1974; both populations have remained fairly stable since the 1950s (Dutcher 1904; Knight 1908; Bent 1919; Palmer 1949; Drury 1973–1974; Korschgen 1979; Nettleship 1980, and unpublished observations).

The recent history in other regions is similar. Puffins were probably abundant in Nova Scotia (Bent 1919), but by 1900 they nested in small numbers only at Seal Island, the Bird Islands (Hertford and Ciboux), and probably Pearl Island (Mahone Bay). The Seal Island population became extinct between 1907 and 1922, and those at the Bird Islands dropped

134 David N. Nettleship and Peter G. H. Evans

from several hundred pairs in 1933 to no more than 50 pairs in 1971 (Macoun and Macoun 1909; Tufts 1961; Nettleship 1980). Only very small numbers (< 10 pairs) nest now on Pearl Island.

Changes in population are best known in the Gulf of St. Lawrence and Labrador. Along the North Shore of the Gulf, continuous disturbance at colonies and excessive exploitation was so great that by 1906 islands 'where auks, murres, gannets and puffins formerly bred in great numbers—are now almost devoid of bird life' (Bent 1919). As early as 1833 Audubon expressed grave concern about the future welfare of seabirds there. The commercial egg industry, developed mainly by entrepreneurs in Nova Scotia, Maine and Newfoundland, systematically collected eggs at all colonies from Sept-Iles to Bradore Bay and on the Labrador coast north to Nain each year. The eggs were sold in the Maritimes and New England until the 1890s when too few birds were left to make it profitable (Frazar 1887; Townsend and Allen 1907; Townsend 1918; Bent 1919). The Common Murre was the major target species (see Section VI,B,1), but at its termination all 'the large breeding colonies of the Alcidae had been nearly, if not quite, annihilated on "the Labrador" ' (Bent 1919). The virtual removal of the murres from this 1800-km coastline (Sept-Iles to Nain) by the turn of the century made the small, relict breeding groups of puffins and other species even more vulnerable to persecution by local fishermen.

Perhaps the worst example of continued persecution after commercial egging had ceased was at Perroquet Island in Bradore Bay, where Audubon (1840–1844) described the puffin population as so immense that 'one might have imagined half the puffins in the world had assembled there'. A careful assessment in 1906, 1909, and 1915 revealed that numbers were 'probably not one hundredth part' of what Audubon had found (Townsend and Allen 1907; Townsend 1918). Even when the population was so much smaller, large-scale shooting and killing of puffins still continued. Fishermen visited the island throughout the summer, in Townsend's (1918) words, to

. . . not only shoot the birds, but also dig them out of the nesting-holes and secure them in nets spread over the holes. In any case the young are left to perish. The Newfoundland fishermen are undoubtedly the worst offenders in egg and bird destruction, but the people of the coast [the North Shore of the Gulf] are not far behind.

Taverner (1922) summarized the status of puffins along the North Shore by stating that 'unless protective steps are taken they will shortly be exterminated'. However, action was under way to provide some protection to the small surviving populations. Ten bird sanctuaries were established soon after the Migratory Birds Convention Act was enacted in 1918

(Lewis 1925), and that probably prevented the complete eradication of puffins in Bradore Bay (Perroquet Island and Greenly Island), the only important colony remaining for the species on the North Shore. Lewis (1925) estimated 51,000 birds in 1925, and numbers remained fairly steady until sometime after 1955 (Tener 1951; Lemieux 1956). Numbers then dropped sharply, and now (1972–1982) appear to have stabilized somewhere around 14,000 birds (Nettleship and Lock 1973; Chapdelaine 1980; Chapdelaine and Brousseau 1984). Illegal egging and killing of adult puffins persists to this day in remote coastal outports along the entire North Shore. A Bradore Bay resident in 1978, when asked about the need for bird conservation, simply stated, 'No matter how many [puffins] are killed, they always seems to be as many left' (Durant and Harwood 1980).

On the Labrador coast, puffins were close to extinction in the early 1900s (Townsend and Allen 1907; Townsend 1918; Bent 1919; Taverner 1922), but around that time the persecution lessened somewhat. The numbers of puffins had become so low that the birds were no longer as vulnerable to eggers and hunters, and a collapse of the cod fishery in the 1920s resulted in an exodus of people which reduced the level of molestation (Austin 1932). Together, these two factors improved the prospects for the puffin population. Puffins showed a slow increase to some hundreds of pairs at seven or eight sites by the late 1920s (Austin 1932). Surveys by Austin (1932) between 1926 and 1928, and Tuck (1953, 1961) between 1952 and 1953 were not directly comparable, but they indicated a continued increase in numbers and expansion of range. Puffins have steadily increased since 1930, and probably quite dramatically since the early 1950s (Brown *et al.* 1975; Nettleship 1977a, 1980, and unpublished observations; Lock 1979; Birkhead and Nettleship 1982a). However, the present population is only a small fraction of the numbers that formerly nested in Labrador and the recent expansion of range is most likely only recolonization of areas used for breeding in the past.

The little early information suggests that the Newfoundland population always had a limited breeding distribution, concentrated along the southeast coast from the Wadham Islands south to Witless Bay. Doubtless puffins were utilized by Portuguese, French, Spanish and English fishing fleets for fresh meat from the 1600s to the 1800s (see Section III on Great Auk and Section VI on Common Murre), as is well documented for Baccalieu Island (Bonnycastle 1842; Innis 1940; Tuck 1961). Many colonies were probably destroyed or severely reduced in size by these activities. By the early 1900s the puffin population in Newfoundland was considered to be much diminished (Bent 1919).

At present, more than half (ca. 61%) the North American population breeds at Witless Bay, but older information on the three largest colonies

(Gull, Green and Great Islands) is meagre and unsatisfactory. Counts from a boat of birds standing on maritime slopes at Gull and Green Islands in 1942 by Peters and Burleigh (1951) are meaningless now that we know that the numbers of puffins visible at a colony on a single day may vary by a factor of a thousand or more (Nettleship 1972, 1976a; Harris 1976a). Puffins always bred on all three islands within memory of the oldest residents in Witless Bay and Bauline East (interviews between 1950 and 1960 by L. M. Tuck and between 1967 and 1969 by D. N. Nettleship), and in fairly large numbers at Great Island since at least the middle of the nineteenth century (firsthand information provided in 1967 by Thomas Reddick, an 80-year-old resident of Bauline East, and details given to him earlier by his father who had also fished in the vicinity of Great Island). Reports of puffins nesting in numbers at Great Island were given to Templeman (1945), but no ground survey was made on any of the islands in Witless Bay until 1951. L. M. Tuck visited Green Island to count and band Common Murres each breeding season from 1951 to 1959; his visits to Gull and Great Islands were infrequent and usually only to view the birds from a boat. Detailed observations of puffins began in 1967. After making the first measurements of burrow density and occupancy rates, Nettleship and Tuck generated preliminary estimates of the three populations: 100,000 pairs on Great, 75,000 pairs on Gull and 20,000 pairs on Green (Nettleship 1970, 1972, and unpublished observations). More detailed surveys were conducted in 1973 and in 1979–1980, but methodologies continue to be developed and refined. Numbers in 1973 were tentatively placed at 148,000 pairs for Great, 60,000 pairs for Gull and 17,000 pairs for Green.

Puffins in Witless Bay appear to have decreased substantially since 1973; provisional results indicate a reduction of 25 to 35% (D. N. Nettleship, unpublished observations). The reductions may be related to the sharp increase in Herring Gulls (133% on Great Island between 1967 and 1979) and contamination by oil in winter, but the most likely factor seems to be a change in the availability of summer or winter food. The development of major fisheries for capelin (the puffin's principal summer food in Newfoundland) may be an important contributing factor (Brown and Nettleship 1984; Carscadden 1984). Much remains to be learned about determinants of seabird numbers, particularly those linked to human activities, but it is clear that what happens to the puffin colonies in Witless Bay will largely determine the future of this species in the western Atlantic (Nettleship 1977a).

There are no baseline data for other colonies in Newfoundland, although the small group (50 pairs) that bred on the Cabot Islands in 1945 (Peters and Burleigh 1951) had gone in 1973 (Brown et al. 1975).

2. GREENLAND

Puffins breed in small colonies scattered along the west coast, and only rarely south of Egedesminde District (Salomonsen 1950, 1967, 1974b, 1981). There are six colonies in the Thule area, from Hakluyt Ø at the mouth of Inglefield Gulf south to the Crimson Cliffs. Numbers probably total only a few hundred pairs, and they nest in cracks on high steep cliffs, associated with high-arctic waters. In the low-arctic zone, puffins breed in burrows dug in grassy turf on small islands, and only occasionally under boulders or in cracks on the cliffs (Salomonsen 1936, 1950, 1967, 1979c). The 25 colonies between Kitsigsorssuit (ca. 74°N) and Qîoqe (ca. 60°N) are mostly <100 pairs except for Torqussârssuk in Upernavik District with 300 pairs in 1974, and Rifkol near Disko Bay, Naujarssuit Islet and Satsigsúnguit, where colony size may reach a thousand pairs. The low-arctic population is between 2000 and 5000 pairs, with the total population provisionally placed at around 4000 pairs (Table 2.7). The information is inadequate to assess population status, although numbers in Upernavik District showed little change between 1965 and 1983 (Joensen and Preuss 1972; Evans 1974a, 1984; K. Kampp, personal communication).

A few pairs were found nesting at Raffles Ø about 20 km north of Scoresby Sound (east Greenland) in the high-arctic zone in the 1920–1930s by A. C. Pedersen and C. Cottam (Salomonsen 1950, 1967; see also Table 2.7). In recent years (1973–1974) there has been no evidence of breeding (de Korte 1973 and personal communication; Meltofte 1975 and personal communication).

3. ICELAND

Iceland has the largest concentration of Atlantic Puffins in the world. The total population is believed to be between 8 and 10 million birds, or about 3 million breeding pairs (Petersen 1982 and personal communica-tion) (Table 2.7). They breed on small coastal islands around the entire country, with the density of colonies lower in the south, where there are long stretches of smooth sandy shore unsuitable for nesting puffins (Gud-mundsson 1953b; Petersen 1982). At the Vestmannaeyjar, off the south-west coast, numbers are around 2 to 3 million birds, and in the mid-west, on the 2000–3000 islands in Breidhafjördhur, the total number of birds approaches a similar level (Petersen 1982 and personal communication). About 60 to 70% of the population breeds in low-arctic waters with the rest in the boreal zone; Iceland is situated at the boundary of the low-arctic and boreal marine zones (Fig. 2.10).

The first attempt to guess the size of the Iceland population was in 1952 by Lockley (1953a). He placed the minimum figure at 5 million breeding adults or 2.5 million breeding pairs (Fisher and Lockley 1954). Those minimum estimates were thought conservative by F. Gudmundsson (Pettingill 1959), and the present population is estimated to be between 8–10 million birds, or roughly 3 million pairs (A. Petersen, personal communication). This is also a guess, although the population is certainly large. While the general pattern of distribution is fairly well known, a systematic survey of the hundreds of individual colonies is not possible with the resources available.

The absence of detailed census data makes it impossible to assess the status of the population. Increases and decreases observed seem to have been temporary local fluctuations rather than trends in the overall population. There has not been any decline in recent years and numbers may have even increased slightly in Breidhafjördhur, where disturbance (farming activity on islands) and persecution (egging and killing of adults and young) by humans have lessened since 1945 (Petersen 1981, 1982, and personal communication). Puffins have been an important source of food in Iceland for centuries. Although the intensity of fowling has decreased, at least 150,000–200,000 puffins are killed annually at colonies (Petersen 1982) which may be significant. There is also a need to assess the potential impact of recent commercial fisheries on puffins and other seabirds breeding in Iceland, for example, the collapse by 1981 of the joint Icelandic–Norwegian capelin fishery. If humans cause fluctuations in fish biomass, what are its implications to seabirds such as puffins and murres, particularly over the long term? Breeding success of adult puffins and body weight of young at fledging (of those that survived to fledge) were low in 1982, apparently owing to food shortage during the chick-rearing period (Petersen 1982 and personal communication). A major effort to monitor changes in the puffin population (numbers, breeding performance, and survival rates) is needed, because the Icelandic population almost certainly represents more than 50% of all Atlantic Puffins in the world (Table 2.7).

4. JAN MAYEN

The Atlantic Puffin is known to be a common breeding bird, nesting in deep rock crevices on the sea-cliffs, often associated with murre colonies (Bird and Bird 1935; Seligman and Willcox 1940; Marshall 1952). No precise numerical information is given, but all investigators report the puffin to be fairly common in many localities around the island. In 1983 van Franeker and Camphuijsen (1984) found them breeding in rock crevices in many areas, usually in small groups (<10 pairs) but sometimes in colonies of some tens of pairs (e.g., Splittodden-Skrinnodden, near Sju-hollendarbukta). They estimated the population to be in order 4, and provisionally place it at 5000 pairs (Table 2.7). Nothing is known on the status of the population.

5. FAEROE ISLANDS

The Atlantic Puffin is perhaps the most abundant breeding seabird in the Faeroes (Joensen 1966). It breeds mainly in large colonies in grassy maritime slopes at the top of steep sea-cliffs or stacks along the coast and sometimes in rock crevices between stones and boulders. There are also a few small colonies on inland slopes more than 1 km from the sea (e.g., Fugloy, Svínoy, Streymoy and Mykines) (Nørrevang 1960; Joensen 1966). The largest populations are in the northwest, particularly in the Mykines, where a total of 150,000 pairs is estimated to breed. Other large colonies (ca. 20,000–60,000 pairs) are found on Tindhólmur, Koltur, Sku-voy, Stóra Dímun, Lítla Dímun, Nólsoy, and Vidhoy. Most of the other colonies are less than 10,000 pairs, although total numbers of birds can be considerable (e.g., Sandoy: perhaps 100,000 pairs distributed over 10 col-onies). No detailed survey of the population in the Faeroes has been made, but in 1979 it was tentatively estimated at 500,000 to 750,000 pairs (E. Mortensen, personal communication). B. Olsen (personal communi-cation) considers it to be around 500,000 pairs (Table 2.7).

Puffins on the Faeroes declined markedly during this century, particu-larly on the larger islands (Sudhuroy, Vágar, Streymoy, Eysturoy, Ku-noy, Bordhoy) where colonies have either decreased or disappeared. The increase and spread of brown rats (since ca. 1900) over many of the islands where puffins have decreased is believed to be one of the most important contributing factors (Joensen 1966). That general population decline appears to have levelled off over the period since the early 1960s, and in 1983 the population was thought to be stable (B. Olsen, personal communication). The present puffin population is probably only half of what it was in 1885, and it will be important to prevent the brown rat from spreading to the remaining rat-free puffin strongholds such as the Mykines. Also other factors were operating to reduce the puffin popula-tion. About 270,000 puffins were caught by fowling each year in the early 1900s (Salomonsen 1935, 1979c), but that large harvest is now much re-duced. Shooting and snaring at colonies increased dramatically during that same period (Salomonsen 1979c). In recent years, no shooting has been allowed from 15 March to 1 September each year and snaring was prohibited (H. Meltofte and B. Olsen, personal communication). A de-tailed investigation of the distribution and abundance of the puffin population is required to monitor and assess adequately future changes in puffin numbers.

6. BRITAIN AND IRELAND

The Atlantic Puffin breeds in colonies distributed mainly on islands and coasts of western Britain and Ireland from the Shetland Isles south to the Scilly Isles, and only very locally in small numbers along the east and south coasts (Fig. 2.10). It has a very clumped distribution, presently centred in north and west Scotland with few important sites elsewhere. Many large colonies in eastern Scotland, England, Wales and Ireland have become extinct or greatly reduced since 1900, particularly in southern areas (Snow 1971; Parslow 1973a; Cramp *et al.* 1974; Harris 1976a; see also below). The total breeding population (based mainly on the 1974–1980 census) is about 720,000 breeding pairs (Table 2.7) with almost 645,000 pairs (90%) in Scotland, 45,000 pairs (6%) in Ireland, 20,000 pairs (3%) in England, 10,000 pairs (1%) in Wales and only 300 pairs in the Channel Islands off the coast of Brittany (figures supplied by M. P. Harris), all in the boreal marine zone. The population in Britain and Ireland makes up 12% of the world population of the Atlantic Puffin.

About 75% of the puffins in Britain and Ireland breed in the Outer Hebrides and the Shetland Isles. Of the 390,000 pairs in the Outer Hebrides, 80% (ca. 310,000 pairs; range: 298,000–324,000) are in the large colonies at St. Kilda: Dùn, 50,000; Hirta, 10,000; Soay, 150,000; and Boreray, 100,000 (using estimates and mid-point of size ranges given in Harris and Murray 1978); 62,000 pairs are at the Shiant Islands (Brooke 1972), with the others spread over a small number of sites (e.g., North Rona: Evans 1978; Mingulay and Flannan Isles: M. P. Harris, personal communication). In the Shetlands with 155,000 pairs, the largest colonies are on Foula, Hermaness (northwest Unst), and Fair Isle, with about 70,000, 50,000 and 20,000 to 30,000 pairs, respectively; the other four major Shetland colonies are of 1500 to 3000 pairs each (Harris 1976a,b, and personal communication; Furness 1981). Elsewhere in Britain and Ireland puffin colonies are mainly small, particularly in the south where there are only relict breeding groups. Surveys between 1969 and 1980 (mainly from 1974 to 1979) indicated about 3500 pairs in the Inner Hebrides and Firth of Clyde (11 major sites, ranging from 20 to 1500 pairs—largest: Lunga), 38,000 pairs in northwest Scottish mainland (5 major sites, ranging from 10,000 to at least 25,000 pairs—largest: Clò Mór), 47,000 pairs in the Orkney Islands (13 sites, ranging from 100 to 44,000 pairs—largest: Sule Skerry), 20,000 pairs in northeast Scottish mainland (northern Caithness to Ord Point; 3 major colonies at Duncansby Head,

Dunnet Head and Ceann Leathad, totalling some 15,000–20,000 pairs), and 12,000–13,000 pairs in east Scotland (many small colonies from 50 to 10,000 pairs—largest: Isle of May). In England, numbers are smaller, about 20,000 to 25,000 pairs on the east coast (three sites, ranging between 1500 and 15,000 to 20,000 pairs on the Farne Islands), 114 pairs on the south coasts (four sites, with 3 to 70 pairs—largest: Scilly Isles), 100 pairs in the Bristol Channel area (six sites in Cornwall, totalling 50 pairs, and Lundy, 50 pairs), 90 pairs in the northern Irish Sea region (three sites, ranging from 10 to 35 pairs—largest: Calf of Man), and 300 pairs on the Channel Islands (eight sites, ranging in size between 2 and 200 to 250 pairs on Burhou). Numbers are also small in Wales, with about 9500 pairs in the south (about 10 sites, ranging in size from ca. 3 to 7000 pairs—largest: Skomer Island) and 1100 pairs in the north (4 sites, between 40 and 500 to 1000 pairs—largest: Gwylan-fawr Island). In Ireland, numbers are relatively small with most birds along the west coast (ca. 40,000 pairs, at 20 sites, ranging between 100 and 7000 to 10,000 pairs—largest: Inishtearaght, 8000 pairs in 1973; Great Skellig, 6000 pairs in 1973; and Puffin Island, 7000–10,000 pairs in 1981). Only 3000 pairs are on the north coast (six sites, from 100 to 2000 pairs—largest: Rathlin Island), 110 pairs on the east coast (100 on Lambay Island, with the others at Irelands Eye), and 1200 pairs on the south coast (three sites, with virtually all on Great Saltee Island). These figures were provided by M. P. Harris, supplemented from Parslow and Bourne (1973), Evans and Lovegrove (1974), Cullen and Slinn (1975), Harris (1976a), Penhallurich (1978), Mudge (1979), and Lloyd (1982). In summary, the breeding distribution of the Atlantic Puffin in Britain and Ireland is centred upon Shetland and the Outer Hebrides, with more than half breeding at St. Kilda, the westernmost islands in the Outer Hebrides.

Accounts from the last century, though possibly given to exaggeration, indicate some very large puffin colonies scattered throughout the western seaboard of Britain and Ireland. First evidence of decline comes from towards the end of the nineteenth century. Since then, puffins have decreased dramatically in Britain and Ireland, especially in the south between 1920 and 1970 (Snow 1971; Parslow 1973a; Cramp et al. 1974; Harris 1976a). These changes are well documented at both large and small colonies. Most colonies in southwest and southern Britain are only remnants of their former size. From the Isle of Wight and the Scilly Isles north to Lundy and the Isle of Man, puffins are either extinct or very much reduced: Isle of Wight (large numbers in 1900, a steady decrease from about 1923 with 300 to 350 birds in 1937, 20 birds in 1968, and a few pairs or none at present), Scilly Isles (100,000 birds in 1908, 'thousands' in 1924, but only 25 pairs in 1945, and never more than 100 pairs since then),

Lundy ('incredible numbers' in 1890—hence its Norse name meaning 'puffin island'—3500 pairs in 1939, 400 pairs in 1953, 60 pairs in 1966, 41 pairs in 1969, about 50 pairs at present), and the Isle of Man ('breeding abundantly' on Man and Calf of Man in the past, less than 100 pairs in 1978 to 1979) (Lockley 1953a; Penhallurich 1969; Parslow 1973a; Cramp *et al.* 1974; Harris 1976a and personal communication). In Wales, the formerly large colonies have undergone dramatic decreases: Skomer (50,000 pairs in 1946, 7000 pairs in 1963 to 1971, 5000–7000 pairs in 1975 to 1979), Skokholm (20,000 pairs from 1928 to 1940, 5000–10,000 in 1953, 6000 in 1955, 2500 from 1969 to 1979), Grassholm (about 500,000 birds in 1890, 200 birds in 1928, 50 pairs in 1946, possibly a few pairs or none at present), St. Tudwal's Islands ('hundreds of thousands' in 1902 to 1907, several thousand in 1935, extinct or only a couple of pairs by 1951) and Puffin Island ('immense numbers' in 1700s and early 1800s, more than 2000 pairs in 1907, 300–400 pairs in 1960, ca. 80 pairs in 1969 to 1970, 100–300 pairs during the 1970s, < 50 pairs in 1980) (Lockley 1953a; Parslow 1973a; Cramp *et al.* 1974; Harris 1976a and personal communication). Those relict populations are still decreasing (Puffin Island) or fairly stable (Skomer and Skokholm).

In Scotland, some decreases occurred from the turn of the century, for example at Ailsa Craig ('immense numbers' in 1871, decreasing by 1900, almost extinct in 1934, 250 pairs in 1950 to 1951, but 15–20 pairs in 1969 to 1979) and Haskeir Rocks ('innumerable' in 1881, fewer than 50 pairs in 1953). It is rather difficult to interpret previous descriptions of the large colonies on St. Kilda, the Shiants and North Rona. At all three sites, declines certainly took place somewhere between the 1930s and 1960s, but it is not possible to say when they began (Brooke 1972; Flegg 1972; Harris 1976a). The St. Kilda population was considered the largest concentration of breeding puffins in Britain and Ireland, with 1 to 3 million birds (Lockley 1953a). In 1971, after the first full survey of puffins at St. Kilda, Flegg (1972) estimated the population to be only about 160,000 pairs, and not larger than 250,000 pairs. That prompted further study. Harris (1976a) reported colonies on Soay and Boreray to be 'still thriving' and concluded that the population at St. Kilda was about 100,000 to 150,000 pairs, but more detailed investigation during 1976 to 1977 resulted in a revision of puffin numbers to a range of 298,100 to 323,500 pairs (Harris and Murray 1978). Those drastic variations in estimates underline how difficult it is to estimate the size of a large puffin population. Whatever the present size of the population, there has been a considerable decline in puffins at St. Kilda during the first half of this century. Although the populations may now be maintaining their numbers (Harris and Murray 1981), they are doing so at a relatively low level. The Shiant Islands, estimated to have been the second largest colony in the Hebrides (Lockley 1953a), also declined from 'hundreds of thousands' to only 77,000 pairs in 1970 and to about 50,000 pairs by 1972 (Brooke 1972; Harris 1976a). The Eilean Mhuire colony decreased from vast numbers in 1888 to only about 15,000 pairs by 1970, 7000 pairs in 1971 and 5700 pairs in 1973 (Harris 1976a). Since then the Shiant population has remained fairly stable (M. P. Harris, personal communication). At North Rona, puffin numbers declined from 100,000 pairs in 1939 to 8000 in 1958, 6200 in 1972, and 6000 pairs in 1976 (Cramp *et al.* 1974; Evans 1978).

Reviews of the 1969–1971 figures for other Scottish colonies with those from earlier times were presented in Cramp *et al.* (1974) and Harris (1976a). Changes were recorded wherever population estimates from the past were available, mostly decreases of uncertain magnitude owing to lack of reliable quantitative baselines. The only increase recorded by 'Operation Seafarer' was from the east coast of Scotland on the Isle of May (Firth of Forth), from 20 pairs in 1884 and 1888, 8–10 pairs in 1934, 5 pairs in 1950, to 2500 pairs in 1969 (Cramp *et al.* 1974; M. P. Harris, personal communication). Since then the population has steadily increased, with 10,000 pairs counted in 1982 (M. P. Harris, personal communication). Almost no numerical information from earlier times existed for populations in Shetland, and it it only conjecture whether populations have changed or remained the same. The information prior to 1970 for most sites in Shetland is qualitative, and so conclusions on population size and status must be considered suspect. Since 'Operation Seafarer' (1969–1971) there appears to have been a levelling-off of the decline throughout west and north Scotland, with most populations now stable or showing slight increases, exceptions being Rhum, Skye, Duncansby Head, and the east coast of Caithness (Harris 1976a and personal communication).

Numbers have also declined in Ireland, particularly since 1925 (Kennedy *et al.* 1954; Ruttledge 1966; Cramp *et al.* 1974). Information on former sizes of the main colonies is almost certainly very limited, but the total number of puffins in Ireland is very much lower than at the turn of the century (Ussher and Warren 1900; Ruttledge 1966). Where numerical estimates from the past exist, they often show marked decreases:

West—the Blasket Islands (Inishtearaght: largest Irish colony around 1900, 20,000–30,000 pairs in 1968, only 7500 pairs in 1969; Great Blasket: 'numerous' around 1900, extinct by 1953 to 1956), Puffin Island (20,000 pairs in 1965, 4000–7000 pairs in 1967 to 1973), Illaunmaistir (2000 pairs in 1966 to 1969, fewer in 1975, but 5500 pairs in 1976), Clare Island–Stags of Broadhaven–Blackrock (totalled 1700 pairs in 1954, far fewer in 1969)

North—Rathlin Island ('densely populated' in the 1940s, 2200 pairs in 1967, 800 pairs in 1969, 1400 pairs in 1974)

East—Lambay Island (1000 pairs in 1939, 100 pairs in 1970), Irelands Eye (300–400 pairs in 1907, 1000 pairs in 1939, only eight birds seen offshore in 1969)

South—Great Saltee Island ('many thousands' in late 1800s, a decline noted between 1912 and 1930, 3000 pairs in 1949, 1500 pairs in 1965, 750 pairs in 1969 to 1975, 1100–1200 pairs in 1979 to 1980) (Lockley 1953a; Ruttledge 1966; Evans and Lovegrove 1974; Harris 1976a and personal communication; Lloyd 1982). Most populations now appear to be stable or showing small increases, but they are mere relicts of what they once were.

The puffin population in the Channel Islands is now about 300 pairs (M. P. Harris, personal communication). There were apparently more than 100,000 puffins as recently as the 1940s (Dobson 1952; Lockley 1953a), but massive declines occurred later (Harris 1976a). On Burhou, their history is well documented: 'great numbers' in 1878 (Smith 1879), about 50,000 pairs in 1946 and 1949 (Lockley 1953a), and only 2500 pairs in 1966 (Potter 1971). The Channel Islands population remained fairly stable in 1969 to 1974 at about 1000 birds, but recent maximal counts of puffins on the water at Burhou were 1080 birds in 1973, 265 in 1978, and 451 in 1979, which suggests that numbers are decreasing again (M. P. Harris, personal communication).

The causes of the general decline in Britain and Ireland between 1930 and 1970 remain obscure. Some of the decline in numbers no doubt has been a result of oil pollution, while climatic changes in the region may have adversely affected the food supply of puffins (see Chapter 10, this volume, for detailed discussion). In summary, the absence of detailed information on the decline of puffins in Britain and Ireland in this century precludes a precise reconstruction of events. However, it is clear that the numbers breeding in Britain and Ireland have decreased enormously, and that small, local increases measured in tens, hundreds or thousands of birds will do little to replace the hundreds of thousands, possibly millions, of puffins that have disappeared during the present century. Many colonies have become extinct or drastically reduced in size since 1900, and no general recovery has occurred despite small local increases since the early 1970s; the reductions in puffin numbers have resulted in a geographic shift of the species which now has relict populations in southern Britain, and its breeding distribution centred upon a very few breeding stations in west Scotland; the puffin population in Britain and Ireland at present (ca. 730,000 pairs) is only a small fraction of what it was 50–100 years ago and certainly below the estimates in the 1950s of about 4 million breeding adults (Lockley 1953a) or 2 million breeding pairs (Fisher and Lockley 1954). Regular monitoring at representative puffin colonies throughout the British Isles must be established and maintained over the long term to allow changes in the population to be detected and evaluated. There is also a need for a thorough and complete historical review of puffin breeding distribution and abundance as a means of estimating the likely size of the population at the turn of this century, and assessing the nature and extent of the decline. Such a review may permit a full evaluation of the biological significance of the crash in the puffin population.

7. BRITTANY, FRANCE

The only puffins in France breed in Brittany where there are now (1980–1981) less than 200 pairs (Henry and Monnat 1981). They nest at Les Sept Iles, 85–120 pairs on Ile Rouzic and fewer than 50 pairs on Ile de Malban in 1981. Relict groups elsewhere (1981) totalled 13 pairs (Ile aux Dames, 4; Beg Lemm, 4; Ile Ricard, 5) in Baie de Morlaix, about 5 pairs on Le Youc'h, Ile d'Ouessant, and possibly a single pair on Ile Bannec, Archipel de Molène (Henry and Monnat 1981). That population breeds in boreal waters at the southern limit of the species' range in Europe.

The puffin population in Brittany was formerly much larger. At Les Sept Iles there were 10,000–100,000 breeding pairs in the 1860s–1870s (Henry and Monnat 1981). However, owing to shooting and hunting at the colony, numbers declined to about 10,000 to 15,000 birds in 1900, and only 1000 birds by 1911 (Yeatman 1976). Legislation in 1912 made Les Sept Iles a sanctuary and the population increased to 3000 pairs in 1921 and about 7000 pairs by 1927, when numbers remained fairly stable until 1950. After 1950 numbers gradually declined to about 4000 pairs in 1956 and 2500 pairs in 1966. The *Torrey Canyon* oil spill in 1967 reduced the population to 400 to 500 pairs, and oil from the *Amoco Cadiz* in 1978 caused further declines to 1981 when there were only 135–170 pairs (Henry and Monnat 1981; P. Penicaud, personal communication). The other populations were already very small (20–60 pairs) at the time of the *Torrey Canyon* wreck and most are now extinct (Guermeur and Monnat 1980; Henry and Monnat 1981).

8. HELGOLAND, GERMANY

The former small population on Helgoland became extinct around 1835. A few puffins are seen each spring, but there is no recent evidence of nesting (Gätke 1895; Salomonsen 1944; Lockley 1953a; Vauk 1982).

9. SWEDEN

Small numbers formerly nested on small islets off the west coast of Sweden: Sösteröyene Skerries (20 pairs in 1944, exterminated soon after), Soteskär (20 pairs in 1920, last pair in 1970), and Stora Knappen in the Väderöarna group (6 pairs in 1944, extinct by 1951) (Salomonsen 1944; Lockey 1953a; Harris 1976a).

10. NORWAY

The Atlantic Puffin is the most numerous seabird in Norway, nesting colonially on coastal islands at 29 locations along the west coast from Storkjør at the south in Rogaland north to Reinøya in eastern Finnmark (Brun 1979). The population is estimated to be about 1.3 million breeding pairs or 21% of the world population (Table 2.7), with 94% concentrated at only 11 sites in Nordland and Troms (Brun 1979; Barrett and Vader 1984). More than half of the puffin population nests on Røst (700,000 pairs, or 56% in 1964) in the Lofoten Islands (Nordland). The next largest colonies are on Nord-Fugløy (218,000 pairs, or 17% in 1967) in Troms, and Vaerøy (70,000 pairs, or 6%, in 1974) and Lovunden (60,000 pairs, or 5%, in 1968) in Nordland. About 3% of the population breeds at 7 sites north of Troms in Finnmark, with most birds on Hjelmsøya (20,000 pairs in 1964) and Gjesvaerstappene (18,000 pairs in 1973). The 11 nesting sites south of Nordland are mostly less than 1500 pairs except for Rundøy where there are at least 30,000 pairs and possibly as many as 50,000 to 100,000 (Brun 1979; Barrett and Vader 1984; A. O. Folkestad, in preparation). The population is concentrated in the northern part of the boreal marine zone (Fig. 2.10).

The puffin population in Norway has declined markedly since surveys began in the mid-1960s (Brun 1979). A dramatic decrease (ca. 30%) occurred between 1964 and 1974, when all alcids except the Black Guillemot were decreasing at Norwegian colonies (Brun 1979). Although the decline in some auks may have slowed or ceased since 1976 (Barrett and Vader 1984), the opposite seems far more likely for puffins. Numbers appear to have increased at the small southern colonies of Hornøya (160 pairs in 1967, 5000 pairs in 1980) and Loppa (180 pairs in 1968, 1000 pairs in 1980), but other positive changes recorded are probably artifacts of census technique. A significant decrease in puffins occurred at the large Lovunden colony (Myrberget 1978) and a crash is expected on Røst owing to reproductive failure since 1969 (Lid 1981). The puffin population may be expected to drop sharply in the next 5–10 years as adults on Røst reach maximum longevity and recruitment of young adults remains virtually zero (Lid 1981; Barrett and Vader 1984).

Most changes since the mid-1960s in the puffin population in Norway appear to be related to the herring fishery. The old-established herring fishery off north-central Norway declined abruptly in 1969 and has not recovered; the average catch in the 1970s was only 3% of that in the 1960s (Anonymous 1962, 1963–1972). The harvest of sardine-sized fish in the Nordland District is now only 0.4% of its former level, and the recent breeding failures of seabirds in Norway, including the large puffin colonies on Røst, coincided with the collapse of the herring fishery there (Myrberget 1978; Tschanz and Barth 1978; Barrett 1981; Lid 1981). Puffins at Røst, which depended on small herring as food for their young, have had only two successful breeding seasons between 1969 and 1983 with virtually all chicks dying of starvation at the colony (Tschanz 1979a; Lid 1981; F. Mehlum, personal communication). Similar breeding failures have been recorded at Lovunden, Anda, Vaerøy and Rundøy during the 1970s and early 1980s, all owing to food shortage believed to be brought about by the reduction in herring stocks through over-fishing (Barrett and Vader 1984). In southern Norway (Møre og Romsdal District), where puffin numbers seem to be stable or increasing slightly, a corresponding increase in certain fish stocks (sprat, sandlance, haddock) has taken place, but these improved conditions are local, involving less than 3% of the Norwegian puffin population. There is an immediate need to complete a monitoring system encompassing all the large colonies and a representative sample of the smaller ones to ensure that changes in population can be measured and assessed with precision.

11. KOLA PENINSULA (MURMANSK COAST)

The small puffin population of the Kola Peninsula is concentrated at 11 colonies along the Murmansk Coast in low-arctic waters. The population was estimated at 16,300 breeding pairs in 1959 to 1961 (Gerasimova 1962; Skokova 1962), mostly on Ostrova Aynovskiye: 8000 pairs on Malyy Aynov and 4000–7000 pairs on Bol'shoy Aynov (Skokova 1962). About 4000 pairs nested at the other nine colonies (Skokova 1962), the largest numbers at Ostrov Malyy Zelenets (1500 pairs) and Ostrov Bol'shoy Zelenets (1000 pairs), with only 10 to 500 pairs at the other sites (Norderhaug *et al.* 1977). No recent estimates for these colonies are available, except for Ostrov Kuvshin where Karpowicz (1970) estimated about 1000 pairs breeding (Golovkin 1984). The population may always have been small, at least at the Ostrova Aynovskiye, where numbers remained fairly stable (16,000 pairs) in 1940 to 1960 (Skokova 1962).

12. BJØRNØYA

Puffins nest in small numbers around the entire coast, usually as single pairs or in small groups, but colonies as large as 100 pairs are known at Tunheim (at Fugleodden and Siloodden) on the northeast coast. The population was estimated to be at least 600 pairs in 1980 (van Franeker and Luttik 1981). There is no information on population status. The difference between the 1970 (Williams 1971) and 1980 estimates is probably related to survey methods used rather than to a real change in abundance.

13. SPITSBERGEN

The puffin breeds in small aggregations or as solitary pairs, with numbers concentrated along the west coast which is normally ice-free in summer. Knowledge of the colonies is very incomplete, but all 18 breeding groups identified by Norderhaug *et al.* (1977) are fairly small (most 11–100 pairs), the two largest being Dei Sju Isfjella at the northwest tip of Vestspitsbergen and Alkefjellet on the northeast side (Løvenskiold 1964). The most recent estimate of the population (1982) by the Norwegian Polar Research Institute places it at less than 10,000 breeding pairs (F. Mehlum, personal communication). Information is not sufficient to assess trends in the population.

14. NOVAYA ZEMLYA

The puffin population on Novaya Zemlya is probably no more than a few hundred pairs (Uspenski 1956). They were known to nest at five locations on the west coast: Ostrova Oranskiye off Mys Zhelaniya at the north tip, Guba Arkhangel'skaya, Gribovaya Guba, Karpinski Poluostrov south of Guba Bezymyannaya, and Pukhovyy Zaliv. The largest breeding groups were in Gribovaya Guba with 64 pairs in 1950; there were also 7 pairs breeding at Pukhovyy Zaliv in 1950 (Uspenski 1956). Some puffins nest as solitary pairs, but usually they are in or close to other seabird colonies.

The status of the population is uncertain. Small colonies at Mys

Shantsa in Guba Mashigina, at Mys Prokof'yeva south of Guba Yuzhnaya Sul'meneva, and on Ostrov Karmakul'skiy in Malaya Karmakul'skaya Guba had disappeared by 1950 when Uspenski (1956) visited those areas. The population probably has always been small. No recent information is available on its present status.

15. FRANZ JOSEF LAND

Puffins have been seen off Franz Josef Land (Lockley 1953a), but there is no evidence of nesting. [See Uspenski (1959) and Norderhaug *et al.* (1977) for a review.]

X. CONCLUSIONS AND INFORMATION NEEDS

Knowledge of the distribution, abundance and status of alcid populations in the Atlantic is necessary for understanding the role of these species in marine ecosystems and for the conservation and management of the species and their ecosystems. Although present information does not provide a precise and accurate measure of these parameters for any species, certain tentative conclusions which emerge identify information gaps and suggest the need and direction for further research. Briefly, the fundamental points revealed by the species reviews are as follows:

1. Alcid populations are not distributed at random. They tend to be concentrated where major water masses meet, that is, towards boundaries of marine zones and in areas where *Polar* water from the Arctic Ocean meets and mixes with *Atlantic* water from the central Atlantic Ocean, and where marine productivity might be expected to be high. Within those areas of suitable marine habitat, patterns of dispersion are limited by ice characteristics (extent and timing of break-up) in northern regions and by the existence of nearby land providing safe breeding sites. Thus the distribution of alcids during the breeding season is a compromise between the oceanographic conditions which provide an adequate supply of food and the existence of breeding sites within range of this food source. Areas meeting both these requirements are scarce.

2. The Dovekie is the most numerous alcid in the Atlantic and the Black Guillemot the least. The numbers of breeding pairs of each alcid species occupying the North Atlantic and adjacent seas are roughly estimated to be (in descending order of abundance): Dovekie, 12 (range: 8–18) million; Thick-billed Murre, 6.8 (range: 4.9–7.5) million; Atlantic Puffin, 5.8 (range: 3.8–8.2) million; Common Murre, 4 (range: 3.0–4.5) mil-

lion; Razorbill, 700,000 (range: 0.3–1.2) million; and Black Guillemot, 270,000 (range: 0.2–0.35) million (see species tables for more exact estimates). Those values are only 'best guesses'; they should be regarded as first-level estimates, which are probably correct in a relative sense both between species (e.g., Dovekie more numerous than puffin and murres, which in turn exceed Razorbill and Black Guillemot) and as a reflection of the breeding distributions of each species over the Atlantic as a whole. They may prove useful as starting points for the examination of the role of alcids in marine ecosystems over large geographic areas. However, although censuses of alcids in some regions allow a reasonably precise measure of population sizes, our understanding of species populations will remain incomplete and uncertain until critical gaps and deficiencies in census information are corrected (see below). That calls for the development of an integrated and cooperative approach to study of the distribution of alcids throughout their breeding ranges (also see Chapter 10, this volume).

3. Table 2.8 summarizes existing information on status and recent changes in species populations, that is, whether populations are presently stable or not, and the degree to which populations have changed over the past century. From the known quantitative and qualitative information available it is clear that alcid populations in many parts of the North Atlantic declined markedly through the 1800s. In the eighteenth and nineteenth centuries these declines were largely owing to the major disturbance associated with human populations expanding rapidly in size and geographic range and to their increased exploitation of seabirds for food. Populations of most alcid species began to recover once the worst disturbances were curbed by the enactment of protective legislation towards the beginning of the twentieth century, and by changes in the numbers and life-styles of island and coastal residents. Until around 1940 alcid populations in areas where numbers had been greatly diminished showed slow, if steady, growth, although none regained their former abundance or geographic distribution. Following that period of limited growth alcid populations began to experience sudden and dramatic declines. Precise causes of those declines are uncertain and probably very complex, but they appear associated with increasing exploitation and pollution of the marine environment by humans. Probably human activity has adversely affected alcids *directly* at sea (e.g., by chronic oil spills and massive oiling such as that which occurred from 1939 to 1945, gill-netting, hunting) and at colonies during the breeding season (through introduced predators, and human disturbance: egging, hunting, tourism), as well as *indirectly* by altering the quantity or quality of their food supply (through commercial fisheries, or toxic chemical poisoning). The relative importance of those

mortality or disturbance factors varies with species and geographic area, but collectively they may explain most of the recent population trends observed, including increases and decreases being recorded concurrently in different parts of the breeding range of a single species (e.g., Common Murre and Atlantic Puffin).

Finally, Table 2.8 underlines how little information exists on the histories of some of the largest existing populations (e.g., Greenland, Iceland, Svalbard, Franz Josef Land, Novaya Zemlya). All of this makes it extremely difficult to attempt substantive historical interpretation of the former sizes and distribution patterns and the role of the Atlantic Alcidae in the natural ecosystem of the North Atlantic before human activities became massive and extensive.

Little can be done to correct deficiencies in information for the past. However, we can encourage investigators to undertake a complete and careful review of the population data (both quantitative and qualitative) for their respective areas of concern in order to develop realistic approximations of population sizes and changes which have taken place in the recent past. Initially, a most important task is the identification of gaps and shortcomings in the available information on present alcid populations, the inefficiencies in our censusing procedures, and how they may be overcome. Such difficulties are important constraints on what can be accomplished in future studies of alcids or on understanding the effects of natural or human-induced perturbations on species populations and their marine ecosystems. The following gaps in existing information or census techniques require careful attention:

1. The measurement of breeding populations in specific areas, particularly those known to have, or suspected of having, large populations of alcids but for which information is limited or non-existent (e.g., northwest and east Greenland, Iceland, Jan Mayen, Spitsbergen, Bjørnøya, Franz Josef Land, and Novaya Zemlya). Special attention should be directed to populations in Iceland, which may include the largest Atlantic populations of several species. To understand adequately the population dynamics of alcid species in the Atlantic as a whole, we must have a complete and precise data base for alcids breeding in Iceland.

2. The use of census techniques and sampling procedures must provide estimates of the size of the *breeding population* of known accuracy and precision. The unit of measurement must be breeding pairs, using eggs or chicks as the criteria of breeding effort (Nettleship 1976a). Counts of total full-grown individuals are of limited value without information on the ratio of total birds present to the number of active breeding pairs in the area, which can only be determined by employing very exacting proce-

David N. Nettleship and Peter G. H. Evans

TABLE 2.8

Estimates of Recent Changes and Present Status of Species Populations of the Atlantic Alcidae[a]

Region	Razorbill 1880–1930	1931–1950	1951–1970	1971–1982	Dovekie 1880–1930	1931–1950	1951–1970	1971–1982	Common Murre 1880–1930	1931–1950	1951–1970	1971–1982
Canada and New England												
E. Arctic												
Labrador	−	−	+	S or +					−	S or +	+	+
Newfoundland	−	−	?	− or ?					−	S or +	+	+
Gulf of St. Lawrence	−	−	−	−					−	−	S or −	− and +
Scotian Shelf– Bay of Fundy– Gulf of Maine	−	−	−	?					−	−	−	S or +
Greenland												
West	?	?	− or ?	− or ?	?	− or ?	− or ?	?	?	?	?	?
East					?	S or ?	S or ?	S or ?				
Iceland	?	?	?	S or ?	−	−	−	−	?	?	S or ?	S or ?
Jan Mayen					?	?	?	?				
Faeroe Islands	?	?	− or ?	− or ?					− and +	S or +	−	−
British Isles												
Scotland	?	− or ?	− or ?	S or +					?	S or −	S or −	S or +
England	?	−	−	S					−	−	−	S or +
Wales	?	−	−	−					−	−	−	S or −
Ireland	?	−	−	S or −					?	−	−	S or +
Channel Islands	?	−	−	−								
Brittany, France	−	S or +	−	−					S or −	S or +	−	−
Spain and Portugal									?	S or ?	−	−
Helgoland, Germany	−	−	−	S or +					?	?	S or −	S or +
Denmark	?	−	+	S or +					+	S or +	S or +	S or +
Sweden and Finland	+ or ?	−	−	S or ?					+	S or ?	S or ?	?
Norway	?	?	−	S or −					?	−	−	− or ?
Kola Peninsula (Murmansk)	?	?	?	?					?	?	?	?
Bjørnøya					?	?	?	?	?	?	?	?
Spitsbergen					?	?	?	?	?	?	?	?
Novaya Zemlya					?	S or ?	?	?	?	?	?	?
Franz Josef Land					?	?	?	?				

[a] +, Species increasing in numbers; −, species decreasing in numbers; S, species numbers relatively stable; ?, status uncertain or unknown. Areas left blank are outside the normal breeding range of the species.

Thick-billed Murre				Black Guillemot				Atlantic Puffin			
1880–1930	1931–1950	1951–1970	1971–1982	1880–1930	1931–1950	1951–1970	1971–1982	1880–1930	1931–1950	1951–1970	1971–1982
?	?	–	S or –	?	?	– or ?	– or ?	?	?	?	?
–	– or ?	–	S or +	–	– or ?	?	?	–	+ or ?	+	+ or ?
?	?	S	S	?	?	?	?	– or ?	+ or ?	S or +	–
–	–	?	?	–	+	S	–	– and +	S or +	–	S or +
				–	+	+	S or ?	–	+	S	S or ?
– or ?	–	–	–	?	?	– or ?	– or ?	?	?	?	?
?	S or ?	S or ?	S or ?	?	?	?	S or ?				
?	?	– or ?	– or ?	?	?	S or ?	– or ?	?	?	S or ?	S or ?
?	?	?	?	?	?	?	?	?	?	?	?
				–	+	+ or ?	S	– or ?	S or ?	S or ?	S or ?
				– or ?	S	S	S or +	– or ?	– or ?	– or S	S or +
				–	S	S	S or ?	–	–	–	S or –
				–	S	S	S or ?	–	–	–	S or –
				?	S or +	S or +	S or +	–	–	–	S or –
								–	–	–	S or –
								–	S	–	–
									Extirpated ca. 1835		
				+	+	+	+				
				–	–	–	–	–	–		Extinct
?	?	?	S	?	?	S	–	?	?	–	–
?	?	?	?	?	?	?	?	?	S or ?	S or ?	?
?	?	?	?	?	?	?	?	?	?	?	?
?	?	?	?	?	?	?	?	?	?	?	?
– or ?	–	–	?	?	?	?	?	?	– or ?	?	?
?	?	?	?	?	?	?	?				

dures (Nettleship 1976a; Birkhead and Nettleship 1980). Attendance of adults and non-breeders varies considerably between years at the same colony (Gaston and Nettleship 1982) making inter-year differences in the total number of birds present almost meaningless for the detection and assessment of changes in effective population size. Methods for estimating population size and monitoring numbers must, to the greatest extent possible, be standardized, agreed upon, and employed in all regions if we are to gather the necessary data on alcid populations and avoid wasting time and monies through inadequate procedures.

3. Population status is best determined through the use of representative plots within selected colonies, and it is essential that investigators take fully into consideration the location, size and number of plots needed to generate statistically useful results. Although this requirement is an obvious one, it is often neglected or given insufficient attention both in the design and in the implementation of monitoring systems.

The effort required to fill data gaps or refine techniques and procedures used to estimate population size and status is substantial. The task ahead is large and formidable. Those needs must be addressed and attained over the longer term, no matter how slowly, if we are to develop an effective base of information from which to understand the biology and ecological requirements of this highly specialized group of marine birds.

CHAPTER **3**

Breeding Ecology of the Atlantic Alcidae

MICHAEL P. HARRIS

Institute of Terrestrial Ecology, Banchory Research Station, Banchory,
Kincardineshire, Scotland

TIM R. BIRKHEAD

Department of Zoology, University of Sheffield, Sheffield, England

155

I. INTRODUCTION

Our aim in this chapter is to provide a concise factual account of the reproductive biology of each Atlantic auk species in turn. Synthesis, interpretation and comparative aspects of alcid breeding biology are presented in Chapter 4. The Atlantic auk species fall into two very distinct groups: the cliff-breeding Common and Thick-billed Murres and the Razorbill, and the hole-breeding Atlantic Puffin, Black Guillemot and Dovekie. Members of the former group are similar in that their young go to sea (inaccurately called fledging) when flightless and weighing only about one-quarter of the adult weight, and are cared for by one parent for several weeks. In contrast, young of the second group have fully developed primaries, are usually capable of some degree of flight and appear to be independent of their parents when they leave the colony. There have been many qualitative accounts of various aspects of these species' breeding biology, but in writing the following account we have relied mainly on the few detailed, quantitative studies listed in Table 3.1.

TABLE 3.1

Main Quantitative Studies Used in Preparing Species Summaries

Species	Location	Number of breeding seasons examined	References
Razorbill	St. Mary I., Gulf of St. Lawrence	Two	Bédard (1969d)
	Skokholm I., Wales	Three	Lloyd (1976a, 1979)
	Kandalakshskaya Guba, U.S.S.R.	Five	Bianki (1967)
Common Murre	Skomer I., Wales	Three	Birkhead (1976a, 1977a,b, 1978a, 1980)
	Stora Karlsö, Baltic Sea	Four	Hedgren (1979, 1980, 1981); Hedgren and Linnman (1979)
Thick-billed Murre	Murmansk Coast, U.S.S.R.	Eight	Belopol'skii (1957)
	Prince Leopold I., N.W.T.	Four	Gaston and Nettleship (1981); Nettleship et al. (1980)
Atlantic Puffin	Lovunden, Norway	Two	Myrberget (1959a, 1962)
	Great I., Nfld.	Two	Nettleship (1972)
	Skomer I., Wales	Six	Ashcroft (1976, 1979)
	Isle of May, Scotland	Eight	Harris (1978, 1979, 1982a, 1983a)
	St. Kilda, Scotland	Four	Harris (1979, 1980, 1982a, 1983a,b)
Black Guillemot	Kent I., Bay of Fundy	Six	Winn (1950); Preston (1968)
	Mickelskären, Finland	Eight	Bergman (1971)
	Nordre Rønner, Denmark	Three	Asbirk (1979b)
	Flatey, Breidhafjordhur, Iceland	Three	Petersen (1979, 1981)
	Brandypot Is. and St. Mary Is., Gulf of St. Lawrence	Two	Cairns (1978, 1980, 1981)
	Hekkingen, Norway	Three	R. Barrett (personal communication)
	Kandalakshskaya Guba, U.S.S.R.	Five	Bianki (1967)
Dovekie	Hornsund, Spitsbergen	Six	Norderhaug (1970, 1980); Stempniewicz (1980, 1981)
	Horse Head I., Upernavik, Greenland	One	Evans (1981a)
	Cape Atholl and Siorapaluk, Thule, Greenland	One	Roby et al. (1981)

II. RAZORBILL, *Alca torda*

A. General Features

1. PRE-LAYING PERIOD

A period of colony attendance prior to egg-laying is a regular feature of Razorbill breeding biology. The duration of this period may be protracted and is related to environmental factors, such as water temperature and ice-cover. In boreal regions, such as Britain, Razorbills begin to return to their breeding sites in late February and early March, about 3 months before the start of egg-laying, but at a few colonies Razorbills may return as early as October or November (Taylor and Reid 1981). At high latitudes and in cold-water areas, such as the Murmansk Coast and eastern Canada, most birds arrive at the colony in late April or early May only about 1 month before egg-laying.

Patterns of colony attendance prior to laying have been recorded only in boreal regions. Lloyd (1973) found that Razorbills were present only on some days and alternated with about 3 days at the colony and 3 or 4 days' absence. At this time Razorbills roost at sea and arrive at the colony at first light, and then depart again several hours later. The birds often spend most of their time at the colony displaying in groups on the sea. It seems likely that birds visit the colony for several days to defend the breeding site with their partner, and then spend several days feeding, away from the colony. The alternating pattern of attendance is influenced by weather conditions: strong winds and heavy seas result in reduced numbers at the colony and a disrupted cycle of attendance. At mixed colonies stormy conditions may synchronize the attendance patterns of different species, since all tend to be absent during consecutive days of bad weather and to return together when weather conditions improve.

2. BREEDING HABITAT

Razorbills breed colonially in rocky, coastal regions, on mainland cliffs and on offshore islands. In most areas breeding sites are situated in boulder scree or on cliff-faces in rock crevices or on ledges. The commonest breeding site is enclosed or partially enclosed. The single egg is usually laid directly on bare rock, but birds may collect small stones, dried droppings, lichen or other bits of vegetation from the immediate vicinity of the breeding site and place them where the egg will be laid. Incubating birds also collect material within their reach and place it under the egg.

3. SITE AND MATE FIDELITY

Pairs generally keep the same breeding site from season to season (Lloyd 1976a). On Skokholm, Wales, 11 of 129 birds changed sites between years and all changes were associated with (actual or presumed) change of mate. Over 95% of mate changes occurred after the death of the partner. Females were more likely to change their breeding site than males. Of the 11 birds which moved 8 were sexed, and 7 were females ($p = .035$) (Lloyd 1976a), suggesting that males own the site.

B. Timing of Breeding

Egg-laying starts earliest in the most southerly parts of the Razorbills' range, but is more closely related to sea-surface temperature than latitude (see Chapter 4, this volume). On Skokholm between 1971 and 1973, the first eggs were laid in the first week of May and laying continued until the first week of June, a spread of about 30 days. Mean laying dates were 17 May in 1971 and 1973, but 29 May in 1972, a year when stormy conditions during the pre-laying period probably disrupted feeding and the females' ability to accumulate reserves for egg formation (Lloyd 1979). At higher latitudes, or where water temperatures are lower, laying is later; for example, on the Murmansk Coast the median laying date was about 8 June (Belopol'skii 1957). (See also Chapter 4, Fig. 4.1, this volume.)

C. The Egg and Incubation

The single egg is 'elliptical ovate' in shape. Eggs vary in colour and markings, but less so than murres'. The background colour may be white, cream, buff or very pale blue and the markings reddish brown through to black. Some eggs are lightly marked with just a few dark spots or blotches, while others have a dense covering of marks. Blotched markings frequently form a ring around the blunt end of the egg. There is no association between egg colour and the type of breeding site occupied (Hudson 1979a). Females produce eggs of similar colour and size in successive years but there is some controversy over whether they use these marks to distinguish their own egg (Birkhead 1978b; Ingold 1980).

The egg constitutes about 14% of adult weight. On Skokholm the mean volume (calculated) of first eggs was 83.3 cm^3 (S.D. = 6.9, $N = 206$) in 1971, and fresh-egg weight (about 90 g) represented 14.5% of mean adult body weight (620 g) (Lloyd 1976a). Corresponding data for the White Sea produce a figure of 14.0% (Bianki 1967). Part of the apparent difference between populations in relative egg size is probably due to seasonal

changes in body weight which occur in Razorbills and other alcids. However, within any particular population, females laying early in the season
lay larger eggs than those laying later: in each of 3 years Lloyd (1979)
recorded a significant negative relationship between egg volume and laying date. Razorbills lay an egg of similar dimensions, relative to other
females in the population, each year, since Lloyd (1979) found significant
correlations between the volume of eggs laid in the same sites in successive years, and site tenacity to be over 90%. There is also a tendency for
egg size to increase with female age, but this may be because older birds
breed earlier than young birds.

Incubation starts immediately after the egg is laid. The egg is incubated
against one of two brood patches situated on the bird's ventral surface,
more or less under each wing. Two patches may either imply that Razorbills once produced two-egg clutches, or that they represent an adaptation
to a particular incubation posture. Lloyd (1979) recorded a mean incubation period of 35.1 days (S.D. = 2.2, N = 239) on Skokholm Island.
Bédard (1969d) and Paludan (1947) obtained values of 36.9 days (S.D. =
1.6, N = 9) and 35.5 days (S.D. = ?, N = 6), respectively. Both sexes
incubate, and although there is no detailed information on the duration of
incubation shifts, each bird probably spends about 12 to 24 hours on the
egg at a time.

If the egg is lost a replacement may be laid, especially if the loss occurs
relatively early in the season. The mean interval between loss and replacement was 14.1 days (S.D. = 1.5, N = 14) on Skokholm (Lloyd 1979),
which is similar to murres. The calculated volume of second eggs was 8
cm^3 less than the eggs they replaced.

D. Chick-rearing Period

Young Razorbills are semi-precocial. At hatching the chick is covered
with down, which is black or pale grey on the dorsal surface, pale grey on
the head and white beneath. During the first few days of life it is closely
brooded since it is unable to regulate its own body temperature. The
information on when auk chicks become homeothermic is confusing, and
different authors report widely different ages for a single species. This is
due to a number of factors: different experimental techniques, inaccurately aged young, and ambiguity concerning the onset and completion of
homeothermy. The most detailed studies are those of Johnson and West
(1975) on Common Murres, and it seems reasonable to assume that Razorbill chicks are completely homeothermic at about the same stage of
development as murres, that is, about 9 to 10 days old (see Chapter 7, this
volume). Once chicks are able to thermoregulate, those in enclosed sites

are occasionally left unattended by their parents, whereas those on open ledges are always guarded by one parent. The chick starts to lose its down and acquire its proper feathers at about day 10. This juvenal plumage consists of well-developed primary coverts and a dense coat of body feathers. The feathers on the ventral surface are particularly dense and provide waterproofing, thermal insulation and some protection during fledging. The primaries and secondaries do not start to emerge until after the chick has left the colony. The primary coverts are used during the chick's 'flight' to the sea, and once on the sea, for propulsion underwater.

Razorbill chicks hatch at a weight of about 60 g, and hatching weight is positively correlated with egg size (Lloyd 1979). The weight of chicks at hatching is about 9 to 10% of adult body weight. The chicks' body weight increases linearly up until the twelfth day, after which it increases more slowly (Lloyd 1979). Razorbill chicks spend about 18 days at the breeding site; the mean value for birds on Skokholm was 17.2 days (S.D. = 2.2, N = 163) (Lloyd 1979), at St. Mary Islands, Gulf of St. Lawrence, 18.2 days (S.D. = 1.5, N = 30) (Bédard 1969d) and 19.3 days (N = 65) at the Lofoten Islands, Norway (Ingold 1974). Chicks leave the colony weighing between 140 and 180 g (i.e., 20–30% of adult body weight). Chicks hatched early in the season fledged at greater weights than those hatched later (Belopol'skii 1957; Lloyd 1979).

E. Departure of Young from the Colony

Chicks leave the colony while they are only partly grown and still flightless. In boreal regions, departure occurs over a 1- to 3-hour period at dusk. At higher latitudes where there is continuous daylight, departure also occurs over a short period of time, usually at 'night' when light intensity is at its lowest (Williams 1975). Where Razorbills breed on ledges above the sea, the chick simply jumps from the breeding site and parachutes down to the water. In boulder colonies the chick scrambles to the sea. In both situations chicks are always accompanied by one parent (the male) which continues to care for the chick for several weeks.

F. Breeding Success

The accurate measurement of breeding success is difficult because most birds breed in enclosed sites where nest-checks disturb the birds with an increased chance of an egg or chick being lost. Consequently, measures of breeding success are minimal. On open sites breeding success can be measured by direct observation, but open sites are less preferred than closed sites so results from such habitats may also be unrepresentative.

TABLE 3.2

Breeding Success of Razorbill, Common Murre and Thick-billed Murre in Various Studies[a]

Species	Colony	Year	No. of eggs laid	No. of eggs hatched[b]	No. of chicks fledged[b]	No. of young fledged per pair	References
Razorbill	Kandalakshskaya Guba, U.S.S.R.	1957	81	69 (85.2)	67 (97.1)	0.83	Bianki (1967)
		1958	48	38 (79.2)	36 (94.7)	0.75	Bianki (1967)
		1959	41	36 (87.8)	35 (97.2)	0.85	Bianki (1967)
	Skomer I., Wales	1976	117	93 (79.5)	76 (81.7)	0.65	P. J. Hudson (personal communication)
		1977	173	116 (67.0)	108 (93.1)	0.62	P. J. Hudson (personal communication)
	Skokholm I., Wales	1971	257	196 (76.3)	181 (92.3)	0.70	Lloyd (1979)
		1972	236	171 (72.4)	164 (95.9)	0.70	Lloyd (1979)
		1973	242	187 (77.3)	175 (93.6)	0.72	Lloyd (1979)
Common Murre	Skomer I., Wales	1973	124	102 (82.6)	90 (87.6)	0.73	Birkhead and Hudson (1977)
		1974	158	116 (70.1)	104 (87.8)	0.62	Birkhead and Hudson (1977)

		Year					Reference
		1975	204	174 (83.4)	155 (88.3)	0.74	Birkhead and Hudson (1977)
	Stora Karlsö, Baltic Sea	1974	287	250 (79.0)	240 (96.0)	0.77	Hedgren (1980)
		1975	372	329 (85.0)	309 (94.0)	0.80	Hedgren (1980)
		1976	389	358 (87.0)	336 (94.0)	0.82	Hedgren (1980)
		1977	427	387 (85.0)	375 (97.0)	0.82	Hedgren (1980)
Thick-billed Murre	Prince Leopold I., N.W.T.	1975	358	309 (86.3)	284 (91.9)	0.79	Gaston and Nettleship (1981)
		1976	359	296 (82.5)	269 (90.0)	0.75	Gaston and Nettleship (1981)
		1977	351	294 (83.8)	270 (91.8)	0.77	Gaston and Nettleship (1981)
		1978	344	280 (81.4)	229 (81.8)	0.67	Nettleship et al. (1980)
	Cape Hay, Bylot I., N.W.T.	1979	513	275 (53.6)	247 (89.8)	0.48	Birkhead and Nettleship (1981)
	Coburg I., N.W.T.	1979	632	503 (79.6)	449 (89.3)	0.71	Birkhead and Nettleship (1981)

[a] Data include replacement eggs.
[b] Percentage of total given in parentheses.

These problems make it difficult to evaluate the results of different workers, and to make intraspecific and interspecific comparisons. The highest values were obtained by Bianki (1967) in the White Sea; in 3 years between 75 and 85% of pairs reared a chick to leave the colony. On Skokholm, the average of 3 consecutive years was 71% (Lloyd 1979). Hudson's values (1982 and personal communication) for neighbouring Skomer Island were lower: 62–64% in 2 years (Table 3.2). Breeding success was 68% in the Baltic (Olsson 1974).

In most studies loss of eggs was greater than the loss of chicks, both on a day-to-day basis and overall; the same pattern occurs in murres (see Table 3.2).

Timing of breeding, age of female and quality of the breeding site all affect breeding success. As in many other birds, Razorbills which lay relatively early in the breeding season are more likely to fledge a chick. Up to 83% of the earliest breeders fledged a young compared with 56% for the latest breeders (Lloyd 1979). Part of this seasonal decline occurs because young birds have low breeding success and tend to lay late in the season.

III. COMMON MURRE, *Uria aalge*

A. General Features

1. PRE-LAYING PERIOD

Common Murres have a longer period of colony attendance prior to egg-laying than many other seabirds. This is longest in the southern extremes of their range and shortest near the northern limits, but the pattern is determined more by water temperature, and ice, than by latitude. At some British colonies birds make irregular, usually brief visits to the colony from immediately after the completion of primary wing moult in October (Taylor and Reid 1981), which results in the pre-laying period lasting 6 months. At colonies in Murmansk, U.S.S.R., near the northern edge of the Common Murre's range, birds return in March about 8 weeks prior to egg-laying. The early return probably occurs because there is severe competition for breeding sites, which would explain the aggression between neighbouring birds in winter. If an early return ensures a breeding territory for the forthcoming season, then natural selection will favour individuals which return early.

At boreal colonies approximately 1 month before egg-laying, attendance at the colony becomes more regular and follows a cyclical pattern.

For example, the general pattern at Skomer Island was a 3- to 5-day period of absence followed by a day on which 60–70% of the breeding population visited the colony. On the following day peak numbers occurred with both members of most pairs at the colony. On the third day numbers were similar to the first, and for the following 3–5 days the birds were absent from the colony. Similar patterns have been recorded at other colonies.

2. BREEDING HABITAT

Common Murre colonies occur on cliffs and offshore islands which provide breeding areas safe from mammalian predators. The birds breed in the open on broad and narrow ledges on steep cliffs and on stack tops and flat, low-lying islands (Fig. 3.1). Less commonly they breed in crevices, under boulders and in caves. No nest is made; the egg is laid on bare rock and held in position against the brood patch by the feet. Murres generally incubate in direct physical contact with their neighbours and the average density on broad, flat rocky areas is about 20 pairs/m².

Fig. 3.1.   Part of the dense, flat-top Common Murre colony at Funk Island, Newfoundland, 11 July 1975. (Photo by D. N. Nettleship.)

3. SITE AND MATE FIDELITY

Despite the tendency to breed at high densities, murres still defend individual territories and over 90% of birds occupy exactly the same spot from year to year (Birkhead 1977a; Hedgren 1980). Birds which fail to rear a chick one year are more likely to change breeding site than successful breeders (Hedgren 1980). The limited data suggest mate fidelity is the rule.

B. Timing of Breeding

The most complete data come from two colonies close to the edge of the species' range, Skomer Island and Stora Karlsö in the Baltic. On Skomer Island the median laying date varied between 16 and 20 May in 3 years (Fig. 3.2), and at Stora Karlsö, it varied from 9 to 19 May in 6 years (Hedgren 1980). At both localities the spread of laying covered 30–40 days. Data for other colonies are less precise: in 1980 at Funk Island, Newfoundland, the first chicks hatched on 22 June, while 560 km farther south, at Great and Green Islands, Witless Bay, first hatching occurred on 13 June. This indicates median laying dates of about 6 June for Funk Island and 26 May for Witless Bay. In northern Norway the first eggs appeared in mid-May, but not until late May (but earliest 11 May) on the Murmansk Coast and the end of May or mid-June in southern Novaya Zemlya (Belopol'skii 1957). (See Chapter 4, Fig. 4.1, this volume.)

Data for Skomer Island and Stora Karlsö indicate that annual median laying dates at a single colony vary by at least 6–10 days. However, within years there may be just as much variation in timing between different parts of the same colony. Members of a breeding colony usually breed

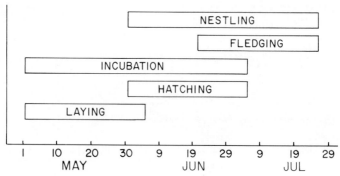

Fig. 3.2. Temporal pattern of egg-laying, hatching and fledging in Common Murres at Skomer Island, Wales (from Birkhead 1980).

synchronously, with most birds laying early in the laying period so that the distribution of laying dates is skewed. There appears to be a multi-tier system of synchrony. At the first level the entire colony (e.g., all the birds breeding on Skomer Island) lays over a period of 30 to 40 days. Within the colony the birds on a single cliff-face may breed over about 20 days, and within a cliff-face, groups of birds breeding at different densities may lay over varying periods of time. On Skomer the highest density groups laid over the shortest time period: where breeding density exceeded 10 pairs/ m^2 the middle 80% of eggs was laid over 9 to 13 days, but at the lowest densities, less than 3 pairs/m^2, the middle 80% of eggs was laid over 20 days (Birkhead 1977a, 1980).

C. The Egg and Incubation

Murres produce a single, pyriform egg which shows remarkable variation in background colour and colour and type of markings. Background colours range from white, blue, green to brown, and the markings (which are dark) may be spots, blotches or pencil-like hieroglyphics. The colour and type of marking are consistent between eggs for a particular female although the distribution of markings can vary. Murres use the colour and type of marking to recognize their own egg (Tschanz 1959, 1968). The fresh weight of Common Murre eggs (100–120 g) is about 12% of adult body weight and egg volume in different populations is positively correlated with adult weight (Fig. 3.3 and Table 3.3).

It has been suggested (Tuck 1961) that the pyriform shape of murre eggs may be an adaptation to prevent eggs from rolling off ledges. Although this may be partly true, the rolling radius varies from 17 cm in fresh eggs to 11 cm in fully incubated eggs (T. R. Birkhead, unpublished observations) and many Common Murres breed on ledges narrower than this. Thick-billed Murres also have pyriform-shaped eggs and characteristically breed on very narrow ledges, whereas Razorbills often breed on ledges yet have more rounded eggs. Ingold (1980) showed that the pyriform egg confers little advantage in terms of egg-rolling and loss. This indicates that the pyriform shape may confer some additional advantage. We suggest that since a sphere-shaped egg has the smallest ratio of surface area to volume from which to lose heat (to the air) and gain heat (from the brood patch), a pyriform egg maximizes the surface area of egg in contact with the brood patch for murres which incubate in a semi-upright position.

In the Common Murre incubation starts immediately after the egg is laid and lasts 32.5 days on average (S.D. = 1.7, N = 43: T. R. Birkhead, unpublished observations). Both sexes incubate in shifts of about 12 to 24 hours (E. Verspoor, personal communication).

In general, eggs lost early in the season are more likely to be replaced than those lost later. The mean interval between loss and replacement was 14.8 days (S.D. = 1.2, N = 9) on Skomer Island (Birkhead and Hudson 1977), 15.1 days (S.D. = 0.9, N = 19) at Stora Karlsö (Hedgren and Linnman 1979) and 15.5 days (N = 30) in Newfoundland (Mahoney 1979). In the Baltic, replacement eggs were 6% smaller in volume than first eggs (Hedgren and Linnman 1979).

D. Chick-rearing Period

Young Common Murres are semi-precocial (see Chapter 7, this volume). The chick takes on average 2.7 days (S.D. = 1.21, N = 53) to emerge from the egg after the first cracks appear (Mahoney 1979). The incubating adult sometimes helps the chick to emerge by breaking away bits of egg shell. Chicks cannot completely maintain their body temperature until they are about 10 days old (Johnson and West 1975), and for the first few days of life are closely brooded against the adults' brood patch. Later they are brooded under one wing and after about the tenth day they spend some time standing beside their parent (Wehrlin 1977). At hatching chicks weigh between 55 and 95 g (according to egg size and adult body size: see Fig. 3.3 and Table 3.3), representing about 6 to 10% of adult body weight (Birkhead 1976a). The chicks' body weight increases linearly up to day 14–16, after which the rate of increase declines (Birkhead 1977b; Hedgren and Linnman 1979). In some cases weight continues to increase

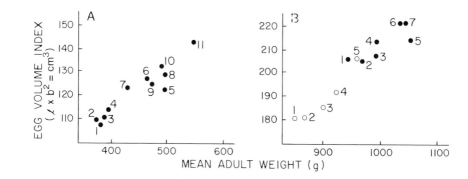

Fig. 3.3.   Relationship between mean adult body weight (g) and mean volume index (length × breadth²) of eggs in (A) Atlantic Puffin and (B) Common Murre (●) and Thick-billed Murre (○). Data for each point are presented in Table 3.3.

until the chick leaves the colony (Johnson and West 1975; see Chapter 7, this volume, for additional information on chick development). Both parents feed the chick although one adult remains at the breeding site with the chick at all times, to brood and protect it from predators. Chicks are fed mainly clupeid fish, smelt or sandlance (see Chapter 6, this volume), brought one at a time about three or four times a day. Feeding rates probably depend on prey size and availability; mean daily food intakes (Clupeidae) of chicks were 28 g on Skomer Island, and 32 g at Stora Karlsö (Birkhead 1977b; Hedgren and Linnman 1979). Chicks leave the colony weighing between 170 and 270 g (ca. 18–28% of adult body weight: Birkhead 1976a; Hedgren and Linnman 1979), usually when 20 or 21 days old (range: 16–30 days). The mean age at departure varies between colonies; for example, it was 19.8 days (S.D. = 2.3, N = 61) at Stora Karlsö (Hedgren and Linnman 1979) and 21.2 days (S.D. = 2.6, N = 42) at Skomer Island (Birkhead 1977b). Age at leaving may also vary between years within the same colony: Hedgren and Linnman (1979) recorded a mean age of 19.0 days (S.D. = 2.3, N = 15) in 1975, and 20.7 days (S.D. = 1.9, N = 22) in 1977.

E. Departure of Young from the Colony

Chicks leave the colony at dusk in boreal regions and at the time of lowest light intensity in the Arctic (Williams 1975). Chicks are accompanied by their male parent at leaving (Scott 1973; Birkhead 1976a) and the male continues to care for the chick for several weeks after leaving the colony (see below). At cliff colonies the chick jumps from the breeding ledge and lands on the water, but at colonies on flat islands or stacks, chicks with their attendant adults may have to walk several metres to suitable jumping places. At Stora Karlsö most chicks jump from ledges, land on a beach, and then run to the sea where their parents wait (Hedgren and Linnman 1979). The adult and chick locate each other by calls and then swim away together. At some colonies a lone chick may be mobbed by other (non-breeding?) murres before the male parent reaches it. In Oregon (Varoujean et al. 1979), chicks reach 90–95% adult weight about 45 to 60 days after leaving the colony and become independent of the male about 25 days later. The female continues to visit the breeding site for up to 2 weeks after the chick has left the colony.

Chicks usually leave the colony over a relatively short period each day, probably using light intensity as a cue for the timing of their departure. Synchronous departure may reduce predation risks (see Chapter 4, this volume). However, levels of predation vary between colonies (Williams

TABLE 3.3

Mean Adult Body Weight and Mean Egg Volume Indices for Common Murre, Thick-billed Murre and Atlantic Puffin

Species and location[a]	Adult weight (g)	Egg volume index (length × breadth²)	References
Common Murre			
1. Cló Mòr, Scotland	945	206	Jefferies and Parslow (1976)
2. N. Shore, Gulf of St. Lawrence	965	205	Johnson (1944)
3. Foula, Scotland	990	207	R. Furness (personal communication)
4. Gull I., Witless Bay, Nfld.	992	214	Mahoney (1979)
5. E. Murmansk, U.S.S.R.	1054	214	Belopol'skii (1957)
6. Hornøya, Norway	1039	222	R. Barrett (personal communication)
7. Novaya Zemlya, U.S.S.R.	1044	222	Uspenski (1956)
Thick-billed Murre			
1. Coburg I., N.W.T.	850	180	Birkhead and Nettleship (1981)
2. Cape Hay, Bylot I., N.W.T.	874	180	Birkhead and Nettleship (1981)
3. Prince Leopold I., N.W.T.	900	185	Gaston and Nettleship (1981)
4. Upernavik, Greenland	923	190	P. G. H. Evans (personal communication)
5. Novaya Zemlya, U.S.S.R.	960	206	Uspenski (1956)
Atlantic Puffin			
1. Skomer I., Wales	385	107	Corkhill (1972); M. P. Harris (unpublished)
2. St. Kilda, Scotland	368	111	M. P. Harris (unpublished)
3. Shetland, Scotland	387	110	M. P. Harris (unpublished)
4. Isle of May, Scotland	400	113	M. P. Harris (unpublished)
5. Novaya Zemlya, U.S.S.R.	501	124	Dement'ev et al. (1951); Uspenski (1956)
6. Great I., Nfld.	476	125	Nettleship (1972)
7. Lovunden, Norway	441	124	Myrberget (1963)

TABLE 3.3 *(Continued)*

Species and location[a]	Adult weight (g)	Egg volume index (length × breadth²)	References
8. Murmansk Coast, U.S.S.R.	504	128	Myrberget (1963)
9. Iceland	484	126	Timmermann (1949)
10. Russia	491	132	Belopol'skii (1957)
11. Spitsbergen	550	142	M. P. Harris (unpublished)

[a] Numbers correspond to those in Fig. 3.3.

1975; Birkhead 1976a), and most losses are due to the failure of adult and chick to remain united during this time.

F. Breeding Success

Two methods have been used to assess breeding success in murres. One, which involves regular visits to breeding areas and disturbance of birds to count eggs and chicks almost certainly gives gross underestimates of breeding success (Tuck 1961; Mahoney 1979). The second method, does not disturb birds, but does require long periods of observation and produces a more accurate measure of breeding success (Birkhead and Nettleship 1980). Like Razorbills, Common Murres have a relatively high breeding success. On Skomer Island, the average proportion of pairs successfully rearing a chick to leaving was 0.72. At Stora Karlsö, hatching success (84.3%), chick success (95.3%) and overall breeding success (0.80 pairs raise a chick) were even higher (Table 3.2).

Murres which breed relatively late in the season are less likely to raise a chick successfully than those breeding early (Birkhead 1977a; Hedgren 1980). On Stora Karlsö, the last 10% of birds to lay had a significantly lower breeding success (0.55) than the first 10% (0.83), or those breeding mid-season (0.83). Hedgren (1980) concluded that this effect was caused mainly by young birds breeding late, rather than to a seasonal decline in environmental conditions. However, he also showed that replacement eggs, most of which were laid by experienced birds and hatched 7–14 days after late first eggs, had low breeding success (0.30), which suggests that both age and date affect breeding success. The effect of breeding density and synchrony on breeding success are discussed in detail in the next chapter.

IV. THICK-BILLED MURRE, *Uria lomvia*

A. General Features

1. PRE-LAYING PERIOD

Like the Common Murre and Razorbill, Thick-billed Murres have a protracted period of colony attendance lasting 4–6 weeks prior to egg-laying (Gaston and Nettleship 1981).

However, because of their more northerly breeding distribution (see Chapter 2, this volume), and the fact that their breeding and feeding areas are often ice-bound until late spring, Thick-billed Murres have a shorter period of pre-laying attendance, on average, than Common Murres. At colonies where both species of murre breed they usually return to the colony at approximately the same time (Swartz 1966). Like Common Murres, pre-laying attendance is characterised by a pattern of alternating presence and absence. This pattern is influenced by environmental factors. For example at Prince Leopold Island in 1976, 82% of the variation in bird numbers present at the colony was explained by changes in barometric pressure (56%), time of year (10%) and wind speed (8%) (Gaston and Nettleship 1981). High numbers of birds occurred at the colony with large changes in barometric pressure, low wind speeds and close to the onset of laying. Maximum numbers, which never exceeded 89% of the breeding adults, occurred about 7 days before the start of laying.

2. BREEDING HABITAT

Thick-billed Murres breed colonially on narrow ledges or, less often, in crevices and caves, on steep sea-cliffs and offshore islands. Unlike Common Murres, they rarely breed more than one rank deep on a ledge, and usually occupy small, narrow ledges, often at sites where there is only sufficient room for one bird. This difference in habitat selection may be related to morphological differences between the two species. Spring (1971) suggested that the enlarged pectoral region of the Thick-billed Murre forces it to adopt a more prone position, and always to rest its breast against the cliff, an isolated stone or a minor break in the ledge surface while incubating (see also Williams 1974). Where birds occupy long, narrow ledges they incubate shoulder to shoulder, in physical contact like Common Murres; however, since they never occupy flat-top surfaces, they do not breed at such high densities. No nest is made; the egg is laid on bare rock and held in position against the brood patch by the feet.

3. SITE AND MATE FIDELITY

Little quantitative information is available but Thick-billed Murres are probably similar to other auks in being site tenacious; they may well be slightly more flexible since they often breed in areas where rockfalls often destroy, and create, breeding sites.

B. Timing of Breeding

Thick-billed Murres have a more northerly distribution than Common Murres (see Chapter 2, this volume), and therefore, on average, commence breeding later than Common Murres. Where both species breed at the same location each species lays at approximately the same time (Belopol'skii 1957; Swartz 1966). As with other alcids, egg-laying is latest among Thick-billed Murres breeding in areas of low sea temperatures (see Fig. 4.1, Chapter 4, this volume). For example, in eastern Murmansk the average date for the start of laying in 12 seasons was 24 May (range: 11–29 May: Belopol'skii 1957), which suggests a median laying date of ca. 1 June. Farther north in Novaya Zemlya, the estimated median laying date was 22 June (Uspenski 1956; Belopol'skii 1957).

Quantitative details of the pattern and timing of laying are available for only a few colonies. At Prince Leopold Island, median laying dates for 1975 to 1977 were between 28 June and 3 July (Gaston and Nettleship 1981). The exceptionally late median laying date of 18 July in 1978 was associated with unusual ice conditions in the Lancaster Sound region (Nettleship *et al.* 1980). At Coburg Island and Cape Hay, Bylot Island, in 1979, median dates were 2 July and 6 July, respectively (Birkhead and Nettleship 1981).

Laying tends to occur synchronously within small areas of the colony but, unlike Common Murres, synchrony is not related to breeding density (see Chapter 4, this volume). Most birds lay early in the laying period, suggesting that in some years at least, part of the population delays laying beyond the date at which they first become capable of laying, resulting in greater overall synchrony. The spread of laying in the high Arctic is about 30 days, very similar to Common Murres breeding in boreal regions.

C. The Egg and Incubation

The clutch is one pyriform-shaped egg which closely resembles that of the Common Murre but Thick-billed Murres' are smaller (Fig. 3.3) and Thick-billed Murre eggs are relatively broader (Table 3.4; see also Upenski 1956; Belopol'skii 1957). Certain types of markings are associated with particular ground colours (Gaston and Nettleship 1981). Eggs with

TABLE 3.4

Shape Indices of Some Atlantic Alcid Eggs

Species	N	Shape Index 1[a] $\bar{x}$	S.E.	Shape Index 2[b] $\bar{x}$	S.E.	References
Common Murre	50	2.597	0.05	63.44	0.66	Hudson (1979a)
Thick-billed Murre	50	2.601	0.01	62.57	0.37	Hudson (1979a and personal communication)
Razorbill[c]	81	2.409	0.01	63.99	0.22	Hudson (1979a and personal communication)
Great Auk	59	2.583	0.01	62.30	0.38	Calculated from photographs of eggs in Tompkinson and Tompkinson (1966)

[a] Shape Index 1, ratio of total width to distance between point of maximum width and blunt end of egg. Pyriform eggs have ratios of >2, elliptical eggs have ratios closer to 2.

[b] Shape Index 2, breath/length × 100; relatively wider eggs have lower values than relatively narrow eggs.

[c] Note: for each shape index (S.I.), Razorbill values are lowest (S.I. 1) or highest (S.I. 2). Great Auk and Razorbill shape indices were significantly different ($p < .001$) for both indices, but differences between Great Auks and both murres were not significant ($p > .05$).

dark ground colours have large, dark markings, while pale eggs tend to have small light markings. Egg volume is related in a complex manner to the ground colour of eggs. In general, very light and very dark eggs are smaller and more variable in size than eggs with an intermediate ground colour (Gaston and Nettleship 1981). The proportion of different egg types does not vary within a colony, but within ledges there is a tendency for eggs of a similar type to occur together. This could arise if female murres returned to breed close to where they were reared, or if birds laying certain egg types preferentially bred on certain ledges.

The shells of the eggs of murres and the Razorbill are disproportionately sturdy compared to those of hole-nesting species (Kaftanovskii 1941). In murres and the Razorbill the egg shells have a higher density of pores to allow gases to diffuse into the embryo, when, as is usual, the egg becomes fouled with moist guano. Belopol'skii (1957) reported that the shells of Thick-billed Murre eggs laid on ledges of sharp-edged slate of Novaya Zemlya were much thicker (mean = 0.50 mm, range: 0.46–0.53) than those of eggs on the granite terraces of Murmansk (mean = 0.30 mm, range: 0.22–0.34).

Fresh-egg weight (ca. 100 g) is about 10 to 12% of adult body weight (Birkhead and Nettleship 1981; Gaston and Nettleship 1981). Egg size is very variable; for example, at Coburg Island and at Cape Hay, there was a 30% difference in the volume of the largest and smallest eggs. In addition, eggs laid early in the laying period were significantly larger than those laid later. Individual eggs lose weight through evaporation during incubation, at a rate of 0.56 g/day (Gaston and Nettleship 1981). Thus, during the 32-day incubation period (Gaston and Nettleship 1981), eggs lose about 18 g, or approximately 20% of their weight.

About 80 to 90% of eggs lost before the median date of laying are replaced, but eggs lost after all first eggs are laid, are not replaced. Gaston and Nettleship (1981) found that, on average, 30% of pairs losing an egg replaced it, the interval between loss and replacement being about 14 days (range: 11–17 days) at Prince Leopold Island. At both Cape Hay (Birkhead and Nettleship 1981) and Novaya Zemlya (Uspenski 1956), a mean interval of 17 days between loss and replacement was recorded. These differences might be due to regional or seasonal differences in food availability. Replacement eggs are about 6% smaller in volume than first eggs laid by the same female (Birkhead and Nettleship 1981, 1984a).

Incubation shifts lasted about 12 to 24 hours at Prince Leopold Island, with a marked sexual difference in incubation patterns; males incubated mainly at 'night' and females during the day (Gaston and Nettleship 1981). Roelke and Hunt (1978) recorded the same pattern among Thick-billed Murres in Alaska.

D. Chick-rearing Period

Young Thick-billed Murres are semi-precocial (see Chapter 7, this volume). Hatching and early life on the ledge is very similar to that of Common Murres. Like Common Murres, Thick-billed Murre chicks start to maintain their body temperature when between 6 and 8 days old, and are completely homeothermic by 9 to 10 days of age (Johnson and West 1975). Juvenal plumage occurs in two basic forms (with some intermediates): one is similar to adult summer plumage with a black throat and chin, and the other is similar to adult winter plumage with a white throat and cheeks, with a dark line running back from the eye. At Prince Leopold Island the proportion of each type varied in different parts of the colony. However, there was no difference in growth or fledging weight between the two forms (Gaston and Nettleship 1981).

Thick-billed Murre chicks weigh between 65 and 70 g at hatching (Gaston and Nettleship 1981; Uspenski 1956), or about 7% of adult body weight. Hatching weight is positively correlated with egg volume

(Birkhead and Nettleship 1982b). Weight increments are greatest in the first week of life and the increase in body weight is linear until days 14–16, after which the rate of weight increase levels off. The shape of the growth curves varies between colonies (Birkhead and Nettleship 1981), between years at the same colony (Gaston and Nettleship 1981), but also between different parts of the same colony in the same year, among chicks hatched on similar dates (Gaston and Nettleship 1981). (See Chapter 7, this volume, for additional information on chick development.) During the chick-rearing period parents take turns to guard the chick and to forage for it. Chicks are fed mainly fish brought to them singly about three or four times during a 24-hour period (see Chapter 6, this volume). Chicks reach their maximum weight a few days prior to leaving the colony; at Prince Leopold Island mean maximum weight was 204.4 g (S.D. = 21.0, N = 18) in 1975, 211.6 g (S.D. = 18.6, N = 28) in 1976 and 221.5 g (S.D. = 28.6, N = 25) in 1977. Departure weights were only slightly lower: 200.5, 209.0 and 215.8 g in 1975, 1976 and 1977 (ca. 22–24% of adult weight) (Gaston and Nettleship 1981).

E. Departure of Young from the Colony

The pattern of colony departure in Thick-billed Murres is very similar to that for Common Murres. In regions with marked light–dark regimes (e.g., Labrador), chicks leave the colony at dusk, while in areas with continuous daylight (i.e., colonies north of 70°N) chicks depart at 'night', when light intensity is lowest. Chicks leave aged between 16 and 30 days old, although most leave when 20–21 days old. Gaston and Nettleship (1981) obtained values of 21.4 days (S.D. = 3.05, N = 400) in 1976, and 20.3 days (S.D. = 2.2, N = 447) in 1977 at Prince Leopold Island. These authors also noted that age at departure was negatively correlated with hatching date so that the latest-hatched chicks had the shortest chick-rearing period. The same effect was recorded at Cape Hay and Coburg Island (Birkhead and Nettleship 1981). This seasonal reduction in departure age results in a more synchronous leaving of the colony and may be an adaptation to high-arctic breeding, since it has not been recorded among Common Murres in boreal waters (Birkhead 1976a; Hedgren 1980).

Thick-billed Murre chicks leave the colony with, and are cared for by their male parent, as in Common Murres. Bradstreet (1979b) collected 47 adults with a chick shortly after departure and in 46 cases the adult accompanying the chick was male.

F. Breeding Success

Breeding success is similar to that for Common Murres, with about 70 to 80% of pairs producing a chick to leave the colony. At Prince Leopold Island between 1975 and 1977, hatching success was ca. 80%, and ca. 90% of young went to sea (Gaston and Nettleship 1981). Similar values were obtained at Coburg Island in 1979, but at Cape Hay in the same year, a low breeding success of only 48% was due to the timing of breeding there being later than average. Success was reduced further by ice and rocks falling onto incubating birds. The combination of these factors resulted in a hatching success of only 54%, although chick success was near normal at 90% (Birkhead and Nettleship 1981) (see Table 3.2). While the breeding success of murres and Razorbills appears to be higher than those of other seabirds, productivity is only calculated up to part way through the chick-rearing period because chicks leave the colony several weeks before they are full grown and independent of their parent. Gaston (1980) estimated from banding recoveries that only 40% of young Thick-billed Murres survived between leaving the colony and reaching the wintering grounds. This indicates that annual productivity is only in the order of 0.25 young per pair.

In common with other alcids, Thick-billed Murres which breed early in the season are more likely to be successful than those breeding late. This has been recorded at Prince Leopold Island (Gaston and Nettleship 1981) and at Cape Hay and Coburg Island (Birkhead and Nettleship 1981). In addition, chicks hatched early in the season are heavier at fledging than late-hatched chicks (see Chapter 4, this volume).

V. GREAT AUK, *Pinguinus impennis*

Little is known of the biology of the extinct Great Auk apart from some generalized and most often second-hand accounts. Here we summarize those and allow ourselves a little reasoned speculation.

The Great Auk bred colonially at a small number of low-arctic and boreal sites, at Bird Rocks in the Gulf of St. Lawrence and at Funk Island, Canada, at the Westmann Islands, Geirfuglasker and at Eldey off southwest Iceland, and at St. Kilda and Papa Westray, off northern Scotland (Grieve 1885; see also Chapter 2, this volume). Most colonies were on offshore islands where these flightless birds could come directly out of the sea and walk to their breeding sites. The largest documented colony was on Funk Island, a low-lying offshore island with a gently shelving shoreline. Great Auks bred in the open and probably at fairly high densities. If the Great Auks on Funk Island occupied the area now used by murres, but bred at only a quarter of the density (which seems reasonable given their larger size), there could have been ca. 100,000 pairs there. About 1800 the Great Auk became extinct in Newfoundland (Peters and Burleigh 1951), and in 1844, the last known breeding pair was collected at Eldey, Iceland. (See Chapter 2, this volume, for details.)

We know very little of its breeding except that it bred in June, at approximately the same time as other auks in the same colony. Martin (1698) stated that on St. Kilda, the Great Auk arrived about the first day of May and left by mid-June. (Note: the change of the calendar in 1752 does necessitate adding 14 days for comparison with modern dates.) The single egg was incubated directly on the bare rock and resembled that of a Razorbill in background colour (dirty white to yellowish buff), but had murre-type black or dark brown markings. Like murres and the Razorbill, the shell was relatively thick, and to judge from 75 eggs illustrated in Tompkinson and Tompkinson (1966), the density of markings was quite low. Bent (1919) describes the shape of Great Auk eggs as ovate-pyriform, indicating that they are intermediate in shape between murre eggs (pyriform) and Razorbill eggs (elliptical ovate). However, two quantitative egg-shape indices (Table 3.4) show that Great Auk eggs more closely resemble murre eggs in shape than Razorbill eggs. This similarity may indicate a closer phylogenetic relationship with murres, or it may represent a common adaptation to similar breeding habitat.

The mean length and breadth of 40 eggs presented by Bent (1919) were 123.7 and 75.5 mm, respectively (range for length: 111–140 mm; for breadth: 69–83.5 mm). Since the shape index of the Great Auk egg does not differ significantly from those of murres, we can use the relationships between volume index (length × breadth^2) and (a) fresh-egg weight, and (b) chick hatching weight for Common Murres (Table 3.5), to estimate these same parameters for Great Auk eggs. The volume index of Great Auk eggs derived from Bent's (1919) values is 705.12, which gives an estimate of 327.1 g for fresh-egg weight, and 236.2 g for the chick at hatching. To check that these values are reasonable, T. R. Birkhead and D. N. Nettleship (unpublished observations) collected the same data for Razorbill eggs and compared predicted values (calculated in the same way as for the Great Auk), with observed values. The close agreement between predicted and observed results (Table 3.5) indicates that the values for the Great Auk are reasonable.

If the average body weight of an adult Great Auk was about 5000 g, as suggested by Bédard (1969a), then fresh weight (327 g) would represent 6.5% of adult body weight. This is consistent with the relationship be-

TABLE 3.5

Egg Parameters for Great Auks and Razorbills

Relationship for Common Murre[a] between volume index and egg weight	Great Auk[b]	Razorbill[c]	
		Predicted	Observed
Fresh-egg wt., $y = 0.44x + 16.85$	327.1 g	96.0 g	96.3 g
Hatching wt., $y = 0.329x + 424$	236.2 g	63.5 g	65.3 g

[a] From T. R. Birkhead and D. N. Nettleship (unpublished observations).
[b] Volume Index, 705.12 (see text).
[c] Volume Index, 180.00 (T. R. Birkhead and D. N. Nettleship, unpublished observations).

tween adult body weight and relative egg weight presented by Sealy (1975b) (see Chapter 4, this volume).

In general, large eggs have longer incubation periods than small eggs (Lack 1968), and although the incubation period is unknown, we can estimate it from Hoyt's (1980) relationship between egg weight and incubation period. This gives a value of 43 days, and although the limits to this estimate are wide (30–65 days) owing to the scatter around Hoyt's regression, the points for murres and the Razorbill fall very close to the predicted line, which indicates that the Great Auk estimate may be approximately correct.

Martin (1698) stated that the Great Auk had a single brood patch 'upon his breast', which suggests that it may have incubated in an upright posture, similar to murres. He also stated that if the egg was taken, no other was laid that year. Martin's statement about the time of arrival and departure of the Great Auk from St. Kilda (if reliable) indicates a 7-week (50-day) breeding cycle. If we assume that egg-laying occurred soon after arrival, and that incubation lasted 43 days, then chicks must have fledged after just 5 days. Grieve (1885, p. 73) stated: ' . . . it is generally supposed that shortly after the young one was hatched it betook itself to the sea, as when it came from the shell it was fitted for swimming and diving'. However, there are no published descriptions or museum specimens of chicks, so it is not clear how reliable Grieve's statement is. Moreover, if relative egg size imposes a constraint on a chick's developmental stage at hatching, as we have suggested for murres (Chapter 4, this volume), then it is unlikely that Great Auk chicks were as precocial as *Endomychura* or *Synthliboramphus*. Since the Great Auk probably had a similar breeding biology to murres and the Razorbill, it may be safest to assume that the chick followed an intermediate post-hatching developmental pattern.

VI. ATLANTIC PUFFIN, *Fratercula arctica*

A. General Features

1. PRE-LAYING PERIOD

Atlantic Puffins return to the colonies later in the spring than murres and the pre-laying period is shorter, lasting only 3–4 weeks in most areas. The mean dates when puffins were first seen on the sea and ashore on Skokholm, Wales, between 1928 and 1979 were 25 March (range: 14 March–3 April) and 5 April (22 March–13 April), respectively (Harris 1982a). The population breeding in eastern Scotland returns slightly earlier with a few birds ashore by 14 to 24 February in 1974 to 1982, and most by early March. They did not arrive so early formerly, and the change may be due to the same conditions which now allow the earlier return of Razorbills to the same colonies (Taylor and Reid 1981). This population is exceptional in that most birds spend the winter within a few hundred kilometres of the colony; other populations are migratory (see Chapter 9, this volume). These east Scottish puffins also moult earlier than other British populations (Harris and Yule 1977), but it is not known whether moult controls the time of return or vice versa. Birds return to colonies in the western Atlantic, south Iceland and the Faeroe Islands in mid-April (e.g., first sighting and first landings on Great Island, Newfoundland, in 1969 were 13 and 17 April), but arrivals to colonies farther north are far less predictable and depend on the weather and amount of ice. Atlantic Puffins are usually present at colonies in east Murmansk by late April, in Greenland by mid-May and in Spitsbergen by early June (Belopol'skii 1957; Salomonsen 1967; Løvenskiold 1964).

The number of puffins present at a colony varies greatly both within and between days. After the birds have come ashore a few times, two well-defined but often unpredictable cycles are built up: first, the number of puffins ashore and on the sea usually increases through the day to an evening peak; second, overall numbers increase over several days to a peak and then decline again. The periodicity of the latter pattern was 4–7 days on Skomer Island (Ashcroft 1976), 5–6 days on Great Island (Nettleship 1972), 4–11 days on Lovunden (Myrberget 1959a), and 4–6 days on the Isle of May. Colony attendance appears most regular at Newfoundland colonies (Nettleship 1972). Attendances may be synchronized at nearby colonies, or even islands, as in southwest Wales (Lloyd 1973), but on the Isle of May different parts of the single colony are usually out of phase. The reasons for these fluctuations are uncertain. Ashcroft (1976) could find no correlation between numbers of puffins present and weather, except that few birds came ashore in storms, but there was a correlation with the numbers 6 days before in 1 year, 2 days before in another year. Presumably birds leave to feed but this does not explain the marked synchrony of attendance. This cycle continues throughout the season and becomes more marked as the number of young birds coming to the colony increases. Four-year-old non-breeders return at the start of the season, 3-year-olds during the laying period, 2-year-olds during the chick period and the very few 1-year-olds which visit land do so near fledging time (Harris 1983a). This pattern is typical of auks and many other sea-birds, and presumably allows immatures to gain experience of the colonies.

2. BREEDING HABITAT

Atlantic Puffins often nest in large colonies, sometimes containing hundreds of thousands of pairs. However, at the fringes of their range the colonies are often small; in the south these colonies were once larger, but high-arctic puffins always nest in small groups in cliff sites. Overall, most colonies are on earthy islands where the birds can burrow, but in the central and northern parts of the range large colonies are found among boulders; only rarely do colonies occur inland. In the extreme north, puffins often nest among rocks, partly because the soil remains frozen until late in the year (although some birds manage to burrow even in Murmansk), and partly because some birds seem to prefer rocky sites. Colonisation of new areas often starts on cliffs, and conversely, populations which are declining often 'retreat' to boulder screes and finally to rocky cliffs. This has occurred at colonies persecuted by humans (Perroquet Island, Gulf of St. Lawrence: Nettleship and Lock 1973) and rats (Faeroe Islands: Williamson 1948) and those which have declined from other causes (Hirta, St. Kilda: Harris and Murray 1977).

Colony size is not usually restricted by lack of habitat and puffins obviously 'chose' to breed at a fairly high density. Although burrow densities of over three per square metre have been recorded, in most colonies mean density does not exceed one per square metre. Densities are highest on sloping ground, because on level ground burrowing is restricted to one level with the tunnels running parallel to the surface, so that burrows almost invariably meet. For example, on a 30° slope three burrows per square metre affects only 12% of the ground whereas on level ground 48% is affected, often causing tunnels to join and the ground to be undermined, leading to erosion (M. Hornung, personal communication). This can result in the collapse of burrowed ground.

Burrow density is easily measured by direct counts and can often be related to physical features such as soil depth, vegetation and nearness to cliff-edge. The breeding success of birds using these burrows can also be measured so the advantage and disadvantage of nesting at different densities and habitats can be examined. On Great Island, Nettleship (1972) found that density was negatively correlated with distance from the cliff-edge and positively correlated with soil depth and the angle of the slope. Over 65% of the variation in burrow abundance was accounted for by distance from the cliff-edge and the addition of the two other variables increased the figure to 81%. Similarly on Skomer Island, burrow density, while much lower, was also greatest near the cliff-edge and away from the edge more burrows occurred in sloping than in flat ground (Ashcroft 1976). Too much should not, however, be made of these two examples as many colonies are far more uniform and do not have such a rigid division between flat and sloping ground. For instance, on the rather flat Isle of May and the Farne Islands soil depth was the main factor influencing burrow density (M. Hornung, personal communication).

The nest burrow is usually about 70 to 100 cm long (extremes vary from 20 cm to many metres). Burrows are dug by loosening soil and stones with the bill and kicking it out with the feet. The tunnel is invariably wider than it is high and ends in a slightly enlarged nest-chamber. The burrow is usually simple, and even if it divides there is only ever a single pair as a pair vigorously defends the burrow entrance. Rarely, several burrows may join to form complicated labyrinths. In a Russian colony 33 burrow entrances in 15 m^2 of ground led to 26 inter-connected nest-chambers (Skokova 1962). Puffins have difficulty in burrowing in thick turf, and readily occupy holes already excavated in that habitat by conspecifics or other species (e.g., rabbits and Manx Shearwaters).

3. SITE AND MATE FIDELITY

An Atlantic Puffin usually retains the same burrow and also the same mate from one year to the next if both survive. On Skomer Island there were only 39 (8%) changes in consecutive years in 502 cases where burrow ownership was known (Ashcroft 1979). Some of these changes occurred because of eviction by other puffins or Manx Shearwaters. Significantly fewer successful breeders moved [19 (6%) of 304 birds] than unsuccessful birds [12 (17%) of 71 birds]. Ashcroft also found that 8% of pairs ($N = 142$) divorced per year. In over half the cases one of the pair was displaced and remained in the area without a burrow for one or more seasons even though there appeared to be suitable sites elsewhere in the colony. Once the bird has chosen a breeding area it usually remains there for life, even if it cannot breed.

The egg is sometimes incubated on the bare earth or rock, but the birds normally line the nest with grass or other vegetation, feathers, seaweed, and other such materials, which help to keep the egg dry, warm and less prone to damage by sharp rocks.

B. Timing of Breeding

There are large geographic differences in laying dates and even within a colony annual median dates vary far more than do those of murres. On the Isle of May, the first eggs are sometimes laid early April or, in exceptional years, the last days of March; the annual median date of laying varied from 18 April to 2 May ($N = 8$ years, mean 25 April) with a mean annual spread of laying of 53 days ($N = 8$ years, range: 41–53 days). Elsewhere in Britain, laying starts during the last week of April with median dates 2 and 22 May for two seasons on Skomer and 1, 5, 6 and 16 May on St. Kilda. The occasional very late young recorded in September presumably came from repeat layings.

Laying is 4 weeks later in southeast Newfoundland and 8 weeks later in southern Labrador (D. N. Nettleship, personal communication); on Great Island, Newfoundland, the median laying dates in 2 years were between 17 and 20 May, and the range of laying dates was 9 May–13 June (Nettleship 1972). In Norway, laying starts in mid-May [the median (and first egg) dates for 2 years at Lovunden being 27 May (17 May) and 8 June (25 May)], but were earlier in western Murmansk [19 May (13 May) and 19 May (8 May)] (Belopol'skii 1957; Myrberget 1962). In eastern Murmansk, the first-egg dates over 7 years ranged from 11 May to 7 June (mean 23 May), and median dates for 3 years spanned 19 May–13 June (Belopol'skii 1957). The last birds to lay are those in northwest Greenland (from early June; Salomonsen 1967) and Novaya Zemlya (mid- to 30 June; Uspenski 1956).

Late snow prevents some northern birds getting to their burrows in certain parts of the colony, and even when they do, the burrows are often plugged with ice. In such colonies there are often consistent differences in laying dates between different parts of the colony (Kaftanovskii 1951). On Great Island, egg-laying dates were similar in sloping and level habitats, but annual variation was greater on level than on slope habitat as was variation within a single year (Nettleship 1972). On St. Kilda, pairs breeding in areas of high burrow density laid significantly earlier (but no more synchronously) than those breeding at low density in the same colony (Harris 1980). Density may also have been important on Great Island, as burrow density was higher in sloping habitat than on the flat. At a very local level, nearby pairs tend to lay on the same dates. Sometimes this is because parts of the colony have been covered with snow or flooded so that adjacent burrows become suitable for laying at approximately the same time (Hornung and Harris 1976). However, local synchrony of breeding is widespread in colonial birds, which suggests a more general reason. Social stimulation is the usual explanation, but how this occurs or the advantages are far from clear.

Some puffins do not breed even though they have nest sites. On Skomer Island in 1973 to 1975, 3 of 54 (6%), 21 of 129 (16%), and 7 of 87 (8%) pairs, respectively, failed to lay. The significantly higher proportion not laying in 1974 was associated with a very late breeding season (median laying date 22 May compared to 2 May 1975) and low numbers attending the colony in the pre-laying period (Ashcroft 1979). On St. Kilda, the proportion of occupied burrows where no egg was found from 1974 to 1978 was, on average (32%), much higher than on Skomer Island (Harris 1980). Although there were no significant differences between the years, the proportion of pairs with burrows which did not lay was signficantly greater where burrow density was low (49%) than where it was high (19%). On Skomer Island 1.85% of breeding adults did not come to the colony at all or returned only late in the season (Ashcroft 1979).

C. The Egg and Incubation

The clutch is one ovate or rounded-elliptical egg, white or cream in colour, and with a relatively rough surface. Many eggs have faint lilac markings which soon fade; very few are boldly marked. These markings serve no apparent purpose as a puffin does not recognize its own egg or young. Two eggs are sometimes found in a burrow, presumably due to a female relaying after misplacing its first egg or, less likely, by a second female laying in the wrong burrow, but only one egg is incubated at a time (even though a puffin has two brood patches) and both embryos die.

In the eastern Atlantic, egg size increases from 60.3 (S.D. = 2.35) × 42.2 mm (S.D. = 1.3) in southern Britain (N = 40) to 67.3 × 45.9 mm in Spitsbergen (N = 4); 150 eggs from Newfoundland were intermediate at 62.9 (S.D. = 2.11) × 44.6 mm (S.D. = 1.13) (Nettleship 1972). On Skomer Island, the mean weight of 28 newly laid eggs was 59.2 g (range: 53–65), 16% of the weight of females weighed at the same time (Corkhill 1972). The mean weight of nine fresh eggs on the Isle of May was 56.9 g (S.D. = 5.4), 14.9% of the mean weight of 12 incubating females, and very similar to Newfoundland (14.7%), where the mean weight of 150 eggs was 65.4 g (Nettleship 1972). At Murmansk, the egg was 13.5% the weight of a female (Kaftanovskii 1951). Thus the egg remains a fairly constant proportion of the female's weight (Fig. 3.3). Eggs laid early in the season are larger than those laid later, but on St. Kilda hatching and fledging success were not related to egg size (Harris 1980).

Incubation starts immediately after laying. Incubating birds hold the egg against the brood patch with one wing while sitting horizontally. Adults share incubation, but the duration of incubation shifts are difficult to determine, as birds frequently leave the egg, but appear to vary from 2 to 50 hours (Myrberget 1962). Incubation takes 40–45 days (Myrberget 1962), including the 3–5 days between the time the egg first becomes pipped and the chick emerges from the shell, but might be reduced to 35 to 37 days by continuous incubation (Kartaschew 1960; Tschanz 1979a).

Lost and deserted eggs are sometimes replaced, the interval between loss and replacement being 13–23 days (Ashcroft 1979). The rate of re-placement is lower than for murres and Razorbills, but is probably higher than published figures suggest as often the only indication that a replace-ment egg has been laid is an unduly prolonged incubation period. Rarely, a replacement egg may be replaced if lost (Sleptsov, in Kaftanovskii 1941). On Skomer Island, at least 7 of 75 eggs (9%) lost were replaced in three seasons (Ashcroft 1979). On St. Kilda the percentage of lost eggs replaced was higher among birds breeding at a high density (19%, $N = 90$) than in birds at low density (6%, $N = 95$) (Harris 1980); 14 (64%) young fledged from 22 repeat eggs. This was not significantly different from the success of first eggs in the same areas.

D. Chick-rearing Period

The newly hatched semi-precocial young is covered with thick down, mostly black and long but white and shorter on the ventral surface. Twenty newly hatched young on Skomer Island had a mean weight of 39.7 g (S.D. = 3.9: Ashcroft 1979), whereas 12 on Lovunden averaged 50 g (S.D. = 5.0: Myrberget 1962)—both about 11% of the weight of the adult. After hatching, the egg shell may be found inside or just outside the entrance, probably accidentally dragged out rather than deliberately ejected. The chick is brooded continuously for the first 6–7 days of life and then left alone. The chick is then homeothermic providing it receives sufficient food (Tschanz 1979a). Chicks move around the burrow and usually defecate in a latrine outside the nest-chamber. Young move away from light and approach the burrow entrance (where they risk being caught and eaten by gulls) only if starving or close to fledging age.

Both adults feed the chick, but on the Isle of May, females fed chicks at a significantly higher rate than did males. Chicks can receive up to 16 meals a day, the actual number varying with age, but the mean daily rate of feeding varies from 2 to 8 meals per day (Nettleship 1972; Harris and Hislop 1978; Ashcroft 1979). Part of the annual difference in feeding fre-quency is offset by variation in the weight of the meal brought to the young as the mean annual feeding frequency is inversely correlated with the mean annual meal weight (N = 24 colony years, r = −.41, p< .05). The amount of food received is presumably related to the availability of fish. However, growth is also influenced by the species of fish delivered to the chicks; the young grow better and fledge at higher weights when fed on oil-rich fish such as sandlance (*Ammodytes* spp.) and sprats (*Sprattus sprattus*) than when fed other fish such as whiting (*Merlangius merlangus:* Harris 1982b). Chicks typically attain a peak of 70 to 80% of the adults when aged 4–5 weeks. From then, the young receives fewer meals but is normally fed up to the day before fledging. If the begging call is played from a tape recorder every time an adult enters the burrow with fish, the adults bring significantly more meals per day. Presumably they are deceived into thinking that the young is still hungry. This suggests that the young can communicate its needs to its parents, and partly influence the adult's rate of delivery of meals (Hudson 1979a; Harris 1983b). Even when given excess food, a chick close to fledging reduces its own intake and loses 10% of its body weight prior to fledging. Post-hatching development patterns are discussed in detail in Chapter 7 of this volume.

E. Departure of Young from the Colony

The young often make brief visits outside the burrow entrance to exercise a day or two before fledging, especially when the adults are present. The young fledge at night (or presumably when light intensity is lowest in the far north: Lockley 1934), but they are fed up to fledging and are not deserted by the adults (Harris 1976c). Most young leave soon after dark and are well away from land by first light the following day. At fledging young can fly and are independent of their parents.

The great variation in the length of the fledging period (Table 3.6) probably reflects feeding conditions. In good conditions the usual period is 38–41 days; in poor conditions it is prolonged to 74 days or more. The longest fledging periods occur in sick or starving young which probably die soon after fledging. In both slope and level habitat on Great Island, chicks that hatched from eggs early in the season survived better, had shorter fledging periods, and fledged at a higher body weight than did those that hatched late (Nettleship 1972). If chicks near fledging are replaced with young chicks, the adults continue to feed them until they fledge. Adults visit the burrow, often with fish, the morning after the young has fledged and may remain in the area for some time. [For example, on the Isle of May, 45 successful adults remained for a mean of 18.6 days (S.D. = 8.3) after their young had fledged.] On the Isle of May, the time breeders spend at the colony after they have finished breeding is positively correlated with the date the young fledged or the egg or chick is lost (Harris 1982a); the birds which fail early remain longest. Non-breeders remain at

TABLE 3.6

Fledging Age (Days) of Young Atlantic Puffin, Black Guillemot and Dovekie

Species	Colony	N	x̄	±S.D.	Range	References
Atlantic Puffin[a]	Skomer I., Wales	241	38	?	34–44	Ashcroft (1979)
	Isle of May, Scotland	312	41	?	34–50	M. P. Harris (unpublished)
	St. Kilda, Scotland	214	44	?	35–57	M. P. Harris (1980)
	Lovunden, Norway	32	47.7	2.4	43–52	Myrbergert (1962)
	Great I., Nfld.	180	53.4	8.3	39–74	Nettleship (1972)
	Murmansk, U.S.S.R.	?	?	?	39–46	Kozlova (1957)
Black Guillemot	Nordre Rønner, Denmark	37	39.5	3.9	31–51	Asbirk (1979)
	Mickelskären, Finland	26	ca. 38	?	36–39	Bergman (1971)
	Flatey, Iceland	213	33.7	2.0	27–40	Petersen (1981)
	Kent I., Bay of Fundy	?	?	?	35–40	Preston (1968)
	Brandypot Is. and St. Mary Is., Gulf of St. Lawrence	16	36.5	1.5	34–39	Cairns (1978)
	Murmansk, U.S.S.R.	37	?	?	33–43	Belopol'skii (1957)
Dovekie	Hornsund, Spitsbergen	34	27.1	0.8	26–29	Norderhaug (1980)
	Spitsbergen	33	27.0	1.8	23–30	Stempniewicz (1981)
	Horse Head I., Greenland	10	28.3	0.6	?	Evans (1981a)

[a] Most puffin ages are ± 1 or 2 days.

the colony until the end of the season so that the majority of birds depart over just a few days leaving only a small number of birds with young. These birds usually rear their young successfully but when conditions are extreme, late-hatched young are, on average, older and lighter at fledging than early young.

Whereas at the start of the season birds arrive at different colonies over a period of several months, most leave in August and only rarely (e.g., at Novaya Zemlya; Uspenski 1956) are birds ashore anywhere after the first week of September. This synchrony is due in part to the fairly abrupt end to the summer in arctic regions. Atlantic Puffins are present at most colonies for 130 to 140 days each season but in Spitsbergen, Novaya Zemlya, north Greenland this is shortened to 110 to 120 days. Belopol'skii (1957) suggested that the season at Novaya Zemlya was reduced to only 70–75 days by greater synchronization of laying and the shortening of the pre-laying period to 10 to 15 days, and the incubation and fledging periods to 30 days each. The reduction of the latter two periods by 30% seems most unlikely. In eastern Scotland the season is extended to 170 days by lengthening of both the pre-breeding and post-fledging periods.

F. Breeding Success

Breeding success if difficult to measure because incubating birds often desert their eggs when disturbed and desertion is the commonest cause of failure. However, annual production is usually in the region of 0.7 to 0.9 fledglings per pair (Table 3.7). Catastrophic breeding failure is occasionally recorded, the most severe cases being in the Lofoten Islands, Norway, where numbers of young were reared in just 2 years between 1968 and 1983, with breeding success very low in all other years. That low productivity has been attributed to failure of the food supply (Lid 1981). Not surprisingly, considering the wide range of habitats occupied, different studies have found different factors to have significant effects on breeding. On Great Island, Newfoundland, birds nesting on sloping ground were most successful because they lost fewer eggs and young to Herring Gulls (Nettleship 1972), whereas on Skomer Island, Wales, competition with Manx Shearwaters reduced breeding success (Ashcroft 1979). On St. Kilda, Scotland, adults nesting at a high density were most successful because they coped better with predatory Great Black-backed Gulls (Harris 1980). These factors are discussed in Chapter 4 of this volume. In each of these three studies, pairs laying early had a higher breeding output than pairs laying late. One advantage to laying early is that there is a greater chance of re-laying if the first egg is lost. Another, suggested by Nettleship (1972), is that the food supply is best early in the season and diminishes as the season progresses; however, there is, as yet, no direct evidence for or against this hypothesis.

The strain of reproduction is probably reflected by the seasonal pattern of weight change. On the Isle of May mean adult weight declined significantly from 415 g in April (before laying) to 384 g in July at the end of the chick-rearing period. Body weight increased significantly after young had fledged (Harris 1979).

VII. BLACK GUILLEMOT, *Cepphus grylle*

A. General Features

1. PRE-LAYING PERIOD

This species is exceptional among Atlantic alcids in breeding in small, scattered colonies, feeding inshore on bottom-living fish and having a

TABLE 3.7

Breeding Success of Atlantic Puffins in Various Studies

Colony	Year	No. of nests before laying	No. of eggs laid[b]	No. of eggs hatched[b]	No. of young fledged[b]	No. of young fledged per pair	References
Great I., Nfld.[a]	1968	—	90	58 (64.4)	25 (43.2)	0.28	Nettleship (1972)
	1969	—	200	151 (75.5)	101 (66.9)	0.51	Nettleship (1972)
Funk I., Nfld.	1969	—	106	?	?	0.87	Nettleship (1972)
Small I., Nfld.	1969	—	147	?	?	0.93	Nettleship (1972)
Skomer I., Wales	1973	54	51 (94.5)	38 (75)	35 (93)	0.66	Ashcroft (1979)
	1974	129	108 (84.0)	84 (78)	61 (74)	0.61	Ashcroft (1979)
	1975	87	80 (92.0)	61 (76)	73 (96)	0.66	Ashcroft (1979)
St. Kilda, Scotland[a]	1974	192	148 (78.6)	113 (76.4)	102 (90.3)	0.69	Harris (1980)
	1975	191	160 (83.4)	130 (81.0)	125 (96.3)	0.78	Harris (1980)
	1976	185	140 (80.5)	124 (88.7)	104 (83.9)	0.74	Harris (1980)
	1977	185	153 (82.7)	?	?	0.84	Harris (1980)
	1978	165	130 (78.8)	?	?	0.69–0.90	Harris (1980)
Isle of May, Scotland	1973	—	58	?	?	0.74	M. P. Harris, (unpublished)
	1977	—	51	?	?	0.73	M. P. Harris (unpublished)
	1978	—	100	?	?	0.87	M. P. Harris (unpublished)
	1979	—	139	?	?	0.90	M. P. Harris (unpublished)
	1980	—	119	?	?	0.76	M. P. Harris (unpublished)

[a] The Great Island and St. Kilda data refer to the best part of the colony (see text). However, the bulk of the population nest in these areas so the results are fairly representative of the population as a whole.
[b] Percentage of total given in parentheses.

clutch of two eggs. It is also the only seabird to over-winter in high-arctic regions, although the proportion of the total population remaining there in winter is small (Renaud and Bradstreet 1980). Adults return to the vicinity of their colonies (e.g., Baltic and Franz Josef Land) in February, or more usually, in March. In parts of Spitsbergen and north Greenland where pack ice remains until late in the spring, return is delayed until the end of April or early May. However, pack ice does not always prevent birds from returning; Black Guillemots made daily visits to a colony in Spitsbergen even where the nearest open water was 70 km away (de Korte 1972). Black Guillemots must be particularly well adapted to extreme conditions as they are the earliest birds to return to Franz Josef Land in the spring (Belopol'skii 1957). Both here and in the Baltic, some birds are present for ca. 110 days prior to laying. This is the longest period of more or less constant occupation among Atlantic auks. In north Iceland birds return 9–10 weeks before laying (Petersen 1981), but in many other places the pre-laying occupation is only 30–40 days.

Communal roosts are used extensively during the pre-laying period. Some roosts are situated on tidal rocks, and if the roost is always in the same place then each pair usually has its own standing area (Asbirk 1979b). In Iceland, non-breeding 1- and 2-year-olds are present at the colonies from up to a month before laying and the proportion of immature, non-breeders declines during the season, in contrast to other alcids (Petersen 1981). Also unlike other auks Black Guillemots do not show a cyclical pattern of attendance; once birds return they visit the colony every day except in extremely bad weather (Petersen 1981). However, each colony has a typical daily pattern of attendance, although the actual pattern varies. In colonies at the southern edge of the species' range, birds are ashore before dawn during the first half of the season to display, copulate and prospect for breeding sites; many remain during the morning, but most return to sea before late afternoon. Prior to laying many birds are also ashore in the evening, but this occurs far less frequently later in the season (Cairns 1978; Asbirk 1979b). Such a cycle occurs even in continuous daylight. At ice-blocked Kapp Lee, Spitsbergen, birds did not return to the breeding station until 30 April, and for the following 6 weeks all birds left the colony each day between 1300 and 1600 hours; the time of return gradually became earlier from 0300 in early May to 2000 in late June, and by mid-June some birds were always present (de Korte 1972). A different cycle was reported at Prince Leopold Island, Lancaster Sound, where prior to laying birds were most abundant between 2300 and 0400 hours; and few or none were visible between 0800 and 1600 hours (D. N. Nettleship, unpublished observations). At colonies in the Gulf of St. Lawrence (Brandypot, St. Mary Islands), and Bay of Fundy (Kent Island), highest numbers ashore occurred at high tide (Preston 1968; Cairns 1979). In Iceland (Flatey) there were morning and evening peaks in numbers present, but the actual numbers at the colony were negatively correlated with the length of the low-tide period in the afternoon. Petersen (1981) suggested that this was because low tides impaired feeding and birds compensated for that by staying longer on the feeding grounds. At Flatey and Brandypot, where breeding density was exceptionally high (but not elsewhere), there were communal displays where all the birds left the colonies for no obvious reason and flew around in circles (Cairns 1978).

At the southern edge of their range, Black Guillemots are far less colonial and less social than the other Atlantic auks, and a colony is often little more than a group of birds forced together by rather restricted suitable breeding habitat. Here 'colony' size reaches the tens or low hundreds of pairs, but in the arctic region there are a few very large concentrations; for instance, 4000 pairs on Prince Leopold Island (Nettleship 1977a) and 10,000 pairs spread over 22 km of coast near Skruis Point, Devon Island (Nettleship 1974; Nettleship and Smith 1975). More typical is Nordre Rønner, where 37% of the 411 pairs bred more than 10 m from their nearest neighbour (Asbirk 1979b), and Brandypot and St. Mary Islands where the mean inter-nest distances of the 90 and 122 nests were 6 and 26 m, respectively (Cairns 1980). This dispersion contrasts with the high breeding density of murres, Atlantic Puffins, and Dovekies, but is similar to that of Razorbills. The Black Guillemot is a good example of how inshore-feeding species tend to breed at low density in small scattered colonies (Lack 1968).

2. BREEDING HABITAT

The Black Guillemot is restricted to rocky shores. Over much of its range it breeds among stones on small islands or rocky skerries where these exist, otherwise among boulders at the bases of large cliffs or, uncommonly, in cracks in the cliffs themselves. Breeding sites are often only just above high-water mark and many get flooded at spring tides and during storms. However, cliff-breeding is the rule in the very large arctic colonies where the bulk of the birds occupy sites in cracks and large cliffs, such as the 75 to 230-m-high sea-cliffs near Skruis Point. Scree-slopes in northern areas are unstable and offer few breeding sites. In Spitsbergen, some colonies occur 2–3 km inland and 600 m up in sandstone mountains (Birulya, in Kaftanovskii 1941). In the Baltic, Black Guillemots breed on afforested islands.

Birds have successfully colonised man-made equivalents to boulder-sites such as holes in breakwaters and harbour walls, and they even breed under the floors and roofs of occupied buildings (Kuyt et al. 1976; Carnduff 1981). In many areas Black Guillemots also breed under fish-boxes and other debris cast ashore by storms; for example, on Nordre Rønner 43% of pairs were in such sites (Asbirk 1979b). Human debris has now allowed the species to colonise parts of Alaska which had previously lacked suitable breeding sites (Divoky et al. 1974). Black Guillemots rarely enlarge the breeding cavity, even where this is possible, and so the few pairs which excavate burrows in steep clay banks alongside Bank Swallows in Denmark (Asbirk 1979b) and in turf-dykes are exceptional. Breeding sites sometimes occur among vegetation, but there is always a large stone nearby which is used for display and take-off; this may be essential for sites in that habitat. Such a wide variety of sites are used that it is hard to believe that numbers can be limited by shortage of breeding sites, particularly since the species virtually always accepts artificial sites if those are offered.

3. SITE AND MATE FIDELITY

Birds usually retain the same breeding site from one year to the next. On Nordre Rønner, 70 of 100 marked individuals used the same site in consecutive years, and only 6 of 34 birds known to have changed moved more than 30 m (Asbirk 1979b); on Flatey there were nine changes of breeding site among 91 birds found in 2 years (Petersen 1981). Similarly pairs usually remain the same from year to year if both birds are alive; on Nordre Rønner and Flatey the annual divorce rate was 7 and 5%, respectively (Asbirk 1979b; Petersen 1981).

Although pairs will breed almost in the open, or under vegetation, the scrape where the egg is laid is usually 25–100 cm under cover. The egg may be laid on bare rock or on a platform of small stones, sometimes partially covered by feathers or pieces of vegetation. While these materials are certainly arranged, the use of nest materials by Black Guillemots is not common.

B. Timing of Breeding

In Britain, eggs are laid in the second half of May and early June. On Flatey, Iceland, the annual median laying dates for 3 years were 30 May 1977 ($N = 368$), 31 May 1975 ($N = 171$) and 2 June 1976 ($N = 311$), with the latest first clutch being laid 1 July; there was a total spread of laying of 6 weeks (but 80% of pairs laid within a 13 to 18-day period) with replacement clutches laid for another 2 weeks (Petersen 1981). Egg-laying is earlier in the Baltic where mean laying dates on Nordre Rønner were 26 May (N = 128), 24 May (N = 142) and 24 May (N = 133); the overall extreme laying dates of first clutches were 3 May–28 June (Asbirk 1979b). The pattern of laying dates is less skewed with a slightly shorter tail of layings late in the season than occurs in many seabirds (see Chapter 4, this volume). In the Gulf of St. Lawrence, median laying dates were ca. 25 May and 15 June at different colonies in different years (Cairns 1981), and farther south on Kent Island, Bay of Fundy, first-egg dates in 5 years varied from 28 May to 8 June (Preston 1968). Laying starts in early May in north Norway, mid-May in west Murmansk, ca. 27 May (range: 13 May– 10 June, N = 11 years) in east Murmansk, 10 June or later in Spitsbergen, 19–23 June in Franz Josef Land, but not until mid-June to mid-July in Novaya Zemlya (Belopol'skii 1957); this variation in laying dates between Norway and Novaya Zemlya is associated with ocean currents which warm the western seas, but have no influence in the east. The median hatching date at Prince Leopold Island, Lancaster Sound, was 29 June (N = 44, range: 14 June–12 July), which indicates a peak of laying about 28 May (D. N. Nettleship, unpublished observations).

Laying date is related to previous breeding experience, and adults which had bred once or more laid significantly earlier than birds which had probably not bred before (mean difference: 4.0 days, S.D. = 10.6, N = 118: Asbirk 1979b). A change of breeding site delayed laying by 1.3 days (S.D. = 10.7, N = 31), but a change of mate had no effect. Layings in 127 new breeding sites on Flatey were significantly later (mean differences in 2 years: 5.4 and 4.6 days) than those in 553 sites which had previously been used; Peterson (1981) suggests that adults need 4–6 years to reach a stable laying date relative to the whole population. Laying date is not influenced by dispersion of breeding sites, as solitary pairs laid at the same time as pairs in groups (Asbirk 1979b), and dispersed and aggregated sub-colonies had the same mean laying dates (Cairns 1980); nor is there greater synchrony within each breeding area than in the population as a whole (Petersen 1981).

C. The Egg and Incubation

Black Guillemot eggs are more ovoid than the elliptical eggs of auks which lay on open ledges, and vary from ovate to elliptical ovate. The ground colour is white, sometimes tinged blue, green or buff and heavily marked with black or ruddy-brown spots. The usual clutch consists of two eggs laid 3 days (rarely up to 10 days) apart, but some pairs lay only one egg (Table 3.8). Black Guillemots have two brood patches and cannot effectively incubate more than two eggs; clutches with three or four eggs

TABLE 3.8

Clutch Size of Black Guillemots at Various Colonies

| | | Clutch size (no. of eggs)[a] | | | | Mean clutch | |
Colony	Year	One	Two	Three	Four	size	References
Kent I., Bay of Fundy	1947	9	39	1	0	1.84	Winn (1950)
	1962–1967	41	148	1	0	1.79	Preston (1980)
Brandypot Is., Gulf of St. Lawrence	1976	19	71	0	0	1.79	Cairns (1980)
St. Mary Is., Gulf of St. Lawrence	1977	6	116	0	0	1.95	Cairns (1980)
Nordre Rønner, Denmark	1975–1977	58	328	5	1	1.87	Asbirk (1979b)
Flatey, Iceland	1976–1977	107	818	10	1	1.90	Petersen (1981)
Norway	1973–1975	13	122	4	1	1.94	R. Barrett (personal communication)
Mickelskären, Finland	1963–1970	3	36	0	0	1.92	Bergman (1971)
Fair Isle, Shetland	1973–1977	——— 104 ———				1.43	R. Broad, in Petersen (1981)
Prince Leopold I., N.W.T.	1977	3	55	1	0	1.97	D. N. Nettleship (personal communication)

[a] Three- and four-egg clutches are uncertain and could have involved more than one female.

are due to two females laying in the same nest (Asbirk 1979b) or a replacement clutch being laid at a site without the addled first clutch being removed or broken (Petersen 1981). The mean clutch size declined with laying date within a season on Kent Island, Bay of Fundy, from 2.00 to 1.00, and on Flatey from 2.00 to 1.68 and from 1.94 to 1.29 in 2 years (Preston 1968; Petersen 1981). This was due, at least in part, to young birds laying later, and laying fewer eggs (Asbirk 1979b).

On Kent Island, Flatey (Iceland) and in Britain, mean egg measurements were 57.7×38.9 mm ($N = 77$: Winn 1950), 58.3×39.3 mm ($N = 1586$: Petersen 1981) and 58.1×39.5 mm ($N = 100$: Witherby et al. 1941), respectively. Eighteen and 14 eggs from Murmansk and Novaya Zemlya were larger, measuring 59.9×40.8 mm and 61.3×41.0 mm, respectively (Uspenski 1956; Kozlova 1957). On Nordre Rønner, Flatey and in Murmansk newly laid eggs weighed 47.9 g (S.D. = 3.4, $N = 106$), 49.7 g (S.D. = 3.9, $N = 1219$), and 53.7 g ($N = 42$), weights which are 12–13% of the weight of the female (Belopol'skii 1957; Petersen 1981; Asbirk 1979b).

On Nordre Rønner the first and second eggs in two-egg clutches were almost the same size (57.5×38.9 mm and 57.7×38.7 mm, respectively)

(Asbirk 1979b). However, on Flatey, first eggs (mean weight = 50.3 g, S.D. = 3.9) were heavier in 63.2% of instances (N = 489), the second (49.3 g, S.D. = 3.2) was heavier in 22.1%, and the eggs were the same weight in the remaining cases; eggs in single-egg clutches weighed 48.0 g (S.D. = 3.8, N = 61: Petersen 1981). Petersen found a strong positive correlation between the sizes of eggs in a clutch; if both were small then the second egg was the larger. There was also a seasonal decline in egg volume.

Both sexes incubate and continuous incubation usually begins with the laying of the second egg. If only a single egg is laid, continuous incubation may not start until 4 to 5 days after it is laid (Preston 1968). In the Pigeon Guillemot, the embryo in the first egg develops slightly before the second egg is laid as a result of intermittent incubation during the day; it is several days after the second egg is laid before the clutch is incubated at night (Drent 1965). The same probably occurs in the Black Guillemot.

Incubation shifts average several hours (Asbirk 1979b), shorter than those for all other auks except the Pigeon Guillemot, where shifts of 2 to 4 hours (maximum 17 hours) have been recorded (Drent 1965). Estimates of the weight loss of eggs during incubation range from 11 to 18% of initial weight. Embryos of Black Guillemots can survive long periods without incubation; for example, Black Guillemot embryos were still alive after the eggs had been left unincubated for 11 and 15 days, and one pipping egg hatched after going without incubation for 43 hours (Bergman 1971). Total 'incubation time' (laying to hatching) for first-laid eggs on Nordre Rønner was 31.1 days (S.D. = 2.9, N = 38) and for second eggs 28.5 days (S.D. = 2.3, N = 41), with extremes of 23 to 39 days for the first egg, and 25 to 36 days for the second egg (Asbirk 1979b). On Flatey, the relevant means were 31.1 days (S.D. = 1.9, N = 147) and 28.8 days (S.D. = 2.0, N = 166) with extremes of 26 and 38 days (Petersen 1981). Infertile eggs are incubated for longer periods. Usually both eggs hatch on the same day, with the first-laid egg usually hatching first, but intervals of 3 days are known.

Clutches lost early in the season are replaced, with mean replacement times being 15.0 days (S.D. = 3.3, range: 12–23 days, N = 8; Asbirk, 1979b) and 14.7 days (S.D. = 4.4, range: 9–32 days, N = 28; Petersen 1981). The proportion of lost clutches which are replaced varies greatly: 8 of 31 (26%) and 17 of 142 (12%) on Nordre Rønner and Flatey, respectively (Asbirk 1979b; Petersen 1981).

D. Chick-rearing Period

Hatching takes 3–4 days and the egg shell is not removed from the nest, although adults have been seen removing unhatched eggs (Preston 1968).

The semi-precocial chick is covered with 8- to 13-mm-long down, black on top, slightly paler and denser underneath. The eyes are open at hatching and the chick moves around as soon as it is dry. It is normally brooded for 3 to 5 days and then left unattended except when fed. Kaftanovskii (1951) reported that the young was not homethermic until the fourth day, but more detailed work showed that Pigeon Guillemot chicks were able to maintain their body temperature in the burrow environment 24 hours after hatching (Drent 1965). During the first 2–3 weeks the chick remains in the breeding site, but later it may wander if there is room, though still remaining under cover (Winn 1950).

Young are fed up to 20 fish per day brought singly to the breeding site. This rate of feeding can be increased, and a mean of 1.38 fish per hour was brought to sites with artificial broods of three chicks compared to 0.57 and 0.87 fish per hour to sites with one and two young, respectively (Asbirk 1979b). Both males and females feed the young, apparently with equal division of labour. Asbirk found no correlation between feeding frequency and the age of the young, although the length of fish brought back did increase so that a chick near fledging received more food than one recently hatched, whereas Petersen (1981) showed an increase in feeding up to day 25–29, then a decline.

The young grow rapidly and reach peak weight at 4 to 6 weeks. On Nordre Rønner, Norway, the average maximum weights of chicks in 1975, 1976 and 1977 were 393 g (S.D. = 42, N = 60), 357 g (S.D. = 57, N = 41) and 407 g (S.D. = 43, N = 37), 105, 95 and 108% of the adult weight, respectively (Asbirk 1979b). Chicks in 1976 were significantly lighter, probably because of a failing food supply (Asbirk 1979b). On Flatey, Iceland, the mean peak weight (381 g, or 95% of the mean adult weight of 400 g) was attained 4 days prior to fledging (Petersen 1981). Young then lose some weight (usually 20–30 g) and fledge at just below adult weight. Single chicks on Nordre Rønner reached significantly higher maximum weights (mean = 400 g, S.D. = 44, N = 43) than chicks with siblings (mean = 382 g, S.D. = 48, N = 84), but the difference in fledging weights (mean = 377 g, S.D. = 53, N = 35, $vs.$ mean = 361 g, S.D. = 48, N = 73) was not significant. In five instances where pairs reared three young, the mean maximum weight (388 g, S.D. = 43) and mean fledging weight (373 g, S.D. = 32) were higher than those of young in normal broods of two (Asbirk 1979b). However, on Flatey there were large differences in fledging weights (Petersen 1981). In 1975, the mean fledging weight of seven artificial triplets was 297 g (S.D. = 44) compared to 343 g (S.D. = 29, N = 25) and 360 g (S.D. = 32, N = 8) for normal twins and singles, respectively; the same pattern occurred in 1976.

E. Departure of Young from the Colony

The fledging period is variable (Table 3.6), but most young leave the safety of the breeding site when aged 30–40 days. Young in broods of two may fledge on the same day, or up to 8 days apart, as adults continue to feed the remaining young. Adults often visit the breeding site and remain at the colony for several days after the young have fledged. The fledging periods of young hatched later in the season appear to be shorter than those of young hatched earlier, but this finding was based on only 20 sites and so needs confirmation (Belopol'skii 1957). On Flatey, artificial triplets had their fledging delayed by a mean of 7 days in 1975 and 5 days in 1976.

There is no desertion period, and typically, the young fledges alone at night or when light intensity is lowest, after which it is independent of its parents. Young Black Guillemots have been seen to return after fledging (P.G.H. Evans, personal communication), but this is exceptional. Winn (1950) saw a chick close to fledging apparently enticed out of its hole with a fish, something that has also been recorded in the Pigeon Guillemot (Thoresen and Booth 1958), but not in other auks. Cairns (1981) and Petersen (1981) noted that fledglings could not fly but scrambled to the water; in the latter instance the young could fly 7–10 days after fledging. However, at many other colonies young fly directly from the breeding site to the sea.

F. Breeding Success

Breeding success among Black Guillemots in a range of geographic locations are summarized in Table 3.9. On Nordre Rønner, Denmark, the mean annual production between 1975 and 1977 was 0.60 young fledged per pair with most losses being due to predation (6–14% and 14–21% of eggs and young, respectively, depending on the year) and flooding (up to 17%); up to 10% of young died of starvation (Asbirk 1979b). In contrast, 1.29 young per pair were fledged on Flatey, Iceland, and most losses of eggs and chicks were due to adverse weather (20 and 49%, respectively) and flooding by high tides (23 and 11%); there was no evidence of predation or starvation (Petersen 1981). In Finland and Sweden mean brood sizes at fledging were 1.4 and 1.6 young, but in one year in Finland no young were reared (Bergman 1971; Olsson 1974). At some Scandinavian colonies, introduced mink often cause more-or-less complete breeding failure (Olsson 1974). In the Bay of Fundy mean production over 6 years was 0.69 fledgling per pair and the main causes of breeding failures were

TABLE 3.9

Breeding Success of Black Guillemots in Various Studies

Colony	Year	No. of eggs laid	No. of young hatched[a]	No. of young fledged[a]	No. of young fledged per pair	References
Kent I., Bay of Fundy	1947	84	44 (52.4)	22 (50.0)	0.48	Winn (1950)
Mickelskären, Finland	1962–1967	337	181 (53.7)	160 (88.4)	0.84	Preston (1968)
	1963–1968	61	58 (95.1)	48 (82.7)	?	Bergman (1971)
	1969	?	?	0	0	Bergman (1971)
Brandypot Is., Gulf of St. Lawrence	1976	161	95 (59.0)	56 (58.9)	0.64	Cairns (1980)
St. Mary Is., Gulf of St. Lawrence	1977	238	126 (52.9)	86 (68.3)	0.73	Cairns (1980)
Nordre Rønner, Denmark	1975	210	125 (59.5)	69 (55.2)	0.59	Asbirk (1979b)
	1976	237	129 (54.4)	61 (47.3)	0.26	Asbirk (1979b)
	1977	236	149 (63.1)	91 (61.1)	0.72	Asbirk (1979b)
Flatey, Iceland	1975	—	(80.8)	(84.6)	1.32	Petersen (1981)
	1976	—	(85.1)	(88.8)	1.42	Petersen (1981)
	1977	—	(74.2)	(83.0)	1.17	Petersen (1981)
Norway	1973–1975	—	(82.1)	(85.8)	1.36	R. Barrett (personal communication)
Kandalakshskaya Guba, U.S.S.R.	1958	28	18 (64.3)	17 (94.4)	1.21	Bianki (1967)
Fair Isle, Shetland	1960	30	26 (86.7)	24 (93.3)	1.60	Bianki (1967)
	1973–1977	149	104 (39.2)	76 (73.2)	0.41	R. Broad, in Petersen (1981)
Prince Leopold I., N.W.T.	1977	93	?	?	0.98	D. N. Nettleship (personal communication)

[a] Percentage of total given in parentheses.

predation and flooding of breeding sites by high tides (Winn 1950; Preston 1968). The production of two Gulf of St. Lawrence colonies was 0.70 young per pair with the main factors contributing to failure being infertility, clutch abandonment and chicks dying soon after hatching (Cairns 1978).

Pairs laying two-egg clutches have far more than twice the reproductive output than those laying just a single egg. For example, in the Gulf of St. Lawrence 0.78 young per breeding pair fledged from two-egg clutches compared to 0.12 from one-egg clutches; on Flatey, the corresponding figures were 1.65 and 0.59 (Cairns 1978; Peterson 1981). This is due mostly to a lower hatching success of one-egg clutches; for instance, 58 and 22% of eggs hatched in two-egg clutches on Kent Island, Bay of Fundy, 62 and 33% on Nordre Rønner, and 82.5 and 59% on Flatey (Preston 1968; Asbirk 1979b; Petersen 1981). When Preston (1968) added artificial eggs to six single eggs, five of the original eggs hatched compared to only one out of nine single eggs left alone as controls. Despite the increased clutch size, breeding success is usually similar to other Atlantic auks at about 0.6 to 0.8 young per pair (i.e., there is apparently little advantage gained from laying two eggs). However, in Iceland and to a lesser extent on Prince Leopold Island, Lancaster Sound, production was increased dramatically (Petersen 1981; D. N. Nettleship, unpublished).

On Kent Island, pairs breeding near other pairs laid more eggs, and experienced higher hatching success, than pairs breeding alone. This resulted in a mean of 0.93 fledged per pair compared to 0.58 for pairs breeding alone (Preston 1968). In the Gulf of St. Lawrence colonies there was no relationship between breeding success and nest density, nor did pairs at high density lay more synchronously (Cairns 1980). However, pairs breeding close to others on Nordre Rønner had a significantly higher fledging success than solitary pairs, but hatching success was similar (Asbirk 1979b). All these studies found that there was much aggression between pairs breeding in close proximity, and this aggression was credited with causing the low clutch size and high frequency of non-laying pairs on parts of Kent Island (Preston 1968). There was a hierarchy among four pairs on Nordre Rønner; the most aggressive pair apparently prevented one other pair from breeding and delayed the laying of another. Over a 3-year period of study the most dominant pair fledged a total of four young, the lowest two in the hierarchy just one each, and the intermediate pair two. Among inshore species competition for food will increase with increasing breeding density, and this may explain why Black Guillemots are less colonial than other auks. The concentrations of breeding Black Guillemots are probably the result of restricted breeding areas rather than the active gathering together of pairs into colonies.

VIII. DOVEKIE, *Alle alle*

A. General Features

1. PRE-LAYING PERIOD

Most Dovekies live in the far north throughout the year. Although some individuals return to the colonies as early as 21 February, the bulk of the birds return to Franz Josef Land in the last third of March, Spitsbergen during the first half of April and north Greenland during early May (Belopol'skii 1957; Løvenskiold 1964; Ferdinand 1969). The date of return is probably influenced by the extent of the pack ice around the land, although Dovekies often start nesting under seemingly severe conditions. Breeding is sometimes prevented in years with extremely heavy snow cover, but this might be due to oceanographic conditions rather than the snow itself.

At the start of the breeding season attendance at the colonies is erratic, and much of the display prior to egg-laying takes the form of spectacular aerial manoeuvres (Ferdinand 1969). Thousands of birds first gather offshore and then flocks take off and circle at about cliff-top level, gradually working their way down to the land. These circling birds call loudly and the sound has been referred to as 'singing'. This contrasts with the normal quiet aerial displays of other Atlantic auks (see Chapter 8, this volume), although some Pacific auklets are also noisy, and displaying groups of Black Guillemots have been recorded vocalizing loudly (A. Petersen, personal communication). Over land the large flocks split up and the flight circle becomes smaller, with a diameter of ca. 400–500 m, before birds start to land on the rocks or snow. Birds usually come ashore a few hours after midnight. The greatest daily activity is when light intensity is lowest, and the birds tend to depart again in mid-day. A similar rhythm of colony attendance occurred during incubation in Greenland (Evans 1981a), but Stempniewicz (1981) found no clear rhythm of diurnal activity at a colony in Spitsbergen during either the incubation or chick periods. Birds are not paired in these flocks and sexual displays take place on the ground. Little is known of the factors influencing colony attendance, but first visits occur when the weather is calm and sunny (Ferdinand 1969). When the weather is inclement (e.g., high winds) the time spent at the colony decreases (Kozlova 1957).

2. BREEDING HABITAT

Most colonies are in steep slopes along fragmented talus or boulder screes. The largest colonies are on mountain sides, but many smaller ones are found in boulders at the bases of cliffs, isolated pockets of rocks on cliff-faces, and even in cracks in the cliff or on isolated rocky skerries. Most colonies are situated on the coast, but a few are known to occur 6 km inland in northern Greenland (Salomonsen 1950), and 1500 m up in the mountains of Spitsbergen (Longstaff 1924). Typically, the species occurs alone, but sometimes, possibly where nesting habitat is restricted, they breed near Black Guillemots, Razorbills and Atlantic Puffins or at the base of murre colonies.

The Dovekie may be the commonest alcid in the North Atlantic (Chapter 2, this volume) and the colonies are often very large, sometimes containing (it is claimed) millions of birds. Such large colonies are typical of species feeding well offshore (see Chapter 9, this volume) but there is doubt as to the normal foraging range of Dovekies. Large numbers have been reported feeding well away from land (Brown 1976), whereas at Horse Head, west Greenland, large numbers were seen feeding close to the colony in 1974 (Evans 1981a). Others have been seen feeding inshore but at considerable distances from the colonies (Roby et al. 1981).

In Dovekie colonies boulders are often covered with a mass of nitrogen-tolerant vegetation (e.g., Alopecurus, Cerastium, Cochlearia and Stellaria) as a result of the manuring by the auks. In large colonies, most macrophytic plants are killed by excessive nitrogen leaving just lichens, and even the lichen flora is influenced by the extent the birds use the area. Black foliose forms are found where there are relatively few auks, bright orange Caloplaca where there are more birds, and no vegetation at all where the greatest densities of birds occur (Roby et al. 1981).

Nest density may exceed one per square metre in suitable substrate, but is usually less (Norderhaug 1980; Stempniewicz 1981). Arctic Fox are common in most colonies, so nests are placed in the rock crevices deep enough (0.5–1.5 m) to protect the adult and its egg or young. The egg is often laid on a bed of rock pebbles 1–4 cm in diameter gathered by the adults (Norderhaug 1980; Stempniewicz 1981); fragments of grasses, lichen and other vegetation are sometimes also present. In Spitsbergen, Dovekies have been recorded as digging tunnels in soil under and between boulders (Birula, in Bannerman 1963).

3. SITE AND MATE FIDELITY

No information is available.

B. Timing of Breeding

There are few data, but in Spitsbergen egg-laying lasted from 18 to 27 June 1974 and from 21 June to 3 July 1975 (Stempniewicz 1981). At the southernmost colony, in Grímsey, Iceland, laying started at the end of May (Hantzsch 1905) and in Greenland eggs were found on 7 June (Bent 1919). In most years and at most colonies the peak of laying seems to occur in the last week of June. The calculated median laying date for 31 eggs on Horse Head Island, west Greenland, in 1974 was 25 June (range: 18 June–10 July; Evans 1981a), and for 54 and 47 eggs in Spitsbergen in 1963 and 1964, 22 June (18 June–1 July) and 27 June (22 June–4 July; Norderhaug 1980). Pairs breeding close together are more closely synchronized than the colony as a whole (Evans 1981a). Throughout the range young fledge by the second half of August and the autumn exodus is complete by early September.

C. The Egg and Incubation

The single egg is oval or pointed-ovate in shape and uniformly bluish-white or bluish-green; rarely eggs are dark. The shell is smooth and lacks lustre (Bent 1919). Many eggs are unmarked, but some have faint patches or streaks of barely perceptible pale-brown spots. These undistinguished eggs suggest that Dovekies do not recognize their own egg. Eggs from Spitsbergen and west Greenland measured 49.1 × 34.2 mm (N = 195: Norderhaug 1980) and 48.2 (S.D. = 1.80) × 33.2 mm (S.D. = 1.12) (N = 24: Evans 1981a). L. Stempniewicz (personal communication) gives a mean weight of 99 fresh eggs as 31.3 g (calculated from the relationship between fresh-egg weight and volume index) for Dovekies in Spitsbergen. This represents 19.2% of adult weight (163 g: Stempniewicz 1980). Dovekies have two lateral brood patches, but only one egg is laid and incubated while being held under a wing. Both adults incubate in turn with (possibly) the male incubating mostly at night and the female by day (Uspenski 1956). In Spitsbergen incubating birds changed over about four times per day (Stempniewicz 1981). In three cases where two eggs were found in a burrow, only one was ever incubated at a time, and neither egg hatched (Norderhaug 1980). The mean incubation period is 29 days (S.D. = 0.80, range: 28–31, N = 38; Stempniewicz 1981). It is not known whether lost eggs are replaced, but chicks still present at the colony in September could be from repeat layings.

D. Chick-rearing Period

Typically a small hole opens up the third day after the first pipping crack appears on the egg, and hatching occurs the next day (Norderhaug 1980). The down of the semi-precocial chick is very dark grey on the upperparts and throat, slightly paler below; published references to brown plumage were not confirmed by Norderhaug in Spitsbergen. The newly hatched young weighed 13% of an adult in Spitsbergen (mean = 163.5 g, range: 136–204, $N = 74$; Norderhaug 1980) and 13.5% in west Greenland (Evans 1981a). The egg tooth is lost 9–19 days after hatching (Evans 1981a). The chick is brooded continuously until it becomes homeothermic when aged 2–4 days, much the same as other hole-nesting auks, but slightly earlier than those which have their young on exposed ledges. After this time the chick is usually left alone except when being fed. The primaries break through the skin when the chick is aged 5–7 days old, and the down is lost from the head, nape and belly at about day 20 and from the back a few days later (Evans 1981a).

The young Dovekie appears to show a stage towards developing a mesoptile plumage as in the Razorbill (Fjeldså 1977 and personal communication). Much down falls off at a relatively early age and the chick then resembles the mesoptile Razorbill and Common Murre chick except that the primaries are longer than the greater coverts (but still much shorter than those of the Atlantic Puffin and Black Guillemot at a comparable stage of development). After leaving the nest, the young Dovekie moults at least some of its body feathers.

Both the adults feed the young with plankton carried in a throat pouch. Stempniewicz (1981) stated that the share of the male and female in parental care at all stages was similar. However, of 95 adults caught with food late in the chick period in northwest Greenland, 60 were male and 35 female, which suggests that there may be unequal division of labour at this stage (Roby *et al.* 1981) or a sexual difference in the diurnal pattern of activity. The chick receives 4–14 meals per day and reaches peak weight when about 3 weeks old. It then loses some weight before fledging. Fledging weights vary greatly; for instance, the mean weights were 67–70, 78 and 82% of the adults' weight (163 g) in Spitsbergen and two northwest Greenland colonies, respectively (Norderhaug 1980; Evans 1981a; Roby *et al.* 1981; Stempniewicz 1981). In Greenland, this weight recession was associated with a slight reduction in feeding frequency (Evans 1981a).

E. Departure of Young from the Colony

At Spitsbergen, and Greenland the mean fledging ages were 27.0 and 28.3 days (Table 3.6). When aged 15 days, young start to leave the crevice and exercise their wings at the entrance where they may also be fed (Stempniewicz 1981). Accounts of fledging vary and are difficult to reconcile. Salomonsen (1950) and P. G. H. Evans (personal communication) saw young fledge alone whereas Løvenskiold (1964) reported that fledglings normally leave their colony with their parents, with several families often departing together in small groups; birds fledging unaccompanied by an adult were almost always caught by Glaucous Gulls. Norderhaug (1980) also described how young were accompanied by one or both adults and they flew out of sight except in one case where a fledgling turned around and flew back to the colony. Stempniewicz (1981) reported that young birds fly out to sea singly or in small groups consisting only of young or in mixed groups, and that fledging was highly synchronized. Bradstreet (1982a) collected 11 adults at sea in August; all were males with chicks (see murres, Sections III and IV) and he therefore concluded that adults abandoned their chicks at sea only sometime after fledging. But the development of the young (i.e., the relatively long time spent in the breeding site and the loss of weight before fledging) suggests that the young Dovekie is independent at fledging just as are the young Atlantic Puffins and Black Guillemots. Obviously further study is needed to clarify these differences.

F. Breeding Success

There are few useful data. However, of 20 eggs followed from incubation to chicks aged 20 days in Greenland, four eggs were deserted, two disappeared, one was broken and three chicks were taken by arctic fox (Evans 1981a). In Spitsbergen in 2 years, 64 of 98 (65%) eggs hatched and of those chicks, two (3%) died, 51 (80%) fledged and the fates of the remainder were undetermined (Stempniewicz 1981).

IX. CONCLUSIONS

This chapter has provided factual accounts of the reproductive ecology of the North Atlantic alcids. The individual species accounts indicate both the extent of our knowledge and the degree of variability in the features of reproduction which exist within species. At one time it was considered sufficient to have just one detailed account of a particular species' breeding biology. As the present chapter has indicated, this has now been achieved for all the living Atlantic species, and is close to being achieved for Pacific alcids. However, as more studies of the same species are published, a remarkable degree of previously unimagined intraspecific diversity is being revealed. Such investigations provide the raw material for comparative studies (Gaston et al. 1983a), from which existing hypotheses can be tested and new ideas generated. To date there have been all too few studies of the same species, and most comparative studies must be made between species. This approach, used extensively by Lack (1968), can provide important clues to the adaptive significance of particular features of a species' biology. In Chapter 4 of this volume we use some of the 'raw material' from this chapter, to make comparisons between North Atlantic alcid species, in order to do just that.

Ecological Adaptations for Breeding in the Atlantic Alcidae

TIM R. BIRKHEAD

Department of Zoology, University of Sheffield, Sheffield, England

MICHAEL P. HARRIS

Institute of Terrestrial Ecology, Banchory Research Station, Banchory, Kincardineshire, Scotland

I. INTRODUCTION

The main features of the reproductive biology of Atlantic alcids have been presented in Chapter 3. In that chapter our aim was to provide a descriptive account of each species' breeding biology with a minimum of interpretation and discussion. In the present chapter we examine alcid

205

breeding biology from a broader perspective, and consider intraspecific and interspecific differences in an attempt to identify important ecological adaptations for breeding. We have selected four aspects of alcid reproduction for discussion: timing of breeding, clutch and egg size, breeding success and the evolution of developmental patterns.

II. TIMING OF BREEDING

A. Geographic Variation in Time of Breeding

Birds which produce only a single clutch in a breeding season are generally thought to time their egg-laying so that they rear young as close as possible to the seasonal peak of food availability (Lack 1954). An important constraint on the timing of laying in some species is the ability of the female to accumulate the necessary reserves for egg formation (Perrins 1970) or for incubation (Brooke 1978). Two sets of factors control the timing of breeding: ultimate and proximate. The most important ultimate factor is likely to be the food supply (Jones and Ward 1976), while the most important proximate factor influencing the timing of laying is probably daylength (Murton and Westwood 1977). However, among arctic birds daylength is unlikely to be an important proximal cue since the time of egg-laying in alcids breeding at different latitudes, and therefore experiencing different photoperiods, may be very similar. For example, Thick-billed Murres in Hudson Strait and those 1300 km (and 12°) farther north in Lancaster Sound, breed on similar dates, despite the fact that they experience very different photoperiods. Any effect of daylength is probably modified by sea-surface temperatures or some other factor closely correlated with sea-surface temperature. Indeed, considering the North Atlantic as a whole, there is only a weak relationship between time of breeding (as measured by median hatching date) and latitude, but a marked relationship between sea-surface temperatures and time of breeding (Fig. 4.1). If alcids use seasonal changes in daylength to time their breeding (for both starting and finishing), then birds breeding at the same latitude but experiencing different sea temperatures must respond to the photoperiod in different ways. The same must also be true for other organisms in the alcid food web. The close correspondence between sea temperature and time of breeding suggests that sea temperatures affect the timing of food availability.

Every 1°C decrease in sea-surface temperature delays breeding by 3.1 days (Fig. 4.1). Warham (1975) found that for Rockhopper Penguins, a 1°C decrease in sea temperature resulted in a 5.2-day delay in time of breeding.

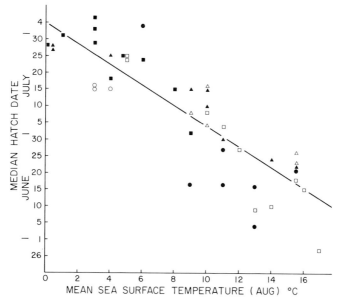

Fig. 4.1.   Relationship between August sea-surface temperatures (°C) and median hatching date. ●, Atlantic Puffin; □, Common Murre; ■, Thick-billed Murre; △, Razorbill; ▲, Black Guillemot; ○, Dovekie. The relationship is significant ($r = -.884$, $p < .001$); regression equation: $y = -3.03x + 63.92$. Sea-surface temperatures are from Sverdrup *et al.* (1942) for low-arctic and boreal regions, and from Anonymous (1958) for high-arctic regions.

B. Interspecific Differences in Time of Breeding

Figure 4.1 also suggests some interspecific differences in timing. For example, both Dovekies and Atlantic Puffins appear to breed relatively early. Perhaps the only way to examine interspecific differences in timing of breeding is to compare species breeding at the same location. Ideally, to do this one needs information on median laying or hatching dates over a number of years. Belopol'skii (1957) presented first-egg dates (which are not the best measure of time of breeding, because the temporal pattern of laying may vary) for five alcid species over 6 to 13 years for eastern Murmansk. Taking average first-egg dates, the order of laying was Atlantic Puffin (23 May), Common and Thick-billed Murre (both 24 May), Black Guillemot (27 May), and Razorbill (29 May). To test whether there was a tendency for species to lay in the same order each year, we produced a correlation matrix (Table 4.1) for the rank order of laying in the 6 years for which Belopol'skii (1957) presented data. A strong tendency for species to lay in the same order each year would result in most correlations being positive, but in our analysis (Table 4.1) 11 were positive and 10 negative, which suggests no consistent order of laying. This may be a

TABLE 4.1

Rank Order of Egg-laying of Five Alcid Species over Several Years[a,b]

Year	1935	1938	1939	1947	1948	1949
1938	.158					
1939	.564	.872				
1947	.108	−.811	−.632			
1948	.975	.154	.500	.105		
1949	−.688	−.229	−.447	−.353	−.671	
1950	.921	−.026	.308	−.834	.975	−.573

[a] Data from Belopol'skii (1957).
[b] Whether r values are significant or not is unimportant, since sample size (i.e., number of species) is only five. If there was a significant tendency for species to lay in the same order each year, most correlations would be positive; that is not the case here.

consequence of using first-egg dates. Bianki (1967) presents frequency distributions of hatching dates over 5 years for Black Guillemots and Razorbills breeding in the White Sea. Here Black Guillemots consistently hatched about 10 days earlier than Razorbills. In addition, the modal hatching dates of the two species were significantly correlated ($r_s = .925$, $p < .05$), which indicates that when one species laid late the other did so too. A similar trend is apparent in Belopol'skii's (1957) data (Table 4.2). Such patterns would occur if all alcids utilized the same prey species,

TABLE 4.2

Correlation Matrix of First-Egg Dates between Five Alcid Species over 6 to 12 Years at Eastern Murmansk Colonies[a,b]

Species	Common Murre	Thick-billed Murre	Razorbill	Atlantic Puffin
Thick-billed Murre	.988**			
Razorbill	.709*	.691*		
Atlantic Puffin	.569	.502	.591	
Black Guillemot	.630	.576	.901**	.706

[a] Data from Belopol'skii (1957).
[b] **$p < .001$, *$p < .05$. Given the small number of years for some comparisons, non-significance is not unexpected. However, it is striking that all correlations are positive.

TABLE 4.3

Median Laying Dates of Alcids in the Same Locality,
Skomer and Skokholm Islands, Wales[a]

Year	Common Murre	Atlantic Puffin	Razorbill
1973	19 May	—	20 May
1974	15 May	22 May	—
1975	16 May	2 May	—

[a] Data for Common Murre, Atlantic Puffin, and Razorbill are from Birkhead (1980), Ashcroft (1976) and Lloyd (1976a), respectively.

which is not true (Belopol'skii 1957), or if a common factor affects the availability of all prey populations similarly. The most likely factor in both Belopol'skii's (1957) and Bianki's (1967) studies is the timing of spring thaw which may affect accessibility of breeding and/or feeding areas.

At lower latitudes ice and snow are rarely a problem, so it should be possible to examine the rank order of laying in different species. Unfortunately there are few long runs of data to look at this. Our qualitative impression (but see Fig. 4.1) is that in Britain, puffins generally breed before other alcids (this was also true at Great Island, Newfoundland: D. N. Nettleship, personal communication). On Skomer Island in 1975, an apparently normal year, puffins laid about 14 days earlier than Common Murres. However, in 1974 puffins laid exceptionally late (Table 4.3) and some failed to lay at all. Common Murres, on the other hand, laid relatively early, which suggests a difference in the availability or abundance of food for the two species. In 1973, the median laying dates of Common Murres on Skomer Island and Razorbills on Skokholm (6 km away) were similar (Table 4.3).

Puffins may lay relatively early because of their protracted incubation period, but even allowing for this (by examining hatching dates), Fig. 4.1 still suggests relatively early breeding by puffins. One possible explanation for this is that since puffins are smaller than murres and Razorbills, they require less food, in absolute terms, and are therefore able to start breeding earlier. The same effect may explain the early breeding by Dovekies (Fig. 4.1), although it may also be explicable in terms of their plankton diet; the peak abundance or availability of food for Dovekies may occur earlier in the season than it does for those alcids which feed their young on fish.

C. Variation in Timing between Years

Despite occasional late years, in both boreal and arctic regions, the time of laying within the same colony is usually fairly constant from year to year. In Table 4.4 we compare the variability in time of breeding in boreal and arctic areas, using first-egg dates as a measure of timing, for lack of better data. The onset of laying in the Arctic tends to be more variable than for the same species in boreal regions. Pooling data for all species, the mean variation in first-egg date for boreal areas is 9 days, and for arctic areas 17 days; this difference is significant ($p < .01$). However, for all species, Belopol'skii's (1957) data give the highest values, possibly because of the longer run of data which is more likely to include the occasional very late year, or possibly conditions in eastern Murmansk may be more variable than elsewhere. Bianki (1967) noted that average laying dates of Black Guillemots and Razorbills in the White Sea were similar to those in eastern Murmansk, but at the latter colony they were considerably more variable than in the White Sea.

Annual variations in laying date in both boreal and arctic regions may result either from changes in food abundance or availability, or the accessibility of breeding areas. In the Arctic a late thaw may result in breeding sites being covered by snow or ice and prevent birds from reaching them (Uspenski 1956; Belopol'skii 1957; Sealy 1975c). The late break-up of sea ice may reduce the birds' feeding area or affect food abundance and thereby delay breeding. Annual variation in the onset of breeding in arctic regions may be high because conditions are more extreme and the onset of spring thaw unpredictable. Inclement weather may also affect laying in boreal regions: Lloyd (1979) attributed late laying in Razorbills on Skokholm in 1972 to stormy sea conditions during the pre-laying period. Hedgren (1979) found that the median fledging date (which presumably reflects laying date) of Common Murres in the Baltic was negatively correlated with spring air temperatures prior to egg-laying. In both cases climatic conditions may have affected the availability of prey species and/ or the energy budgets of females so that they had to expend more energy on self-maintenance than on egg formation.

D. Boreal and Arctic Breeding Seasons

If laying is delayed in the Arctic, conditions later in the season may be unsuitable for chick rearing. It is also important for birds to know (in an evolutionary sense) when to stop laying. Despite the abrupt seasonal changes and the greater variability in the onset of breeding in polar regions, there is little evidence that the time needed for breeding (from

TABLE 4.4

Variation in Time of Breeding in Boreal and Arctic Regions[a]

Species	Oceanographic zone[b] Boreal	Arctic	References
Razorbill	—	13 (10)	Belopol'skii (1957)
	—	15 (5)	Bianki (1967)
	15 (3)	—	Lloyd (1976a)
Common Murre	—	18 (12)	Belopol'skii (1957)
	—	8 (3)	Drury *et al.* (1980)
	—	16 (3)	Swartz (1966)
	10 (4)	—	Hedgren (1980)[d]
	10 (3)	—	T. R. Birkhead (unpublished)
Atlantic Puffin	—	27 (7)	Belopol'skii (1957)
	—	15 (5)	Skokova (1967)
	8 (4)	—	Ashcroft (1976); Corkhill (1972)
	7 (5)	—	Harris (1982a)[e]
	11 (8)	—	Harris (1982a)[f]
Black Guillemot	—	28 (10)	Belopol'skii (1957)
	—	20 (5)	Bianki (1967)
	4 (3)	—	Asbirk (1979b)
	4 (3)	—	Petersen (1981)
	12 (5)	—	Preston (1968)
Thick-billed Murre[c]	—	18 (12)	Belopol'skii (1957)
	—	14 (4)	Gaston and Nettleship (1981); Nettleship *et al.* (1980)
	—	15 (3)	Swartz (1966)

[a] Values are number of days variation in date of first eggs, and number of years in parentheses.

[b] *Zones* as defined by Freuchen and Salomonsen (1958) and Salomonsen (1965, 1972a); see also Chapter 2, this volume.

[c] Thick-billed Murre included for comparison with Common Murre.

[d] Based on first fledging dates.

[e] St. Kilda based on hatching dates.

[f] Isle of May, hatching dates.

laying to fledging) is less than it is in boreal areas. Both Thick-billed Murres at Prince Leopold Island, and Common Murres on Skomer Island (high-arctic and boreal colonies, respectively) laid over a period of about 40 days. Belopol'skii (1957) suggested that synchrony of laying of Atlantic Puffins breeding at Novaya Zemlya was greater, and incubation and nestling periods reduced (to 30 days each) as adaptations for high-arctic breeding; increased synchrony is possible, but a reduction in incubation and chick-rearing periods by 30% seems unlikely (see Chapter 3, this volume). Evans (1981a) also thought that the breeding season of Dovekies was compressed, but the incubation and chick-rearing periods total 56 days (Stempneiwicz 1981), which is greater than for murres and the Razorbill (53 days). In addition, synchrony of breeding in Dovekies was similar to murres. The only way a compressed season could be achieved would be through a reduction in the pre-laying period. This is exactly what occurs in murres and Razorbills (but not puffins—see Chapter 3, this volume): the pre-laying period of colony attendance is much reduced at arctic colonies (Belopol'skii 1957). Furthermore, departure at the end of the season may be more synchronous in arctic colonies than in boreal ones. Some alcids breeding at colonies in boreal waters continue to visit the colony for 1 or 2 weeks after their chicks have fledged (e.g., puffins on the Isle of May; Common Murres on Skomer Island). The reduction of this post-fledging period of colony attendance in the Arctic may explain the more synchronous departure at the end of the season.

E. Temporal Patterns of Laying

For most alcid species which have been studied in detail, the distribution of laying dates within a single colony are skewed to the right. Generally there is a rapid increase in the number of birds laying at the beginning of the season followed by a more gradual decrease (Gochfeld 1980). The pattern of laying in the two least colonial alcids, the Razorbill and Black Guillemot, are less skewed, and follow a more normal distribution (Lloyd 1976a; Asbirk 1979b).

Gaston and Nettleship (1981) suggested that a skewed pattern of laying occurs because some birds, capable of laying, 'hold back' to optimize the timing of the chick-rearing period, or so that they lay when most other birds lay. Other individuals are unable to lay at the optimum time because they have not accumulated the necessary reserves. These differences in laying date presumably reflect differences in the quality of females.

Both patterns may be adaptive, although few studies have attempted to distinguish between these two alternatives. In Herring Gulls, when synchrony and calendar date were experimentally changed, breeding success

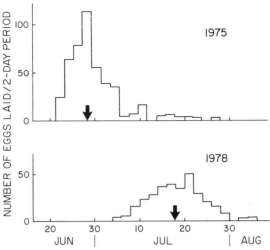

Fig. 4.2.   Temporal pattern of laying in Thick-billed Murres at Prince Leopold Island, N.W.T., in 1975, a year in which laying was early, and 1978, when laying was late. Arrows indicate median laying dates (from Nettleship *et al.* 1980).

was affected more by synchrony within the colony than by calendar egg-laying date (Parsons 1975). A similar effect has been recorded in Common Murres: groups with similar degrees of synchrony, but with different median laying dates, had approximately the same breeding success. On the other hand, less synchronous groups laying at any time had lower breeding success (Birkhead 1977a).

For alcids breeding in the Arctic, calendar egg-laying date may be more important than intra-group synchrony. If laying is late, synchrony is also reduced (Birkhead and Nettleship 1981), probably because once the optimal calendar egg-laying date is past birds cannot afford to delay laying in order to synchronize their breeding with other colony members. Low temperatures which resulted in late ice break-up at Prince Leopold Island in 1978 meant that the median laying date occurred 18 days later, and laying was less synchronous than in previous years in which temperatures and ice conditions were 'normal' (Fig. 4.2).

III. CLUTCH AND EGG SIZE

A. Clutch Size

Lack's (1954) hypothesis that birds produce clutch sizes that leave the most survivors has been modified in recent years to become more comprehensive and intimately bound up with the theory of life-history strategies (Stearns 1976, 1977). Although Lack's basic idea is supported by several studies, discrepancies occur and the most frequent clutch size is sometimes smaller than that which fledges the most young (Klomp 1970). A number of theoretical models (mainly modifications of Lack's original hypothesis) predict clutch sizes smaller than the most productive ones (Stearns 1976). For example, Cody (1966) and Skutch (1967) suggested that there is a trade-off between the demands for resources for reproduction *versus* other functions. Charnov and Krebs (1974) also suggest a trade-off, but between clutch size and mortality. This was an extension of Williams' (1966) point, that the number of young surviving to breed must be considered in relation to adult survival. Charnov and Krebs (1974) also suggested that the effect of adult survival on fitness will be more important for long-lived species like seabirds, than for short-lived species.

In species with nidicolous young, clutch size has evolved in relation to the amount of food which the parents can provide for the young. In those species with precocial young predation is the most important factor affecting clutch size (Safriel 1975; Perrins 1977). Relative egg size is greater in precocial species, but in both groups there is probably a compromise between the size and number of eggs. The mean clutch size in both nidicolous and precocial species is that which over an individual's lifetime results in birds leaving the greatest number of surviving offspring (Lack 1968; Williams 1966).

Four alcid species have precocial young and even these are probably fed to some extent by their parents, so in most alcids clutch size is probably determined by the number of young they can feed. Most alcids, like many other seabirds, produce a single-egg clutch, presumably because the food supply is distant from breeding areas. The precocial Xantus', Craveri's, Ancient and Japanese Murrelets greatly reduce the travel time between feeding areas and their young by taking their chicks to feeding areas just 2 days after hatching. These species produce a two-egg clutch (see Chapter 7, this volume). The problem of food availability is also less pronounced for the Black, Pigeon and Spectacled Guillemots which feed inshore; they also produce a clutch of two eggs.

Species which feed offshore produce a single-egg clutch because they can provide less food for their young than inshore-feeding, or precocial species (Lack 1968). There is some experimental evidence to support this view. Pairs of alcids, given an additional chick (or where one parent was removed), usually failed to rear both chicks (Table 4.5). However, those cases where additional chicks are successfully reared as in the Black Guillemot (see also Nelson 1964; Harris 1970a) do not necessarily provide evidence contrary to Lack's ideas on clutch size. Most seabirds are long-

TABLE 4.5

Summary of the Results of Alcid Chick Twinning Experiments

Species	Location	Experiment	N	Outcome	References
Atlantic Puffin	Great Island, Nfld.	One extra chick added	10	Five of 20 chicks fledged.	Nettleship (1972)
		One parent removed	12	Four chicks died and 8 disappeared prematurely.	Nettleship (1972)
	Skomer Island, Wales	One extra chick added	4	Six of 8 chicks fledged.	Corkhill (1973)
		One parent died	2	Chicks fledged.	Ashcroft (1976)
	Isle of May, Scotland	One parent removed	10	Four of 10 chicks fledged.	Harris (1978)
		One extra chick added	7	Five of 14 chicks fledged.	M. P. Harris (unpublished)
Razorbill	Skokholm Island, Wales	One extra chick added	12	Fourteen of 24 chicks (including two pairs of twins) fledged.	Plumb (1965)
		One extra chick added	14	Sixteen of 28 chicks (including two pairs of twins) fledged.	Lloyd (1977)
Black Guillemot	Nordre Rønner, Denmark	Brood increased from one to two	7	Twelve of 14 chicks fledged.	Asbirk (1979b)
		Brood increased from two to three	9	Ten of 18 chicks fledged.	Asbirk (1979b)
	Flatey, Iceland	Brood increased from two to three	14	Thirty-three of 42 chicks fledged.	Peterson (1981)
Rhinoceros Auklet	Cleland Island, B.C.	One extra chick added	13	Eight of 26 chicks fledged.	Summers (1970)

lived and there may be a trade-off between reproductive effort (e.g., clutch size, egg size, chick-feeding rates) and adult survival (Stearns 1976, 1977). Presumably natural selection will have favoured those individuals whose overall life-history strategy has resulted in the highest fitness (Goodman 1974). Twinning experiments tell us little about the evolution of clutch size unless we also measure factors like adult survival or chick survival to breeding age. Asbirk's (1979b) data for Black Guillemots provide some evidence for this type of argument for alcids. He found that the survival rate of birds laying two eggs and rearing one or two chicks was 83%, whereas parents laying two eggs and rearing no young had a survival rate of 92%. A decrease in adult survival from 92 to 83% reduced the expectation of further life by 6.7 years, from 11.5 to 4.8 years. These data are in the predicted direction, but the difference between the two groups was not statistically significant.

B. Variation in Egg Size

Clutch size is a measure of reproductive effort, as is egg size, in those species producing a single-egg clutch. Egg weight as a proportion of body weight is inversely related to adult body weight, and varies from 1.5 to 27% of adult weight (Lack 1968). Alcids lay relatively large eggs (range: 12–24% of adult weight), and show the same trend with adult weight (Fig. 4.3). The largest eggs relative to adult size are laid by the precocial murrelets (Sealy 1975b), whose young must be particularly well developed at hatching in order to go to sea 2 days later.

Egg size varies between populations of the same species, and Fig. 3.3 (Chapter 3, this volume) indicates that much of this variation can be explained by adult body size. Within populations, egg size may also vary considerably. For example, in Thick-billed Murres, Razorbills and Atlantic Puffins the largest eggs may be 25–30% more in volume than the smallest (Lloyd 1976a; Birkhead and Nettleship 1981). Part of this variation is undoubtedly explained by variation in body size, but the date of laying also has an important effect. Birds laying late in the season tend to produce relatively small eggs (Chapter 3, this volume).

A significant negative relationship between laying date and egg size has been recorded in Thick-billed Murres (Gaston and Nettleship 1981; Birkhead and Nettleship 1982b), Razorbills (Lloyd 1976a), Atlantic Puffins (Ashcroft 1976; Harris 1980), and Black Guillemots (Petersen 1981). Clutch size in other birds follows a similar seasonal trend (Murton and Westwood 1977). A number of factors might produce such an effect. Female age affects laying date as well as egg size and clutch size (Coulson et al. 1969; Lloyd 1976a; De Steven 1978), with young females generally laying later and producing smaller eggs or clutches than older females.

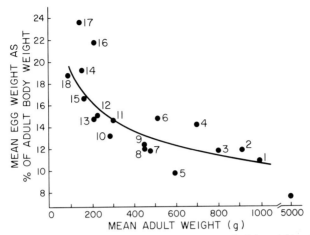

Fig. 4.3.   Relationship between egg weight as a percentage of adult weight and adult body weight. The line of best fit is a log · log plot ($r = -.855$, $p < .001$), including the Great Auk point (unnumbered point, far right). The regression equation is $\log y = 1.801 - 0.251 \log x$. Note that although the x axis is broken to accommodate the Great Auk point, this point falls close to the fitted curve. Numbers beside points are as follows: 1, Common Murre; 2, Thick-billed Murre; 3, Tufted Puffin; 4, Razorbill; 5, Horned Puffin; 6, Rhinoceros Auklet; 7, Atlantic Puffin; 8, Black Guillemot; 9, Pigeon Guillemot; 10, Parakeet Auklet; 11, Crested Auklet; 12, Kittlitz's Murrelet; 13, Marbled Murrelet; 14, Dovekie; 15, Cassin's Auklet; 16, Ancient Murrelet; 17, Xantus' Murrelet; 18, Least Auklet (modified and redrawn from Sealy 1975b).

However, several studies have shown that females of all age classes produce smaller clutches when they lay late (Coulson *et al.* 1969; Finney and Cooke 1978). There have been no studies of alcids with sufficient birds of known age to demonstrate this effect. There is, however, some indirect evidence; comparisons of mean egg size in the same population of Thick-billed Murres in years when the timing of laying varied have shown that mean egg size was smallest in the years when laying was latest (Nettleship *et al.* 1980). That is, when laying of the whole population was delayed, the average egg size was reduced. Both Bianki (1967) and Lloyd (1976a) recorded significantly smaller mean egg size in Razorbills in years when laying was late. This same effect occurs in clutch size among passerines, although Perrins (1979) suggested that the inter-seasonal effect is produced by factors which are different from those controlling the intraseasonal decline.

Another factor contributing to the seasonal decline in egg size is the increasing number of replacement eggs laid late in the season (see Chapter 3, this volume). Replacement eggs are smaller than first eggs and tend to follow the seasonal change in egg size. There was a correlation between the size of first and replacement eggs in Razorbills, Common Murres and

Thick-billed Murres (Birkhead and Nettleship 1984a), which supports the idea that female size (or some other characteristic such as quality) contributed to the variation in egg size.

C. Seasonal Reduction in Egg Size

Perrins (1970) suggested two advantages for a seasonal reduction in clutch size. First, a smaller clutch among late-breeding individuals is an adaptation to a worsening food supply for the young. By starting with a smaller clutch and having fewer chicks, each chick can be given more of the available food. It is unlikely that the reduced clutch size of late breeders is a result of food shortage during egg formation since late breeders are laying when the earliest breeders are finding enough food to rear young. Second, a reduced clutch size results in a time-saving mechanism. Since eggs are laid at intervals of 1 or more days, by laying fewer eggs birds can make an earlier start to incubation and hatching.

The first advantage may apply to murrelets and guillemots (*Cepphus* spp.), which generally lay two-egg clutches, but clearly cannot apply to the other alcids which lay only one egg. Birkhead and Nettleship (1982b) have considered the seasonal reduction in egg size in single-egg clutch species as a time-saving mechanism. The problem can be stated as follows, and applies to females which are unable to lay on time. Should a female delay laying even further in order to produce a larger egg or should she lay a minimum viable-sized egg as soon as possible? This problem was examined in Thick-billed Murres, by considering the effect of hatching date and hatching weight (which is closely related to egg size) on fledging weight. Fledging weight was used as a measure of breeding success, and although survival and fledging weight may be closely related in some species (Perrins *et al.* 1973), there is little evidence for this in murres (Hedgren 1981) and Razorbills (Lloyd 1979). This may be because parental care after fledging off-sets any disadvantage of low fledging weights. In Thick-billed Murres both date and egg size had a significant effect on fledging weight, but of the two, the hatching date was more important. In other words, the best strategy for a female unable to lay on time would be to minimize the delay in laying by producing a smaller egg. A model based on the multiple regression between fledging weight (dependent variable) and (1) hatching weight and (2) hatching date, is shown in Fig. 4.4. It seems unlikely that females can ever choose between the various options shown in Fig. 4.4, because the maximum rate of egg development is slower than the average rate of chick growth. Although the overall energetic cost of chick production may be higher than the cost of egg production, the cost of rearing the chick (unlike the cost of egg production) is shared between the male and female.

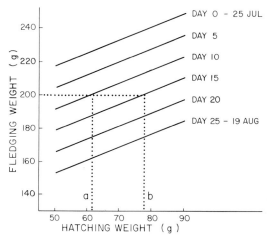

Fig. 4.4. Relationship between hatching date (x_1) and hatching weight (x_2) and effect on fledging weight (y), based on the multiple regression equation: $y = 178.66 - 2.5x_1 + 0.777x_2$. The diagonal lines represent the relationship between hatching weight and fledging weight at 5-day intervals, where day 0 = 25 July and day 25 = 19 August. Dotted lines illustrate an example of two possible options open to a female in order to produce a 200-g chick at fledging: produce an egg of a size which will give rise to (a) a 61-g chick at hatching on day 10, or (b) a chick of 77.5 g at hatching on day 15. (From Birkhead and Nettleship 1982b.)

Female Thick-billed Murres which lay 'on time' and produce large eggs do better than those laying on time and producing small eggs, which in turn do better than females laying late with large or small eggs. Clearly, both laying date and egg size are important. Egg size is important because large eggs can produce chicks which are large and well developed at hatching, and/or standard-sized chicks with larger food reserves. An interspecific comparison of alcids (Fig. 4.3) shows that the murrelets adopt the first strategy, while an intraspecific comparison of Common Murres indicated that they adopt the second strategy: chicks from large eggs have heavier yolk sacs at hatching, but are of similar size to chicks from small eggs (Birkhead and Nettleship 1984a).

D. Composition of Alcid Eggs

The composition of eggs of different bird species varies according to the pattern of chick development (Ricklefs 1974; Carey *et al.* 1980); the more precocial the chick at hatching the greater proportion of yolk in the egg, and the greater proportion of lipid in the yolk. The composition of eggs of the Common Murre, Razorbill and Atlantic Puffin are similar to those of species with precocial young (Fig. 4.5), with about 30 to 35% of egg weight made up of yolk, and 33 to 35% of the yolk made up of lipid. These

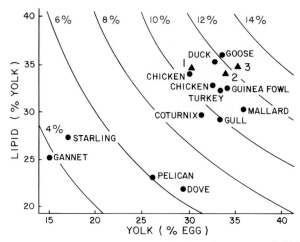

Fig. 4.5. Scatter diagram of the relative size of yolk and percentage lipid in yolk, in the eggs of several bird species. Diagonal curves represent different levels of lipid as a percentage of the whole egg. ▲, Alcids: 1, Common Murre; 2, Razorbill; 3, Atlantic Puffin (other data from Ricklefs 1974; Montevecchi and Porter 1980).

values are equivalent to 9 to 12% lipid in the whole egg, and are similar to the value of 10.8% for Cassin's Auklet (Carey *et al.* 1980). The energetic cost of egg production and laying are difficult to measure directly, but can be estimated relative to the standard metabolic rate (S.M.R.) of adults, from the energy content of the egg, clutch size and the number of days over which the yolk is deposited, that is, the rapid phase of yolk formation (Ricklefs 1974). The energy content of Common and Thick-billed Murre eggs are similar, 1.99 kcal/g wet weight (Uspenski 1956), and the cost of production estimated at 85% of adult S.M.R. This is considerably higher than in the Northern Gannet (50% of adult S.M.R.; Ricklefs and Montevecchi 1979), but lower than in gulls (100% of adult S.M.R.), which produce clutches of three eggs, and Anatidae (149–180% of adult S.M.R.), which produce large broods of precocial young (Ricklefs 1974). It seems likely that the energetic cost of egg production in murrelets, which produce two relatively large eggs, will be higher than in any other alcid.

IV. FACTORS AFFECTING BREEDING SUCCESS

A. Habitat Selection

All animal species occur in a limited range of habitats, and habitat specificity is generally considered to be adaptive. The evolutionary mechanism of habitat selection can be divided into proximate and ultimate factors. The ultimate factors are those directly influencing individual fitness, while the proximate factors are those stimuli which result in settling behaviour. Proximate factors can be divided into (a) mechanisms by which a habitat is selected, and (b) which parts of the environment the animal uses to select a habitat. The identification of these proximate factors is best done by looking for correlations between population density and features of the habitat, assuming that most individuals select the habitat which provides optimum conditions for survival and reproduction (Hilden 1965; Partridge 1978). However, abundance alone is not necessarily a reliable measure of habitat suitability since density could be low in a particular area because there are few individuals available to invade the habitat (Fretwell 1968, 1969). Habitat selection has important consequences in determining the reproductive success and survival of individuals.

For seabirds, habitat selection can operate at a number of levels. At the first, selection of a colony location is important. The two main factors which affect selection at this level are that (a) the area contains suitable breeding sites (see below), and (b) it is within the range of good feeding areas. The present discussion is concerned only with breeding habitats. (Selection of feeding habitats is discussed in Chapter 6 of this volume.) Second, birds must 'decide' between habitats within a colony (Buckley and Buckley 1980). For example, puffins in some colonies must decide between sloping and level ground (Nettleship 1972). Third, birds must discriminate between breeding sites within a particular habitat. These last two levels of habitat selection have been described in a qualitative way by many workers, in that the main characteristics of each species' breeding site are well known (see Chapter 3, this volume). In only a few cases have habitat or breeding-site characteristics for alcids been examined quantitatively, and in such studies it has been assumed that habitat selection is adaptive and that breeding success (and adult survival) reflects habitat quality.

Nettleship (1972) used multivariate statistics to determine which factors affected habitat selection in Atlantic Puffins in Newfoundland, and found that density of nesting burrows was negatively correlated with distance from the cliff-edge and positively correlated with soil depth and angle of slope. Over 65% of the variation in burrow density was accounted for by distance from the cliff-edge and the addition of the other two variables increased the figure to 81%. Similarly on Skomer Island, Wales, burrow density, while much lower, was also greatest near the cliff-edge, and away from the edge more burrows occurred in sloping than on flat ground (Ashcroft 1976). The puffin population on Skomer declined this century, accompanied by a shift in distribution, so that now most birds are concen-

222   Tim R. Birkhead and Michael P. Harris

trated in a narrow band near the cliff-edge. Too much should not, however, be made of these two examples as many colonies are much more
uniform and do not have such a marked division between flat and sloping
ground. For instance, on the rather flat Isle of May (Scotland) and the
Farne Islands (England) soil depth was the main factor influencing burrow
density (M. Hornung, personal communication). There is no indication of
what influences the position of nest sites in boulder colonies; such colonies, and the birds which live in them, have proved extremely difficult to
study (but see Myrberget 1962).

A comparison of the three main population studies of Atlantic Puffins
serves as a good example of how habitat selection in some colonies can
play a major role in determining breeding success, and also how the
factors affecting success differ between colonies. On Great Island, Nettleship (1972) found that puffins nesting on steep slopes raised at least twice
as many young per pair as pairs nesting nearby on level ground (Table
4.6). Hatching success was significantly higher in nests on the slope
mainly due to the higher proportion of eggs which disappeared and which
were infertile on level ground. Chicks on the slope grew and survived
better than those on level ground, and most chicks which failed either
died or disappeared early in the nestling period; fledging success and

TABLE 4.6

**Data on Breeding of Atlantic Puffins on Slope and Level Habitats on Great Island, Nfld., in
1968 and 1969**[a]

		Slope		Level		
Character	Year	N	Mean	N	Mean	p
Hatching success (%)	1968	90	64.4	60	46.6	<.05
Eggs infertile (%)	1968	90	3.3	60	10.0	n.s.
Eggs disappearing (%)	1968	90	32.3	60	43.4	n.s.
Hatching success (%)	1969	200	75.5	202	54.4	<.001
Eggs infertile (%)	1969	200	2.0	202	12.9	<.001
Eggs disappearing (%)	1969	200	22.5	202	32.7	n.s.
Fledging weight (g)	1968	25	261.4	6	247.5	n.s.
	1969	101	261.8	47	248.2	<.001
Age at fledging (days)	1968	25	59.7	6	55.5	n.s.
	1969	101	52.3	48	52.2	n.s.
Meals/day	1969	17	3.6	15	2.4	<.01
Meal size (g)	1968	30	14.2	19	11.9	n.s.
	1969	125	12.0	75	12.9	n.s.
Meals lost to gulls (%)	1968–1969	601	4.4	775	13.5	<.001

[a] From Nettleship (1972).

fledging weight were strongly related to time of hatching. There were obvious advantages to breeding on the slope and breeding early. Young on sloping ground received more meals per day than those on level ground because many fewer adults lost their fish to kleptoparasitic Herring and Great Black-backed Gulls, probably because they could escape attack more rapidly on the slope. Starving young were more likely to come to the burrow entrance and risk being caught by gulls. Nettleship concluded that the difference in breeding success in the two habitats was due to higher exposure of eggs and chicks to gull predation on the level ground. Puffins nesting elsewhere in Newfoundland where there was little interference from gulls had a much higher success rate. For example, at Funk and Small Islands breeding success was 0.87 and 0.93 chicks fledged per burrow, respectively, compared to 0.37 at Great Island for slope and level breeding pairs combined or 0.51 in nests on the slopes where more than 80% of the population breeds (Nettleship 1972). In addition, young were heavier at fledging (mean: 351.3 g $\pm$ 24.0 S.D. compared to 261.8 g $\pm$ 36.0 S.D. on sloping ground at Great Island).

For puffins on St. Kilda, Scotland, density of conspecifics was probably the most important aspect of habitat selection, and pairs nesting in areas of high burrow density bred earlier and reared significantly more young (0.77 young per egg laid $\pm$ 0.06 S.D.) than those breeding at low density (0.51 young $\pm$ 0.11) (Harris 1980). Although pairs breeding early had a higher success than those breeding late, the annual difference in laying dates between birds in the two areas was only 1.6 $\pm$ 4.7 days, insufficient to explain the difference in chick production. The main advantage in laying early was a greater chance of re-laying if the first egg was lost. Young in the high-density area attained higher peak weights and fledging weights than young in the low-density area, but there was no clear-cut relationship linking weights of chicks and their hatching date. At this colony the most important factor influencing breeding success (and adult survival) was predation by Great Black-backed Gulls. Puffins breeding at low density were most affected, and at least 4.2% of adults (almost equal to the total annual mortality at other colonies; see Chapter 5, this volume) were killed by gulls each season, compared to only 0.9% of adults from high-density areas. Birds in the low-density areas spent far less time at the colony than those breeding at higher densities, which may explain the reduced breeding success recorded at low densities. On Great Island, the density of burrows was positively correlated with the angle of slope of the ground, so it is possible that there, nesting density, as well as slope, had some effect on breeding success.

On Skomer Island, puffins which laid in the first half of the laying period fledged more young (83%) than those which laid later (63%) (Ashcroft

1976). There was no correlation between breeding success and the position of burrow, slope of ground, density of burrows, burrow length or depth. However, there were more total successes or complete failures in individual burrows in all 3 years than would be expected by chance, which was probably due to the failure or success of particular birds rather than the characteristics of the burrow (see below).

In Common Murres the proximity of conspecifics is important in habitat selection, as birds prefer to breed in close physical contact with their neighbours (Birkhead 1977a). Moreover, murres breeding on broad rock ledges had very different breeding success according to the density of conspecifics on that habitat. On Skomer Island, breeding success was greatest at high densities on broad ledges. This is what one might expect since most birds breed under such conditions (see Fig. 3.1 and Chapter 3, this volume). On Skomer Island, the murre population has declined, and consequently there is only a weak relationship between breeding success and abundance in particular habitats. Most birds now breed on narrow ledges, even though birds at high densities on broad ledges are more productive. When the population was higher, a greater proportion of the population bred on broad ledges at high density. This suggests that as numbers declined there were disadvantages associated with the formation of a few dense groups. For such a reorganization to be successful, all birds would have to move simultaneously, since isolated pairs on broad ledges are especially vulnerable to predatory gulls (Birkhead 1977a).

In Thick-billed Murres at Prince Leopold Island, arctic Canada, rock ledges with certain characteristics were used in preference to others, and the most frequently used sites tended to be the most successful (Gaston and Nettleship 1981). The most productive sites were those with one or two walls, with neighbouring birds on level ledges. However, this combination may not be the most productive in all colonies, since the physical characteristics of ledges are dependent on rock type and weathering, and these differ between colonies. As in Atlantic Puffins and Common Murres, the presence of neighbouring conspecifics was important, although the effect was less marked than in Common Murres because Thick-billed Murres do not breed at such high densities.

Gaston and Nettleship (1981) found a significant tendency for birds at the same site to fail or be successful in successive years. Sites at which birds failed to rear a chick were occupied less consistently than those sites at which birds were successful, which suggests a higher turnover rate of birds at these sites. Such sites are more likely to be occupied by young, inexperienced birds, which exaggerates the low success of those sites. Breeding-site quality and bird quality are unlikely to be independent. In all species, high-quality sites are likely to be occupied by high-quality birds. In Thick-billed Murres, site quality and bird quality (as measured by hatching date) were inter-related (Gaston and Nettleship 1981). Similarly, in Atlantic Puffins at Great Island, males on maritime sloping ground (the most productive habitat) were significantly heavier than those on level ground (Nettleship 1972).

The situation in Black Guillemots is rather different from the other alcids discussed, since Black Guillemots usually breed at relatively low densities and the proximity of conspecifics is less important. Asbirk (1979b) found that birds breeding in rock crevices (the most frequently used type of site) were more successful than those breeding under driftwood. The annual survival of birds breeding under driftwood was lower (80%) than those breeding in rock crevices (87%). Although crevice breeding sites were abundant on Nordre Rønner, the territorial behaviour of site-holders prevented others from settling in such areas, forcing them to accept sites under driftwood.

Since there is good evidence among Atlantic alcids for certain habitats or breeding sites being more productive than others, we might expect the average breeding success of a population to be controlled in a density-dependent manner. An increase in population density would result in an increase in the proportion of poor sites occupied with a corresponding reduction in overall breeding success (Gaston and Nettleship 1981). This effect has been clearly demonstrated in Shags (Potts *et al.* 1980).

B. Interspecific Competition

Although many alcids breed in mixed-species colonies, there have been no detailed investigations of interspecific competition for breeding sites. Indeed many authors have commented on the clear segregation in the type of breeding site used by different species (Lack 1971; Bédard 1969a; Buckley and Buckley 1980). We will consider breeding-site competition between alcid species first, and then between alcids and other species.

The Common Murre and Thick-billed Murre often breed in similar habitats. In Murmansk, Common Murres outnumber Thick-billed Murres, and have apparently pushed Thick-billed Murres onto narrow cliff-ledges or the edge of larger ledges, while they occupied broader ledges (Belopol'skii 1957). Other authors (Sergeant 1951; Lack 1968) imply that the two species compete for breeding sites, but also point out the differences in site preferences in the two species. Both Sergeant and Lack state that where only one species occurs it may occupy the whole range of murre breeding sites. However, this is not correct: while Common Murres can breed on either broad or narrow ledges, Thick-billed Murres very rarely breed on broad flat ledges and never at the same densities as Common Murres (Williams 1974). Since Common Murres can use the same type of site used by Thick-billed Murres, there may be situations, for example, when Common Murre numbers are increasing relative to Thick-billed Murres, when the latter are excluded from their optimum breeding areas. Williams (1974) described interspecific aggression between the two species and found that among pairs with established breeding sites, the outcome of aggressive encounters depended on which species owned the site. He suggested that Common Murres could displace Thick-billed Murres from breeding areas in two ways. First, prospecting Thick-billed Murres were harassed by Common Murres and prevented from remaining on ledges. This may be because of the difference in the post-landing displays of the two species (see Chapter 8, this volume); Common Murres did not attack conspecifics which displayed, but did attack Thick-billed Murres, which performed a different display. Second, on ledges where both species had breeding sites, a Thick-billed Murre which loses its mate may be thwarted in its attempts to attract a partner, because of the aggression of adjacent Common Murres. The dominance of Common Murres over Thick-billed Murres may be due to their greater size and weight: in all areas of sympatry Common Murres are heavier than Thick-billed Murres (Uspenski 1956; Belopol'skii 1957; Swartz 1966; R. Barrett, personal communication). In addition, on the basis of anatomical studies Spring (1971) suggested that Common Murres are more agile than Thick-billed Murres, which gives them an additional advantage in aggressive encounters. Williams' (1974) study showed that competition for breeding sites does occur between the two murre species, and that they do not provide such a clear example of ecological segregation, as Lack (1968) suggested.

The most detailed investigation of interspecific competition involving alcids is Ashcroft's (1976) study of Atlantic Puffins and Manx Shearwaters on Skomer Island. Breeding success of both species was reduced by competition for nesting burrows. Shearwaters affected puffins in two ways. First, some puffins were prevented from breeding because they could not obtain a burrow. Second, even those puffins with burrows suffered reduced breeding success because the frequent nocturnal visits by prospecting shearwaters caused between 5 and 10% of all puffin eggs to be broken or deserted. Puffins which failed in their breeding attempt were more likely to lose their burrow to a shearwater, than those which bred successfully. A similar pattern occurred in shearwaters. Ashcroft concluded that the same proportion of puffin burrows were taken over each year by shearwaters, as were shearwater burrows taken over by puffins. This balanced situation occurred because puffins had a competitive advantage over shearwaters in their (puffins) optimal habitat (i.e., close to the cliff edge—see above), whereas shearwaters were at an advantage elsewhere. Despite this balance, puffins were probably affected more by shearwater competition, than vice versa (Ashcroft 1976).

Other records of interspecific competition for breeding sites are anecdotal and can be summarized as follows. Murres of both species may displace Black-legged Kittiwakes from breeding areas (Uspenski 1956; Tuck 1961). Northern Gannets may displace Common Murres (Nelson 1978b). Black Guillemots and Razorbills at Roskaren in the Baltic compete for breeding sites since this is one of the few places where mink are absent. A similar situation apparently exists on Flatey, Iceland, where Black Guillemots and puffins compete for sites (Petersen 1979).

C. Timing of Breeding

In most alcids, as in many other bird species, individuals laying relatively early in the season are more successful in fledging young than late breeders. Seasonal declines in breeding success have been reported for all alcids which have been studied in detail. Seasonal declines in breeding success support Lack's (1954) ideas on the evolution of timing of breeding, and there are at least two explanations for this pattern. First, young birds tend to breed relatively late and because they are inexperienced, are able to rear fewer young on average than older birds (Coulson and White 1960). However, in long-lived species like auks only a small proportion of the population at any time will comprise young, inexperienced breeders, which suggests that some other factor is important. Birds which lay late may miss the peak of food abundance and be forced to rear their young when food is relatively scarce. This may affect the energy budgets of both adults and their young. Relatively poor food supplies may result in reduced parental attentiveness during incubation or brooding, which in turn may mean increased egg or chick loss as well as reduced growth rates of the young. Birds which lay late may be poor-quality individuals and less likely to rear young successfully, irrespective of the food supply. Several studies have shown that late-breeding birds produce fewer young, and also ones which are lighter in weight, or less well developed. However, as yet, the data on post-fledging survival in relation to fledging weight or fledging date do not indicate any disadvantage for light or late-hatched chicks (Hedgren 1981; Harris 1982a).

V. CORRELATES OF CHICK DEVELOPMENTAL PATTERNS

This section considers some of the selective pressures which have been important in the evolution of reproductive patterns within the Alcidae and are summarized in Table 4.7. However, to examine trends between alcid species it is necessary to include the Pacific species since the entire family apparently originated from a single North Pacific stock (see Chapter 1, this volume). By examining features which tend to be positively or negatively associated we try to explain why certain breeding patterns have evolved.

Alcids can be separated into three groups on the basis of their chick developmental patterns (see Chapter 7, this volume), which are associated with several other factors (see Table 4.8). Species with precocial

TABLE 4.7

Summary of Breeding Biology of Atlantic Auks at Certain Locations[a]

Character	Razor-bill	Common Murre	Thick-billed Murre	Dovekie	Black Guillemot	Atlantic Puffin
Adult weight (g)	628	875	899	160	400	373
Diurnal at colony	Yes	Yes	Yes	Yes	Yes	Yes
Adult diet[b]	F (C)	F	F + C	C	F + C?	F + C?
Chick diet[b]	F	F	F	C	F	F
Solitary or colonial[c]	C	C	C	C	S + C	C
Breeding site[d]	L, C	L	L	C	B, C	B, C
Chick development[e]	I	I	I	S	S	S
Incubation period (days)	35	32	32	29	28	40
Chick-rearing period (days)	17	21	21	27	34	38
Hatching weight (g)	60	67	65	21	35	40
Hatching weight as % adult weight	9.5	7.7	7.2	13.1	8.7	11
Fledging weight (g)	157	215	200	114	353	290
Fledging weight as % adult weight	25	25	22	71	88	78

[a] Razorbills on Skokholm Island, Wales (Lloyd 1976a, 1979), Common Murres on Skomer Island, Wales (Birkhead 1976a, 1977b), Thick-billed Murres on Prince Leopold Island, N.W.T. (Gaston and Nettleship 1981), Dovekie in Spitsbergen (Norderhaug 1980; Stempniewicz 1981), Black Guillemot in western Iceland (Petersen 1981), and Atlantic Puffin on Skomer Island, Wales (Ashcroft 1976, 1979).

[b] F, Fish; C, crustaceans.

[c] S, Solitary; C, colonial.

[d] L, Ledge; C, crevice; B, burrow.

[e] I, Intermediate; S, semi-precocial.

TABLE 4.8

Features of Breeding Biology of Auks, Associated with Patterns of Post-hatching Development

	Developmental pattern		
Character	Precocial	Intermediate	Semi-Precocial
Nocturnal or diurnal at breeding colony	Nocturnal	Diurnal	Diurnal (except Rhinoceros Auklet and Cassin's Auklet)
Clutch size (no. of eggs)	Two	One	One (except *Cepphus* spp.)
Breeding site	Enclosed	Open	Enclosed
Adult size	Small	Large	Intermediate
Consequences of size:			
Vulnerability to predators	High	Low	Intermediate
Relative egg size (% adult weight)	Large (22–24%)	Small (12–15%)	Intermediate (15–20%)
Relative meal size for chicks	—	Small	Medium-large

young are small, nocturnal, have enclosed breeding sites and produce a clutch of two relatively large eggs (Fig. 4.3). Intermediate species are large, diurnal and use open breeding sites. Semi-precocial species are intermediate in size, most are diurnal and all use enclosed breeding sites. Overall, there appears to be a close association between the pattern of chick development and adult body size. Alcids range in weight from 90 g (Least Auklet) to ca. 1000 g (murres); the Great Auk probably weighed ca. 5000 g. This diversity in body size probably arose as a result of interspecific competition for food and breeding sites (Bédard 1969a; Lack 1968). There are several allometric consequences of body size. There are inverse relationships between (a) body size and egg size (Fig. 4.3), (b) body size and wing loading [because the wings are used both for aerial flight and as paddles underwater, large auks have relatively small wings and high wing loadings (Watson 1968)], (c) body weight and the load which a bird can carry (Pennycuick 1969): the largest auks deliver the smallest meals (relative to adult body weight) to their chicks (Cody 1973; and see Fig. 4.6). Further consequences of size are energetic (Dunn 1979) and that small birds are more vulnerable to predators than larger ones. Because of these various effects, precocial development occurs only in the smallest auks, because the largest species would probably be physically or physiologically unable to produce an egg sufficiently large to hatch a precocial chick.

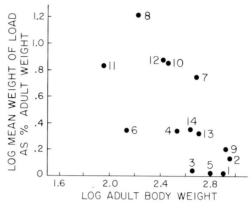

Fig. 4.6. Relationship between meal weight as a percentage of adult body weight and adult body weight in alcids. The relationship is significant ($r = -.682$, 12 df, $p < .01$), and is described by the log · log equation, $\log y = -.869 \log x + 2.69$. Numbers beside points refer to species as follows: 1, Common Murre (Birkhead 1977b); 2, Thick-billed Murre (Gaston and Nettleship 1981); 3, Pigeon Guillemot (Koelink 1972); 4, Black Guillemot (Asbirk 1979b and personal communication); 5, Razorbill (Lloyd 1976a); 6, Dovekie (Roby *et al.* 1981); 7, Rhinoceros Auklet (Vermeer *et al.* 1979; Vermeer 1980); 8, Cassin's Auklet (Manuwal 1974a); 9, Tufted Puffin (Wehle 1980); 10, Parakeet Auklet (Bédard 1969b); 11, Least Auklet (Bédard 1969b); 12, Crested Auklet (Bédard 1969b); 13, Horned Puffin (Wehle 1980); 14, Atlantic Puffin (Myrberget 1962).

The intermediate developmental pattern may be a compromise between the precocial and semi-precocial strategies. At one extreme large body size limits relative egg size (preventing precocial development), while at the other, it limits chick meal size. In both murres and the Razorbill, the mean meal size represents only 1–2% of adult body weight (whereas in the Crested Auklet it is about 7%). Partly as a consequence of this, it is impossible for these species to have semi-precocial chicks and for adults to rear them to 70 to 90% of adult body weight at the nest site (Lack 1968; Sealy 1973b; Birkhead 1977b). However, large body size does reduce heat loss and vulnerability to predators, enabling those species to use open breeding sites.

The semi-precocial species form the least homogeneous group. In body size they overlap both precocial and intermediate species, although the majority are of medium size. While small body size and nocturnal habits are linked in precocial species, this is not the case in semi-precocial auks, mainly because all but one (Cassin's Auklet) breed at high latitudes in continuous daylight. Cassin's Auklet is relatively small (ca. 160 g) and is nocturnal. The other nocturnal species, the Rhinoceros Auklet, is relatively large (ca. 520 g). All semi-precocial species breed in enclosed breeding sites which provide protection from predators and environmental conditions, and this reduces heat loss in both incubating adults and in chicks. Enclosed breeding sites offer relatively constant thermal environments for chicks to develop in. Since chicks are relatively safe from predators and from fluctuations in air temperatures, they can be left unattended, allowing both parents to forage simultaneously (unlike the intermediate species).

We have used comparative methods to produce, post hoc, adaptive explanations for the patterns in reproductive biology which occur in alcids. However, while this provides some insight into the evolution of different species' reproductive ecologies, such a discussion must remain somewhat speculative because it is impossible to test the hypotheses directly, and because of the limits of the comparative approach (Clutton-Brock and Harvey 1979; Krebs 1978).

VI. CONCLUSIONS

Our discussion has centered to a large extent on adaptive trends between species, mainly because of the nature of the available data. The type of information which we have is a result of the type of question which alcid biologists have been satisfied with answering. This has come about partly because alcids are relatively difficult to study, and partly because it is only in the last 10–20 years that study techniques have been developed. Now that we know the main features of most auks' breeding biology, we should address ourselves to questions with broader biological implications.

The most obvious gaps in our knowledge concern 'normal' variability in breeding parameters, both between seasons at the same colonies, and between colonies in different areas. We also need more information on how closely related species cope with the same environmental conditions, that is, interspecific comparisons at the same colonies at the same time. Finally, recent advances in theoretical ecology have been made by considering differences *between individuals* of the same species, by integrating studies of breeding ecology, social behaviour and population dynamics to consider reproductive regimes, and overall life-history strategies. The few long-term studies of individually marked seabirds are now yielding exciting results in this field.

CHAPTER 5

Population Parameters for the Atlantic Alcidae

PETER J. HUDSON

The Game Conservancy, Leyburn, North Yorkshire, England

I. INTRODUCTION

The auks in the North Atlantic are currently at risk from humanity's pollution and exploitation of the marine environment. Before conserva-

THE ATLANTIC ALCIDAE

tion and management techniques can be implemented, it is necessary to understand the factors which influence the survival, recruitment and productivity of these species and to know how such factors interact so that predictions can be made of future population trends. This and the preceding two chapters review and summarize the data currently available in an attempt to highlight areas requiring further research and to act as a source of information to those conducting comparative studies or constructing management plans for alcid species under threat.

II. POPULATION TRENDS

A. Censusing Auk Populations

The location and size of many auk colonies has been well documented (Chapter 2, this volume), but the accuracy of censusing techniques has only recently been investigated. It is now apparent that standardized methods (Birkhead and Nettleship 1980; Wanless *et al.* 1982; Stowe 1982a) are essential if counts are to be meaningful and comparable (also see Chapter 10, this volume). The auks are a difficult group to census with precision as numbers vary with the time of day, weather and phase of the breeding cycle (Corkhill 1971). Even during the period of least variation counts of some species can vary by as much as 46% away from the mean (Lloyd 1975). In some instances the structure and size of a colony can make detailed counts impossible.

Census work has two objectives: first, to provide an estimate of population size, and second, if repeated at regular intervals, to detect any change in bird numbers. Assessing the size of a population requires the location and plotting of all breeding pairs or breeding sites. Changes in population status are more difficult to determine and require regular counts, conducted in a standardised manner at selected study colonies (Stowe 1982a). Any change in the methods used could invalidate results as observed differences may be attributable to changes in technique. Further information on the census techniques used in the field can be found in Nettleship (1976a), Birkhead and Nettleship (1980), Evans (1980) and Chapters 2 and 10 of this volume.

B. Population Changes

At a number of auk colonies a series of single counts has been conducted and—bearing in mind the biases outlined above—may indicate population trends. A selection of these counts is presented in Table 5.1.

The data in this table were chosen to represent the best estimates available taken over a time span of several years, from wherever possible, large colonies in different areas of the Atlantic. Generally, the alcid population in the southeast Atlantic and Greenland show declines in numbers whereas many colonies in the Baltic and Newfoundland–Labrador have increased (see Chapter 2, this volume).

Given the limitations of the data available, Table 5.1 indicates that auk populations have rarely been stable for long periods during this century. Most appear to be slowly increasing or decreasing, although these gradual trends are frequently punctuated with sudden declines. These decreases tend to be associated with mass mortalities caused by natural or human-induced disasters. The frequency of human-induced disasters seem to be increasing, with oiling incidents frequently killing large numbers of birds (see Chapter 10, this volume). Tull et al. (1972) record that the mortality of Thick-billed Murres, caused mostly by hunting and salmon nets, off the west coast of Greenland probably exceeds the annual production of young in that region so it is hardly surprising these colonies are declining rapidly. Sudden declines in a population may also cause some kind of secondary effect and so accelerate a population decline. For example, Birkhead (1977a) suggests the decline of the Common Murre on Skomer Island, Wales, has reduced the density of breeding groups and exposed the eggs and chicks of the remaining birds to gull predation.

Some gradual changes in alcid populations may relate to natural, climatic or oceanographic changes. Tuck (1961) notes that since the decline of many Common Murre colonies in Atlantic Canada, only those influenced by the Labrador Current (southern Labrador and eastern Newfoundland) have subsequently increased. Similarly, Harris (1976a) recorded population trends of the Atlantic Puffin in British waters and suggested recent increases could be associated with the cooling-off of ocean temperatures and an increase in the abundance of cold-water marine species, although direct evidence for such a relationship is weak. (See Chapter 10 of this volume for details.) However, these small and localised increases in both murres and puffins do not off-set the major declines which have occurred since the turn of this century (Bourne 1968; Nettleship 1977a).

III. MORTALITY FACTORS

Information on the factors associated with the death of alcids tends to come from two sources. The first reports birds dying from specific causes such as oil fouling (e.g., Greenwood 1969), the ingestion of rubber thread

TABLE 5.1

Recent Population Changes at Some Auk Colonies in the Atlantic[a]

Species and colony area	Estimated number of pairs[b]	Period	Percentage change per annum[c]	References
Common Murre				
Funk I., Nfld.	10,000 → 400,000	1936–1972	+10	Tuck (1961); Nettleship (1980)
Stora Karlsö, Sweden	35,000 → 6,400	1950–1974	−7	Hedgren (1975)
Sør Fugløy, Norway	10,000 → 10	1940–1974	−28	Brun (1979)
Handa I., Scotland	38,390 → 30,790	1962–1970	−3	Cramp et al. (1974)
Great Saltee I., S. Ireland	14,500 → 9,670	1967–1970	−13	Cramp et al. (1974)
Bempton, England	12,950 → 12,600	1964–1970	0	Cramp et al. (1974)
Skomer I., Wales	5,000 → 1,600	1930–1978	−2.4	Hudson (1979a)
Thick-billed Murre				
Guba Bezymyannaya, Novaya Zemlya	822,250 → 290,000	1934–1948	−7	Tuck (1961)
Guba Bezymyannaya, Novaya Zemlya	290,000 → 371,000	1948–1950	+12	Tuck (1961)
Kipako, Greenland	30,000 → 5,700	1935–1974	−4	Evans and Waterson (1976)
Sanderson Hope, Greenland	100,000 → 18,000	1935–1974	−4	Evans and Waterson (1976)
Razorbill				
Roskaren, Sweden	15 → 55	1954–1973	+7	Olsson (1974)
Handa I., Scotland	5,340 → 8,370	1962–1970	+6	Cramp et al. (1974)

Great Saltee I., S. Ireland	10,000 → 5,800	1960–1970	−6	Cramp et al. (1974)
Bempton, England	2,130 → 1,730	1964–1974	−3	Cramp et al. (1974)
Skomer I., Wales	1,966 → 1,572	1963–1978	−1	Hudson (1979a)
Black Guillemot				
Nordre Rønner, Denmark	100 → 450	1920–1977	+3	Asbirk (1978)
Kent I., Bay of Fundy	40 → 43	1935–1965	0	Preston (1968)
Priest I., Scotland	85 → 10	1938–1969	−7	Cramp et al. (1974)
Cape Clear, S. Ireland	44 → 39	1963–1969	−2	Cramp et al. (1974)
Flatey, Iceland	1 → 417	1966–1977	+5	Petersen (1981)
Atlantic Puffin				
Disko Bay, Greenland	300 → 1,500	1960–1975	+11	Harris (1976a)
Ostrova Aynovskiye, Murmansk	20,000 → 11,980	1928–1960	−2	Harris (1976a)
Les Sept Iles, France	7,000 → 400	1950–1973	−12	Harris (1976a)
N. Rona I., Scotland	8,000 → 6,200	1957–1972	−2	Evans (1975)
Great Saltee I., S. Ireland	437 → 375	1968–1972	−2	Harris (1976a)
Isle of May, Scotland	35 → 3,000	1883–1975	+5	Harris (1976d)
Skomer I., Wales	50,000 → 5,850	1946–1973	−8	Birkhead and Ashcroft (1975)

[a] Colonies given represent general population trends in different parts of the Atlantic.

[b] Where sources referred to number of individuals, these figures were divided by two to present the estimates in pairs.

[c] Percentage change calculated as r from the exponential equation: $N_t = N_o e^{rt}$ where N_t = number of pairs after period t (in years) and N_o = initial population size. This assumes an exponential increase or decrease between the first and second estimate of bird numbers.

(Parslow and Jefferies 1972), and the drowning of birds in nets (King *et al.* 1979). The second reports the proportion of banded birds recovered and the factors associated with death. Data from both sources can be informative, but may not indicate the relative importance of mortality factors since the recovery of a corpse can be associated with one or several factors. For example, starving birds are likely to be more vulnerable to predators, pollution, oiling and disease so an incidental factor rather than starvation may be recorded as the cause of death. Obviously further research is required to elucidate the significance of ultimate and proximate factors influencing death.

A. Reports of Causes of Death

Many reports exist on the factors associated with the death of auks and a number of more significant ones are summarized in Table 5.2. Lack of space does not allow a detailed discussion of these and the reader should consult the references therein or review papers by Bourne (1968, 1976) and Nettleship (1977a). Not surprisingly the factors often reported are those associated with human activities.

B. Factors Associated with the Recovery of Banded Birds

There are four main mortality factors frequently recorded with the recovery of a banded bird, namely, oiled, shot, found dead, and caught in fishing gear. Most recoveries fall into the 'found dead' category and this includes all birds where the cause of death cannot be discerned and as such will include a number from the other categories. Banding recoveries are influenced by many biases and a number of these are discussed in Section IV on adult survival.

The data available from the analysis of banding returns is summarized in Table 5.3. This consists primarily of the extensive analysis of British banded auks by Mead (1974), Lloyd (1974) and Birkhead (1974), and includes Petersen's (1981) collation of Icelandic and Scandinavian recoveries for Black Guillemots. A number of other workers (Olsson 1974) have published banding recoveries, but so few birds have been recorded, and details are often lacking, that these have not been included.

The results from the banding recoveries of the Razorbill, Common Murre and Atlantic Puffin are very similar: the majority of birds are found dead, few birds are caught in nets, and there is a tendency for young birds to be shot and older birds oiled. These findings reflect the interaction of three factors: (1) a variation in mortality from one region to another, (2)

TABLE 5.2

A Summary of Factors Recorded Causing Death of Auks

Mortality factor	Frequency of occurrence	Region of Atlantic[a]	Species[b]	References
Natural factors				
Predation	Abundant	SE, NE, N, NW, SW	CM, TBM, R, AP, BG, D	Uspenski (1956); Tuck (1961): Evans (1975); Petersen (1981)
Disease and predators	Several	SE, NE	CM, TBM, R, AP, BG	Uspenski (1956); Bourne et al. (1970); Bourne (1971); Threlfall (1971)
Starvation	Many	SE, NE, NW	CM, D	Uspenski (1956): Bailey and Davenport (1972)
Poor weather	Several	NE, SE, NW	CM, TBM, D	Dement'ev et al. (1951); Sergeant (1952); Tuck (1961); Holdgate (1971)
Human-induced factors				
Fishing nets	Many	NE, N, NW	CM, TBM, R, AP, BG	Tull et al. (1972); Evans and Waterson (1976); King et al. (1979)
Hunting	Numerous	NE, N, NW	CM, TBM, R, AP, BG, D	Dixon (1970); Ainley and Lewis (1974); Salomonsen (1979c); Wendt and Cooch (1984)
Oil pollution	Numerous	SE, NE, NW, SW	CM, TBM, R, AP, D	Bourne (1968); Greenwood et al. (1971)
Toxic chemicals	Few	SE, SW, NW	CM, AP	Parslow et al. (1972); Bourne (1976); Harris and Osborn (1981)
Ingestion of artifacts	Few	SE, NE	AP	Berland (1971); Parslow and Jefferies (1972)

[a] Areas of report: SE, British Isles and south of Netherlands; NE, Scandinavia and Russia; N, Greenland and Iceland; NW, Canada; SW, United States.

[b] Species: CM, Common Murre; TBM, Thick-billed Murre; R, Razorbill; AP, Atlantic Puffin; D, Dovekie; BG, Black Guillemot.

TABLE 5.3

Percentage Recovery of Banded Auks Relative to Age and Recovery Method[a]

		Recovery method (%)			
Species and age	Number of recoveries	Found dead	Oiled	Nets	Shot
Common Murre					
First year	248	42	20	5	33
Immature	135	47	39	4	10
Adult	121	49	34	5	12
Razorbill					
First year	283	47	8	11	34
Immature	155	46	23	5	26
Adult	173	60	29	1	10
Atlantic Puffin					
Immature	43	46	21	5	28
Adult	133	75	17	3	5
Black Guillemot					
All ages	515	27	2	38	33

[a] Results for the Razorbill, Common Murre and Atlantic Puffin come from Mead (1974) and the Black Guillemot from Petersen (1981).

differential movement of birds of different ages, and (3) the relative experience of birds with respect to age.

The variation in cause of recovery by region within the northeast Atlantic is demonstrated for the Razorbill and Common Murre in Fig. 5.1. This shows that in Scandinavian waters both species are more likely to be shot, whereas in British waters they are more likely to be oiled. In the northwest Atlantic the major cause of death is by shooting and drowning in fishing gear (Nettleship 1977a and personal communication; Kampp 1982; Piatt et al. 1984; Wendt and Cooch 1984).

In the northeast Atlantic young auks tend to be shot and old birds oiled (Table 5.3), indicating that young birds move into northern waters while the adults remain close to the breeding colony. However, young birds are less experienced and may therefore be more vulnerable to mortality factors such as hunting. In their first year of life alcids tend to be recovered within the months September–November after fledging, while the peak mortality for adults is several months later between January and March. These differences may be associated with the adults' experience and being able to withstand poor conditions for a longer period of time (Mead 1974).

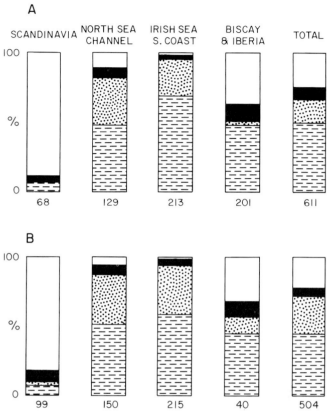

Fig. 5.1. Bar charts indicating recovery method (%) by locality for (A) the Razorbill and (B) Common Murre. ⊟, Found dead; ⊞, oiled; ■, drowned in nets; □, shot (after Mead 1974). Numbers indicate number of birds recovered for each locality. Note that regional patterns for the two species are very similar.

C. Auk Wrecks

Occasionally large numbers of seabirds are washed ashore in what is generally termed a 'wreck'. These consist predominantly of auks and petrels, and in many instances only a single species is involved. Many wrecks of the Dovekie have been recorded on both sides of the Atlantic, and these tend to occur during January and February, usually further south than their normal range (e.g., Florida: Murphy and Vogt 1933; British Isles: Sergeant 1952). The birds have been observed moving south in large numbers and subsequently found blown ashore, usually in an emaciated condition after a period of inclement weather (Sprunt 1938). Sergeant (1952) suggested the initial southerly movement may be due to the plankton food supply failing in the Arctic.

Wrecks of the larger auks are less frequent (Holdgate 1971) and usually occur in August and September when the birds are moulting and flightless. Again, these wrecks are often associated with poor weather conditions (Tuck 1961; Dement'ev, *et al.* 1951) which may be a major determinant (Bailey and Davenport 1972) or contributive cause of a wreck (Holdgate 1971). Birkhead (1976b) observed that Common Murres had difficulty in obtaining food for their chicks during heavy seas. Conceivably, adult murres may also find it difficult locating food for themselves during poor weather. Starvation in conjunction with poor weather is probably the most important single cause of natural mortality for the Atlantic alcids, but the effects of malnutrition can become accentuated by other factors such as oiling, disease and the effects of organic and metallic residues.

IV. SURVIVAL RATES OF ADULT AUKS

The annual adult survival rates of auks have been estimated by a number of methods, but most frequently from analyses of banding recoveries or the marking and subsequent resighting of individually colour-banded birds. The colour-banding technique tends to produce a more accurate estimate, but both procedures suffer from a number of biases. Some of these are reviewed below before survival estimates are presented.

A. Biases Influencing the Estimation of Survival Rates

1. BAND WEAR

Coulson and White (1955) indicated that the bands put on seabirds are often subjected to a great deal of wear and can fall off within a few years of banding. This problem is exacerbated in the murres and Razorbill, which tend to shuffle over rocks on their tarsii, an action which leads to rapid band wear and loss. For example, Lloyd and Perrins (1977) found that many of the early bands used on Razorbills did not last for more than 2 years.

One way of minimizing the bias caused by band wear is to use Haldane's (1955) method of analysis for 'middle-aged' birds only, as Mead (1974) has done for British alcids. He used only those birds recovered after the high mortality experienced by immature birds, but before band wear among old birds became important. Mead's results indicate that band wear may overestimate mortality by as much as 50% in some auk species (e.g., 12% as opposed to 6.3% in the Common Murre).

2. BREEDING-SITE FIDELITY AND COLONY INTERCHANGE OF ADULTS

In a study of banded birds, the movement of adults from one breeding area to another may result in birds being assumed dead and mortality rates over-estimated. Lloyd and Perrins (1977) did not record any breeding Razorbills emigrating from the colony, nor did Harris (1976d) for breeding Atlantic Puffins or Asbirk (1979b) and Petersen (1982) for breeding Black Guillemots, although all recorded the movement of immatures between colonies. Fidelity to the breeding site is high in all species: 91.5%, Razorbill (Lloyd 1976a); 96%, Common Murre (Birkhead 1977a); 93.2%, Atlantic Puffin (Ashcroft 1979); 57–79%, Black Guillemot (Asbirk 1979b); and probably high in the Thick-billed Murre (Gaston and Nettleship 1981). A number of factors can result in birds changing breeding sites such as reproductive failures, loss of mate or disturbance. To minimize the effects of banding disturbance in estimating adult survival, it is probably best if data from the first year after banding are excluded from the analysis.

A number of factors will influence whether an established breeder will not only change breeding sites but also emigrate from a population. One such factor will be the state of the local population; birds may be expected to move from a decreasing population to an expanding population if they are likely to contribute more to future generations by doing so. It is possible that such a move may result in a short-term decrease in reproductive output, but the change can be considered profitable if the lifetime production of offspring is increased.

3. FACTORS INFLUENCING THE RECOVERY OF DEAD BIRDS

Several factors may influence whether a banded bird is subsequently recovered: (1) where the bird dies: the density and vigilance of observers will vary around the coastline, and a large proportion of birds that die will probably not be washed ashore; (2) how the bird dies: birds shot or caught in nets are more likely to be recovered than birds dying far out at sea; and (3) the age of a bird: different-aged birds tend to be recovered in different regions (Mead 1974). In reality, a combination of these factors determine whether a banded bird is likely to be recovered or not.

B. Adult Survival Estimates

The survival estimates for adult auks are presented in Table 5.4. They come from a number of different studies utilising different methods, so the

TABLE 5.4

Annual Survival Estimates for Adult Atlantic Auks

Species and study area	Method of estimate	Survival estimates (%)	References
Razorbill			
British Isles	Banding recoveries	89.0	Lloyd (1974)
British Isles	Corrected banding recoveries	91.4	Mead (1974)
Skokholm I., Wales	Colour bands	80.7	Lloyd and Perrins (1977)
Bluffs, Skokholm I., Wales	Colour bands	89.0	Lloyd and Perrins (1977)
Clò Mór, Scotland	Colour bands	96.0	Parslow, in Lloyd and Perrins (1977)
Skomer I., Wales	Colour bands	89.8	Hudson (1979a)
Shiant Is., Scotland	Capture–recapture	92.0	Steventon (1979)
Common Murre			
British Isles	Banding recoveries	87.9	Birkhead (1974)
British Isles	Corrected banding recoveries	93.7	Mead (1974)
Helgoland, Germany	Corrected banding recoveries	87.0	Mead (1974)
Skomer I., Wales	Colour bands	90.4	Birkhead and Hudson (1977); Hudson (1979a)
N.E. Scotland	Colour bands	87.0	Southern et al. (1965)
Thick-billed Murre			
N.E. Canada	Banding recoveries	91.0	Birkhead and Hudson (1977)
Atlantic Puffin			
British Isles	Corrected banding recoveries	90.1	Mead (1974)
Skomer I., Wales	Colour bands	88.8	Ashcroft (1979); Hudson (1979a)
Skomer I., Wales	Colour bands—burrow owners	95.0	Ashcroft (1979)
Isle of May, Scotland	Colour bands	94.4	M. P. Harris (personal communication)
Great I., Nfld.	Colour bands	95.0	Nettleship (1972 and personal communication)
Ostrova Aynovskiye, Murmansk	Colour bands	95.0	Skokova (1967)
Black Guillemot			
Kent I., Bay of Fundy	Colour bands	94.4	Preston (1968)
Nordre Rønner, Denmark	Colour bands	85.3	Asbirk (1979b)
Flatey, Iceland	Colour bands	83.3	Petersen (1981)

biases differ and make direct comparisons difficult. The variation within each species is approximately 10%. Although that appears reasonably low, variation in life expectancy will, however, be large. For example, a bird with a mean adult survival rate of 85% could expect to live for a further 6.2 years, whereas a bird with a 95% survival rate could expect a further 19.5 years of life.

The survival rates for all species are relatively similar (ca. 90%) with the exception of the Black Guillemot (81–85.3%). The lower survival rate for Black Guillemots may be associated with its large clutch size and its younger age at time of first breeding.

C. The Incidence of Non-breeding among Adult Auks

A number of long-term studies on seabirds have noted that proportion of experienced breeders (i.e., excluding those that have lost their mate or breeding site) will refrain from breeding during one or more seasons during their life (Wooler and Coulson 1977; Ainley and DeMaster 1980). Ashcroft (1979) found that 5–16% of adult Atlantic Puffins, known to have bred previously and still occupying a breeding site, did not attempt to breed every year. Similarly, Lloyd and Perrins (1977) found that in each year a small but variable proportion of adult Razorbills did not breed.

One explanation for this phenomenon comes from some theoretical studies which indicate that there is likely to be a balance between the production of young and the costs of breeding to the adult (Williams 1966; Gadgill and Bossert 1970; Wiley 1974). In long-lived species like the alcids, the cost of breeding may be measured in terms of reduced survivorship, as any small decrease in the probability of survival will reduce life expectancy and, consequently, the number of years available for breeding. The costs of breeding and their influence on the probability of survival have not been investigated in detail among the auks. However, Asbirk (1979b) found that Black Guillemots laying two eggs, but not feeding any chicks to fledging, had a survival rate of 92%, a value greater than that for birds laying two eggs and feeding the chicks to fledging (85%). Although this difference was not statistically significant (S. Asbirk, personal communication), these results suggest the process of breeding may have some effect on adult survival in Black Guillemots. The work by Ainley and DeMaster (1980) provides an interesting way in which breeding costs influence the survival of adult Adelie Penguins. The annual survival rate of breeding Adelies was 60.5%, significantly lower than the 78.2% of the non-breeding adults. The reason for this difference is due in part to predation by Leopard Seals which patrol near the colony and take penguins as they enter or leave the water. As the breeders must obtain food for their offspring, they pass the seals more frequently than the nonbreeders, and are thus exposed to predation more often. In this example, some of the costs of breeding are borne out during the breeding season, but it is possible that the energetic costs of breeding may not become apparent until a later date when the birds are subjected to extreme conditions. Ashcroft (1979) recorded non-breeding in Atlantic Puffins in each of the 3 years studied, but the greatest proportion did not attempt to breed in one year when feeding conditions prior to egg-laying were probably poor and egg-laying late. Similarly, in the season following poor weather conditions or a seabird wreck, the size of the breeding population present at the colony often falls dramatically, but then increases in the following 2–3 years. This subsequent increase is often assumed to be due to an increase in immigration or increased recruitment into the breeding population (e.g., Common Murres on Skomer Island; Birkhead and Hudson 1977), but it may also be related to experienced breeders missing one or more breeding seasons and rejoining the population in the following years.

V. AGE OF FIRST BREEDING

Like many long-lived bird species, the alcids do not commence breeding until several years old. Most records for the age of first breeding are obtained from birds banded as chicks and subsequently found breeding; in some instances it may be possible to age a young bird by plumage (e.g., Black Guillemot: Asbirk 1978) or physical characteristics (e.g., Atlantic Puffin; Petersen 1976a).

Data for the age of first breeding in Atlantic auks are summarized in Table 5.5. In general, the Common Murre, Razorbill and Atlantic Puffin begin to breed when about 5 years old, whereas Black Guillemots start at an earlier age. There are three records of Black Guillemots breeding at 2 years of age. Asbirk (1979b) indicates this difference may be related to differences in feeding habits; he suggests that breeding costs for the alcids may be related to the distance between the breeding site and feeding location; among Atlantic alcids this distance is least in the Black Guillemot (see Chapter 6, this volume). Another approach is to consider the relationship between survival and age of first breeding where there is a tendency for species with high survival rates to defer maturity for longer than species with a lower survival rate. Excluding Dovekies, for which there are no data, the Black Guillemot has the lowest survival rate of all Atlantic alcids and commences breeding at a younger age. As these features probably arose together to balance reproductive output and costs, it is not possible to say what may have influenced one and not the other.

TABLE 5.5

Records for the Age of First Breeding for Some Atlantic Auks

Species and study area	Number breeding for first time at age (years)[a]							References
	2	3	4	5	6	7	8+	
Razorbill								
Skokholm I., Wales	0	0	7	12	1	0	0	Lloyd and Perrins (1977)
Common Murre								
Skomer I., Wales	0	0	2	1	3	–	–	Hudson (1979a)
Stora Karlsö, Sweden	0	0	0	+	?	?	?	S. Hedgren (personal communication)
Atlantic Puffin								
Vestmannaeyjar, Iceland	0	0	0	5	9	0	6	Petersen (1976b)
Skomer I., Wales	0	1	4	–	–	–	–	Ashcroft (1979)
Isle of May, Scotland	0	1	5	7	15	12	14	Harris (1981)
St. Kilda, Scotland	0	0	3	7	1	2	–	Harris (1981)
Farne Is., England	0	0	0	3	5	8	26	Harris (1981)
Black Guillemot								
Kent I., Bay of Fundy	0	0	1	–	–	–	–	Preston (1968)
Nordre Rønner, Denmark	2	–	–	–	–	–	–	Asbirk (1979b)
Denmark	–	–	–	1	–	–	–	Andersen-Harild (1969)
Fair Isle, Scotland	–	–	2	1	3	3	1	Broad, in Petersen (1981)
Sweden	1	–	–	–	–	–	–	Unger, in Petersen (1981)

[a] –, no birds available to breed; +, single cohort only observed.

In some seabird species male and female may commence breeding at different ages (Richdale 1957; Wooler and Coulson 1977). Lloyd and Perrins (1977) found no evidence of this among a small sample ($N = 20$) of Razorbills breeding for the first time. Petersen (1976b) inspected the oviduct (female) and bursa fabricus (male) of 91 Atlantic Puffins and found some evidence that males may commence breeding at a younger age than females.

The fact that auks do not breed until they are several years old may appear maladaptive at first sight since the production of even a small number of young during this period may be selectively advantageous. It seems unlikely that physiological reasons alone would prevent young birds breeding. As discussed earlier, a number of theoretical studies expect long-lived species to balance the costs of breeding (measured in terms of reduced survivorship) against the long-term production of young, in order to maximize their contribution to future generations (Fisher 1958). If the relative costs of breeding decrease with age and, perhaps experience, then the optimal age of first breeding may not be until an individual is several years old (Goodman 1974). The optimal age will vary depending on the condition, experience and sex of the individual. It may also depend on the state of the population; for example, birds may commence breeding at a younger age in an expanding population (Coulson and White 1960; Williams and Joanen 1974) or when favourable breeding sites become available (Potts *et al.* 1980).

VI. RETURN OF IMMATURE AUKS TO THE
BREEDING COLONY

In common with other seabirds exhibiting deferred maturity, immature auks return to the colony several years before attempting to breed for the first time. These immature birds are frequently seen interacting with other immatures close to areas occupied by breeders. This section presents information on the age and behaviour of these immature birds at the breeding colony.

A. Date and Percentage Return by Age

Occasionally alcids in their first year of life are observed at the breeding colony, but these are rare. Out of more than 700 Atlantic Puffins banded, Harris (1983a) recorded only nine (1%) sightings of yearlings. Asbirk (1979b) states that small numbers of 1-year-old Black Guillemots were seen at a breeding colony in Denmark. In studies of the Razorbill and Common Murre in Wales (Birkhead and Hudson 1977; Lloyd and Perrins 1977; Hudson 1979a), no 1-year-old birds were recorded at the breeding colony, although occasionally birds in winter plumage were seen and these may have been in their first year of life.

The pattern of return by age is similar in all species studied (Table 5.6), but there may be some variation between colonies (e.g., 2- and 3-year-old Atlantic Puffins on the Isle of May, Scotland, have been recorded at the colony earlier in the season than birds of similar age on Skomer Island, Wales). Generally, 2-year-old birds return during late incubation, 3-year-olds during early incubation, and older birds before laying. Many 4- and 5-year-old birds are present at the colony sufficiently early in the season to attempt breeding.

The percentage of chicks banded and observed at the colony in subsequent years is shown in Table 5.7, and is similar in each species. Few 2-

year-olds are observed, and the percentage of banded birds seen increases with age. In the Common Murre and Razorbill the values for the older birds are likely to be underestimates as band wear and loss increases with age. It is possible that a greater proportion of the young birds were present than actually recorded, as 2- and 3- year-olds tend to spend less time per visit at the colony than older birds (e.g., Razorbill; Lloyd and Perrins 1977). No quantitative data exist on the return of Black Guillemots to the natal colony, but Asbirk (1979b) recorded yearlings at the colony.

B. Behaviour of Immatures at the Breeding Colony

Immature Common Murres are frequently observed in gatherings on tidal rocks in what Birkhead and Hudson (1977) refer to as 'clubs'. At Skomer Island, 72% of birds in clubs were 3 years old, with fewer 2- and 4-year-olds (Hudson 1979a). Attendance at the clubs commenced before egg-laying and slowly increased until peak numbers were reached during the time relating to the mid-incubation period of the breeding populations (Birkhead and Hudson 1977; Hudson 1979a). Immature murres on clubs performed sexual behaviour more frequently than immatures on breeding ledges (Hudson 1979a). Only the older birds are seen on the breeding ledges and the proportion of 3-year-olds visiting ledges increased as the season progressed (Birkhead and Hudson 1977). The percentage of immatures observed in temporary pairs also increased with age (Hudson 1979a). These results suggest that immature Common Murres may meet prospective mates in clubs prior to visiting the breeding ledges.

Pennycuick (1956) noted that in Thick-billed Murres in Greenland, non-breeders congregated on rocks near breeding sites where they performed sexual behaviour. However, Gaston and Nettleship (1981) reported no congregations of Thick-billed Murres similar to those in Common Murres.

C. Discussion on the Return of Immatures

It is common among those seabirds exhibiting deferred maturity for the immature birds to return to the breeding colony several years before attempting to breed (Belopol'skii 1957; Lack 1968). The following discussion identifies some of the possible advantages and disadvantages in returning to the colony prior to breeding.

The return to the breeding colony by immatures may be considered adaptive if this behaviour contributes to the animals' reproductive success. This could be achieved if the returning birds obtained information on prospective breeding sites, mates, neighbours, and the profitability of

TABLE 5.6

Date of First Sighting for Known-aged Auks[a]

Species and study area	Year	Age of birds (years)					References
		1	2	3	4	5	
Razorbill							
Skokholm I., Wales	1963–1973	0	9 June	15 May	1 May	6 May	Lloyd and Perrins (1977), estimated from Fig. 3
Common Murre							
Skomer I., Wales	1974	0	8 June	—	—	—	Birkhead and Hudson (1977); Hudson (1979a)
	1975	0	27 May	13 May	—	—	
	1976	0	11 June	28 May	10 April*	—	
	1977	—	17 June	18 May	21 April	12 April	
	1978	—	—	26 May	23 April	12 April*	
	x̄ dates		9 June	21 May	18 April	11 April	
Atlantic Puffin							
Skomer I., Wales	1973	0	20 July	9 June	16 April	—	Ashcroft (1979); Hudson (1979a)
	1974	0	16 July	16 June	23 April	—	
	1975	0	18 July	28 June	11 April	6 April*	
	1977	0	23 June	23 June	23 April	16 April*	
	1978	0	19 June	16 June	23 April	23 April*	
	x̄ dates		7 July	18 June	18 April	15 April	
Isle of May, Scotland	1975	0	17 June	—	—	—	Harris (1983a)
	1976	29 July	4 July	17 May	—	—	
	1977	0	15 June	30 April	11 April	—	
	1978	16 July	1 June	13 April	30 March	29 March	
	1979	0	16 May	8 May	10 April	9 April	
	1980	3 July	27 June	16 April	7 April	31 April	
	x̄ dates	16 July	9 June	29 April	9 April	14 April	

[a] 0, no birds sighted; *, first observations of the year, birds may have been present earlier; —, no birds available for sighting.

TABLE 5.7

Percentage Return of Immature Auks to Their Natal Colony in Relation to Age[a]

Species and study area	1	2	3	4	5	6	References

Species and study area	Age of birds (years) 1	2	3	4	5	6	References
Razorbill							
Skokholm I., Wales	0	3.2	11.0	17.8	—	—	Lloyd and Perrins (1977)
Common Murre							
Skokholm I., Wales	0	3.9	13.5	19.3	12.7	16.3	Birkhead and Hudson (1977); Hudson (1979a)
Atlantic Puffin							
Skokholm I., Wales	0	4.2	10.8	12.8	13.0	—	Ashcroft (1979)[b]
Isle of May, Scotland	Few	5.1	6.4	9.2	5.1	4.3	Harris (1983a)

[a] Figures are mean percentage of chicks banded, seen in subsequent years. —, No birds available for resighting.

[b] Ashcroft (1979) presents figures as a range; these figures represent the centre of this range.

feeding areas. Such information may help to alleviate the costs of breeding and improve future survival chances. Peak mortality in adult alcids occurs during mid-winter (Mead 1974), and may be considered the period of greatest danger for all birds. As immature birds do not have any restrictions from breeding, we can expect them to maximize their survival chances during winter by visiting areas of profitable feeding and delaying any biological process that may endanger their future survival chances. In boreal regions such as Britain, immature auks tend to move farther from the breeding colony than the adults in winter (Lloyd 1974; Mead 1974); but whether they visit more productive feeding areas is not known. Adult Atlantic Puffins moult during mid-winter, but the immatures do not moult until the early summer, perhaps to reduce the energy demand during the critical winter months. A consequence of delaying the moult until spring or early summer may be that young birds are prevented from returning earlier to the colony. Indeed, differential movement and moulting according to age may account for the observed differences in return times of different ages.

A major disadvantage to the birds returning to the colony, but not breeding, is the increased risk of predation. At some colonies predation pressure can be severe and many inexperienced immature birds are killed. For example, at St. Kilda, Scotland, Great Black-backed Gulls kill about 2600 Atlantic Puffins each year from a population of ca. 40,000 pairs, and of those killed, 43% are immatures (Harris 1980). Immature puffins spend a lot of time circling the colony (Petersen 1976b; Hudson 1979a; D. N. Nettleship, personal communication), perhaps to gain information on flight lines and escape routes.

VII. SURVIVAL OF IMMATURES TO BREEDING AGE

Direct estimates of immature survival are often difficult to make and subject to a number of biases. Some of these have already been discussed in Section IV (Survival Rates of Adult Auks), but perhaps the most important bias in estimating survival is emigration, a factor rarely monitored in population studies. This section first examines the problem of emigration, and then presents a number of survival estimates calculated in different ways.

A. Emigration and Intercolony Movements of Immature Auks

It has become apparent from a number of recent seabird studies (Brooke 1977; Harris 1983a) that the emigration of immature birds can greatly influence estimates of survival to breeding age. It is therefore necessary to monitor the degree of emigration and immigration before any detailed life tables for the species are constructed. The main difficulty with this is that observers tend to concentrate their search efforts at the colonies where birds were banded. Ideally, neighbouring colonies should be visited regularly, or at least until no new sightings or recoveries are recorded.

A number of alcid studies have recorded rapid population increases. Those increases are often thought to be too large to have come from the populations' own productivity, and can probably be accounted for only by large-scale immigration (Leslie 1966). The Atlantic Puffin population on the Isle of May increased from 5 to about 3000 breeding pairs within only 16 years; part of this increase was due to immigration of immature and failed breeders from neighbouring islands (Harris 1976d). Petersen (1981) recorded a population increase in Black Guillemots on Flatey, Iceland, and by using a simple computer model concluded that the increase seemed likely to have been due to immigration. The model estimated that the percentage of immigrants recruited into the population decreased from 100% (in 1970) to 82% (in 1977), as more birds produced by the resident breeding population reached maturity and, presumably, as the colony increased in size. Petersen concluded that some of the immigrants came from mainland colonies where predation by feral mink was high.

Immature auks are frequently recorded at great distances from their natal colonies, and this seems to be the case during both the breeding season and the winter months. Analyses of banding recoveries demonstrate that immatures are recovered farther away from their natal colony than adults from their breeding colony (Lloyd 1974; Mead 1974). A number of studies have also recorded immature birds visiting other breeding colonies (Lloyd and Perrins 1977; Asbirk 1979b; Ashcroft 1979; Harris 1983a). However, the only study to provide quantitative estimates of emigration among alcids has been by Harris (1983a) on the Atlantic Puffin. He examined recoveries of immatures banded on the Isle of May, Scotland, where numbers are rapidly increasing, and estimated that about 23% of fledglings produced at that site subsequently bred at other locations.

The probability that an immature bird will visit other colonies depends on the number and location of other breeding stations relative to its natal site. Those colonies close to the natal colony, and in areas that birds pass regularly on migration, will be visited more often. Whether an individual eventually breeds in another colony will depend on the status of the population. Advantages in returning to, and breeding in, the natal colony include the fact that the bird's parents (similar genetic constitution) were successful there, and that the bird may well be related to its neighbours. Advantages in moving to another colony may include contributing proportionately more offspring to future generations if the colony is increasing or more productive breeding sites are available.

B. Survival Estimates for Immature Auks

In this section, a number of survival estimates to breeding age are presented. Age of first breeding is considered to be 5 years (see Section V) for all species other than the Black Guillemot, where it is taken as 4 years (Petersen 1981). Techniques for estimating survival include the analysis of banding recoveries (e.g., Haldane 1955) and observations of the percentage return of colour-marked immature birds (see Section VI). For the larger alcid species (Razorbill and murres) survival to 4 years of age is calculated and, due to band loss at this age, adult survival to 5 years assumed. But other methods do exist including the following three. First, the technique devised by Birkhead and Hudson (1977) and used by Hudson (1979a) for Common Murres where chick production in year 'N' is compared with the proportion of 4-year-old birds in the clubs during year '$N + 4$'. Second, the use of Gaston and Nettleship's (1981) estimate of nonbreeding Thick-billed Murres, and assuming the ratio of immatures present to be similar to the Common Murre (after Hudson 1979a), the number of 4-year-old birds present can be compared with the average

chick production. And third, the method used by Harris (1983a) to calculate the survival of immature Atlantic Puffins from extensive retrapping
data and a model derived by Rothery [see Appendix to Harris (1983a) for
details]; this model produces two survival estimates, one which does not
include a correction for emigration and another which does.

The estimates for survival to breeding age are presented in Table 5.8.
The large variation within each species may be related to regional differences in survival. The figures from the western Atlantic tend to be greater
than those from the eastern Atlantic. Within the eastern Atlantic, the
colonies at the southern extreme (southern Britain) are lower than those
farther north. This variation may reflect regional differences, but could
also be associated with differences in technique.

C. Life Tables and Estimates of Expected Immature Survival

A useful method when considering immature survival is to calculate an
expected survival rate for immatures and compare this with observed
estimates. This expected value is the survival value for immatures from
fledging to recruitment necessary to balance adult mortality and so maintain a stable population. For different colonies this can be estimated from
annual productivity and adult survival, where rates of emigration and
imigration are assumed to be equal.

The expected values of immature survival calculated from adult survival and breeding production are presented in Table 5.9. In the strict
sense of the term, these are not life tables as only average values for
mortality and productivity are used. Those colonies that were increasing
in population size when the study was conducted tended to have observed
estimates greater than the expected values.

VIII. POPULATION PARAMETERS, CONSERVATION
AND FUTURE RESEARCH

Similar to many seabird species, the Atlantic Alcidae exhibit high adult
survival, low clutch size, high breeding success and delayed maturity.
The significance of this life-history strategy has been discussed by several
authors (Lack 1968; Ashmole 1971; Goodman 1974; Wiley 1974). With the
exception of the Dovekie and the Black Guillemot, there is apparently
little difference in the population parameters of the Atlantic auks. This
similarity is probably associated with the birds similar life-styles, but
insufficient data for each species may prevent small differences being

detected. This final section concentrates on the interaction of the major population parameters and their significance to the conservation of the Atlantic auks.

Average population parameters for a typical, stable alcid population has adult survival at approximately 90% per annum, annual production of 0.7 chicks per pair, and post-fledging survival to breeding age (taken as 5 years) to be 29%. The significance of the mortality in these three parameters to future population trends can be shown if each is halved in turn and future population trends projected. For example, if adult mortality was halved (survival increased to 95%), then with suitable breeding sites available, a population of 100 breeding pairs could be expected to increase at 4% per annum (Fig. 5.2A). Halving the mortality of eggs and young would result in a 1% per annum increase (Fig. 5.2B), while halving immature mortality would result in a 7% rate of increase (Fig. 5.2C). Another approach is to examine what change in each parameter in turn is necessary to bring about a population increase of 5% per annum; adult survival would need to be 97% (a 70% decrease in mortality), immature survival about 51% (a 31% decrease in mortality), and breeding production would require a clutch or two eggs to produce an average of 1.24 chicks per pair. These figures serve to demonstrate that small changes in the mortality of immature birds can have important consequences on future population trends. Unfortunately, few studies have concentrated on immature survival, and further work is needed on the mortality factors influencing these birds. Mead (1974) indicates that immatures disperse further from natal colonies than adults from the breeding colonies and are probably subjected to different mortality factors. The extent and severity of these mortality factors, far from the breeding colonies, may have serious long-term repercussions on population trends.

Many of the large colonies of alcids are constantly threatened by an oiling incident which could kill a large proportion of the breeding population. The significance of such a disaster depends on when it occurs; probably the worst time for a murre colony would be immediately after fledging when the chicks and adults are flightless and in the sea. After such an incident, the future of a colony depends on a number of factors including recruitment rate and the relative productivity within the population. A study by Birkhead (1977a) has shown that breeding success in Common Murres is density dependent; at high densities, the tightly packed murres successfully defended their eggs and chicks from predatory gulls, whereas at low densities, the breeding groups were 'opened up' and therefore more vulnerable to predators. Consider a population of 100 breeding murres at high density which is subjected to an oiling incident early in the breeding season that kills off a proportion of the breeding birds. Using

TABLE 5.8

Estimates of Survival to Breeding Age for Atlantic Auks

Species and study area	Method of estimate	Number of re-coveries	Survival estimate (%)	References
Razorbill				
British Isles	Band recoveries	9	48.0	Lloyd (1974)
Skokholm I., Wales	Percentage return	—	16.2	Lloyd and Perrins (1977)
Common Murre				
Green I., Nfld.	Band recoveries	301	41.1	Birkhead and Hudson (1977)
Funk I., Nfld.	Band recoveries	319	37.1	Birkhead and Hudson (1977)
Outer Gannet I., Labrador	Band recoveries	43	29.5	Birkhead and Hudson (1977)
Gulf of St. Lawrence	Band recoveries	32	36.0	Birkhead and Hudson (1977)
S. British Isles	Band recoveries	70	27.0	Birkhead and Hudson (1977)
Helgoland, Germany (1933–1943)	Band recoveries	153	31.3	Mead (1974)
Helgoland, Germany (1955–1966)	Band recoveries	143	30.2	Mead (1974)
Norway	Band recoveries	157	28.6	Birkhead and Hudson (1977)
Skomer I., Wales	Percentage return	—	17.4	Hudson (1979a)
Skomer I., Wales	Club counts	—	22.9	Hudson (1979a)

Thick-billed Murre				
Cape Wolstenholme, Digges Sd., N.W.T.	Band recoveries	55	52.9	Birkhead and Hudson (1977)
Cape Hay, Bylot I., N.W.T.	Band recoveries	53	34.5	Birkhead and Hudson (1977)
W. Greenland (1958–1962)	Band recoveries	39	33.0	Birkhead and Hudson (1977)
W. Greenland (1965–1969)	Band recoveries	70	19.0	Birkhead and Hudson (1977)
Prince Leopold I., N.W.T.	Non-breeders	—	33.3	Gaston and Nettleship (1981)
Atlantic Puffin				
Skomer I., Wales	Percentage return	—	13.3	Ashcroft (1979)
British Isles	Band recoveries	28	28.0	Mead (1974)
Isle of May, Scotland	Band recoveries (excluding emigration)[a]	218	30.0	Harris (1983a)
Isle of May, Scotland	Band recoveries (including emigration)	230	39.0	Harris (1983a)
Black Guillemot				
Greenland	Band recoveries	657	27.0	Petersen (1981)
Norway	Band recoveries	53	16.0	Petersen (1981)
Sweden	Band recoveries	111	21.0	Petersen (1981)
Denmark	Band recoveries	141	25.0	Petersen (1981)
Finland	Band recoveries	174	32.0	Petersen (1981)

[a] Recovery of living, banded birds that were subsequently released.

TABLE 5.9

Life Tables and Estimates of Expected Immature Survival for a Number of Auk Colonies in the Atlantic[a]

Species and study area	Adult survival (%)	No. of chicks per pair	Immature survival (%) Observed	Immature survival (%) Calculated	Observed population trend at time of study[b]	References
Razorbill						
Skokholm I., Wales	89.0	0.71	16.2	31.0	–	Lloyd and Perrins (1977)
Skomer I., Wales	89.8	0.62	16.2	33.0	–	Hudson (1982)
Common Murre						
Skomer I., Wales	90.4	0.71	17.4	26.3	–	Birkhead and Hudson (1977)
Stora Karlsö, Sweden	87.1	0.82	36.0	32.0	+	Hedgren (1980)
Thick-billed Murre						
Prince Leopold I., N.W.T.	91.0	0.74	33.0	24.0	–	Gaston and Nettleship (1981)
Cape Hay, Bylot I., N.W.T.	91.0	0.48	34.5	37.0	–	Birkhead and Nettleship (1981)
Coburg I., N.W.T.	91.0	0.71		25.0	–	Birkhead and Nettleship (1981)
Atlantic Puffin[c]						
Skomer I., Wales	95.0	0.51	13.3	19.5	0	Ashcroft (1979)
St. Kilda, Scotland	95.0	0.54	No data	19.0	+	Harris (1983a)
Funk I., Nfld.	95.0	0.63	No data	16.0	+	Nettleship (1972)
Great I., Nfld.	95.0	0.28	0.39	36.0	?	Nettleship (1972)
Isle of May, Scotland	95.7	0.56	0.39	15.0	+	Harris (1983a)
Black Guillemot						
Nordre Rønner, Denmark	85.3	0.60	25.0	48.7	0	Asbirk (1979b)
Flatey, Iceland	87.0	1.29	25.0	48.7	0	Petersen (1981)
Finland	85.3	1.5	32.0	20.0	?	Bergman (1971)

[a] Where certain estimates for adult survival or productivity are missing, then figures for the region or a neighbouring colony are used.
[b] Population trends: +, increasing; 0, stable; –, decreasing; ?, status uncertain.
[c] Includes estimates of non-breeding adults.

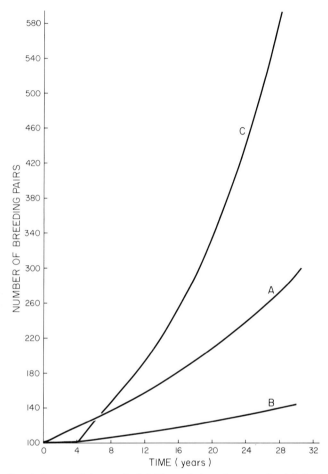

Fig. 5.2.   Population trends in a typical alcid population after mortality is halved. (A) Adult mortality, (B) breeding mortality, (C) immature mortality.

Birkhead's (1977a) data relating to breeding success and the average survival estimates used above, it is possible to project population numbers with respect to the proportion killed. The time taken for the population to return to initial levels depends on the proportion of adults killed, but as a result of density-dependent breeding success there is a threshold where productivity is lower than survival and the breeding population decreases and becomes extinct (Fig. 5.3A); with predator control, breeding success at low densities would be high, and the population would return to high densities rapidly (Fig. 5.3B). If the oiling incident occurred at the peak of fledging, and killed all adults and young produced that year, then with no

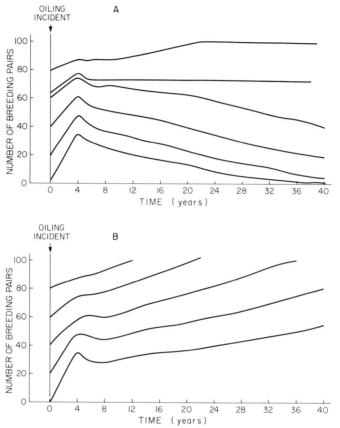

Fig. 5.3. Population projections for a hypothetical Common Murre colony after an oiling incident in early spring, (A) with density-dependent breeding success and (B) with predator control. In (A) a threshold level exists below which the population will become extinct; in (B) no such threshold exists when predators are controlled. The lowest line in both (A) and (B) represents the population change following an oiling incident soon after the peak of fledging.

predator control, the population would become extinct; with predator control, the population could survive on recruitment. Thus, although the examination of population parameters made above indicated that changes in breeding success did not constitute a major factor influencing population trends, under certain circumstances, it can be important and in some instances may warrant the careful control of predators.

It is clear from this discussion that before any sound, practical recommendations can be given on the management of alcid populations, further information is needed on several population parameters. Many of the figures presented in this chapter have come from studies on the eastern side of the Atlantic, usually at the edge of a species' breeding range. Obviously, further comparative studies are required to see whether such studies reflect the situation elsewhere. Harris (1983a) has shown that immigration is a significant factor in the population dynamics of the Atlantic Puffin colony on the Isle of May, Scotland. It is possible that emigration, and hence immature survival, have been underestimated in many studies, so further work is needed to determine whether the Isle of May situation is typical. Moreover, what is truly required is a long-term study of recruitment and age-related mortality factors at several of the large auk colonies backed up with detailed studies of the birds' movements and survival at sea.

CHAPTER 6

Feeding Ecology of the Atlantic Alcidae[1]

MICHAEL S.W. BRADSTREET

LGL Limited, environmental research associates, King City, Ontario, Canada

RICHARD G. B. BROWN

Seabird Research Unit, Canadian Wildlife Service, Bedford Institute of Oceanography, Dartmouth, Nova Scotia, Canada

[1] This chapter was prepared in association with the program "Studies on Northern Seabirds", Seabird Research Unit, Canadian Wildlife Service, Environment Canada (Report No. 142).

I. INTRODUCTION

This chapter summarises what is known of the feeding and foraging habits of the Atlantic Alcidae: the planktivorous Dovekie (*Alle alle:* high arctic, during the breeding season) and the other six fish-eating species— Thick-billed Murre (*Uria lomvia:* high and low arctic), Common Murre (*Uria aalge:* low arctic, boreal), Atlantic Puffin (*Fratercula arctica:* high and low arctic, boreal), Razorbill (*Alca torda:* low arctic and boreal), the recently extinct Great Auk (*Pinguinus impennis*), and the anomalously coastal Black Guillemot (*Cepphus grylle:* high and low arctic, boreal). (See also Chapters 2 and 9 of this volume for more detailed information on distributions.) The chapter tries to bring together the many recent studies of alcid biology in the North Atlantic, especially in eastern Canada and the British Isles. The treatment is inevitably uneven and often sketchy, and, in the case of the Great Auk, frankly speculative. However, our aim is not just to outline existing knowledge, but also to draw attention to the requirements of future research to fill in the many gaps.

The seven species are discussed in an order dictated by convenience. The species with the most specialised feeding habits, Dovekie and Black Guillemot, are treated apart from the remaining, more generalised fish-eaters. To avoid repetition among the latter, the best-known species, the murres and Atlantic Puffin, are taken before the less well-known Razorbill and the largely hypothetical discussion of the diet of the Great Auk. The section dealing with each species is divided into three topics: Adult Diet, Chick Diet, and Foraging. Adult and chick diets are treated separately because, while they obviously overlap a great deal, there are significant differences between the two in most of the species, apparently related to the maintenance of a more-or-less stable metabolic regime in the adults against the rapidly changing requirements of the growing chicks. The differences are important, and have often been obscured in the literature when the two topics are treated together. 'Diet' here covers the prey species and the proportions in which they are taken in different regions, their size and energetic quality, and the birds' daily food requirements, where these are known. 'Foraging', on the other hand, deals with the ways in which the birds actually catch their prey: diving behaviour, the ranges at which the birds forage from their colonies, and the extent to which they maximise their hunting efficiency by exploiting locally dense concentrations of prey of suitable quality.

The results of diet studies are usually presented in three ways:

1. 'Percentage occurrence', the simplest, shows the proportion of the sampled stomachs which contained at least one item of a given type of prey.
2. 'Percentage frequency' expresses the number of items of the prey in question as a proportion of the total number of items of all types of prey in the sample.
3. 'Percentage biomass' allows for differences in the sizes of prey items of different types by multiplying 'percentage frequency' by a factor based on the volume or wet or dry weight of each item. This is an important correction in any estimate of energetic intake because it is likely that a bird receives more energy from a single large item—a fish, for example—than from a dozen small items of the size of copepods.

Each method has its limitations. Biomass values give a better estimate of the energetic importance of the various taxa in the diet than do values based on occurrence or frequency, although those indices are useful in determining the importance of certain types of food. Ideally, results should be presented in all three ways and standardised to compensate for variations in the amounts of food present in individuals stomachs. However, this is rarely attempted. These points should be borne in mind in the discussions of alcid diets which follow.

II. DOVEKIE, *Alle alle*

A. Adult Diet

The Dovekie is the only Atlantic alcid which feeds primarily on zoo-plankton. Its winter diet is little known. The stomachs of three birds collected in March and April off southeast Baffin Island all contained the pelagic amphipod crustacean *Parathemisto libellula* (Smith and Hammill 1980). Farther south, Sergeant (1952) suggested that they fed on *Calanus finmarchicus*, a large copepod crustacean, and also on pelagic amphipods, and that when these disappeared from the surface waters the Dovekies either starved or migrated (see also Murphy and Vogt 1933; Fisher and Lockley 1954). The well-known 'wrecks' of birds driven far out of their normal ranges may occur when winter storms break up local concentrations of zooplankton, and churn them down to depths which the Dovekies cannot reach.

On their northward migration through Baffin Bay in spring, adult Dovekies feed mainly on copepods, especially *Calanus glacialis* (Table 6.1). Bradstreet (1982a) found seasonal changes in the diets of both adults and subadults, with copepods the principal food from May through June (74–100% of diet dry wt.), but with amphipods and the young of the arctic cod *Boreogadus saida* (Gadidae) becoming important in August (90–99.9% of dry wt.). At that time the adults fed mainly on the free-swimming *Parathemisto* spp., while the subadults were taking *Apherusa glacialis,* an ice-associated amphipod. This change in diet coincided with the increased availability of the larger stages of these amphipods in August (Dunbar 1946; Cross 1982), and their higher calorific value relative to copepods may also have been important (Bradstreet 1982a).

Little is known of the diet of breeding adult Dovekies. Copepods, hyperiid amphipods, euphausiids and other crustaceans are the principal foods in the Spitsbergen area (Hartley and Fisher 1936; Duffey and Sergeant 1950; Løvenskiold 1964). The stomachs of five adults collected on Jan Mayen contained a few fish vertebrae and many calanoids (Seligman and Willcox 1940). In Franz Josef Land two-thirds of the food consumed by Dovekies was crustaceans and the remainder fish (Demme 1934 cited in Belopol'skii 1957), but it is not clear whether this refers to the adult or chick diet, or both. More generally, it is not known whether the adults eat the same foods as they bring to their chicks (see below).

B. Chick Diet

The main prey fed to Dovekie chicks is planktonic crustaceans, brought back to the colony in the parents' throat pouches; mainly *Calanus finmarchicus, C. glacialis* and *C. hyperboreus,* along with occasional pteropod molluscs and larval fish—for example, arctic cod, *Leptoclinus* sp. (Stichaeidae) and others (Duffey and Sergeant 1950; Salomonsen 1950; Løvenskiold 1964; Norderhaug 1970, 1980; Bruemmer 1978; Golovkin *et al.* 1972a; Zelickman and Golovkin 1972; Stempniewicz 1980; Bradstreet *et al.* 1981; Evans 1981a; Roby *et al.* 1981). Other crustaceans recorded in the diets of Dovekie chicks include *Euchaeta* and *Metridia* (copepods); *Parathemisto, Hyperia* and *Hyperoche* (hyperiid amphipods); *Acanthostephia, Anonyx, Apherusa, Gammarus, Gammarellus,* and *Onisimus* (gammarid amphipods); *Mysis* (mysid), *Thysanoessa* (euphausiid), and larval *Crangon, Eualus, Hyas, Pagurus, Sabinea, Sclerocrangon* and *Spirontocaris* (decapods). There are regional differences in the chick diet. Those from colonies at or just south of the southern limit of the high-arctic

TABLE 6.1

Percentage Importance of Various Taxa in the Diets of Adult Alcids during the Breeding Season

Species and marine zone[a]	Period in breeding cycle	Number of stomachs	Source of % determination[b]	Copepods	Amphipods	Euphausiids	Other invertebrates	All invertebrates	Smelt (Osmeridae)	Cod (Gadidae)	Sandlance (Ammodytidae)	Sculpins (Cottidae)	Unidentified fish remains	All fish	References
Dovekie															
HA	Pre-hatching	67	EDW	99.8	0.2	—	—	100.0	—	—	—	—	—	—	Bradstreet (1982a)
HA	Post-fledging	21	EDW	5.8	50.7	—	—	56.5	—	43.5	—	—	—	43.5	Bradstreet (1982a)
Thick-billed Murre															
HA	Pre-hatching	213	EDW	—	14.1	—	3.0	17.1	—	82.3	—	0.6	—	82.7	Bradstreet (1977, 1980); Bradstreet and Cross (1982)
HA	Chick-rearing	250	EDW	—	7.1	—	—	7.1	—	92.7	—	0.2	—	92.9	Bradstreet (1976, 1979b)
Common Murre															
LA	Pre-hatching	16	OWW	<0.1	<0.1	—	<0.1	<0.1	32.5	—	4.9	—	62.4	99.9	Bradstreet (1983)
LA	Chick-rearing	9	OWW	—	9.2	9.0	12.1	30.3	26.4	—	—	—	40.8	67.2	Bradstreet (1983)
Razorbill															
LA	Pre-hatching	5	OWW	—	—	—	—	—	51.0	—	2.3	—	46.5	100.0	Bradstreet (1983)
LA	Post-fledging	9	OWW	—	0.1	10.9	1.5	12.5	<0.1	—	—	21.3	62.1	83.7	Bradstreet (1983)
Atlantic Puffin															
LA	Pre-hatching	17	OWW	<0.1	1.3	0.2	4.6	6.1	12.9	—	—	<0.1	80.8	93.7	Bradstreet (1983)
LA	Chick-rearing	7	OWW	<0.1	0.9	—	0.2	1.1	0.1	—	5.0	1.2	92.4	98.7	Bradstreet (1983)
Black Guillemot															
HA	Pre-hatching	47	EDW	0.1	1.0	—	0.3	1.4	—	98.5	—	0.1	—	98.6	Bradstreet (1977, 1980)
HA	Chick-rearing	56	EDW	<0.1	14.9	—	1.1	16.0	—	84.0	—	—	—	84.0	Bradstreet (1976)

[a] HA, high arctic; LA, low arctic.
[b] Percentage determination from: EDW, estimated dry weight; OWW, observed wet weight

zone (Spitsbergen, Novaya Zemlya and Horse Head, west Greenland: Norderhaug 1970, 1980; Golovkin *et al.* 1972a; Evans 1981a) were mainly fed *Calanus finmarchicus, Thysanoessa inermis* and *T. longicaudata*, typical low-arctic species; those from northwest Greenland (Bradstreet *et al.* 1981; Roby *et al.* 1981) received the characteristically high-arctic *Calanus glacialis* and *C. hyperboreus, Parathemisto libellula* and *Spirontocaris* spp. (plankton data from Stephensen 1933a,b; Jespersen 1934; Dunbar 1942, 1972; Grainger 1961, 1965). Although Dovekies are primarily high-arctic birds, they do not specialise on high-arctic prey but take whatsoever is available close to their colonies.

In terms of numbers, copepods were the commonest prey items (Table 6.2). In terms of biomass, however, amphipods were more important than copepods at Kap Atholl, northwest Greenland, in 2 years (56 to 59% of diet dry wt., against 28 to 39%), and almost as important at Siorapaluk (45 against 48%: Bradstreet *et al.* 1981), even though amphipods made up only 3.5% of the diet items at Siorapaluk (Table 6.2). It is likely that they also form a significant fraction of the diet biomass at other colonies, even though only small frequencies have been reported in chick diets there (Golovkin *et al.* 1972a; Evans 1981a; Norderhaug 1980).

The lengths of the items in northwest Greenland chick diets varied from under 2.0 mm (small copepods) to 16.5 mm (*Parathemisto*) (Bradstreet *et al.* 1981). The lengths of *Parathemisto* and *Spirontocaris* brought to the young increased significantly in the course of the chick-rearing period, presumably reflecting the growth of the crustaceans themselves (Dunbar 1957), although it is also possible that the adult Dovekies select larger prey for older chicks. The diet biomass of copepods and decapods also increased relative to that of amphipods during the chick-rearing period, which suggests that these became more acceptable prey as they grew larger.

Food loads contain many individual prey items. At Guba Arkhangel'skaya, Novaya Zemlya, and at Kap Atholl in 1978 and Siorapaluk, Greenland, the mean numbers of prey items per load were, respectively, 564, 618 and 927 (Golovkin *et al.* 1972a; Bradstreet *et al.* 1981). The maximum number in a Novaya Zemlya load was 2868 items of which 2840 were copepods; separate, single Novaya Zemlya loads contained maxima of 980 euphausiids, 863 mysids and 545 hyperiid amphipods. Meal weights increased with the age of the chick (Norderhaug 1970, 1980; Roby *et al.* 1981). Roby *et al.* found no significant differences between the weights carried by males and females but, as meal size was significantly correlated with adult weight and winglength, the birds' body size may influence the amount they bring to the chicks at each visit. Average meal weights during the last week of the chick-rearing period ranged from 3.0 g

TABLE 6.2

Diet of Dovekie Chicks

Marine zone and location	Year	Frequency in diet[a] (%)								Sample size		References
		Amphipods	Copepods	Mysids	Euphausiids	Decapods	Ostracods	Pteropods	Fish	Number of items	Number of meals	
High arctic												
Kap Atholl, N. W. Greenland	1978	13.0	84.8	–	–	2.0	+	+	0.1	68,052	110	Bradstreet et al. (1981)
	1979	6.9	84.5	–	–	8.5	0.1	–	+	12,404	56	Bradstreet et al. (1981)
Siorapaluk, N. W. Greenland	1978	3.5	94.7	–	–	1.7	+	+	+	82,473	89	Bradstreet et al. (1981)
Guba Arkhangel'skaya, Novaya Zemlya	1967	4.9	77.0	2.7	14.7	0.4	–	–	0.3	41,807	74	Golovkin et al. (1972a)
Hornsund, Vestspitsbergen	1962–1965	+	95.0	+	–	+	–	–	–	?	116	Norderhaug (1970, 1980)
Low arctic												
Horse Head, W. Greenland	1974	6.0	94.0	–	–	–	–	–	–	?	460	Evans (1981a)

[a] –, not recorded in diet; +, present in diet in unrecorded amounts.

at Guba Arkhangel'skaya to 3.4 g at Spitsbergen and 3.8 g at Siorapaluk (Golovkin *et al.* 1972a; Norderhaug 1980; Bradstreet *et al.* 1981, respectively). Feeding rates at Spitsbergen (8.5 meals/day) were somewhat higher than at Horse Head (5.25 meals/day), west Greenland (Norderhaug 1980; Evans 1981a, respectively). On this basis the Spitsbergen chicks were being fed ca. 28.9 g/day for the first 19 days after hatching, or ca. 17.7% of adult weight (163.5 g) per day. On average, chicks gained 1 g in body weight for every 5.5 g of food.

The diet of 184 recently fledged Dovekies collected in Lancaster Sound and western Baffin Bay in 1976 through 1979 consisted mainly of amphipods: *Parathemisto* (59.8% of dry wt.), *Apherusa* (13.6%) and *Onisimus* (5.6%); young arctic cod (14.5%) and calanoid copepods (5.5%) were also taken (Bradstreet 1982a). However, the diets of these juveniles varied between areas and years. In one of the years in which samples were collected, the *Parathemisto* and *Apherusa* taken by the birds in one of the water-types were significantly smaller than they were in the two other years and three other water-types. The birds apparently compensated for this by taking more copepods. The diet of the juveniles later in the fall and in the winter is not known, but presumably zooplanktonic organisms are important.

C. Foraging

Many species of zooplankton remain at depth during the day but rise towards the surface at night (e.g., Hardy 1956; Mauchline and Fisher 1969), where they would be more accessible to diving seabirds such as Dovekies. *Calanus finmarchicus* spends the day at depths of ca. 15 m or more but rises to the surface at night, and many euphausiids do the same. During the continuous daylight of the arctic summer copepods in the Barents Sea apparently maintain a constant level, although they perform a limited amount of vertical migration in Vestspitsbergen (Bogorov 1946; Digby 1961); *Thysanoessa* spp., however, maintain their migration (Zelickman *et al.* 1979). The activity rhythms of Dovekies at some colonies seem more intense at night, which suggests that they might be exploiting these vertical movements; not only at low-latitude colonies in Iceland and east Greenland (Foster *et al.* 1951; Meltofte 1976), but also at Horse Head at 73°N (Evans 1981a). However, there were no obvious differences between 'day' and 'night' feeding rates in Spitsbergen (Norderhaug 1980) nor, probably, at Guba Arkhangel'skaya (Golovkin *et al.* 1972a), although at the latter colony the males apparently foraged during the 'day' and the females at 'night'.

Dovekies may travel considerable distances from their colonies to feed:

25–30 km in northwest Greenland (Ekblaw cited in Bent 1919); 30 km in Franz Josef Land (Collett and Nansen 1900); over 32 km near Horse Head (Evans 1981a); ca. 100 km in Spitsbergen (Kolthoff 1903). Birds off Parker Snow Bay, northwest Greenland (76°N) were travelling ca. 100 km and ca. 60 km in late July 1974 and 1980, respectively, but only 25–30 km in mid-August 1976 (Brown 1976, and unpublished observations). It is likely that foraging ranges depend of the location of concentrations of prey, but it is also possible that they contract after the chicks hatch at the end of July or early August. Few of the birds off Parker Snow Bay were carrying back pouches filled with food to the colony, and none at all were seen farther offshore than 17 km (1976) or 9.5 km (1980); their highly syn-chronised flight and diving behaviour suggested that most of the birds seen well offshore were non-breeders (Marshall 1952). By contrast most of the birds seen with full pouches in 1980 were inside the bay itself: 82% (N = 137 birds) and 28% (N = 260) on two separate counts, against only 5% (N = 126) as little as 2.8 to 9.5 km offshore. Similarly, Kap Atholl Dovekies foraged only ca. 3.5 km from the colony after their chicks hatched (Bradstreet et al. 1981), and Horse Head birds only ca. 2.5 km (Evans 1981a). There may therefore be a contraction in range after hatch-ing, as has also been suggested for related auklets in the Bering Sea (Bédard 1969b, and personal communication). Further investigations of this and other aspects of foraging ranges are clearly needed.

  Potentially, at least, a Dovekie can supply its chick efficiently by forag-ing as far as 100 km from the colony. The energetic requirements of Dovekie flight are not known but, compared with the other Atlantic Alci-dae, it appears to be an efficient flyer with a relatively large wing area in proportion to its weight (Warham 1977). This, and the fact that smaller species of birds can carry relatively heavier loads than can larger ones, suggest that the Dovekie, of all the Atlantic alcids, is the species most likely to forage at long distances. In time-and-motion terms a bird could forage 100 km offshore, bring back four meals a day to its chick, and still spend only 16 out of the 24 hours in flight (Brown 1976). Given the greater energetic requirements of swimming compared to flying (Prange and Schmidt-Nielsen 1970), such behaviour would be most economical if the prey was so densely concentrated in the foraging area that the birds needed to spend little time in the water collecting it once they arrived there. The birds from Parker Snow Bay were feeding offshore at an oce-anic 'front' in 1974 and at the edge of broken pack-ice in 1980 (Brown 1976, and unpublished observations)—both situations in which zooplank-ton is likely to be found in dense local concentrations (Brown 1980a; Bradstreet and Cross 1982; see also Fig. 6.1)

  The Dovekies' foraging area has a third dimension, depth. Little is

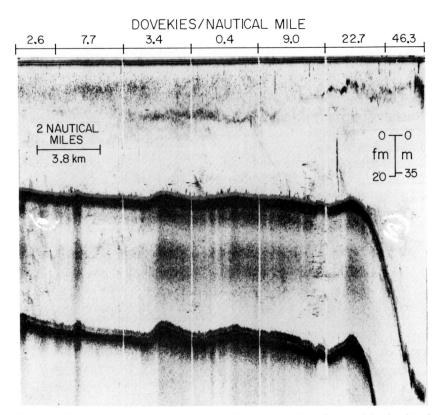

Fig. 6.1. The relation between the numbers of Dovekies at the surface, and the density of zooplankton in the surface layers, on a transect across the southern Scotian Shelf (42°43′N, 64°49′W to 42°32′N, 64°38′W) on 25 February 1980. Note that the plankton trace becomes denser, and rises to within 20 m of the surface, at the shelf-break (right-hand side). A net-haul over the shelf-break from 130 m to the surface showed that swarms of euphausiids, copepods and amphipods were probably responsible for the trace. Plankton densities were recorded on an ELAC LAZ-7-AGPVR echo-sounder.

known of their diving behaviour. The only systematic work on seabird diving has been done with penguins (Kooyman *et al.* 1971), and it is difficult to compare these large, anatomically specialised divers with the small and relatively unspecialised Dovekie. Bédard (1969b) believed that Bering Sea auklets, related to Dovekies and similar in size, were taking zooplankton as deep as 35 m, and so it is likely that Dovekies can do the same. Figure 6.1 suggests that they can certainly reach ca. 20 m. The only direct observation, a bird believed to be a Dovekie and seen through a submarine's periscope at 50 m (Menzies 1965), needs confirmation.

We can, however, make deductions from what is known of Dovekie diving times. Dewar (1924) recorded an average dive time of 14.1 seconds in water up to 2 m deep and 22.3 seconds (maximum 27 seconds) in 2 to 4 m. The pauses between dives averaged only 3.1 seconds for an average dive/pause ratio of 5.9, which indicates that the Dovekie was a more efficient diver than the other alcids and diving birds in Dewar's survey. Other observers report similar average diving times: 25–30 seconds, with pauses of 10 to 20 seconds (Salomonsen 1950); 33 seconds (maximum 68 seconds for birds diving to escape a ship (Ekblaw cited in Bent 1919); 24.5 ± 9.0 seconds (maximum 41 seconds; N = 35) with pauses of 6.0 ± 11.0 seconds (N = 8) in northern Baffin Bay (R. G. B. Brown, unpublished observations). Thirteen of 24 of Brown's birds dived 'vertically', surfacing at the spot where they went under, which suggests a fairly deep dive; the rest emerged ca. 10–25 m away. If we assume an average diving time of 30 seconds, how far down could the birds go in that time on a 'vertical' dive? Their speed underwater is not known, but the Little Penguin, the smallest penguin, can attain 1.72 m/second (Clark and Bemis 1979) and the Black Guillemot 1.5–2 m/second (Uspenski 1956) in horizontal underwater movement, while the very large Emperor Penguin can change depths at a rate of 2 m/second (Kooyman *et al.* 1971). At 1 m/second, a Dovekie diving 'vertically' could reach 15 m and surface again in 30 seconds, and dive to over 30 m in Ekblaw's maximum time of 68 seconds.

Dovekie colonies are very large; there are perhaps 30 million birds in the species' principal breeding area in northwest Greenland (Freuchen and Salomonsen 1958; see also Chapter 2, this volume). These birds must therefore have access to a very large quantity of food within the horizontal and vertical limits of their foraging range. Two rough estimates, which need refinement, give an impression of the quantities required. Zelickman and Golovkin (1972) estimated that the 11,000 birds breeding in the colony at Guba Arkhangel'skaya consumed 110 tonnes(t) of zooplankton—the biomass underlying ca. 2 km of sea surface. Norderhaug (1980) estimated that the 200,000 birds at Hornsund, Spitsbergen, brought back 70 t during the 4-week chick-rearing period, or 280–1120 if extrapolated to Spitsbergen as a whole. Clearly, the waters off the large colonies in Greenland, Spitsbergen and Novaya Zemlya must be rich in zooplankton—as the data of Zelickman and Golovkin (1972) demonstrate.

However, it is important to realize that this richness is not uniformly distributed. The mean zooplankton biomass off Guba Arkhangel'skaya is 0.56 g/m^3, ranging from a minimum of ca. 0.1 to a maximum of 1.9 g/m^3 (Golovkin *et al.* 1972a; Zelickman and Golovkin 1972). The general advantages of foraging where plankton is densest have already been outlined. More specifically, these authors estimate that a foraging Dovekie must collect ca. 100 g of food a day for itself and its chick. Dovekies feed underwater by seizing individual prey items (Keats 1981), so on this basis the bird must hunt through ca. 1000 m^3 of water a day at the lowest plankton density, ca. 180 m^3 at the mean, but only ca. 50 m^3 at the maximum. There is evidence that Dovekies do indeed feed where prey is most concentrated: 75% of the birds foraging off Guba Arkhangel'skaya were doing so over dense swarms of crustaceans (Zelickman and Go-lovkin 1972). The throat pouches of these birds usually contained either a single species of prey, or sandwiched layers of several species, but never a random species mix; this suggests that the Dovekies were either feeding on a single swarm, or moving from swarm to swarm, but were not forag-ing at random in the water column. Concentrations of Dovekies observed in association with pack-ice, continental slopes and oceanic 'fronts' sug-gest that the birds also exploit the locally dense patches of prey associated with these phenomena (Pingree et al. 1974; Bradstreet 1980, 1982a; Brad-street et al. 1981; Brown 1980a). This is true outside the breeding season as well (Fig. 6.1). However, Bradstreet et al. (1981) found no 'layering' of prey species in the pouches of birds collected off northwest Greenland, so it appears that Dovekies are also able to forage away from very dense single-species patches of plankton.

Dovekies could increase their foraging efficiency further by specialising in prey which gave them the greatest return for their foraging effort. They could, for example, take the largest available prey species. Dovekies in northern Baffin Bay fed mainly on the largest age-stages of the largest potential prey—usually *Calanus hyperboreus* (Bradstreet 1982a). Those off Guba Arkhangel'skaya fed on swarms of *Calanus finmarchicus* (maxi-mum adult female length 2.7–5.0 mm), but not on those of the smaller *Pseudocalanus elongatus* (1.2–1.6 mm) (Zelickman and Golovkin 1972; measurements from Farren and Verwourt 1951a,b). In Baffin Bay, in spring, the birds ignored the amphipod *Apherusa glacialis,* small and inactive at that season, although large, active *Apherusa* concentrated near the undersurface of the ice were an important prey later in the summer (Bradstreet 1982a).

Prey species differ in their nutritional quality as well as in their size, and Dovekies may also select for high-quality items. *Parathemisto* spp. pro-vides a higher energetic return than do copepods in late summer in Baffin Bay, and newly independent juvenile Dovekies selected these amphipods out of all proportion to their abundance in the water column (Bradstreet 1982a). *Parathemisto* made up 60% of the diet dry weight, but contrib-uted only 4 to 5% of the biomass of the zooplankton against 79 to 94% for the copepods. Adult birds also changed their diet from mainly copepods in the spring (when *Parathemisto* is apparently not readily available) to *Parathemisto* later in the summer—a shift which was also consistent with a preference for this amphipod. In this example selection for both quality and size were probably operating together, but in others it was clear that the Dovekies were virtually ignoring large, abundant but low-quality prey species: chaetognaths, ctenophores and pteropods in Spitsbergen (Norderhaug 1980), and pteropods off Novaya Zemlya and northwest Greenland (Golovkin et al. 1972a; Zelickman and Golovkin 1972; Bruemmer 1978; see also Table 6.2). All three groups are significantly lower in calorific value and lipid content than are the copepods, amphipods and euphausiids which are the birds' preferred foods in these areas (Percy and Fife 1981; Bradstreet 1982a).

III. THICK-BILLED MURRE, *Uria lomvia*

A. Adult Diet

The diet of adult Thick-billed Murres throughout the year consists mainly of fish and crustaceans, and to a lesser extent polychaetes and molluscs (Montague 1926; Sutton 1932; Hartley and Fisher 1936; Cottam and Hanson 1938; Duffey and Sergeant 1950; Salomonsen 1950; Sergeant 1951; Storer 1952; Wynne-Edwards 1952; Tuck 1961; Løvenskiold 1964; Swartz 1966; Spring 1971; de Korte 1972; Bradstreet 1976, 1977, 1979a,b, 1980; Ogi and Tsujita 1977; Birkhead and Nettleship 1981, 1982a; Gaston and Nettleship 1981; Gaston et al. 1981; Bradstreet and Cross 1982). Invertebrates play a more important part in their diet than they do in that of the Common Murre (see below).

Most of the information about the birds' winter diet comes from specimens collected off Newfoundland; of 614 stomachs, 93% contained capelin (*Mallotus villosus*, Osmeridae), with Atlantic cod (*Gadus morhua*, Gadidae) in 4%, haddock (*Melanogrammus aeglefinus*, Gadidae) in 2% and arctic cod in less than 1% (Tuck 1961). Three stomachs collected off southeast Baffin Island in March–April all contained arctic cod, two contained unidentified sculpins (Cottidae) and one a sculpin (*Icelus* sp.: Smith and Hammill 1980). Pteropods (*Limacina helicina*), amphipods, euphausiids, cephalopods and polychaetes also occurred.

The diet in spring, up to the early incubation period, is similar: *Hippolyte* (Caridae), and *Gammarus locusta* and other amphipods, in Spitsbergen (Walter 1890 cited in Storer 1952); *Calanus* spp., euphausiids and other invertebrates in Novaya Zemlya (Uspenski 1956); crustaceans and fish, and to a lesser extent polychaetes and molluscs in Franz Josef Land (Demme 1934 cited in Belopol'skii 1957). In Lancaster Sound and Barrow Strait in the spring, the most important foods at Prince Leopold Island

and at the edge of the landfast ice in terms of diet dry weight were arctic cod and crustaceans (mainly the amphipods *Parathemisto* and *Onisimus;* Table 6.1); at a conservative estimate, the birds took as many as 3.5 million *Onisimus* and 1.5 million arctic cod from a 150-km length of ice-edge during a 35-day period in 1976 (Bradstreet 1977, 1980; Gaston and Nettleship 1981; Bradstreet and Cross 1982). Arctic cod were important at both coastal and offshore ice-edges, comprising, respectively, 96 and 74% of diet dry weight. (The difference partly reflects the fact that the offshore fish were smaller: Bradstreet 1980.) The rest of the diet there was made up of crustaceans: mainly *Gammarus setosus* and *Onisimus littoralis* at coastal ice-edges—benthic species presumably taken off the bottom in shallow water; *O. glacialis* and *Parathemisto* offshore, taken from the undersurface of the ice and the upper water column, respectively. In the Russian Arctic, adult Thick-billed Murres ate more crustaceans in spring than later in the summer (Uspenski 1956; Belopol'skii 1957), but this was very variable in Canadian waters (Bradstreet 1980; Bradstreet and Cross 1982). These birds preferred arctic cod in the spring but they switched to crustaceans, mainly *Parathemisto,* when the cod were less abundant. Amphipods are not only smaller but they have a lower calorific content than cod (Bradstreet and Cross 1982), so the birds' energetic requirements probably account for this preference. The average length of arctic cod taken early in the season by Prince Leopold Island birds was ca. 75 mm, against ca. 160 mm from late July onwards (Gaston and Nettleship 1981).

The relative importance of fish and crustaceans in the adult diet later in the summer, during the chick-rearing period, is unclear and seems to vary regionally. Crustaceans are very important in Hudson Strait (Tuck and Squires 1955; Gaston *et al.* 1981); they made up 85% by volume of the food in 34 stomachs from Akpatok Island. (Note: however, this figure underestimates the quantity of the more readily digestible fish; see Gaston and Nettleship 1981, pp. 220–225.) Fish predominate elsewhere. In the years 1976 and 1978 (85 and 165 stomachs, respectively), arctic cod made up 85–95% of diet dry weight of Thick-billed Murres collected in Lancaster Sound and northern Baffin Bay, even though the smaller invertebrates—mainly amphipods—made up 84–98% of the diet *items* (Bradstreet 1976, 1979b). Fish also predominated in adult diets at Prince Leopold Island (Gaston and Nettleship 1981) and Guba Bezymyannaya (Uspenski 1956; Belopol'skii 1957) at this season. The species varied with the location. Arctic cod was the principal fish taken by birds from the high-arctic colony on Prince Leopold Island (Gaston and Nettleship 1981); arctic and Atlantic cod were important at the low-arctic colonies at Guba Bezymyannaya, Novaya Zemlya, and on the Murmansk Coast (Belopol'skii 1957), and at Akpatok, with the addition of sculpins and prickle-backs (Stichaeidae) (Tuck and Squires 1955). Five adult stomachs collected during the chick-rearing period on Jan Mayen contained fish vertebrae (probably herring, capelin and stichaeids; see below), and the remains of crustaceans and squid (Seligman and Willcox 1940). The species also varied from year to year. There was a rough inverse correlation between the frequency of occurrence of arctic and Atlantic cod in the stomachs of adults from Guba Bezymyannaya in July–August between years, and in one summer the birds took significant quantities of Atlantic herring (*Clupea harengus,* Clupeidae: Belopol'skii 1957). This undoubtedly reflects annual variations in the extent to which the warm Norwegian Current, the usual habitat of Atlantic cod and herring, penetrates into the Barents Sea. In general, adult Thick-billed Murres in summer seem to feed on whatever fish are available close to their colonies, and with an average length of roughly 100 mm (based on Swennen and Duiven 1977, on the Common Murre; see below). Belopol'skii (1957) indicated differences in the diets of male and female Thick-billed Murres at the same colony, both in Novaya Zemlya and on the Murmansk Coast; however, the differences were small, and not tested statistically. Bradstreet (1977, 1979b) found no such differences in the diets of adult birds collected in spring and summer in Lancaster Sound and northern Baffin Bay.

From the rate at which fish otoliths passed through the digestive systems of Thick-billed Murres, Uspenski (1956) estimated that an adult required ca. 10–20% of its body weight daily. Experiments with captive birds indicated an intake of ca. 320 g, or ca. 34% of body weight (Johnson and West 1975). This is broadly comparable to the daily requirements of Common Murres of similar size (see below).

The experiments of Golovkin (1963) and Johnson and West (1975) on the consumption rates of mixed, captive groups of Thick-billed and Common Murres are described in Section IV, below.

B. Chick Diet

The principal food of Thick-billed Murre chicks on the breeding site is fish—brought one at a time by the parent and usually held lengthwise, tail-forward, in its bill. This position may allow pre-digestion of the tough skull bones before the fish is fed to the chick (Tuck and Squires 1955). Fish of five families have been identified in the diets of chicks at high-arctic colonies (Table 6.3), and arctic cod have been dominant in all of them, ranging from ca. 78% of all items brought in at Prince Leopold Island (Gaston and Nettleship 1981), through ca. 90% at Cape Hay (Tuck 1961), to 100% at fledging time at Coburg Island, and Cape Hay and Cape

TABLE 6.3

Diet of Thick-billed Murre, Common Murre, Atlantic Puffin, Razorbill and Black Guillemot Chicks

Rank in diet[a,b]

Species	Marine zone and location	Year	Herring (Clupeidae)	Smelt (Osmeridae)	Lanternfish (Myctophidae)	Sticklebacks (Gasterosteidae)	Cod (Gadidae)	Wrasse (Labridae)	Gobies (Gobiidae)	Sandlance (Ammodytidae)	Mackerel (Scombridae)	Gunnel (Pholidae)[c]	Pricklebacks (Stichaeidae)[c]	Eelpouts (Zoarcidae)[c]	Rockfish (Scorpaenidae)	Sea robins (Triglidae)	Weevers (Trachinidae)	Sculpins (Cottidae)	Sea-snails (Cyclopteridae)	Halibut (Pleuronectidae)	Sample size (Number of items)	References
Thick-billed Murre	High arctic																					
	Prince Leopold I., N.W.T.	1975–1977	—	—	—	—	1	—	—	—	—	—	—	—	—	—	—	2	3	—	178	Gaston and Nettleship (1981)
	Coburg I., N.W.T.	1978	—	—	—	—	1	—	—	—	—	—	—	+	—	—	—	+	—	—	29	Bradstreet (1979b)
		1979	—	—	—	—	1	—	—	—	—	—	—	—	—	—	—	—	—	—	—	Birkhead and Nettleship (1981)
	Cape Hay, Bylot, I., N.W.T.	1957	—	—	—	—	1	—	—	—	—	—	—	—	—	—	—	—	—	—	—	Tuck (1961)
		1978	—	—	—	—	1	—	—	+	—	—	—	—	—	—	—	+	—	—	33	Bradstreet (1979b)
		1979	—	—	—	—	1	—	—	—	—	—	—	—	—	—	—	—	—	—	—	Birkhead and Nettleship (1981)
	Cape Graham Moore, Bylot I., N.W.T.	1978	—	—	—	—	1	—	—	—	—	—	—	—	—	—	—	—	—	—	52	Bradstreet (1979b)
	High arctic–low arctic																					
	Digges I., Digges Sound, N.W.T.	1981	—	+	—	—	1	—	—	2	—	3	+	3	—	—	—	+	+	+	173	Gaston et al. (1981)
	Low arctic																					
	Akpatok I., N.W.T.	1954	—	+	+	—	1	—	—	+	—	3	3	3	—	—	—	2	+	+	2702	Tuck and Squires (1955)
	Gannet Is., Labrador	1981	—	1	—	—	+	—	—	3	—	—	—	2	+	—	—	—	—	—	91	Birkhead and Nettleship (1982a)

Table (rotated on page) — colony-specific data for Common Murre, Atlantic Puffin, and Razorbill.

Species / Region	Colony	Years	n	Reference
Common Murre	Novaya Zemlya	1937	—	Krasovski, in Uspenski (1956); Uspenski (1956)
Low arctic	Gannet Is., Labrador	1942, 1944–1950	37	Birkhead and Nettleship (1982a)
	Great I., Nfld.	1981	294	D. N. Nettleship (unpublished)
	Gull I., Nfld.	1980, 1982,1983	—	Mahoney (1979)
		1977, 1978	520	
Boreal	Skomer I., Wales	1973–1975	1190	Birkhead (1976a)
	Farne Is., England	1961–1963	139	Pearson (1968)
	Stora Karlsö, Sweden	1972–1976	176	Hedgren (1976)
	Orkney Is., Scotland	1976	—	Slater (1980)
Atlantic Puffin				
Low arctic	Great I., Nfld.	1968–1969	249^d	Nettleship (1972)
		1982–1984	—	D. N. Nettleship (unpublished)
Boreal	Skomer I., Wales	1967–1970	1387	Corkhill (1973)
		1973–1975	957	Ashcroft (1976)
		1977	—	Hudson (1979b)
	Farne Is., England	1961–1963	258	Pearson (1968)
	10 Scottish colonies	1971–1976	10016	Harris and Hislop (1978)
	Puffin I., Ireland	1973	78	Harris and Hislop (1978)
	N. Norway	1955	460	Myrberget (1962)
		1974	—	Lid (1981)
Razorbill				
Low arctic	St. Mary Is., Gulf of St. Lawrence	1962–1963	35	Bédard (1969d)
	Kandalakshskaya Guba, White Sea	1957–1959	—	Bianki (1967)
	W. Greenland	1930s?	'few'	Salomonsen (1950)
	Gannet Is., Labrador	1981	409	Birkhead and Nettleship (1982a)
Boreal	Skokholm and Skomer Is., Wales	1962–1963	12	Harris (1970b)
	Skokholm I., Wales	1972–1973	—	Lloyd (1976a)
	Skomer I., Wales	1973–1975	22	Ashcroft (1976)

279

TABLE 6.3 (Continued)

Species / Marine zone and location	Year	Herring (Clupeidae)	Smelt (Osmeridae)	Lanternfish (Myctophidae)	Sticklebacks (Gasterosteidae)	Cod (Gadidae)	Wrasse (Labridae)	Gobies (Gobiidae)	Sandlance (Ammodytidae)	Mackerel (Scombridae)	Gunnel (Pholidae)[c]	Pricklebacks (Stichaeidae)[c]	Eelpouts (Zoarcidae)[c]	Rockfish (Scorpaenidae)	Sea robins (Triglidae)	Weevers (Trachinidae)	Sculpins (Cottidae)	Sea-snails (Cyclopteridae)	Halibut (Pleuronectidae)	Sample size (Number of items)	References
Black Guillemot																					
High arctic																					
Prince Leopold, I., N.W.T.	1977	−	−	−	−	(3)	−	−	−	−	−	−	(1)	−	−	−	(3)	(2)	−	58[d]	Gaston and Nettleship (1981); D. N. Nettleship (unpublished)
Wollaston Is., N.W.T.	1957	−	−	−	−	1	−	−	−	−	−	−	−	−	−	−	−	−	−	—	Tuck and Lemieux (1959)
Low arctic																					
Nuvuk Is., Digges Sound, N.W.T.	1981	−	+	−	−	2	−	−	−	−	−	−	−	−	−	−	3	−	−	554	Cairns (1982)
St. Mary and Brandypot Is., Gulf of St. Lawrence	1976, 1977	−	−	−	−	2	−	−	−	3	−	−	+	−	−	−	+	−	−	375	Cairns (1981)
Kandalakshskaya Guba, White Sea	1954–1960	+	−	−	−	3	−	−	+	−	+	2	−	−	−	−	−	−	−	356	Bianki (1967)
Flatey, Iceland	1975–1977	+	−	−	−	−	−	1	3	−	1	+	−	+	−	−	2	+	+	609	Petersen (1981)
Boreal																					
Porkkala, Finland	1963–1970	−	−	−	−	−	−	−	2	−	1	−	1	−	−	−	−	−	−	433	Bergman (1971, 1978)
N. Denmark	1975–1977	−	−	−	−	−	−	−	2	−	1	−	3	−	−	−	−	−	−	274	Asbirk (1979b)
Kent I., Bay of Fundy	1946–1947	−	−	−	−	−	−	−	−	−	1	−	−	−	−	−	2	−	−	—	Winn (1950)
Fair Isle, Scotland	1964–1967	+	−	−	−	−	+	−	−	−	1	3	3	−	−	−	2	+	−	500+	Preston (1968)
	1970	−	−	−	−	2	−	−	3	−	1	−	−	−	−	−	−	−	+	544	Slater and Slater (1972)

[a] −, Not recorded in diet; +, present in diet in unrecorded amounts.
[b] Rank determined as percentage of weight in diet.
[c] "Blennies".
[d] Sample based on number of meals, *not* number of items.

Graham Moore, Bylot Island (Bradstreet 1979b; Birkhead and Nettleship 1981). The next commonest items at Prince Leopold Island were sculpins (*Triglops* spp., ca. 18%) and *Gammarus* amphipods (ca. 3%). Other invertebrates brought to the young at these colonies include *Parathemisto*, *Gonatus* squid and *Harmothoe* polychaetes, but invertebrates never exceeded 7% of the food items.

Fish of nine families have been identified at low-arctic colonies (Table 6.3) and arctic cod are still important in the diet of chicks in the northern part of this zone, though less so than in the high arctic: 51% of the items brought in at Digges Island (Gaston *et al.* 1981) and Guba Bezymyannaya, Novaya Zemlya (Uspenski 1956); 35% at Akpatok (Tuck and Squires 1955), but only 2% on Gannet Islands, Labrador (Birkhead and Nettleship 1982a). Blennies (Stichaeidae, Pholidae and Zoarcidae) and sculpins were also significant in chick diets at Akpatok, and Atlantic cod and herring at Guba Bezymyannaya. The principal fish at Gannet Islands in 1981 were capelin and blennies (Blennioidea: Birkhead and Nettleship 1982a), and blennies and other benthic fish in 1982 (Birkhead and Nettleship 1983), but the main diet item found in a less detailed study there in 1952 was sandlance (*Ammodytes* spp., Ammodytidae: Tuck 1961). The chick diet on Jan Mayen was herring, capelin and daubed shanny (*Lumpenus maculatus*, Stichaeidae: Seligman and Willcox 1940). Only 6% of the diet items at Akpatok were invertebrates, while only ca. 5% and ca. 8% of the stomachs of Guba Bezymyannaya chicks contained, respectively, crustaceans and polychaetes. The invertebrates identified at these two colonies included *Eunoe* and *Nereis* polychaetes, *Parathemisto*, *Gammarus* and *Anonyx* amphipods, the decapods *Argis*, *Lebbeus*, *Pandalus* and *Sclerocrangon*, *Gonatus* squid and one gastropod, *Onchidiopsis*. The scarcity of invertebrates in chick diets here and in the high-arctic areas may reflect their poor nutritional quality; an Akpatok chick fed exclusively on gammarid amphipods quickly lost weight and died (Tuck and Squires 1955).

The diet of Akpatok chicks changed in the course of the season, with arctic cod decreasing in importance, mailed sculpin (*Triglops pingeli*) increasing, and with no change in the frequency of the blennies *Eumesogrammus*, *Lumpenus* and *Gymnelis* (Tuck and Squires 1955). This probably reflects changes in the availability of one or more of these prey species rather than in the preferences of the foraging adults; most of the sculpins were gravid females and thus may have been sluggish and easily caught. There is also evidence of year-to-year variations. Those at Gannet Islands have already been described (see above). Sculpins were commonest in chick diets at Prince Leopold Island in 1977, but were scarce or absent in the two preceding summers (Gaston and Nettleship 1981). At Guba Bezymyannaya in 1942 and from 1947 to 1950, 51% of the 37 chick stomachs examined contained arctic cod, Atlantic cod and Atlantic herring both occurred in 27%, and sandlance in 8% (Uspenski 1956). But in 1934, 58% of the fish found abandoned on the chick ledges were Atlantic cod, only 16% arctic cod, 11% capelin, 10% sandlance and 5% arctic alligator-fish (*Ulcina olriki*, Aspidophoroididae: Krasovski 1937 cited in Belopol'skii 1957). Such variations also occur in adult diets (see above).

The fish fed to 1- or 2-day-old chicks at Prince Leopold Island were significantly smaller than those brought to older chicks (Gaston and Nettleship 1981). The average length of items, mostly arctic cod, fed to the older chicks was 125 mm (range: 28–193 mm), the smaller items being all *Gammarus wilkitzkii*. However, there was some evidence that fish lengths declined to less than 100 mm at the end of August, just before the chicks left the colony. The arctic cod fed to chicks just about to fledge at Cape Hay, Cape Graham Moore and Coburg Island were also small (Fig. 6.2), averaging only 89 mm (range: 40–170 mm; Bradstreet 1979b). On the Gannet Islands, Labrador, the mean lengths of fish fed to chicks were as follows: capelin, 128 mm (N = 42); blennies, 121 mm (N = 34); and

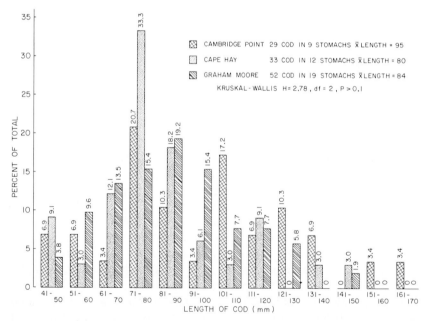

Fig. 6.2. Length–frequency distribution of *Boreogadus saida* (arctic cod) in Thick-billed Murre chicks on the day they fledged at three high-arctic colonies (after Bradstreet 1979b). For the statistical comparison, the mean length of all cod in a stomach was considered to be a unit of observation.

sandlance, 113 mm (N = 13) (Birkhead and Nettleship 1982a). These suggest prey weights of ca. 5 g and ca. 12 g for the sandlance and capelin, respectively (Scott 1972; Jangaard 1974).

Feeding rates were variable. Chicks at Guba Bezymyannaya were fed about once a day between the ages of 3 and 8 days and two to three times daily from 9 to 18 days, with a slackening in feeding rate after that (Uspenski 1956). They sometimes received food from adults other than their parents. Uspenski put the daily food requirement for a chick at 35 to 40 g. On the basis of feeding experiments Tuck and Squires (1955) estimated that Akpatok chicks ate 13.4 g of food for every 1-g gain in body weight, about half their body weight in food a day. The daily intake averaged 94.8 g (range: 48–131 g). Coburg Island and Cape Hay chicks received around four to five meals a day (Birkhead and Nettleship 1981). The chicks on Prince Leopold Island were fed at rates which varied between years, increasing from 3.5 to 6–8 meals/day in the 1975–1976 seasons, but declining from ca. 7 to ca. 5.5 meals/day in 1977 (Gaston and Nettleship 1981). There were no consistent changes in feeding rates as the chick grew older. Gaston and Nettleship (1981) estimated an intake of 25.9 g on day 1 after hatching, 30.1 g on day 2 and an average of 57.8 g/day for days 3–20, with the chicks eating 23–26% of their body weight daily to gain 1 g of body weight for every 4–4.5 g of food. This conversion rate is three times more efficient than that at Akpatok and probably reflects differences in the nutritional quality of the principal prey species at these two colonies. The energetic content of arctic cod, the principal prey on Prince Leopold Island, is ca. 6.8 kJ/g (wet wt., based on Bradstreet and Cross 1982); that of sculpins, which along with arctic cod were the main prey at Akpatok, is only ca. 5.1 kJ/g (wet wt.: Dunn 1975a). The Prince Leopold Island figures are consistent with the daily intake of 22 to 25% of adult body weight which seems characteristic of most fish-eating birds (Spaans 1971).

Nothing is known of the diet of young Thick-billed Murres after they leave their colonies.

C. Foraging

Thick-billed Murres often forage at considerable distances from their colonies, especially at the start of the breeding season. Just after they arrived at Cape Hay, in May–June, large numbers of birds were foraging as far as 100 km away, mainly at the ice-edge (McLaren 1982). Farther west in Lancaster Sound, murres from Prince Leopold Island were common at or near the edge of the landfast ice as far as 110 to 175 km from the colony (Bradstreet 1979a), and there was an inverse relationship between the numbers of birds at the colony and at the ice-edge at that time (Gaston and Nettleship 1981). Individual birds were absent for as long as 24 hours at a time from this colony, which suggests that the murres had enough time available to travel considerable distances.

It is possible that the foraging range narrows after the chicks hatch at the end of July but the great variation from colony to colony makes this hard to assess. The range contracted from ca. 80 to ca. 30 km or less at Cape Hay (Fig. 6.3). During the same stage in the cycle, in early August 1980 and mid-August 1976, most murres from Agpat, northwest Greenland, were foraging only ca. 20 km offshore, although a few went as far out as 100 km (R. G. B. Brown, unpublished observations). Akpatok birds fed only 2–8 km offshore, unusually close to the colony (Tuck and Squires 1955): 'The presence of murre colonies in that region could not be detected until the observer came within ten miles [16 km] of a colony' (Tuck 1961, p. 176). Cody (1973; modified by Bédard 1976) estimated a foraging range of ca. 10 km from Grímsey, northeast Iceland. However, the evidence from Digges Sound, in western Hudson Strait, is conflicting. Tuck (1961) found that most Digges birds foraged in two shallow-water areas ca. 25 km from the Sound, while Brown (1980b, Fig. 2), much farther offshore, found that Digges birds in late July were foraging 80 km or more from their colony. Large numbers of birds from Prince Leopold Island were foraging on the far side of Lancaster Sound in August 1976 and 1977, ca. 50–100 km away (Nettleship and Gaston 1978; Gaston and Nettleship 1981), and many of these were bringing fish back to the colony to feed their chicks. Of the 270 birds observed heading back to Prince Leopold Island on 17 August 1980 from Maxwell Bay (ca. 75 km northeast), 53% were carrying fish (R. G. B. Brown, unpublished observations). There is clearly no general trend to forage close to the colony during the chick-rearing period. Foraging areas are presumably determined by such factors as ice-cover and the movements of the prey, and they can change very rapidly (Nettleship and Gaston 1978, Figs. 14 and 15). Foraging close to the colonies may, for example, be in response to the inshore movement of arctic cod which occurs at this season (Craig et al. 1982).

It is difficult to relate foraging behaviour to prey abundance because, unlike the plankton on which Dovekies feed (see above), the fish which are the prey of the murres are hard to sample, and not much is known of their distributions near the large Thick-billed Murre colonies in the Canadian Arctic. However, the fact that long-distance foragers from Lancaster Sound colonies (McLaren 1982) and also from Spitsbergen (Løvenskiold 1964) were feeding at ice-edges is suggestive. There is a very large population of phytoplankton, grazed on by zooplankton, on the underside of the pack-ice (Dunbar 1981; Bradstreet and Cross 1982; Cross 1982). These

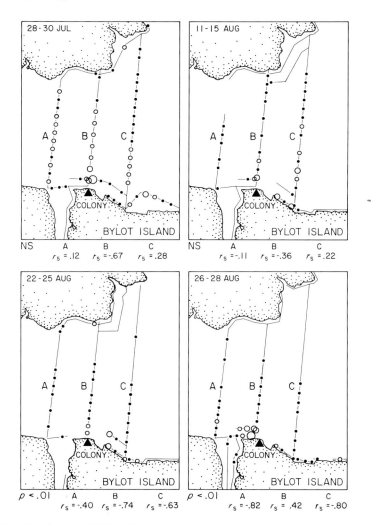

Fig. 6.3.   Distribution of Thick-billed Murres in Lancaster Sound in relation to distance from the colony near Cape Hay, Bylot Island (after McLaren and Renaud 1979). The black dots and the largest circles represent 0–5 and 250–1000 individuals per square km, respectively. The significance of the relationship was assessed by applying the Spearman rank correlation procedure to the southernmost 12 transect segments along each north–south line (but omitting the southernmost segment from the middle transect in order to exclude sightings immediately adjacent to the Cape Hay colony). Each transect was considered separately, and the resultant probabilities were pooled using the 'method of adding Z' (see Rosenthal 1978 for details). Trends were considered significant only when $p < .01$; NS, not significant.

Michael S.W. Bradstreet and Richard G.B. Brown

diatoms contribute as much as a quarter of total primary production in arctic waters, and since this process begins before the ice breaks up, it allows the herbivorous zooplankton a grazing season twice as long as that available to them away from the ice-edge zone. This in turn benefits the arctic cod at the next trophic level, a species central to the food web at the ice-edge both as the principal predator of the zooplankton, and as the principal prey of almost all the high-arctic seabirds and also of many marine mammals (Bradstreet and Cross 1982, Fig. 4). It is possible that the local concentrations of these fish make ice-edges economical foraging areas even at considerable distances from the murres' colonies, along the lines suggested for Dovekies (see above).

Thick-billed Murres are also known to exploit other local concentrations of prey to a limited extent—for example, the swarms of euphausiids at a glacier face in Spitsbergen (Hartley and Fisher 1936). In Novaya Zemlya hundreds of thousands of murres fed at a narrow 'front' between fresh and saline water where swarms of polychaetes and other zooplankton were concentrated, and large numbers also fed on dense schools of capelin (Uspenski 1956).

Average dive times have been estimated at 40 to 50 seconds (Uspenski 1956, Novaya Zemlya), 29.0 seconds ($N = 212$, maximum 75 seconds: R. G. B. Brown, unpublished observations, Lancaster Sound and Baffin Bay), 83 seconds (maximum 192 seconds: Bradstreet 1982b, Lancaster Sound). It is hard to say what these times mean in terms of depths achieved, but if the birds dived 'vertically' and changed depths at a rate of 1 m/second (see the discussion on Dovekies, above), they might reach ca. 90 m during a dive time of 192 seconds. Thick-billed Murres have in fact been taken on baited hooks set on the bottom at ca. 75 m (Tuck and Squires 1955), although such evidence is always suspect since the birds could have been caught as the line was being raised or lowered. If the benthic blennies and sculpins fed to Akpatok chicks were taken on the bottom near the colony (Tuck and Squires 1955), the birds may have been diving as deep as 100 m to catch them. Foraging depths of only 20 m or less have been suggested for birds in Novaya Zemlya and in the North Pacific (Uspenski 1956; Ogi and Tsujita 1977), but these are certainly underestimates; even the Short-tailed Shearwater, a relatively unspecialised diver, has been observed feeding at 20 m (Skira 1979).

More generally, the prevalence of benthic fish in the diets of Thick-billed Murres at many colonies suggests that this species regularly feeds at or near the bottom, in contrast to the Common Murre (see below), which usually takes pelagic fish. The difference is consistent with Spring's (1971) conclusions, based on anatomical comparisons, that the Common Murre is adapted to pursuit-swimming, but the Thick-billed Murre to deep diving.

IV. COMMON MURRE, *Uria aalge*

A. Adult Diet

The diet of adult Common Murres at all seasons of the year is principally fish; molluscs, crustaceans, polychaetes and fish eggs are also taken, but only to a small degree (Salomonsen 1935; Kaftanovskii 1938; Witherby *et al.* 1941; Uspenski 1956; Belopol'skii 1957; Madsen 1957; Tuck 1961; Swartz 1966; Scott 1973; Ogi and Tsujita 1973, 1977; Wiens and Scott 1975; Birkhead 1976a; Reinert 1976; Anonymous 1980a). Almost 92% of a sample of 44 Common Murre stomachs taken off Newfoundland in winter contained capelin, and most of the remainder Atlantic cod and haddock (Tuck 1961). Birds wintering off Denmark fed only on fish: sprats (*Sprattus sprattus*, Clupeidae), Atlantic mackerel (*Scomber scombrus*, Scombridae), gadids, gobies and eelpouts (Madsen 1957). Sandlance occurred in 44 of 48 stomachs of birds breeding in Shetland, with gadids in 8 and polychaetes in 2 (Anonymous 1980a), while sprats, herring and sandlance were the principal foods of Faeroese birds (Salomonsen 1935 cited in Tuck 1961; Reinert 1976). Of the stomachs with food matter in them from the Murmansk Coast, 95% contained fish, against only ca. 2% with crustaceans and even smaller numbers with molluscs, polychaetes, insects and plant matter (Belopol'skii 1957). Sandlance, capelin, Atlantic herring and Atlantic cod were the principal species. In Guba Bezymyannaya, Novaya Zemlya, 17 of 20 stomachs contained arctic cod and 3 contained sandlance; Atlantic cod, capelin and sculpins each occurred in 2, and the remains of bivalve molluscs in 1 (Uspenski 1956). The birds may be selecting for fish and against invertebrates in their diet, and it is interesting that captive Common Murres rejected crustaceans even when they were given no other food (Golovkin 1963; Swennen 1977). In Labrador, however, Common Murres increased their use of invertebrates between the pre-hatching and chick-rearing periods of the breeding cycle (Table 6.1).

Common Murres, like other fish-eating alcids, use body depth rather than length in selecting fish of a suitable size (Swennen and Duiven 1977). Experiments have shown a preferred body depth of Atlantic herring of 23 mm (14 g, or ca. 100 mm long) and a maximum of 44 mm (96 g, or ca. 200 mm); the preferred size of poor cod (*Trichopterus esmarkii*, Gadidae) was also 23 mm (16 g, or ca. 100 mm) and the maximum 41 mm (96 g, or ca. 180 mm). [Depth/length conversions follow Leim and Scott (1966), using Atlantic cod as a model for *Trichopterus*.] However, the birds readily accepted larger, but thinner, sandlance up to 220 mm long [ca. 22.5 g (Scott 1972), or ca. 17 mm in body depth]. The maximum size of fish a murre will take is obviously limited by its gape size, but other factors are also important; captive birds often rejected large fish which they were physically capable of swallowing (Swennen and Duiven 1977). Under natural conditions the time taken to 'handle' large fish must be one such factor, since these take longer to catch and swallow (Brown *et al.* 1981). A large fish, weighing 3–10% as much as the bird and at a temperature some 25–20°C colder, might also have a significant cooling effect on the bird's metabolism (Swennen and Duiven 1977). A large fish would also be energetically expensive for a bird to carry back to its chick if it was foraging at any distance from its colony.

Daily food intake is about a quarter to a third of the adult body weight (ca. 950–990 g: Bédard 1969a; Johnson and West 1975). A captive Common Murre maintained at an ambient temperature of 11°C had a daily intake of ca. 184 g of young trout (*Salmo gairdnerii*, Salmonidae), ca. 28% of its body weight (Sanford and Harris 1967). The daily intake of fish by a group of captive birds varied in the course of the year from 90 to 300 g/bird, of ca. 10–33% of body weight (Swennen and Duiven 1977). Another group had a daily intake of sprats of ca. 200 g/bird (ca. 20% of body weight), but increased this during the moult when their metabolic requirements were higher, and also when the fat content of the sprats was low (Marsault 1975). A mixed group of seven Common and seven Thick-billed Murres were fed 4.5 kg of smelt (*Osmerus* sp., Osmeridae) daily, or ca. 320 g/bird (Johnson and West 1975). The Common Murres maintained a mean body weight of 957 g, indicating a daily intake of ca. 34% of body weight.

Captive adult Thick-billed and Common Murres from colonies on the Murmansk Coast preferred sandlance, gadids and nine-spined sticklebacks (*Pungitius pungitius,* Gasterosteidae) to gobies and flounders, and refused gammarid amphipods even when fasting (Golovkin 1963). The birds were able to maintain their body weight on a daily ration of 300 to 350 g of fish (sandlance and gadids), or ca. 28.5% of normal body weight. They lost weight but stabilised at ca. 85–90% of normal weight on a ration of 200 g, but died after 9 to 10 days, at 75% of normal weight, on a ration of only 100 g. Birds given no food at all died after 6 to 8 days, at ca. 60% of normal weight. These captive birds could take up to 200 g at a meal, and individual fish weighing as much as 113 g, but they normally took only 55–65 g at a meal if fed regularly. Digestion was rapid; the birds took only 3 hours to consume ca. 60 g of fish.

B. Chick Diet

Common Murres bring fish to their young (Table 6.3)—almost always one at a time, held lengthwise in the bill with the tail forward—although

invertebrates have been recorded occasionally (Salomonsen 1935; Johnson 1940; Perry 1948; Uspenski 1956; Belopol'skii 1957; Nørrevang 1958;
Pearson 1968; Birkhead 1976a; Hedgren 1976; Mahoney 1979). About
94% of the food items brought to chicks at Gull Island, Newfoundland,
were capelin, against only 2.7% sandlance and 3.6% short-finned squid
(*Illex illecebrosus,* Ommastrephidae: Mahoney 1979); the squid were not
eaten by the chicks, perhaps because they were too big. Capelin was also
the principal prey at the Gannet Islands, Labrador, in 1981 and 1982,
although a few blennies were taken (Birkhead and Nettleship 1982a,
1983); however, the principal food there in 1952 was apparently sandlance
(Tuck 1961). Sprats are the main food both in the Faeroe Islands and in
the southern Baltic (Salomonsen 1935; Hedgren 1976); pricklebacks and
Atlantic mackerel have also been recorded in chick diets in the Atlantic
(Johnson 1940; Perry 1948). In general, the fish fed to the chicks are
usually of species high in fat content and calorific value, such as Atlantic
herring, sprat, sandlance and capelin (Harris and Hislop 1978).
    The rates at which the chicks are fed vary: 2.1 meals/day at Great
Island, Newfoundland (D. N. Nettleship, unpublished observations), 2.4
at Stora Karlsö in the Baltic (Hedgren and Linnman 1979), 2.7 at Gannet
Islands (Birkhead and Nettleship 1982a), 3.0 at Gull Island, Newfoundland (Mahoney 1979), 3.2 at Skomer Island, Wales, in the Irish Sea
(Birkhead 1976a), and as high as 4.2 to 5.8 at Copinsay, Scotland (Slater
1980). The rates are highest between days 3 and 16 after hatching, but
they are generally low during stormy weather, presumably because foraging is more difficult then (Birkhead 1976b). There is a peak in feeding rate
shortly after first light (Birkhead 1976a; Hedgren and Linnman 1979;
Birkhead and Nettleship 1982a). However, the chick is not fed at night,
presumably because murres are unable to catch fish in the dark (Sanford
and Harris 1967).
    The average length of fish fed to the chicks is 120 mm ($N = 340$, range:
93–139 mm; Table 6.4), although fish as large as ca. 150–180 mm have
been recorded (Tuck 1961; Hedgren 1976; Birkhead and Nettleship
1982a). Very small sandlance (ca. 30–70 mm in length, or ca. 1 g) were
only fed to very young chicks, 3 days old or less, on Skomer Island
(Birkhead 1976a), but the average length of clupeids, the principal chick
food at this colony, was 104 mm (ca. 8.8 g). The adults tended to bring in
large clupeids for their chicks, but a higher proportion of small sandlance
for their mates at the fish-presentation display on the breeding ledge earlier in the season. Such variations probably reflect variations in the sizes
and species of prey available to the foraging birds during the course of the
breeding season.
    The average weight of food provided daily to the Skomer Island chicks

TABLE 6.4

Mean Lengths of Fish Brought to Common Murre Chicks

	Mean length (mm)			
Location	Capelin	Sandlance	Sprat	References
Gannet Is., Labrador	122 (259)[a]	96 (14)	—	Birkhead and Nettleship (1982a)
Great I., Nfld.	139 (18)	—	—	Birkhead and Nettleship (1984b)
Skomer I., Wales	—	—	104 (46)	Birkhead (1976a)
Stora Karlsö, Sweden	—	—	132 (32)	Hedgren (1976)

[a] Sample size in parentheses.

was sufficient for an average daily weight increase of 9.25 g during days 3–16 after hatching, or ca. 3.2 g of food for 1 g of body weight (Birkhead 1976a, 1977b). The figures for Stora Karlsö chicks are very similar: ca. 32 g/day producing an average increase of ca. 9.28 g/day over the first 19 days or ca. 3.5 g of food for 1 g of body weight (Hedgren 1976; Hedgren and Linnman 1979). In southeast Newfoundland, chicks on Gull Island grew at a rate of 8.8 g/day for the first 16 days after hatching (Mahoney 1979; Mahoney and Threlfall 1981). These authors assumed that each chick received three capelin a day, average weight 26.5 g, for a total of 79.5 g food per day, and thus received ca. 9 g of fish to produce 1 g of body weight. Birkhead and Nettleship (1984b) have questioned this apparently inefficient conversion ratio. Their own work on Common Murres at Great Island nearby indicated an average of 2.1 meals/day of fish, mainly capelin, for a total of 19.3 g/day, which gave a growth rate of 9 g/day; 2.1 g food for 1 g of body weight, a conversion figure closer to that for the chicks at Skomer Island and Stora Karlsö, above. Birkhead and Nettleship showed that the average weight of the capelin in the Gull Island study was almost certainly overestimated and instead suggested an average of 9 g, for a total of 27 g food per day, or 3 g food for 1 g in body weight. Mahoney and Threlfall suggested that Common Murre chicks need a greater intake of food to maintain their body temperatures in the cold climate of Newfoundland than in the warmer one of Skomer Island, but this clearly is not the case.

    In all four cases, however, the conversion ratios were between 1.5 and 4 times as efficient as those for Thick-billed Murre chicks (see above), even though the two species have similar growth rates and fledging periods (cf. Birkhead 1976a; Gaston and Nettleship 1981). The daily feeding rates of the Common Murres were also lower (see above). In other words, Common Murres were more efficient at raising chicks than are Thick-billed Murres, in terms of the quality of the prey and the effort they themselves spend in providing it. The staple foods at these Common Murre colonies were fat, oily species of high calorific value like sprats and capelin, compared to the nutritionally poorer gadids on which the Thick-bills feed (see above and Harris and Hislop 1978).

Golovkin (1963) reports conversion ratios of ca. 6–9 g fish (sandlance, gadids) to 1 g increase in body weight for captive chicks of Common and Thick-billed Murres. The chicks gained weight when fed ca. 36–46% of their body weight per day, but lost weight and died after only 4 days when given a ration of only ca. 27–29% of body weight. Unfortunately the precise constituents of the diet and the murre species used in these experiments are not given.

Young murres in captivity can feed themselves on both live and dead prey at ca. 25 days after hatching, although they can at first catch only the slower moving living fish (Oberholzer and Tschanz 1969; Swennen 1977). The age at which chicks are able to catch live fish in the wild is not known: presumably they are fed before this by the parent which accompanies them (Tuck 1961).

C. Foraging

The foraging ranges of breeding Common Murres are not well known. They are absent from the colonies for 3 to 5 days at a time at the beginning of the breeding cycle before the eggs are laid, probably because food is scarce and hard to find at that time (see Chapter 3, Section IIIA). The interval is much shorter after the chicks hatch: an average of 65 minutes ($N = 24$) at Gannet Islands (Birkhead and Nettleship 1982a) and 86 (range: 6–226) minutes at Skomer Island (Birkhead 1976a). At a flight speed of 78 km/hour (based on Vaughan 1937; Tuck 1961) a bird could in theory fly 56 and 146 km out and back to the colony in, respectively, 86 and 226 minutes. But such estimates leave no time for it to locate and catch the prey, rest, and so forth, and they are undoubtedly exaggerated. However, a Common Murre carrying a fish, presumably for its chick, has been observed in the North Sea ca. 50 km from the nearest colony (Joiris 1978). On the other hand, dye-marked birds from Fair Isle, Scotland, fed only as far as 6 to 8 km from the colony (Anonymous 1980a), as did most birds at Cape Thompson, Alaska (Swartz 1967). Birkhead (1976a) counted Common Murres along a 10-km transect leading away from their colony on Skomer Island. The largest numbers—presumably 'loafing' birds—were seen close to the island. The numbers then declined abruptly, but gradually increased out to the limit of the transect. The implication is that Skomer Island murres were travelling at least 10 km to catch their food. In Witless Bay, Newfoundland, from 1980 to 1983, J. F. Piatt (personal communication) found that birds foraged closer to colony sites in a year with high capelin abundance than in a year when capelin were less common.

The birds' attendance patterns early in the season at Copinsay, Orkney Islands, were correlated with the tidal cycle and Slater (1977, 1980) attributed this to the influence of the strong and complex local tidal streams on the availability of food. With the possible exception of the Black Guillemot (see Section VIII), this is the only Atlantic alcid for which such an association has been reported. Foraging patterns may be interrupted by strong winds and high seas (Birkhead 1976b; Slater 1980), which either reduce the birds' efficiency in searching for prey, or disperse the schools of fish or force them to go deep and thus make foraging less successful.

In Scottish coastal waters Dewar (1924) found that most Common Murre dives close to shore occurred in water ca. 3.6–5.5 m deep, over a range of depths from 0 to 11 m. The birds' behaviour suggested that they were often going down to the bottom. The longest dive took 68 seconds, and the birds increased their dive times from 15 seconds over ca. 0.3–1.8 m of water to 61 seconds at ca. 7.6–9.1 m. The dive/pause ratio averaged 3.6, almost as high as the Dovekie's (see above). Unlike the Razorbill (see below) whose dive/pause ratios rapidly declined with increasing depth, those of the Common Murre actually increased—to 4.8 over water ca. 8.4 m deep—an indication that these relatively shallow depths were well within the birds' diving capablilities. However, there were no significant changes in the ratio in Common Murres feeding over rather greater depths off Oregon (Scott 1973). Two Oregon birds brought flatfish to the surface, presumably taken off the bottom, in water 31.7 and 60.4 m deep. The species is regularly taken in gill-nets set off Newfoundland in ca. 10–180 m of water (Piatt et al. 1984; Piatt and Nettleship 1985). Mean and maximum diving times of 41 and 71 seconds have been recorded off Iceland (Cody 1973), 71.3 and 140 seconds off Oregon (Scott 1973), and up to 60 seconds in a captive bird (Sanford and Harris 1967). At an assumed descent/ascent rate of ca. 1 m/second (see Dovekie, Section II, C) the birds could be diving as deep as 70 m if these dives were 'vertical'. However, the Common Murre is structurally adapted more to horizontal pursuit than deep diving underwater (Spring 1971). Slower fish, swimming at less than 0.5 m/second, are caught head-first but faster fish are seized by the tail; in both cases the prey is swallowed head-first, however (Sanford and Harris 1967; Oberholzer and Tschanz 1969; Swennen 1977). The birds may surface to swallow their prey, but they may also swallow several fish underwater in the course of a dive. The birds' speed underwater is not known, but an underwater speed of 1.5 to 2.0 m/second, based on Uspenski's estimates (1956) for the Black Guillemot (see Section VIII), would be equal to or faster than the maximum, short-term 'burst' of speed of ca. 1.9 m/second or less of which small clupeids and osmerids are capable (Beamish 1978).

Golovkin (1963, Table 3) estimated from his experiments with captive birds that an adult Thick-billed or Common Murre requires 300 g of fish daily, and a chick 100 g/day. He calculated from this that the 2.05 million adults and 0.34 million chicks at the colonies in southeastern Barents Sea, present for 120 and 30 days, respectively, consumed a total of ca. 74.9 million t of fish during that period. It is not clear what fraction this represented of the total fish biomass, but it was ca. 13% of the total commercial catch there in the late 1950s. It was ca. 7% of the commercial catch in 1979 (Nikolaev 1982), but, in contrast to the 1950s, over 70% of that catch is now capelin, an important food of murres (see above). It remains to be seen to what extent competition with the fishery for this common resource has affected the populations of the birds. The birds subsequently return ca. 10,000 t of guano to the sea, and this enhances phytoplankton production in the vicinity of colonies both in Novaya Zemlya and on the Murmansk Coast (Golovkin 1963, 1967; Golovkin et al. 1972b). Golovkin et al. (1972b) suggest that the increase in nutrients from this source may be detected as far away as 240 km from the colony. It is not clear, however, whether this leads to enhanced zooplankton and fish production as well, and if the birds are, so to speak, helping to produce part of their own food supply. Tuck (1961) has suggested that guano from murre colonies in Hudson Strait may influence production as far downstream as the Grand Banks, over 1200 km away, but this is almost certainly an exaggeration.

V. ATLANTIC PUFFIN, *Fratercula arctica*

A. Adult Diet

In summer adult Atlantic Puffins feed mainly, but not exclusively, on fish; the importance of invertebrates apparently varies both geographically and seasonally. However, sampling has generally been poor. The principal foods of the birds breeding on the Murmansk Coast of northwest Russia, the most detailed study, were sandlance, capelin, Atlantic herring and young gadids, with sandlance and capelin declining relative to the other two as the season progressed; invertebrates were only rarely taken

(Belopol'skii 1957). A single adult from east Greenland contained 99% gadids by volume, and only 1% polychaetes (Cottam and Hanson 1938). Of a sample of 15 Scottish birds from the Isle of May, 11 contained small fish, 3 contained nereids and 1, euphausiids; the occurrence of pink-stained droppings, a sign of predation on crustaceans, suggested that crustaceans might have been more important prey early in the season (Harris and Hislop 1978). Adult puffins breeding in southeast Labrador fed principally on fish (Bradstreet 1983; see also Table 6.1). The proportion of invertebrates in the diet declined in the course of the season at this colony and it is possible that early sampling, before the eggs were laid, might have shown that invertebrates were important at that period. The evidence from Jan Mayen is conflicting. Ten birds taken there in July and August 1934, during the chick-rearing period, had been feeding almost exclusively on crustaceans—*Mysis relicta* and a calanoid copepod—and the only fish recorded was a single Atlantic herring (Bird and Bird 1935). However, seven adult birds collected at the same season in 1938 contained the remains of fish and squid as well as small crustaceans (Seligman and Wilcox 1940). A sample of 10 birds collected towards the end of the breeding season at a glacier face in Spitsbergen had all been feeding on crustaceans swarming in the area—*Thysanoessa, Parathemisto* and *Mysis*—although 7 of them had been feeding on gadid and stichaeid fish as well (Hartley and Fisher 1936). Løvenskiold (1964) suggests that crustaceans and other invertebrates are the principal diet of adult puffins in Spitsbergen, but no detailed studies have been made. Nothing is known of the diet of Atlantic Puffins in winter.

    The puffins' preferred and maximum body depths for Atlantic herring are 15 mm (4 g, or ca. 70 mm long) and 26 mm (18 g, or ca. 120 mm long); those for poor cod are 15 mm (6 g, or ca. 70 mm long) and 23 mm (16 g, or 100 mm long), respectively [Swennen and Duiven (1977); depth/length conversions follow Leim and Scott (1966)]. However, they will take longer fish of narrow-bodied species like sandlance.

    A full-grown captive puffin required 56 g of sprats a day (equivalent to 543 kJ of energetic input) to maintain its body weight (Harris 1978)—a daily consumption of ca. 15% of its body weight. However, the bird was in wing-moult, and so its requirements may have exceeded those needed for minimum maintenance.

B. Chick Diet

    The food brought to Atlantic Puffin nestlings is almost exclusively fish and invertebrates are very rare (Lockley 1953a; Myrberget 1962; Pearson 1968; Nettleship 1972; Corkhill 1973; Evans 1975; Ashcroft 1976; Harris and Hislop 1978; Hudson 1979b; Lid 1981). For example, only 6 of 10,100 items delivered to chicks at colonies in the British Isles were invertebrates: 5 squid (*Alloteuthis subulata*) and a planktonic crustacean (Harris and Hislop 1978). A few crustaceans (mainly *Calanus* spp.), polychaetes and molluscs were included in the predominantly fish diet fed to young birds on the Murmansk Coast (Kartaschew 1960).

Fish from 10 families have been recorded in chick diets in various parts of the North Atlantic (Table 6.3). There have been no studies in the high arctic. In the low arctic, off Newfoundland, capelin was the principal food in the late 1960s, but in 1981 when these fish were scarce, the adults were mainly feeding small gadids to the chicks (Nettleship 1972, and unpublished observations; Brown and Nettleship 1984a). In the boreal zone of northern Norway the principal foods were sandlance and the young of Atlantic herring and Atlantic mackerel and of gadids (Myrberget 1962; Tschanz 1979a; Lid 1981). The most extensive studies have been done on the British Isles, where sandlance and sprat, usually in that order, were the dominant prey, with gadids of several genera—*Ciliata, Gaidropsarus, Melanogrammus, Merlangius, Micromesistus, Pollachius* and *Trisopterus*—usually third in importance (Corkhill 1973; Ashcroft 1976; Harris and Hislop 1978; Hudson 1979b). Sticklebacks (Gasterosteidae), flatfish (Pleuronectidae), sea robins (Triglidae) and gobies (Gobiidae) were also recorded; on the Farne Islands (Pearson 1968), weevers (*Trachinus vipera,* Trachinidae) came second to sandlance in frequency, although sprats were second in biomass. There may, however, be considerable variations in the species and sizes of the fish brought to the young, both within and between years at a given colony, and even between neighbouring colonies during the same season (Belopol'skii 1957; Myrberget 1962; Pearson 1968; Nettleship 1972; Corkhill 1973; Ashcroft 1976; Harris and Hislop 1978), presumably reflecting fluctuations in the various fish populations (see below).

The species most prevalent in the chick diet tend to have the highest calorific values. Large, oily sprats had a calorific value of 10.9 kJ/g (wet), compared to 6.7 and 5.6 kJ/g, respectively, in young and larval fish; large sandlance averaged 6.5 kJ/g (Harris and Hislop 1978). On the other hand, gadids such as saithe (*Pollachius virens*) and whiting (*Merlangius merlangus*) averaged only 5.1 and 4.05 kJ/g, respectively. Adult puffins seemed actively to select against these gadids, bringing back far fewer than would be expected from their abundance at sea (Harris and Hislop 1978). The calorific values of invertebrates, even less preferred, are also low: ca. 3–5 kJ/g for euphausiids (Mauchline 1980) and ca. 4–5 kJ/g for squid (Morejohn *et al.* 1978; Croxall and Prince 1982). [These averages are given only as relative indices of the calorific value of the various preys, and take no account of seasonal fluctuations in chemical composition (Mauchline and Fisher 1969; Jangaard 1974).] The importance of the energetic quality of the food is shown by the reduced fledging weights and fledging success of puffin chicks in seasons when the preferred high-quality prey is scarce and the parents bring low-calorie gadids or other lower quality prey instead (Nettleship 1972, and unpublished observations; Harris and Hislop 1978; Brown and Nettleship 1984a).

There are also seasonal changes in the composition of chick diets, and these are apparently due more to changes in the availability of different prey species than to changes in the parents' foraging behaviour geared to the changing requirements of the growing chicks (Myrberget 1962; Pearson 1968; Ashcroft 1976). The main food brought to puffin chicks at British colonies (mainly in northern and eastern Scotland) is sandlance at first, but sprats later. Sprats are offshore in deep water at the start of the puffins' breeding season and do not move inshore until about the time that the chicks hatch—just as the sandlance begin to move away offshore (Pearson 1968). The adults' shifting 'preferences' are thus mainly responses to the changing availability of these two prey species, although active selection for sprats against sandlance probably also takes place (Harris and Hislop 1978). But even without active selection, the incidental effect is to provide the young puffins with an energy-rich food supply— sprats—during their period of maximum growth. The timing of the hatch may well be geared to the timing of this inshore migration. This is known to occur for puffins in east Newfoundland with capelin (Nettleship 1972, and unpublished observations).

The size of fish brought to the young in the British colonies averaged ca. 60 mm (Table 6.5), and ranged from ca. 30 to 90 mm; the largest recorded prey was a 207-mm sandlance (Harris and Hislop 1978). Prey length tended to increase during the season (Myrberget 1962; Ashcroft 1976; Harris and Hislop 1978). This is probably because the fish themselves are growing as the summer progresses, but it is also possible that the adults may be selecting larger prey as their chicks increase in size. On average, the chicks received between 3.8 and 15.7 meals/day at Scottish colonies, for example (Harris and Hislop 1978). These Scottish adults usually brought back 5–10 fish (range: 1–62) in a meal. This is similar to the average of 8.3 to 11.9 fish in Wales (Corkhill 1973), but rather larger than that of only 5.2 fish in Norway (Myrberget 1962). Meal weights increased during the first few days after the chicks hatched but remained constant thereafter (Ashcroft 1976; Harris and Hislop 1978). However, the *frequency* of meals was greatest during the middle 2 weeks of the 6-week period that the young were in burrows—during their period of maximum growth. There are limits to the amount which a very small chick can

TABLE 6.5

Mean Length (mm) of Fish Fed to Atlantic Puffin Chicks at Boreal European Colonies

				Location			
Species	N. Norway	Skokholm and Skomer Is., Wales	Skomer I.	Skomer I.	10 Scottish colonies	N. Rona, Scotland	Grand mean (all studies)
Sandlance (*Ammodytes, Hyperoplus*)	78 (337)[a]	64 (66)	56 (758)	61 (551)	66 (4627)	72 (46)	65 (6385)
Sprat (*Sprattus sprattus*)	—	52 (10)	39 (626)	47 (380)	50 (2841)	—	48 (3857)
Atlantic herring (*Clupea harengus*)	79 (102)	—	—	29 (24)	—	—	69 (126)
Saithe (*Pollachius virens*)	87 (18)	—	—	—	53 (129)	—	57 (147)
Atlantic cod (*Gadus morhua*)	57 (3)	—	—	—	—	—	57 (3)
Rockling (*Gaidropsarus, Ciliata*)	—	—	—	—	33 (1687)	42 (48)	33 (1735)
Whiting (*Merlangius*)	—	—	—	—	55 (579)	—	55 (579)
Haddock (*Melanogrammus*)	—	—	—	—	65 (34)	—	65 (34)
References	Myrberget (1962)	Harris (1970b)	Corkhill (1973)	Ashcroft (1976)	Harris and Hislop (1978)	Evans (1975)	

[a] Sample size in parentheses.

eat—hence, presumably, the low initial feeding frequency (Ashcroft 1976). Adults on Skomer Island, Wales, reduced their feeding visits towards the end of the fledging period even though the chicks would accept additional food presented to them by the experimenter (Hudson 1979b). This suggests a diminishing of the food supply at this colony towards the end of the chick-rearing period.

Young puffins will readily accept supplementary food during the first month after hatching, and experiments have shown that this significantly increases their growth rates (Harris 1978). Under natural conditions there is obviously an upper limit to the amount of food which a parent can bring, set by its own foraging efficiency and by the amount of food in the vicinity of the colony. The adult birds can adjust their provisioning rates to increased demands by their chicks, but only to a limited extent, as 'twinning' and 'single-parent' experiments have shown (Nettleship 1972; Corkhill 1973; Ashcroft 1976; Harris 1978; see also Chapter 4, this volume). In all these cases there is a significant reduction in fledging success, and also in the weights of the chicks which do survive until fledging.

The daily intake of food by young puffins varies from colony to colony. Birds on Skomer Island in 1974 to 1975 had an average intake of 46.0 to 50.7 g/day (Ashcroft 1976), equivalent to 283 to 312 kJ/day (Harris and Hislop 1978, Table X). That of chicks at St. Kilda, northwest Scotland, was smaller—43.2 g/day or 252.3 kJ/day—but at the Isle of May, eastern Scotland, it was ca. 61.6 g/day or 497 kJ/day (Harris 1978; Harris and Hislop 1978, Table X). The rate for puffins breeding in optimal habitat on Great Island, Newfoundland, was 43.2 g/day; no calorific equivalent is available (Nettleship 1972). This variability is reflected in differences in growth patterns between different colonies, as one would expect from the supplementary feeding experiments (see above and Chapter 4, this volume). The peak weight of control chicks on the Isle of May was greater than that at St. Kilda, and was attained ca. 4 days earlier. Newfoundland birds, by contrast, had a much slower growth rate and took much longer to fledge than did chicks from Skomer Island or either Scottish colony. This in turn presumably reflects differences in the availability and quality of prey at these colonies—capelin in Newfoundland, compared to clupeids in Britain.

Puffin chicks on St. Kilda and Skomer received, respectively, 5.8 and 5.9 g of food for every 1 g of weight gained up to the time they reached peak body weight (Ashcroft 1976; Harris 1978). Captive chicks from Vedøya, northern Norway, fed on similar food to that given chicks in the wild and growing at a similar rate, had a conversion ratio of 7.7:1 (Tschanz 1979a). By contrast the conversion ratio for the slow-growing Great Island birds was over 10:1 (Nettleship 1972). The conversion ratio at Skomer Island is markedly lower than that for the Common Murre and Razor-bill chicks on the island (3.2:1 and 2.5–3.4:1, respectively: Birkhead 1976a; Lloyd 1976a, 1977), although all three species were feeding on clupeids. The Great Island figure is also lower than that of Common Murres on Gull Island nearby although the principal food of both alcids was capelin.

Nothing is known of the diets of young puffins from the time they leave the colony until they return as adults to breed.

C. Foraging

Adult Atlantic Puffins often forage very close to their colonies. At Skomer Island most of them did so within 3 to 5 km of the island, and none were seen returning with fish for the chicks at distances of over 13 km (Corkhill 1973; Ashcroft 1976; Birkhead 1976a). On the Isle of May the shortest intervals between alternate deliveries of food to the chick (i.e., meals presumed to have been brought by the same parent) were only 6 and 14 minutes, and at St. Kilda they were only 14 and 18 minutes (Harris and Hislop 1978). The fish which the parents brought back were often still alive (Harris 1970b; Corkhill 1973). Puffins breeding on the Murmansk Coast and in northern Iceland also foraged close to their colonies (Belo-pol'skii 1957; Cody 1973).

However, this is by no means universally true. A puffin carrying a fish has been seen ca. 50 km from the nearest colony in the North Sea (Joiris 1978). The extremely low provisioning rate of birds on Great Island, Newfoundland, only 3.0 meals/day (Nettleship 1972; see also Table 6.6) suggests that the foraging parents were travelling some distance from the colony; they were in fact observed carrying food over 16 km away (D. N.

TABLE 6.6

Average Numbers of Meals per Day Fed to Atlantic Puffin Chicks

No. of meals/day	Location	References
2.5	N. Norway	Myrberget (1962)
2.8	Greenland	Evans, in Harris and Hislop (1978)
3.0	Great I., Nfld.	Nettleship (1972)
4.0	Puffin I., Ireland	Evans, in Harris and Hislop (1978)
4.4	N. Rona, Scotland	Evans (1975)
6.1, 6.9	Skomer I., Wales	Corkhill (1973); Ashcroft (1976)
7.0	Isle of May, Scotland	Harris and Hislop (1978)
8.9	St. Kilda, Scotland	Harris and Hislop (1978)

Nettleship, unpublished observations). Flying puffins have been timed at speeds of 48 km/hour (Corkhill 1973; see also Pennycuick 1969), and at 82 km/hour (Meinertzhagen 1955). A Great Island puffin bringing two meals back to the nest in the course of a 16-hour day might therefore, in theory, be foraging over 200 km from the colony. The average interval between alternate meals on Skomer Island is 1.4 hour (Corkhill 1973), and so at the two speeds quoted the parent could have travelled 34–58 km out from the colony and back. The potential ranges at Scottish colonies are 36–61 km at St. Kilda (1.5 hour interval), 49–83 km at Hermaness (2.0 hours), and 57–97 km at the Isle of May (2.4 hours) (Harris and Hislop 1978), and 83–141 km (3.4 hours) at the Farne Islands in the North Sea (Pearson 1968). With puffins as with Common Murres (Section IV), however, these theoretical ranges are undoubtedly overestimates, since they allow no time for the adult bird to locate and catch its prey, or to perform its own maintenance activities.

Puffins breeding at low latitudes do not feed their young at night. The first birds to return with food in the morning to colonies in the eastern Atlantic do not arrive until ca. 0.3 hour after first light; their highest delivery rates are in the early morning, with a smaller peak in the early evening (Myrberget 1962; Corkhill 1973; Ashcroft 1976; Harris and Hislop 1978). This diurnal pattern may be interrupted by stormy weather, but it is apparently not influenced by the tidal cycle (Corkhill 1973; Ashcroft 1976). Puffins breeding on Great Island, Newfoundland, have a similar bimodal pattern of provisioning activity, with a well-defined peak between 0500 and 0900 hours, local time, and a less well-defined one between 1600 and 2000 hours (D. N. Nettleship, unpublished observations). The pattern in both cases suggests that the birds are exploiting fish which are available, or are concentrated in the surface waters, only after dark and in the twilight. This is very probable. There are many schools of clupeids, on which the Skomer Island birds depend, at the surface in the daytime (Birkhead 1976a, Fig. 4.11), but others stay near the bottom and only rise towards the surface at dusk, sinking again at dawn (Woodhead 1966). Capelin show a similar rhythm of vertical migration in offshore Newfoundland waters (Devold et al. 1972).

Foraging puffins apparently exploit schools of fish, as opposed to single individuals. The prey brought back in a meal to the colony almost always consists of fish of the same species and similar in size, although there may be small but significant differences in the lengths of fish brought back by different birds at the same place and time (Harris and Hislop 1978). This suggests that the birds stay with a school until they have collected a full load, with individual puffins staying with different schools. Some authors have observed that the fish are arranged alternately, head to tail, in the puffin's bill (Perry 1940; Lockley 1953a). Nash (1975) has suggested that this would come about if the bird made alternate lunges, left and right, when it was in the middle of a school of fish. However, the ordering of the fish in the bill may also be random (Myrberget 1962).

Little is known about the behaviour of the puffin underwater. Bird and Bird (1935) noted that birds in Jan Mayen dived only for ca. 5–10 seconds and did not go deep, but travelled up to 30 to 50 m in that time. However, either the speed or the distance here seems exaggerated, given Uspenski's estimate (1956) of an underwater speed of only 1.5–2 m/second in the Black Guillemot (see below). Dewar (1924) recorded submersion times of 26 and 33 seconds for two birds wintering in shallow water. Lockley (1953a) gives an average of 21 seconds (N = 45 birds) off Skokholm Island, Wales, but these were all newly fledged chicks; experienced adult birds might be expected to dive for longer periods. The mean dive time for the closely related, slightly bigger Horned Puffin in the North Pacific was 37 seconds (N = 16: Cody 1973). These times suggest that puffins do not dive very deeply. In support of this Piatt et al. (1984) found that puffins off eastern Newfoundland were never drowned in gill-nets set at depths of more than 60 m, but were commonly caught in those set 0–30 m below the surface (see also Piatt and Nettleship 1985).

VI. RAZORBILL, Alca torda

A. Adult Diet

Adult Razorbills wintering off Newfoundland fed mainly on crustaceans (Tuck 1961), and those in the Baltic on fish (Madsen 1957; Andersson et al. 1974). About 90% of the diet of Madsen's birds was fish—30% clupeids, 25% gobies and also some garfish (Belone sp., Belonidae), gadids and sticklebacks; the remainder was crustaceans (mysids and Gammarus amphipods). Single stomachs contained as many as ca. 1400 mysids and ca. 78 small, 25- to 30-mm-long sticklebacks. Of the birds examined in summer on the Murmansk Coast, 80% contained fish (sandlance, capelin, Atlantic herring and Atlantic cod), supplemented by small numbers of crustaceans and polychaetes (Belopol'skii 1957). Atlantic herring was the commonest species; these and young Atlantic cod increased in frequency during the summer, while capelin declined and sandlance remained constant. Sandlance, followed by capelin and to a lesser extent Atlantic herring, are the principal foods in the White Sea (Bianki 1967). In Labrador the diet of adult Razorbills early in the season was largely, if not totally, fish (mainly capelin), but after the chicks hatched the adult birds took few capelin but large numbers of small *Myxocephalus* sculpins and euphausiids (Bradstreet 1983; see also Table 6.1).

Experiments with captive birds showed that Razorbills had the same prey-size preferences as Atlantic Puffins (see above and Swennen and Duiven 1977), taking Atlantic herring and poor cod no longer than ca. 120 and ca. 100 mm, respectively. At sea, however, birds wintering in the Baltic took clupeids and gadids as long as 150 and 200 mm, respectively, and the longer but thinner garfish up to 250 mm (Madsen 1957).

Captive Razorbills ate ca. 15 sprats a day each—some 25% of their adult body weight (Marsault 1975). Like Common Murres (see above), they adjusted their consumption to allow for the quality of the prey, and for seasonal variations in their own metabolic requirements.

B. Chick Diet

The diet of young Razorbills consists of fish (Table 6.3); the species vary regionally. West Greenland chicks were fed only capelin (Salomonsen 1950), but the principal food elsewhere in the low arctic, in the Gulf of St. Lawrence, the White Sea and Labrador, is sandlance with capelin of secondary importance, while gadids, eelpouts and Atlantic herring are also taken (Bianki 1967; Bédard 1969d; Birkhead and Nettleship 1982a). Birds in boreal colonies in the Irish Sea mainly took sprats, followed by young Atlantic herring (Harris 1970b; Ashcroft 1976; Lloyd 1976a). Baltic birds fed their young almost entirely on sprat and herring, though sandlance was recorded once (Andersson *et al.* 1974).

The parents usually bring 1–6 fish (occasionally up to 20) at a meal, holding them crosswise in the bill (Perry 1940; Bédard 1969d; Lloyd 1976a; Birkhead and Nettleship 1982a); the number of fish brought in a meal decreases as their size increases. There was no correlation between the age of the chicks and the weight of the meals or the number of fish brought in them (Lloyd 1976a, 1977). The average feeding rate in Labrador was only 1.6–2.5 meals/day ($N = 13$: Birkhead and Nettleship 1982a). Up to a point the parents can adjust their provisioning to the chicks' requirements, as the birds' partial ability to raise artificially 'twinned' broods demonstrates (Plumb 1965; Lloyd 1976a, 1977; see also Chapter 4, this volume). Lloyd's (1976a, 1977) normal, one-chick broods on Skomer Island, Wales, received an average of 4.7 meals/day, against 9.0 (or 4.5 per chick) for experimental two-chick broods; this, along with an increase in the weight of the meals, provided, respectively, 22.0 and 20.1 g food/chick/day. Even so there was a shortfall in food, and the two-chick broods grew more slowly and fledged fewer chicks. There was no apparent relationship between the feeding frequency and the state of the tidal cycle but, as with the Atlantic Puffin (see Section V), feeding rates were highest just after dawn. Bianki (1967) found morning and evening activity peaks in White Sea birds. Meals were not always spread evenly through the day; one chick at a colony in the Gulf of St. Lawrence was fed five times in as little as 1.5 hour (Bédard 1969d). Bédard suggests that the feeding rate may be determined as much by the local abundance of prey as by the age or appetite of the chicks. On average, Lloyd's Skomer Island birds (1976a) received three to five meals a day, equivalent to 2.5 to 3.4 g of food for every 1 g of body weight gained during the first 19 days after hatching.

The average length of sandlance brought to chicks in Irish Sea colonies was 53–79 mm (Harris 1970b; Corkhill 1973; Ashcroft 1976; Lloyd 1976a), against 108 mm (N = 329) in Labrador (Birkhead and Nettleship 1982a) and 137 mm (N = 3) in northern Scotland (Evans 1975), up to a maximum of 130 mm in the Gulf of St. Lawrence (Bédard 1969d), 158 mm in the Irish Sea (Harris 1970b), and ca. 180 mm in Labrador (Birkhead and Nettleship 1982a).

The diet of young Razorbills after they leave the colony is not known.

C. Foraging

The foraging ranges of breeding Razorbills are poorly known. Most birds seen on the water (and thus potential foragers) near colonies in Iceland and the Irish Sea were only 2 km away (Cody 1973; Birkhead 1976a). However, neither observer went more than 10 km offshore and so the birds could have been travelling farther; nor need the birds on the water have been actual foragers. Murmansk Coast birds apparently forage within a radius of 15 km (Kaftanovskii 1951 cited in Bianki 1967; Kartaschew 1960). The largest concentrations off Skokholm Island, Wales, in the Irish Sea, were ca. 9–13 km away and the birds may have been foraging even closer, since the fish were sometimes still alive when brought to the breeding site (Lloyd 1976a). The intervals between meals may be as long as 1.9 hour (Lloyd 1976a), and at the maximum recorded flight speed of 86 km/hour (Meinertzhagen 1955; but see also Pennycuick 1969) Razorbills could have travelled 130 km out and back, although, as with the other alcids (q.v.), such an estimate is certainly exaggerated.

Razorbills diving in coastal waters preferred to do so over depths of ca. 1.8–3.6 m, with a range of 0 to 11 m (Dewar 1924); many of these were diving 'horizontally', not going down to the bottom (although Razorbills also make 'vertical' dives in deeper water; R. G. B. Brown, unpublished observations). The longest dive was 52 seconds; the average times increased from 18.9 seconds over ca. 1.7 m of water to 48.7 seconds over ca. 6.8 m. The average dive/pause ratio of 3.3 indicated that the Razorbill was almost as efficient a diver as the Dovekie and Common Murre (see Sections II, C and IV, C). However, the ratio decreased rapidly when the birds were in water deeper than 3 m, suggesting that the Razorbills were approaching the limit of their diving capabilities at that depth. However, other reports indicate that they fed off the bottom at ca. 5 m, though preferring to do so at 2 to 3 m (Madsen 1957; Paludan 1960 cited in Bianki 1967), and that they can almost certainly reach 10–15 m (Belopol'skii 1957; Bianki 1967). Several fish may be caught and eaten in the course of a single dive (Lloyd 1976a; Swennen and Duiven 1977).

VII. GREAT AUK, *Pinguinus impennis*

A. Diet

The last known Great Auks were killed in Iceland in 1844 (Newton 1861; Grieve 1885). Any attempt to describe the species' diet and feeding habits must necessarily be speculative, but it is worth summarising the little evidence available.

The only direct evidence of the Great Auk's diet comes from specimens collected ca. 1770 off Frederikshåb, southwest Greenland, in the fall (O. Fabricius cited in Salomonsen 1950). These were probably juvenile or subadult birds (Chapter 9, this volume), and they had been feeding on shorthorn sculpins (*Myoxocephalus scorpius*) and lumpsuckers (*Cyclopterus lumpus,* Cyclopteridae). The former is a benthic fish, and the latter largely benthic when adult (Leim and Scott 1966).

Olson *et al.* (1979) have tried to reconstruct the Great Auk's diet in another way. The species' last stronghold in North America was on Funk Island, Newfoundland (Chapter 2, this volume), and the only soil found there today has been formed from the corpses of Great Auks and other seabirds slaughtered on the island in the late 1700s (Lucas 1890). One would expect that the remains of any fish found in this soil would have come from the stomachs of the dead birds. Olson *et al.* (1979) examined a sample of soil adhering to a collection of bones, almost all of Great Auks, which Lucas (1890) collected on the Funks in 1887. They discovered scales and bone fragments of several species of fish (asterisk indicates species represented only by scales): menhaden (*Brevoortia tyrranus**, Clupeidae; estimated standard length range of the sample: 140–190 mm); shad (*Alosa* sp.*, Clupeidae; 120 mm); capelin (80–100 mm); unidentified gadids (120–150 and ca. 250 mm); three-spine stickleback (*Gasterosteus aculeatus;* 100–120 mm); striped bass (*Morone ?saxatilis**, Percichthy-

idae; 280–320 mm); an unidentified flatfish (Pleuronectidae); and also the
remains of several unidentified teleost fish.

Unfortunately this ingenious reconstruction is not completely convincing. Capelin, sticklebacks, gadids and pleuronectids all occur in the area
of Funk Island today (Leim and Scott 1966). But Funk Island is at, or just
beyond, the extreme northern edge of *Alosa sapidissima* and *A. pseudo-
harengus,* the only Newfoundland shads; striped bass occur no closer
than Cape Breton, Nova Scotia, ca. 900 km away by sea; the nearest
menhaden are in the Bay of Fundy (ca. 1500 km), but the species is rare
north of Cape Cod, Massachusetts. Olson *et al.* (1979) postulate a contraction in bass and menhaden ranges since the late eighteenth century.
But the maximum sea-surface temperature off Funk Island today is only
ca. 15°C (Anonymous 1967), with average summer temperatures much
below this, while the minimum preferred by menhaden is 21°C (Bigelow
and Schroeder 1953). If Olson *et al.* (1979) are right, there must have been
a radical change either in the species' temperature preferences or in the
water regime off Funk Island, and neither seems very probable. On the
other hand, contamination of the soil sample is a distinct possibility. The
three anomalous, warm-water species—bass, shad and menhaden—are
represented only by scales and not by the bony fragments which are more
likely to have survived the Great Auk's digestion. These scales might well
have been brought up from Massachusetts adhering to old fishing nets or
other gear used to corral the Great Auks before the birds were slaughtered. They might also have been brought up on the crate which held the
soil sample, although this seems unlikely (S. L. Olson, personal communication).

However, these data still make a useful basis for some speculations
about the size of prey which the Great Auk took. The largest item of
probable Newfoundland origin was the 250-mm gadid. If this was an
Atlantic cod, the commonest local species, it must have had a maximum
body depth of ca. 50–60 mm and a weight of ca. 150 g (Kohler 1964; Leim
and Scott 1966). The birds would undoubtedly also have been capable of
swallowing full-sized capelin (length ca. 210 mm, weight ca. 50 g: Jangaard 1974), much larger than the 80- to 100-mm fish (ca. 10 g) found in the
soil sample.

Body depth, not length, is the key to prey-size selection by the extant
fish-eating alcids, and this is at least partly related to the sizes of the birds'
gapes (Swennen and Duiven 1977). The Razorbill, the Great Auk's closest
extant relative, has a bill width of 9.07 mm and a gape of 52.40 mm; the
comparable measurements for the Great Auk are 16.73 and 107.95 mm
(Bédard 1969a). The maximum and preferred body depths of fish (herring
and poor cod) accepted by Razorbills are, respectively, 23–26 and 15 mm

(Swennen and Duiven 1977): bill depth/fish body depth ratios of 1:2.7 and
1:1.7, or gape size/fish body depth ratios of 1:0.5 and 1:0.3. If these
ratios are extrapolated to fit the bill measurements of the Great Auk they
suggest a maximum and preferred fish body depth of ca. 50 mm and ca. 30
mm, respectively. In an Atlantic cod these are equivalent to a fish ca. 225
mm long and ca. 75-100 g in weight, and ca. 135 mm and ca. 20 g,
respectively (Leim and Scott 1966; Swennen and Duiven 1977).

Again, one can compare the body weights of the birds and fish. Razorbills weigh 580-740 g (Bédard 1969a; Swennen and Duiven 1977) and their
maximum and preferred prey weights (16-18 and 4-6 g) are, respectively,
ca. 2.2 and ca. 0.75% of this. If Great Auks weighed ca. 5000 g (Bédard
1969a), extrapolation from the Razorbill percentages suggests maximum
and preferred prey weights of ca. 110 and ca. 37.5 g for this species.

Obviously these are only quantified guesses which cannot now be
checked. But, taken together, they suggest a maximum prey size of at
least 100-150 g and a preferred prey size of perhaps a quarter or a third of
that.

B. Foraging

The most detailed description of the habits of the Great Auk at sea
comes from the *English Pilot* of 1767 (but referring back to ca. 1715;
facsimile in Lysaght 1971, Fig. 4). This sets out 'Some Directions which
ought to be taken Notice of by those sailing to *Newfoundland*', one of
which was the appearance of '*Pengwins*':

> I have read an Author that says, in treating of this Coast, that you may know this by
> the great quantity of Fowls upon the Bank, *viz. Sheer-waters [Puffinus* spp.], *Willocks*
> [alcids, probably murres], *Noddies* [Northern Fulmars], *Gulls* [probably Black-legged
> Kittiwakes] and *Pengwins* [Great Auks], &c. without making any Exceptions; which is
> a mistake for I have seen these Fowls 10 Leag. off this Bank, the *Pengwins* excepted.
> It's true that all these Fowls are seen there in great quantities, but none are to be
> minded so much as the *Pengwin*, for these never go without [i.e., away from] the Bank
> as the others do, for they are always on it, or within [inshore of] it, several of them
> together, sometimes more, other times less, but never less than 2 together . . .

It is clear from the context that the *Pilot* is referring to the northern Grand
Banks on the route between England and St. John's, Newfoundland (ca.
46°N–48°N), and during the regular sailing season—say, May–October.
Nicholas Denys (1672), writing of the Great Auk in the mid-seventeenth
century, adds: 'It is claimed that it dives even to the bottom to seek its
prey upon the Bank. It is found more than a hundred leagues (ca. 550 km)
from land.' The distance of 'a hundred leagues' does not necessarily mean
that, contrary to the *Pilot,* the bird was found away from the bank. Parts

of the Grand Bank are as much as 450 km from the nearest part of New-foundland, and ca. 800 km from Denys' own base in Cape Breton, Nova Scotia. Taken together, these accounts suggest a preference for waters 75 m deep or less—the average depth of the Grand Bank. There is nothing improbable in the statement that Great Auks fed off the bottom at such depths. Gentoo Penguins, birds of similar size, can reach 100 m (Conroy and Twelves 1972), and even the much smaller Common Murres are regularly taken in gill-nets set on the bottom at ca. 180 m deep (see Section IV).

Otho Fabricius' observations off Frederikshåb (Salomonsen 1950) agree with those of Denys and the *Pilot*. His Great Auks were never seen on land and only occasionally among the offshore skerries; they usually occurred well out to sea. This suggests that they were on the offshore fishing banks there, ca. 55–75 m deep. As they were apparently taking benthic fish there (see above), this too suggests a deep-diving habit.

Olson *et al.* (1979) suggest that Great Auks from Funk Island must have foraged in water less than ca. 18 m deep and within ca. 2 km of the Newfoundland coast—or at least 65 km from the colony. They deduce this inshore niche from the occurrence of the remains of anadromous fishes—bass, shad—in their soil sample, but the evidence is suspect (see above). However, it is quite possible that Great Auks could have had a 65-km foraging range; they were strong swimmers, well able to outdistance rowing boats (Bent 1919). Macaroni Penguins, birds of similar size, forage as far as 115 km from their colonies (Croxall and Prince 1980). Eye-witnesses in Iceland told Newton (1861) that Great Auks were regularly seen in the tide race off Reykjanes, ca. 15–20 km inshore of the last surviving colony on Eldey, Iceland.

VIII. BLACK GUILLEMOT, *Cepphus grylle*

A. Adult Diet

The diet of Black Guillemots during the breeding season reflects their coastal habitat. They feed on many of the fish and invertebrates found on or near the sea bottom in shallow water, although they also feed on prey associated with pack-ice in the Arctic. Their prey spectrum is wider than that of the other Atlantic alcids: small demersal and pelagic fish and the young of larger fish (Tables 6.1 and 6.7), and a wide range of inverte-brates: polychaetes, pteropods and other molluscs, jellyfish, oedicerotids, lamellibranchs, sponges, ctenophores and such crustaceans as decapods, amphipods, mysids, euphausiids, isopods and copepods (Sutton 1932;

TABLE 6.7

Diet of Adult Black Guillemots during the Breeding Season[a]

	Marine zone and location			
	High arctic		Low arctic	
Prey taxa	Barrow Strait, N.W.T. (N = 681 items/ 47 stomachs)	Lancaster Sound, N.W.T. (N = 1190 items/ 56 stomachs)	Nuvuk Is., Digges Sound, N.W.T. (N = 290 items/ 22 stomachs)	Flatey, Iceland (N = 651 items/ 69 stomachs)
Invertebrates				
Polychaetes	+	−	10.0	37.3
Molluscs	7.5	+	−	6.8
Crabs	−	−	−	3.4
Decapods	0.9	−	1.4	29.2
Amphipods	62.6	92.9	2.4	8.3
Mysids	0.4	3.6	62.1	−
Barnacles	+	−	−	−
Copepods	15.3	0.3	−	−
Isopods	−	+	−	−
Cumaceans	−	0.1	−	−
Fish				
Herring	−	−	−	0.2
Cod	12.9	3.3	20.3	0.3
Sandlance	−	−	−	5.5
Gunnel	−	−	−	4.5
Pricklebacks	−	−	3.8	1.2
Rockfish	−	−	−	0.2
Sculpins	0.3	−	−	0.9
Sea-snails	−	−	−	0.2
References	Bradstreet (1977, 1980)	Bradstreet (1976)	Cairns (1982)	Petersen (1981)

[a] Values given are percentage frequency; −, not recorded in diet; +, present in small amounts.

Bird and Bird 1935; Degerbøl and Møhl-Hansen 1935; Hartley and Fisher 1936; Cottam and Hanson 1938; Duffey and Sergeant 1950; Storer 1952; Gudmundsson 1953a; Uspenski 1956; Belopol'skii 1957; Madsen 1957; Macpherson and McLaren 1959; Løvenskiold 1964; de Korte 1972; Bradstreet 1976, 1977, 1980; Smith and Hammill 1980; Petersen 1981; Cairns 1982).

Table 6.7 summarises quantitative aspects of adult diets in the high- and low-arctic regions. Most of the items are invertebrates, mainly amphipods, mysids, decapods and polychaetes. In the high-arctic region, fish (mostly arctic cod) made up only 13% of the items up to the end of the incubation period (Bradstreet 1977, 1980), and only 3% during the chick-rearing period (Bradstreet 1976); only 13–24% of those found in birds at low-arctic colonies were fish (Petersen 1981; Cairns 1982). There is no quantitative information on the diets of adult birds breeding farther south.

The numerical preponderance of invertebrates is, however, very misleading, since most of these items are small. In the high-arctic area, arctic cod made up 84% of the *biomass* of adult diets during the chick-rearing season even though 97% of the items were invertebrates (Table 6.1; see also Bradstreet 1976). If this applies to the other feeding studies based on numerical indices (Petersen 1981; Cairns 1982), it is probable that breeding adult Black Guillemots derive a significant proportion of their diet energy from fish.

Little is known of adult diets outside the breeding season. The stomachs of 15 birds collected off Southampton Island, Hudson Bay, in late February contained crustaceans, probably *Parathemisto libellula;* two birds collected in mid-May contained crustaceans and molluscs (Sutton 1932). Two-thirds of the diet of birds (N = 26) collected in Denmark in winter was fish (mostly gobies but also Atlantic herring, Atlantic cod, eelpout, sculpins and others); the remainder was crustaceans, mainly crabs and shrimps (Madsen 1957). Of the stomachs of birds collected off southeast Baffin Island in late winter, 83% contained larval cottid and liparid fish, 57% *Parathemisto libellula,* 43% mysids and 17% squid (*Gonatus fabricii*), as well as a few other crustaceans (Smith and Hammill 1980). Polychaetes and amphipods predominate in the stomachs of Black Guillemots collected in late winter and early spring in Franz Josef Land, in contrast to the summer diet which consists only of fish (Gorbunov 1932 and Demme 1934 cited in Belopol'skii 1957).

B. Chick Diet

Black Guillemots feed their young mainly on fish, and it is only in the high-arctic areas that invertebrates are more than a minor fraction of the chick diet [25% by weight, mainly crustaceans at Prince Leopold Island (Gaston and Nettleship 1981; D. N. Nettleship, unpublished observations); crustaceans 28% by number in west Greenland (P. G. H. Evans, cited in Petersen 1981)]. Blennies, along with gobies, sculpins and arctic cod, predominate in chick diets (Table 6.3), along with sea-snails (Cyclopteridae) in the high- and low-arctic areas, and sandlance at boreal colonies; clupeids, osmerids, rockfish (Scorpaenidae), flatfish and wrasse (Labridae) have also been recorded.

Each meal consists of a single item, almost always a fish, held cross-wise in the bill. Average daily feeding rates range from ca. 3 per day in Novaya Zemlya, Barents Sea (Uspenski 1956), to 7 to 15 in the White Sea (Robardzei, cited in Bianki 1967), to 12.4 in the Gulf of St. Lawrence (Cairns 1982) and 15 in Iceland (Petersen 1981). In many, but not all cases, these rates increase as the chicks grow older (Bianki 1967; Petersen 1981; but see also Asbirk 1979b). The rates may also vary from year to year, presumably reflecting the abundance of prey: the average for a colony in southwest Finland was only 5.3 meals/day in 1963 to 1968, but increased to 14 in 1970 (Bergman 1971, 1978). They also vary with the number of young in the brood, since the Black Guillemot is the only Atlantic alcid which may lay two eggs in a clutch (see Chapter 3, this volume). Broods of two chicks were fed more than those of only one, and experimental broods of three at a higher frequency still (Cairns 1978, 1981; Asbirk 1979b; Petersen 1981). However, this higher frequency was still not enough to maintain a constant ration for each chick; Petersen's two-chick broods received ca. 30% fewer meals than his single chicks. It is not known whether the adults compensate for this shortfall by increasing the size or calorific quality of the fish. The average size of fish brought to Icelandic chicks was 124 mm long or 7.6 g ($N = 554$); the heaviest, a gunnel, weighed 37 g, ca. 9% of the average adult weight (Petersen 1981). Petersen's birds received an average of 10.0 g of food for every 1 g of weight gained during the first 30 days after hatching. Average prey lengths elsewhere were comparable: 108 mm in the White Sea ($N = 172$; Bianki 1967) and 137 mm at Nuvuk Islands, Digges Sound ($N = 92$; Cairns 1982). Sizes increased as the chicks grew older (Asbirk 1979b; Petersen 1981; Cairns 1982). Like the other fish-eating alcids (see above), Black Guillemots apparently used body depth rather than length in selecting prey of suitable size (Petersen 1981). Sandlance were mainly fed to the smaller chicks in Petersen's colony rather than to older birds, even though these fish were available all summer, and he suggests that small chicks may be unable to swallow broad-bodied or spiny prey such as sculpins. In extreme cases Black Guillemot chicks have died in attempting to swallow over-large prey (Divoky et al. 1974).

The fish fed to Black Guillemot chicks tend to be larger than the fish and invertebrates found in the stomachs of breeding adults. Small (ca. 5.5 g) arctic cod made up over 75% of the items in the adult diet at Nuvuk Islands, but only 13% of the chicks'—the rest being mainly large (15–20 g) blennies (Cairns 1982). Small invertebrates made up 84% of the adult diet items in Iceland, but only 6% of the chicks' (Petersen 1981). Presumably an adult bird will catch and eat any prey it finds underwater, however small, since that would provide a better energy return than nothing at all.

On the other hand, it would be more advantageous to reserve large items of prey for the chicks, since the larger the food package brought back to the colony, the fewer trips the adult will have to make in the long run. The higher calorific values of fish over crustaceans (see Atlantic Puffin, Section V) are probably also factors here. Those of gunnel and sculpins have been estimated at 5.9 and 5.1 kJ/g, respectively (Dunn 1975a). The relative proportions of large and small fish and of crustaceans in the diets of adult and young Black Guillemots no doubt reflect compromises between quantitative and qualitative factors such as these, and what is actually available in the waters around the colony. The degree of flexibility in the adults' ability to change from one prey to another must therefore vary with the region. The main fish fed to Icelandic chicks—gunnel, sandlance and sculpins—were present in all 3 years of Petersen's study (1981) although their relative proportions varied a little from year to year, much as Harris and Hislop (1978) describe for Atlantic Puffins. Petersen (1981) concluded that his birds were generalised feeders which could switch to a different species if one prey was not available. On the other hand, the main fish brought to chicks in southwest Finland was the eelpout (*Zoarces viviparus*), and there was apparently no acceptable substitute for it; breeding success was reduced in summers when sea temperatures were below average and this fish was scarce or absent (Bergman 1971, 1978).

Little is known of the diet of young Black Guillemots after they leave the breeding site. Juveniles collected in Lancaster Sound in late August to early September had been feeding mainly on *Parathemisto* and *Apherusa* amphipods (M. S. W. Bradstreet, unpublished observations).

C. Foraging

Adult Black Guillemots show three diurnal activity patterns in feeding their young: a fairly constant feeding rate throughout the daylight hours (Asbirk 1979b; Cairns 1982); a morning peak followed by a steady decline for the rest of the day (Bianki 1967); a strong morning and a weaker evening peak (Bergman 1971; Cairns 1981). Birds in western Iceland showed a fairly constant rate in one year but a morning peak in another (Petersen 1981). The reasons for these variations are not clear. They may reflect the requirements of the chicks, since adult birds with two-chick broods make more afternoon feeding trips than those with only one (Petersen 1981), and the movements of prey may also be important (Sealy 1973a). In the latter case one would expect the tidal cycle to be important in this, the most coastal of the Atlantic alcids, but the evidence is conflicting; tidal correlations may occur in the Barents Sea and the Bay of Fundy

(Belopol'skii 1957; Preston 1968), but not in Denmark or the Gulf of St. Lawrence (Asbirk 1979b; Cairns 1981, 1982).

Black Guillemots tend to forage closer to their breeding sites than do the other alcids: out to ca. 1.5 km (Preston 1968, Bay of Fundy); 1.5–4.0 km away (Bergman 1971, Finland); 0.5–4.0 km (Asbirk 1979b, Denmark); 2 km or more (Bianki 1967, White Sea); usually 2–4 km, but up to 7 km or more (Petersen 1981, Iceland). Birds have been recorded as much as 15 to 20 km away from the nearest site in western Lancaster Sound in summer (Nettleship and Gaston 1978), and ca. 30 km in eastern Hudson Bay (R. G. B. Brown, unpublished observations), but these may not have been active breeders. However, they regularly forage in deep water, away from the coast, at other times of year, close to icebergs or the pack-ice (Sutton 1932; Salomonsen 1950; Johnson et al. 1976; Brown 1980a; Renaud and Bradstreet 1980; McLaren 1982). They are often found in very narrow leads (or cracks) in the ice; as small as ca. 0.3 m wide by 6 m long off Prince Leopold Island, Lancaster Sound, in May 1977 (D. N. Nettleship, personal communication). The fact that they can take off from a strip of water only 6 m long shows that they are agile flyers; more so than Thick-billed Murres, for example, which require ca. 8–10 m (Uspenski 1956) and which, unlike Black Guillemots, are regularly trapped when sudden shifts in the pack-ice reduce the amount of open water (Freuchen and Salomonsen 1958, pp. 42–43).

Average diving times vary from 25–40 seconds (Bianki 1967), through 30–35 seconds, maximum 75 seconds (Nicholson, cited in Salomonsen 1950), to 36.2 seconds, maximum 68.8 seconds (Scott 1973, for the sibling Pigeon Guillemot of the North Pacific). Birds in Lancaster Sound, mainly feeding 'horizontally' under the ice, averaged 60 seconds, maximum 146 seconds ($N = 9$: Bradstreet 1982b) and this may well be an underestimate, given their ability to forage in relatively dense pack-ice where there may be few openings into which they may come up to breathe. A bird diving 'vertically' in Lancaster Sound, away from the ice and in 110 m of water, remained underwater for ca. 60 seconds (R. G. B. Brown, unpublished observations); given an underwater swimming speed of 1.5 to 2 m/second (Uspenski 1956), it is possible that it could have dived to the bottom in that time. However, most accounts stress the Black Guillemot's association with the shallow sublittoral zones (Salomonsen 1950; Bianki 1967). Cairns (1982) concluded that most birds foraging along the northeastern coast of Hudson Bay did so in water less than 18 m deep. This agrees with Scott's observations (1973) on the Pigeon Guillemot in Oregon, although his birds foraged as deep as 37 m on occasion.

Individual Black Guillemots differ in the food they bring back to their young, even at the same colony (Slater and Slater 1972; Cairns 1981, 1982;

Petersen 1981). Petersen shows that this is at least partly the result of individual differences in foraging area, even between the members of a pair.

IX. DISCUSSION

The information on the feeding and foraging behaviour of the Atlantic alcids, set out in the individual species sections, has ranged rather widely, and it is useful to conclude by summarising the principal points (see also Table 6.8).

What the alcids have in common, in the Atlantic as in the Pacific, is that they are all diving birds which catch their prey by pursuing it underwater. They are, perhaps, the most efficient diving birds in the North Atlantic (Dewar 1924). Common and Thick-billed Murres and Black Guillemots have the longest dive times of the extant species, and the two murres also dive the deepest: regularly, perhaps, to over 100 m. The Black Guillemot is restricted by the shallow waters of its preferred coastal habitat, but it is probable that it too dives deeply farther offshore. However, Razorbills and Atlantic Puffins apparently do not go very deep, and the Razorbill, at least, may be poorly adapted physiologically for deep diving.

The foraging ranges of breeding birds may be very wide—50 km or more in the Dovekie, murres and puffin, although the puffin and Razorbill usually forage closer inshore, as does the coastal Black Guillemot. The birds exploit local 'patches' of prey at higher concentrations than the average density in the area—at oceanic 'fronts', for example, or ice-edges—presumably because these allow them to collect food while expending the minimum amount of energy in energetically expensive swimming. They seem able to trade this off against the relatively lower costs of long flights to such areas. Dovekies, at least, further improve their foraging efficiency by selecting prey items which are not only locally concentrated, but also of relatively large size and high nutritional quality.

Dovekies are planktivorous but the other species are primarily fish-eaters, although Razorbills, Black Guillemots and, to a lesser extent, Thick-billed Murres and Atlantic Puffins may at times take significant quantities of invertebrates. Black Guillemots feed on fish in the littoral and sublittoral zone, such as sculpins and blennies; Thick-billed Murres in the Arctic in summer take demersal species such as arctic cod, the dominant small fish of the high-arctic area, and sculpins, blennies and also the pelagic capelin farther south. However, the dominant foods of the other extant fish-eating alcids are pelagic species such as clupeids, sandlance and capelin.

TABLE 6.8

Comparative Aspects of Food and Foraging Behaviour in the Atlantic Alcidae[a]

Character	Dovekie	Thick-billed Murre	Common Murre	Atlantic Puffin	Razorbill	Great Auk	Black Guillemot
Foraging habitat (summer)[b]	ON	ON	ON	N	N	ON?	L
Range (km) of birds foraging for chicks							
Normal	<17	2–25	<10?	5?	10	?	≤4
Maximum	100?	75	50	50	15	15–20?	7
Dive time (seconds)							
Normal	22–33	40–83	41–71	20–30	19–49	?	25–40
Maximum	68	192	140	?	52	?	146
Dive depth (m)							
Normal	?	?	30?	6–10	<5	?	<18
Maximum	35?	75–100	60–100	?	10–15	75?	37
Principal foods[c]							
Adult	dI	BDPi	bDP	DPI	dPI	BDP	BDpI
Chick	I	BDP	P	dP	dP	?	BDpi

Prey length (mm), 'medium' fish[d]							
Preferred	—	70–160	100	70	70	135?	
Maximum	—	193	200	120	100–200	250?	
Prey length (mm), 'thin' fish[e]							
Preferred	—	113	?	76–145	53–137	?	108–137
Maximum	—	?	220	207	250	?	290
Average no. items/chick meal	ca. 600	1	1	5–12	1–6	?	1
Method of transport[f]	po	bt	bt	bx	bx	?	bx
Chick growth: food (g) for 1 g body weight increase	5.5	4.0–13.4	3.2–3.4	5.9–ca. 10	2.5–3.4	?	10.0
Adult daily consumption as % of body weight	?	10–33	10–34	?	25	?	?

[a] For further details see the species sections in the text.

[b] O, Offshore; N, nearshore; L, littoral zone.

[c] I, Invertebrates. Fish: B, benthic species (e.g., sculpins, blennies); D, demersal (e.g., gadids); P, pelagic (e.g., clupeids, sandlance, capelin). Lower case indicates a group which is relatively unimportant.

[d] Species with relatively deep bodies (e.g., gadids, clupeids).

[e] Species with slender bodies (e.g., sandlance, blennies).

[f] po, Throat pouch; bt, fish tail-foremost in the bill; bx, fish crosswise in the bill.

The food brought to the chicks is not necessarily the same as that which the adults themselves eat. Dovekie chicks are fed on invertebrates. However, the chicks of the other extant species are fed almost exclusively on fish even though the adults may, on occasion, feed extensively on invertebrates. In temperate marine environments, where there is a relatively large community of fish species, the Common Murre, Razorbill and puffin usually feed their young on pelagic rather than demersal species. Invertebrates usually have a lower calorific content than fish, and pelagic fish tend to be richer in fat and oil than demersal ones. It is therefore likely that a fish diet, especially one made up of pelagic species, would be well adapted to the energetic requirement of the rapidly growing chicks. The ability of the chicks to convert their food into body weight varies between the species. The two species which are fed mainly on demersal fish, Thick-billed Murre and Black Guillemot, do so less efficiently than do the Common Murre, Razorbill and puffin, fed on clupeids and similar species; of the last three, puffin chicks appear to have the least efficient conversion ratios. The adult birds also vary in their ability to increase the size and frequency of the meals to cope with the additional demands of the chicks when these are experimentally increased. Of the three species which have been investigated the Black Guillemot, the only Atlantic alcid which regularly has more than one chick to a brood, is the most adaptable, while Razorbills can sometimes raise an additional chick but puffins usually fail to do so.

All in all, the brief survey in this chapter has probably revealed more gaps than information about our knowledge of the feeding and foraging habits of the Atlantic alcids, for all the intensive fieldwork of the last 15 years. We will conclude by proposing some topics for future research:

1. It goes without saying that we need more quantitative studies of the diets of adult and young birds, but these should be selective. The ideal is to study the whole alcid community in a given area, and to choose the areas carefully so that they are representative of a variety of marine habitats. The surveys in the Irish Sea (Corkhill 1973; Ashcroft 1976; Birkhead 1976a; Lloyd 1976a) and in eastern Canada (Nettleship 1972; Mahoney 1979; Gaston and Nettleship 1981; Gaston et al. 1981; Birkhead and Nettleship 1982a) show the advantages of the comparative approach. However, it would be interesting to match the geographic spread of the Canadian investigations with others in Europe: so as to compare the birds breeding in Spitsbergen–Murmansk Coast–Norway–Shetland–Irish Sea, for example, with those in Lancaster Sound–Hudson Strait–Labrador–Newfoundland. Within such a framework, certain species and areas de-

serve particular attention. We need to know more about the feeding ecology of Atlantic Puffins and Black Guillemots breeding in the Arctic, with their greater apparent dependence on invertebrate foods compared to colonies farther south. We also need more information on alcids breeding at the extreme limits of their ranges, whether these are the very numerous Dovekies, Thick-billed Murres and Black Guillemots of Franz Josef Land (Norderhaug et al. 1977), or the very small Common Murre populations of Spain and Portugal (Bárcena et al. 1984); knowing what limits the birds at the edges of their range is an important part of an understanding of their feeding ecology where they are most abundant.

2. We also need more information, quantitative or qualitative, about the diet of the Great Auk, but of course we are unlikely to get it. It would be interesting to repeat the analyses of Olson et al. (1979) of fish remains in fresh samples of soil from Funk Island. However, this would mean damaging the nesting habitat of the present puffin population there, and the extant birds obviously have priority over the extinct. It is highly unlikely that the slaughter of Great Auks has left similar soil deposits at any other of their former colonies. The remaining possibility is the examination of the remains of fishes associated with Great Auk bones in prehistoric middens.

3. A better understanding is needed of the relationships between the Atlantic Alcidae and their prey at sea; for example, by correlating bird numbers with the densities of fish and plankton recorded by sonar surveys, continuous sampling devices and satellite imagery, along the lines of Anderson et al. (1982) and Briggs et al. (1984) (see also Fig. 6.1). Such surveys would be basic to our understanding of where the prey is, how the birds locate it, and its maximum local density, depth and distance from the colony for efficient foraging by the alcids in question. The ultimate aim would be a predictive model to account for the birds' distributions throughout the year, as Brown (1980b; see also Chapters 2 and 9, this volume) has provisionally attempted for Dovekie distributions.

4. We need to be able to define foraging areas and ranges at different times during the breeding season; is there a contraction of foraging ranges around alcid colonies after the chicks hatch and, if so, to what extent is this the result of coincident inshore movements of prey, or is a limitation imposed by the feeding requirements of the chicks? Specifically, if Dovekies foraging for chicks in Greenland colonies do so mainly very close inshore, why do birds which are *not* foraging for chicks travel so far offshore to feed?

5. To what extent do adult birds feed themselves on prey different in size and/or species from that which they bring to their chicks? How do

such differences reflect the differing metabolic requirements of adults and young? To what extent can the chicks adjust their growth rates, and the adults their provisioning, if prey of suitable quality is scarce or absent?

6. Almost nothing is known of the alcids' behaviour underwater. We need information about such basic topics as dive times and depths, and both horizontal and vertical speeds underwater, and to relate these to the speeds and depths of the prey species in question. The ultimate aim, of course, is an understanding of the physiology of diving in these birds, and the telemetric techniques for acquiring this are probably already available.

7. Very little more is known of the biology of the birds' prey species either, even when these are commercially fished species such as capelin and sandlance. It is particularly important to study the arctic cod, central to high-arctic food webs on both sides of the Atlantic, and also the many non-commercial fish such as sculpins and blennies which are very important in the diets of many alcids. Such surveys should include the collection of information on the energetic content of these species as food, not more or less at random as has been done up to now in most cases, but in the form of *systematic* sampling of the prey spectrum available at each colony, throughout the term of the birds' occupancy. These surveys must go beyond the establishment of calorific values and must include chemical analyses of the proportions of fat and other constituents in the birds' foods.

8. Input from the quality and density of the prey, the costs of the birds' foraging and the metabolic requirements of adults and chicks should be used to draw up an energy budget for both breeding and non-breeding alcids, along the lines of other models for seabird communities (Wiens and Scott 1975; Furness 1978b). This would have the theoretical value of allowing us to understand, and make predictions about the role of seabirds in marine communities. It would have the additional, practical advantage of writing the birds' requirements into the assessments of allowable catches for the fisheries in which humans and birds compete (Brown and Nettleship 1984a).

CHAPTER 7

Development of the Young in the Atlantic Alcidae[1]

ANTHONY J. GASTON

Canadian Wildlife Service, Ottawa, Ontario, Canada

I. INTRODUCTION

Most alcids are oceanic birds feeding out of sight of land throughout the year. Like other oceanic birds they face the perennial problem of having to return to land to reproduce. The effects of this constraint have undoubtedly influenced the evolution of many of their physical and behavioural adaptations but we can observe the interaction of feeding ecology and breeding requirements most clearly in the growth and development of the young.

The Alcidae are unusual, among families of birds, in including species exhibiting a considerable diversity of behaviour during the period immedi-

[1] This chapter was prepared in association with the program "Studies on Northern Seabirds", Seabird Research Unit, Canadian Wildlife Service, Environment Canada (Report No. 132).

319

ately after hatching (see Sealy 1973a for review). These differences in behaviour are frequently referred to as different patterns of development, but strictly speaking this is not the case; the stage of development at which young alcids hatch and the plumages through which they subsequently pass are, with one important exception, quite similar. The exception involves the genera *Uria* and *Alca* in which the development of the rectrices and remiges is delayed relative to the development of the contour plumage. Otherwise, variation within the family occurs mainly in the timing of departure from the breeding site, with some young auks leaving within a few days after hatching (precocial), others completing a part of

TABLE 7.1

Age and Proportion of Adult Weight Attained at Fledging among Species of Alcidae: Selected Examples

Species	Age (days at) departure from breeding site	% Adult weight at departure from breeding site	References
Precocial			
Xantus' Murrelet	2	14	Murray *et al.* (1983)
Craveri's Murrelet	*ca.* 2	?	Sealy (1973a)
Ancient Murrelet	2	14	Sealy (1976)
Japanese Murrelet	*ca.* 2	?	Sealy (1973a)
'Intermediate'			
Razorbill	15–20	20–25	Bédard (1969d)
Common Murre	18–25	20–27	Hedgren (1979)
Thick-billed Murre	15–30	15–30	Gaston and Nettleship (1981)
Semi-precocial			
Dovekie	26–29	71–74	Norderhaug (1980)
Black Guillemot	34–39	88	Cairns (1978)
Pigeon Guillemot	29–39	91	Drent (1965)
Marbled Murrelet	21	70	Sealy (1974)
Cassin's Auklet	35–46	90	Manuwal (1974a)
Parakeet Auklet	35	79	Sealy and Bédard (1973)
Crested Auklet	33	80	Sealy (1972)
Least Auklet	29	88	Sealy (1972)
Rhinoceros Auklet	50–60	51–69	Vermeer and Cullen (1979)
Atlantic Puffin	34–44	69–75	Harris (1978)
Horned Puffin	38	67	Sealy (1973b)
Tufted Puffin	43–51	67–70	Vermeer and Cullen (1979)

their growth at the breeding site (intermediate) and some remaining until almost fully grown (semi-precocial) (Table 7.1). Differences in patterns of development among species are largely behavioural, rather than physical, therefore.

In terms of physical development, co-ordination and thermoregulatory abilities, the development of the Alcidae is broadly similar at a given age. The striking variation in the age and state of development of the chick on departure from the breeding site has led to considerable speculation regarding the adaptive significance of different behavioural strategies. To clarify this issue it is necessary to view the predicament of the alcid chick in its correct ecological and evolutionary context.

This, in turn, requires us to distinguish those aspects of development that are determined by factors intrinsic to the chick itself and those which are, in a sense, imposed by constraints operating on the adult. It is these latter forces which are presumably responsible for the present diversity of strategies in the timing of departure from the breeding site.

Before addressing the case of the Alcidae, it is necessary to review the main ideas concerning the selection pressures operating on growth and development of the young at the natal site. I shall also discuss methods used in measuring, recording and analysing growth because it is quite possible to draw very different conclusions about parameters such as 'growth rates', depending on the way that they are calculated. We are only safe in making comparisons when we have a rigorous and appropriate definition of the parameter that we wish to compare.

II. GROWTH AND HOW TO MEASURE IT

A. Growth and Development in Their Evolutionary Context

Patterns of development can be viewed as a compromise between a number of selection pressures acting on both chick and parent (Ricklefs 1977a). From the point of view of the parent, the first compromise is between the investment required for reproduction, and the possible decrease in its own chance of survival that such an investment might entail, at the expense of future reproductive attempts (see reviews in Goodman 1974; Stearns 1976). This consideration may influence the choice of breeding site, the size of egg laid, the intensity of incubation, the amount of time spent brooding and the rate at which the chick is provisioned. The adaptations of the chick evolve within the framework of these constraints; hence the size of the egg, or more specifically the size of the yolk, governs the initial size of the chick, while the rate of provisioning affects its subsequent growth. It has been common to discuss breeding adaptations as though the optimum strategies of chick and parent were identical, but there are good theoretical grounds for distinguishing between them (Alexander 1974; Trivers 1974; O'Connor 1978).

During the period when young non-precocial birds are dependent on their parents for food, their increase in weight is determined by an interaction between intrinsic physiological constraints and the rate of provisioning by their parents. The weight–age curves of chicks approximate the logistic or similar curve, with an early accelerating phase, a linear phase, and a decelerating phase terminating at the asymptote. This is, in some cases, followed by a fourth phase of weight recession. As the existence energy needs of the chick are a function of its weight, it follows that the amount of food it requires must increase, at least up to the end of the linear phase, unless there is a progressive change in its digestive efficiency. In practice, for a range of species, maximum food requirements have been found to occur at or close to the time of fledging (Drent and Daan 1980). This suggests that up to the end of the linear phase, the parents are capable of supplying food in excess of the chick's requirements and hence, up to this point, the shape of the growth curve has been

TABLE 7.2

Predicted Relationship between Chick Weight and Age, from the End of the Linear Growth Phase to the Asymptote

Assumption 1

That when the chick reaches asymptotic weight (t_a), the food supplied by the parents is exactly balanced by the metabolic requirements of the chicks for maintenance. Hence,

$$I = \gamma \, (\beta W_a^\alpha) \tag{1}$$

where W_a is the asymptotic weight of the chick (kg), I is the daily energy intake (kcal/day) and γ, β and α are constants relating chick weight to metabolic rate (Kendeigh 1970).

Assumption 2

That at the end of the linear growth phase (t_i) the food supplied by the parents is just enough to sustain growth at the rate maintained during the linear growth phase plus the metabolic requirements of the chick for maintenance at the weight (W_i). Hence,

$$I = \beta(W_i^\alpha) + g_0 \tag{2}$$

where g_0 is the energy expended on growth during the linear phase.

The shape of the curve from t_i to t_a can then be predicted from the formula:

$$\frac{dw}{I - \gamma(\beta W^\alpha)} = t \tag{3}$$

Hypothetical curves based on Lasiewski and Dawson (1967) for values of β and α and estimating γ at 1.5 for quiescent chicks being brooded for most of the time are shown in Fig. 7.1.

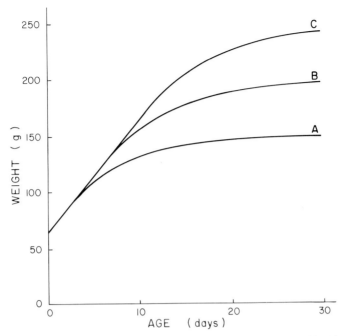

Fig. 7.1. Hypothetical curves generated from the formula given in Table 7.2. Parameters given are as follows: rate of increase in the linear phase, 10 g/day (fixed); asymptotes, A = 150 g, B = 200 g, and C = 250 g.

determined by intrinsic factors, presumably the result of selection operating on the chick.

If parental feeding continues to exceed the requirements of the chick the growth curve will continue to reflect only intrinsic effects, but if feeding falls below the level required to maintain the rate of growth characteristic of the linear phase, the rate of provisioning will begin to affect the observed growth curve. Lack (1954, 1966, 1968) has argued that clutch size is adjusted to the number of offspring that can be fed by the parents. With minor modifications (Cody 1966; Williams 1966; Charnov and Krebs 1974; Perrins 1977; Ricklefs 1977b) this hypothesis has been substantiated for a wide range of species. Among alcids it has been experimentally demonstrated in the case of Atlantic Puffins (Nettleship 1972; Harris 1978), Razorbills (Lloyd 1977) and Rhinoceros Auklets (Summers and Drent 1979). Using this assumption, the shape of the growth curve from the end of the linear phase to the asymptote can be predicted [Table 7.2, Eq. (3); and Fig. 7.1]. We should anticipate that physiological processes will be adapted to coincide with this curve to optimize the use of available food. The extent to which an actual growth curve coincides with this prediction will depend on how accurately the actual clutch laid approximates to the optimum clutch size.

Growth curves can therefore be expected to be made up of two components; in the first phase growth will be adjusted to match the maximum possible growth rate of the chick, while in the second it will be adjusted to match the constraints imposed by the maximum rate of provisioning that the parents can achieve. The shape of the latter phase is therefore determined by selection operating on the parental genotype. This selection will tend to maximize the residual reproductive potential of the parent and during this period we may anticipate some conflict between the optimum requirements of the chick and the level of provisioning that optimizes the present and future reproductive output of the parents (Trivers 1974).

For most species of birds internal mechanisms in the female allow adjustment of the clutch size so that asymptotic weights are fairly similar among different broods, seasons and years (Coulson and White 1961; Perrins 1965; Lack 1966; Cody 1971). Where food supplies during the chick-rearing period cannot be predicted accurately at the time of laying, brood reduction also occurs (O'Connor 1978; Werschkul and Jackson 1979). For species laying only a single egg, which include the majority of the Alcidae, no adjustment is possible and asymptotic weights vary widely among populations and between years. The ability of alcids laying a single-egg clutch to rear two young has been tested in a number of experiments involving brood manipulation or the removal of one parent. In all cases it was clear that the parents were capable of increasing feeding rates to only a limited extent and the result was that in most instances one of the chicks starved or both were severely underweight (Plumb 1965; Nettleship 1972; Corkhill 1973; Lloyd 1976a; Harris 1978; Petersen 1981).

Changes in the availability of food during the breeding season which affect the rate at which the parents provision their chicks may affect rates of growth. As the requirements of the chick are greatest just before fledging, there is a selective advantage in timing the breeding cycle so that this period coincides with the maximum availability of food, provided that other constraints allow it (Lack 1950, 1968; Perrins 1970; Murton and Westwood 1977). We can predict from this that food will usually be less readily available during the growth phase than just prior to fledging. For given species we can estimate the approximate magnitude of variations in food availability that might begin to affect observed growth rates, although the calculation is complicated by variations in foraging range and the consequent travel time involved. The extent to which chick growth rates may be adapted to regular seasonal changes in the availability of food is an area which has been little explored, although it may have a bearing on the slow growth rates of certain pelagic seabirds.

Where asymptotic weights attained on the breeding site are significantly lower than adult weights, we can regard these as the product of selection on the adult phenotype and as a measure of parental investment. The evolution of fledging weights in the case of non-precocial chicks can therefore be treated as the product of the same selective forces that operate on clutch size. From this point of view it is reasonable to regard reduced fledging weights as the reduction of clutch size by other means. Variation in clutch size has received much more attention, from a theoretical standpoint, than fledging weight. (For reviews of the subject see Cody 1966; Lack 1966; Brockelman 1975; Stearns 1976.) However, O'Connor (1977) and Ricklefs (1979) have contributed to the integration of data on growth rates into theories of life-history strategy. A large clutch size can be regarded as a large parental investment and, hence, is generally associated with an 'r' type of life-history strategy (MacArthur and Wilson 1967; Pianka 1970). Similarly a large chick, relative to the parent can be regarded as a large parental investment (Jarvis 1974). However, rate of growth is more difficult to classify in these terms because while a fast-growing chick indicates a high *rate of investment* by the parents, the *total investment* by parents of a slower-growing chick which reaches the same asymptotic weight will usually be greater because the maintenance needs of the chick must be supplied over a longer period of time.

In any inter-specific comparisons of growth rates, parental investment and life-history strategy, it is important to recognize the crucial role of adult size. Large birds lay larger eggs than small birds, but smaller eggs in proportion to adult weight (Huxley 1923–1924; Rahn *et al.* 1975). The incubation period is positively correlated with egg weight (Rahn and Ar 1974; Rahn *et al.* 1975) and, among nidicolous birds, incubation periods are positively correlated with nestling period (Lack 1968). For flying birds there is an inverse relationship between size and the amount of extra weight that can be carried, in relation to body weight (Pennycuick 1975). This affects the capacity of adult birds to provision their chicks. Adult size is, in itself, part of the compromise between survival and reproduction (Pianka 1970; Southwood 1977), but for comparisons within related groups such as the Alcidae, this can probably be ignored; a necessary procedure in any case, as the adaptive value of size has not been quantified. The result of these general relationships is that within any group of birds, comparisons of chick size and chick growth rates can only be made after controlling for the effects of adult size.

B. Methods and Some Problems of Interpretation

Very few authors who have presented data on growth in alcids have discussed the problems of sampling and analysis. Most have followed

Ricklefs (1967, 1969) in regarding weight as the most important single measure of growth, and in many cases simple weight–age curves are presented along with sample sizes. A few problems with this type of data are generally recognized; others are more cryptic. I shall discuss those associated with field studies since the majority of work carried out in the past has been done in the field.

1. SAMPLING

Studies on many species of colonial birds have shown that breeding success is not uniform throughout the colony, but varies among different areas. In many species (Black-legged Kittiwakes: Coulson 1968; Shags: Potts *et al.* 1980; Northern Gannets: Nelson 1978a) birds breeding in the centre of the colony are more successful than those on the periphery, this effect being related to the distribution of inexperienced breeders. For some colonial alcids different types of breeding sites within the colony have been found to influence breeding success, either directly, through physical characteristics, or indirectly, through the proximity of neighbours (Nettleship 1972; Birkhead 1977a; Asbirk 1979b; Gaston and Nettleship 1981). Where breeding success is influenced by characteristics of the breeding site, we may anticipate that good-quality parents will obtain good-quality sites, and hence, those sites which are physically most suitable are also likely to be those where the chicks receive the most food. In fact, where comparisons have been made among different parts of an alcid colony, significant differences in fledging weights have frequently been detected (Atlantic Puffin: Nettleship 1972; Ashcroft 1976; Thick-billed Murre: Gaston and Nettleship 1981). Wherever possible, sampling of chicks for growth studies should be randomized in relation to variations in the quality of breeding sites.

Variation in the timing and frequency of sampling is another matter which can reduce the comparability of different studies. The weight of chicks is affected by whether or not they have been recently fed, and where the frequency of feeding varies over the course of the day this needs to be taken into account (Common Murre: Birkhead 1976a; Mahoney 1979; Thick-billed Murre: Gaston and Nettleship 1981; Black Guillemot: Petersen 1981; Atlantic Puffin: Corkhill 1973; Harris and Hislop 1978). Variation in the frequency with which weighing is performed also reduces comparability among studies. Most researchers weigh and measure their chicks daily, but when a longer interval is chosen, maximum weights will be lower because there is a lower chance that a particular chick will be weighed at its peak. Estimates of fledging weights will be similarly affected. Chicks subject to handling may tend to fledge prematurely and in this case measured fledging weights and ages may underestimate the true population mean.

The subject of weight recession in alcids has been slightly confused by using a comparison of maximum and fledging weights (Tuck 1961; Sealy 1973a). In practice, of course, 'maximum weights' are always equal to or greater than fledging weights, by definition. Furthermore, it is possible to calculate a 'recession' for a sample of chicks which, on average, continue to increase in weight right up to fledging, if light chicks are older at fledging than heavy chicks.

2. PROCEDURES FOR MEASUREMENT

Evidence from several studies suggests that disturbance associated with the measurement of growth in alcids may affect peak and fledging weights. Both M. P. Harris (personal communication), working on the Isle of May, Scotland, and T. R. Birkhead and D. N. Nettleship (unpublished observations) at Gannet Islands, Labrador, found that Common Murre chicks weighed regularly were lighter just prior to fledging than those of a similar age weighed only once and aged on the basis of their winglength. A similar effect was found by me (unpublished observations) for Thick-billed Murres at Digges Island, N.W.T., and by Evans (1981a) for Dovekies at Horse Head, Greenland.

In most cases the differences detected were within the range of variation occurring among different study plots on the same colony, but M. P. Harris (personal communication) was able to compare two adjacent groups of Common Murres, one where the adults always left the chicks while they were being weighed, the other where the chicks could be removed and weighed without the adults flying off. Weights of chicks with undisturbed parents were generally higher than those with parents that panicked. There is a clear indication from all these observations that growth rates of alcid chicks measured regularly may be lower than those found in undisturbed young. To make comparisons between chicks subject to similar amounts of disturbance this difference can probably be ignored, but it needs to be accounted for where comparisons are made between weights obtained by different methods.

3. PRESENTATION OF RESULTS

The processes of growth presumably proceed continuously, but successive weighings of individual chicks do not usually provide a picture of smooth development; the increases in weight between successive weighings fluctuate widely. Most authors choose to present average data for

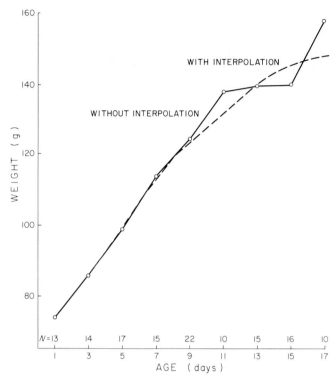

Fig. 7.2.   Comparison of growth curves with (dashed line) and without (solid line) inter-
polation for Thick-billed Murre chicks weighed at Digges Island (Plot R), N.W.T., in 1980.

their entire sample in order to reduce these, presumably random, fluctuations. Growth curves are smoothed even further if 'missing values' for
days on which chicks were not weighed are interpolated and included in
the sample (Hussell 1972; and Fig. 7.2). This concentration on comparisons between average growth curves is understandable if authors merely
wish to show general relationships between age and weight, but some
potentially valuable information may be obscured. The extent to which
weight changes vary at a particular age is, in part, a measure of how
predictable the chick's food supply may be, and this is not wholly described by including standard deviations. If growth processes have to be
geared to a particular level of food intake, then the fact that, on average,
weight is increasing at a particular age may be less important than the fact
that, for part of the population, weight decreased, which indicates a shortage of food.

  Systematic biases may also be introduced by the presentation of com-
posite growth curves, particularly where there is wide variation in the age

at fledging. If age at fledging is related to rate of growth, then chicks fledging first are likely to be heavier at a given age than those fledging later. In that case, growth curves plotted beyond the age at fledging of the first chick will show a systematic bias reducing the apparent growth rate of chicks (Fig. 7.3). If the asymptotic weights of later chicks are lower than those of early chicks, a spurious recession can be produced. The elegant method for obtaining growth curves from only two weighings proposed by Ricklefs and White (1975) may also suffer from a systematic bias where winglength and weight for a given age are correlated, a relationship observed in the case of Thick-billed Murres (Birkhead and Nettleship 1981; Gaston and Nettleship 1981), and the same applies to curves constructed from weighings on a single day where winglength is used as the criterion for age.

In a perfect world everyone would weigh chicks in the same way. However, the constraints imposed by field conditions force us to adopt methods suited to local conditions. I do not suggest that comparisons between studies are invalid; merely that we should make them with care.

4. INTERPRETATION

In describing patterns of weight increase many authors have followed Ricklefs (1967, 1968) in fitting their data to mathematical equations such as the logistic, Von Bertalanffy or Gompertz equations and then deriving

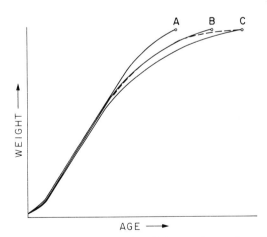

Fig. 7.3. Hypothetical growth curves for chicks growing at three different rates. The dashed line represents the mean growth curve derived from lumping data containing equal proportions of these three types.

the growth constant K and the inverse measure $t_{10\text{-}90}$ (the time taken to grow from 10 to 90% of asymptotic weight). For calculating growth rates at a particular period of development Brody's (1945) 'instantaneous growth rate' has also been widely used to express the rate of growth at specific times during the chick-rearing period. The procedure of fitting a mathematical equation to the data has the virtue of standardizing the data, but, as Hussell (1972) has pointed out, neither the growth constant nor $t_{10\text{-}90}$, which both provide measures of the rate at which the asymptote is achieved, are appropriate for comparisons between species or samples where the asymptote varies as a proportion of adult weight.

As noted by Sealy (1973a), this is particularly pertinent in the case of alcids where asymptotic weights achieved at the breeding site vary tremendously in relation to adult weights. Comparison of growth constants under these circumstances may produce paradoxical results, in the case of auks suggesting that murres, which grow from 80 to 200 g in about 15 days, have a higher rate of growth than Atlantic Puffins which cover the same range of weight in 10 days but continue growing for twice as long to reach a much higher asymptote. Nor is the procedure of fitting curves meaningful where chicks continue to grow right up to the point of fledging and beyond, because, in this situation, often encountered in murres and in the Razorbill, there is no asymptote.

In reality the family of curves which include the logistic differ mainly in the position of the point of inflection. It is earliest in the Gompertz curve and latest in the Von Bertalanffy, while the logistic is symmetrical about the inflection (Kaufmann 1981; Ricketts and Prince 1981). The smaller the difference between initial and asymptotic weights of chicks, the more likely it is that the point of inflection will occur early in the growth period; hence, as this difference narrows, there is an increasing likelihood that the growth curve will resemble the Gompertz curve. This effect probably accounts for an alteration in growth curve from Gompertz to logistic observed by Vermeer and Cullen (1979) for Rhinoceros Auklets cross-fostered by Tufted Puffins. The Tufted Puffins provided more food than the natural parents so that the young Rhinoceros Auklets reached a higher asymptotic weight than under normal conditions, and this probably altered the shape of the growth curve.

The instantaneous growth rate at the point of inflection of the fitted curve represents the maximum rate of growth (Hussell 1972), and probably provides the best measure to be derived from a fitted curve for the purpose of intra-specific comparisons. Converting this rate, or the absolute increment in weight per day, to a percentage of adult weight permits inter-specific comparisons, as illustrated by Drent and Daan (1980).

III. GROWTH PATTERNS IN ATLANTIC ALCIDAE

A. General Features

1. WEIGHT

Chicks of all genera begin to take food from their parents within 24 hours of hatching and increase in weight begins immediately (*Alca:* Lloyd 1976a; *Uria:* Gaston and Nettleship 1981; *Alle:* Stempniewicz 1980; *Cepphus:* Petersen 1981; *Fratercula:* Ashcroft 1976). The initial phase involving an acceleration in the rate of increase lasts no more than 5 days (10–20% of the period at the breeding site), and though obvious in the example shown, is scarcely detectable in many cases (Fig. 7.4). The linear phase that follows lasts in most cases from 30 to 50% of the time that the chick

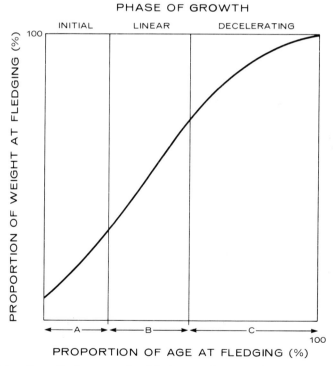

Fig. 7.4. Generalized pattern of weight increase for alcid chicks; example based on Black Guillemots at Brandypot Is., Gulf of St. Lawrence (Cairns 1978). Phases: A, accelerating; B, linear; C, decelerating.

spends at the breeding site. Following this, the decelerating phase occupies the remainder of the time and it is during this period that inter- and intra-specific variation is most evident. Actual weight reduction just prior to leaving the breeding site has been recorded for certain populations of several species and is the normal pattern in the Atlantic Puffin (Harris 1976c). Generalizations about growth in weight, either between or within species, are complicated by the large amount of variation that occurs, presumably determined by differences in feeding conditions, between different colonies and different years. This variation is expressed most obviously during the period when the energy requirement of the chick is greatest, just prior to leaving the breeding site.

2. PLUMAGE

At hatching all young alcids are covered in down. Feather development begins at once and, in the case of Atlantic species, the total replacement of the down is completed before the chicks leave their breeding site. The timing of important events is indicated in Table 7.3. There is a fundamental division between the 'normal' semi-precocial species, in which the whole juvenile plumage develops simultaneously, being practically fully grown at fledging, and the intermediate species which do not develop rectrices or remiges until after they have left the breeding site. For the latter, there is a partial post-juvenile moult of the body plumage, coinciding with the growth of the tail and flight feathers and beginning soon after their departure from the breeding site (Salomonsen 1944). The semi-precocial species also moult parts of their juvenile body plumage immediately after leaving the breeding site, but retain their flight feathers until the period of the annual adult moult; in spring for *Fratercula* and in late summer for *Alle* and *Cepphus*. (See Chapter 1 of this volume for details.)

Experiments by several researchers who have manipulated the food intake of chicks have shown that the rate of growth of the wing feathers is unaffected by nutrition (Razorbill: Lloyd 1976a; Black Guillemot: Asbirk 1979b; Atlantic Puffin: Nettleship 1972; Harris 1978; Hudson 1979b). In the case of Thick-billed Murres there is a correlation between winglength and weight at 14 days of age (Birkhead and Nettleship 1981; Gaston and Nettleship 1981) and this applies also after controlling for the effect of initial weight. In the Dovekie weight and winglength of the chick are also correlated almost to the age of fledging (Stempniewicz 1980). There is evidence that, at least for very light chicks, the state of nutrition has an effect on the growth of the wing feathers in Thick-billed Murres (A. J. Gaston, unpublished observations).

TABLE 7.3

Timing of Various Events in the Post-hatching Development of the Atlantic Alcidae

Species	Age (days)					References
	First emergence of quills	Bursting of feather quills	Thermo-regulation (complete)	Brooding ceases	Leaves breeding site	
Razorbill	3–4	7–9	4–5[a]	5–6	16–20	Bédard (1969d); Lloyd (1976a)
Common Murre	4–5	6–7	6–8	At fledging	18–30	Pearson (1968); Birkhead (1976a); Mahoney (1979)
Thick-billed Murre	4–5	6–7	6–8	At fledging	15–30	Gaston and Nettleship (1981)
Dovekie	4–6	8–9	3–5[a]	5–7	26–29	Norderhaug (1980); Evans (1981a)
Black Guillemot	6–8	12–15	3–4[a]	5	31–51	Asbirk (1979b); Hudson (1979b); D. N. Nettleship and A. J. Gaston (unpublished)
Atlantic Puffin			6–7	9	34–60	Kaftanovskii, in Kartaschew (1960); Nettleship (1972); Ashcroft (1979)

[a] Based on age at which brooding ceases.

3. PROPORTIONS

In common with all precocial and semi-precocial birds (Ricklefs 1979), alcid chicks show uneven development of different parts of the body at hatching, with the legs and feet, in particular, being much larger than other organs, in proportion to their adult size. Consequently, the hind limbs grow less rapidly than other parts of the body after hatching, linear measurements increasing by a factor of only 1.22 to 1.67 from hatching to the time of departure from the breeding site, compared with increases of 1.28 to 2.16 for bill length, 2.55 to 6.85 for winglength (this is mainly a feather increase, however), and 2.24 to 10.76 for weight (Table 7.4).

Chicks of the three intermediate species leave the breeding site with bills and feet similar in proportions to the adults. The ratio of bill length to the cube root of weight (weight is generally proportional to the cube of linear measurements) for adult Thick-billed Murres and for chicks on departure from the breeding site, for example, are 3.5 and 3.1. The same ratios for tarsus length are 3.7 and 4.6. For winglength, however, the corresponding ratio for adults is almost double that for the chick (22.3 vs. 12.4), owing to the lack of primary feathers in the chick (A. J. Gaston, unpublished observations).

None of the Atlantic alcids undertake sustained flights immediately after leaving the breeding site, but Dovekies and Atlantic Puffins may fly

TABLE 7.4

Ratios of Measurements at Departure from the Breeding Site to Those at Hatching for Atlantic Alcidae

Species	Ratio: departure condition/ hatching condition				References
	Weight	Wing	Culmen	Tarsus	
Razorbill	2.24	2.68	1.28	1.22	Bédard (1969d)
Common Murre	3.22	2.55	1.69	1.63	Mahoney (1979)
Thick-billed Murre	2.82	2.77	1.33	1.47	A. J. Gaston and D. N. Nettleship (unpublished)
Dovekie	5.29	5.54	1.41	1.25	Norderhaug (1980)
Black Guillemot	10.76	6.5	2.16	1.67	Asbirk (1979b)
Atlantic Puffin	5.67	6.85	—	—	D. N. Nettleship (unpublished)

several kilometres before alighting on the water (D. N. Nettleship and M. P. Harris, personal communication). The Black Guillemot, which reaches 85–90% of adult weight at departure, can probably fly within a few days of leaving its site (Petersen 1981). Murres, at the other extreme, are probably incapable of flight for at least the first 6 weeks (M. S. W. Bradstreet, unpublished observations). It is difficult to get information on growth after chicks have left the colony, but Bradstreet (1982a) has given data on growth rates of Dovekies immediately after going to sea, showing that adult weights are achieved within about 1 month.

In all species the bill, and probably other skeletal parts, continue to grow throughout the first winter (Storer 1952). In the genus *Uria,* development of the bony ridges above the orbits does not take place until the first summer (personal observation), and hence the process of physical development continues for at least a year. The horny ridges on the bill of the adult Atlantic Puffin continue to increase in extent up to at least 6–7 years old (Petersen 1976a; Harris 1981). This rather gradual attainment of skeletal maturity is probably associated with the prolonged pre-breeding period of most Atlantic alcids (see Chapter 5, this volume).

4. THERMOREGULATION AND LOCOMOTOR ABILITY

All species are capable of a wide range of muscular activities at hatching, including wing movements and food manipulation. The semi-precocial chicks are capable of only very limited locomotion for the first 3–4 days, but 'intermediate' chicks can walk within 2 days. Murre chicks 1–2 days old shiver their wing and leg muscles after brief exposure to temperatures below 0°C but are not capable of sustained thermoregulation until 6 to 8 days old. Razorbills are apparently capable of thermoregulation by 4 to 5 days (Lloyd 1976a). Semi-precocial chicks, on the other hand, though slower to develop locomotor ability, can thermoregulate at a younger age (Table 7.3). In these species the parents cease brooding their chicks after 5 to 10 days. Both species of murres normally brood and/or guard their chicks more or less continuously throughout the chick-rearing period, but the Razorbill broods only intermittently after the chick is 5 days old; although older chicks are often attended by a parent, they may also be left alone for several hours at a time where the breeding site affords protection from predators (Lloyd 1976a). Such desertion by both parents is very unusual in arctic-breeding Thick-billed Murres, irrespective of the type of site (personal observation), but this difference may be a function of the different temperatures prevailing.

B. Interspecific Variation

1. FLEDGING STRATEGY AND LENGTH OF TIME SPENT AT THE BREEDING SITE

Of the three strategies found within the Alcidae (Table 7.1), only two are found among the Atlantic species: the intermediate and the semi-precocial. Truly precocial fledging occurs only in the Pacific genera *Synthliboramphus* and *Endomychura*. The duration of the chick-rearing period is generally shorter among intermediate species than among semi-precocial species, but growth rates are slower relative to adult weight with intermediate chicks leaving their breeding sites at 15 to 35% of adult weight, compared with 60 to 75% for the Atlantic Puffin and Dovekie (Fig. 7.5). In the Black Guillemot, which usually lays two eggs and rears two chicks, the young fledge at close to adult weight.

The exact selection pressures determining the adoption of the intermediate fledging strategy by *Uria* and *Alca* have been the subject of some

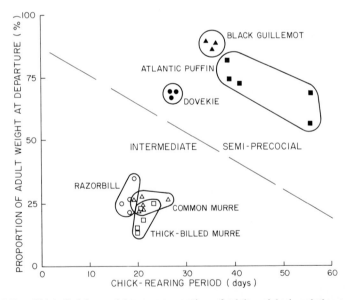

Fig. 7.5. Chick fledging weight as a proportion of adult weight in relation to age at fledging for Atlantic alcids. [Data from: Razorbill—Kaftanovskii, cited in Kartaschew (1960); Bédard (1969d); Lloyd (1976a); Common Murre—Pearson (1968); Cody (1973); Birkhead (1976a); Johnson and West (1975); Hedgren (1979); Mahoney (1979); Thick-billed Murre—Uspenski (1956); Birkhead and Nettleship (1981); Gaston and Nettleship (1981); A. J. Gaston (unpublished observations); Dovekie—Norderhaug (1980); Stempniewicz (1980); Evans (1981a); Black Guillemot—Cairns (1978); Petersen (1981); P. G. H. Evans (personal communication); Atlantic Puffin—Nettleship (1972); Harris (1978); Ashcroft (1979).]

speculation, but the consensus is that the strategy is a result of the inability of adults to supply sufficient food to allow chicks to reach heavier weights on the site. (See Chapter 4 of this volume for details.) The ratios of wing area to weight for the genera *Uria* and *Alca* are the lowest of any flying birds (Greenwalt 1962). The result is that murres and Razorbills can carry smaller amounts of food for their chicks, relative to their size, than other alcids (Cody 1973; Sealy 1973a). This is partly an allometric effect of size, since large birds are normally heavier relative to their wing area, than small birds (Pennycuick 1969). However, the most important reason for the poor load-carrying ability of murres and Razorbills is probably the need for a compromise between the optimum wing-span needed for flight and the best dimensions for underwater propulsion. Where underwater speed is particularly important, as in the Common Murre and Razorbill, which feed mainly on pelagic schooling fish (see Chapter 6, this volume), this constraint must be particularly pertinent.

The existence of fully precocial murrelets in the Pacific raises the question of why no Atlantic alcid has adopted this strategy, given the problems in chick-rearing already noted for 'intermediate' species. The eggs of precocial murrelets are much larger, relative to adult body weight, than those of murres and Razorbills, a character apparently associated with their precocial behaviour (Sealy 1975b). However, the eggs of murres and Razorbills are larger in absolute terms, and it is not obvious why, given such large eggs, the chicks could not evolve adaptations allowing them to leave the breeding site soon after hatching. At present, however, most murres and Razorbills breed on cliffs from which the chicks must be able to glide down to the water. For this they need to develop feathers that allow them to plane. Adoption of precocial fledging would therefore make it necessary to alter the type of breeding site selected—an option that may not be viable over these species' present range.

2. PATTERNS OF WEIGHT INCREASE

In the two genera with 'intermediate' fledging strategies (*Uria, Alca*) the weight increase of chicks normally continues right up to fledging, with no recession. In the other three genera some genuine weight recession occurs in the last few days before fledging (see references in Table 7.5). Atlantic Puffin chicks, which show the largest recession (Fig. 7.6A), lower their rate of food intake after 30 days of age when food is provided *ad lib.* (Harris 1978). Hudson (1979b) presented evidence that the most important factor in creating the weight recession is a reduction in the amount of food delivered by the parents which occurs at a predetermined date relative to the chicks hatching, and irrespective of the true age of the

TABLE 7.5

Maximum Growth Rates of Alcid Chicks, Weights at the Mid-point of Growth on the Colony and Adult Weights

Species	Locality	Year	A Max. growth rate[a] (g/day)	B Chick weight at mid-point (g)[b]	A/B%	C x̄ Adult weight (g)	A/C%	References
Razorbill	Skokholm I., Wales	1972	10.33	116	8.9	630	1.6	Lloyd (1976a)
		1973	13.75	116	11.9		2.2	Lloyd (1976a)
		1974	12.80	126	10.2		2.0	Lloyd (1976a)
	Gulf of St. Lawrence	1963	8.33	109	7.6	686	1.2	Bédard (1969d)
	Gannet Is., Labrador	1981	11.67	130	9.0	726	1.6	T. R. Birkhead and D. N. Nettleship (unpublished)
Common Murre	Farne Is., England	1965	12.58	152	8.3	925	1.4	Pearson (1968)
	St. Lawrence I., Alaska	1972	8.60	135	6.4	956	0.9	Johnson and West (1975)
	Skomer I., Wales	1974	11.83	142	8.3	875	1.4	Birkhead (1976a)
	Gull I., Nfld.	1977	14.10	167	8.4	992	1.4	Mahoney (1979)
		1978	14.22	167	8.5		1.4	Mahoney (1979)
	Stora Karlsö, Sweden	1974	15.50	165	9.4	?		Hedgren and Linnman (1979)
		1975	15.67	160	9.8	?		Hedgren and Linnman (1979)
		1976	12.33	160	7.7	?		Hedgren and Linnman (1979)
		1977	13.11	165	7.9	?		Hedgren and Linnman (1979)
	Gannet Is., Labrador	1981	13.75	140	9.8	928	1.5	T. R. Birkhead and D. N. Nettleship (unpublished)
Thick-billed Murre	St. Lawrence I., Alaska	1972	8.60	130	6.6	989	0.9	Johnson and West (1975)
	Prince Leopold I., N.W.T.	1975	14.40	136	10.6	900	1.6	Gaston and Nettleship (1981)
		1976	8.53	144	5.9		0.9	Gaston and Nettleship (1981)
		1977	11.60	149	7.8		1.3	Gaston and Nettleship (1981)

	Location	Year						Reference
	Coburg I., N.W.T.	1979	13.00	146	8.9	850	1.5	Birkhead and Nettleship (1981)
	Cape Hay, N.W.T.	1979	11.43	135	8.5	874	1.3	Birkhead and Nettleship (1981)
	Digges I., N.W.T.	1980	8.42	110	7.7	940	0.9	A. J. Gaston (unpublished)
		1981	6.83	105	6.5		0.7	A. J. Gaston (unpublished)
Dovekie	Hornsund, Spitsbergen	1963–1964	7.14	72	9.9	163	4.4	Norderhaug (1980)
	Hornsund, Spitsbergen	1974–1975	7.90	73	10.0	163	4.8	Stempniewicz (1980)
	Horse Head, Greenland	1974	6.48	75	8.6	160	4.0	Evans (1981a)
Black Guillemot	Denmark	1975–1976	15.11	200	7.6	?		Asbirk (1979b)
	Flatey, Iceland	1975	13.50	202	6.7	400	3.4	Petersen (1981)
		1976	15.99	207	7.7	400	4.0	Petersen (1981)
	Brandypot Is., Gulf of St. Lawrence	1976	14.83	200	7.4	401	3.7	Cairns (1981)
	St. Mary Is., Gulf of St. Lawrence	1976	15.00	227	6.6	407	3.7	Cairns (1981)
	Prince Leopold I., N.W.T.	1977	13.16	160	8.2	382	3.4	D. N. Nettleship (unpublished)
	Nuvuk Is., N.W.T.	1981	12.63	182	6.9	406	3.1	D. Cairns (unpublished)
Atlantic Puffin	Farne Is., England	1965	12.82	171	7.5	380	3.4	Pearson (1968)
	Skomer I., Wales	1973	12.00	178	6.7		3.0	Ashcroft (1979)
		1974	11.00	176	6.2	406	2.7	Ashcroft (1979)
		1975	11.87	179	6.6		2.9	Ashcroft (1979)
	St Kilda, Scotland	1975	6.90	164	4.2	376	1.8	Harris (1978)
	Isle of May, Scotland	1975	11.86	174	6.8	399	3.0	Harris (1978)

[a] Determined from the steepest tangent to the growth curve, fitted by eye to published curves.
[b] Determined by calculating the median of the hatching and peak weights.

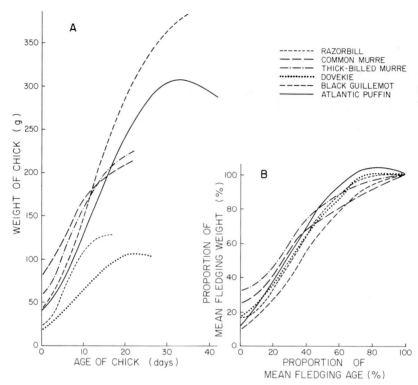

Fig. 7.6. Growth curves for representative populations of Atlantic alcids: (A) actual weights, and (B) standardized by converting weights to percentages of mean fledging weight and ages to percentages of mean fledging age. Populations used: Razorbill—Skokholm I., Wales, 1971–1973 (Lloyd 1976a); Common Murre—Gull I., Nfld., 1977 (Mahoney 1979); Thick-billed Murre—Prince Leopold I., N.W.T., 1977 (Gaston and Nettleship 1981); Dovekie—W. Greenland, 1974 (Evans 1981a); Black Guillemot—Brandypot Is., Gulf of St. Lawrence, 1976 (Cairns 1978); Atlantic Puffin—Isle of May, Scotland, 1975 (Harris 1978).

(experimentally manipulated) chick. This finding contrasts with evidence presented by Harris (1983b), who found that the feeding rate of the parents could be manipulated by playing recordings of the hunger calls of the young. Although these findings are not necessarily incompatible, it appears that the question of whether weight recession in puffin chicks results from voluntary restraint on the part of the chick or reductions in the amount of food brought by the parent is not completely resolved. Similar effects may occur in the Dovekie where feeding rates are significantly lower in the last 3 days before fledging than during the preceding period (Evans 1981a). The presence or absence of a recession period is one of the most prominent variations among standardized growth curves (Fig. 7.6B).

The significance of the recession period in alcids is not understood. In Procellariiformes, many of which show a prolonged period of weight recession, the phenomenon is associated with greatly reduced feeding rates during the latter part of the chick-rearing period (Lack 1968). At peak weight the chicks contain large quanities of stored fat; Ricklefs (1979) has suggested that these fat stores are accumulated by the chicks as 'energy sinks' to allow the chicks to take in large quantities of energy-rich but nutrient-poor food. This is unlikely to be the case in the Atlantic Puffin, however, where chicks are fed mainly on fish, a diet high in proteins (Harris and Hislop 1978). Weight recession in chicks is generally associated with reduction of water content as tissues mature (Ricklefs 1968; O'Connor 1975; Dunn 1975b). Overall reduction of water content in the last stages of growth has been demonstrated for the Pigeon Guillemot by Koelink (1972). The process may be intensified by increased exercise in the last few days before fledging, and by a reduction in the amount of food delivered by the parents.

Little information is available on the growth of intermediate chicks after they have left the colony. Common Murre fledglings are accompanied by one of their parents for 70 to 85 days after leaving the colony. During this period they reach an asymptotic weight of about 90 to 95% mean adult weight (Varoujean et al. 1979). The growth of Thick-billed Murres is probably similar. Chicks collected in September in Lancaster Sound, N.W.T., ranged up to 650 g in weight (M. S. W. Bradstreet, personal communication); these birds had probably left their colonies about a month earlier. A single captive Common Murre given unlimited food reached 500 g at 61 days old and 700 g at 100 days (W. Montevecchi, personal communication). A Razorbill chick, under the same conditions reached a peak weight of 580 g after 82 days (W. Montevecchi, personal communication). Weights of first-year birds during winter are significantly lower than those of adults, and most of that difference is contributed by differences in the weight of the pectoral muscles, which suggests that muscular development continues throughout the first year of life (A. J. Gaston, unpublished observations).

3. MAXIMUM GROWTH RATE

The maximum rate of growth is probably controlled by intrinsic factors (Ricklefs 1979), and hence, it seems a useful measure to compare among species if we want to detect adaptive trends in rates of growth. To estimate maximum rates of weight increase from published data I have fitted the steepest possible tangents to smoothed growth curves, a procedure similar to that adopted by Drent and Daan (1980). I estimated the size of chicks at maximum rate of growth by taking the mean of the hatching weight and the maximum weight attained prior to leaving the breeding site.

Rates thus calculated were very variable, suggesting that if intrinsic constraints operate, they do so only occasionally (Table 7.5). When expressed as a percentage of adult weights, the maximum daily weight increments of chicks are inversely correlated with adult weight (r_s = .97, $p <$ .05): highest for the Dovekie (4.0–4.8% per day), somewhat lower for the two medium-sized auks (Black Guillemot, 3.1–4.0% per day; Atlantic Puffin, 1.8–3.4% per day), and lowest for the large species with intermediate fledging strategies (Razorbill, 1.2–2.2% per day; Common Murre, 0.9–1.5% per day; Thick-billed Murre, 0.7–1.6% per day).

In comparison with median chick weights, maximum daily weight increments are very similar with a great deal of overlap among species. Highest rates have been recorded for Razorbill and Dovekie chicks and lowest rates among Thick-billed Murres and Atlantic Puffins. No relationship was apparent between growth rates calculated in this manner and adult body weight. The fact that chicks of intermediate species grow just as fast as semi-precocial species, in relation to their weight, suggests that these species have not adopted a slow growth rate as an adaptive strategy. Instead, they have adopted premature fledging allied to a very flexible growth rate.

Comparing the maximum growth rates of Atlantic alcids with the general regression of maximum growth rate on adult body weight for non-passerine birds presented by Drent and Daan (1980), the majority of populations studied show slower growth rates than predicted by adult weights (Fig. 7.7). Dovekies and Black Guillemots lie close to the general regression, while most Atlantic Puffin populations are not far below it. The most striking deviations occur among the intermediate species, particularly the Thick-billed Murre, emphasizing the small amount of food delivered by the adult birds to their chicks relative to their own body weight.

4. PARENTAL INVESTMENT IN CHICK REARING

If we consider only the amount of food delivered to chicks, then it appears that intermediate species make a much smaller energetic investment in reproduction than semi-precocial species, because the amount of food that they must bring to their chicks is smaller relative to the amount of food they consume for their own maintenance. Harris (1978) noted that Atlantic Puffin chicks at St. Kilda, Scotland, had an average daily energy intake of 381 kJ compared with an adult puffin in captivity which required

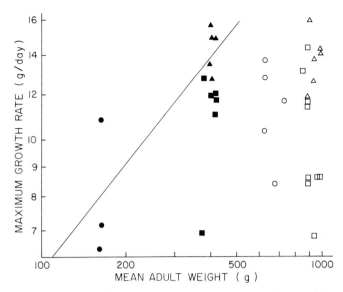

Fig. 7.7. Maximum daily weight increments of chicks in relation to adult weight for populations given in Table 7.5. Both axes are plotted on log scales. The straight line shows the general regression for non-passerine birds given by Drent and Daan (1980). Symbols are as follows: Dovekie (●); Black Guillemot (▲); Atlantic Puffin (■); Razorbill (○); Common Murre (△); Thick-billed Murre (□).

573 kJ to maintain its weight (ratio 1 : 1.5). In contrast, Sanford and Harris (1967) found that a captive adult Common Murre required about 250 g (wet wt.) of fish while Common Murre chicks receive only about 30 g (wet wt.) of fish per day (Birkhead 1976a; Hedgren and Linnman 1979), which gives a ratio of 1 : 8.3.

The apparent difference in parental investment in chick-rearing is less striking if the time spent finding and transporting food to the chicks is taken into account. For example, in the case of some populations of murres, time spent travelling to and from the colony during the chick-rearing period may account for up to 50% of total foraging time (Gaston and Nettleship 1981). That, added to the energy expended in flight, may raise daily energy consumption related to chick-rearing to the levels found in semi-precocial species (A. J. Gaston, unpublished observations). The time devoted to brooding chicks in the two murre species also halves the potential time available for foraging during the chick-rearing period, compared to the other species which leave their chicks unattended during most of their growth period. Total investment in intermediate species is impossible to evaluate, however, because one parent accompanies the chick after leaving the colony for at least a month in the case of the Thick-

344   Anthony J. Gaston

billed Murre (Gaston 1982); the energetic cost of this behaviour cannot be estimated at present. Among semi-precocial species, only Dovekies may sometimes accompany their chicks after they leave the breeding site (see Chapter 3 of this volume for details.)

C. Intraspecific Variation

1. WITHIN-SEASON VARIATION

A seasonal decline in maximum and fledging weights of alcid chicks has been noted for Razorbills (Lloyd 1976a), Common Murres (Hedgren 1979), Thick-billed Murres (Gaston and Nettleship 1981), and Atlantic Puffins (Nettleship 1972; Harris 1982b). For the Common Murre, Hedgren (1979) has demonstrated that the decline in weights at departure from the colony is not uniform, but that chicks leaving before the median date for the population are similar in weight, the decline beginning only thereafter. That effect was found over 5 consecutive years, although the point at which the decline in fledging weights began, in relation to the proportion of chicks fledged, varied somewhat.

The seasonal decline in chick weights is probably related to a reduction in the availability of food close to breeding colonies (Birkhead and Nettleship 1982b), either because of seasonal trends in the abundance of prey species, or because food supplies in the immediate vicinity of the colony are exhausted by the concentration of feeding birds. Other factors which may contribute to the seasonal decline are as follows:

1. The seasonal trend in egg weights, which also show a seasonal decline and which may be related in some cases to fledging weights (Gaston and Nettleship 1981; Birkhead and Nettleship 1982b)
2. Seasonal decline in temperature which may affect the maintenance energy requirements of the chick, particularly high-arctic species which hatch after the annual thermal maximum (Uspenski 1956)
3. Seasonal reduction in the photoperiod and hence the time available to the adults for foraging
4. A reduction in the effort invested by parents due to the fact that late chicks, if less likely to survive, represent a smaller return for a given level of investment than early chicks do

Not all alcid populations show a seasonal decline in fledging weights, and no such effect was found over 2 years for the Thick-billed Murre population of Digges Island, N.W.T. (A. J. Gaston, unpublished observations) or in 5 of 8 years for Atlantic Puffins at St. Kilda, Scotland (Harris 1982b). Thus, seasonal declines in fledging weights cannot be regarded as inevitable, and there is some evidence that such effects may be colony-specific, reflecting seasonal changes in food that are peculiar to particular marine areas.

2. BETWEEN-YEAR VARIATION

Significant inter-year variation in maximum and fledging weights of chicks has been demonstrated for: Razorbills at Skokholm Island, Wales (Lloyd 1976a); Common Murres on Gull Island, Newfoundland (Mahoney 1979); Thick-billed Murres at Prince Leopold Island (Gaston and Nettleship 1981), Digges Island (A. J. Gaston, unpublished observations) and Novaya Zemlya (Uspenski 1956); and Atlantic Puffins on St. Kilda (Harris 1978). Fledging weights among murre and Razorbill chicks are related to fledging age, because chicks continue to increase in weight up to fledging, and in the case of the variation described by Mahoney (1979), differences in fledging age may explain the observed differences in weight. In other studies, differences in fledging weights were not related to differences in age at fledging and presumably reflect inter-year variation in the availability of food and/or differences in the mean ambient temperature during the chick-rearing period.

Not all multi-year studies have found significant variation among years. Nettleship (1972) found no difference in the mean fledging weights of Atlantic Puffins at Great Island, Newfoundland, between two consecutive years (1968–1969). Hedgren (1979) found no significant variation in weights of Common Murre chicks at Stora Karlsö in the Baltic Sea over 5 years (1972–1976), and Ashcroft (1979) found no significant variation in the fledging weight of Atlantic Puffins at Skomer Island, Wales, over 3 years (1973–1975). It is probably no coincidence that the greatest inter-year variation was recorded for Thick-billed Murres at Prince Leopold Island and Novaya Zemlya, in the most extreme arctic environments yet studied over several years. This suggests that high-arctic marine ecosystems are less predictable from year to year than those at lower latitudes (Gaston and Nettleship 1981). Mean maximum weights at Prince Leopold Island varied from 165 to 221 g over 4 years (1975–1978: Nettleship et al. 1980), and at Novaya Zemlya from 124 to 150 g over 3 years (1948–1950: Uspenski 1956).

3. WITHIN-COLONY VARIATION

Variation within colonies probably arises from two groups of effects:

1. Those associated with the quality of breeding sites and the sorting of birds according to their own quality through competition for the best sites

2. Those arising through non-random distribution of age and genotypes within the colony which cause a mosaic unrelated to the quality of sites

These two effects are probably linked and difficult to analyse separately in the majority of situations.

For the Atlantic Puffin, Nettleship (1972) found that chicks occupying good-quality nest sites (those which reduced the intensity of kleptoparasitism by gulls) were heavier at fledging than those in poor sites. Similarly, Lloyd (1976a) found that Razorbill chicks from sites among boulders were heavier at fledging than those reared on open ledges, perhaps because the parents of the former group needed to spend less time in attendance at the site and hence had more time available for feeding. Hudson (1982), on Skomer Island, Wales, found a similar effect for Razorbills, though statistically significant in only 1 of 3 years. In this case, however, the chicks reared on open ledges were heavier than those reared in enclosed sites or under boulders in 2 of 3 years.

For Atlantic Puffins on St. Kilda, Harris (1978) found that chicks reared in the densest, central part of the colony reached higher maximum weights than those in less densely settled areas. Uspenski (1956) mentions a similar effect for colonies of Thick-billed Murres in Novaya Zemlya. On Digges Island, Thick-billed Murres from different parts of the colony varied in maximum and fledging weights, but here the chicks at the edge of the colony were heavier than those in a more central area (Table 7.6). Where colonies are very large there may be a whole range of factors creating within-colony variation; not all of these are susceptible to an analysis based on one or a small number of seasons, because determinants of breeding success may vary in intensity from year to year.

TABLE 7.6

Mean Maximum and Fledging Weight of Thick-billed Murre Chicks in Two Areas of the Digges Island Colony in 1980

Study plot[a]	Maximum weight (g)			Fledging weight (g)		
	N	$\bar{x}$	S.D.	N	$\bar{x}$	S.D.
R	44	161.8	24.5	44	156.9	15.3
T	24	144.2	23.0	22	137.1	14.4
	$t = 3.19$			$t = 3.67$		
	$p = .002$			$p = .001$		

[a] Plot R, on extreme southern edge of colony; Plot T, ca. 0.5 km from north end of colony.

4. BETWEEN-COLONY VARIATION

Because of the between-year and within-colony variation already discussed, it is difficult to evaluate the considerable variation that has been
described among colonies for several species of Atlantic Alcidae. For
example, the 8.1% difference in mean fledging weights described by
Birkhead and Nettleship (1981) between the Thick-billed Murre colonies
at Cape Hay, Bylot Island, and Coburg Island, N.W.T., in 1979 is actually
smaller than the differences between study areas within the Digges Island
colony (Table 7.6: 14.4%). Some differences are much larger than this,
however, and others are consistent from year to year, making it clear that
inter-colony variation is an important component of the total variation
within species in maximum and fledging weights.

Particularly striking inter-colony variation occurs among Thick-billed
Murres, where mean fledging weights reported for single-year samples
vary from 125 (Uspenski 1956) to 250 g (Kaftanovskii 1951), a range of
+200% of the minimum. Sufficient information is available for Thick-
billed Murres to suggest that these extremes are not unusual, and that
some colonies regularly produce young which are consistently lighter at
fledging than others and consistently different as a proportion of adult
weight (Table 7.7).

Uspenski (1956) attributed differences in the fledging weight of Thick-
billed Murres at Novaya Zemlya and in Ostrova Sem'ostrovov on the
Murmansk Coast to differences in air temperatures during the chick-rearing period; he also used that hypothesis to explain inter-year variations.
However, in comparing the nine colonies for which fledging weights are
available, there is little indication of a temperature effect (Table 7.7).
There is, however, a significant negative correlation between mean fledging weights and colony size (Fig. 7.8). This correlation probably results
from a reduction in the amount of food available close to the colony due to
the density of the population so that birds from large colonies have to
travel farther to forage than those from smaller colonies (Gaston and
Nettleship 1981). However, in the absence of data on the foraging ranges
of birds at most colonies this remains speculative.

Significant inter-colony variation in fledging weights has also been recorded for Atlantic Puffins. Weights recorded by Nettleship (1972) in two
seasons at Great Island, Newfoundland, were considerably lower than
those recorded by Harris (1978) and Ashcroft (1979) over several years at
British colonies, despite the fact that adult puffins were larger in Newfoundland. Furthermore, Harris (1978) showed that maximum and fledging weights at St. Kilda, off the west coast of Scotland, were consistently
lower than those recorded at the Isle of May off eastern Scotland. Harris
and Hislop (1978) were able to relate that to differences in the amount of

TABLE 7.7

Mean Fledging Weights, Adult Weights, Air Temperatures and Total Numbers of Breeding Pairs for Thick-billed Murre Colonies in Different Geographic Areas

| Locality | Year | Weight at fledging (g) | | | $\bar{x}$ adult weight (g) | Chick fledging wt. as % adult wt. | $\bar{x}$ August air temp.[a] (°C) | Colony size[b] (breeding pairs) | References |
		$\bar{x}$	S.D.	N					
Lancaster Sound									
Cape Hay, Bylot I.	1957	195	(median)	?	?	—	1	?	Tuck (1957)
	1979	191	14.4	24	874	21.9	1	140,000	Birkhead and Nettleship (1981)
Coburg I.	1979	206	21.2	36	850	24.2	1	160,000	Birkhead and Nettleship (1981)
Prince Leopold I.	1975	204	21.8	18		22.7	1		Gaston and Nettleship (1981)
	1976	212	18.6	28		23.6	1	86,000	
	1977	221	28.6	25	900	24.6	1		
	1978	164	32.9	18	863	19.0	−1	86,000	Nettleship et al. (1980)

	Year								Reference
Hudson Bay									
Digges I.	1979	150[c]	—	—	941	15.9	3 }		A. J. Gaston (unpublished)
	1980	157	23.0	44	936	15.6	3 }	300,000	
	1981	146[c]	17.4	61		15.6	3 }		
Coats I.	1981	250[c]	—	—	990	25.3	4	24,000	A. J. Gaston (unpublished)
Barents Sea									
Guba Bezymyannaya	1948	140	?	?	1002	14.0	4 }		Uspenski (1956)
	1949	124	?	?	1008	12.3	4 }	257,000	
	1950	150	?	?	966	15.5	4 }		
Ostrova Sem'ostrovov	1948	250	?	?	?	—	10	10,000	Kaftanovskii (1951)
Alaska									
Cape Thompson	1960	121	?	6	970	12.5	6	196,000	Swartz (1966)
St. Lawrence I.	1972	200	—	44	989	20.2	7	25,000	Johnson and West (1975)

[a] Temperatures from Vowinckel and Orvig (1970).
[b] Figures for Canadian colonies from Gaston (1980) and for the Barents Sea from Norderhaug et al. (1977), including for Guba Bezymyannaya two colonies close by and probably foraging over the same area.
[c] Estimated from growth curves based on ages determined from wing length.

349

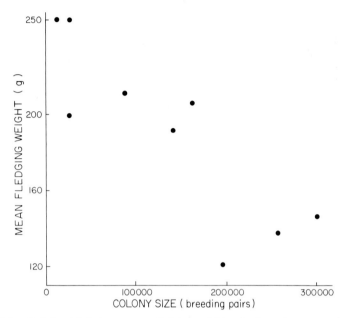

Fig. 7.8. Relationship between mean fledging weight and colony size among nine populations of Thick-billed Murres. Correlation coefficient: $r = -.857$, df 7, $p = .002$. Data derived from Table 7.7, taking mean values for colonies with more than one annual sample.

food fed to the chicks; those at the Isle of May received approximately 25% more food (in energy units) than those at St. Kilda. There is a significant correlation between colony size and fledging weight in Atlantic Puffins, similar to that demonstrated for Thick-billed Murres ($r = .757$, $N = 6$, $P = .04$: Table 7.8), but the probability level is too high to draw any firm conclusions.

Considerable variation among fledging weights has also been recorded for Black Guillemots, but there are insufficient data to rule out inter-year effects completely. However, weights observed at Prince Leopold Island, N.W.T., in 1977 are considerably lower than those recorded elsewhere and may be due to colony-specific effects (Table 7.5 and Fig. 7.9). The Prince Leopold Island colony, with 4000 pairs, is among the largest Black Guillemot colonies known (Nettleship 1974, and personal communication). If we ignore the possible effect of temperature during the chick-rearing period, then consistent intra-specific differences in fledging weights among different colonies are most readily explained by differences in the availability of food. This may be related either to regional differences in the abundance of certain prey organisms, or to differences in the balance between population density and food supply. Where colonies are increasing in numbers, it seems reasonable to assume that food supplies are in excess and we might therefore anticipate that expanding colonies will rear heavy chicks. This prediction is fulfilled in the case of Atlantic Puffins. At the Isle of May, where the population is increasing, chicks are significantly heavier than at St. Kilda where the population has recently stabilised after considerable declines (Harris 1976c, 1977).

Evidence from other seabirds suggests that weight at fledging may be positively correlated with the subsequent survival of the chick (Perrins *et al.* 1973; Jarvis 1974). However, the evidence available for alcids gives no indication of such an effect (Lloyd 1976a; Hedgren 1979; Harris 1982b). We might expect that in species where the chick is completely independent after leaving the colony (Black Guillemot, Atlantic Puffin), weight at fledging should be important in determining survival during the transition to independent feeding. The situation for species which are accompanied by a parent during the immediate post-fledging period may be different,

TABLE 7.8

Mean Fledging Weights Reported for Atlantic Puffins from Different Colonies and Size of Colonies Involved

Locality	Year	N	$\bar{x}$	S.D.	Colony size (pairs)	References
Newfoundland						
Great I.	1968	25	261[a]	32.3	148,000[b]	Nettleship (1972, 1980)
	1969	101	262[a]	35.9		
Small I.	1969	58	346	28.6	10,000	Nettleship (1972, 1980 and unpublished)
Funk I.	1969	33	361	31.6	1,000	Nettleship (1972, 1980 and unpublished)
Britain						
St. Kilda, Scotland	1974	21	269	37.2	310,000	Harris (1978); Harris and Murray (1978)
	1975	37	279	19.3		
	1976	30	272	25.7		
Isle of May, Scotland	1974	41	289	27.9	3,000	Harris (1976a, 1978)
	1975	65	293	28.9		
	1976	13	304	42.4		
Skomer I., Wales	1973	63	290	28.0	6,000	Ashcroft (1979)
	1974	110	287	22.2		
	1975	68	297	24.7		

[a] For only chicks reared in good-quality (slope) sites.
[b] Total number of birds foraging over the same area increases to 225,000 pairs if adjacent colonies on Gull and Green Islands are included.

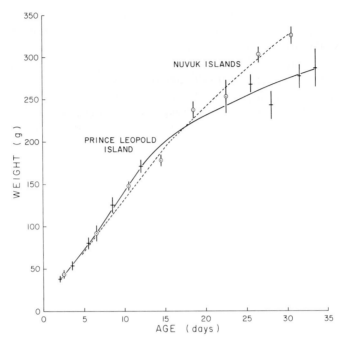

Fig. 7.9.   Growth curves for Black Guillemot chicks from two arctic populations: Prince Leopold I., N.W.T. (D. N. Nettleship, unpublished observations) and Nuvuk Is. (A. J. Gaston, unpublished observations). The curve for Nuvuk Is. is based on ages determined from wing length.

and for these species, we might anticipate that condition at fledging has little effect on subsequent survival provided that the chick exceeds some basic threshold of viability. In either case, data are too few to permit firm conclusions.

IV. CONCLUSIONS

The growth of young alcids has received considerable attention because it is an aspect of their biology relatively easily accessible to investigation. Certain growth parameters are important because they provide information on the amount of food available during the chick-rearing period. They also provide an interesting instance of evolutionary radiation in the degree of precociality exhibited by the chicks which represent different solutions to the problem of being an aquatic organism forced to return annually to reproduce.

Among birds as a whole, fledging behaviour is relatively uniform within avian families (Lack 1968). The Alcidae appear unusual in the variety of their approaches, even in comparison with their ecological counterparts in the southern hemisphere, the penguins, which are uniformly nidicolous and semi-precocial in their development (Lack 1968). Inter-specific differences in the timing of departure from the breeding site is best explained by differences in feeding ecology. This explanation, however, is considerably weakened by the existence of fully precocial murrelets, which begs the question of why this pattern is not adopted by intermediate species. It is interesting to speculate that if no precocial alcids existed, we should almost certainly adopt a different attitude to explaining the existence of intermediate species.

If we assume that the intermediate fledging strategy has evolved because parents find it hard to supply enough food to rear their chick to full size at the colony, then it follows that this effect will be exacerbated in large colonies where birds have to fly long distances to feed. Clearly, where birds have to spend a long time travelling to and from their feeding grounds, it is more difficult to maintain high rates of feeding (Ricklefs 1979). The compression of the population into a small number of very large breeding colonies, therefore, will intensify selection for behaviour that reduces the frequency with which parents have to visit the colony. This, in turn, increases selection on the chicks for adaptations allowing them to fledge at lower weights. At present, more than 90% of Atlantic murres breed in colonies of more than 10,000 pairs; hence, for the majority of individuals, there is selection for adaptations conferring fitness in large colonies. Such colonies are typical of offshore rather than inshore feeding among seabirds (Diamond 1978). It may therefore be permissible to view the intermediate fledging strategy as an adaptation to pelagic feeding.

Interest in the growth and development of alcid chicks has increased in recent years as a result of research aimed at improving the welfare of alcid populations, some of which are believed vulnerable to current human activities impinging on marine ecosystems (see Chapter 10, this volume). Measurements of chick weights, where they are related to differences in the chicks' nutrition, provide a clue to the availability of food and may therefore provide evidence that changes in breeding success or population sizes are related to changes in food supplies. For such predictions to be useful, we need to know more about the normally occurring variation among and within regions and colonies.

Because the energy requirements of the chick are at a peak when it reaches its maximum weight, comparisons of mean maximum or fledging weights are likely to be more useful in predicting the availability of food than growth rates, either calculated by fitting data to standardized curves or by calculating instantaneous growth rates. For species in which individuals vary considerably in their age at fledging, comparisons based on their weights just before the age at which chicks begin to fledge may be more useful than those based on fledging weights where variability is exacerbated by differences in age. For those in which growth typically includes a pre-fledging recession in weight, mean maximum weights may be more useful for comparison than mean fledging weights.

The large intra-specific variations in maximum and fledging weights observed under apparently natural conditions suggest that inter-colony and inter-year variation in the availability of food during the breeding season may be typical of the ecology of many alcid species. Similar variability has been observed for some Pacific species (Sealy 1973a; Vermeer and Cullen 1979; Vermeer et al. 1979; Vermeer 1980). However, it is important to remember that marine ecosystems throughout most of the world's oceans have been drastically altered by human harvesting of fish and marine mammals, which probably have resulted in huge, but in most cases unmeasured, compensatory adjustments in marine animal communities (Idyll 1973; Bonner 1981). Also, many seabird colonies are still recovering from reductions caused by earlier hunting and egg-collecting (see Chapters 2 and 10, this volume). All of these effects will have altered the balance between alcid populations and their prey species, and in the case of commercial fisheries, such perturbations persist (Brown and Nettleship 1984a). It is impossible to assess the extent to which alcid growth parameters measured today reflect the results of these human-induced changes. However, it is worthwhile to note that one of the most striking examples of intra-specific variation in fledging weight involves the Thick-billed Murre colonies of the eastern Canadian Arctic. In the Lancaster–Jones Sounds region (Prince Leopold Island, Cape Hay and Coburg Island), chicks generally fledge at 180 to 250 g, whereas at Digges Sound in Hudson Strait weights at fledging mainly fall between 130 and 160 g (Table 7.7). There has never been any form of commercial fishery within the foraging range of any of the colonies, and commercial whaling had ended by 1915 (Mitchell and Reeves 1982). This startling variation therefore exists in an essentially 'untouched' marine environment and offers us hope that at least some of the phenomena that we investigate result from natural biological processes rather than from reactions to human-induced disturbances.

CHAPTER **8**

Coloniality and Social Behaviour in the Atlantic Alcidae

TIM R. BIRKHEAD

Department of Zoology, University of Sheffield, Sheffield, England

I. INTRODUCTION

Most alcids are colonial; 14 of the 22 living species are truly colonial, 6 are either loosely colonial or form colonies at least occasionally and two species are solitary (Table 8.1). This chapter examines two related prob-

355

TABLE 8.1

Degrees of Coloniality in the Alcidae

Species	Colonial	Intermediate	Solitary
Razorbill	+		
Common Murre	+		
Thick-billed Murre	+		
Dovekie	+		
Black Guillemot		+	
Pigeon Guillemot		+	
Spectacled Guillemot		+	
Marbled Murrelet			+
Kittlitz's Murrelet			+
Xantus' Murrelet		+	
Craveri's Murrelet		+	
Ancient Murrelet	+		
Japanese Murrelet	+		
Cassin's Auklet	+		
Parakeet Auklet		+	
Crested Auklet	+		
Least Auklet	+		
Whiskered Auklet	+		
Rhinoceros Auklet	+		
Atlantic Puffin	+		
Horned Puffin	+		
Tufted Puffin	+		

lems: the evolution of colonial breeding and the evolution of social signals which enable alcids to breed in large and often dense colonies.

II. COLONIALITY

A. Introduction

Lack (1968) showed that for birds as a whole there is a strong association between breeding dispersion and food distribution: seabird species which feed on clumped food sources, tend to feed and breed in groups. Alcids show a similar pattern, with colonial species feeding offshore on clumped prey such as mid-water schooling fish or zooplankton (see Chapter 9, this volume), and loosely colonial or solitary species feeding inshore on prey which are probably more evenly dispersed (Table 8.1). Lack explained this association among seabirds by the presence of water, which creates colony sites that are free from predators. In other words, he concluded that the effect of predators was the major factor in the evolution of coloniality, while any feeding advantages were secondary adaptations. Krebs (1978) attempted to disentangle the effects of predators and food in the Ciconiiformes (herons, storks, etc.) and found a marked association between coloniality and vulnerability to predators. He concluded that coloniality in these species had evolved in relation to food dispersion rather than in response to predators. Our lack of knowledge and the relatively low diversity of colony sites in alcids makes it difficult to use this type of approach to assess the relative roles of food and predators in the evolution of alcid coloniality. An additional possibility is that coloniality occurs primarily because of a shortage of suitable colony sites (Lack 1968; Ashmole 1971; Snapp 1976; Walter 1979).

Since Lack's (1968) analysis, interest in the theoretical aspects of group living, including avian coloniality (Alexander 1974; Bertram 1978; Wittenberger and Hunt 1985), has resulted in a number of alternative hypotheses to explain coloniality. Here I examine these hypotheses and their predictions in relation to the data from alcid studies.

There are several potential benefits of group living (see below), but Alexander (1974) has argued that none are automatic advantages of sociality, whereas there are several automatic disadvantages. A cost–benefit approach has been successfully applied to avian territoriality (Brown 1964; Davies and Houston 1981), but to date there has been no analogous theory for the evolution of coloniality. This is probably because in studies of territoriality it has been possible to measure costs and benefits in energetic terms, whereas the only currency available for coloniality studies is fitness. Measuring benefits of coloniality in terms of fitness (e.g., breeding success) is relatively straightforward, but measuring costs is much more difficult. Consider the effect of predation on a colonial breeding seabird: increased numbers of birds breeding in a colony may enable individuals to detect a predator sooner, so that they are better prepared for an attack and therefore less likely to lose eggs or chicks. By comparing birds breeding in dense and sparse colonies it may be possible to measure the benefits of colonial breeding in terms of number of young reared. But we must also consider the cost of coloniality: large aggregations of breeding seabirds are conspicuous and probably attract predators, but it is extremely difficult to measure this type of cost in order to examine the overall effect of coloniality.

The main effects of coloniality can be summarised as follows:

1. EFFECTS CONCERNED WITH FOOD

a. Colony Location. A centrally placed colony minimizes the travel distance to feeding areas (Horn 1968).

b. Information Centre Hypothesis. Colonies (and communal roosts) serve as information centres and individuals determine the location of good feeding sites by following others. Unsuccessful birds return to the colony (the information centre) and follow successful foragers (Ward and Zahavi 1973). The term 'information centre' implies mutual cooperation (as in some social insects), but this is not so; successful birds probably cannot prevent others from following them. In any case, it is also assumed that sufficient food is available so it is not disadvantageous to be followed.

c. Competition for Food. Increased colony size is probably associated with increased productivity, but also increased competition among colony members for food (Gaston and Nettleship 1981; see also Chapter 7, this volume).

2. EFFECTS CONCERNED WITH PREDATION

a. Concealment versus Clumping in Safe Sites. Wittenberger and Hunt (1985) refer to this as the 'critical density hypothesis', and suggest that beyond a certain local population density concealment from predators is no longer possible. Once this critical threshold is reached, birds do better by forming colonies in inaccessible sites.

b. Increased Vigilance. The greater number of individuals in a colony means that predators are more likely to be detected sooner.

c. Increased Mobbing. The effectiveness of predator mobbing will be greater if the area over which an individual mobs overlaps with that of other individuals, so that several birds, rather than one, mob a predator (Kruuk 1964; Veen 1977).

d. Predator Swamping. Spatial clumping, together with temporal synchrony in breeding, may result in a concentration of food which predators cannot fully exploit, such that the risks of predation per individual are reduced.

e. Position within a Colony. The argument here is that birds at the centre of breeding groups, or in dense as opposed to sparse groups, suffer less predation.

f. Attraction of Predators. Predators are undoubtedly attracted to breeding colonies, but as Wittenberger and Hunt (1985) have pointed out, the key question is whether predation rates per individual are increased or decreased by coloniality. This is the only negative predation effect.

3. INCREASED COMPETITION FOR SPACE

Within a colony there will be a continuum of breeding-site quality; individuals which are unsuccessful in competing for sites will either obtain only poor-quality sites, or no site at all (Brown 1969).

4. INCREASED COMPETITION FOR MATINGS

The opportunities for extra-pair matings and risks of cuckoldry are greater among individuals breeding colonially than those breeding solitarily.

5. INCREASED TRANSMISSION OF DISEASE AND ECTOPARASITES

Increased proximity increases the risk of transmission.

6. INCREASED RISK OF MISDIRECTED PARENTAL CARE

Increased proximity increases the chances of intraspecific brood parasitism (Yom-Tov 1980), of cuckoldry (see above), or of eggs or chicks being accidentally exchanged between neighbours.

B. Coloniality and Food

1. COLONY LOCATION

There is little evidence to test this idea in alcids because in only a few cases have the foraging areas for particular colonies been examined. Hunt *et al.* (1980, 1981) found that for most island seabird colonies in Alaska, the foraging distribution around the colonies was 'markedly asymmetrical'. On the other hand, data for Thick-billed Murres, presented by Nettleship and Gaston (1978), show a fairly symmetrical distribution around the colony. Wittenberger and Hunt (1985) suggest that this hypothesis is unlikely to apply to very large colonies, like those formed by many alcids (see Chapter 2, this volume), because the feeding area around a large colony could be exploited more efficiently if the area was partitioned among a number of smaller colonies. However, this presupposes that colony sites are not limiting.

2. INFORMATION CENTRE HYPOTHESIS

In order to demonstrate that colonies serve as information centres it must be shown that (a) birds are exploiting a food supply which is patchy and unpredictable in space and time; (b) colony members are not behaving independently of each other in their feeding trips; (c) the distance, and hence travel time, between the colony and feeding areas is large (otherwise the cost of returning to poor areas would be minimal); (d) individuals foraging in groups have a higher food intake than solitary individuals; and (e) unsuccessful individuals tend to follow successful ones.

The evidence to support the information centre hypothesis comes from a variety of sources (Krebs 1978). The major studies are those of Krebs (1974), working on Great Blue Herons in the field, and De Groot (1980), working on Red-billed Weavers in captivity (see also Waltz 1982). In addition, there is a large amount of indirect evidence for the idea, some of it derived from observations of auks. First, most, if not all, offshore auks exploit patchily distributed prey: either fish or plankton (see Chapter 6, this volume). Second, data for Thick-billed Murres (Gaston and Nettleship 1981), Common Murres (Birkhead 1976a) and Atlantic Puffins (Ashcroft 1976) show that birds do not leave their respective colonies independently of conspecifics. Interestingly, the pattern observed in Thick-billed Murres differed from that of the Common Murre and Atlantic Puffin. In the latter two species, observed on Skomer Island, Wales, individuals left their colonies in small groups and flew directly from breeding areas out to sea. The non-random, temporal (Fig. 8.1) and spatial distribution of departures (Birkhead 1976a) indicates that some birds follow others to feeding areas. Among Thick-billed Murres at Prince Leopold Island, a different pattern occurred; birds left breeding ledges at random, showing no tendency to follow each other, but instead of flying directly to feeding areas, birds alighted on the sea below the breeding cliffs. They later left this area, in a non-random way, in flocks of between 10 and 50 individuals. Gaston and Nettleship (1981) suggested that two inter-related processes may be operating in food location in Thick-billed Murres at this colony. First, birds congregate on the sea near breeding areas, rather than departing directly from breeding ledges, in order to obtain a better view of incoming birds so that they have the choice of following out-going birds or orientating to incoming flocks. Birds leave in flocks because some individuals which are uncertain about which way to fly, follow others. Once airborne the flock can orientate to incoming birds. In other words, 'information transfer' can occur either by some individuals following others as they leave the vicinity of the colony, or by following the flight paths of birds returning to the colony, or both. Such a system

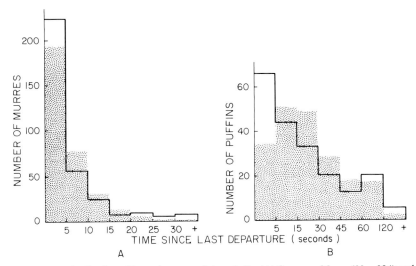

Fig. 8.1.   Distribution of inter-departure intervals for (A) Common Murre (N = 324) and (B) Atlantic Puffin (N = 200) departures from their respective colonies (open histogram). The stippled histogram is the expected frequency if departures occurred at random. In both cases observed values are significantly (p < .001) different from expected (from Ashcroft 1976; Birkhead 1976a).

is possible only if the rate of incoming birds is sufficiently high, and Gaston and Nettleship (1981) have shown, using a theoretical model, that given the size of the Prince Leopold Island colony (ca. 86,000 pairs), this idea is highly plausible (see below).

The difference in the way murres at Skomer Island and Prince Leopold Island leave their colonies may be more closely associated with colony size than with a species-specific difference. At large colonies of either species, high-flying, linear flocks of murres returning to the colony are a characteristic feature (Sergeant 1951). I have observed such flocks at the Cape Hay, Bylot Island, and Coburg Island Thick-billed Murre colonies, both of which hold 100,000–200,000 pairs, and at Common Murre colonies, at Funk Island (400,000 pairs) and Green Island (74,000 pairs), Newfoundland, and the Gannet Islands (47,000 pairs), Labrador (Nettleship 1980; also see Chapter 2, this volume). However, no such flocks were observed at Skomer Island (2500 pairs). Moreover, in contrast to Prince Leopold Island, murres returning to Skomer did so over a wide area, and did not use obvious flight paths. The combination of this, plus the small population size, probably meant that there were insufficient incoming birds for departing birds to orientate to. Consequently, if birds breeding at small colonies are to use conspecifics to help them find feeding areas then they must rely on departing individuals.

The large size of high-arctic murre colonies may be specifically associated with food location, and Gaston and Nettleship (1981) argued that colony size and the spatial predictability of food should be negatively correlated. Food predictability cannot be measured directly, but we know that for Thick-billed Murres food distribution can be closely associated with the distribution of floating ice pans (see Chapter 6, this volume). In areas where mean ice cover exceeds 10% during the chick-rearing period, colonies tend to be relatively large, numbering 10,000 or more pairs. In other words, birds breeding in regions where food supplies are highly unpredictable need to be part of a large colony in order to obtain sufficient information on the location of food.

We can conclude that, although the information centre hypothesis has not been rigorously tested with any bird species, there is some circumstantial evidence from alcid studies to support it.

3. COMPETITION FOR FOOD

Gaston and Nettleship (1981) have suggested that the availability of food close to large colonies is reduced by intraspecific competition, consequently birds must travel farther to feeding areas. Large colonies owe their size to the fact that food is more abundant in the area as a whole, so that increased travel costs are offset by an increased rate of food intake. A. J. Gaston (Chapter 7, this volume) has shown that for Thick-billed Murres, using chick fledging weight as a measure of food availability, fledging weights are inversely related to colony size, indicating that competition for food is increased around large colonies. Although these data suggest increased competition for food, we cannot exclude the possibility that differences in food availability caused by other factors produce this effect.

C. Coloniality and Predation

1. CONCEALMENT VERSUS CLUMPING

If inaccessible sites are clumped in space, then local population densities will be high, and concealment from predators impossible. The evidence is equivocal regarding the availability of alternative colony sites for alcids (see Chapter 4, this volume). If Wittenberger and Hunt's (1985) critical density hypothesis is correct, then concealment should be the best form of defence at low population densities. There is some evidence to support this prediction for Common Murres. Gulls (*Larus* spp.) are well-known predators of Common Murre eggs and young (Johnson 1938, 1941; Kaftanovskii 1938; Birkhead 1977a), and losses to predators are higher when breeding density is low (Birkhead 1977a). At the Farallon Islands, California, where the Common Murre population has undergone a marked decline (Ainley and Lewis 1974), birds retreated into crevices and under boulders, to breed, to avoid predatory gulls (Chaney 1924). As the population density increased birds bred in the open in dense groups, as they had done prior to the decline (Bent 1919; Ainley and Lewis 1974).

2. INCREASED VIGILANCE

Vigilance may be beneficial in that birds are less likely to be taken by surprise by a predator. Even in situations where predators take only eggs and young (and not adults), vigilance may be important. Among Common Murres, those breeding at low densities and hence vulnerable to egg and chick predation by gulls, spent more time alert and less time sleeping then did birds in dense groups (Birkhead 1977a). Both murre species have a specific alarm signal: a short, low-amplitude call together with a rapid bowing of the head and neck, which alerts nearby conspecifics. An early warning of a predator's approach may result in birds being better prepared for an attack. For example, chicks or eggs may be more closely brooded. Other alcids respond to some predators by flying away, and such 'panic flights' (e.g., Atlantic Puffins) may alert others to a predator's presence.

3. INCREASED MOBBING

Alcids do not mob predators, probably because they risk being caught.

4. PREDATOR SWAMPING

The results of several studies have shown that groups of animals breeding synchronously are more successful than those breeding asynchronously, and in some cases this is apparently due to predator swamping, for example, Black-headed Gull (Patterson 1965), Common Tern (Nisbet 1975). Most seabirds exhibit local synchrony of breeding in different parts of the colony (see Chapter 4, this volume), and this effect has been recorded in Common Murres (Birkhead 1980), Thick-billed Murres (Gaston and Nettleship 1981), Dovekies (Evans 1981a), Razorbills (Lloyd 1976a), and Atlantic Puffins (Ashcroft 1976). In the Common Murre at least, synchronous breeding is adaptive since, in conjunction with high-density breeding, it reduces egg and chick loss to predators (Birkhead 1977a; see

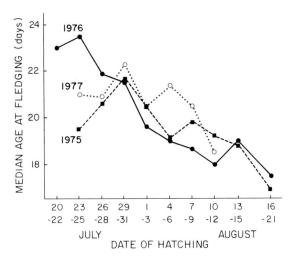

Fig. 8.2.   Seasonal decline in age at fledging in Thick-billed Murre chicks at Prince Leopold Island (from Gaston and Nettleship 1981).

also Chapter 4, this volume). Most auk chicks are vulnerable to predation from gulls during fledging and this may be why some species fledge synchronously. In Thick-billed Murres, fledging occurs more synchronously than egg-laying because of a seasonal decline in age at fledging (Fig. 8.2). Chicks hatched early in the season fledge at about 20 days, whereas late-hatched chicks fledge at about 17 days of age, resulting in the overall spread of fledging being reduced (Gaston and Nettleship 1981). Williams (1975) found that on Bjørnøya, murre and Razorbill chicks fledging asynchronously, either relatively early or late in the evening, were more likely to be killed by gulls than those fledging synchronously. Daan and Tinbergen (1979) recorded the same effect among Thick-billed Murres at Spitsbergen.

Synchrony may also be important for reasons other than predator avoidance. Emlen and Demong (1975) showed that breeding success in different colonies of Bank Swallows was positively correlated with the degree of synchrony within the group. They attributed this to an information centre-type effect since birds at the same stage of the breeding cycle will benefit most from the information on the location of food.

5. POSITION WITHIN A COLONY AND BREEDING
   DENSITY

Studies of several alcids have shown that losses through predation are lower among individuals breeding at the most frequent density. In most of these cases the commonest density is the highest density. The situation for Common Murres (Birkhead 1977a) and Atlantic Puffins (Nettleship 1972; Harris 1980) has already been described (see Chapter 4, this volume). However, in each of these studies it was not possible to separate the effects of breeding density from other factors. For example, in Common Murres, density was closely associated with breeding synchrony, and in Atlantic Puffins, density was associated with angle of slope of the ground (Nettleship 1972).

6. ATTRACTION OF PREDATORS

There is little doubt that predators are attracted to alcid colonies. Most large alcid colonies also contain breeding populations of one or more gull (*Larus*) or corvid (Corvidae) species, which may obtain much of their food from the birds. Similarly, arctic fox tend to be concentrated around large colonies of Thick-billed Murres (Tuck 1961). Tuck (1961) also records a temporal increase in the number of predatory species visiting murre colonies, from egg-laying through to fledging, when chicks are most vulnerable. However, these anecdotal accounts tell us nothing about the predation rates per individual colony member.

D. Increased Competition for Breeding Sites

There is good evidence that breeding-site quality influences breeding success in alcids. Data for Common and Thick-billed Murre, and Atlantic Puffin have been presented in Chapter 4 of this volume. All auks are territorial and defend just a small area around the breeding site. Territories are usually defended for several consecutive years, and birds compete vigorously for good sites. Among Cassin's Auklets breeding on the Farallon Islands, California, much of the breeding habitat is fully occupied and, as for murres and puffins, there are marked differences in habitat quality (Manuwal 1972, 1974b) so that some birds breed in optimal areas, some in suboptimal areas, and others (floaters) are excluded from breeding. Thus, some individuals which are physiologically capable of breeding are unable to do so because they cannot compete successfully for breeding sites. When burrow owners were experimentally removed they were rapidly replaced by new individuals which bred successfully (Manuwal 1974b). Most alcid populations contain a non-breeding segment (see Chapter 5, this volume), but this is the only study of alcids in which the existence of a floating population has been experimentally demonstrated. It seems likely that 'floaters' also exist among the rapidly expanding Atlantic Puffin population on the Farne Islands, England (M. P. Harris, personal communication).

Among Atlantic Puffins, Nettleship (1972) recorded that fights were more frequent in the best habitat (i.e., sloping ground; see Chapter 4, this volume), and males breeding in this habitat were significantly heavier than those on level ground. This suggests that heavy males were more likely to win fights for good-quality sites. Competition for breeding sites may also explain the early return, and protracted pre-laying period in murres at some colonies (see Chapter 3, this volume); in boreal-water regions, Common Murres return to their colonies several months prior to egg-laying. The frequency of fighting among murres was highest soon after birds returned to the colony, which suggests that this was associated with the re-establishment of breeding sites (Birkhead 1978b). In Common Murres, Thick-billed Murres and Razorbills there is also a peak of fighting during the chick-rearing period: this coincides with the time when immature, prospecting birds are most common at the colony. In addition, the females of these species may remain at the colony, for up to 14 days, after their chick has fledged, possibly in order to guard the site from other birds.

E. Increased Competition for Matings

Males of monogamous species which fertilize females in addition to their own mate may gain a genetic advantage. However, while males may benefit from securing extra-pair copulations, they must also ensure that their own mate is not fertilized by another male. Males must spend time and energy guarding, and they may also risk injury while defending females; in Common Murres some of the most intense fighting occurs in mate defence (Birkhead 1978b). Females may, or more likely may not, benefit from extra-pair copulations. The main potential benefit is increased genetic diversity of their off-spring. The main potential disadvantages are time spent in extra-pair copulations, or in resisting extra-pair copulations, and the chance of reduced male parental assistance if the copulation is detected (Trivers 1972). Knowlton (1979) suggested that breeding synchrony may be a female strategy to minimize the chances of male cuckoldry, and this might explain the local breeding synchrony found in so many colonial species.

Extra-pair matings have been recorded in several alcid species, for example, Common and Thick-billed Murres (Birkhead 1978b; Gaston and Nettleship 1981) and Dovekies (P. G. H. Evans, personal communication). Male Atlantic Puffins will attempt to mount a model puffin (P. J. Hudson, personal communication), indicating that extra-pair copulations occur as suggested by Lockley (1953a). Recently, extra pair copulation has been examined in Common Murres (Birkhead et al. 1985a).

Female Common Murres usually resisted extra-pair copulation attempts; in only 1 of 121 incidents did the female appear to 'cooperate'. In all other cases females attempted to stand upright, to throw off the male. On some occasions extra-pair matings were apparently successful: females usually initiated copulation by adopting a prone posture and calling. If the female's partner was engaged in some other activity (e.g., fighting with a neighbour), another male would mount the female. In such cases the female apparently did not distinguish between her partner and another male. However, such matings were often cut short by the male partner attacking the mounting male (Birkhead 1978b, Birkhead *et al.* 1985a).

F. Increased Transmission of Disease and Ectoparasites

There is some evidence (mostly anecdotal) that the frequency of disease and ectoparasite infestation is correlated with colony size (Wittenberger and Hunt 1985). Colony density may also be important; in both murres and puffins (which form large, dense colonies), ticks are much more frequent than they are among Razorbills, which breed at lower densities and in smaller colonies (personal observation). There have, however, been no systematic examinations of the occurrence of ticks in alcid colonies (but see Duffy 1983).

G. Increased Risk of Misdirected Parental Care

It would clearly be disadvantageous for an individual to rear another's off-spring, so we would expect egg and chick recognition to be well developed in those species in which the risks of misdirected parental care are high. Alexander (1974) has suggested that these will be higher among colonial than non-colonial species. In addition, within colonial species we would expect the risks to be greater in species and individuals breeding at high densities. Among alcids, the species most likely to experience misdirected parental care are murres. Both species breed in physical contact with their neighbours, and neither species makes a nest which might reduce the chances of eggs rolling between breeding sites. Detailed studies by B. Tschanz and co-workers have shown that the high degree of egg-colour polymorphism in Common Murres is associated with the ability of parents to recognise their own egg. In addition, individual differences in the voice of chicks and parents are used for recognition (Tschanz 1959, 1968). In Common Murres adult–chick recognition starts before the chick has emerged from the shell. Hatching may take several days and during this time the chick calls from within the shell and the adult birds call to the chick.

In the Razorbill the evidence for egg recognition is equivocal; Birkhead (1978b) found no evidence for recognition, whereas Ingold (1980) did. The available evidence suggests that Razorbills can recognise their own egg when given a choice if the difference between the two eggs is very marked (P. Ingold, personal communication). However, it is clear that egg recognition in Razorbills is less well developed than it is in Common Murres. Just as in Common Murres, adult Razorbills and their chicks recognise each other by their calls, but only after the chick is several days old (Ingold 1973). For both murre species and the Razorbill, adult–chick recognition is important because the two must maintain contact with each other when the chick leaves the colony. However, for Common Murres, which breed at much higher densities than Razorbills, adult–chick recognition is essential throughout the time the chick is at the breeding site.

There is now good evidence that in murres and Razorbills it is the male parent which accompanies the chick when it leaves the colony (see Chapter 3, this volume). However, we do not know whether there are any differences in the way male and female parents respond to their chick while at the breeding site. There have been no behavioural studies of Thick-billed Murres equivalent to those on Common Murres and Razorbills, but it seems likely that the situation in Thick-billed Murres is similar to that in Common Murres.

III. MIXED COLONIES

Many alcids breed in colonies with other alcid species and with other seabirds. In fact, single-species colonies appear to be quite rare (see below). There are two main explanations for the occurrence of mixed alcid colonies. The first is that they occur simply as a consequence of suitable colony sites being limited. The second explanation, proposed by Burger (1981; see also Ward and Zahavi 1973), is that mixed colonies have evolved because competition among individuals for resources is reduced (e.g., food, mates, space) and some of the advantages of coloniality (e.g., anti-predator behaviour, food-finding) are maintained. Burger suggests that the costs of coloniality are reduced because the relative number of conspecifics (with whom resource competition would be greatest) is small, but that many of the advantages of coloniality occur irrespective of the species composition of the colony.

Burger (1981) has produced a model to explain the evolution of mixed colonies and has derived a number of predictions from the model, among them the following:

   1. There should be a positive correlation between the number of species and total number of individuals at particular colonies, because

the greater the number of species the higher the number of individuals can be supported because competition for resources is reduced.
2. There should be more colonies with a large number of species than one would expect if species distributed themselves randomly.

However, if colony sites were limiting, as seems likely for many seabirds (Wittenberger 1981), then both the above predictions would be fulfilled. Clearly, it is essential to determine whether alcids form mixed colonies because they have to (i.e., colony sites are limiting), or because individuals doing so are at some advantage over those which do not.

IV. COLONY INFRASTRUCTURE AND SOCIAL BEHAVIOUR

Because adult alcids usually retain the same breeding site from one year to the next, and because young birds tend to return to breed close to where they were reared (see Chapters 3, 4 and 5 of this volume), genetically related birds may tend to occur in local concentrations within a colony. There is some evidence to support this for murres: bridled Common Murres (Birkhead *et al.* 1980), egg-colour type in both species (Gaston and Nettleship 1981; T. R. Birkhead and D. N. Nettleship, unpublished observations) and chick-colour type in Thick-billed Murres (Gaston and Nettleship 1981) are all clumped in their distribution within a colony. Jefferies and Parslow (1976) have shown, through a study of hand-reared birds, that bridling in Common Murres is genetically determined, and that the bridled condition is almost certainly a recessive variant of the normal form, carried by a single gene on one of the autosomes.

Egg colour and type of marking may also be genetically determined: observations of females which laid eggs in captivity showed that they laid the same colour egg each year (Marsault 1975, and personal communication). In addition, first and replacement eggs in both species of murre are very similar in colour and markings (T. R. Birkhead and D. N. Nettleship, unpublished observations).

If murre colonies comprise local concentrations of genetically related individuals, then the potential for cooperative forms of behaviour to evolve through kin selection exists. Common and Thick-billed Murres show two behaviours which might be explicable in these terms. Both species will shelter young of neighbours, if the approach of a predator causes the parents to leave the breeding area; this reduces the probability of the chick being taken by the predator (Birkhead 1977a; Tschanz 1979b; Gaston and Nettleship 1981). Second, both species frequently allopreen their neighbours. I have examined the distribution of allopreening by neighbouring Common Murres and found that birds did not alloppreen each other at random (χ^2 = 42.7, 10 df, p < .001), and that the number of preening bouts given was correlated with the number of bouts received (r_s = .759, N = 12, p < .01). Allopreening is probably advantageous in removing dirt and ectoparasites from the plumage in areas which a bird cannot preen itself. For example, R. Lambeck (personal communication) noted that in a captive group of Common Murres one individual with a heavy tick infestation was alloppreened more frequently than other birds.

There are several possible explanations for cooperative behaviours such as these (e.g., Trivers 1971; Wilson 1975), so these data do not confirm the operation of kin selection. Nevertheless, they do suggest that further studies would be rewarding.

V. MATING SYSTEMS

All alcids, like most seabirds, are monogamous (Hunt 1980). However, as stated above, males of some alcid species adopt a 'mixed strategy' of pairing with one female, with whom they help to rear the young, but exploiting any opportunity to copulate with other females. Monogamy in alcids has probably evolved because male parental care is essential for female reproductive success (Lack 1968; Wittenberger and Tilson 1980). In only two situations is male parental care essential: (a) where continuous breeding-site attendance is vital for successful reproduction, and (b) where species rear only a single chick at a time. The argument here is that a larger clutch would have evolved if one parent could rear the young alone. In other words, for single-egg clutch species the food supply is such that it takes both parents to rear one chick. Both these factors are relevant to cliff-breeding alcids (murres and Razorbills); they produce only one egg, and one parent must remain at the breeding site to guard the chick for the entire rearing period. Situation (b) probably explains monogamy in other single-egg clutch alcids, and the data from twinning experiments (see Chapter 4, Table 4.5, this volume) support this. The situation in alcids which produce two-egg clutches (e.g., Black and Pigeon Guillemots, and some murrelets) is less clear, since in theory at least, the female could rear a single young, if both parents can rear two.

VI. SOCIAL SIGNALS

A. Introduction

Relationships of any sort, whether they are friendly, sexual or agonistic, long or short term, are based on information provided by participating individuals. The information upon which a particular relationship is based is presented through communication. In most vertebrates communication is complex (Smith 1977), and for the auks we have, as yet, only a poor understanding of their communication system and social relationships. However, because most species are relatively easy to observe, we have more or less complete ethograms for all Atlantic alcid species (see references in Table 8.2). For some species we also have details of the context in which particular displays are used (see below), so it has been possible to formulate some hypotheses about their functions.

One reason alcid behaviour has not previously been considered in detail, is that compared with other seabird families whose social signals have been studied (larids: Tinbergen 1959; sulids: Nelson 1978b), the social signals of alcids are less ritualised and relatively diverse. The diversity in behavioural repertoire is probably associated with the greater diversity of body form and life-styles found in alcids (Bédard 1969a). In both gulls and sulids, counterparts of the same visual display can be seen in most or all species, for example, the long-call in gulls.

Within the alcids only a few displays are common to all species. The similarities and differences in social signals and other behaviours used by alcids are summarised in Table 8.2. One of the objectives of this section is to provide the reader with an idea of the social meaning of the various displays they are likely to observe at an alcid colony. Studies of this type were pioneered by N. Tinbergen in the 1950s, and although this aspect of social behaviour is no longer fashionable, it is included here in order to provide as complete a picture as possible of the social life of Atlantic alcids.

It is often convenient, though not always biologically sound, to distinguish sexual and agonistic behaviour. The aim in the following sections has been to outline the sexual and agonistic behaviour of the Atlantic alcids and to identify the main differences and similarities between species. However, I have not offered explanations for why such differences should exist because at the present time there is insufficient quantitative information for all species to be able to do this.

B. Sexual Behaviour

Sexual behaviour comprises formation, re-formation and maintenance of pair bonds. All auks, like most other seabirds, are monogamous with long-term pair bonds which are renewed each year at the breeding site. We know very little about pair formation in alcids, but we know that it probably does not take the form seen in some other species (e.g., sulids) in which a male establishes a territory and then advertises for a female. In

TABLE 8.2

Summary of Behaviour Patterns and Social Signals Used by Atlantic Auks

Behaviour	Razorbill	Common Murre	Thick-billed Murre	Dovekie	Black Guillemot	Atlantic Puffin
Territorial defence and site-ownership	Post-landing display; fighting	Post-landing display; fighting	Post-landing display; fighting	? Post-landing display; fighting	Nest song; head-tossing; fighting	?Post-landing display; head-flicking/ shaking; foot-stomp, fighting
Greeting ceremony	Yes	Yes	Yes	Yes	Yes	No
Allopreening	Yes	Yes	Yes	No[a]	No	No[a]
Copulation frequency	Low	High	High	?	Low	Low
Extra-pair copulation	Rare	Common	Common	Occurs	Occurs	Occurs
Alarm signal	None	Alarm-bowing	Alarm-bowing	?	Scream	None
Aerial display[b]	Yes	No	Yes	Yes	No	Yes
Adults perform social behaviour on sea	Yes	Infrequent	Infrequent	Infrequent	Yes	Yes
References[c]	1	2	3	4	5	6

[a] Occurs, but is extremely rare.

[b] Referred to as 'butterfly/moth' flight.

[c] References: 1. Perry (1940); Paludan (1947); Conder (1950); Bédard (1969d); Birkhead (1976a). 2. Selous (1901, 1905); Perry (1940); Conder (1950); Nørrevang (1958); Williams (1972); Birkhead (1976a, 1978b). 3. Pennycuik (1956); Williams (1972); Gaston and Nettleship (1981); T. R. Birkhead (personal observation). 4. Ferdinand (1969); Evans (1981a). 5. Preston (1968); Asbirk (1979c). 6. Perry (1940); Conder (1950); Myrberget (1962); M. P. Harris (personal communication); D. N. Nettleship (personal communication)s K. Taylor (personal communication).

Common Murres pair formation may occur in clubs, which contain mainly young birds which show relatively high levels of sexual and agonistic behaviour (Birkhead 1976a). Male murres in clubs perform a head-vertical display, which is only rarely seen among birds on breeding areas. This display may be part of the early stages of pair formation since it often precedes two birds forming at least a temporary association. Observations of colour-marked individuals are necessary to confirm this.

Most alcids perform behaviours concerned with the maintenance of the pair bond at or near the breeding site. In addition, though, Black Guillemots, Atlantic Puffins, Razorbills and Thick-billed Murres display communally on the sea near the colony. The behaviours described below are those performed by pair members at or near the breeding site. All six species perform a billing or mutual fencing display with their partner, either as a greeting or in a few other contexts. Common Murres perform a protracted greeting ceremony in which the male and female clash their open bills together, calling loudly for several seconds. They perform the same display after either one of them, or a neighbour, has been involved in an aggressive encounter, or when a neighbour returns with a fish to feed its chick. Thick-billed Murres perform fencing which is similar in form to the Common Murres', but which rarely occurs as a greeting. It is given after they, or a neighbour, have been involved in aggressive interaction. In the Razorbill and Dovekie, billing occurs both as a greeting and apparently spontaneously at other times. Razorbills sometimes perform another display, bill-vibrating, immediately prior to billing when a partner returns to the breeding site. Two forms of billing have been recorded in Dovekies: one in which the head is moved up and down occurs during incubation, and the other, which occurs during the chick-rearing period in which the head is moved from side to side (Evans 1981a). In the Atlantic Puffin, billing comprises lateral head shaking in which birds strike their bills together. In contrast to other species no vocalizations are made. Although allopreening is very rarely seen in the Atlantic Puffin, birds sometimes nibble each others' bills or rictal rosettes after billing.

Among breeding alcids, billing occurs mainly in the pre-laying period, so it may be associated with pair formation, or re-formation. Billing does not occur as a greeting ceremony in puffins, but it is performed mainly by pair members. As in murres, pairs may bill in response to a nearby fight or the arrival of a neighbour. In the Black Guillemot the greeting ceremony consists of birds adopting the hunch–whistle posture followed by billing, in which there is little or no actual bill contact, in contrast to other species. The hunch–whistle component of greeting may be agonistic since the hunch–whistle is also used in more obviously aggressive situations (Asbirk 1979c). Billing in all auks appears to contain elements of aggression. The same is true in other seabirds, and Nelson's (1978b) explanation

TABLE 8.3

Frequency and Duration of Allopreening between Partners during the Incubation Period in Common Murres, Thick-billed Murres and Razorbills[a]

Species[b]	Frequency[c]			Duration[d]		
	$\bar{x}$	S.E.	N	$\bar{x}$	S.E.	N
Common Murre	1.35	0.05	10	14.31	1.16	152
Thick-billed Murre	0.21	0.05	7	18.94	2.70	49
Razorbill	0.93	0.17	3	9.60	1.12	139

[a] Values are means ±1 S.E.

[b] Data for Common Murre and Razorbill from Skomer Island, Wales (Birkhead 1976a); data for Thick-billed Murre from Gannet Islands, Labrador (T. R. Birkhead and D. N. Nettleship, unpublished observations).

[c] Frequency given as number of allopreens/pair/minute; N = number of 50-minute observation periods. Difference between murres: $p < .001$.

[d] Duration given in seconds; N = number of allopreening bouts. Difference between murres: $p > .1$.

of meeting ceremonies in sulids may be applicable to auks. He suggests that there is a correlation between aggressiveness of the male and the 'strength' of the meeting ceremony, and as a result, the pair bond. A well-developed pair bond is important in site defence, since both members of the pair defend the site. Nelson also suggests that where male and female are forced to remain close to each other, because of the restricted breeding site (as in most auks), an elaborate meeting ceremony is an important outlet for the pair members' aggression; the agonistic element of billing in auks seems to agree with Nelson's idea. Nelson ascribes a similar aggression-outlet function to allopreening in sulids, and this may also be applicable to auks. Indeed there appears to be a correlation between greeting displays and allopreening. If we rank species according to the 'strength' of their greeting ceremony (i.e., duration, degree of ritualisation, number of components), then the Common Murre has the most elaborate greeting and the highest frequency of allopreening of any alcid. The Razorbill ranks second, the Thick-billed Murre third, both with frequent allopreening (see Table 8.3). The Dovekie and Black Guillemot have less intense greeting ceremonies and very rare allopreening. The Atlantic Puffin ranks sixth, with no greeting ceremony and extremely rare allopreening.

Compared with most other birds, copulation in seabirds is protracted and frequent. All but one Atlantic alcid copulate on land, at or near the breeding site. The Atlantic Puffin is the only exception, and this species copulates on the sea. Quantitative details are available for only a few species: in both murres, copulations last about 17 seconds on average, with between one and four cloacal contacts. Other alcids probably also perform multiple cloacal contacts during copulation, a feature which they share with gulls, terns and skuas (Brown 1967a). In murres and the Razorbill, the male and female utter (different) calls during copulation, the female flicking her head back as she calls. In the Atlantic Puffin it is the male who head-flicks as a preliminary to copulation. We have little information for the Dovekie or Black Guillemot, but in the Pigeon Guillemot calling and head flicking by the female are rare (Drent 1965). In murres and the Razorbill, copulation most often occurs when one bird returns to the other at the breeding site (Williams 1972; Birkhead 1976a; Gaston and Nettleship 1981). In murres, copulation occurs regularly throughout the pre-laying period, and in some areas, several months before egg-laying. In Thick-billed Murres, copulation reaches its highest level about 3 weeks before egg-laying (Gaston and Nettleship 1981). However, since fertilization in birds occurs very soon (within 30 minutes) after ovulation (Howarth 1974) and since fresh sperm are most likely to fertilize the ovum (Warren and Kilpatrick 1929; Lake 1975), a 3-week interval between the peak of copulation and egg-laying is unexpected. An alternative explanation is that 3 weeks prior to egg-laying the sex ratio at the colony is closest to 1 : 1, and although the overall rate of copulation is highest at this time, the rate per individual female may peak some time later. Observations of Common Murres show copulation rates per female peak a few days before egg-laying (Birkhead *et al.* 1985a).

Nonetheless, the early start to copulation in murres suggests that it serves some purpose other than insemination. Behaviours of this sort whose function are obscure are sometimes said to 'strengthen the pair bond', but labelling behaviour in this way does little to increase our understanding of it. Williams (1972) suggested that in Thick-billed Murres copulation had become ritualised and served as a greeting ceremony during the pre-laying period. Another explanation is that regular copulation serves to obscure the females' fertile period, and may be important in mate-guarding and cuckoldry avoidance (Birkhead 1979). Extra-marital copulation is common in both murres and may be a consequence of breeding colonially at high densities, in that opportunities for extra matings are relatively high. Males appear to defend their partners from the sexual advances of other males and vigorously attack would-be rapists (Trivers 1972; Birkhead 1978b; Birkhead *et al.* 1985a).

C. Agonistic Behaviour

Animals may compete by threat and fighting for resources, like good breeding sites and mates, which are often in short supply. This section is concerned mainly with social signals associated with obtaining and maintaining a territory. Competition for mates and matings have already been discussed. The acquisition of a breeding place by auks is usually achieved by a bird repeatedly returning to the same place in the colony. This may occur in the year prior to the first breeding attempt. Most immature Atlantic Puffins return to the general area where they were reared and confine their attempts to secure a nest site to an area of just a few square metres (Ashcroft 1976). Some Atlantic Puffins acquire a site but do not breed in their fourth year; others obtain a site and breed for the first time in their fifth year (Ashcroft 1979). Immature Common Murres at Skomer Island, Wales, start to visit breeding ledges towards the end of their third year and may visit several parts of their natal colony before returning to establish a territory close to where they were reared (Birkhead 1976a). There are no obvious displays associated with territory acquisition; birds simply spend an increasing amount of time at a particular place in the colony. Initially, immature birds are submissive to established breeders and rarely initiate aggressive interactions, but as they become more attached to a site they become more likely to defend it against conspecifics.

Fighting in all auk species is unritualised and usually comprises grasping with the bill an opponent's bill, neck, wing or tail and vigorous wing-beating. In the Atlantic Puffin and Black Guillemot fighting birds also scratch with their feet. Fights are usually of short duration, but a few may last several minutes, or very occasionally, may last, on and off, for several hours.

Territories are maintained by threat and fighting, and in all auks both members of the pair defend the site. Fighting results in the spacing out of individuals within the colony; Veen (1977) has demonstrated this experimentally in Sandwich Terns. In Common Murres, high-density breeding is important for successful reproduction, but at the same time increases the rate at which individuals encounter each other. Aggressive interactions per bird are more frequent among individuals which are completely surrounded by other murres, than those breeding at lower densities, on narrow ledges with just one neighbour on each side. High-density breeding in the Common Murre is maintained, despite high rates of aggression, by a range of appeasement signals (see below). In dense groups of murres, neighbouring birds have an aggressive interaction about once every 20 minutes on average, during the incubation period (Birkhead 1978b), a rate which is similar to that reported for the Northern Gannet (Nelson 1978b). However, unlike gannets, aggressive interactions in murres are short, averaging 4.5 seconds, with few developing into fights (Birkhead 1978b). Aggressive interactions generally comprise one murre threatening another, which either performs an appeasement signal, or retaliates briefly and then performs an appeasement display.

Threat consists of individuals lunging at each other; in murres this is done with a closed bill, but in the Razorbill the beak is open. Puffins threaten each other by head waving, with an open bill. In Black Guillemots the attacker runs towards its opponent with its neck stretched forward and head held low; the bird calls and has a slightly open bill. At lower intensity, threat comprises a hunch–whistle display (Asbirk 1979c).

In addition to these threat displays, which in most auk species are unritualised, some alcids also perform what may be ritualised, site-ownership signals. All species, except the Black Guillemot, perform post-landing displays (Fig. 8.3). Displays which are similar in form and occur in the same context are performed by some sulids, and Nelson (1978b) suggests that these are aggressively motivated, site-ownership displays. It is not clear whether these signals in auks are aggressively motivated, although they may signal site-ownership: in Common Murres and Razorbills immature, non-breeding birds do not perform these displays, which suggests that they may be associated with site-ownership (Birkhead

Fig. 8.3.   Post-landing and ritualised walking postures in Atlantic auks: (A) Razorbill, post-landing posture; (B) Thick-billed Murre, post-landing and ritualised walking posture; (C) Common Murre, post-landing posture, also used when walking through dense groups of conspecifics; (D) Atlantic Puffin, post-landing posture, the low-profile ritualised walk (see text) is similar but the wings are not raised; (E) Black Guillemot, posture which occurs as part of the twitter–waggle display; and (F) Dovekie, head-down form of ritualised walking.

1976a). However, post-landing displays are very similar in form to ritualised walking displays, and there is some evidence to indicate that these are agonistic displays, which serve an appeasement function.

Ritualised walking is one of the few displays used by all six species of Atlantic auks. The display has two components: the posture of the head and that of the wings (Fig. 8.3). These displays are given by birds as they walk through the colony. In Common Murres the display occurs in two forms, dependent upon the proximity of conspecifics. When walking between birds which are just a few centimetres away, the head is held up, but when neighbours are about 0.5 m away, the head is held down. In Thick-billed Murres only the head-down form occurs, and is commonly performed immediately prior to a bird leaving the colony. Ritualised walking may occur prior to take-off in the Common Murre, but only if the bird has to walk past conspecifics to a take-off point. Ritualised walking in the Thick-billed Murre seems to be specifically associated with departure from the colony.

Razorbills perform ritualised walking with the head up. The display is used less often than in Common Murres, and its performance is not related to a bird's proximity to others as it is in Common Murres. In the Dovekie the wings are not raised above the back, but both head-up and head-down forms of the display occur; the latter is most frequently used (Evans 1981a). Two forms of ritualised walking occur in the Atlantic Puffin: the low-profile walk (in which the body is held horizontally), which is similar to the post-landing display (Fig. 8.3D), and the 'pelican walk', in which the body is held erect and in which the feet are moved in an exaggerated manner. The pelican walk may serve as site-ownership, whereas the low-profile walk probably serves as an appeasement. In the Black Guillemot, the ritualised walking posture (Fig. 8.3E) occurs as part of the twitter–waggle display, which occurs in agonistic encounters (Asbirk 1979c). Ritualised walking in all alcids contains an agonistic element and in all species may class as an appeasement display, since its main function may be to draw attention to the performer, to signal 'I am moving, but have no aggressive intentions' (Van Tets 1965).

Common and Thick-billed Murres possess three additional appeasement signals: side-preening, stretch-away and turn-away. Quantitative details are available only for the Common Murre (Birkhead 1978b). Side-preening occurs mainly among non-incubating birds in several contexts: (a) after or during a fight; (b) after a bird returns to its site and has performed a post-landing display, it is most likely to side-preen if its partner is absent and if it has neighbours closer than 0.5 m; (c) after ritualised walking, again, particularly if conspecifics are closer than 0.5 m. Stretch-away occurs mainly among incubating birds, mainly in response to conspecifics moving or fighting nearby. Turn-away is performed by all birds, either during a fight or in response to neighbours fighting. Thick-billed Murres perform the same displays in similar contexts, except that in this species, when a bird returns to its partner, it performs side-preening on at least 50% of occasions. The corresponding value for Common Murres is 5%.

These three displays are classical appeasement signals in that they remove the bill (the main weapon) from a position in which an attack could be launched. No other auks have such appeasement signals or breed at such high densities. The close proximity of conspecifics in murres has obviously been important in the evolution of inter-pair appeasement displays. The main differences in social signals between the two murre species are summarised in the following section.

D. A Comparison between Common and Thick-billed Murres

Of all the Atlantic auks the Common and Thick-billed Murres are perhaps the most closely related; they are similar in form, have similar life-styles and are considered to be ecological counterparts (Chapter 1, this volume). They are also the species whose social signals have been studied in most detail. In general terms the two species of murre use similar visual and vocal displays in similar contexts, and these signals probably have very similar functions in each species (Table 8.4). However, there are some marked differences in the form and function of certain signals, and the frequency of interactions. In Thick-billed Murres, the frequency of social interactions between pair members and between neighbours is much lower than in Common Murres. This is partly because Thick-billed Murres breed at lower densities than Common Murres and partly because off-duty Thick-billed Murres spend less time at the colony than Common Murres. Although the repertoire size of each species is similar (Table 8.2), I have the impression that Common Murres have a more complex social system since the rate of social interaction is so much higher. Indeed, Wilson (1975) has used the frequency of interaction as a measure of sociality. One of the most frequent behaviours between pair members in murres is allopreening. The data in Table 8.3, which were collected to control for density effects and presence of off-duty partner, show that allopreening is significantly less frequent in Thick-billed Murres than in Common Murres, although the mean length of allopreening bouts in each species was similar. Other differences include:

1. Form and intensity of the greeting ceremony—when a Common Murre returns to its mate, both birds engage in several seconds of mutual fencing and calling; in Thick-billed Murres usually only one bird calls, for a shorter time, and there is no fencing.

TABLE 8.4

Comparison of Social Signals Used by Common and Thick-billed Murres[a]

Social signal	Common Murre (U. aalge)	Thick-billed Murre (U. lomvia)	Function	Comments
Fighting	+	+	Defence of territory and mate	More frequent in lomvia, escalation more rapid
Side-preening	+	+	Appeasement	Given when returning to partner in lomvia
Head-turn	+	+	Appeasement	
Stretch-away	+	+	Appeasement	
Post-landing	+	+	Site-ownership/ appeasement?	In aalge head up and wing up; in lomvia head down and wing up
Ritualised walking	+	+	Appeasement?	In lomvia prior to departure from site
Mutual fencing	+	+	aalge: greeting; see text	Less frequent in lomvia and not as greeting
Allopreening	+	+	'Friendly behaviour'	Less frequent in lomvia
Butterfly flight	−	+	?	
Copulation	+	+	See text; insemination	
Extra pair copulation	+	+	Insemination	
Fish presentation	+	−	Pair maintenance?	
Head vertical	+	+	Pair formation	
Hawing	−	+	?	
Mutual bowing	+	+	Pair maintenance?	
Alarm bowing	+	+	Signals alarm	Shorter bow in lomvia

[a] Based on Williams (1972) and Birkhead (1976a, 1978b, and personal observation).
[b] +, signal occurs; − signal does not occur.

2. Behaviour of pre-breeders at the colony—immature Common Murres congregate in clubs at the base of breeding cliffs, whereas no such clubs form among Thick-billed Murres; instead, immature Thick-bills simply fly along breeding cliffs and alight at the edge of breeding areas, or rest on the sea.

VII. CONCLUSIONS

A. Coloniality

Although there is a large amount of information on alcid coloniality, some of which supports the various hypotheses presented, none of the hypotheses have been adequately tested. There are at least two reasons for this. First, there is the difficulty of disentangling inter-related effects, and second, the problems concerned with the measurements of costs and benefits. The best measure of fitness is life-time reproductive success, but since alcids live at least 10 years on average (see Chapter 5, this volume), it is unlikely that we will ever be able to measure this. We are therefore forced to assume that success measured over one or a few years accurately reflects life-time success. It may be possible to check this from long-term studies of individually marked birds, such as the Black-legged Kittiwake (Coulson 1968; Wooler and Coulson 1977).

There is evidence from alcid studies that supports the information centre hypothesis, to some extent. Doubtless there are difficulties of testing this idea adequately (Hailman 1975), but there are several possibilities for further work. For example, observations on the spatial and temporal distribution of colony departures and, in particular, comparisons of large versus small, and synchronous versus asynchronous colonies. If birds obtain information from colony neighbours, then adjacent chicks should receive more similar food, and should show synchronous weight changes, compared with non-neighbours. It may be possible to show that less successful birds follow more successful ones by examining the relationship between feeding success (weight of food per unit time) on the last trip, with the time spent at the colony before departing. The assumption here is that unsuccessful birds should spend longer at the colony, waiting to follow a more successful one. It may also be worth comparing some measure of reproductive success, between small versus large, and asynchronous versus synchronous colonies. If there is information transfer, then small and asynchronous colonies would be expected to do less well than large synchronous ones (Krebs 1978). It may even be possible to manipulate synchrony experimentally (see, e.g., Parsons 1975) to test these ideas.

There is also some evidence for both predator swamping and density effects in several alcid species, although for both effects confounding variables make interpretation difficult. Until recently, most alcid biologists have relied entirely on observation. However, the effect of different variables can be assessed either by the use of multivariate statistics or by adopting an experimental approach. The cost of attracting predators to colonies can probably be assessed in those species, like the Black Guillemot, which breed both colonially and solitarily. It may be possible by careful measurement of predator (e.g., gull or fox) and prey (alcid) population sizes, or attack rates together with predator food requirements, to assess the cost per individual in each situation.

The factors which are important in the evolution of mixed colonies should also be examined further. The most important initial step is to make a systematic analysis of alcid colony-site characteristics, in order to assess the extent to which site limitation controls intraspecific and inter-specific coloniality.

An examination of some of the costs of coloniality would also repay further study. The available information suggests high rates of tick infes-tation in species which breed in dense colonies, compared with those breeding less densely. A study of tick densities in large versus small and dense versus sparse colonies of the same species, and a comparison be-tween species, could be made relatively easily (Hoogland and Sherman 1976; Hoogland 1979).

B. Social Signals

A species' repertoire of social signals and degree of coloniality it ex-hibits are closely linked, and almost certainly evolved hand in hand. Clearly, species such as murres which breed in large, dense colonies have a larger range of social signals and appear to have more complex social relationships than alcids which typically breed in smaller or less dense colonies.

We now have fairly complete descriptions of the social signals used by Atlantic auks, but these provide only the starting point to understanding alcid social behaviour. Most of what we know about the behaviour of auks is at the species level; for example, Common Murres perform a particular display more or less frequently than another species. We know nothing about sexual differences in behaviour, nor do we know very much about individual differences in behaviour. If we are to make any progress in our understanding of alcid social behaviour we need to conduct studies of individually colour-marked birds, which would provide information in both these areas.

CHAPTER 9

The Atlantic Alcidae at Sea[1]

RICHARD G. B. BROWN

Seabird Research Unit, Canadian Wildlife Service, Bedford Institute of Oceanography,
Dartmouth, Nova Scotia, Canada

[1] This chapter was prepared in association with the program "Studies on Northern Seabirds", Seabird Research Unit, Canadian Wildlife Service, Environment Canada (Report No. 141).

383

I. INTRODUCTION

This chapter summarises what is known of the distributions and move-ments of the Atlantic Alcidae at sea. It is based on direct observations from ships and aircraft, banding returns, the species composition of the alcids killed in various oil spills and, in the case of the Great Auk, archae-ological findings as well. The sections on pelagic ecology for each species attempt to interpret these distributions through a series of rather specula-tive scenarios which link the birds with the distributions and movements of some of their prey species. Finally, the discussion summarises the migration and dispersal routes of the seven species, and suggests how these routes may have evolved since the end of the last glaciation. In this scheme there is a certain amount of unavoidable overlap with topics dealt with in other chapters of this volume—in particular, with the discussions on breeding distributions (Chapter 2) and feeding ecology (Chapter 6).

The seven species are described in an order dictated by convenience, beginning with those whose pelagic distributions and ecology are the best known. Discussions of subspecies refer to Salomonsen (1944) and Storer (1952)—but see Chapter 1 of this volume for a critique of these and other studies of geographic variation in the alcids. Descriptions of currents, ice-cover and other oceanographic phenomena refer to Anonymous (1958, 1967, 1968). The principal place-names are shown in Figs. 9.1–9.3.

II. DOVEKIE, *Alle alle*

A. Pelagic Distribution and Movements

The Dovekie is one of the most northerly of the Atlantic Alcidae, breed-ing almost as far north as there is land. The majority of the population breeds in the Thule District of northwest Greenland, and substantial num-bers breed elsewhere in the high-arctic area: Jan Mayen, Spitsbergen, northern Novaya Zemlya, Severnaya Zemlya, Franz Josef Land, and the Scoresby Sound region of east Greenland. There are also small colonies in the low-arctic area: Bjørnøya, northern Iceland, and west Greenland south of 75°N (see Chapter 2, this volume).

In the western Atlantic the Dovekie is commonest in summer close to its enormous colonies in northwest Greenland, although there are also smaller numbers, presumably of non-breeders, in the pack-ice zone off southeastern Baffin Island, as well as stragglers off eastern Labrador (Brown 1980a, and unpublished observations). The birds abandon their colonies in the Thule District by the end of August and move south, reaching northern Newfoundland by early October (Salomonsen 1967; Brown *et al.* 1975; Johnson *et al.* 1976; McLaren and Renaud 1979; Renaud *et al.* 1982). In winter they are commonest on the southern Grand Banks, especially near the edge of the continental shelf, and to a lesser extent at the shelf-edge east of Nova Scotia, but are scarce farther south (Brown *et al.* 1975; Brown 1980b; see also Table 9.1). They return to the Thule District in the first half of May (Salomonsen 1967) and very large numbers are seen on passage near the ice-edge east of Lancaster Sound at this time (Renaud *et al.* 1982). Renaud *et al.* estimated from aerial surveys that there were some 14 million birds in the region of this ice-edge on 14 May 1978—perhaps half of the Thule population, which is of the order of 30 million birds (Freuchen and Salomonsen 1958). In addition, many Dovekies are still moving north in Newfoundland waters at this season (Brown 1968).

The normal distribution limits in the eastern Atlantic are not well defined. Since Dovekies are regular visitors to the Norwegian coast in winter, but are rare in British waters (Cramp *et al.* 1974; Norderhaug *et al.* 1977), their southern limit is probably ca. 55°N–60°N. They occur as far south as ca. 54°30′N in January to March, well offshore in the tongue of warm, saline Atlantic water which enters the North Sea between Shetland and Norway (Joiris 1983). They are largely confined to Fraser's (1965) North Atlantic and northern North Sea zooplankton community regions, and to that part of the North Sea which has the greatest abundance of oceanic zooplankton from the open Atlantic. However, the southern limit in the Norwegian Sea in March 1982 was at ca. 64°N (Brown 1984). As in the western Atlantic, Dovekies are often associated with the edge of the pack-ice (Salomonsen 1950; Løvenskiold 1964; Brown 1984).

However, Dovekies are notorious for their tendency to be driven well outside the normal limits of their range by winter storms, as the occurrence of many 'wrecks' of Dovekie flocks in Britain and along the eastern seaboard of the United States has shown (Fisher and Lockley 1954). Stray birds have been reported as far south as Cuba and the Canary Islands.

More detailed information about Dovekie movements has come from intensive banding programmes in northwest Greenland and west Spitsbergen. Nearly 10,000 adult birds have been banded at colonies in the Thule District, yet none have been recovered in Greenland outside their colonies despite an intensive winter hunt for Dovekies off southwest Greenland (Salomonsen 1971a, 1979b). The only foreign recoveries have been three birds found in eastern Newfoundland in November to January. Salomonsen (1967) concludes that most if not all of the Thule birds winter off Newfoundland, but that they are too far offshore for there to be much chance of recovering banded birds. Brown (1980b, Fig. 1) supports this last point.

TABLE 9.1

Numbers of Alcids Killed by Some Winter Oil Spills in the Western North Atlantic[a]

Species	New England—Nantucket Shoals Dec. 1976–Jan. 1977	Eastern Nova Scotia					S.E. Newfoundland	
		Chedabucto Bay Feb.–March 1970	Sable Island		Cabot Strait March–May 1979	Burin/St. Shotts Feb.–March 1970	Placentia Bay	
			Feb.–March 1970	March–May 1979			March 1956	Jan. 1981
Razorbill	26 (29.9)	0 —	1 (0.2)	0 —	5 (0.4)	0 —	0 —	0 —
Common Murre	49 (56.3)	5 (5.8)	7 (1.2)	0 —	0 —	0 —	0 —	0 —
Thick-billed Murre	10 (11.4)	0 —	137 (24.2)	2 (0.6)	12 (1.0)	0 —	322 (93.7)	0 —
Murre spp.[b]	1 (1.1)	56 (65.1)	297 (52.5)	56 (16.1)	684[c] (59.1)	36 (57.1)	0 —	72[d] (71.3)
Black Guillemot	0 —	8 (9.3)	6 (1.1)	0 —	27 (2.3)	25 (39.7)	5 (0.2)	12 (11.9)
Dovekie	1 (1.1)	17 (19.8)	114 (20.1)	290 (83.3)	430 (37.1)	2 (3.2)	16 (4.6)	17 (16.8)
Atlantic Puffin	0 —	0 —	4 (0.7)	0 —	0 —	0 —	1 (0.3)	0 —
References	Powers and Rumage (1978)	Brown et al. (1973)	Brown et al. (1973)	Brown and Johnson (1980)	Brown and Johnson (1980)	Brown et al. (1973)	Tuck (1961)	I. M. Goudie (personal communication and unpublished; CWS files)

[a] Figures in parentheses show the percentage of the total alcid kill made up by the species in question.
[b] The Thick-billed Murre is the dominant murre species inshore in winter in Newfoundland waters, making up an average of 87% of the murre hunting kill (Gaston et al. 1983b); 314 of 384 (82%) murres positively identified as to species, at sea off Newfoundland and Nova Scotia in winter (November–March 1969–1983), were Thick-billed Murres (R. G. B. Brown, unpublished observations).
[c] Includes both Common and Thick-billed Murres.
[d] About 90% Thick-billed Murres.

The birds which winter off west Greenland apparently come from the eastern Atlantic. There have been 14 recoveries of Spitsbergen birds from there, almost all in November to January and from the extreme southwest coast south of ca. 65°N (Norderhaug 1967; Salomonsen 1967, 1971b; Holgersen 1980). The only other recovery, a bird from northeast Iceland in March, was presumably returning to Spitsbergen on spring migration (Holgersen 1969). It is not clear what proportion of the Spitsbergen Dovekies reach west Greenland. Salomonsen (1967) suggests that only the earliest migrants get so far before the time comes for them to return, and that many, perhaps most Spitsbergen birds winter along the ice-edge off east Greenland—a sparsely populated region where the chances of recovering banded birds are slight. The regular occurrence of Dovekies in November to January on this coast at Angmagssalik (ca. 65°N) supports this suggestion (Helms 1926). The absence of Dovekie recoveries from the well-populated coasts of Norway and Russia to the south of Spitsbergen also supports the suggestion of a southwesterly dispersal.

Nothing is known of the movements of Dovekies from Scoresby Sound or from Jan Mayen; they might winter off southwest Greenland, or fly directly to the Grand Banks. Farther east, there is a massive westerly movement of Dovekies past the Murmansk Coast of northwest Russia in October, and a return movement in April (Meinertzhagen 1938). These are presumably birds from Novaya Zemlya, possibly even from Severnaya Zemlya. The absence of Dovekies from the tally of birds killed in a winter oil spill off northeast Norway, and their presence in one off western Norway (Table 9.2) suggests that these Russian birds winter in the Atlantic rather than in the Barents Sea. On the other hand, Dovekies breeding in Franz Josef Land, their most northerly colony, return as early as the end of February (Collett and Nansen 1900; Dement'ev et al. 1951). This suggests that these birds are wintering fairly close to the archipelago, perhaps at the ice-edge in the northeast Barents Sea which, in March, is usually as far north as 73°N (Norderhaug et al. 1977). There is no evidence of any major eastward movement from the colonies in the Russian Arctic (Collett and Nansen 1900), but some undoubtedly occurs. Dovekies identified as *A. a. polaris,* the subspecies endemic to Franz Josef Land, have been collected as far east as the New Siberian Islands (ca. 142°E: Dement'ev et al. 1951). This may explain how this Atlantic alcid has established a very small breeding population in the Bering Sea (Breckenridge 1966).

In summary, then, Dovekies show two principal migratory patterns. Birds from northwest Greenland winter off Newfoundland, while many of those from the European Arctic winter off southwest and, possibly, southeast Greenland. Both populations belong to the subspecies *A. a.*

TABLE 9.2

Numbers of Alcids Killed by Some Winter Oil Spills in the Eastern North Atlantic[a,b]

Species	Brittany March–May 1967	Brittany March–May 1978	S.W. England March–May 1967	N.W. Netherlands Feb. 1969	N.E. England–S.E. Scotland Jan.–Feb. 1971	N.E. Scotland Jan.–Feb. 1971	Kattegat Dec.–March 1969–71	W. Norway Jan.–Feb. 1981	N.E. Norway March 1979
Razorbill	390 (65.0)	978 (31.5)	237 (19.8)	193 (39.6)	388 (9.5)	1211 (29.3)	13 (27.7)	30 (3.6)	4 (0.2)
Common Murre	110 (18.3)	731 (23.6)	957 (79.8)	271 (55.6)	3182 (78.3)	1939 (46.9)	14 (29.8)	27 (3.2)	40 (2.5)
Thick-billed Murre	0 —	0 —	0 —	1 (0.2)	0 —	0 —	0 —	1 (0.1)	1477 (93.7)
Murre spp.	0 —	0 —	0 —	0 —	300[c] (7.4)	30[c] (0.7)	0 —	0 —	0 —
Black Guillemot	0 —	0 —	0 —	0 —	0 —	0 —	20 (42.5)	447 (53.2)	3 (0.2)
Dovekie	0 —	0 —	0 —	<10 (<2.0)	132 (3.2)	823 (19.9)	0 —	240 (28.6)	0 —
Atlantic Puffin	100 (16.7)	1391 (44.9)	5 (0.4)	12 (2.5)	60 (1.5)	127 (3.1)	0 —	95 (11.3)	52 (3.3)
References	Bourne et al. (1967); Hope Jones et al. (1978)	Hope Jones et al. (1978)	Bourne et al. (1967); Hope Jones et al. (1978)	Swennen and Spaans (1970)	Greenwood et al. (1971)	Greenwood et al. (1971)	Joensen (1972a)	Røv (1982)	Barrett (1979)

[a] Figures in parentheses show the percentage of the total alcid kill made up by the species in question.

[b] In addition, Mead (1981) notes a major oil spill in the North Sea–English Channel area in January 1981 which killed the following species: Skagerrak—≥55% Common Murres and 'large numbers' of Razorbills and Dovekies; Netherlands, Belgium and English Channel—mainly Common Murres and Razorbills. In February 1983 a massive 'wreck' of alcids along the North Sea coast of Britain included an unexpectedly large proportion of Razorbills: ca. 60%, against ca. 32% Common Murres, ca. 4% each of Dovekies and Atlantic Puffins, and a single Black Guillemot (Mead and Cawthorne 1983).

[c] Includes all unidentified alcids.

alle, so the two patterns are not obviously related to subspecific differences (Salomonsen 1944). However, the subspecies *A. a. polaris* is endemic to Franz Josef Land, and it seems likely that birds of this form may not undertake long migrations but winter in the Barents Sea close to their colonies instead.

B. Pelagic Ecology

Dovekies feed primarily on copepods, amphipods, euphausiids and zooplankton of similar size (Norderhaug 1980; Bradstreet 1982a). For maximum foraging efficiency they tend to seek out areas where such prey is not only generally abundant, but also locally concentrated—near the edge of the pack-ice, for example, at oceanic 'fronts', or at upwellings at shelf-breaks (Zelickman and Golovkin 1972; Brown 1980a,b; see also Chapter 6, Fig. 6.1, this volume). The seasonal pattern of their movements seems to be a series of journeys between such areas. For example, when the birds migrate north in spring, the overwhelming majority travel to high-latitude regions where there is pack-ice, but where the sea either never freezes over, or where the ice breaks up very early in the spring (Brown 1980b; see also Chapter 2, this volume). This gives them immediate access to the rich zooplankton fauna directly or indirectly associated with ice-edges (Bradstreet 1982b; Bradstreet and Cross 1982; Renaud *et al.* 1982). In the longer run it also gives them early access to the summer zooplankton bloom, since this occurs earlier in ice-free than in ice-covered waters at comparable latitudes (Pavshtiks 1968). When the birds abandon their colonies in Thule District at the end of August, they cross to the ice-covered waters of western Baffin Bay and Davis Strait, where they have access to the epontic fauna under the ice and also to the late zooplankton bloom, which does not occur until September in those waters (Salomonsen 1967; Pavshtiks 1968; Johnson *et al.* 1976; McLaren and Renaud 1979; Brown 1980a, and unpublished observations). This ice-edge is also an extremely important feeding area in the spring (Renaud *et al.* 1982), and many birds spend the whole summer there (Brown 1980a, Fig. 3).

The Dovekies' principal winter quarters on the Grand Banks are in another region where plankton is exceptionally abundant (Pavshtiks *et al.* 1962; Vladimirskaya 1965; Edinburgh Oceanographic Laboratory 1973), and where the annual bloom of *Calanus finmarchicus,* the dominant species of copepod and an important food of Dovekies (see Chapter 6, this volume), begins as early as February (Vladimirskaya 1965). There is little pack-ice in this area (Anonymous 1968), but the birds are commonest at the edges of the continental shelf (Brown *et al.* 1975; Brown 1980b; see also Chapter 6, Fig. 6.1, this volume). Both 'fronts' and upwellings occur in such areas (Yentsch 1974; Houghton et al. 1978; Fournier et al. 1979), and these would both bring food up to the surface where the birds can reach it, and concentrate it there to allow for more efficient foraging.

III. THICK-BILLED MURRE, Uria lomvia

A. Pelagic Distribution and Movements

The Thick-billed Murre breeds from Newfoundland north to the head of Baffin Bay on both the Canadian and Greenland sides, in the Scoresby Sound District of east Greenland, Jan Mayen, Iceland, Bjørnøya, Spitsbergen, Franz Josef Land, Novaya Zemlya, Severnaya Zemlya, the Murmansk Coast and the extreme north of Norway, as well as in the Pacific sector of the Arctic (Tuck 1961; see also Chapter 2, this volume).

In the western Atlantic Thick-billed Murres are not confined to the vicinity of their colonies in summer, but occur all through Baffin Bay, as well as in Hudson Strait west to ca. 80°W and in Lancaster Sound west to ca. 93°W (Brown et al. 1975; Brown 1980b, 1984). They are also found over the whole width of the continental shelf south to ca. 47°N off Newfoundland and as far east as Flemish Cap (ca. 47°N 45°W), the most easterly of the Newfoundland Banks. The more southerly and offshore of these sightings are probably of immature birds, which may spend the summer well south of their natal colonies (Salomonsen 1967). The birds withdraw in winter from Labrador and northern Newfoundland waters, which become ice-covered from January on. Their range extends down to the waters off eastern Nova Scotia and broadly overlaps with that of the Common Murre (see below), although the proportions of the two species in winter oil kills off eastern North America (Table 9.1) show that the Thick-billed Murre is the more northerly species.

Not much is known about the pelagic distribution of Thick-billed Murres in the eastern Atlantic. Like the Dovekie, this species reaches northern Norway in winter but it is very rare in Britain (Cramp et al. 1974; Norderhaug et al. 1977; see also Table 9.2). The southern limit of its winter range must therefore be at ca. 60°N or even farther north. Murres were very scarce in the Greenland and Norwegian Seas in March except in the vicinity of their colonies on Jan Mayen, Spitsbergen and northern Norway (Brown 1984).

Banding returns have shown that the general pattern of movements of Thick-billed Murres in the North Atlantic is similar to that of Dovekies. However, birds from many more populations have been banded, and so we know more about the finer points of detail. The movements of the principal populations may be summarised as follows.

1. HUDSON STRAIT

The Thick-billed Murres which winter in the polynyas and other open-water areas in Hudson Strait and northern Hudson Bay (Brown and Nettleship 1981) probably come from local colonies there. However, the banding returns indicate that the bulk of this population winters off Newfoundland, where it makes up ca. 53% of the Thick-billed Murres which winter in that region (Tuck 1961; Gaston 1980). The birds pass out of the eastern end of the Strait in early September (Gaston 1982; Orr and Ward 1982), and large numbers of murres, perhaps from this population, occur close inshore off central Labrador in late October (unpublished CWS files). The banding returns show that Hudson Strait birds reach northern Newfoundland in November and December. These birds, and also birds from the colonies in Labrador, remain in Newfoundland waters at least until the end of March. A few birds from Hudson Strait have been recovered in late winter off west Greenland, and Tuck (1961) suggests that part of this population winters there too. However, Gaston (1980) suggests instead that these are spring migrants en route to the Strait via Greenland.

2. WEST GREENLAND

All the first- and second-winter birds from west Greenland colonies, and perhaps 25% of the adults also winter off Newfoundland (Tuck 1961; Salomonsen 1967, 1971a, 1979a; Gaston 1980). Gaston estimates that these make up ca. 27% of the Thick-billed Murres which winter off Newfoundland. The first-winter birds begin to move down the Greenland coast in October and November, and have left the country altogether by December; older birds do not reach Newfoundland until January or February. The return migration begins in March. Thick-billed Murres are still returning to colonies in west Greenland or elsewhere in the western Atlantic sector of the Arctic as late as early May (Brown 1968).

3. LANCASTER AND JONES SOUNDS

After the end of the breeding season most Thick-billed Murres from colonies in Lancaster Sound move initially towards west Greenland and arrive there in November (Tuck 1961; Salomonsen 1967). Both these authors believe that the birds remain off Greenland all winter, at ca. 66°N. However, in a subsequent analysis Gaston (1980) concluded that about

75% of them move on later in the winter to Newfoundland, where they make up ca. 19% of the wintering Thick-billed Murre population. It is too soon to say how the recent intensive banding programme carried out by the Canadian Wildlife Service will alter this picture. However, there is already some evidence that these birds may move directly, and very rapidly, to Newfoundland. A chick banded prior to fledging in the colony on Coburg Island, Jones Sound, on 20 August 1979 was shot off Twillingate, northeast Newfoundland, on 18 October 1979 and may have arrived even earlier (D. N. Nettleship, personal communication).

To judge from the banding data (Tuck 1961, 1971; Salomonsen 1971a, 1979a; unpublished CWS files), the winter ranges of the Hudson Strait, west Greenland and Lancaster Sound populations overlap considerably off eastern and southeastern Newfoundland. However this applies only to the coastal areas where banded birds are recovered. It is possible that differences in wintering areas may be more apparent farther offshore on the Newfoundland Banks.

4. SOUTHEAST BAFFIN ISLAND

In geographic terms the large Thick-billed Murre colony near Reid Bay, southeast Baffin Island (ca. 67°N) is intermediate between the high-arctic populations in Lancaster and Jones Sounds and the low-arctic ones in Hudson Strait. In terms of climate—especially ice-cover—it is closer to the high arctic (Anonymous 1958; see also Fig. 9.3 and Chapter 2, Figs. 2.2 and 2.3). The colony is virtually inaccessible and in the absence of any banding one can only speculate over whether the birds follow the Hudson Strait murres' route direct to Newfoundland, or go via Greenland, like those from the high-arctic region. In late summer murres accompanied by chicks are seen quite commonly between Reid Bay and the Greenland coast, north of ca. 65°N, but there are very few sightings south of ca. 65°N (Stemp 1980; Orr and Ward 1982; R. G. B. Brown, unpublished observations). This suggests that Reid Bay birds migrate to Greenland. Gaston (1980) thought that they moved south towards Labrador. However, he based this hypothesis on that fact that young Thick-billed Murres (like young Common Murres and Razorbills) leave the breeding site before they can fly, and swim off accompanied by parents which are themselves moulting their flight feathers and are unable to fly (Birkhead 1977b; Birkhead and Taylor 1977). One would expect such birds to travel with the prevailing current, which sets southwards from Reid Bay towards Labrador (Anonymous 1958). However, swimming adult and young murres can in fact make headway against the current; Salomonsen (1979a,

p. 186) observed them moving south against the northward flow of the West Greenland Current on the east side of Davis Strait. The passage from Reid Bay to Greenland is in any case *across* rather than *against* the currents for the most part (Anonymous 1958). One can only hope that a banding programme will resolve this problem.

5. SCORESBY SOUND, JAN MAYEN AND ICELAND

The Scoresby Sound region of east Greenland (ca. 70°N) has a large population of Thick-billed Murres, and large numbers of birds have been banded there. However, there have been only three recoveries: first-winter birds in January from eastern Newfoundland and from Julianehåb District in the extreme southwest of Greenland, and a subadult in September from south of Scoresby Sound (Salomonsen 1979b). This is a recovery rate of only 0.1%, against 5% for birds from west Greenland colonies. Salomonsen concludes from this that the bulk of the population cannot be wintering off west Greenland or Newfoundland, where murres are regularly hunted and bands recovered. He suggests that they are wintering in the deep waters between Greenland and Newfoundland, while admitting that this seems improbable in a species which normally prefers relatively shallow water. However, preliminary surveys do not indicate an abundance of murres in that region (Brown 1968 and unpublished observations). One alternative is that the birds are wintering in the pack-ice off southeast Greenland, where the chances of recovering banded birds are slight; if so, however, one would expect more recoveries from Julianehåb District, where the pack-ice extends west around Cape Farewell and into inhabited country, and where many Thick-billed Murres from Europe are recovered in winter (Salomonsen 1971b). Another possibility is that the Scoresby Sound birds move directly southwest to Flemish Cap (see above), 700 km east of Newfoundland and thus well beyond the range of hunters. There is a report of flocks of Thick-billed Murres in breeding plumage migrating east-northeast in March past a weather ship at 62°30'N 33°W, ca. 550 km southwest of Iceland (Agnew 1975). The direction of this movement would be appropriate for birds returning from Flemish Cap to colonies in Scoresby Sound, or farther northeast in Jan Mayen or Spitsbergen.

There are no banding data for birds from Iceland or Jan Mayen and one can only speculate about the movements of these populations. The birds could be wintering off west Greenland, like Thick-billed Murres from Spitsbergen and the Russian Arctic, or on Flemish Cap, as has been suggested for the birds from Scoresby Sound.

6. BARENTS SEA

Many Thick-billed Murres from the colonies in the Barents Sea apparently winter there (Norderhaug et al. 1977). The precise limits of this wintering area are not known but it would appear to include northeast Norway, where Thick-billed Murres were the main alcids killed in a winter oil spill (Table 9.2), and the west coast south to ca. 69°N, where birds banded in colonies on the Murmansk Coast have been recovered. Birds banded in Spitsbergen, and to a lesser extent the Murmansk Coast and Novaya Zemlya, are frequently recovered in southwest Greenland in November through February (Salomonsen 1967, 1971b). It is not known whether all these westerly migrants press on to west Greenland or whether, as Salomonsen suggests, many of them also winter at the ice-edge off east Greenland. Salomonsen (1967) estimates that the ratio of Spitsbergen to Greenland birds off west Greenland in winter is 16:1. The southwesterly movement of the Spitsbergen birds is also apparent from the most recent Norwegian banding returns; Holgersen (1974, 1980) reports 15 recoveries from west Greenland [all made since Salomonsen's (1971b) review] and one from northeast Newfoundland, but none at all from northern Norway.

Many, perhaps most Thick-billed Murres from colonies in the eastern Barents Sea probably winter in the ice-free parts of that area (Uspenski 1956), and the fact that birds return to their colonies on Franz Josef Land as early as the end of February (Dement'ev et al. 1951) supports this. Løvenskiold (1964) quotes reports of murres swimming south between Franz Josef and Spitsbergen immediately after the end of the breeding season, so it seems likely that Franz Josef birds initially disperse to the south or southwest.

7. SUMMARY

The general pattern for Thick-billed Murre movements is therefore for birds from the North American Arctic to move down to Newfoundland, either directly or via west Greenland, while birds from the European Arctic move southwestwards towards west Greenland. These two migratory paths roughly follow, respectively, the Labrador and East–West Greenland Currents (see below, Fig. 9.3). In quantitative terms, Newfoundland waters are the most important wintering area in the western Atlantic. Gaston (1980) estimates that something of the order of 4 million birds go there, against a combined total of only ca. 1.75 million Greenland and Canadian birds wintering off west Greenland. The latter will be augmented by birds from the European Arctic, mainly Spitsbergen. However, the order-of-magnitude figures given by Norderhaug *et al.* (1977) suggest that the Spitsbergen population would be unlikely to add more than 2 million birds even if all of them were to winter in west Greenland. But west Greenland has a special importance to the Atlantic populations of the Thick-billed Murre as a migratory crossroads or stopover, because birds from all the high-arctic populations in North America probably pass through its waters on migration, and many birds from the European high- and low-arctic populations occur there as well. Almost all of the Atlantic Thick-billed Murre population belongs to the subspecies *U. l. lomvia,* and so the two principal migration routes do not reflect subspecific differences (Salomonsen 1944). *U. l. arroides* is endemic to Franz Josef Land, but the movements of this population are virtually unknown.

B. Pelagic Ecology

Thick-billed Murres, like the remainder of the Atlantic Alcidae, are primarily predators of small fish (see Chapter 6, this volume). The murres, like the plankton-feeding Dovekies, have the same need to forage economically, and they too tend to exploit ice-edges and other phenomena where food is locally concentrated (Hartley and Fisher 1936; Belopol'skii 1957; Meltofte 1976; Ogi and Tsujita 1977; Bradstreet and Cross 1982). Unfortunately it is often difficult to make direct comparisons between the distributions of the murres and their prey, for lack of quantitative information about the latter. This is because small fish are usually too large to be sampled in plankton surveys, and too small to be the subject of a commercial fishery. For example, important prey of the Thick-billed Murre such as arctic cod and sculpins (Cottidae) are either not fished commercially at all, or are fished only in very limited areas (Nikolaev 1979, 1980; Anonymous 1980b). Others, such as capelin, sprat, sandlance, and the small clupeids marketed as 'sardines', are indeed harvested commercially. But there are many pitfalls in using the statistics from such fisheries as indices of the abundance and distribution of the birds' prey, since they are often distorted by extraneous factors such as the weather, previous under- or over-fishing of the stock, the value of the fish in comparison with alternatives which might be caught, restricted fishing seasons, and so on.

The interpretations put forward in this chapter to explain the movements of the fish-eating Atlantic alcids are therefore little more than speculative scenarios, and should be treated as such. They are presented here merely as plausible hypotheses which need to be examined in a great deal more detail.

One such hypothesis would link the movements of Thick-billed Murres to those of capelin, the principal food of the birds which winter off New-foundland and northern Norway (Tuck 1961; Barrett 1979; see also Chapter 6, this volume). Capelin are abundant off southeast Labrador and northeast Newfoundland in August through December (Jangaard 1974), and the fishery there peaks in October to November (Anonymous 1980b). This suggests that it is one of the factors influencing the timing of the arrival of murres from arctic colonies. This food supply is probably available all winter; Jangaard (1974) notes that the fish also school south of Newfoundland and on the Grand Banks from February through May. Farther east, the timing and direction of the southwesterly dispersal of murres from Spitsbergen colonies may be linked to the occurrence of capelin in commercial quantities in September and October in the waters west of Jan Mayen, and the wintering of birds in the southern Barents Sea to a capelin spawning season there in February through March (Nikolaev 1979, 1980).

It would be an obvious oversimplification to think of murre movements in terms of the availability of only one type of prey. Birds wintering in the North Pacific, for example, feed mainly on crustaceans and small fish but *not* on capelin, which are apparently too deep for them to reach (Ogi 1980). The murres which take capelin on the Grand Banks in winter, feed mainly on sculpins and arctic cod when they return north in summer (Tuck and Squires 1955; Gaston and Nettleship 1981; Bradstreet 1982b). The birds are to an unknown extent flexible in their choice of prey, and we will have to take in the whole spectrum of possibilities for a complete interpretation of their movements. We are very far from knowing enough about either the birds' feeding habits or the ecology of their various preys to be able to do that. Nonetheless the capelin scenario outlined here fits just well enough to show a little of the adaptations which must underlie the migratory patterns of the Thick-billed Murre.

IV. COMMON MURRE, *Uria aalge*

A. Pelagic Distribution and Movements

The Common Murre breeds in the Gulf of St. Lawrence, Newfoundland and southeast Labrador, west Greenland, Iceland, Faeroe Islands, the British Isles, Brittany, northwest Spain, Portugal, Helgoland, the southern Baltic, Norway, the Murmansk Coast and Bjørnøya, as well as in the North Pacific (Tuck 1961; see also Chapter 2, this volume).

Common Murres tend to occur farther south in summer in the western Atlantic than do Thick-billed Murres (Brown *et al.* 1975). Most sightings at sea are between ca. 46°N and 55°N, off the strip of coast along which most eastern North American colonies are situated. The birds occur from the coast out to the edge of the continental shelf, across the whole width of the Grand Banks and on Flemish Cap beyond. In January to March they largely withdraw from Labrador waters and are commonest on the southern Grand Banks and off Nova Scotia. The relative frequencies with which the two murre species occur in winter oil kills off eastern North America show that Common Murres winter farther south than Thick-billed Murres (Table 9.1). The southern limit of their regular occurrence in the western Atlantic is on Georges Bank off New England, ca. 41°N.

In January through April in the eastern Atlantic, Common Murres were abundant west of the Outer Hebrides at ca. 58°N (Brown 1984, and unpublished observations) and also in the northern North Sea (Joiris 1983). Most North Sea birds occurred north of ca. 55°N and were in breeding plumage; south of this they were scarce and in winter plumage—probably subadults. However, the winter distribution of Common Murres in this region is best indicated by the banding returns (see below): the birds are found from northern Norway to northwest Spain, and occasionally as far south as Gibraltar (Mead 1974; Norderhaug et al. 1977). Here, as in the western Atlantic, the winter oil kill data show a more southerly distribution than that of the Thick-billed Murre. The limits of distribution away from the coast are not known, but Common Murres have been seen in March as far north as ca. 71°N near Jan Mayen in the Greenland Sea, and ca. 73°30′N in the western Barents Sea (Brown 1984).

The movements of the various breeding populations of Common Murres in the North Atlantic are complex, and may be summarised as follows.

1. EASTERN NORTH AMERICA

Banding returns show that birds from Newfoundland, the breeding centre in the western Atlantic, do not move very far but winter off the south and southeast coasts of the island (Tuck 1961; unpublished CWS files)—and presumably also out on the Grand Banks. Tuck suggests that the birds initially disperse northwards after they leave their colonies and move as far north as the Strait of Belle Isle. However a re-analysis of Tuck's and more recent data does not confirm this, but indicates instead a general dispersal, to the south as well as the north (A. J. Gaston, personal communication). Those birds which do disperse northwards move south again in December, when the pack-ice reaches northern Newfoundland. First-winter birds from southeast Labrador begin to reach Newfoundland in October, and recoveries from December onwards are all from southern and eastern Newfoundland (Tuck 1961). Presumably these birds too are driven south by the pack-ice. Birds from Cape Whittle, in the northeast Gulf of St. Lawrence, have been recovered in their first winter from both south and northeast Newfoundland (Johnson 1940), which suggests that they may disperse both south into the Gulf and northeast through the Strait of Belle Isle.

Murres are not legally hunted south of Newfoundland, so it is hard to judge from the banding returns what proportion of the Common Murre population moves farther south still. Two first-winter birds from Newfoundland colonies have been recovered off northeastern Nova Scotia (November, December), and a third off southern Nova Scotia (November), while two older birds were recovered in April off southern Nova Scotia, and off Rhode Island (Tuck 1961; unpublished CWS files). Evidently at least part of the Newfoundland population moves farther south, and one would judge from the virtual absence of Common Murres from winter oil kills north of New England (Table 9.1) that the proportion which does so is a large one.

Finally, two birds banded as chicks in southeast Newfoundland have been recovered in the Disko Bay area of west Greenland (ca. 69°N), one in June of its second summer and the other as an adult in September (unpublished CWS files). It is likely that both birds came north among the flocks of Thick-billed Murres returning to Greenland after wintering off Newfoundland (see above). No doubt accidental movements of this kind explain how a Common Murre colony came to be established among breeding Thick-billed Murres near Sukkertoppen, west Greenland (ca. 65°N)—over 1100 km from the nearest Common Murre colony in Labrador and even farther from those in Iceland (Salomonsen 1967). It is not known whether the Sukkertoppen birds winter in Newfoundland, but Salomonsen believes that the Common Murres which winter off southwest Greenland may be from that colony.

2. ICELAND AND FAEROE ISLANDS

Very few Common Murres have been banded in Iceland, and there have been only five recoveries (Björnsson 1940, 1941; Mead and Cawthorne 1983; A. Petersen, personal communication). Three juveniles banded at a colony in southwest Iceland were recovered in their first winter in eastern Iceland (October), northeast Iceland (December) and Faeroe (May); two Icelandic birds were recovered in northeast Britain in February. This suggests an eastward dispersal from the colonies, but more information is clearly needed. It is possible, for example, that the Common Murres which winter off southwest Greenland (Salomonsen

1967) come from Icelandic colonies—a migration similar to that of Icelandic Black Guillemots (see Section VII,A,4). The banding of Faeroese birds, however, shows a definite eastward dispersal (Reinert 1976; N. O. Preuss, personal communication). There have been 23 recoveries from western Norway, mainly between ca. 62°N and 70°N and from September to January, although there have been a few recoveries from later in the winter. This wintering area is similar to that of birds from colonies in southern Norway, but is a little farther north from where most north British birds have been recovered (see below). Three birds have also been recovered from northern Britain at this season. There is some evidence that Faeroese birds undertake a southerly or westerly movement from February onwards, indicated by 10 recoveries from the western North Sea and one from the western English Channel in March through June; many north British Common Murres also move westward at this season (see below). On the other hand, other Faeroese birds migrate west to Iceland in winter; an adult bird has been recovered in December from northeast Iceland, and there have been four recoveries of adults in April, from the northwest, northeast, southwest and southeast coasts (A. Petersen, personal communication). Most Faeroese murres are banded as non-pulli (N. O. Preuss, personal communication), so it is not possible to analyse the movements of birds of different ages along the lines of Mead (1974; see below).

3. BRITISH ISLES

Common Murres breeding in the British Isles show two sharply contrasting patterns of movement. Birds from colonies in Scotland and northeast England (for simplicity, 'north British' birds) behave like Faeroese murres, and disperse east to southwest Norway and the Skagerrak in August through November (Mead 1974; see also Fig. 9.1). Many remain there until March but others, mainly adults, return to the northeast coast of Britain in December through March. At the same time many first-winter and subadult birds spread up the coast of Norway to ca. 68°N, while others move southwest into the English Channel. As in the Faeroes, some north British birds go northwest instead; a first-winter and a subadult bird have been recovered in December through March, and two adults in April through July, from the Faeroes (Mead 1974), and a first-winter bird reached northeast Iceland in January (A. Petersen, personal communication).

By contrast, first-winter birds from colonies in the Irish Sea move to southwest England, Brittany and the Bay of Biscay in August to November, although others remain in the Irish Sea (Mead 1974). Their distribu-

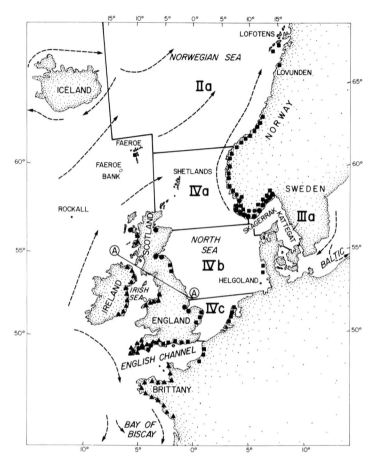

Fig. 9.1. The dispersal of first-winter Common Murres (*Uria aalge*) from British colonies at the end of the breeding season (adapted from Mead 1974, Figs. 18, 21). The symbols indicate where and when banded birds have been recovered but do not mark every recovery: North Britain (● August–November; ■ December–March); Irish Sea (▲ August–November). Ⓐ—Ⓐ marks the boundary between 'North British' and 'Irish Sea' colonies (see the text). Arrows indicate the principal currents (after Anonymous 1967). Roman numerals indicate ICES sub-areas (see Table 9.3).

tion later in the winter, in December through March, is the same with the addition of an eastward movement up the English Channel towards the southern North Sea. Subadult birds show the same patterns, although few get as far as the Bay of Biscay, and then not until December to March. Adults do not move as far as subadults. However, there is a great deal of inter-colony variability within this general pattern. In the Irish Sea the colonies on the Isle of Man and Puffin Island, Wales, are less than 100 km apart, yet the Isle of Man birds spend December–March along the north side of the English Channel while most Puffin Island birds remain in the northeast Irish Sea. To add to the complexity, murres from Great Saltee Island, at the southeast corner of Ireland and only 100 km from Puffin Island, mainly winter on the *south* side of the English Channel.

4. HELGOLAND

There is an isolated Common Murre colony on Helgoland in the southeastern North Sea. The birds are of the same subspecies (*U. a. albionis*) as those in the Irish Sea but their migration patterns are different. First-winter birds spend December–March in the North Sea, going as far north as southwest Norway, and down the English Channel as far west as Brittany, but they do not reach the Bay of Biscay (Stechow 1938; Schloss 1969; Mead 1974). Adults also disperse in these directions, but they never move more than ca. 200 km from Helgoland. They remain within the limits of the Eastern North Sea zooplankton community (Fraser 1965).

5. NORWAY AND BARENTS SEA

Common Murres from colonies in the Barents Sea apparently winter in that region (Holgersen 1961; Norderhaug *et al.* 1977). Birds from colonies along the Murmansk Coast disperse westward to northern Norway in the course of the winter and a few have been recovered as far south as the Skagerrak. Both first-winter and older birds from colonies in northern Norway move away from the exposed outer coast and into the fjords at the end of the breeding season; they tend to move north and east and to winter in northern Norway. First-winter birds from the small population breeding in southwest Norway mainly disperse northwards, and birds have been recovered in winter from as far away as the Murmansk Coast. By contrast, some first-winter and all adult birds move south, and winter in the Skagerrak area. As in Britain and Helgoland, the adult birds do not move as far away from their colonies as do the younger birds.

6. BALTIC SEA

Common Murres from the colonies off the south coast of Sweden disperse westwards to the coasts of northeast Germany and southeast Denmark (Mathiassen 1962; Preuss 1981). The first-winter birds travel further than the older ones. As a rule Baltic birds do not reach the Kattegat and Skagerrak, although there have been a few recoveries from there. There have also been three recoveries from the North Sea, beyond: two from the west coast of Denmark and one from southeast Scotland.

7. SUMMARY

There are seven trends in the dispersal of Common Murres after the end of the breeding season:

1. Newfoundland birds are resident, or move a little way south.
2. Birds from north British and Faeroese colonies, and possibly also Iceland, move east to western Norway and the North Sea. Young birds from Britain and southern Norway tend to move up the Norwegian coast in the course of the winter, while adults tend to move southwest into the western North Sea.
3. Some north British and Faeroese birds move westward instead, towards Iceland, and it is possible though not proven that some Icelandic birds move west to Greenland.
4. Birds from Irish Sea colonies either remain there or move south into the English Channel. First-winter birds tend to move on to the Bay of Biscay, occasionally farther south, and towards the southern North Sea.
5. Helgoland birds mostly stay in the southern and central North Sea.
6. Birds from the south-central Baltic move to the southwest Baltic and the Kattegat.
7. Barents Sea and northern Norwegian birds probably remain in the Barents Sea, although there is some tendency for them to spread southwest down the Norwegian coast.

Unlike Dovekies, Thick-billed Murres and Atlantic Puffins (q.v.), there is no evidence that Common Murres undertake transatlantic migrations. So many birds have been banded in Europe by now that one would expect some to have been shot in Newfoundland or Greenland if such migrations were at all regular (Tuck 1971; Salomonsen 1971b). It is just possible, however, that European birds, from Iceland perhaps, might reach Flemish Cap or the extreme eastern edge of the Grand Banks, so far offshore that the chances of band recovery are negligible.

These migration patterns partly reflect subspecific differences. The first three concern the subspecies *U. a. aalge* (Newfoundland, north Britain, Iceland) and *spiloptera* (Faeroes), the next two *albionis* (Irish and North Seas), the sixth *intermedia* (Baltic) and the last *hyperboreus* (Barents Sea) (Salomonsen 1944). Nothing is known of the movements of *ibericus,* the subspecies found in Portugal and northwest Spain. The possible origins of the patterns will be dealt with in the discussion (Section IX,A).

B. Pelagic Ecology

Sandlance and small clupeid fish are the principal foods of the Common Murres which breed in the British Isles (see Chapter 6, this volume), and

TABLE 9.3

Landings of Sprat (*Sprattus sprattus:* tonnes, wet wt., × 10³) in 1976 in Norwegian and North Seas and the Skagerrak, Divided by Season and ICES Sub-areas[a,b]

ICES sub-area		Landings	Percentage of total landings		
			Aug.–Nov.	Dec.–March	April–July
IIa[c]	Norwegian Sea	4.3	56.9	0.5	42.6
IIIa	Skagerrak	44.2	51.6	20.1	19.9
IVa	N. North Sea				
	Norway	28.7	99.4	0	0.C
	Scotland	12.6	11.6	88.4	0
IVb	Central North Sea	519.4	41.8	48.2	10.0
IVc	S. North Sea	1.2	1.8	77.1	21.0

[a] From Nikolaev (1979); see also Fig. 9.1.
[b] ICES, International Commission for the Exploration of the Sea.
[c] Almost all landed in the part of the sub-area immediately adjacent to IVa (Anonymous 1979).

the movements of the birds from north British colonies coincide quite closely with the movements of suitable prey in that area. Table 9.3 (based on Nikolaev 1979; see also Lee and Ramster 1981) shows that the fishery for sprat off southwest Norway takes place mainly during August through November, the season in which Common Murres from north British colonies move to that coast (Fig. 9.1). There is also a sprat fishery in the Skagerrak and Kattegat at this time of year, but which extends into the spring as well. By contrast the sprat fishery off the east coast of Scotland is mainly in December through March. The movements of the birds can therefore be seen as journeys to food resources. Southwest Norway and the Skagerrak provide abundant food for the young birds, still growing to adult size, and for adults in moult (which occurs mainly from August to October; Birkhead and Taylor 1977). The adults can then move back to Scotland in December through March to be ready to return to their colonies, and at the same time take advantage of the abundance of sprat in the western North Sea in spring. Young birds may also move back there, or they may move into the southern North Sea where there is also a sprat fishery in the spring. The very large sprat fishery in the central North Sea is spread evenly throughout the winter. The Common Murre colony on Helgoland is in the middle of this area, and it is not surprising that the young birds have no need to travel far from there in winter, and that the adults are virtually resident.

The northward movement of north British, Faeroese and southern Norwegian birds up the Norwegian coast would, by contrast, take them away from the area where sprat are abundant. It would, however, take them into an area where there is a fishery for sardine-sized young herring and, farther north, for capelin (Jangaard 1974; Dragesund et al. 1980).

The sprat scenario fits less well for the birds from the colonies in the Irish Sea. Sprat occur in the western English Channel and the Bay of Biscay, where the birds go at the end of the breeding season, but they are not fished commercially there so it is difficult to make any correlations between the distributions of fish and murres (Wheeler 1969; Nikolaev 1979). The main clupeid fishery there is for adult pilchards and these, ca. 15 cm in length, are appreciably larger than the size of fish preferred by these birds (Swennen and Duiven 1977; see also Chapter 6, this volume). Nevertheless, suitable prey exists in the area in the form of sprat (Mead 1981) and immature pilchards. Lockley (1953b) suggests that the Manx Shearwaters which breed in the Irish Sea feed at a 'nursery' for young pilchards in the southeast corner of the Bay of Biscay, and that they follow the fish as these migrate north along the coasts of Gascony and Brittany in the spring. The Common Murres from Irish Sea colonies may do the same, after the end of the breeding season. Similarly, the northeast Irish Sea is a 'nursery' for young herring in December through March (Bowers 1980), and this may explain why murres from the colony on Puffin Island nearby spend the winter in that area.

V. RAZORBILL, *Alca torda*

A. Pelagic Distribution and Movements

The Razorbill is exclusively an Atlantic species, with no counterpart in the North Pacific. It breeds in Atlantic Canada from the Bay of Fundy to Hudson Strait, in west Greenland north to ca. 75°N, in Iceland, the Faeroes, the British Isles, Brittany, Helgoland, the Baltic, Bjørnøya, and along the coast from southwestern Norway to the White Sea (Lloyd 1976b; Petersen 1982; see also Chapter 2, this volume). The bulk of the population is in the eastern Atlantic, in British and Icelandic waters.

In the western Atlantic Razorbills are most commonly seen in summer off Labrador, the centre of the species' range in North America. In January through March they occur off southern Nova Scotia and farther south. They are the only large auks regularly seen on Georges Bank, off the New England coast (K. D. Powers and R. G. B. Brown in preparation), and they have been recorded fairly regularly as far south as North Carolina (Lee and Booth 1980). Razorbills, along with Common Murres, were severely affected by a winter oil spill off Cape Cod, but were virtually absent from the tallies of alcids killed by winter spills farther north (Table 9.1). In addition, there is a report that the bird is common in February on the Flemish Cap (ca. 47°N 45°W), ca. 700 km east of the Newfoundland coast (Bourne and Dixon 1975).

There is little information about the Razorbill's pelagic distribution in the eastern Atlantic, and this must be inferred from the banding data, below. The winter oil kill statistics (Table 9.2) show that, as in the west, it has a southerly distribution. In January through March Joiris (1983) saw Razorbills in the North Sea only south of ca. 54°N in water cooler and less saline than that farther north and west. These are the areas occupied by the Channel Water and English Coastal Water zooplankton communities (Fraser 1965). In the western Mediterranean, near the southern limit of the species' wintering range, Razorbills appear to be fairly common in December to January off the west coast of Corsica (Marzocchi 1982).

The movements of Razorbills outside the breeding season are broadly similar to those of Common Murres, although they tend to go farther south. The migrations of the various populations may be summarised as follows.

1. WESTERN ATLANTIC

There have been few recoveries of Razorbills in the western Atlantic, partly because few have been banded, and partly because the species winters south of Newfoundland and Greenland, where alcids are regularly hunted. A first-winter bird banded in Labrador was recovered in the Strait of Belle Isle in October, another off eastern Newfoundland in November, and a third in the southeastern Gulf of St. Lawrence in August (unpublished CWS files). This suggests that Labrador birds disperse southwards down both coasts of Newfoundland at the end of the breeding season. There are only six winter recoveries, December–March, from farther south: one each from eastern Newfoundland and eastern and southern Nova Scotia, and three off Cape Cod.

Salomonsen (1967) believes that all or most of the Greenland Razorbill population winters off Atlantic Canada or farther south. The only recovery was of a subadult in April from the Strait of Belle Isle.

2. BARENTS SEA, WHITE SEA AND WESTERN NORWAY

Birds from the colonies along this coast winter off southwest Norway and in the Skagerrak and Kattegat, although there are stragglers farther north along the Norwegian coast (Bianki 1967; Norderhaug et al. 1977). Some of these birds reach eastern and southwestern Britain in March

(Mead 1974). Stray birds may also move west; a White Sea Razorbill was recovered in southwest Greenland in January 1961 [Bianki (1967, p. 217); not listed in Salomonsen's (1971b) review]. Bianki suggests that this bird was carried westward among flocks of migrating Thick-billed Murres (see above). The same may be true of a bird collected on Jan Mayen in February (Bird and Bird 1935).

3. ICELAND AND FAEROE ISLANDS

Three Razorbills from Grímsey, northeast Iceland, have been recovered in their first winter from the Faeroes (A. Petersen, personal communication). Two Icelandic birds were recovered in northeast Britain in February (Mead and Cawthorne 1983). There is no information about the movements of Faeroese birds.

4. BRITISH ISLES

The movements of British and Irish Razorbills, like those of Common Murres and Atlantic Puffins (q.v.), are complex. Birds of all ages from north British colonies cross to southwest Norway and the Skagerrak in August through November (Lloyd 1974; Mead 1974). The adults and subadults then tend to move down to the southern North Sea in December through March, while first-winter birds virtually abandon the North Sea altogether and migrate south, apparently through the English Channel, to the Bay of Biscay, Portugal, western Morocco (ca. 30°30'N) and the western Mediterranean. However, two adults and three subadults banded in north British colonies have been recovered in the Faeroes in April to July.

By contrast, first-winter birds from the colonies in the Irish Sea move directly south and reach the Bay of Biscay and Portugal by November (Lloyd 1974; Mead 1974). Many move farther south in December through March, reaching western Morocco (ca. 33°N) and the western Mediterranean east to ca. 10°E. Most subadult birds follow the same pattern although a few, like those from the north British colonies, go to southwest Norway instead, and on later to the southern North Sea. Most adults winter in the Irish Sea and the English Channel, although a few move down to the Bay of Biscay and beyond.

5. BRITTANY AND CHANNEL ISLANDS

Two first-winter birds were recovered in August through November on the north side of the English Channel near the Isle of Wight (Mead 1974).

This suggests that birds from the western channel initially disperse to the northeast.

6. BALTIC SEA

Finnish Razorbills winter in the ice-free parts of the Baltic south of ca. 60°N, along the Swedish, Polish and German coasts, and some birds reach the Kattegat and Skagerrak (Nordström 1963; Bianki 1967; Pfister 1980, Fig. 23). Two birds have been recovered from the North Sea. Birds from southeast Sweden mainly winter along the Swedish coast from ca. 55°N to 60°N, although a few reach southeast Denmark (Mathiassen 1962). Birds from the Bornholm area, south of Sweden, winter in the southwest Baltic (Salomonsen 1972b).

7. SUMMARY

Northern Razorbills, on both sides of the Atlantic, move south or southwest; Labrador and Greenland birds go to Newfoundland and farther south, and those from the Barents and White Seas to the Skagerrak. Baltic birds also move southwest. Irish Sea birds move south to Biscay and the western Mediterranean. Birds from north British colonies initially move to southwest Norway and the North Sea, but the younger birds later move down to Biscay. There is a rough division here along subspecific lines: the northern birds, on both sides of the Atlantic are of the form *A. t. pica,* Baltic birds are *A. t. torda* and British birds are *A. t. islandica* (Salomonsen 1944). Note that elements of all three subspecies meet in winter in the region of the Skagerrak.

B. Pelagic Ecology

The scenarios suggested as interpretations of the movements of Common Murres in the eastern Atlantic (see above and Fig. 9.1) can be applied to Razorbills too. Where the Razorbills differ is in the young birds' tendency to go farther south late in the winter. The fact that Irish Sea birds penetrate deeper into the Mediterranean than do those from north Britain presumably comes about because their initial dispersal is southwards, not east towards Norway. This allows them to travel farther before the end of the winter. There are insufficient data either on the comparative diets of Razorbills and Common Murres or on the distributions and movements of potential prey species in the southern parts of their winter ranges for it to be worth interpreting this southern movement in any detail.

VI. GREAT AUK, *Pinguinus impennis*

The last Great Auks were killed on Eldey off southwest Iceland in 1844 (Newton 1861; Steenstrup 1868; Grieve 1885) and it is not now possible to determine how this unique flightless alcid fitted in to the marine environment of the North Atlantic. Nonetheless, there remain a few tantalising clues about its distribution and movements at sea, and this chapter would be incomplete without an attempt to summarise what little information we possess.

A. Pelagic Distribution and Movements

The breeding distribution of the Great Auk is reviewed in Chapter 2 of this volume. During the last century before its extinction it bred in Newfoundland, Iceland, Scotland and, probably, the Faeroes (Grieve 1885)—a range very similar to that of the Razorbill today, although the Great Auk did not go quite so far north. Archaeological data and casual contemporary observations suggest that it occurred at sea along the North American seaboard from eastern Florida to Saglek Bay, Labrador (ca. 58°30′N), as far north as Disko Bay (ca. 69°N) in west Greenland and up to Angmagssalik (ca. 65°N) on the east coast, opposite its last surviving colonies in southern Iceland (Bent 1919; Salomonsen 1950; Godfrey 1966; Lysaght 1971; Tuck 1975, 1976). In Europe, Great Auk remains have been found in post-glacial sites in southwest and west-central Norway, the Kattegat area, northeast England, both coasts of Scotland, northern and southern Ireland and Brittany, and from earlier sites in Gibraltar and southern Italy (Clark 1948). Løvenskiold (1964) adds a record from the extreme north of Norway, but rejects an erroneous record from Spitsbergen. [Given the bird's occurrence in the tongue of warm water which extends up the west Greenland coast (Salomonsen 1950), there is however no *a priori* reason why it should not also have occurred in the similar tongue which reaches Spitsbergen (Norderhaug *et al.* 1977).]

Martin (1698) visited St. Kilda, northwest Scotland, in 1697. Great Auks probably no longer bred there but the islanders told him that the birds used to return to the colony in mid-May and leave at the end of June, by the modern calendar. Other dates cited by Grieve (1885; see also below, and Fisher and Lockley 1954) for the capture of birds at other colonies confirm this general breeding season for both sides of the Atlantic. But where did they go after that? Casual sightings and archaeological finds can tell us only where the birds were, but very little about the direction of their migration and nothing at all about its timing. Fortunately, the fairly detailed observations which Otho Fabricius made in west Greenland and George Cartwright in southeast Labrador in the late eighteenth century give us some clues about the birds' movements in the western Atlantic.

O. Fabricius (cited in Salomonsen 1950) lived in Frederikshåb, southwest Greenland (ca. 62°N) from 1768 to 1774. Among much else, he noted that Great Auks occurred there fairly regularly, some distance offshore, from September through January. Skeletal material from archaeological sites in Greenland suggests that these birds were immature (Salomonsen 1950). They may, of course, have been subadult birds spending their whole summer at sea; if so, one would expect Fabricius to have seen them earlier in the summer—say, May–June when capelin (a prey of Great Auks: Olson *et al.* 1979; see also Chapter 6, this volume) spawn off southwest Greenland (Jangaard 1974). But their arrival in September suggests instead that this was a post-breeding dispersal from a colony, perhaps of young of the year. The nearest surviving colonies at that late date were in southwest Iceland (Chapter 2, this volume). If these birds, like those on St. Kilda (see above), went to sea at the beginning of July, they could easily have reached southwest Greenland by September, covering the distance of ca. 1400 km at ca. 22 km/day, and assisted by the East Greenland Current which flows in the same direction at ca. 18 km/day (Anonymous 1958). Other alcids breeding in Iceland or farther northeast—Dovekies, Thick-billed Murres, Black Guillemots and Atlantic Puffins (q.v.)—also disperse southwestwards in the western Atlantic at the end of the breeding season.

The alternative, as Salomonsen (1950) points out, is that Great Auks migrated northwards to Frederikshåb from Funk Island, Newfoundland, their last surviving colony in the western Atlantic. There were still enough birds left on Funk for a boatload to have been collected from there at the beginning of July 1785 (Cartwright 1792). Cartwright lived on the Labrador coast north of Funk at ca. 54°N from 1770 to 1786. The traditional season for the fishery and for boat travel off Labrador was from June to November (Smith 1938), and so if there was a regular northward movement of Great Auks to Greenland at the end of the breeding season, Cartwright could not have failed to see or hear about it. As it is he only recorded Great Auks three times in his 16-year stay on that coast: the boatload described above, and single birds off northeast Newfoundland on 4 August 1771 and 10 June 1774. The inference is that Newfoundland Great Auks did *not* disperse northwards, and that the birds which Fabricius saw in the fall off Frederikshåb came from the eastern Atlantic, almost certainly from Iceland.

It is a further inference that the Funk Island birds either stayed on the Newfoundland Banks or dispersed southwards, much as Newfoundland

Razorbills and Common Murres do today (q.v.). Certainly, the evidence from the archaeological sites (see above) indicates that Great Auks from *somewhere* used to travel as far south as Florida, and Newfoundland seems a likely point of origin for these birds. Moreover, an old hunter told J. J. Audubon (cited in Steenstrup 1868) that Great Auks used to be common in winter in Massachusetts Bay in the late 1700s. This too suggests a southward dispersal along the east coast of North America after the end of the breeding season (see also Bent 1919).

It must be noted, however, that Great Auks undoubtedly also migrated southeast from Iceland. The birds collected in southeast Ireland in 1834 and St. Kilda in 1840 (Greive 1885) must have come from Eldey, the last surviving Great Auk colony.

The archaeological evidence summarised by Clark (1948; see also above) suggests that European Great Auks dispersed southwards towards Biscay and farther south, much as Razorbills, Atlantic Puffins and Common Murres from Irish Sea colonies do today (q.v.). Scottish birds might have moved east to the Norwegian coast, again like the small flying alcids, although the remains found there might equally have been of local breeding birds. Unlike the western Atlantic, however, there are no direct observations from which the timing and route of the migration may be inferred.

In summary, then, Great Auks from Newfoundland probably migrated south, as far as Florida, after the breeding season; young birds from Iceland probably initially moved to west Greenland; but Icelandic birds also migrated southeast to the British Isles. Movements in the eastern Atlantic are obscure, but dispersal of British birds towards Norway and to Biscay and farther south are both possible.

B. Pelagic Ecology

The little which can be inferred about the pelagic ecology of the Great Auk has been set out in Chapter 6 of this volume, and need not be repeated here. In summary, observations made in the late eighteenth century in Greenland and Newfoundland (Salomonsen 1950; Lysaght 1971) suggest that when it was at sea the Great Auk was a bird of the shallow offshore fishing banks, absent from the deeper waters offshore and seldom seen close to land. It may at times have fed on benthic fish, at depths perhaps as great as 75 m. More generally, the broad coincidence between the breeding and pelagic ranges of the Great Auk and its closest surviving relative, the Razorbill (q.v.), suggests that the two species may have been influenced by the same set of physical and biological oceanographic factors, partitioning the resource so that one took large and the other small prey. But since we know very little more about the pelagic ecology of the Razorbill than we do of the Great Auk, such speculation is not very informative.

VII. BLACK GUILLEMOT, *Cepphus grylle*

A. Pelagic Distribution and Movements

The Black Guillemot is the most coastal of the Atlantic alcids, seldom seen far from shore, and so its pelagic distribution is essentially the same as its breeding distribution. In the North Atlantic this extends from Maine to Labrador, Hudson Strait and Hudson Bay, Lancaster and Jones Sounds, both sides of Baffin Bay, east, northeast and northwest Greenland, Iceland, the Faeroes, Ireland, Scotland, Scandinavia from the Kattegat to the White Sea, the Baltic, Jan Mayen, Bjørnøya, Spitsbergen, Franz Josef Land, Novaya Zemlya and Severnaya Zemlya (see Chapter 2, this volume). It also breeds all around the Arctic Ocean and it, or closely related forms, occur in the North Pacific.

The Black Guillemot is also the most sedentary of the Atlantic alcids. Nonetheless, banding has shown that there is a tendency to move away from the nesting area at the end of the breeding season, and that this is especially marked in newly fledged young birds. The movements of the various populations may be summed up as follows.

1. WEST GREENLAND AND EASTERN CANADIAN ARCTIC

The west Greenland population of Black Guillemots has been extensively banded (Salomonsen 1967). There have been two foreign recoveries of birds from northwest Greenland, both subadults recovered in spring from western Hudson Strait. Salomonsen suggests that birds from this region remain at the ice-edge all winter and gradually work their way southwards along it towards Hudson Strait. A few birds over-winter in the North Water polynya at the head of Baffin Bay and in smaller ice-free areas in that region, and the birds are common in spring at the ice-edge in Lancaster Sound (Salomonsen 1967; Bradstreet 1980; Renaud and Bradstreet 1980; Brown and Nettleship 1981; McLaren 1982). However, Black Guillemots are much commoner in winter in the open-water areas in Hudson Strait and Hudson Bay (Brown and Nettleship 1981; A. J. Gaston, personal communication). Presumably these are a mixture of local birds and immigrants from farther north. These birds are assigned to the subspecies *C. g. ultimus* (Salomonsen 1944).

On the other hand, the Black Guillemots which breed in west Greenland south of ca. 72°N belong to a separate subspecies, *C. g. arcticus,* and this population seems to be more sedentary. The coasts of the northern part of its range, from Umanak District to Disko Bay (ca. 71°N–69°N) become icebound in winter and the adult birds then move a little way south into ice-free areas. Salomonsen (1967) describes a serial southward shifting of populations, with Umanak birds moving down to Disko Bay and farther south to Egedesminde District, Disko birds to Egedesminde and farther south still, and so on. Birds from these northern populations begin to move back as early as March. By contrast, young birds from west Greenland leave the breeding area as soon as they fledge. Their initial dispersal, in September and October, is northwards, and they show in reverse the same serial displacements that the adults make later in the winter. They move south again later. Their initial dispersal follows the north-flowing West Greenland Current, although Salomonsen shows that at least part of their migration must be by flying, as opposed to passive drifting.

2. ATLANTIC CANADA

Most of the recoveries of Black Guillemots in Atlantic Canada, of the subspecies *C. g. atlantis,* come from birds banded at Cape Whittle in the northeast Gulf of St. Lawrence (Fig. 9.2). The initial dispersal of the young birds is westward although, as in west Greenland, they are also going with the prevailing current. Young Black Guillemots are prized by hunters in Newfoundland, so the absence of recoveries from northeast of Cape Whittle, despite the recovery there of banded alcids of other species, confirms this westward trend. The birds apparently reach the lower St. Lawrence Estuary in October and November. Some birds probably winter there, in leads in the ice. However, others either move on from the estuary, or never go there at all, and winter along the Atlantic coast of Nova Scotia and as far south as Cape Cod. Recoveries of birds banded in Labrador (probably of the subspecies *arcticus:* Fig. 9.2) suggest that part of this population also enters the Gulf of St. Lawrence, while the rest moves down the east coast of Newfoundland.

3. EAST GREENLAND, BARENTS SEA AND WHITE SEA

Black Guillemots occur in winter in leads in the ice off Spitsbergen, and this suggests that many birds remain up there all winter at the edge of the pack-ice. However, there were a few birds, also at the ice-edge, in the northwest Greenland Sea (ca. 75°N 0°W–10°W) in March (Brown 1984). This suggests a southerly movement along the edge of the pack-ice, similar to that in northern Baffin Bay. A first-winter bird of the subspecies *C.*

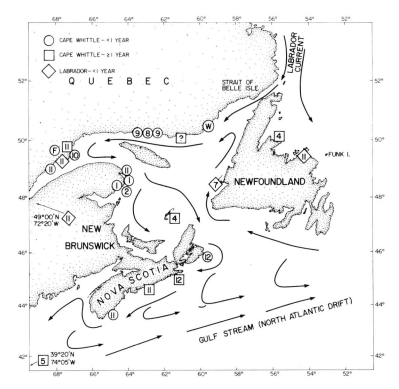

Fig. 9.2. Recoveries away from the colony of Black Guillemots (*Cepphus grylle*) banded near Cape Whittle, Québec (W), and in Labrador between ca. 53°N and 56°N. Symbols: Cape Whittle (○ <1 year; □ ≥1 year); Labrador (◇ <1 year). Numbers within the symbols indicate months of recovery (F, October–December; ?, month unknown; note that the July recovery occurred ca. 11 months after banding). Data from unpublished CWS files. Arrows indicate the principal surface currents (after Anonymous 1967).

g. mandti, the form found in northeast Greenland and farther east (Salomonsen 1944), was collected off eastern Iceland as early as October (Petersen 1977), and this suggests a fairly rapid southerly or southwesterly movement of newly fledged birds, in the direction of the East Greenland Current.

White Sea birds also belong to the subspecies *mandti,* but they are resident and winter in the polynya in Kandalakshskaya Guba (Bianki 1967).

4. ICELAND AND FAEROE ISLANDS

The Icelandic and Faeroese populations belong, respectively, to the endemic subspecies *C. g. islandicus* and *faeroensis,* and one would suppose from this that both populations are sedentary. However a first- and a second-winter bird from northwest Iceland have been recovered in winter off southwest Greenland, and Petersen (1977) believes that a significant fraction of the Icelandic Black Guillemot population may undertake this migration.

Black Guillemots occur all year in the Faeroes (Joensen 1966).

5. BALTIC SEA

Baltic Black Guillemots belong to the endemic subspecies *C. g. grylle* and are apparently almost completely isolated from other populations. They winter for the most part along the east coast of Sweden, south of ca. 60°N, which is largely ice-free in winter (Nordström 1963; Myrberget 1973a; Bianki 1967; Pfister 1980, Fig. 22; see also Anonymous 1968). There have been a very few recoveries from eastern Denmark and the southwest Baltic.

6. NORTHEAST ATLANTIC

Black Guillemots in the northeast Atlantic, of the subspecies *atlantis,* resemble *arcticus* in west Greenland in that the more northerly populations tend to move farther than do those farther south. First-winter birds also tend to move farther than older ones. Again as in Greenland, newly fledged birds from northern Norway tend to move northwards at first, in the direction of the North Atlantic Drift, and return south later in the year (Myrberget 1973a). This movement can be very rapid; Myrberget cites a banded bird which travelled 210 km north-northeast in only 8 days. Adult movements are usually shorter, although some birds have been recovered as far south as Denmark, 700 km from the point of banding. Southern Norwegian birds and those from northern Scotland move very little (Myrberget 1973a; Mead 1974) although there are some exceptions: a first-winter bird from southern Norway has been recovered in Brittany, and one from Scotland in southeast England.

Birds from the Kattegat and Skagerrak region are also more or less sedentary, although a chick from the Kattegat was recovered 850 km away, on the east coast of England, only 18 days later (Andersen-Harild 1969; Myrberget 1973a).

7. SUMMARY

In general, young Black Guillemots move away from their breeding site as soon as they are fledged, and in the direction of the prevailing current:

northwards up the west coasts of Greenland and Norway, west or south-west from Cape Whittle into the Gulf of St. Lawrence, and from Iceland to Greenland and in the Baltic. The recovery of a Labrador bird off eastern Newfoundland, of birds from northwest Greenland in Hudson Strait, and the *mandti* specimen from eastern Iceland are also consistent with a 'downstream' dispersal. On the other hand, the currents in the North Sea are variable and tidally dominated (Anonymous 1967), and there is no obvious 'downstream' pattern to the movements of birds from Scotland and the Kattegat to eastern England. Where dispersal is 'downstream', it is clear that the birds' movement is at least partly by flight and not just by passive drifting. However, the possible functions and origins of 'downstream' dispersal, in the Black Guillemot and in the other alcids, will be dealt with more fully in the discussion, Section IX.

B. Pelagic Ecology

Since the Black Guillemot is a coastal species and, as an adult, largely sedentary, the pelagic ecology of the species has already been covered in the discussions in this volume of the ecological aspects of its breeding distribution (Chapter 2), and of its feeding ecology (Chapter 6). If the movements of the various populations have any common factor, it appears to be in response to the formation of sea-ice in winter. However, the movements of the young birds begin long before the sea freezes—and, in such regions as the Norwegian coast, where it does not freeze at all. Why these movements should take place, and why they are more extensive than those of the adults, are questions whose answers remain obscure.

VIII. ATLANTIC PUFFIN, *Fratercula arctica*

A. Pelagic Distribution and Movements

The Atlantic Puffin is endemic to the Atlantic. It breeds from Labrador to the Gulf of Maine, in west, northwest and northeast Greenland, Jan Mayen, Iceland, the Faeroes, the British Isles, Bjørnøya, Spitsbergen, Novaya Zemlya, the Murmansk Coast, and along the Atlantic coast of Scandinavia from the Kattegat northwards (see Chapter 2, this volume).

In the western Atlantic the puffin is widely distributed in summer over the continental shelf from eastern Newfoundland to southeast Labrador, although it is only abundant close to its colonies and very few birds are seen farther offshore (Brown *et al.* 1975; R. G. B. Brown, in preparation). It is likely that these offshore birds are non- or post-breeders, although foraging by active breeders has been reported as far as 50 km from the nearest colony (Joiris 1978). There are very few observations of birds after the end of the breeding season. There have been only a few sightings, mainly from south of Nova Scotia. Puffins are also virtually absent from the tallies of birds killed by winter oil spills off eastern North America (Table 9.1). Flocks of birds have, however, been reported in December through February from the deep waters east of the Newfoundland Banks at ca. 47°N 40°W (Bourne and Dixon 1973; see also Rankin and Duffey 1948).

Winter oil kills in the eastern Atlantic (Table 9.2) indicate that the puffin has a southerly distribution there in winter, although some birds winter as far north as ca. 70°N in northeastern Norway. The species was completely absent from the Greenland and northern Barents Seas, and from most of the Norwegian Sea, in March (Brown 1984); they were also scarce west of the Outer Hebrides (ca. 58°N) at this time. Joiris (1983) saw small numbers in the North Sea, mainly in the warm, saline Atlantic waters north of ca. 54°N. Like Dovekies, but unlike Razorbills (see above), this distribution coincides with those of the North Atlantic and northern North Sea zooplankton communities in the region (Fraser 1965). However, most of what is known about the pelagic distribution of puffins in the eastern Atlantic comes from the banding returns.

The movements of the various populations are perhaps more complex than those of any other Atlantic alcid, and they are not yet fully understood. They may be summarised as follows.

1. WESTERN ATLANTIC

Puffins winter off west Greenland as far north as ca. 66°N and, since no foreign-banded birds have been recovered from north of 60°40′N, it seems likely that these are from Greenland colonies (Salomonsen 1967, 1971b). However, Salomonsen (1967) suggests that most Greenland birds leave the country in winter. Single first-winter Greenland and Newfoundland birds have been recovered (December, January) off eastern Newfoundland, as have two adult Newfoundland birds in December and March (Salomonsen 1971a; D. N. Nettleship, personal communication; unpublished CWS files). Despite the absence of sight records, some puffins clearly do winter in that area.

2. ICELAND AND FAEROE ISLANDS

Large numbers of puffins have been banded in the Vestmannaeyjar in southwest Iceland (Petersen 1976b). There have been 33 foreign recoveries of first-winter birds: 30 from Newfoundland, 1 from Greenland, 1 from the Bay of Biscay and 1 from the Azores (Tuck 1971; A. Petersen, personal communication). The birds arrive off Newfoundland in October and remain until March. One of these birds was recovered at most 38 days after it was banded, and in that time it had travelled ca. 2000 km; this speed suggests a directed migration rather than a general, gradual dispersal from the Icelandic colonies.

Older birds from Vestmannaeyjar seem to move eastwards, by contrast; there have been 11 recoveries of birds 2 years old or more from the Faeroes (A. Petersen, personal communication). However, all these birds were recovered during the breeding season, so it is hard to say whether this is a true migration, a wandering of subadult birds, or the adoption of new colonies.

Puffins are scarce in the Faeroes in winter (Joensen 1966). However, there is no published account of the banding returns from this area, so nothing is known about where this population winters.

3. GREENLAND SEA AND BARENTS SEA

Puffins from the Murmansk Coast, on the south shore of the Barents Sea, have only twice been recovered in Norway, the most southerly of the two reaching ca. 64°N (Norderhaug et al. 1977). The absence of recoveries south of ca. 62°N, where many birds from north British colonies have been recovered (see below), suggests that this population disperses westwards into the Atlantic. On the other hand, the absence of recoveries of Murmansk Coast birds from Newfoundland and Greenland (Salomonsen 1971b; Tuck 1971) suggests that the birds do not go all the way across. Puffins do winter in small numbers in northern Norway (Table 9.2), and Norderhaug et al. (1977) believe that these are a mixture of local and Murmansk Coast birds.

There are no recovery data for puffins from the European high Arctic. Birds breeding in Spitsbergen abandon the area from December to May, and presumably move out into the Barents Sea; a bird of the high-arctic subspecies, *F. a. naumanni*, has been collected in winter in northern Norway (Løvenskiold 1964; Norderhaug et al. 1977).

4. WESTERN NORWAY

There is a fairly sharp division between the wintering areas of the puffins which breed on the Lofoten Islands, ca. 68°N on the north-central coast of Norway, and those at Lovunden, ca. 150 km farther south (Myrberget 1973b). Lofoten birds apparently move west. Two first-winter birds and an adult have been recovered from the Faeroes, a first-winter and an adult from Iceland, and single first-winter birds from Newfoundland and Greenland. Only one bird has been recovered from southwest Norway. By contrast, 13 Lovunden birds have been recovered from southwest Norway, along with three from Britain and one from Germany. Over 6000 puffins have been banded in the Lofotens against only ca. 300 at Lovunden and so, as Myrberget (1973b) points out, the absence of recoveries of Lofoten birds from the well-populated coast of southwest Norway seems particularly significant in comparison.

5. BRITISH ISLES

The winter quarters of British puffins are also sharply divided, along rather similar lines to those of British Common Murres and Razorbills (see above). Mead (1974) shows that birds from the east coast, south of ca. 57°N, remain in the North Sea and, if they travel at all, go no farther than the coasts of southwest Norway, Denmark and the Netherlands. By contrast, birds from Irish Sea colonies disperse southwards after the end of the breeding season, reaching Brittany by November and the southeast corner of the Bay of Biscay by March; some go farther still and enter the Mediterranean. In neither population is there any clear evidence that the young birds travel farther than the adults.

On the other hand, the movements of north British puffins are intermediate between those from the North and Irish Seas and those from the Lofotens (Mead 1974). Some remain in the North Sea, while others go to southeast Biscay and the Mediterranean; both movements involve individuals of all ages. But some first-winter birds also cross the Atlantic; two were recovered in eastern Newfoundland in December and one in southwest Greenland in November. A puffin banded in Iceland has been recovered in northeast Britain in February (Mead and Cawthorne 1983).

6. SUMMARY

In general, then, Atlantic Puffins show four patterns of dispersal after the end of the breeding season:

1. Greenland and Newfoundland birds probably remain in the western Atlantic. The dearth of banding recoveries may mean that the birds are well offshore, but it probably also reflects the fact that not many puffins have been banded in the western Atlantic.
2. Irish Sea and some north British puffins move south to Biscay, and may reach the Mediterranean.
3. Birds from the east coast of Britain, southwest Norway, and some from north British colonies winter in the region of the North Sea.

4. Puffins from the Murmansk Coast, northern Norway, Iceland, possibly the European high Arctic, and some of those from north British colonies move west or southwest. The north British contingent appears to consist of first-winter birds and these, and the younger birds from other areas travel farthest, reaching Newfoundland and Greenland.

These patterns partly, but not wholly, reflect subspecific differences. Salomonsen (1944) recognizes *F. a. arctica* in eastern Canada, west Greenland, Iceland, Bjørnøya and along the Norwegian coast; *naumanni* in northwest Greenland, Spitsbergen and Novaya Zemlya, and *grabae* in the Faeroes, the Skagerrak and most of the British Isles. Birds from Orkney, Shetland and the extreme southwest of Norway are intermediate between *grabae* and *arctica,* and those in Jan Mayen and on the Murmansk Coast between *arctica* and *naumanni.* In the eastern Atlantic, then, *arctica* birds and those on the *arctica–grabae* and *arctica–naumanni* borderline, and possibly *naumanni* as well, tend to disperse westwards; *grabae* birds, along with other *arctica–grabae* intermediates, either stay in the North Sea or move south towards Biscay. However, there are no subspecific differences in the current taxonomy of the species between Lofoten and Lovunden puffins, nor between those in the North and Irish Seas, yet both pairs have sharply divergent dispersal patterns. A taxonomic appraisal of the various populations of the Atlantic Puffin is long overdue, and should include both the qualitative and quantitative comparisons used in classic taxonomic studies of birds, and the more modern biochemical techniques (see Chapter 1, this volume).

B. Pelagic Ecology

The principal foods of Atlantic Puffins from the more southerly populations are small pelagic fish such as capelin, sprat and sandlance (see Chapter 6, this volume). The scenarios put forward in previous sections in which the movements of Common Murres and Razorbills in the North Sea are associated with those of sprat, and of birds from the Irish Sea with those of young pilchards and, probably, sprat, may also apply to the puffins breeding in those regions. In fact all the colonies of *F. a. grabae* are in areas where sprat occur (Lee and Ramster 1981; see also Chapter 2, this volume). Most colonies of *arctica,* on the other hand, are in areas where there is a capelin fishery (Jangaard 1974), and the movements of the birds from these low-arctic colonies are at least to some extent associated with movements of capelin. For example, the capelin fishery off Iceland slackens off in October, just as that off northeast Newfoundland and Labrador is reaching its peak (Nikolaev 1979, 1980; Anonymous 1980b).

This seasonal and geographic shift in abundance might lie behind the movement of first-winter puffins from Iceland to Newfoundland, from October onwards (Tuck 1971).

Unfortunately, it is difficult to say very much about the pelagic ecology of puffins without knowing where most of them spend the winter. Puffins are very rarely seen at sea either by observers in transit (Wynne-Edwards 1935; Rankin and Duffey 1948; Brown et al. 1975; see also Fig. 9.3 below), or on weather ships (G. S. Tuck 1967, 1970; Agnew 1973, 1974, 1975, 1976, 1977, 1978, 1979, 1980). This might mean that the birds are scattered across much of the North Atlantic, in both cool and temperate waters, subsisting on small patches of plankton or on sporadic schools of the young of warm-water fish such as sauries (Leim and Scott 1966). This would make the puffin the Atlantic alcid adapted to exploit the more barren parts of the ocean in winter, in much the same role that Harcourt's Storm-petrel seems to play among hydrobatids in tropical seas (Brown 1979). The fact that an Icelandic puffin has been recovered in the Azores (see above) would support this suggestion.

Alternatively, puffins are concentrated in winter very locally at ice-edges or along oceanic 'fronts'. Gudmundsson (1953b) notes that puffins sometimes enter the fjords in northern Iceland when the pack-ice moves into the coast. This suggests that the birds might be feeding at the edge of the ice, although they certainly do not appear to do so farther north in the Greenland Sea (Brown 1984; see also above). Puffins are also known to feed at 'fronts' in the western English Channel (Pingree et al. 1974), in the Bay of Fundy (Brown 1980a, and unpublished observations), and at a Spitsbergen glacier face (Hartley and Fisher 1936). In this connection it is interesting that birds should have been reported in winter east of the Grand Banks at ca. 47°N 40°W (Bourne and Dixon 1973), because this is in the general area of the boundary between the warm North Atlantic Drift and the cooler waters to the north (Dietrich 1969). 'Fronts' undoubtedly occur in this boundary zone (see Brown 1980a, Fig. 5 for an example from a little farther north). If substantial numbers of puffins winter there the chances of locating them would be small, because there is almost no possibility of banding recoveries there and, since 'fronts' are very narrow, it would be easy for a shipboard observer to overlook them.

IX. DISCUSSION

A. Patterns of Movement

The descriptions of alcid movements have shown several patterns which are common to more than one species. These can be summarised as follows (numbers refer to Fig. 9.3):

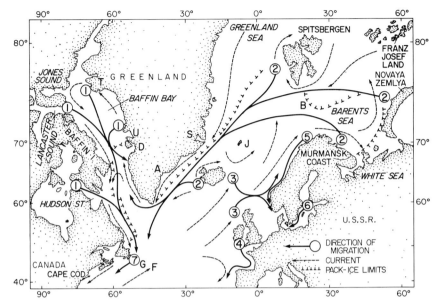

Fig. 9.3. The principal migrations of the North Atlantic Alcidae. The heavy arrows show the routes; the numbers refer to the list of routes in the discussion (Section IX). Light arrows show the principal sea surface currents in summer (after Anonymous 1967, 1968). February pack-ice limits are from Anonymous (1958, 1968). A, Angmagssalik; B, Bjørnøya; D, Disko Bay; F, Flemish Cap; G, Grand Banks; J, Jan Mayen; S, Scoresby Sound; T, Thule District; U, Umanak.

1. Baffin Bay, Hudson Strait and west Greenland to Newfoundland (Dovekie, Thick-billed Murre; probably Razorbill and Common Murre)
2. Spitsbergen, Novaya Zemlya, the Murmansk Coast, northern Norway and Iceland to the west and southwest, with many birds reaching Newfoundland or west Greenland (Dovekie, Thick-billed Murre, northern Norwegian Atlantic Puffins; and Icelandic Black Guillemots and possibly also Great Auks)
3. Iceland, Faeroe Islands, and north and east Britain towards western Norway and the North Sea (Common Murre, Razorbill, Great Auk, Atlantic Puffin)
4. Irish Sea to Bay of Biscay and the western Mediterranean (Common Murre, Razorbill, Atlantic Puffin; possibly Great Auk)
5. Northern Norway to southwest Norway and the Skagerrak and Kattegat (Razorbill, Atlantic Puffin and, to some extent, Common Murre)
6. Central and eastern Baltic to southwest Baltic (Common Murre, Razorbill, Black Guillemot)

7. Newfoundland and southern Labrador south and southwest towards Nova Scotia, New England and the Gulf of St. Lawrence (Common Murre, Razorbill, Black Guillemot, possibly Atlantic Puffin and Newfoundland Great Auks)

The directions of movement vary but the movements themselves have several features in common:

1. They tend to take birds to regions where food is abundant (Grand Banks of Newfoundland, North Sea, Bay of Biscay, ice-edges), or away from areas which are ice-covered in winter (Baffin Bay, Greenland and eastern Barents Seas, east and central Baltic).
2. The migrations of young birds, especially those in their first winter, are more extensive than those of adults.
3. The initial direction of dispersal after the end of the breeding season is 'downstream', following the prevailing currents. This applies both to the species whose young are unable to fly when they leave the breeding site (Thick-billed and Common Murres, Razorbill and Great Auk), and to those which can (Dovekie, Black Guillemot, Atlantic Puffin). The main exceptions are the southerly dispersal of Thick-billed Murres from northwest to southwest Greenland, and of Common Murres and Razorbills from northern Norway and the Murmansk Coast towards the Skagerrak, which run counter to the Norwegian and West Greenland Currents (Anonymous 1967).

The tendency for movements to be away from ice and towards known food supplies are self-evident and have been dealt with already in the various sections on pelagic ecology. There is no need to repeat this here.

In the second case, it is not difficult to see why adults should spend the winter closer to their colonies than should younger birds. Breeding birds must return to their colonies as early as possible in order to claim the best-quality breeding sites (Gaston and Nettleship 1981; see also Chapter 8 of this volume). If they winter any distance away they not only risk returning too late to take up a good territory, but must also expend energy reserves needed for the breeding season in the long flight back. Pre-breeding birds are not tied to their colony in this way. First-winter birds must learn to hunt efficiently (Birkhead 1976b) and their high mortality in their first year of life (e.g., Chapter 5, this volume), suggests that they face many hazards while they do so. In their case it may be an advantage to fly as far south as possible to winter in a mild climate (contrast, for example, the North Sea and the Mediterranean Sea; Lamb 1982).

The possible advantages of 'downstream' dispersal are less obvious. The distributions of many species of zooplankton and young fish are determined by the currents (Cushing 1975; Dooley and McKay 1979; Dragesund *et al.* 1980). By following the currents the dispersing alcids could maintain their position relative to a constant, drifting food supply. Dispersal by this means would also be energetically economical; the advantages to Great Auks of following the East and West Greenland Currents in moving from Iceland to west Greenland have already been outlined, and could also apply to other alcids. The adult birds would have the opportunity to rebuild their energy reserves as they moult after the breeding season (Birkhead and Taylor 1977), and the young birds could learn to forage efficiently, as they drifted along with their food supply.

But it is not immediately obvious how this tendency to disperse 'downstream', along with the often complex and interweaving routes of the various populations, could have evolved in the first place. The phenomenon is not confined to permanently or temporarily flightless species, as one would expect. In fact, the flightless species are physically capable of making headway 'upstream' against the current (Salomonsen 1979a, p. 186), while some of the very rapid transits of banded birds, quoted above, suggest that both 'flightless' and 'flying' alcids may disperse 'downstream' by flight. However, the 'downstream' tendency and the complicated migration routes make rather more sense if we think of the North Atlantic not as it is today, but as it was after the end of the last, Würm glaciation some 18,000 years ago.

The North Atlantic was rather different then. Ice sheets covered North America south to Cape Cod, Greenland, Iceland and the Faeroes, all land in Europe north of southern England and northern Denmark, and the Baltic and northwest Russia. Consolidated pack-ice extended north of an arc from Newfoundland through southern Greenland, Iceland, the Faeroes and northern Scotland, and drift ice occurred south to ca. 40°N. The sea level fell by ca. 120 m and this exposed ice-free land on the Grand, Georges, Rockall and Faeroe Banks and in Biscay, the English Channel and the southern North Sea. The boundary between arctic and temperate water, which lies between Iceland and Greenland today, extended then from Flemish Cap to northwest Scotland, and was sometimes much farther south. The general pattern of ocean circulation was similar, with cold water coming south off Labrador and the temperate North Atlantic Drift flowing east towards Europe, but the drift approached Europe at ca. 45°N instead of ca. 55°N and, although it split into a northern and southern branch there as it does today, the northern one curved back west towards Iceland instead of flowing up the Norwegian coast. [Summary based on Ruddiman (1977), Ruddiman and McIntyre (1977), Alvinerie *et al.* (1978), and Kellogg (1980); see also Salomonsen 1972a, Figs. 1 and 4.]

Salomonsen (1972a) suggested that the present-day migration routes of Dovekies and Thick-billed Murres—Greenland to Newfoundland, and northern Europe to Greenland—evolved as the ice retreated and these birds began to extend their ranges northwards from the refuges they had been occupying at the height of the glaciation. Birds breeding in whatever ice-free refuge that was open to them in the European Arctic went to feed at the edge of the pack-ice when the breeding season was over, and were drifted more or less passively south by the East Greenland Current. As the climate improved, the waters off southwest Greenland opened up and became their regular winter quarters, and they kept on returning there as the climate improved further and their breeding ranges expanded into what is now the high-arctic region. He further suggested that birds from the Old World colonised first west Greenland and then, as the retreat of the ice continued, Baffin Bay and Hudson Strait. Birds from these new colonies, in their turn, went to feed at the ice-edge at the end of the summer, were carried south by the Labrador Current and established a second wintering area off Newfoundland. Alternatively, birds could have spread northwards up the Labrador coast from a Newfoundland refuge as the ice retreated, formed colonies there, and returned 'downstream' to Newfoundland in winter. If this was so, however, the New World and Old World populations of Dovekies and Thick-billed Murres would have been isolated for some 85,000 years since the start of the last glaciation, and one would expect them to have developed some subspecific differentiation. As it is, the southerly movements of the present-day Newfoundland alcid populations suggest that they also originally dispersed south or southwest, with the Labrador Current and also along the ice-edge, towards the permanently ice-free zone south of Cape Cod, much as Salomonsen (1972a) has suggested for the high-arctic alcids.

The dichotomy of migration patterns showed by the Common Murres, Razorbills and Atlantic Puffins breeding in north Britain and the Irish Sea could have evolved in a similar way, although the likely refuges there— Rockall and Faeroe Banks and the Biscay–English Channel region—were probably too far south for the ice-edge to have been as important. The key factor here was perhaps the North Atlantic Drift, whose bifurcation would take Rockall–Faeroe Bank birds northeast, and Biscay–Channel birds south. As the ice sheets retreated and the sea level rose, Rockall– Faeroe Bank birds would have been able to expand eastwards into the North Sea and up the Norwegian coast, with the birds returning in winter from their new colonies to their old wintering area off southwest Norway, even though this was no longer 'downstream'. Similarly, birds from the Biscay–Channel region would have been able to expand eastwards into the newly flooded Irish and southern North Seas via the English Channel, while still returning to winter in Biscay.

However, this still leaves unexplained the movements of young north British Razorbills which apparently combine both patterns, moving first to southwest Norway and later, apparently via the English Channel, to Biscay (Mead 1974). This population has evidently developed a new migration route since the Channel was flooded and the northern North Sea became free of ice, and it could not have done so by migrating 'downstream' because the currents in the Channel and the North Sea are weak, variable, and tidally dominated (Anonymous 1967). So while alcid migration patterns are conservative on the whole, it would be a mistake to overestimate the degree of this conservatism. Two other alcid populations have certainly evolved new patterns since the end of the last glaciation. The Common Murres on Helgoland belong to the subspecies *albionis,* the form occurring in the Biscay–Channel refuge, and the colony was presumably repopulated from there, some 7000 years ago when that part of the North Sea was flooded by the rising sea level (Lamb 1982, Fig. 40). Yet the Helgoland birds no longer migrate down to Biscay, even as subadults. Again, the Common Murres, Razorbills and Black Guillemots which breed today in the Baltic are not relics from a refuge there but must have arrived after the Baltic ice sheet retreated (Løppenthin 1963b), perhaps from the north British populations which, in the case of the first two species, winter today in the Kattegat region. If so, the Baltic populations show no signs of these origins but have evolved a migratory pattern which effectively confines them to the Baltic.

The allohiemy of the various populations of Atlantic alcids—their tendency to winter in separate areas—would therefore appear to have arisen more or less passively, the birds' patterns of migration having been determined by such oceanographic accidents as the pattern of currents in the North Atlantic and by the position of its ice-edges.

B. Recommendations for Future Work

I have stressed information gaps all through this chapter and so it is useful to finish by summarising the most important of them, along with some suggestions for future research on the movements of the Atlantic alcids.

1. In certain strategic areas we need to band more birds, although we must be selective about this because banding alcids can be both expensive and dangerous. It is unlikely that banding more Thick-billed Murres in Scoresby Sound will yield many more recoveries if, as seems likely, they winter far out at sea and away from land. On the other hand, more banding in the Canadian Arctic would help to build up our understanding of the movements of the various alcid populations to the level it has reached in

Greenland. The problem of the migration routes of the Thick-billed Murres near Reid Bay is a case in point. We also need to know more about the movements of alcids from the mid-Atlantic colonies (Jan Mayen, Iceland, the Faeroes), from the eastern Eurasian high Arctic (Franz Josef Land, Severnaya Zemlya), and from the very small Common Murre colonies still surviving in Spain and Portugal.

2. Existing analyses need to be updated: for example, Holgersen's (1961) and Tuck's (1961) reviews of, respectively, the movements of Norwegian and Newfoundland Common Murres. Reviews are also needed for Iceland and the Faeroe Islands, and published in journals easily accessible to ornithologists. It is clear from Reinert's (1976) review, for example, that a great deal is known about the movements of Faeroese Common Murres, yet his results have appeared only in a series of articles in Faeroese in a Tórshavn newspaper. Ideally, we should take this further and aim for an integrated analysis of alcid banding returns from the populations of the Atlantic as a whole, something which modern computer technology is well equipped to handle.

3. We need more observations at sea, especially east of ca. 40°W. This would help us to resolve, among other things, such problems as the wintering grounds of the Razorbill in the western Atlantic, of the puffin in the Atlantic as a whole, and the use which alcids make in winter of the Greenland and Barents Seas and their ice-edges.

4. We should develop and test scenarios to explain and interpret the movements of the various Atlantic alcid populations, along the lines of those suggested in some of the pelagic ecology sections of this chapter. We should make the fullest use of the results of fisheries research cruises to obtain information on the distribution and abundance of the crustaceans and the species of small, non-commercial fish which are the birds' principal foods, and supplement them with better data on the birds' feeding ecology from studies at their colonies *and* at sea.

5. The preliminary analyses of the alcid migration patterns presented here have shown some wide divergences in the behavior of different populations of the same species. In some cases these coincide with taxonomic differences at the subspecific level, but in others they do not. It is important to reappraise the taxonomic status of the populations of the Atlantic alcids, using both the classic museum procedures and the modern biochemical techniques, as J. Bédard has stressed in Chapter 1 of this volume.

CHAPTER **10**

Conservation of the Atlantic Alcidae[1]

PETER G. H. EVANS

Edward Grey Institute of Field Ornithology, Department of Zoology, University of
Oxford, Oxford, England

DAVID N. NETTLESHIP

Seabird Research Unit, Canadian Wildlife Service, Bedford Institute of Oceanography,
Dartmouth, Nova Scotia, Canada

[1] This chapter was prepared in association with the program "Studies on Northern Seabirds", Seabird Research Unit, Canadian Wildlife Service, Environment Canada (Report No. 180).

I. INTRODUCTION

Many consider that conservation is the maintenance of a status quo. In a changing world this must be more than simply the preservation of a state inherited from the past. Unfortunately the concept of conservation means different things to different people: to the warden of a nature reserve it may be the protection of a piece of land and the animals and plants within it from human disturbance and exploitation; to a forester or fisherman it is the safeguarding of a renewable resource to provide a sustained yield. Here, we use the broader definition that conservation is 'the wise principle of coexistence between man and nature, even if it has to be a modified kind of nature' (Jeffers 1979). If conservation of the biological environment is to be carried out successfully, biologists must take full account of the differences of outlook within the community and try to resolve many conflicts of interest that may occur, particularly those associated with immediate socio-economic needs.

Conservation practice requires an understanding of the relations between animals and plants and other aspects of their environment, principles of competition, systems analysis, population dynamics and population genetics, sociobiology and evolutionary theory. All these fields have developed at great rates in recent years, but sadly often distant from conservation practice itself. There is a strong need for conservation biology to develop, encompassing these fields [see Soulé and Wilcox (1980) and Frankel and Soulé (1981) for moves in this direction]. Too often there is a reluctance on the part of professional biologists to involve themselves in this subject, despite the fact that it will invariably impinge upon their work. The destruction of a habitat may be the loss of their study site, or the loss of a study animal or plant, so that on selfish grounds alone they should be more aware of their responsibilities. For their part, organizations such as World Wildlife Fund (WWF), International Union for the Conservation of Nature and Natural Resources (IUCN), and the International Council for Bird Preservation (ICBP), need to recognize the role that conservation biology must play in determining their policy decisions. It is all very well to advocate tighter controls to protect auks from human-induced disturbances such as oil pollution and toxic chemical poisoning, but without the evidence that auk populations are being affected negatively by these factors, industry can rightfully argue that no strong case exists for further regulation. This requires detailed knowledge of the populations at risk; it requires information on the following key parameters: (1) the size and geographic limits of that population, and extent of gene flow between it and other populations; (2) age and breeding structure of the population; (3) age-specific fecundity and survivorship; and (4) the effects of inter- and intra-specific competition for resources and relative importance to that population of all human-made and 'natural' perturbations of the system.

But why bother to conserve seabirds? The coexistence of human beings and nature is desirable not simply out of deference for other living things. We depend upon animals and plants for food, clothing, medicines and a host of less vital products. We also cannot live in isolation from our environment, and perturbations of that environment, which includes the animals and plants within it, will affect our well-being. Arguments are rarely against conservation *per se,* but more the extent to which it should encroach upon ordinary people's lives. Besides the philosophical aspects of this issue, which will yield different answers for different people (depending on how they view quality of life), it is not easy to evaluate the extent to which a particular conservation policy (which might conflict with other interests) is necessary. The task of a conservation biologist should be to provide the information that leads to a wiser evaluation.

In this chapter we briefly review the biological features of the Alcidae, and highlight those which might make this seabird family vulnerable to environmental change. To accomplish this we first briefly summarize the present status of each of the North Atlantic species so far as is known, and discuss in turn each of the specific factors (climatic changes, human-made changes, and interactions between them) which may negatively affect the sizes of their populations, and their relative importance. Finally we propose some courses of action, bearing in mind the need for practical suggestions in the face of possible conflicts of interest.

II. FEATURES OF THE ALCIDAE

Top predators in a food chain are always more susceptible to the consequences of environmental change. In the marine ecosystem this position is primarily held by seabirds, cetaceans, seals and humans. All of these share a number of features. They are relatively long-lived with high adult survivorship, they mature slowly, and have low reproductive rates, often bearing no more than single young annually. The consequence of those features is that recovery from environmental perturbations is slow and large increases in adult mortality have a much greater impact on the population than it does on a species which normally has high reproductive rates and relatively high adult mortality.

Among seabirds, alcids are towards the vulnerable end of the scale with usually single clutches annually, first breeding at 3 to 5 years, low juvenile survivorship (ca. 30% to breeding), but high adult survivorship (ca. 90%)

TABLE 10.1

Biological Features of Alcids and Other North Atlantic Marine Bird Families

Family	Normal clutch size	Usual age of first breeding (years)	Average survival to breeding (%)	Average adult survival (%)	References
Alcidae	1[a]	4–6	13–53	80–96	See Chapters 3 and 5 (this volume)
Procellariidae	1	5–9	30	90–97	Perrins *et al.* (1973); Dunnet and Ollason (1978a,b)
Hydrobatidae	1	4–5	?	87–88	Scott (1970); Huntington and Burtt (1972)
Sulidae	1–2	5–6	20	94–98	Nelson (1966); Simmons (1967)
Phalacrocoracidae	2–5	4–5	35–40	84	Kortlandt (1942); Potts (1969)
Stercorariidae	2–3	4–8	35–50	79–94	Carrick and Ingham (1970); Wood (1971); Andersson (1976); Furness (1977, 1978c); O'Donald (1983)
Laridae					
Larinae	2–3	3–4	36–73	80–95	Brown (1967b); Onno (1968); Harris (1970c); Flegg and Cox (1975); Coulson and Wooller (1976); Kadlec (1976); Lebreton and Isenmann (1976); Chabrzyk and Coulson (1976); Sørenson (1977)
Sterninae	1–3	3–5	7–57	79–92	Soikkeli (1970); Coulson and Horobin (1976); Nisbet (1978b); Gill and Mewaldt (1983)

[a] Clutch normally one egg except for *Cepphus* spp.

(see Table 10.1 and Chapter 5, this volume). However, these features are not necessarily a recipe for disaster; if conditions are good, such a species may rapidly increase: for example, the Northern Fulmar, at present a successful and spreading species, lays a single clutch annually, reaches sexual maturity over 9 years, has high annual adult survivorship (97%) and is long-lived (42–45 years) (Dunnet and Ollason 1978a,b). Even among alcids there are instances of rapid increase—for example, puffins in eastern Britain have increased at an annual rate of 9% between 1969 and 1979 (Harris 1983a).

The auks are a highly specialised group of seabirds, their short wings more adapted for underwater swimming than for long-distance flying. Although their diet may include a number of prey species (see Chapter 6, this volume), usually only one or two species predominate (with the possible exception of the Black Guillemot). Like many other seabirds, most auks are colonial during the summer, often occurring in large breeding concentrations. In winter all but the Atlantic Puffin show a clumped distribution, often in shallow seas not very far from land. Thus if humans upset the marine ecosystem by polluting the seas with toxic chemicals or oil, or by over-fishing common prey organisms, auks tend to be more vulnerable than many of the more dispersed pelagic seabirds such as the Procellariiformes.

A number of generalizations can be derived from the relative abundance, breeding and wintering distributions of the six extant Atlantic alcid species (see Chapters 2 and 9 of this volume for details). All species have a primarily cool temperate or arctic distribution and except for Black Guillemot show clumped breeding distributions (with a high proportion of the total breeding populations occurring in a rather few colonies); all but the Atlantic Puffin also have a clumped distribution in winter. Colony size tends to be greater farther north in the range of a species and the majority of the very large colonies occur either in the high-arctic area or where cold polar and warmer Atlantic waters meet. (A summary of the best population estimates available for each region of the North Atlantic is given in Table 10.2 and Chapter 2, this volume.)

Wintering areas for populations from particular regions tend to be similar across a number of species (see Chapter 9, this volume). Where there are sufficient banding data, recoveries suggest that juveniles move farther than adults. Movements usually follow major ocean currents; for example, murres and Dovekies travel with the Labrador Current in autumn from colonies in Baffin Bay south to the Grand Banks of Newfoundland.

TABLE 10.2

Summary Totals of Atlantic Alcid Populations[a]

	Population size (millions of breeding pairs)	
Species	Estimate	Range
Razorbill	0.7	0.3–1.2
Dovekie	12.0	8–18
Common Murre	4.0	3.0–4.5
Thick-billed Murre	6.8	4.9–7.5
Black Guillemot	0.27	0.20–0.35
Atlantic Puffin	5.8	3.8–8.2

[a] See Chapter 2 for details.

Such movements probably result from the flightless, or near-flightless, condition which birds are experiencing during wing moult in autumn, so that their migration is essentially a passive movement. They may, however, also be in part to avoid ice cover and very low sea temperatures (at least in the north). With the exception of the Atlantic Puffin, they appear to seek out specific sea areas, such as the Skaggerak and Kattegat off southern Scandinavia or the Newfoundland Grand Banks in eastern Canada. Little is known of winter food availability in those areas.

This clumped pattern of distribution throughout the year makes the alcid group particularly vulnerable to human activities. An oiling incident or intensive fishing activity actually leading to incidental drownings in nets, could have severe impact on the population of a large geographic region, not necessarily only the nearest breeding population, since winter movements often take members of a population some distance from their breeding colonies. For example, the concentrations of murres and other seabird species wintering on the Grand Banks of Newfoundland include birds breeding as far away as the eastern Canadian high Arctic, both west and east Greenland, and even Iceland.

III. CHANGES IN STATUS

A review of changes in population size of any species depends greatly upon the quality of the counts. Alcids are not easy to count as they breed in relatively inaccessible locations, sometimes out of sight, and their numbers fluctuate in response to a variety of factors. For the present section we shall only summarize status changes (or lack of them) for which we consider there is good supporting evidence either in the form of well-documented quantitative changes (bearing in mind inaccuracies of population estimates) or, in the case of older accounts where this is lacking, qualitative changes involving an increase or decline of an order of magnitude.

The quality of information varies considerably between regions. Generally speaking, colonies in boreal water areas (Britain, Ireland, North Sea countries, New England) have the best historical documentation, while information is scanty throughout most arctic water regions. Since the 1960s, data from eastern Canada and Scandinavia has greatly improved, and so for these areas we have some idea at least of *recent* status changes. Those variations in coverage should be borne in mind in the following brief review of population changes (a more detailed review is contained in Chapter 2 of this volume).

A. Razorbill

Widespread declines have taken place on both sides of the North Atlantic since the last century. These have continued to the present day in the south of the Razorbill's range, but farther north (Labrador, Canada; West Greenland; north and east Britain; and Scandinavia), there has been little evidence of declines between 1940 and 1960, since which time a number of colonies have shown increases in numbers (see Chapter 2, this volume).

B. Dovekie

Estimates of the population size of this species are either very approximate or lacking altogether and so we are not yet able to determine whether there have been any changes in status. In most instances early accounts have described the high-arctic colonies in superlative terms with descriptions such as 'immense numbers', 'swarms', or 'countless numbers'. Since these epithets still apply to those colonies, it is impossible to assess whether any have changed in population size, with the exception of a definite decline this century in Iceland (Timmermann 1949; Hantzsch 1905; Gardarsson 1982) and southwest Greenland (Salomonsen 1967).

C. Common Murre

Status changes of the Common Murre mirror, in many ways, those of the Razorbill, with declines on both sides of the Atlantic in the last 100 years, first over much of its range, but later continuing primarily in the southern parts. The timing of the declines is difficult to evaluate since they are influenced by the timing of surveys by ornithologists. In the southern parts of its northeastern Atlantic range, declines have occurred fairly steadily from the last century. They also appear to have occurred elsewhere in the northeastern Atlantic from the late 1950s at least to 1970. In the northwestern Atlantic the picture is more complicated, with declines checked in many areas between 1920 and 1970, followed by rapid increases at least into the 1950s when numbers began to stabilize. In the last decade a number of areas on both sides of the Atlantic are showing increases, for example, east Newfoundland and Labrador in the western Atlantic and northern Britain, Denmark, Finland and northern Norway in the eastern Atlantic (see Chapter 2, this volume).

D. Thick-billed Murre

Information from colonies from the last century is both scarce and qualitative. Since then, although population estimates remain only very approximate, it is clear that large declines have taken place in many parts of its range, notably west Greenland, Novaya Zemlya and, at least since the mid-1950s, in the eastern Canadian Arctic. In Novaya Zemlya, these declines were recorded between the 1920s and 1940s, although in most areas elsewhere they have continued to the present day (Evans and Waterston 1976; Nettleship 1977a; Salomonsen 1979a,c; see also Chapter 2, this volume).

E. Black Guillemot

Population sizes of this species are scarcely better known than for the Dovekie, and there is little that can be said about possible status changes in the Arctic. Farther south, declines have been recorded in western Norway (Folkestad 1982; Barrett and Vader 1984) and eastern Canada (Nettleship 1980) since the mid-1930s. In the southern part of the species' range, populations appear to be stable or increasing, with extensions or recolonisations around the Irish Sea and Firth of Clyde in the British Isles since 1945. We thus see a reverse situation to that observed in the Common Murre and Razorbill since 1935, with populations stable or increasing at the southern edge of the range but declining farther north, although we have little information for arctic regions.

F. Atlantic Puffin

Early information for this species comes primarily from the British Isles where accounts of the last century, though possibly given to exaggeration, indicate some very large puffin colonies scattered throughout the western seaboard of Britain and Ireland. First evidence of decline comes from around the turn of the century, and at many sites which continued to decline until the 1960s. Such decreases appear to have been widespread, occurring in eastern Canada and northeastern United States, many parts of western Britain, the Channel Islands and Brittany. In the last decade, however, although declines continued in southern parts of the range of the puffin (southeastern Canada and northeastern United States; British Isles—southwest and southern England, southwestern Ireland; the Channel Islands; and Brittany, France), the trend has reversed farther north with increases in northern Britain (from North Wales northward) (Harris

1976a), northeast Canada (Labrador) (Nettleship 1977a, 1980), and northern Norway (Barrett and Vader 1984). In the northern parts of the range
(e.g., Iceland, Greenland, Jan Mayen, and Spitsbergen) of the puffin,
there is little information on status changes.

G. Conclusions

All auk species except the Dovekie (for which we have insufficient
information anyway) have shown widespread declines during the first half
of this century, changes which probably began in the nineteenth century.
The decline has continued for Razorbill, Common Murre and Atlantic
Puffin in the southernmost parts of their range up to the present day, and
throughout its western North Atlantic range for the Thick-billed Murre. In
contrast, the Black Guillemot has recently shown a decline in some northerly parts of its range (although there is little information from arctic
regions), remaining stable or increasing in the south. The Razorbill, Common Murre and Atlantic Puffin are all showing increases in northerly parts
of their range over the last decade.

IV. CAUSES OF STATUS CHANGES

Many factors may influence status changes among auks. We may divide
these into two main groupings: natural factors (i.e., climatic changes) and
human-induced or 'artificial' factors. In the context of this chapter we
shall consider negative influences of humans and recognize seven major
threats (i.e., human-made causes of disequilibrium in the population of a
species): human exploitation, incidental kills in fishing nets, competition
with fisheries, disturbance and habitat destruction, natural and introduced
predators, oil pollution and chemical poisoning. We shall conclude this
section with a discussion of the relative importance of natural and unnatural (human-made) causes for changes in population status.

A. Climatic Changes

1. NORTH ATLANTIC AS A WHOLE

Since the recovery of the earth from the last Pleistocene glaciation,
8000–10,000 years ago, climate in the North Atlantic (and indeed the
globe as a whole) has not been static, but instead has fluctuated within

narrower limits. The major cycling of 2000–3000 years' duration, has been described as neo-glacial cycles. The 'Little Ice Age', a period of temperatures 1–2°C lower than today and stormy conditions in the North Atlantic, lasting from about 1550 to 1850 A.D., was a part of such a cycle. At that time the Gulf Stream was farther south than now and tended to turn away south before reaching the coast of Europe; the Polar Stream and Labrador Current in the western Atlantic were also broader than now. Since that period, the world has generally warmed about 1°C, although the rate of warming has been irregular. It was especially pronounced during the first half of the twentieth century, with temperatures rising most rapidly (several degrees Celsius in 50 years) in the Atlantic sector of the Arctic. Wind belts and storm tracks of the northern hemisphere appear to have contracted somewhat towards the Arctic at that time. Since 1950, the climatic trends have reversed direction with ambient temperatures falling in the Arctic and Atlantic low-Arctic (by several degrees Celsius in some areas; 0.1–0.2°C per decade between 1950 and 1975) when the extent of sea ice had again been increasing. Since 1975 there has been some indication of a further reversal with increasing temperatures. The atmospheric circulation of the northern hemisphere appears to have reverted to a pattern resembling that of the last part of the nineteenth century, with a tendency towards greater variability of weather conditions in many areas (particularly in the eastern sector of the North Atlantic). There have been slight differences in timing between regions of the North Atlantic. In 1971, the Canadian Arctic became, for the first time, involved in the cooling that had set in sharply in other sectors of the far north in 1961 with cooling events occurring rather later in the northwest Atlantic. This has resulted in a great increase in the south-to-north thermal gradient between the western Atlantic and northern Canada, particularly in the winter months. That has resulted in a great increase in the energy of atmospheric circulation over the North Atlantic, driving mild air towards Europe and more saline water to Iceland. This in turn may influence the volume of polar water transported by the East Greenland Current. The southward penetration of this water into the East Iceland Current may have further consequences on the development of cool periods in the North Atlantic, including 'ice age' conditions (Lamb 1972, 1975, 1982; Rodewald 1975; Cushing 1982).

The climatic changes outlined above may have important influences upon organisms, their abundance and distributional range. To understand the possible role that they may play in the changing status of alcid populations, we shall consider in further detail the changes in the climate that have taken place in the northeast Atlantic, where meteorological records and accounts of alcid population changes are more detailed.

2. NORTHEAST ATLANTIC

Climates fluctuate in both the short and long terms (Lamb 1966, 1972, 1982; Bray 1971). After the last Ice Age in Europe, there was a post-glacial climatic optimum between 4000 and 2000 B.C., followed by a deterioration. A second optimum of dry, warm and storm-free weather occurred between A.D. 400 and 1200, the time of the Celtic and Viking voyages to new lands with settlement in Iceland and Greenland, and the growing of vineyards in England. This was followed by unsettled weather over a couple of centuries with a partial recovery between 1400 and 1550 before a further decline into the Little Ice Age between 1550 and 1850. Over this period, winters were very cold and there was even some spread of glaciation in Scandinavia and the European Alps. Mild summers appeared around the end of the eighteenth century, followed by mild winters in the mid-nineteenth century, but deteriorated slightly towards the end of the century, in northwest Europe. During the present century (except for the 1920s) the climate slowly ameliorated (warmed), becoming warmest during the 1930s and 1940s. A further cooling then took place until the 1960s, with a reversal of this trend in the 1970s. Although some of the short-term secondary cycling described for the present century also appears to have taken place in previous centuries, the recent period of warming is possibly a much more notable event (Cushing 1982, Fig. 39).

These climatic fluctuations also affect the sea-surface temperatures, though usually with some time lag. Smed (1965) plotted the trends in surface temperatures for sea areas around the British Isles between 1880 and 1960, and found that in each area the sea was coolest during the 1880s and the first 20 years of this century, but subsequently became warmer (by about 1°C) from the 1930s to 1960. Dietrich (1954) compared monthly sea-surface temperatures for west Denmark over the period 1849 to 1950 and found that a period of cold winters and mild summers towards the end of the nineteenth century also gave way to a period of mild winters and warm summers in the North Sea during the 1930s and 1940s. However, since about 1960, sea-surface temperatures have been declining (Kukla *et al.* 1977). Bjerknes (1963, 1964) explained the earlier warming of the northeast Atlantic by showing that as westerly winds diminished in strength, the quantity of heat remaining in the sea increased and the temperatures rose. The westerlies slackened as the pressure difference between the Iceland low and the Azores high declined. The differences were large in the 1880s, resulting in strong westerly winds, but declined giving slack westerlies by the 1930s and 1940s.

The strength of westerly winds (and alternating southerlies) may also affect the salinity of coastal waters. Such temporal changes in salinity were identified by Dickson (1971), who expressed monthly salinity values for the period 1905–1970 for different regions in the northeast Atlantic (western approaches to the British Isles, English Channel, North Sea, and German Bight). He found that peaks of high salinity occurred in the following years: 1904–1906, 1920–1921, 1925–1926, 1930–1931, 1934–1935, 1939, 1950, 1954–1955, 1959–1960, and 1964–1965. These salinity peaks coincide not only with sea-surface temperature peaks, but also with periods of southerly winds, which draw more saline waters from the south (Namias 1959, 1964; Dickson 1971). At the same time as these peaks, there were records of the invasion of warm-water indicator plankton species (Glover 1957; Southward 1963; Russell *et al.* 1971; Cushing 1975, 1982; Southward *et al.* 1975). (It should be noted that events in the northeast Atlantic may not be the same in the northwest.) Dickson (1971) showed, for example, that the same pressure system generates warm water in the eastern Atlantic and cool water in the west so that effects on marine life in these areas may be rather different. This probably relates to the fact that fish tend to spawn relatively close to the coast and differences in wind strength and direction can be modified by the aspect of the coast, simply by the way the coast affects the degree of fetch (i.e., the length of open water across which the wind is blowing, which largely determines the height of the waves). Thus a westerly wind provides a long fetch to the west Norwegian coast, whereas a southerly one provides a long fetch to the east English coast.

3. EFFECTS OF CLIMATE ON MARINE ORGANISMS

An assessment of the impact of climatic fluctuations on marine life, including seabirds, is complicated by the interactions of many factors in the marine ecosystem. Changes in water temperature may cause a shift in the range of some planktonic or fish species which may by competitive release affect the abundance of others. Predator–prey relationships may thus be altered, while human impact through commercial fisheries may alter the balance of these relationships, independently of climate (see below, Section IV,C).

In the North Atlantic, long-term changes in plankton have been examined by three separate studies. The first began off Plymouth in 1925, and examined both annual and seasonal variation in plankton (including fish eggs and larvae) for the western English Channel (Cushing 1961; Russell *et al.* 1971; Southward *et al.* 1975; Southward 1980). The second was based on a line of transects in the North Sea from 1935 to 1960 (except 1940–1946: Wimpenny 1944; Cattley 1950, 1954). The third was the plankton recorder network established in the 1930s, and extended since 1945 to cover fixed transect lines (recorders towed by merchant ships) across the North Sea and North Atlantic (Hardy 1936, 1939, 1956, 1959). Besides some of the changes in indicator species referred to above, the results showed a decline in recruitment to the Atlantic herring stock in the western English Channel starting in the 1920s and a replacement by the more southerly pilchard, so that by the early 1930s, pilchard had become the dominant pelagic fish in the area, a condition that lasted until the late 1960s when a reversal of that trend occurred (Cushing 1961; Russell and Demir 1971; Southward *et al.* 1975). There was no evidence that fishing had caused the decline of recruitment in the herring stock. There were correlations with the abundance of macroplankton and winter phosphorus levels, both of which declined at the same time as the declines in spring-spawned herring larvae. There is also some evidence of competition between herring and pilchard involving separate age classes (Cushing 1961; Russell and Demir 1971). Other temporal changes involving replacement of one fish stock by another have been well documented for the Norwegian and Swedish herring stocks. Those stocks have alternated in a periodic manner of 50 to 70 years' duration since the fourteenth century, in parallel with changes in the extent of ice cover north of Iceland where Norwegian herring migrated to feed (Beverton and Lee 1965). Superimposed upon adverse climatic changes are the effects of over-fishing by humans, and that almost certainly led to the collapse of the Norwegian herring stocks around 1967 (Cushing 1975, 1982). Pelagic fish, such as herring, with low fecundity are considered more vulnerable to long-term climatic changes than demersal fish such as Atlantic cod because of the consequent relationship between density dependence and fecundity. When heavy fishing pressure is also imposed upon a pelagic population, particularly reducing recruitment, the result can be a catastrophic decline in numbers with changes in abundance orders of magnitude greater than for demersal stocks (Cushing 1975, 1982).

Relationships for a number of plankton and fish species have been found between the magnitude of recruitment and climatic factors, particularly wind strength and direction, and heat radiation (Cushing 1975, 1982). These include cod in west Greenland (Hermann and Hansen 1965), New Brunswick (Martin and Kohler 1965), and the North Sea (Dickson *et al.* 1974); herring in the English Channel and North Sea (Carruthers 1938; Rae 1957); and *Calanus* in the North Sea (Cushing 1966).

In boreal waters fish tend to spawn at fixed seasons in the same place from year to year, whereas the production of the larval food varies in timing. The extent of the match or mismatch of the production of fish larvae to that of their food is thought to determine the magnitude of recruitment, but that is in turn affected by the above climatic factors

(Cushing 1975). These may influence a number of fish species simultaneously. Thus, an analysis by Templeman (1965) of cod, haddock and
herring stocks from 1902 to 1962 revealed particular year classes that
were abundant for many different stocks of different species throughout
the North Atlantic. Those included the years: 1904, 1922, 1934, 1942,
1950, and 1956 (though with variations in the extent and degree of abundance) with the great year classes of atlanto-scandian herring occurring in
1904 and 1950. Although one cannot make direct comparisons since those
years often involve different peaks of abundance in different areas, it will
be noted that a number of those years correspond to those recorded
earlier when associated climatic changes were highlighted.

   The relationships between climatic change and changes in abundance of
marine life are essential to a proper examination of their possible influence upon alcid populations. This has not been attempted in any depth
previously other than to identify it as a possible factor influencing alcid
numbers (Lockley 1953a; Tuck 1961). Unfortunately, we have little information on the diet of auks in boreal waters except for the period since
1965 (although there is some evidence that herring figured more highly in
the diet in some areas in the 1950s and 1960s—Myrberget 1962; Reinert
1976). However, those recent studies indicate which are the main food
items taken and possible preferences, while calorific estimates give some
idea of the relative energy value of different species. Harris and Hislop
(1978), for example, have suggested that juvenile Atlantic Puffins are
better fed upon high-calorific fish such as sprats, sandlance and young
herring, than upon saithe or whiting (which in any case tend to live a bit
deeper, even in the young stages). The same probably applies to the other
auks, Common and Thick-billed Murres and Razorbill (with the exception
that capelin and arctic cod are likely to replace sprat and sandlance as the
more important fish species in colder waters), since they feed on the same
species, although size classes may differ. Alcid productivity is likely to be
affected by the availability of abundant food in the vicinity of breeding
colonies, which will be dictated also by the need for breeding sites suitable for incubating eggs and growing young, and secure from predators.
However, outside the breeding season, survival is probably less tied to
the need to winter in a particular area and the birds should, at least in
theory, be able to adjust to changes in the distribution of available food.
Since we have no information on the past distribution and abundance of
sprats and sandlance in the eastern North Atlantic, we have to confine our
examination to any correlations of temporal changes in alcid numbers
with those of recruitment to herring stocks. The relationship, if any,
would almost certainly be a complicated one. Time lags, interactions
between species, and additional influences of over-fishing are all likely to

affect the results of such a comparison. However, we can expect some periodicity in population size, perhaps comparable to those suggested by Reinert (1976) when he related climatic fluctuations for the period 1200–1970 to cycles of peak catches of Atlantic pilot whales and herring spawning. He also reported the qualitative observations of the Faeroese fowlers on the occurrence of very good and bad periods of catches of Atlantic Puffins, Common Murres and harvests of their eggs since 1800. Those data are combined with information from Nørrevang (1977) and presented in Fig. 10.1. Although they suffer from the lack of a quantitative base for auk population size increases, it is likely that an extended period of poor fowling-years can be taken as reflecting smaller population sizes. The results indicate strong relationships between periods of herring spawning and good years of catches of auks, and the converse, but with a time lag for its effects upon the breeding population to be observed.

B. Influences of Humans: Threats to Alcid Populations

1. HUMAN EXPLOITATION

Alcids have for past centuries been harvested for food and feathers. Bone fragments of puffins, murres, and even the Great Auk have been found in archaeological sites from northern Norway and northern Britain (Orkney and Shetland) west to eastern Canada (Labrador, east New-foundland, Nova Scotia) and the Gulf of Maine, dating as far back as 3000 B.C. (Grieve 1885; L. M. Tuck 1961, 1967; Tuck 1975, 1976; Barrett and Vader 1984; Groundwater 1974; Lea and Bourne 1975). Moreover, in Greenland, Iceland and the Faeroes, there is a long tradition of fowling for eggs and full-grown birds which probably started soon after human immigrants arrived (ca. 3000 to 2500 B.C. in the case of Greenland, and in the ninth or tenth centuries in the case of Iceland and the Faeroes: Salomonsen 1970; Nørrevang 1977). Human exploitation has continued in some areas (e.g., North Shore of the Gulf of St. Lawrence, West Greenland, Faeroes, Iceland, Bjørnøya, Novaya Zemlya) until the present century, probably as a result of the dependence of the local community on meat and eggs, supplied by the large quantities of seabirds, marine mammals, and fish in those regions. Elsewhere, the development of agriculture allowed humans to find alternative foods in the form of domestic animals and crops, and such exploitation no longer remained an essential part of their living.

Until the nineteenth century we have little idea of the extent of the impact local communities had on alcid colonies, but it was probably only of local importance, since the human populations were invariably small

(A)

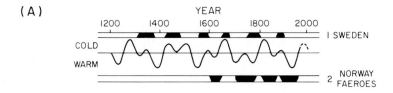

(B)

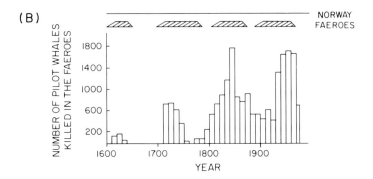

(C)

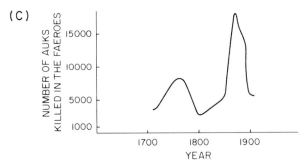

Fig. 10.1. Climatic changes since 1200 and the relationship between fluctuations of climate, periods of abundance of herring, and the catches of pilot whales and auks in the Faeroe Islands. (A) Changes in climate from 1200 to 1970, obtained by isotopic analysis of glacier ice from the Greenland ice cap (from Johnsen *et al.* 1970). Fluctuations above the line indicate periods of cooler climate, and those below the line, periods of warmer climate. Bar 1 (Sweden) indicates the periods when herring were found at Bohuslän, Sweden. Bar 2 indicates the periods when herring spawned on the Norwegian and Faeroese coasts. (B) Periods of time when herring spawned along the Norwegian and Faeroese coasts (indicated by horizontal bars) compared with numbers of pilot whales killed in the Faeroes. (C) Fluctuations in the estimated numbers of auks (mainly Atlantic Puffin, but also Common Murres) collected from the Faeroes between 1710 and 1910. Estimates derived by Svabo on the basis of exports of seabird feathers: 20–25 puffins and 10–12 Common Murres taken to equal 1 pound of feathers; since the great majority of the catches are puffins, a figure of 15 birds per pound was used (adapted from Reinert 1976 and Nørrevang 1977).

and confined to particular areas. It is probable that the pressures were greatest along accessible coastlines in eastern Canada and northeastern United States (New England, Gulf of St. Lawrence, Labrador and east Newfoundland) and southern Britain (west Wales, Cornwall and Devon). Where depletion of seabird populations might have a direct impact on the community, for example on isolated island groups such as the Faeroes and St. Kilda, a complex set of rules developed to allow the sustained harvesting of the resource. The annual 'fleyg' netting of puffins and murres flying around their colonies in these regions tended to select for non-breeding young birds, while areas where eggs or breeding birds were removed from ledges or burrows were left undisturbed for 2 or 3 years (Nørrevang 1977). These practices probably helped to provide a sustained harvest, although it is likely that they were as much an economic strategy as one of conservation.

As human populations became less dependent upon seabirds for survival, they also became less in balance with local seabird populations and more exploitative. With rapid increases in the sizes of human populations, putting greater pressure on food resources, and the development of more efficient means of boat travel (particularly motor power) and more effective ways of killing (notably firearms) in the nineteenth and early twentieth centuries, the impact upon seabirds increased dramatically. The nineteenth century saw extensive travel to remote unpopulated areas (such as the Arctic), and seabird colonies that until that time had remained relatively undisturbed, suffered depredation at the hands of humans with no ties to those regions. Although marine mammals such as whales, seals and sea otters suffered most with some populations being greatly reduced or even extirpated (e.g., Steller's sea cow), seabird populations were apparently less affected, perhaps due to their sheer large numbers and also to the inaccessibility of a proportion of colonies. A notable exception, however, is that of the Great Auk, the most specialised of all recent Alcidae, which in its development to efficient swimming ability, had become flightless, bearing only vestigial wings. This flightless habit left the species very vulnerable to human persecution for meat, feathers and oil, and the last Great Auk was killed in Iceland in 1844 (see Chapter 2 of this volume for details).

In temperate regions, pressures upon seabird colonies increased, particularly during periods when alternative sources of food were scarce. In western Ireland, for example, the potato famine of the mid-1800s almost certainly resulted in greater exploitation of offshore seabird colonies (Evans and Lovegrove 1974). In other regions, even where human populations were thriving, massive commercial egging enterprises were initiated (e.g., North Shore of Gulf of St. Lawrence and Labrador) to supply food for southern markets (see Chapter 2 of this volume for details).

Many of the known declines of alcids (and other seabird species such as the Northern Gannet) appear to have been the direct result of human exploitation. In northeast North America, those took place primarily in many parts of Labrador, the Gulf of St. Lawrence, Bay of Fundy and Gulf of Maine (Nettleship 1977a). The best documented declines took place in the Gulf of St. Lawrence and on Funk Island among Great Auks, Razorbills, Common Murres and Atlantic Puffins with very large populations being greatly reduced (some colonies extirpated) from the late 1700s well into the present century. In Britain and Ireland, these declines occurred over the same time period throughout the western seaboard but particularly on islands either inhabited by humans or readily accessible to them, for example: Mull and other Inner Hebridean islands, Ailsa Craig, Bardsey Island, Grassholm Island, Lundy, and the Scilly Isles. Farther north, the effects of human depredations came rather later. In west Greenland, Thick-billed Murres have been intensively hunted at the breeding colonies since the 1880s, with recent estimates amounting to an annual take of ca. 250,000–750,000 birds (Salomonsen 1970; Kampp 1982 and personal communication), a kill toll which together with the number drowned in fishing nets off southwest Greenland, is almost certainly responsible for the drastic declines in this species noted over the last half century (Salomonsen 1970, 1979a,c; Tull et al. 1972; Evans and Waterston 1976; Nettleship 1977a).

At Guba Bezymyannaya, the largest of all the seabird colonies in Novaya Zemlya, massive harvesting of the eggs and the young of Thick-billed Murres since 1927 probably caused a decline from an estimated 1.64 million birds in 1933–1934 to 290,000 birds in 1948 (Portenko 1931; Krasovski 1937; Uspenski 1956). Only when protective measures came into force did the population begin to recover, increasing to 371,000 murres by 1950 (Uspenski 1951), but still remaining only a fraction of its former size by 1967 (Zelickman and Golovkin 1972). In the Faeroes, Common Murre declines were first recorded from late in the 1950s (Dyck and Meltofte 1973, 1975; Olsen 1980, 1982), probably as a result of over-exploitation as the human population became more affluent and the need for a sustained harvest lessened. Olsen (1982) also suggested that food shortage may have played a part, particularly in the sudden decline of immature birds which accompanied the overall decline at the start. In 1980, Common Murres became legally protected from 1 April to 15 August (Olsen 1982).

Those alcid species breeding in large, dense colonies have been the most vulnerable so long as the colonies were relatively accessible. Thus the Common Murre, Thick-billed Murre, Razorbill and Atlantic Puffin have all suffered heavily, while the Black Guillemot and Dovekie were probably less affected, the former because of its more dispersed breeding habit and the latter because of the enormous colony sizes in relation to the very small human population sizes in the vicinity. However, we should be cautious before concluding that the Dovekie has not suffered, since population estimates are very rarely available for comparison. It is possible that the declines in southwest Greenland and Iceland are due to human persecution where colonies are more accessible, although it may also be due to a climatic amelioration which could be affecting the distribution of the Dovekie's food as proposed by Salomonsen (1967).

During this century most countries have enacted protective legislation to safeguard North Atlantic seabird populations. In 1916 the Migratory Bird Treaty was signed between Canada and the United States prohibiting the taking of adult migratory birds or their eggs in most areas. However, seabirds may still be legally hunted by native peoples in certain regions of Canada, and both Common and Thick-billed Murres may be hunted in winter (1 September to 31 March) off Newfoundland and Labrador by all residents of that province (Nettleship 1977a). The scope of the Newfound-land–Labrador hunt has been expanded by the use of high-powered rifles and speedboats, and is no longer for subsistence, and has no bag limits (Nettleship 1977a, 1980; Brown and Nettleship 1984b). Recent estimates have put the annual murre kill in Newfoundland and Labrador at 450,000 birds (Wendt and Cooch 1984). Those will include not only birds from the eastern Canadian Arctic, but also from west Greenland (Salomonsen 1967, 1970, 1971b; Nettleship 1977a; Gaston 1980). Unfortunately even where legislation does exist, often it is not observed, particularly in the more remote parts of Canada where it is virtually unenforceable (Nettleship and Lock 1973; Nettleship 1977a, 1980; Brown and Nettleship 1984b).

The west Greenland populations continued to be hunted through this century. In 1955 F. Salomonsen advocated protection of all murre colonies in Greenland with a prohibition on shooting and any disturbance within at least 1 km of the colony. The Greenland Assembly eventually accepted his proposals and, in 1961, legislated accordingly. However, those laws were rarely taken seriously and the depredations continued (Salomonsen 1970). Further proposals for seabird conservation were put forward (Salomonsen 1974a), and after widespread concern was expressed for the bird populations, they were finally adopted in December 1977 (Salomonsen 1979a,c). Those laws still permit the taking of murres (the most seriously threatened alcid in Greenland) and, with the usual difficulties of enforcement in these remote areas, it remains to be seen whether they have any positive effect (Kampp 1982; Evans 1984). Hunting in winter along the southwest coast of Greenland will be of birds from west Greenland (mainly adults), the eastern Canadian Arctic, and Spitsbergen (Salomonsen 1967, 1970, 1971b; Gaston 1980; Kampp 1982).

Moving to the northeast Atlantic, legislation protecting seabird colonies in Britain first came into force in 1868, and now the hunting of all alcid species in Britain and Ireland is prohibited. To a large degree these laws appear to be observed. In Iceland, Norway, Spitsbergen and Bjørnøya, the taking of eggs and hunting of adult auks with nets, snares or guns continues; only very recently, in 1980, were protection laws imposed in the Faeroes (Olsen 1982). Human exploitation is probably less important now that plastics have replaced feathers for insulation, while deep freezers and high prices of cartridges and fuel have effectively restricted the market for eggs and meat (Barrett and Vader 1984). However, all the auk species may be hunted from 21 August to 1 March in Norway and since 1945, hunting them has become increasingly popular. Brun (1979) estimated the annual kill of murres and Razorbills to be an absolute minimum of 5000 individuals, while Barrett and Vader (1984) noted 30,000–40,000 auks of all species taken annually between 1971 and 1979. The hunting of murres and Razorbills was banned in 1979 and the following winter the number of puffins, Black Guillemots and Dovekies taken declined to ca. 7000 (Barrett and Vader 1984). Birds shot each winter are derived from the populations of the Faeroes and Britain and Ireland (Mead 1974; Olsen 1980, 1982; Baillie and Mead 1982).

To conclude, it appears that populations of Common and Thick-billed Murres, Great Auk, Razorbill and Atlantic Puffin have all suffered heavy exploitation at the hands of humans in the eighteenth, nineteenth and early twentieth centuries. This resulted in widespread declines of most species, with the extinction of the Great Auk. At the present time, it is likely that among the alcids, only the Thick-billed Murre (notably in west Greenland and eastern Canada) and possibly the Razorbill (eastern Canada) are greatly affected by exploitation, giving cause for serious concern.

2. INCIDENTAL KILLS IN FISHING NETS

The accidental capture of seabirds in fishing nets has in recent years become a serious problem. Although noted at the end of the last century off the east coast of Scotland when annual losses in drift-nets numbered in the thousands (McIntosh 1903), and the coast of northern Norway in the 1950s (Holgersen 1961), it was with the introduction of inconspicuous monofilament nylon nets to capture salmon that the incidental kills became much more regular an occurrence. In northern Norway, annual mortality from the long-line fishery was estimated to be 21,000 murres and 18,000 puffins on the basis of sample figures from the 1969 season (Brun 1979). Though considered less damaging to seabirds, the drift-net fishery in Norwegian waters almost certainly increased the total annual kill through drowning. A third source of mortality in this area arose from the use of pound nets set close inshore, often near the colonies of diving seabirds. However, although at least 40,000 birds were estimated to be lost by this means in 1969, the extent of mortality to alcids in particular is unknown (Brun 1979). Long-line fishing is now prohibited, although monofilament drift-nets and land-based pound nets continue to be used (Barrett and Vader 1984).

In Britain, drift-nets are illegal (though still used), but some mortality occurs in fixed nets. In western Ireland where drift-netting for salmon still widely takes place, 5000 alcids (mainly Razorbills) were caught in Galway Bay in 1976 and similar numbers elsewhere along the west coast (Bibby 1972; Melville 1973; Whilde 1979).

The greatest mortality undoubtedly occurs in eastern Canada and west Greenland where monofilament drift-netting for Atlantic cod and Atlantic salmon started in the 1960s and rapidly increased in intensity (Anonymous 1969; Tull et al. 1972; Piatt et al. 1984). These nets are inconspicuous and also virtually indestructible so that nets which are lost at sea may continue to be a hazard (Bourne 1976). In southwest Greenland the mortality was estimated to be 500,000 murres per year on the basis of by-catches during salmon-tagging operations in the region between 1969 and 1971 (Tull et al. 1972). A re-examination of the data collected in 1970 to 1972 on the basis of further surveys by Christensen and Lear (1977) indicated a lower annual kill of between 215,000 and 350,000 birds. However, as with all mortality estimates from fishing net takes, a good deal of extrapolation takes place from sample surveys. In this region, most birds were probably caught during night fishing (with 97% of by-catches sampled from night fishing—Christensen and Lear 1977) mainly from September to October, and mainly in the Disko Bay area; few were caught in the previous 2 months probably because the bulk of the autumn 'rafts' had not reached the region by this time (Evans and Waterston 1976). Furthermore, salmon netting close inshore was likely to catch many fewer birds than the offshore fishery since auk numbers are relatively small close to the coast (Evans and Waterston 1976; Piatt and Reddin 1984). Murre by-catches within a particular region are extremely variable, probably owing in part to the timing of the murre migration and the prevailing weather conditions and sea state, but also to the coincidence of murres and salmon to feed on capelin which form dense post-spawning schools on offshore banks in autumn (Jangaard 1974; Christensen and Lear 1977; Lear 1980). The imposition in 1976 of salmon quotas which effectively terminated the fishing season by mid-September almost certainly provided some respite since many birds would not have reached the area by then (Evans and

Waterston 1977; Salomonsen 1979c). Piatt and Reddin (1984) estimate that for 1976 through 1980 the by-catch was reduced to about 10 to 20% of the numbers taken between 1969 and 1971 (i.e., 50,000–100,000 per year). However, recent changes in the operation and type of fishing gear (notably a greater *offshore* fishery with larger vessels operated both day and night and fishing effort concentrated on the northern banks around Disko that are occupied also by murres), used by Greenlandic fleets, and the imposition of later fishery opening dates from 1981 is predicted to result in a renewal of heavy net mortality for murres (Piatt and Reddin 1984).

The timing of the salmon netting season appears to be critical in determining the extent of murre mortality, with the crucial period being from mid-September to mid-October. If the fishery is terminated by early September, mortality is presumably lower since most of the west Greenland murre population from the large colonies in the Upernavik District have left their breeding cliffs between mid-August and the first week in September and not yet reached the Disko area by that time (Evans and Waterston 1976; Kampp 1982; Evans 1984). Judging by the by-catch figures for Disko Bay in 1972 (Christensen and Lear 1977), murres move into the area in early September and any netting carried out after this date will likely result in heavy mortality. The west Greenland wintering population comprises not only local birds but also a proportion of the eastern Canadian arctic and Spitsbergen populations. It is therefore likely that fishing net mortality in September will be made up primarily of west Greenland birds, but that by October, those drowned will include birds from the Lancaster–Jones Sounds and Davis and Hudson Straits populations of the eastern Canadian Arctic (Brown *et al.* 1975; Nettleship and Gaston 1978; Gaston 1980; Kampp 1982). In November, a portion of the west Greenland populations (all 1- and 2-year-old birds, and 25% of the adult population) and most, if not all, of the Lancaster–Jones Sounds population apparently move across Davis Strait to winter off Newfoundland, while birds from Spitsbergen move northwards up the southwest coast of Greenland (Salomonsen 1967; Brown *et al.* 1975; Gaston 1980; Kampp 1982; see also Chapter 9, this volume). In west Greenland, puffins, Black Guillemots and Dovekies (and marine mammals such as porpoises and seals) are also caught, but in lower numbers. The principal reason for that is probably that they do not form large, dense flocks in the vulnerable area.

Off Newfoundland, there are major inshore fisheries for herring in April, salmon in mid-May to July, and cod in early June to October. In this region, murre mortality in cod and salmon gill-nets increased dramatically from the 1950s to the early 1970s as murre populations increased and inshore fishing effort intensified in the vicinity of the major colonies (Piatt *et al.* 1984). On the basis of banding recoveries and two surveys of alcid by-catches, annual mortality of Common Murres was estimated to average 4400 birds between the years 1954 and 1956 and 15,400 birds between 1967 and 1971. Of all the immature murres recovered from nets, about 25% were 1-year-olds, 50% 2-year-olds, and 25% 3- or 4-year-olds (Piatt *et al.* 1984). In recent years (1977–1980), the mortality has apparently decreased due to a marked decline in the abundance and inshore spawning of capelin on which murres and puffins, and cod and salmon all feed, although fishing effort continues to increase (a fivefold increase estimated since 1975; see Brown and Nettleship 1984a). At present there are restrictions on the capelin fishery to allow the stocks to recover, but one may anticipate a continued high by-catch, particularly in view of the increased emphasis on the inshore fishery (Piatt *et al.* 1984).

Banding recoveries indicate that close to 90% of mortality occurs in gillnets rather than cod traps, trawl lines or herring nets (pound nets are not used in this region), and that twice as many murres are killed in cod gillnets as in salmon gill-nets; 86% of net recoveries occurred between May and July with the majority of them in June (Piatt *et al.* 1984). Those findings suggested that locally breeding Common Murres and Atlantic Puffins form the bulk of the net by-catches, with murres caught primarily in cod gill-nets and puffins mainly in salmon gill-nets (murres dive more deeply than puffins and therefore are probably more likely to become entangled in the deeper-set cod nets—Piatt and Nettleship 1985).

In addition to the inshore fishery, there is an offshore gill-net fishery operating between May and December east of Newfoundland, encompassing all known alcid wintering grounds in eastern North America. The nets are generally set at depths ranging from 50 to 200 m. Although both murre species, Dovekies and puffins are all known to suffer mortality in this fishery, it is likely to be highest in murres since they dive more deeply than the other two species, which makes them more vulnerable. During the months of June, and September to December, there is overlap in the use of these water areas by alcids and commercial gill-net fisheries, with most birds from eastern Canadian and west Greenland populations.

Incidental kills in fishing nets are clearly an important source of mortality in particular regions. Thick-billed Murres incur the greatest mortality, notably off west Greenland, but Common Murres predominate farther south off Newfoundland and the Norwegian coast. Along the west coast of Ireland, Razorbills are the main species in by-catches. In all regions small numbers of other alcids are also taken. Off Newfoundland, birds drowned are mainly puffins but also Dovekies and Black Guillemots, with numbers killed apparently dependent upon bird density in the region of the fishery and the depths to which the nets are set.

3. COMPETITION WITH COMMERCIAL FISHERIES

This century has seen widespread increases in the exploitation of fish stocks by highly developed commercial fisheries (Graham 1956; Hardy 1956, 1959; Cushing 1976). In the North Atlantic these have concentrated upon the larger species such as Atlantic cod, Atlantic herring and Atlantic mackerel and often have resulted in the depletion of their stocks and subsequent decline in numbers. In the northeast Atlantic catches of herring reached a peak in 1965 of 1.3 million tonnes (t) for the North Sea and 2 million t in the Norwegian Sea, but declined after that date (particularly in the latter region) and despite a regulated fishery the spawning stocks have been slow to recover (Cushing 1976; Saville and Bailey 1980). Mackerel landings in the North Sea rose to a peak in 1967 while sprat landings increased rather later, from 1972. West of Britain the catches of pelagic fish only rose after 1960. Those catches, though bearing some relationship to changes in stock size, are also influenced by variations in fishing effort. In eastern Canadian waters, the traditional catch was Atlantic cod, but with declines in this stock during the 1960s, a commercial fishery for capelin started in 1972 and landings steadily increased until 1976 when there was a sudden decline from 326,000 t reported in 1976 to only 11,000 t in 1979. The offshore fishery was closed from 1978 to 1981, although an inshore fishery was allowed to continue (Pinhorn 1976; Nettleship 1977a; Le Messurier 1980; Carscadden *et al.* 1981; Brown and Nettleship 1984a; Carscadden 1984).

While the target of the earlier fisheries were generally above the size range taken by alcids, they may have had an indirect effect on alcid populations since these fish are predators of smaller species such as capelin, sprats, and sandlance which form important parts of the diet of a number of the auk species. The absence of some of this predation pressure may have led to increases in the population sizes of capelin, sprats and sandlance, which in turn would be likely to benefit Atlantic alcids in general. However, the spread of offshore fisheries using seiners, for fishmeal (and taking fish of many sizes and species), and increasing emphasis since the late 1950s on the smaller species, pose serious threats to alcid populations. The main industrial fisheries are in the North Sea (sandlance, Norway pout and sprat), the north Norwegian and Barents Seas (capelin) and off eastern Newfoundland (capelin), and all of these have likely come into direct competition with alcids.

During the 1950s young herring formed the main food of Atlantic Puffin chicks on Lovunden in west Norway (Myrberget 1962). However, since the collapse in the herring stocks (abrupt decline in 1969 so that the average catch in the 1970s was only 3% of that in the previous decade— Anonymous 1962, 1963–1972), few herring have been brought to young puffins, Razorbills or murres on Røst, Lofoten Islands (150 km north of Lovunden). From 1969 to the present, widespread breeding failure has taken place on Røst with most puffin chicks starving to death (with the exception of 1974 and 1983 when breeding success was normal and sandlance, young mackerel and herring were fed to the chicks: Tschanz 1979a; Lid 1981; F. Mehlum, personal communication). So far, those breeding failures have not resulted in a measurable decline in the population size of puffins on Røst (owing to insufficient data prior to 1969). However, the almost complete lack of immatures in the population indicates that recruitment to the population is virtually zero (Lid 1981; Barrett and Vader 1984), and unless there is a change in circumstances, we can expect to see a marked decline when the adults in the population reach maximum longevity. Similar partial or complete breeding failures in the Common Murre and Atlantic Puffin (and Black-legged Kittiwake) populations have taken place on Rundøy in southwest Norway, and this is also presumed to be due to the lack of herring, their main prey, in the area. Since 1978, however, there have been reports of large stocks of sprats, sandlance and haddock as well as a slight increase in herring stocks along the southwest coast of Norway, and those may have resulted in the improvement in breeding success of seabirds recently observed on Rundøy (A. Folkestad, in preparation; Barrett and Vader 1984). In northern Norway, the alcid populations show no sign of low breeding success and are increasing. This is attributed to the availability of other fish prey species during the breeding season, particularly capelin which comprise the main item in the diet of puffin and murre chicks in this region (Barrett and Vader 1984).

On the southeast coast of Newfoundland, the inshore capelin fishery has increased sharply since 1978, after regulations were imposed on the offshore fishery to allow stocks to recover from over-exploitation. In the summer of 1981, puffins on Great Island, the largest colony of this species in North America, experienced a serious breeding failure with many chicks starving to death and others fledging significantly underweight (Homer 1982; W.G.A.S. 1982; Brown and Nettleship 1984a). Diet of the chicks which normally comprised capelin was made up mainly of small gadoid fish, and chick meals were fewer in number and smaller in size than in previous years (Nettleship 1972, and in preparation); Common Murres and Razorbills may have been similarly affected (Brown and Nettleship 1984a). In 1982, 1983, and 1984, however, production and condition of young puffins at fledging have been similar to those recorded in 1967 through 1969 (Nettleship 1972), although numbers of adult puffins attending the colony have continued to decline (D. N. Nettleship, unpublished observations).

Recently, attention has been directed at the possible impact of fisheries upon the seabird community, using bioenergetic models (see, e.g., Wiens and Scott 1975; Wiens *et al.* 1984; Furness 1977, 1978b, 1982, 1984). Application of these models suggested that seabirds were serving an important (sometimes controlling) role in the marine energy web with, for example, the five main seabird communities in Shetland requiring 20–35% of annual food-fish production (Furness 1978b; but see Bourne 1983 for reinterpretation of data). Bailey and Hislop (1978) on the basis of figures for annual production of sprats and sandlance and mortality due to fisheries in the Shetland–Orkney region estimated that seabirds take only 5–10% of the natural mortality, but their calculations also depend upon very imprecise estimates. Clearly we need to improve our estimates for a number of parameters—fish abundance and production, and mortality due to seabirds, and other factors, with break-downs according to species since changes in the proportions of species could have important effects upon the values obtained. Attempts to model interactions between seabirds, fisheries and other predators are important and should be encouraged; but at present considerable caution is necessary in their interpretation since the accuracy of the data upon which the calculations are based is largely unknown and that could lead to quite misleading results.

Bailey and Hislop (1978) also compared recent trends in seabird numbers with the development of pelagic and industrial fisheries. They considered that there was no evidence for any competitive relationship between them. Declines in Atlantic Puffins and other auks had occurred in western Britain, whereas the major industrial fisheries had developed in the North Sea where Atlantic Puffins, Common Murres, and Razorbills have all shown recent increases in numbers. Nevertheless, we should be cautious before concluding that commercial fisheries had little or no effect on changes in the size of alcid populations in the past. Although auks do not take adult herring, they do take immatures, and when herring are abundant, that age group forms an important part of the diet of young puffins and other auks (Myrberget 1962; Tschanz 1979a; Lid 1981). Over-exploitation by the pelagic herring fishery has probably resulted in a reduction in recruitment of young fish to the adult breeding population. Although this may have been partly compensated for by density-dependent juvenile mortality, there must have come a time when that could no longer offset the high adult mortality and the fish stocks declined. Thus, the general declines recorded in alcid populations between 1950 and 1970 may be attributable to over-fishing (at least in part), but in other cases declines occurred before the pelagic herring fishery could have had much impact (e.g., late 1800s to early 1900s). Alcid population fluctuations do not therefore necessarily match the fluctuations in local herring stocks (e.g., immature herring declined in North Sea areas such as the Firth of

Forth from the 1960s, yet puffins have been steadily inceasing at that location). The recent increases in northern British alcid populations could be due to an increase in sandlance and sprat populations owing to a relaxation of predation pressures from herring, once their populations had declined through over-fishing. Furthermore, we know very little about the diet of alcid populations outside the breeding season, and the effects that reductions in fish stocks might have on their winter survival and ability to reach the condition necessary for reproduction by spring.

Unfortunately, our lack of knowledge of the population sizes of preferred alcid prey since the 1880s will probably prevent us from ever knowing what impact the commercial fisheries have had on auk populations. It is likely that effects would be greater in regions having a more simple food web. This would apply to cold-water systems (both high- and low-arctic zones) comprising much of eastern Canada south to Newfoundland, Greenland, northern Iceland, Greenland Sea, northwest Norway and Barents Sea. In high-arctic waters the primary alcid food is arctic cod whereas in the low-arctic zone it is capelin. In boreal-water regions (northeast United States, Faeroes, British Isles, and southern Scandinavia) there is a much higher diversity of prey species which tends to buffer the reduction or removal of a single fish species, although in the western Atlantic the numbers of alcids present are low. At the present time there is good evidence for negative effects on alcids, particularly puffins in western Norway and east Newfoundland, both areas where the birds appear to be dependent on single fish species (Atlantic herring in west Norway; capelin off Newfoundland).

The development since the 1880s of trawling methods which process fish at sea and the disposal of waste into the ocean as fish offal, have been considered important factors in the increase of scavenging species such as fulmars, gulls and stercorarids. Some of these species may then kleptoparasitise or prey directly upon other seabirds, notably terns, alcids and kittiwakes and so become a direct threat to these birds (Nettleship 1972, 1977a; Nisbet 1973). The possible effects of increases in these species will be considered in the section on natural and introduced predators (Section IV,B,5).

To summarize, there are two instances to date where fisheries may be directly implicated as having a negative effect upon alcid populations (west Norway and Newfoundland), with the threat in both cases being a very recent one. This is not to say that some past status changes may not also be due to fisheries practices, but we do not have the data to test this adequately. Fisheries, particularly for sandlance, sprats and capelin, pose potentially serious threats in the future, possibly more so than any other single factor. Those alcid species most likely to be adversely affected at the present time are Atlantic Puffins, Common Murres and Razorbills. We have insufficient information on the winter diet of Thick-billed Murres to assess how this species may be affected; Black Guillemots and Dovekies are probably little affected at present, either because they do not take the same food exploited by the fishery or because there is no fishery in the region of its breeding colonies. However, since fisheries can have a series of effects upon other marine organisms in the food web besides those directly fished, possible indirect effects should not be overlooked. Any fisheries developments in the future should give careful thought to the possible interactive effects of depleting a particular prey species within a marine food web. [See Beddington and May (1982), Furness (1982) and Nettleship *et al.* (1984) for a review of the problem.]

4. DISTURBANCE AND HABITAT DESTRUCTION

Disturbance by humans or human-made objects such as motor boats, airplanes, etc., can adversely affect auk populations in two ways:

1. On land it may cause fish-carrying adults to feed their young less frequently (which may reduce their growth rates or leave them more vulnerable to predation) or it may cause actual desertion.
2. In the sea it may deter birds from congregating in rich feeding areas or in areas with low predation.

Evidence for either of these is very scanty, partly because of the difficulty of actually monitoring the effects. The increase in tourism and other forms of recreation in coastal regions and on offshore islands must have resulted in increased disturbance to seabird colonies, although its effect is little known. On Bonaventure Island in eastern Canada, the number of tourists (about 100,000 annually—an increase of at least 100% since 1965) visiting the Northern Gannet colony on foot during the breeding season, and the still greater volume of boat traffic is thought to have contributed in a small way to the 19% decline of the breeding population between 1966 and 1976; most of the decrease appears related to toxic chemical poisoning (Nettleship 1975a, 1976b, 1977a). Terns are known to be vulnerable to disturbance at their breeding sites and this has been well documented by Nisbet (1973). Recently there has been an increase in wildlife tours by boat and airplane, often to areas rarely visited by humans, so that seabird colonies there may also be subjected to unaccustomed disturbance.

Many alcid colonies occur at sites undisturbed by humans and this could be taken as the most telling evidence for its negative effects. However, since these colonies were more likely to have been exploited than merely disturbed by human presence, this argument is not so strong.

Where exploitation takes place by the removal of eggs and adult birds, disturbance is almost certainly an additional problem. In northwest Greenland, for example, it was very clear in 1974 that Eskimos and Danes were adversely affecting feeding rates to young Atlantic Puffins, Razor-bills and Thick-billed Murres, and adult attendance at the colony, which was increasing the risk of predation by Glaucous Gulls, Ravens and arctic fox (Evans and Waterston 1976). Thus estimates of the number of eggs or adults taken in a season amount to only part of the damage to those colonies (the actual effects being very much higher).

In southern Norway, human disturbance is considered particularly serious with very large numbers of pleasure craft around islands and offshore skerries, and the collapse of the Common Murre and Atlantic Puffin populations here has been attributed to this (Norderhaug et al. 1977; Barrett and Vader 1984). Habitat destruction has been implicated as the key factor resulting in declines of the Atlantic Puffin along the North Shore of the Gulf of St. Lawrence, and tourism looms as a potential threat to colonies in Witless Bay, east Newfoundland (Nettleship and Lock 1973; Nettleship 1977a). Tourist boats have frequently been observed to disturb breeding murres (e.g., west Greenland and Iceland) by passing close underneath their breeding ledges and by sounding horns nearby. Aircraft (particularly helicopters) flying over or near seabird cliffs during the incubation period of murres may cause a great deal of damage by initiating panic flights of adults which as they fly off may accidentally dislodge their eggs. Disturbance at auk colonies may also leave eggs and young unattended and vulnerable to predation. However, if aircraft flights are regular, it appears that some seabird species will acclimate to them (Evans 1974b; Dunnet 1977), although they may still cause high loss of eggs and young of species breeding in exposed situations at large colonies (e.g., murres on narrow ledges: Nettleship 1977a, 1980, and personal observation; G. L. Hunt, Jr., personal communication).

At the present time there is no evidence that disturbance away from the breeding colony has had any major effect upon alcid populations. One might expect this to occur where boat traffic is greatest and, although general declines have taken place on both sides of the Atlantic in southern populations of the Atlantic Puffin, Razorbill and Common Murre which winter in such areas (e.g., the Gulf of St. Lawrence, eastern Newfoundland, English Channel and southern Irish Sea), all three species are increasing in northern Britain where shipping associated with the oil industry has rapidly increased in the last decade. This does not preclude disturbance at sea from having a negative effect, but indicates that it may not be a primary cause for status changes.

Habitat destruction occurs where breeding or feeding habitats are removed or are modified to such an extent that birds can no longer use them, or when the birds' efficiency is considerably reduced. One such example, referred to above, is the destruction of puffin breeding habitat along the North Shore of the Gulf of St. Lawrence where burrows have been systematically dug up to remove adult birds (Nettleship and Lock 1973). On Sule Skerry, northern Scotland, the building of a helicopter pad within a puffin colony of 60,000 pairs destroyed some breeding burrows (A. Blackburn and D. Budworth, personal communication). Offshore oil drilling operations and the pollution they cause is a special form of habitat modification to feeding areas and will be considered in the section on oil pollution.

We should not underestimate the possible harm that biologists themselves may cause at seabird breeding colonies, inadvertently affecting feeding rates and growth rates of young by their disturbance. The damage may be greatest to terns and gulls, but auks are also vulnerable. Adverse effects on breeding success (through desertions) of Atlantic Puffins (Lockley 1934; Nettleship 1972), and growth rates of young Common Murres (Harris and Wanless 1985) and Dovekies (Evans 1981a) have been reported by the biologists concerned. One aspect that does need to be stressed is that both between and within colonies, and between species, individuals may vary greatly in their tolerance and susceptibility to disturbance. All seabird biologists should monitor and document the disturbance caused by their own activities.

In conclusion, although disturbance and habitat destruction probably has not resulted alone in overall status changes of any alcid species, their effects may be of local importance and are likely to increase as access to once-remote breeding and feeding areas increases.

5. NATURAL AND INTRODUCED PREDATORS

Alcids face a number of predators besides humans, but in most cases they are distributed in areas where predation is not an important factor. Where predation may cause an imbalance in the population of an auk species, it can usually be attributed to the indirect influence of humans, either by providing food which results in an increase in the predator (e.g., *Larus* gulls, stercorarids) or by introducing a predator to islands previously free of it (e.g., mink, cats, rats).

Gulls suffered human persecution during the nineteenth century on both sides of the Atlantic, and in many areas this is thought to have resulted in the widespread decline observed in many species (Lewis 1925; Gross 1951; Mörzer-Bruyns 1958; Kadlec and Drury 1968; Harris 1970c). However, with the help of protection and the provision of extra food either at sea as fish offal or inland as garbage or rubbish dumps, most gull species have steadily increased during this century to the 1970s, though some populations may now have stabilized (Kadlec and Drury 1968; Drury 1973–1974; Drury and Kadlec 1974; Nisbet 1978a; Chabrzyk and Coulson 1976). In the temperate North Atlantic, the Herring Gull and Great Black-backed Gull probably represent the greatest threat among gull species to alcids, to be replaced by the Glaucous and Iceland Gulls in arctic regions. Their damage ranges from the taking of eggs and young, predation on adults, kleptoparasitism of food-carrying adults, and displacement of potential breeding birds from suitable nesting habitat (Nettleship 1972, 1975b, 1977a; Nisbet 1973; Drury 1973–1974; Evans 1975). Although Common and Thick-billed Murres, Razorbills and Black Guillemots are not exempt from Herring and Great Black-backed Gulls, it is the Atlantic Puffin which is usually reported as the species most affected. This is probably due to its nesting habitat being on sloping ground compared with the vertical cliffs used by Common and Thick-billed Murres and often the other species noted above. The result of this is that puffins have more difficulty in taking off and are more vulnerable to attack. They may also be taken by surprise on emergence from their breeding burrows. In the northeast Atlantic, usually only a very small proportion of a gull colony (usually pairs away from the main colony area) is responsible for predation and kleptoparasitism, the rest feeding mainly upon surface-shoaling fish, and offal (Evans 1975; Beaman 1978). However, in the northwest Atlantic, Nettleship (1972, 1975b) has reported a much greater impact by Herring Gulls at the largest puffin colonies in North America. On North Rona and St. Kilda (Scotland) and Great Island (Newfoundland), puffins nesting on flattish ground experienced greater predation or kleptoparasitism, and their colonies showed higher proportions of unoccupied burrows (Nettleship 1972; Evans 1975, and personal observation; Harris 1980). There appears to be little relationship between the number of gulls breeding at a site and the intensity of food-robbing and predation of puffins. The size of the breeding puffin population appears to have a greater effect on the number predated than the number of gulls present, but other factors such as alternative seabird species (e.g., kittiwake), and other food prey (notably shoaling fish), as well as weather conditions which could affect feeding at sea, may play important roles.

   Although in any one season puffin mortality attributable to gull predation (mainly by Great Black-backed Gulls) at the breeding colony has been estimated at 1.5 to 3% of the adult population at St. Kilda and North Rona, north Scotland (Evans 1975; Beaman 1978; Harris 1980), there seems to be little relationship between the timing of major declines of puffins at these sites and increases in the gull populations there. For example, on both St. Kilda and North Rona, puffins declined most markedly before the 1950s whereas Great Black-backed Gulls were present in very low numbers until after this time. It is possible that gulls at low population size cause relatively more damage than do larger populations since they tend to nest solitarily and may also have more difficulty finding alternative food. However, their overall effect upon puffin populations in the British Isles is in most cases thought not to be significant (Taylor 1982).

Farther north in arctic regions, populations of Glaucous and Iceland Gulls show little sign of major increases, and predation levels probably have remained fairly constant since the mid-1960s. Great Skuas and Parasitic Jaegers, however, have shown most increases, particularly in the northeast Atlantic (British Isles: Cramp *et al.* 1974; Everett 1982; O'Donald 1983; Norway: Vader 1980). The Parasitic Jaeger is primarily a kleptoparasite of puffins, kittiwakes and Arctic Terns, but together with the Great Skua will also prey directly upon these species, young and adults alike. All such increases have taken place since 1970 and there are few localities with colonies exceeding 20 pairs (Everett 1982; O'Donald 1983). Although some local damage in the form of predation and kleptoparasitism occurs, mainly to Atlantic Puffins, nowhere is it considered to be responsible for changes of status in populations of any alcid species.

Other natural predators such as Ravens, Gyrfalcons, and arctic and red fox are thought to have little effect upon alcid populations, although they can cause local damage. Breeding colonies of auks generally occur on small islands or stretches of coastline relatively inaccessible to disturbance by humans and by associated mammals such as rats and cats. However, a number of these colonies have experienced introductions of potential ground predators, sometimes inadvertently (e.g., rats and mink) and sometimes purposely to remove other pests (e.g., cats). Those alcids which nest among boulder or vegetated slopes are the most vulnerable— notably the Atlantic Puffin and Black Guillemot. On the Shiant Islands, Ailsa Craig, Puffin Island (Wales), and Lundy in Britain, rats are thought to have caused declines in the puffin colonies there (Lockley 1953a), although in all these cases there is no direct evidence to support this and other factors cannot be excluded. On the Shiants, rats arrived in 1900 but major declines may not have occurred until the 1950s (Harris 1984); rats arrived on Ailsa Craig in 1889 but the most marked decline was not until between the 1900s and 1930s (McWilliam 1936; Baxter and Rintoul 1953); on Lundy rats arrived around the middle of the nineteenth century, but the major part of the decline in puffins was also sometime between the 1900s and 1930s (Lockley 1953a). However, perhaps the most telling indication of rats being responsible for a decline exists on Puffin Island, where puffins were apparently exterminated by rats in 1835, when only 60 years previous they were described as occurring like 'swarms of bees' (Pennant 1778; Price, cited in Forrest 1907). The rats were then said to be exterminated from the island and soon after 1880 puffins recolonised the area, increasing to a peak of 2000 pairs by 1907. However, rats returned in the 1970s and the puffins again declined to the present level of less than 50 pairs (M. P. Harris, personal communication). Finally, on the east coast of Ireland, declines in the puffin colonies on Lambay Island and Irelands Eye have been attributed in part to rats (Harris 1984).

However, we should not necessarily dismiss the lack of concordance in timing between the introduction of rats and the reported puffin declines, since there may be a time lag before rat populations have built up sufficiently to cause extensive damage, and a further delay before a decline in recruitment affects the breeding population size. A number of islands with puffin colonies do nevertheless also have rats without a marked negative effect being noted. These include Great Saltee Island, southern Ireland (Lloyd 1982), and the Shiants which still have very large populations of puffins and rats.

A more recent threat from an introduced mammal comes from the mink which has escaped from mink farms and caused serious harm to Black Guillemot (and Common Eider) populations since the mid-1970s in Iceland and western Norway (Petersen 1981, 1982; Folkestad 1982; Barrett and Vader 1984). The widespread decline of the Black Guillemot in Nordland, Trøndelag, Møre og Romsdal, in western Norway has been attributed to the increase and spread of mink (Folkestad 1982). In this region, breeding colonies of the Black Guillemot have withdrawn to outer skerries or steep-sided cliffs where they are safe from mink. Folkestad (1982) also noted mink predation of puffin and Common Murre colonies, although those were generally rare. Recent attempts to have mink farms on the Shetland and Orkney isles, north Scotland have caused serious concern, but fortunately both proposals were denied permission by the local council. However, continued vigilance is clearly required to minimise the likelihood of mink predation where seabird colonies exist. Despite precautions taken to prevent mink escaping from farms, they have not been successful, and wherever farms exist, feral mink have before long been recorded in the vicinity.

Elsewhere, the introduction of red fox (escaping from fox farms) has caused considerable damage to alcid populations (notably Cassin's Auklet, Ancient Murrelet and Rhinoceros Auklet) in the Aleutian and Pribilof Islands, Alaska (Sowls *et al.* 1978). Although feral cat predation of puffins at Faraid Head, Sutherland, has been observed (P. G. H. Evans, unpub-

lished observations), and they may have taken numbers on Lundy (Lockley 1953a) and other breeding localities in southwest Britain, there is no
evidence that declines of any auk populations have been caused by cats
(unlike the situation on many tropical islands involving other seabirds; see
Garnett 1984; Moors and Atkinson 1984).

To summarize, avian predators such as Great Black-backed Gulls and
Herring Gulls, and mammalian predators such as rats and mink, may
cause local damage to alcid populations, particularly those such as the
Atlantic Puffin and Black Guillemot which nest in flattish or sloping
ground, readily accessible to these predators. Although some declines in
those two alcid species have been attributed to one or other of the above
predators, they are not likely to have caused any of the widespread declines in auk species noted earlier. However, they represent potential
local threats and in this context possible effects should be monitored
carefully. The control of gull populations by large-scale culls at breeding
sites has recently had great success (e.g., Isle of May, Scotland: Duncan
1978), and this should be more effective if their winter food supply is
limited by the introduction of more modern and efficient refuse disposal
methods, as used, for example, in some areas in eastern North America
(Drury and Kadlec 1974).

6. OIL POLLUTION

Pollution of the seas by oil has occurred from the time that humans used
oil to power ships. There is a record of oil pollution in the Caspian Sea in
1753 (Hawkes 1961) but it is likely that except in local areas such as the
Firth of Clyde, southwest Scotland (Anonymous 1876), seabirds did not
suffer from such pollution until the widespread introduction of oil-burning
engines for shipping in the early part of this century. Although seabird
mortality was recorded after a natural oil seep off the coast of California
(Ventura and Wintz 1971), the first serious incident was the wreck of the
Thomas W. Lawson spilling 1500 t in 1907 on the Scilly Isles, off southwest England (Mothersole 1910). Since then there has been a steady
number of oiling incidents in the main shipping lanes, particularly off the
coasts of northwest Europe (Mackay and Harrison 1973; Johnston 1976;
GESAMP 1977; Gerlach 1981; Sprague *et al.* 1982). The total extent of oil
pollution of the world's oceans has been estimated at between 3 and 25
million t per year (Mileykowskiy 1979).

Marine birds are the most conspicuous casualties of oil pollution. Oil
floats on water, where it comes into contact with swimming birds; if it is
liquid it soaks their plumage, destroying their insulation and buoyancy so
that they tend to become chilled and sink lower in the water (Portier and

Raffy 1934; Holmes and Cronshaw 1977). Their increased efforts to maintain their body temperature and buoyancy impose further stress, using up fat and muscular energy reserves (Hartung 1967; McEwan and Koelink 1973); poisoning may also occur if they inhale fumes from fresh oil, or ingest oil after trying to preen it out of their feathers, although the effects of the latter are still unclear (Hartung and Hunt 1966; Clark and Kennedy 1968; Gorman and Milne 1971; Holmes and Cronshaw 1977; Peakall *et al.* 1981).

Experimental dosing of Black Guillemots and other seabirds indicate that even quite small doses of oil (e.g., a single dose of 0.1 to 1.0 ml) can lead to physiological stress, affecting adult foraging performance, and growth rates of young (Miller *et al.* 1978; Butler and Lukasiewicz 1979; Peakall *et al.* 1981). Small amounts of oil (10–25 ml) placed on the surface of eggs is embryotoxic during the first half of incubation (Szaro and Albers 1977; Albers 1978). Transfer of enough oil from plumage to cause mortality has been demonstrated (Albers 1980). Among marine birds, alcids together with other divers, seaducks and grebes are most vulnerable to oil pollution, partly because they spend long periods of time on the seasurface, and dive rather than fly up when disturbed, and partly because they tend to be gregarious, concentrating in particular marine areas.

Most incidents of high seabird mortality attributable to oil have occurred in boreal-water regions (Joensen 1972a,b; Bourne 1976; Andrews and Standring 1979; Brown 1982). This must in part reflect the intensity of shipping in those areas and the coincidence of large numbers of surface-diving birds. However, it may also relate to sea-surface temperatures, since oil loses its more volatile and soluble toxic components more quickly in warmer waters, to form a solid inert residue which is apparently less damaging to birds (Bourne 1974; Bourne and Bibby 1975).

Although it is the major oil spills such as the *Torrey Canyon* (1967), *Arrow* (1970), *Amoco Cadiz* (1978), *Kurdistan* (1979), and *Esso Bernicia* (1979), which hit the headlines, the majority of oil-induced seabird mortality probably results from the routine and deliberate discharge of black fuel oils and crude oil from the tanks of oil-fired vessels and oil tankers (Bourne 1976; Andrews and Standring 1979). A review of the major incidents of mortality of seabirds at sea in the North Atlantic is given in Table 10.3. These figures show that a high proportion of the incidents could not be attributed to a single source, such as the sinking of a vessel. An analysis by the Royal Society for the Protection of Birds (RSPB) of 46 incidents, reported in British waters between 1971 and 1979, indicated that 63% could not be ascribed to any source other than unreported discharges by ships at sea (Andrews and Standring 1979). Table 10.3 also illustrates how the number of birds affected need not reflect the amount of

TABLE 10.3

Recent Major Bird Mortality Incidents in the North Atlantic[a]

Date	Bird mortality Total number	Bird mortality Number of auks	Location	Cause of mortality (name of vessel when known, in case of oil spill)	Amount of oil spilled (t)	References
Jan. 1966	805	627	N.E. Britain	?	?	Bourne (1969, 1976)
Sept. 1966	2,772	5	Medway (Kent), England	*Seestern*	1,700	Bourne (1969, 1976)
Jan.–March 1967	1,000	0	Lancashire, England	?	?	Bourne (1969, 1976)
March 1967	9,851	ca. 9,650	Cornwall, England, and France	*Torrey Canyon*	119,000	Bourne (1969, 1976); Gill et al. (1967)
Feb.–March 1968	1,368	5	Tayside, Scotland	*Tank Duchess*	?	Bourne (1969, 1976)
Feb. 1969	14,564	476	Netherlands	?	?	Swennen and Spaans (1970)
Feb. 1969	10,000	0?	Kattegat, Denmark	Oil	?	Joensen (1972a)
May 1969	4,407	4,175	Irish Sea, Britain	*Hamilton Trader*	700	T. J. Stowe, personal communication
Sept.–Oct. 1969	12,000	ca. 2,000	Irish Sea, Britain	Bad weather, starvation, oil	?	Holdgate (1971)
Dec. 1969	5,000	0?	Kattegat, Denmark	Oil	?	Joensen (1972a)
Jan.–Feb. 1970	12,856	8,264	N.E. Britain	Probably oil	?	Greenwood et al. (1971)
Feb. 1970	12,000	0?	Kattegat, Denmark	Oil	?	Joensen (1972a)
Feb. 1970	>5,500	82	Newfoundland, Canada	*Irving Whale*	27	Brown et al. (1973)
Feb.–May 1970	>7,100	652	Nova Scotia, Canada	*Arrow*	9,000	Brown et al. (1973)
Nov. 1970	3,150	3,000	Cornwall, England	?	—	Stowe and Underwood (1985)
Dec. 1970	15,000	0?	Kattegat, Denmark	Oil	?	Joensen (1972a)
Jan. 1971	>500	'Mainly auks'	Dorset, England	?	?	T. J. Stowe, personal communication
Jan. 1971	528	'Mainly auks'	Dorset, England	?	?	T. J. Stowe, personal communication
May–June 1971	1,102	1,035	Shetland, Scotland	Probably oil	?	T. J. Stowe, personal communication; Andrews and Standring (1979)
March 1972	>30,000	0?	Kattegat, Denmark	Oil	?	Joensen and Hansen (1977)
Dec. 1972	>30,000	0?	Waddensea, Denmark	Oil	?	Joensen and Hansen (1977)
Jan.–Feb. 1974	2,140	1,170	Irish Sea, Britain	?	—	T. J. Stowe, personal communication; Andrews and Standring (1979)
Nov. 1975	>800	0	Lancashire, England	*Victorious Coloctronis*	?	T. J. Stowe, personal communication; Andrews and Standring (1979)
Jan. 1976	1,644	ca. 1,500	Northumberland, England	?	?	T. J. Stowe, personal communication; Andrews and Standring (1979)
Feb. 1977	513	364	Highlands, Scotland	*HMS Vulcan*	?	T. J. Stowe, personal communication; Andrews and Standring (1979)
Feb. 1977	920	920	Humberside, England	?	?	T. J. Stowe, personal communication; Andrews and Standring (1979)
April 1977	1,455	1,455	Humberside, England	?	?	T. J. Stowe, personal communication; Andrews and Standring (1979)

Date			Location			Source
Jan. 1978	5,044	4,228	Northumberland, England		?	T. J. Stowe, personal communication; Andrews and Standring (1979)
Feb. 1978	802	178	Lothian–Fife, Scotland	ICI fertiliser plant	?	T. J. Stowe, personal communication; Andrews and Standring (1979)
March 1978	4,572	3,100	N.W. Britanny, France; Channel Islands	*Amoco Cadiz*	220,000	Andrews and Standring (1979)
Oct. 1978	2,541	2,182	S. Wales–Devon, Britain	*Christos Bitas*	?	Andrews and Standring (1979)
Dec. 1978	573	448	Orkney–Highland, Scotland		?	T. J. Stowe, personal communication; Andrews and Standring (1979)
Nov. 1978	5,000	?	Kattegat, Sweden		?	T. Larsen, personal communication
Jan. 1979	35,100	0?	Kattegat, Denmark		?	Clausager (1979)
Jan. 1979	3,704	1,064	Shetland, Scotland	*Esso Bernicia*	?	T. J. Stowe, personal communication; Andrews and Standring (1979)
Jan. 1979	923	869	Galicia, Spain	*Andros Patria*	?	Seccion de Ornitoloxia (1979)
Feb. 1979	6,000	?	Latvia–Baltic Sea–Russia–Sweden	Oil	?	Lloyds List (31/3/79)
Feb. 1979	504	465	Orkney, Scotland		?	T. J. Stowe, personal communication; Andrews and Standring (1979)
Feb. 1979	1,765	1,459	Shetland, Scotland		?	T. J. Stowe, personal communication; Andrews and Standring (1979)
March 1979	>2,600	1,872	Cape Breton, Nova Scotia, Canada	*Kurdistan*	7,500	Brown (1982)
March 1979	5,000	'Mainly auks'	Varanger, Norway	Oil	?	Barrett (1979)
April 1979	792	661	Orkney–Highland, Scotland		?	T. J. Stowe, personal communication; Andrews and Standring (1979)
Dec. 1979–Jan. 1980	2,990	2,056	Cornwall, England		?	T. J. Stowe, personal communication
March 1980	2,122	1,735	Northumberland, England		?	T. J. Stowe, personal communication
Jan. 1981	1,615	1,527	Norfolk, England	*Ems*	?	T. J. Stowe, personal communication
Jan. 1981	>8,500	'Many auks'	Netherlands, Belgium, France	Oil and weather	?	T. J. Stowe, personal communication; Mead (1981)
Jan. 1981	45,000	'Mainly auks'	Skaggerak, Denmark–Sweden–Norway	Oil	?	Mead (1981); N. Røv, personal communication
Jan. 1981	1,500–2,000	'Few auks'	W. Denmark	Oil	?	N. Røv, personal communication
March 1981	10,000	0?	Helgeland, Norway		?	R.S.P.B. (1981)
Dec. 1981–Jan. 1982	1,126	1,001	E. England		?	T. J. Stowe, personal communication
Dec. 1981–Feb. 1982	850	746	S. Devon, England		?	T. J. Stowe, personal communication
March 1982	745	709	N.E. Grampian, Scotland		?	T. J. Stowe, personal communication
Feb. 1983	34,026	31,643	E. Britain	Bad weather, starvation	—	T. J. Stowe, personal commnication

[a] Involving at least 500 birds.

oil released into the sea. For example, in 1970, a spill of about 450,000 gallons of bunker oil from the *Arrow* in eastern Canada, resulted in the death of at least 7100 birds, but a mere 7000 gallons of oil from the oil barge *Irving Whale* killed at least 5500 birds along the south coast of Newfoundland (Brown *et al.* 1973).

Our knowledge of the extent of seabird mortality from oil is dependent upon counts of dead or dying birds ashore. In Britain these beached-bird surveys were initiated jointly by the RSPB and the British Seabird Group in 1966, and modified 5 years later to take the form of systematic national surveys of beaches on five pre-arranged weekends from September to March. Since 1969, counts in February have been extended to other northwest European countries: Denmark, West Germany, the Netherlands, Belgium, France, and more recently including Norway and Spain (Bourne 1976; Andrews and Standring 1979; Stowe 1982b). No such monitoring scheme exists to date elsewhere in North Atlantic countries, although less intensive monitoring after oiling incidents has taken place in eastern North America, notably after the *Argo Merchant* oil spill in 1976 (Powers and Rumage 1978).

Interpretation of results of beached-bird surveys suffer from a number of limitations. The finding of corpses depends upon the accessibility of the shore and intensity of searching; birds may be buried in the sand or hidden among algae and escape attention, or be revealed sometime later (Goss-Custard *et al.* 1977). Furthermore, corpses of some species such as gulls appear to disintegrate more quickly than those of others such as loons and auks (Hope Jones 1980), and oil on corpses may have occurred only after the bird had died [5–7% of corpses estimated oiled after coming ashore for Belgian beaches by Kuyken and Zegers (1968), and between 11 and 52% of corpses used in drift experiments, although this oil may have contaminated the corpses at sea before becoming beached; see Stowe (1982b)]. Probably most important, however, is the unknown proportion of oiled birds which may die at sea but not reach the coast (Tanis and Mörzer-Bruyns 1968; Bourne 1976). The eventual recovery rate with large groups of marked unoiled bodies placed in the Irish Sea away from the coast have varied between 5 and 59% along well-watched coasts (Hope Jones *et al.* 1970; Bibby and Bourne 1974; Bibby and Lloyd 1977). A similar large experiment in the North Sea resulted in only 0.3% being recovered over a long period, mainly along the poorly surveyed coasts and islands of Norway (Bibby 1981). Most of these drift experiments involved gull corpses and it has been estimated that they drift downwind at 2.5 to 4.0% of the wind speed (Bibby and Lloyd 1977; Bibby 1981). Similar experiments need to be repeated on alcids to determine whether they drift in the same manner, and preferably should compare different auk species such as Atlantic Puffin, Razorbill and Common Murre.

Perhaps the most detailed analysis to date of beached-bird survey results has been carried out by Stowe (1982b), based upon an average of 1905 km of coastline walked per count in Britain during autumn and winter between 1971 and 1979, with additional data from the February international counts in other west European countries. Systematic counts were made in September, November, January, February and March with wide coverage over most of Britain, although a greater proportion of the coastline has been surveyed in south and east England than in north and west Scotland. The results of those beached-bird surveys may be summarized as follows:

1. The five most numerous species recorded are in descending order: Herring Gull and Common Murre, followed some way behind by Black-headed Gull, Razorbill and Common Gull (but bear in mind the relative abundance of each species).
2. The proportion oiled is highest in Red-throated Loon (66.8%), Razorbill (60.8%), Common Murre (58.3%), Common Scoter (50.7%) and Atlantic Puffin (47.0%).
3. Densities of corpses and proportion oiled are highest in winter (particularly February) for auks and most other species.
4. Densities of alcid corpses (and most other species) were highest in east Scotland, although the highest proportion oiled occurred between southwest and northeast England inclusive (the regions which border the busiest shipping routes).
5. The highest proportion of beaches recorded oiled were in southwest and southern England, and in February.
6. Regional densities of corpses (but not proportions of oiled birds) were positively correlated with periods of onshore wind prior to the count and negatively with overall national sea temperatures (these results were more clear-cut for east Scotland than elsewhere).
7. Significant increases in auk corpse densities were observed between 1971 and 1979 in parts of northeast England and east Scotland only, whereas the proportion of birds found oiled either remained the same or declined over this period in nearly all regions.
8. When beached-bird data are re-examined incorporating the effects of weather and sea-surface temperatures, any significant trends disappear, both in numbers found and proportions oiled.
9. The number of beaches oiled decreased over the period 1971–1979 in the south and west, but increased in the east and north.

10. About 40% of oiling incidents have occurred in Orkney and Pentland Firth, Firth of Forth—northeast England and east Norfolk, and primarily in winter—the largest incidents (over 1000 birds affected) have all occurred since 1976, with the exception of one incident in northeast England in January to March 1970.
11. Comparing British results with those from other west European countries, alcids were most represented in the English Channel, but also high in the Irish Sea and west side of the North Sea.
12. Overall densities of beached birds in Britain and Ireland were generally lower than those in continental Europe, while the proportion of alcids found oiled was highest in the Netherlands.

These results emphasize the need for careful interpretation of beached-bird surveys. Whereas the observed trends indicate an increase in numbers of corpses along beaches in Britain between 1971 and 1979 but declines in the proportion of birds oiled, those findings can be attributed to the effects of weather. Cold weather appears to increase the density of unoiled birds, reducing the proportion oiled, and onshore winds may increase the overall numbers beached (although there are regional differences). However, the precise effects of weather are still poorly understood. An increase in numbers of corpses may also reflect increased population sizes with mortality remaining constant, and in northern Britain, for example, we have good evidence that many of the alcid populations are indeed increasing (Harris 1976a; Stowe 1982a; Stowe and Harris 1984).

Despite all those qualifications, the beached-bird survey is undoubtedly the best method we have available for monitoring seabird mortality from oil pollution. The results provide a picture of the regional patterns of the occurrence of oiled birds which generally reflects the distribution of shipping intensity. If weather effects are taken into account, they can monitor trends in mortality and oiling with time. They help to identify major pollution incidents, and if combined with corpse drift experiments at the time, together with careful examination of weather effects, they are likely to provide the best available estimates of total mortality. Further information on the age and origin of birds (from banding recoveries) affected in these incidents would help to identify the possible impact to different auk populations.

There has been much discussion as to whether oil pollution has led directly to declines in seabird populations (Tanis and Mörzer-Bruyns 1968; Advisory Committee on Oil Pollution of the Sea 1971–1980; Bourne 1976; Harris 1976a; Joensen and Hansen 1977; Andrews and Standring 1979; Royal Commission on Environmental Pollution 1981). In recent years there are two alcid populations whose declines have been directly attributed to oil pollution: (1) the Atlantic Puffin population on Les Sept Iles off the Brittany coast, which is said to have declined drastically after the *Torrey Canyon* disaster in March 1967 (Monnat 1969; Brien 1970; Bourne 1976; Henry and Monnat 1981); and (2) the Black Guillemot population of Yell Sound, Shetland, following the spillage from the *Esso Bernicia* in December 1978 (Heubeck and Richardson 1980; McKay *et al.* 1981). As Baillie and Mead (1982) have demonstrated, the problem is that the present level of accuracy of our monitoring schemes at breeding colonies is insufficient to detect even quite extensive mortality from oiling unless it persists over a number of years, particularly since most birds dying from oil appear to be immatures. However, the indications are that there has been continued mortality from oiling over and above natural mortality from other sources, particularly in the southern North Sea and English Channel since about 1915, with the problem apparently increasing as shipping increased. The detailed review in Chapter 2 of this volume and summary earlier in this chapter of status changes of auks indicate general declines in all temperate regions of the North Atlantic of the Razorbill, Common Murre and Atlantic Puffin from at least the middle of the last century until the early part of this century. Those declines, though checked or even reversed since then in many northern parts of the species' breeding range on both sides of the Atlantic, have shown little recovery in southern areas. The majority of Razorbill and Common Murre populations winter south of their breeding quarters (see Chapter 9, this volume). In the northeast Atlantic they concentrate in the North Sea, English Channel and Bay of Biscay, with more northerly populations tending to winter farthest north and breeding adults dispersing shorter distances from their colonies. Thus the wintering populations coincide to a large extent with those areas receiving most chronic pollution. Adult birds of at least the more southerly populations on the northeast side of the Atlantic should be the most affected, since immatures are usually wintering farther south.

However, if oil pollution is responsible for these declines, other factors are probably also important. The lack of recovery in the southern populations is explicable if oil is an important mortality factor, but most of the populations farther north (on both sides of the Atlantic in northern boreal, low- and high-arctic waters) are presently stable or increasing (with the exception of Thick-billed Murres where over-exploitation and incidental kills in fishing nets almost certainly account for their declines). There are three possible explanations (excluding that oil is not involved):

1. The wintering areas of these populations are more dispersed and generally north of the main areas of chronic pollution (with adults

less vulnerable than juveniles, since the latter are more likely to winter in polluted areas).

2. There is a density-dependent effect such that increased breeding productivity at lower population levels has compensated for increased mortality by relaxed competition.

3. Survival and/or productivity of food fish has increased in these areas.

The first of these, though correct, does not explain why the populations continued to decline in the first half of this century, unless the wintering areas have shifted either as a response to changing food availability in winter or to avoid increased shipping and associated pollution. We have no information at present to test this adequately, but there is certainly evidence that adult auks have shown an increasing tendency to return to their breeding cliffs early in the northeast Atlantic, during the winter, while most of the declines at northern colonies in Britain during the last century may be attributed to human exploitation.

There is circumstantial evidence to support the second and third explanations. Populations in northern and western Britain and Ireland are almost certainly much smaller than they were at the turn of the century, while total numbers have since the 1880s always been much higher than in southern and southeast regions. If seabirds (particularly alcids) take anything like the proportion of available fish (19–29%) estimated by recent studies (Furness 1978b, 1982—although, as noted earlier, this has been questioned), then one might expect a density-dependent effect through competition for food. However, since we have no information on the relative quantities of available food in the two regions, it is difficult to draw any conclusions about competition or its effects. Finally, over-exploitation of predatory fish such as herring during the first half of this century, or climatic change, may be responsible for increases in numbers of sandlance and sprats in north and northwest Britain, which form an important part of the diet of Razorbills, Common Murre and Atlantic Puffin (Furness 1978b; Harris and Hislop 1978; Sherman et al. 1981). However, as before, we have insufficient data on sprat or sandlance numbers (either past or present) and no information on possible changes in productivity for any alcid population in this region.

Another difficulty for attributing twentieth-century auk population declines primarily to oil-induced mortality is the fact that the Atlantic Puffin has declined in parallel with the Razorbill and Common Murre, but is only poorly represented among beached birds. If puffin concentrations coincide with inshore pollution incidents, we know that they are vulnerable to oiling. [See Seccion de Ornitoloxia 1979 for an account of mortality of 900

birds, 90% of which were Atlantic Puffins; also Hope Jones *et al.* (1978) re
Amoco Cadiz incident.] A high proportion of beached Atlantic Puffins are
indeed oiled (Stowe 1982b), but our present knowledge indicates that the
puffin usually disperses over large areas in winter in contrast to the other
two species. Again, we cannot distinguish between a possible lower vulnerability to oiling and a lower recovery rate of dead birds to account for
the relatively low numbers of puffins found dead during beached-bird
surveys. At this point it may be pertinent to note that few puffins were
found dead after the *Torrey Canyon* disaster despite a number of southern
colonies, notably Les Sept Iles, Brittany, showing marked declines immediately after.

To summarize, oil pollution can, and indeed does, cause mortality of
auks, particularly in winter; Common Murres and Razorbills are apparently the most affected. This may be due to the lower probability of
finding corpses or to the lower vulnerability to oiling of other species
(Atlantic Puffins and Black Guillemots being dispersed over wide areas in
winter, while Dovekies and Thick-billed Murres generally winter away
from heavily polluted areas; however, when oiling occurs, large numbers
may die, viz. Varangerfjorden, Norway; see Barrett 1979). This mortality
may in part be responsible for the widespread declines in alcid populations during this century, although other factors such as increased food
availability in northern populations could complicate the picture and account for the present regional differences in changes of status. We have
insufficient data to examine these influences critically or to determine
whether the similar decline in Atlantic Puffins might have been due to oil.

Much of this section has concentrated upon the areas of the northeast
Atlantic and North Sea around Britain and Ireland, and continental western Europe. This is partly due to the resulting greater attention paid to the
problem. Recently, however, the oil industry has focused its attention
upon other areas, notably in the northwest Atlantic, arctic Canada and
east Newfoundland. As has occurred in the northern North Sea, this will
result in an increase in the probability of oil spillage not only from rig
blow-outs but more importantly also from associated shipping transport.
Furthermore, oil spilled in these cold polar waters will remain liquid for
longer periods instead of becoming tar balls relatively harmless to birds
(Bourne and Bibby 1975; Vandermeulen 1980); auk concentrations in
summer may therefore be more vulnerable than those in more temperate
regions. Oil frozen into sea ice and released later during the thaw will also
prolong the effects of a spill. Combined with the present large size of the
breeding populations in those regions, concentrated at a few very large
colonies in summer and localised areas in winter, and the difficult weather
conditions which may change suddenly for the worse, these pose major

threats to a number of alcid species. From present experience with North Sea oil developments (Dunnet 1974, 1980; Bourne 1976; Andrews and Standring 1979), we can expect heavy mortality of auks, although as yet we cannot determine the extent to which it might cause population declines.

Whatever the long-term impact of oil pollution upon alcid populations, every effort should be made to minimise it. This requires much tighter legislation than we have at present, at both national and international levels, with schemes developed whereby violators pay heavily for their pollution and are held responsible for clean-up operation costs (Nettleship 1977a; Nisbet 1979). A continuation and expansion of vigilance through ever more refined monitoring schemes (breeding population changes, and beached-bird surveys) is essential. Efforts to rehabilitate oiled seabirds, though very worthy, have not been shown to be very successful (Clark and Kennedy 1968). Measures to prevent mortality by chemical dispersion, protection by the use of booms, and the scaring of birds from the path of oil slicks (Koski and Richardson 1976; Bourne 1976; Andrews and Standring 1979) are also likely to be of limited value. If we are to reduce the amount of seabird mortality from oiling, we must first and foremost reduce the amount of oil spilled. This can only be achieved by governments attaching greater importance to the problem than they do at present, providing more investment in research and development of preventative oil pollution systems, and improving anti-pollution controls by legislation and education.

7. CHEMICAL POISONING

During the late 1940s, chlorinated hydrocarbon insecticides were introduced into the environment in North America and northern Europe as sprays and dressings to combat the damage to forests and crops by insect pests. Soon after, it became apparent that these insecticides were killing non-target species, particularly seed-eating landbirds and their predators (R.S.P.B. 1962; Borg et al. 1969; Moriarty 1975). Widespread declines in a number of raptor species, due largely to pesticide-induced effects on reproduction rather than direct mortality, were documented by the late 1960s (Hickey 1969; Ratcliffe 1970; Moriarty 1972; Stickel 1973). At the same time, residues were detected in the eggs of British seabirds (Moore and Tatton 1965) and relatively high levels in birds and their eggs in both the Arctic (Bogan and Bourne 1972) and Antarctic (Sladen et al. 1966; George and Frear 1966; Tatton and Ruzicka 1967), thousands of miles from industrialised areas, highlighted their widespread dispersal in the marine environment (see also Risebrough 1969; Pearce et al. 1973). In autumn 1969, a large wreck of seabirds, mostly Common Murres and Razorbills, occurred in the Irish Sea and post-mortem analyses revealed very high levels (up to 800 ppm) of polychlorinated biphenyls (PCBs) in the livers of some of the corpses (Holdgate 1971; Parslow and Jefferies 1973), as was the case with massive kills of murres off California in 1969 (Scott *et al.* 1975). The mobilization of fat containing these PCBs may have been encouraged by starvation after a period of bad weather, so that their deaths were probably not directly due to PCBs. However, this incident served to draw attention to the increasing presence in animal tissues of PCBs, which had been introduced for a variety of industrial uses in the 1930s. These also received wide distribution, occurring throughout the world, even in the Antarctic (Bourne and Bogan 1972; Risebrough and Carmignani 1972). Recent reviews of levels of pollutants and their effects upon seabirds are given by Ohlendorf *et al.* (1978) for North America and N.E.R.C. (1983) for Britain and Ireland.

There is only one well-documented case of the decline of a seabird population which can be attributed to toxic chemical poisoning. In the Gulf of St. Lawrence, eastern Canada, organochlorine levels in Northern Gannets sampled in the late 1960s and early 1970s were high; the species showed reduced breeding success, particularly low hatchability of eggs, and the population at Bonaventure Island (50% of the North American population) declined in contrast to virtually all populations of this species elsewhere (Keith 1969; Nettleship 1975a, 1976b). Pearce *et al.* (1979) reviewed the data for a number of other species of seabirds in eastern Canada. They concluded that only in the case of Double-crested Cormorants were DDE residues high enough to cause effects on reproductive success via eggshell thinning. Elsewhere reduced growth rates during the early 1970s in populations of Double-crested Cormorants in the Gulf of Maine (Drury 1973–1974) and declines of Common Terns in Long Island Sound (Hays and Risebrough 1972) were believed to be due to the effects of DDE on reproduction, but supporting evidence is more circumstantial.

With increasing attention paid to chlorinated hydrocarbons, analysts also looked more closely at heavy-metal levels in a variety of animal species, including seabirds. Heavy metals tend to be comparatively soluble in water and insoluble in fat so that they are not transported around the body in the same way as organic compounds. They tend to accumulate in some organs more than they do in others; for example: mercury in birds' feathers, lead in bone, cadmium in the liver and kidneys, and mercury in the adrenal glands (Anderlini *et al.* 1972; Parslow *et al.* 1972; Jones *et al.* 1972; Bourne 1976). Essential metals like zinc and copper occur in all tissues, their levels being largely regulated by physiological needs. Some metals can enter the environment from agriculture or industry. Mercury, for example, is used as a seed dressing against insect pests. However, all these metals occur naturally and may be routinely taken up by birds; indeed many, for example zinc, iron, copper, cobalt, chromium, manganese and molybdenum, are probably as physiologically essential for seabirds as they are for other animals (Anderlini *et al.* 1972; Osborn *et al.* 1979). High levels of cadmium in seabirds, particularly Procellariiformes, collected at St. Kilda, northwest Scotland, almost certainly originate naturally, probably from seabed rocks where it is carried to the surface by upwelling ocean currents and then incorporated into marine life (Parslow *et al.* 1972; Bull *et al.* 1977; Murton *et al.* 1978; Osborn 1980). Much of this metal is bound to a metallothionein-type protein which may detoxify the cadmium (Osborn 1978), although its presence in both gonad and pancreas (two organs whose functions can be disrupted by cadmium) may have an adverse effect (Osborn 1980), especially as recent work on kidney ultrastructure has shown that kidney damage occurs in apparently healthy birds from St. Kilda (Nicholson and Osborn 1983). Cadmium levels in puffins sampled at the same time were much lower, although levels were higher at the more pelagic northwest Scottish colonies than those farther inshore (Osborn 1980).

A review of toxic chemical levels obtained from analyses of North Atlantic alcids is given in Table 10.4. Although quantities are often higher from samples collected close to industrial or agricultural activities, this does not necessarily mean that the birds suffer detrimental effects. Indeed, most of those birds were collected in apparently good condition while breeding, and although toxic chemicals, particularly persistent hydrocarbons, may cause sub-lethal effects such as increased eggshell thinning, infertility and embryo death, the levels recorded here are generally much lower than those which have in the past been shown to cause such effects (Ratcliffe 1970; Jefferies 1973; Cooke 1973; Peakall *et al.* 1973; Peakall 1975; Dobson *et al.* 1977). Walker (1980) showed that Atlantic Puffins have very active liver enzymes capable of metabolizing organochlorines, which may help to explain their relatively low levels. Harris and Osborn (1981) experimentally increased levels of PCBs in puffins to far higher than those recorded in normal birds, and yet could detect no adverse effect on survival or breeding.

A comparison of pollutant concentrations in the eggs of Common Murres collected from 1969 to 1972 and in 1980 from a variety of sites in the British Isles showed significant reductions in mercury at the three colonies sampled on both occasions, and in DDE (from the insecticide DDT), HEOD (from the insecticides aldrin and dieldrin), and PCBs for one site, Scar Rocks, which in 1969 to 1972 had among the highest levels of the sites sampled (Parslow and Jefferies 1975; Newton *et al.* 1982). The

TABLE 10.4

Review of Toxic Chemical Levels in Atlantic Alcids[a]

Species	Tissue	Location	Toxic chemical (range of concentrations in ppm)						
			Mercury (dry wt.)	PCBs (wet wt.)	DDE (wet wt.)	Dieldrin (wet wt.)	DDD (wet wt.)	pp′-DDT (wet wt.)	HEOD (wet wt.)
Razorbill	Liver	Atlantic Canada	0.31–0.34[b]	6.16	0.67	0.03	0.06	0.00	0.02
	Liver	Faeroes	4.00–7.5	0.3–1.2	0.04–0.4	—	—	—	—
	Liver	Britain	0.8–1.6	2.7–120	0.18–11.8	—	—	—	—
	Egg	Atlantic Canada	0.01–0.25	6.29–132	1.47–45.3	0.04–0.94	0.00–1.55	0.00–0.30	0.02–0.27
	Egg	Baltic	3.5–6.3[c]	590–1300[c]	—	—	—	590–1600[c]	—
	Egg	Britain	—	—	—	<0.05	—	—	—
Dovekie	Muscle	Canada	—	—	0.013–0.03	0.004–0.01	0.001–0.003	0.002–0.009	0.007
	Liver	Bjørnøya	—	0.70	0.23	—	—	—	—
	Liver	Massachusetts, U.S.A.	—	0.31–3.33	0.42–0.96	—	—	—	—
	Liver	Britain	5.5[d]	0.20–11.4	0.10–1.60	—	—	—	—
Common Murre	Liver	Atlantic Canada	0.14–0.21[b]	—	—	—	—	—	—
	Liver	Faeroes	—	0.6–1.1	0.15–0.23	—	—	—	—
	Liver	Bjørnøya	—	0.8	0.2	—	—	—	—
	Liver	Britain	0.00–23.0	0.0–126	0.3–22.3	—	—	—	0.07–1.2
	Egg	Atlantic Canada	0.08–0.17	0.94–7.0	—	—	—	—	—
	Egg	Faeroes	—	15.0[d]	6.5[d]	—	—	—	—
	Egg	Britain	0.69–9.42	0.26–216	0.55–28.8	<0.05	—	—	—
Thick-billed Murre	Liver	Canadian Arctic	—	0.0–0.92	0.01–0.46	0.00–0.02	0.00–0.01	0.00	0.00–0.02
	Liver	Bjørnøya	—	0.10–0.30	0.05–0.15	—	—	—	—
	Egg	Canadian Arctic	—	0.37–1.26	0.20–0.56	0.01–0.03	0.00	0.00	0.00–0.01
Black Guillemot	Liver	Britain	0.20	0.07–0.20	0.03–0.05	0.01–0.05	—	—	—
	Egg	Atlantic Canada	0.10–0.17	1.62–2.99	0.75–1.27	0.01–0.05	0.00	0.02–0.03	0.01–0.03
Atlantic Puffin	Whole body	Atlantic Canada	0.16	0.35–6.55	0.19–2.13	0.02–0.08	0.00–0.02	0.00–0.03	0.00–0.04
	Liver	Atlantic Canada	—	0.10–0.60	—	—	—	—	—
	Liver	Faeroes	—	0.20–0.70	0.01–0.15	—	—	—	—
	Liver	Spitsbergen	—	0.20–0.50	0.07–0.10	—	—	—	—
	Liver	Davis Strait	—	0.02–0.03	0.01	—	—	—	—
	Liver	Britain	0.06–7.70	<0.10–31.10	0.10–3.42	—	—	—	0.17
	Egg	Atlantic Canada	0.10–0.34	1.48–8.19	0.38–5.36	0.028–0.13	0.00–0.064	0.00–0.087	0.00–0.04
	Egg	Britain	—	—	—	<0.05	—	—	—

[a] Sources: CWS Pesticide Unit's unpublished reports, 1968–1982; Jensen et al. (1969); Bourne and Bogan (1972); Parslow et al. (1972); Dale et al. (1983); Parslow (1973b); Parslow and Jefferies (1973); Andersson et al. (1974); Bourne (1976); Newton et al. (1982); Osborn et al. (1979); Osborn (1980, 1982).
[b] Muscle.
[c] Range of $\bar{x}$ in lipid fat.
[d] Mean value.

declines in pesticide residues were consistent with known reductions in agricultural usage, particularly of dieldrin and aldrin in the 1970s. Declines in PCBs were consistent with restrictions in industrial use, and declines in mercury with its reduction in industrial effluents.

To summarize, present levels of toxic chemicals in alcids do not suggest that these contaminants are having a pronounced negative effect upon the populations of any alcid species. Past declines in alcids cannot be attributed to toxic chemicals since the declines occurred principally before their introduction into the environment. Despite that fact, it is important that levels continue to be monitored in a variety of seabird species (including alcids) in a number of regions to sample varying proximity to the discharge of these chemicals. Insecticides are known to persist in the environment for long periods of time and continue to be used in agriculture in western Europe and North America, despite tighter legislation. The separate lethal and sub-lethal effects of each of these chemicals need to be further investigated in the context of the birds' annual cycle, and a greater understanding is required of their physiological relationships.

C. Relative Importance of Natural and Human-induced Factors in Status Changes

In an earlier section it was concluded that in the southern part of their range on both sides of the Atlantic, the numbers of Razorbills, Common Murres and Atlantic Puffins underwent widespread declines from at least the middle of the nineteenth century (see Chapter 2, Table 2.8, this volume). In some areas at least, these declines have continued to the present day. In the northern part of their range, parallel declines appear to have taken place since the mid-1800s, but in many cases populations in the northeast Atlantic stabilized from about 1920 onwards, and indeed have shown signs of increase since 1970, particularly in the British Isles. These status changes have generally been mirrored across all three species. If auk population changes are generally related to changes in climate mediated through sea-surface temperatures, salinity and periods of westerly winds which influence recruitment of suitable food fish, then we should expect to see similar patterns in three species for which there are some data since the 1880s. We shall examine this with particular reference to population changes in the northeast Atlantic for which there are more data.

Air temperatures in northern Europe were relatively cool over the period 1880–1910 (though slightly warmer than the minimum reached around 1810). There followed a marked increase until about 1950 when the trend was reversed and cooling took place. Smed (1965), plotting sea-surface temperatures around the British Isles from 1880, also recorded relatively cool periods around the turn of the century with distinct periods of warming in the 1930s–1950s; and Bjerknes (1963, 1964) noted corresponding periods of relatively strong westerly winds at the turn of the century but weak westerlies (replaced by southerlies) during the 1930s and 1940s. Thus between 1870 and 1900 Atlantic herring spawning in the North Sea centred upon the east British and Swedish coasts, whereas between the 1920s and 1960s, it switched to the Norwegian coast (and the Faeroes), since when it has switched back again (although over-fishing of herring during the present century has considerably reduced recruitment). In the western English Channel, herring spawning declined between the 1920s and 1930s, being replaced entirely by pilchard, a warmer water species, by the mid-1930s. Although fluctuations in Faeroese and west Norwegian alcid populations appear to coincide with spawning years in those areas, populations in north and east Britain were relatively stable between the 1920s and 1960s, and since 1970 have been increasing, contrary to the above predictions. Furthermore, west British alcid populations should have benefitted from conditions during the 1930s and 1940s, but so far as we can tell, they were undergoing widespread declines at this time (see Chapter 2, Table 2.8, this volume). Whether one compares longer-term periodicities of 120 years' duration, mid-term ones of 50 to 70 years, or short-term ones of 6 to 11 years, there is no obvious general relationship with observed population fluctuations of North Atlantic alcids since 1850. Some local populations (e.g., in the Faeroes) may vary in conjunction with climatic changes that affect fish spawning, but this may be because of their coincidence with particular fish stocks (such as the alternation between Norwegian–Faeroese and Swedish spawning of herring). None of these can account *alone* for the fact that alcid populations almost certainly were much larger in 1850 than they are today, nor the steady declines observed through this century, particularly in the southern regions of their range on both sides of the Atlantic. If cooler periods are likely to provide the most favourable feeding conditions for auks in the boreal zone of the North Atlantic (and farther north so long as it is not constrained by ice cover), then we might suppose that alcid populations would be at a maximum around 1810 (particularly in the northwest Atlantic where temperatures were lowest), or perhaps a bit later if there is a time lag. They would then naturally decline to a minimum during the 1930s with a subsequent increase to a peak towards the end of the present century. Population changes in the northwest Atlantic can be expected to be 10–15 years later than the northeast Atlantic since there appears to be a corresponding time lag in temperature decline. If such a natural fluctuation were operating, the trends observed in the populations of different alcid species must be subjected to additional constraints otherwise they would by now be increasing everywhere in the North Atlantic.

Possibly with a better understanding of the complexities of interacting factors in the North Atlantic marine ecosystems, we shall identify ways in which climatic changes may have played a role in regulating alcid population sizes, but until then we must use the most parsimonious explanations and conclude the following from the available facts:

1. During the nineteenth century, Razorbills, Common Murres and Atlantic Puffins probably existed in much greater numbers than they do now. Declines occurred during that century, although their timing is obscure. One obvious negative factor over this period was exploitation by humans, which led to the extinction of the Great Auk, and in the case of the Thick-billed Murre, almost certainly also plays an important part in their decline in the eastern Canadian Arctic and west Greenland during the present century. It is unlikely that oil and toxic chemicals, predators, habitat destruction or disturbance, drowning in fishing nets, or competition with fisheries were important over this period. Changes in food supply resulting from climatic fluctuations may have contributed to these declines and the indirect effects of the whaling industry may also have had a negative effect (although it is difficult to see how the latter would be mediated).

2. Declines have continued during the twentieth century in the southernmost parts of the range (on both sides of the Atlantic) of the Razorbill, Common Murre and Atlantic Puffin, but in northern parts (Labrador and, later, Newfoundland, in the northwest Atlantic; northern Britain, Scandinavia and Novaya Zemlya in northeast Atlantic) they were checked sometime around the 1920s and since the 1970s many populations here have increased. With the exception of the Thick-billed Murre which is also declining, and the Razorbill and Atlantic Puffin in the western Atlantic, exploitation by humans can no longer be an important negative factor, except on a local basis (e.g., Faeroese murre hunts; hunting of Razorbills, Common and Thick-billed Murres and Atlantic Puffins in Newfoundland and Labrador). Nor is it considered that toxic chemicals, predators, habitat destruction or disturbance, have had more than a local effect, although the Newfoundland capelin fishery may be having a significant impact since 1972. Fishing net mortality, though usually of local importance, almost certainly is partly responsible for the decline of the Thick-billed Murre in west Greenland and Arctic Canada. On the other hand, oil pollution since the mid-1920s is the most obvious explanation for the continued decline of the southern populations of Razorbill and Common Murre, and may also account for the decline of Atlantic Puffins (although this is less

easily understood). Other factors such as changes in food supply arising from climatic changes and/or intensity of fishing may contribute to these population changes but cannot explain the population changes on their own.

3. North Atlantic alcid populations in the 1980s face the continued threat of oil pollution, while increasing competition with commercial fisheries is likely to be even more important than it is today. Thick-billed Murres continue to be threatened by hunting and drowning in fishing nets (as do some other local auk populations). On a local level, Dovekies and Black Guillemots may be affected by oil pollution and drowning in fishing nets, while Black Guillemots are also particularly vulnerable to introduced ground predators such as mink.

4. Presumably alcid populations fluctuate in the long term along with fluctuations in food supply caused by climatic changes, although the ever-increasing human exploitation of marine resources (both vertebrate and invertebrate) makes it difficult to discern with confidence. If the population is naturally increasing, when humans impose additional mortality, this may be compensated for to the extent that no population decline is observed. However, if humans impose additional mortality when the population is already declining, the result will be a precipitated decline which may endanger species populations both locally and/or over a wide geographic area. This is thought to have occurred when the North Sea herring fishery collapsed and it is not unreasonable to suppose that it may not happen to other marine organisms, even auks.

V. COURSES OF ACTION

A. Education and Legislation

In an enlightened world, we should not need legislation, and the problems we have described through this chapter would be alleviated with better education. This should begin with children in the schools but must also extend to their parents, to industry and fisheries, to politicians, and to aboriginal peoples, preferably with local members of the community providing the teaching. It should include all forms of communications: books, magazines, newspapers, lectures, films, television and radio. Only in this way can we safeguard the health of marine ecosystems and their habitats, and by doing so ensure that the intricate relations among species in such ecosystems are not altered by human activities to cause the reduction or extermination of species and markedly limit our capability both to conserve marine organisms *per se* (including seabirds) and to utilize some of those living resources for human needs. However, if these goals are to be achieved now when they are needed, it will only come by a combined effort through public education, public pressure and the enactment of suitable legislation (i.e., laws, regulations and controls) followed by the initiation or increase in research and management.

Conservationists are rarely legislators, but they may canvass for laws where they are appropriate and necessary. Three areas are recognized as priorities for legislation.

1. OIL POLLUTION LAWS

The need for tighter oil pollution laws and the form that these should take have been presented in detail by Andrews and Standring (1979) for Britain's Commission on Environmental Pollution. Though aimed at preventing pollution in British waters, their recommendations are applicable elsewhere. Those of particular relevance to the international scene include:

1. Attention to the prevention of oil pollution arising from routine ship operations
2. International agreement to prevent discharge of all types of oil and mixtures containing oil from all sources within 100 km of the coast with national jurisdiction extended to 20 km where it is less at the present time (e.g., in the British Isles it is limited to 5 km)
3. International agreement for the mutual application of port–state jurisdiction over oil pollution offences within designated national maritime zones and to consider the implications of joint action against ships of all flags, for the same purposes
4. Establishment of a compensation fund for unattributable oil spills which affect national or local interests, financed at an international level
5. Markedly improved law enforcement at sea with higher detection and prosecution rates of violators, severe penalties and sanctions imposed against ship-owners, and unlimited powers to inspect and arrest ships where appropriate

2. HUNTING QUOTAS

Although there is legislation applied to the hunting of alcids in Canada, Greenland, Norway and the Faeroes, those laws need to be revised with harvest quotas established and enforced. This applies particularly to the west Greenland and eastern Canadian Arctic populations of Thick-billed

Murre which have declined most markedly during this century. The new Game Act in Greenland (Salomonsen 1979c) which, in theory, prohibits shooting at the colonies from 15 June to 15 August inclusive should be extended to 15 September (many individual birds are still present on the cliffs until that time in the northwest; see Evans 1984) and enforced. Important colonies (e.g., Kap Shackleton and Sanderson's Hope in Upernavik District) should receive total protection at all times. Elsewhere most legal hunting occurs in the winter, and although less damaging than when concentrated at breeding colonies, it nevertheless may be imposing severe stress on some auk populations, particularly Thick-billed Murres in eastern Canada (Wendt and Cooch 1984). It is therefore recommended that quotas be imposed on the harvest of birds in Newfoundland and Labrador (Canada), west Greenland and west Norway.

3. FISHING NET LIMITATIONS

Much of the problem of incidental drowning in fishing nets relates to the material of which these nets are made, and the time of day and period of the year when they are in use. Monofilament gill-netting is inconspicuous (particularly at night) and virtually indestructible. Auk mortality occurs when these nets are set near the surface in areas where concentrations of birds occur, particularly when auks are flightless in moult. One way to reduce mortality would be to restrict the periods over which the nets are set. This was done in west Greenland (to safeguard salmon stocks) between 1976 and 1980 with quotas imposed that resulted in the fishery terminating by mid-September, before most alcids reach the area. Unfortunately since 1981 extended fishing seasons have been introduced which has very probably increased the incidental mortality once more. The crucial period of overlap here is between mid-September and mid-October (and later if it were applicable) and the need is for legislation to limit fishing to earlier periods.

In Newfoundland waters, various fisheries operate with most incidental alcid by-catch in cod (mainly murres) and salmon (mostly Atlantic Puffin) gill-nets affecting local breeding birds inshore during the summer, but a number of populations do occur offshore between May and December. Although some restrictions have been imposed recently to allow fish stocks to recover, there is increased emphasis on the inshore fishery. It is recommended that restrictions be imposed upon this inshore fishery, particularly during the period May–September in areas within 50 km of major breeding colonies (Brown and Nettleship 1984a,b; Piatt *et al* 1984). Whether or not such a regulation is acceptable to the fishing industry, attention should be paid to developing the use of a net which is more conspicuous to alcids, either by using a material other than monofilament or by attaching warning buoys, particularly if nets are set overnight.

B. Monitoring Systems

If we are to recommend practical ways to safeguard alcid populations, we need first to identify the major factors influencing productivity and survival. This requires schemes for monitoring changes in population size, breeding success, and levels of mortality. Those have started to a varying extent in different countries bordering the North Atlantic. Although in an ideal world we should wish for the most refined scheme developed, this will depend upon the resources of finance and work force available. A priority in one region may be simply to survey remote stretches of coastline and islands for an estimate of initial population size whereas in another region that phase may already have been completed. If so, the priority would then be to set up detailed study plots within breeding colonies and monitor annual changes in the breeding population and their reproductive performance (Nettleship 1976a; Birkhead and Nettleship 1980; Evans 1980).

Ford *et al.* (1982) emphasize in their novel attempt to model the effects of different types of environmental perturbation (in this case, chronic and one-time mortality from oil spills) on the demography of Common Murres and Black-legged Kittiwakes, the urgent need for improved data on a number of population parameters. These include an estimate of the size of the non-breeding part of the population; the movement patterns of individuals as they forage, and the spatial and temporal availability of food to them; the relationships between feeding rates to chicks of various ages and their growth rates and probability of survival; and the degree of density-dependence in various population parameters. With respect to the modelling of the effects of oil spills, Ford *et al.* (1982) highlight four parameters as most important: the mortality probabilities associated with encounters of various spill types by individuals of different breeding status; age-specific mortality schedules characterizing local populations under 'normal' conditions; the rate at which a population responds to a perturbation and regains an equilibrium at-sea distribution; and the effect of a spill on the short-term availability of food. Monitoring during and outside the breeding season are considered separately below.

1. BREEDING COLONIES

Alcids are not easy to count and much attention has been paid to census methods (O'Connor 1967; Cramp *et al.* 1974; Nettleship 1976a; Birkhead and Nettleship 1980; Evans 1980). Many factors affect the numbers of birds counted at a colony and there is considerable literature on the subject (Myrberget 1959b; Corkhill 1971; Evans 1973, 1974a; Lloyd 1973, 1975; Kinnear 1975, 1977; Harris 1976a; Slater 1976, 1980; Birkhead 1978a; Hope Jones 1978; Cairns 1979; Gaston and Nettleship 1981; Harris and Murray 1981; Richardson *et al.* 1981). These include climatic factors such as wind speed and direction, sea conditions and rainfall (which can influence time spent at sea feeding or at the breeding site on land), time of day (since feeding for many species tends to peak shortly after dawn and again late in the afternoon or evening), and time of season (some breeding birds will fail and others may join the colony late). Usually counts of birds (as opposed to nests or breeding sites) include both breeders and non-breeders, and the difficulty is that it is generally not possible to distinguish between the two. Furthermore, the factors described above may cause one (the non-breeding element) to vary over and above the other. Counts of cliff-breeding auks such as murres and Razorbills most closely represent the breeding population when they are made between laying of last egg and hatching of first chick (Birkhead and Nettleship 1980) and around the period of lowest light intensity (dawn and dusk in temperate regions). However, it is often not practicable to expect observers to concentrate their counts at these times, and so it is necessary to calculate correction values (termed k values) obtained by accurately determining the number of breeding pairs spanning the entire laying period in sample areas (N_p) and relating this to total counts of numbers of individuals (N_i). This ratio ($k = N_p/N_i$) may thus be used to calculate the total number of pairs breeding in the colony (Nettleship 1976a), while maximum values of N_i provide an estimate of the proportion of non-breeders. Typical k values that have been obtained are 0.67 (Skomer: Birkhead 1978a) and 0.70 (Baltic: Hedgren 1975) for the Common Murre, 0.75 for the Thick-billed Murre (eastern Canadian Arctic: Gaston and Nettleship 1981), and 0.56 for the Razorbill (Skomer: Lloyd 1976a,b), but it should be emphasized that one needs to calculate k for each colony at the time of counting since that value may vary according to the varying influence of the factors noted above, and these correction factors often can only be obtained by detailed study (Birkhead and Nettleship 1980).

The level of intensity one provides depends upon the time available to the counter, and so recommendations for auk consusing are divided into the following three levels:

1. Whole-colony assessment—a single visit to a colony when initial population estimates are required for remote, rarely visited regions (methods designed to reduce variation in attendance with or without k values calculated)

2. Study plot estimates—counts at selected small sample areas within a colony, preferably repeated several times in one season and annually (these provide a more accurate measure of the population size and may be used to detect status changes over a period of years)
3. Studies of breeding success and adult survival—counts of numbers of eggs laid, young hatched and fledged for sample plots and repeated preferably annually to monitor productivity and, where possible, adult survival also (see, e.g., Birkhead *et al.* 1985b) using marked (Nettleship 1972) and unmarked (Birkhead *et al.* 1985b) breeding birds on separate sample plots

Table 10.5 provides a review of North Atlantic regions already receiving or still requiring attention at each level of intensity.

Monitoring schemes at present can probably detect only gross changes in population status. Richardson *et al.* (1981) showed that significant changes of 8 to 10% in Common Murre populations, but of only 25 to 30% in Razorbill populations, could be detected from counts carried out in Orkney and Shetland in 1976 and 1977. Stowe (1982a,b) analyzed the results of the RSPB's monitoring scheme for the British Isles from 1971 to 1979, following some of the methods described in Evans (1980). He considered that relatively small annual changes (2–3% for Common Murres and 3–4% for Razorbills) could be measured accurately if a minimum of five counts per year were made in at least 4 years, but wondered whether study plots necessarily reflected overall colony change. Harris *et al.* (1983) examined census data from the monitoring scheme set up in Orkney (1976–1980) and concluded that study plots indeed did not always reflect status changes in the colony as a whole. The selection of study plots to be representative of the whole colony is critical if conclusions are to be drawn on changes of the population as a whole (Nettleship 1976a; Birkhead and Nettleship 1980; Evans 1980). It should include areas at the centre and on the periphery of the colony, although it may be that population changes affect the latter differentially. The compromise between number of individuals counted per study plot and number of study plots will depend upon a variety of circumstances (species, colony size and extent, cliff topography, and the time available) and has yet to be investigated in detail. However, preliminary recommendations are for sample size to be a minimum of 50 for the former and 5 for the latter. At present we do not have sufficient information to say whether it is more important to monitor a number of colonies in the region with fewer study plots per colony or the converse, and this too needs to be investigated. When considering burrow- and crevice-breeding alcids such as the Atlantic Puffin and Dovekie, it is necessary to adopt different methods to monitor

TABLE 10.5

Atlantic Regions Receiving or Requiring Surveys of Breeding Populations of Auk Species

Areas currently receiving reasonably adequate attention	Areas requiring further attention
Whole-colony assessment	
Lancaster Sound region, Canada	Greenland
Hudson Strait, Canada	
Labrador, Canada	Iceland
Gulf of St. Lawrence, Canada	
Newfoundland, Canada	Faeroes (except Common Murre)
N.E. United States	
Britain	Jan Mayen
Ireland	
	Spitsbergen
Portugal	Bjørnøya
Spain	
	Murmansk Coast
France	
Germany	Novaya Zemlya
	Franz Josef Land
Denmark	
Finland	
Sweden	
Norway	
Annual surveillance[a]	
Labrador, Canada[b]	E. Canadian arctic
Newfoundland, Canada	Gulf of St. Lawrence, Canada
	N.E. United States
Britain	
	Greenland
France	
Germany	Iceland
N. Norway[b]	Faeroes (except Common Murre)
	Ireland (mainly SW)
	Portugal
	Spain
	Denmark
	Finland
	Sweden
	W. and S. Norway
	Murmansk Coast
	Jan Mayen
	Spitsbergen
	Bjørnøya
	Franz Josef Land
	Novaya Zemlya

[a] Monitoring of seabird numbers on an annual basis over 5 years.
[b] Currently only 4 years, but monitoring continuing.

status changes, and these usually require greater intensity of effort than those required for cliff-breeders. Nettleship (1972, 1976a) in eastern Canada and Harris (1976a) and Harris and Murray (1981) in northern Britain used such methods to good effect to detect population changes for the Atlantic Puffin, and similar procedures need to be adopted elsewhere.

Although greater intensity of effort is required to obtain estimates of both the true breeding population and its non-breeding component (as opposed to the total population comprising breeders and non-breeders) at study locations, and estimates of reproductive output, these are quite essential if we are to understand properly factors affecting population change. At the present neither of those aspects is being monitored to any extent in the North Atlantic with the exception of studies by the Canadian Wildlife Service on Common and Thick-billed Murres, and Atlantic Puffins in Canada, and by the Natural Environment Research Council on Atlantic Puffins in northern Britain. However, even on a small scale, monitoring of this nature would amply repay the extra effort. Without these efforts, it will be impossible to evaluate changes in fecundity or recruitment into the breeding population, or adult survival, and all three are necessary to identify the relative effects of different threats.

2. WINTERING AREAS

The distribution of different alcid populations during winter is best known for the Common Murre and Razorbill in the northeast Atlantic around the British Isles, and the Common and Thick-billed Murres, Razorbill and Dovekie in the northwest Atlantic around Newfoundland. It requires detailed information from studies at sea to identify localities used by auks (e.g., British Isles: Bourne 1976, Evans 1981b, Hope Jones 1982, Blake *et al.* 1983; Canada: Brown *et al.* 1975) and intensive banding programs at breeding sites, preferably to include known-aged birds (e.g., British Isles: Mead 1974, Baillie 1982; Canada: CWS files, Gaston 1980; West Greenland: Salomonsen 1967, Kampp 1982), bearing in mind that birds may breed some distance from their wintering areas (see Chapter 9 of this volume for details). This form of data needs to be collected from other areas (notably Bay of Biscay, north and west Norway, west and southeast Greenland, and central Atlantic) and from other species (notably the Black Guillemot for all regions, Dovekie and Thick-billed Murre for the European Arctic), and even in the better known regions, there is a need for further data with particular emphasis upon the banding of juvenile and adult birds (Kampp 1982).

Our knowledge of the diet of adult auks throughout the annual cycle is very poor (see Chapter 6 of this volume for details) and methods should be developed which will efficiently capture individuals at sea. Preferably an emetic should be used so that birds will regurgitate food remains which can be examined without recourse to killing the birds.

Causes of mortality outside the breeding season can be monitored, including hunting, oil fouling and drowning in fishnets. Systematic surveys of corpses along beaches, as described earlier for the British Isles (Bourne 1976; Andrews and Standring 1979; Stowe 1982b) and also operative now in other west European countries (Kuyken 1978; Stowe 1982b), should be extended to western and southern Norway, and to the western Atlantic, particularly eastern Canada (Gulf of St. Lawrence and Atlantic provinces) and the Gulf of Maine. It requires long stretches of coastline to be walked at least once in February and preferably also in January and March (Stowe 1982b). Counts from September to December may be less useful for monitoring mortality from oiling, but they obviously do provide additional data on natural causes of death. If counts were extended to include July and August, they might give a better measure of juvenile mortality. All oiled and unoiled corpses should be recorded separately, and they should be checked for bands. During analysis, account should be taken of sea-surface and ambient temperatures, the strength of onshore winds, and the fate of corpses on beaches. Corpse-drift experiments, particularly during major mortality incidents, should be carried out to determine the proportion of dead birds recovered on beaches and hence provide an estimate of total mortality.

3. OTHER MONITORING PROGRAMS

Although toxic chemicals, such as insecticides, PCBs, and heavy metals, do not appear to be important in determining status changes of alcids, we cannot be certain this will be the case in the future. Small numbers of individuals (both alive and apparently healthy, and dead) from each alcid species should be collected at regular intervals (perhaps every 2–4 years) from a wide area (encompassing both remote areas and regions close to industry and intensive agriculture). This should be supplemented with experimental studies of sub-lethal effects, and of the relationship between toxic chemicals and the physiology of the bird. Such a monitoring scheme exists in the northeast United States and eastern Canada (Peakall et al. 1978) and in the British Isles (Newton et al. 1982; Osborn 1979, 1980), and there is a need to extend this to west European countries such as Belgium, the Netherlands and Denmark (where already some analyses have been carried out) as well as less industrial areas including Scandinavia, Iceland and Greenland.

Other negative factors also require monitoring, notably the drowning of auks in fishing nets and levels of hunting and disturbance, particularly in west Greenland and eastern Canada. To date there have been few attempts to monitor the effects of these activities (Christensen and Lear 1977; Piatt *et al* 1984; Piatt and Reddin 1984; Wendt and Cooch 1984) and no recent information collected directly from west Greenland.

A major potential threat to alcid populations was identified as the recent increase in commercial fishing (sandlance, sprats and capelin) in areas such as Shetland Isles and Newfoundland. Monitoring fish catches is complicated by variations in fishing effort and efficiency, and is more the domain of the fisheries biologist. However, there is a need to liaise closely with the fisheries to ensure that possible effects can be detected, particularly where fish species far down in the food chain are being exploited (e.g., capelin). This is facilitated if information is available on the localities of fish catches. At present such information is rarely recorded or reported. Obviously there are conflicts of interest here as there were with the monitoring of hunting and fishnet mortality. However, in all cases, there is no reason why ways should not be devised either to allow sustained yields (such as taking mainly non-breeders in hunting activities) or to minimise alcid mortality (such as by making fishing nets observable to auks), or to reduce competition for food either by reducing the fishing catches or restricting the areas over which fishery activities may take place. All of that requires closer contact between the individual interest groups involved and better understanding of each other's requirements.

VI. CONCLUSIONS

At present, approximately 700,000 pairs of Razorbills, 12 million pairs of Dovekies, 4 million pairs of Common Murres, 6.8 million pairs of Thick-billed Murres, 5.8 million pairs of Atlantic Puffins and 270,000 pairs of Black Guillemots breed in the North Atlantic (see Table 10.2 and Chapter 2, this volume, for details). Information is insufficient for Dovekie and Black Guillemot to determine whether they have undergone a general change in status. However, all other alcid species were almost certainly at population levels at least an order of magnitude greater during the nineteenth century than they are today. Declines in these species in the last century were probably mainly attributable to excessive human exploitation (egging and killing of adults). During the present century, the same factor, combined with excessive mortality from fishing nets, has resulted in the continued decline of the Thick-billed Murre. Razorbills, Common Murres and Atlantic Puffins continued to decline during the twentieth century in the southern parts of their range, but in the southern part of the low-arctic (Labrador, Newfoundland) and northern boreal (Iceland, Faeroes, north Britain, much of Scandinavia) marine zones these declines were checked in the first half of the century. Since the 1970s, many of those populations have increased except for Atlantic Puffins in Newfoundland, and Common Murres and Razorbills in the Faeroes. Oil pollution since the 1920s is the most likely cause for the continued decline of the populations of Razorbill and Common Murre, and may also explain the decline of puffins, although this is less clear. Other factors such as changes in food supply (possibly through both climatic changes and over-fishing by humans) may contribute to those population changes.

Today, alcid populations in the North Atlantic continue to face the threat of oil pollution with potential dangers to arctic populations as oil exploration spreads to those regions. In addition, the negative effects of competition with commercial fisheries are likely to be of increasing importance. Although not endangered as a species, the Thick-billed Murre at the present time faces the greatest threats of unnatural mortality of all alcids. Priorities should be as follows:

1. Improve our knowledge of breeding populations of alcids in Greenland, Iceland, Faeroes, Jan Mayen, Spitsbergen, Bjørnøya, Novaya and Severnaya Zemlya, and Franz Josef Land; particular attention should be given to surveys of the Dovekie and Black Guillemot, and to the Razorbill, Common and Thick-billed Murres, and Atlantic Puffin in Iceland.
2. Extend monitoring schemes at breeding colonies to Greenland, Iceland, and Svalbard, and where appropriate, to include Dovekie, Black Guillemot and Atlantic Puffin in those and existing schemes.
3. Introduce into existing monitoring schemes at breeding colonies a sample of sites from which data on the proportion of breeding and non-breeding birds, and reproductive output, can be obtained (starting with, perhaps: two to three sites each in Atlantic Canada and the eastern Canadian Arctic; one site each in west and north Norway; two to three sites each in north, east and southwest Britain; one site in Brittany; and one site on the Iberian Peninsula).
4. Start regular beached-bird surveys to monitor winter mortality in northeast United States (Gulf of Maine), eastern Canada (especially Newfoundland, Nova Scotia, and the Gulf of St. Lawrence), Norway (west and south coasts) and Sweden (south and east coasts), supplemented with corpse-drift experiments.
5. Collect further data on the distribution of birds at sea throughout the annual cycle, in particular to understand better the factors influenc-

ing their distribution and survivorship outside the breeding season,
including:

A. *Important areas where information is most lacking*—the coastal
waters off southwest and southeast Greenland, southern and
western Norway, southern Ireland and southwest England, the
Skagerrak, Kattegat, Bay of Biscay and western Mediterranean;

B. *Other better known areas still requiring further information*—
east Newfoundland, Hebrides, Shetland, Orkney, eastern England, the Netherlands, and Belgium; and

C. *Some additional sampling of more offshore regions*—the North
Atlantic, Baffin Bay and Greenland Sea, Barents Sea, and North
Sea.

6. Examine more closely the extent of hunting and mortality by drowning in fishnets and their significance to populations of Thick-billed
Murres in west Greenland and eastern Canada.

7. Push for stronger legislation on:

A. *Oil pollution*—particularly for the Gulf of St. Lawrence and Gulf
of Maine, English Channel, Bay of Biscay, North Sea and Baltic;

B. *Hunting Regulations*—particularly in west Greenland and eastern Canada, where bag limits do not exist and enforcement of
existing restrictions is poor;

C. *Limitations on gill-net fisheries which cause auk mortality*—by
the introduction of closed seasons and ways to make nets more
conspicuous to the birds.

Often apparent conflicts of interest in conservation are due to a lack of
realisation of the consequences of an action, when that action does not
directly affect those who have initiated it. The history of humanity has
seen a whole series of such misunderstandings—the discovery of a food
resource whether it be whale or seal, seabird or fish, its over-exploitation,
subsequent decline and in some cases extinction. Unfortunately hard economics mean that in a free-trading society it is more profitable to over-
exploit in the short term and then invest the spoils than to regulate one's
harvests for a sustained yield (Clark 1975). Until there is direct feedback
to humans as hunters, developers, and polluters, there will always be this
conflict.

Bibliography

Adams, C. G. 1981. An outline of Tertiary palaeogeography. *In* L. R. M. Cocks (ed.), "The Evolving Earth," pp. 221–235. British Museum of Natural History, London and Cambridge University Press, Cambridge, England.

Addicott, W. O. 1970. Latitudinal gradients in Tertiary molluscan faunas of the Pacific coast. *Palaeogeography, Palaeoclimatology, Palaeoecology* **8,** 287–312.

Advisory Committee on Oil Pollution of the Sea. 1971–80. "Annual Reports." Her Majesty's Stationery Office, London.

Agnew, J. H. 1973. Seabird observations from O. W. S. ships in North Atlantic—1970, 1971. *Sea Swallow* **22,** 20–26.

Agnew, J. H. 1974. Seabird observations from ocean weather ships in North Atlantic. *Sea Swallow* **23,** 29–33.

Agnew, J. H. 1975. Seabird observations from ocean weather ships in North Atlantic. *Sea Swallow* **24,** 27–29.

Agnew, J. H. 1976. Seabird observations from ocean weather ships in North Atlantic. *Sea Swallow* **25,** 15–17.

Agnew, J. H. 1977. Seabird observations from ocean weather ships in North Atlantic. *Sea Swallow* **26,** 14–15.

Agnew, J. H. 1978. Ocean weather ship reports 1976/1977. *Sea Swallow* **27,** 16–17.

Agnew, J. H. 1979. Ocean weather ship reports, 1977/1978. *Sea Swallow* **28,** 19–20.

Agnew, J. H. 1980. Ocean weather ship reports, 1978/1979. Seabirds—narrative summary of sightings. *Sea Swallow* **29,** 14–15.

Åhren, P. M. 1982. "Fåglar i Sodra Halland 1981," Halmstads Ornithologis Klubb, Stockholm. 28 pp.

Ainley, D. G. and D. P. DeMaster. 1980. Survival and mortality in a population of Adelie Penguins. *Ecology* **61,** 522–530.

Ainley, D. G. and T. J. Lewis. 1974. The history of Farallon Island marine bird populations. *Condor* **76,** 432–446.

Albers, P. H. 1978. The effects of petroleum on different stages of incubation in bird eggs. *Bulletin of Environmental Toxicology* **19,** 624–630.

Albers, P. H. 1980. Transfer of crude oil from contaminated water to bird eggs. *Environmental Research* **22,** 307–314.

Alexander, R. D. 1974. The evolution of social behavior. *Annual Review of Ecology and Systematics* **5,** 325–384.

Alexander, W. B. and D. L. Lack. 1944. Changes in status among British breeding birds. *British Birds* **38,** 42–45, 62–69, 82–88.

Alvinerie, J., M. Caralp, J. Latouche, J. Moyes and M. Vigneaux. 1978. Apport a la connaissance de la paleohydrologie de l'Atlantique nord-oriental pendant le Quaternaire terminal. *Oceanologica Acta* **1,** 87–97.

American Ornithologists' Union. 1957. "Check-list of North American Birds," 5th Ed.

American Ornithologists' Union, Baltimore, Maryland. 691 pp. (also 32nd supplement,
    Auk **90**, 411–419, 1973).
Anderlini, V. C., P. G. Connors, R. W. Risebrough and J. H. Martin. 1972. Concentrations
    of heavy metals in some Antarctic and North American sea birds. *In* R. C. Parker
    (ed.), "Proceedings of the Colloquium on Conservation Problems in Antarctica," pp.
    49–61. Allen Press, Lawrence, Kansas.
Andersen-Harild, P. 1969. Nogle resultater af ringmaerkningen af Tejst (*Cepphus grylle*) i
    Danmark. *Dansk Ornithologisk Forenings Tidsskrift* **63**, 105–110.
Anderson, D. W., F. Gress and K. F. Mais. 1982. Brown pelicans: influence of food supply
    on reproduction. *Oikos* **39**, 23–31.
Andersson, Å. 1979. "Natur i Stockholms Lan, 4. Kustfagelfauna." Stockholms Lans
    Landsting, Stockholm.
Andersson, Å. and N. Rosenlund. 1973. Tobisgrisslorna på Hallands Väderö. (The Black
    Guillemots on Hallands Väderö.) *Meddelanden Skånes Ornitologiska Foerening* **12**,
    46–51.
Andersson, Å., T. Odsjö and M. Olsson. 1974. Häckningsresultat hos Tordmule i Stock-
    holms skärgård i relation till aggskalstjocklek och halter av DDT, PCB och kvicksilver
    i agg. (Breeding success of Razorbill in the Archipelago of Stockholm in relation to
    eggshell thickness and levels of DDT, PCB and mercury in eggs.) *Statens Naturvårds-
    verk* No. PM 483, 1–30. (English summary.)
Andersson, M. 1976. Population ecology of the Long-tailed Skua (*Stercorarius longicaudus*
    Vieill.). *Journal of Animal Ecology* **45**, 537–559.
Andrews, J. H. and K. T. Standring (eds.). 1979. "Marine Oil Pollution and Birds." Royal
    Society for the Protection of Birds, Sandy, Bedfordshire. 126 pp.
Anonymous. 1876. Report on "specimens exhibited" at Anderson's University buildings,
    February 27, 1872. *Proceedings of the Natural History Society of Glasgow* **2**, 181–182.
Anonymous. 1958. "Oceanographic Atlas of the Polar Seas. Part II: Arctic." U.S. Navy
    Hydrographic Office, Washington, D.C. 149 pp.
Anonymous. 1962. "Norges Fiskerier 1960," Norges Offisielle Statistikk XII, p. 89. Fiskeri-
    direktøren, Bergen.
Anonymous. 1963–1972. "Fiskeristatistikk 1961–1969," Norges Offisielle Statistikk XII.
    Fiskeridirektøren, Bergen.
Anonymous. 1967. "Oceanographic Atlas of the North Atlantic Ocean. Section I: Tides and
    Currents." U.S. Naval Oceanographic Office Publication No. 700. Washington, D.C.
Anonymous. 1968. "Oceanographic Atlas of the North Atlantic Ocean, Section III, Ice."
    U.S. Naval Oceanographic Office Publication No. 700. Washington, D.C.
Anonymous. 1969. Seabird slaughter. *Sport Fishing Institute Bulletin* **203**, 5.
Anonymous. 1979. "Fiskeristatistikk 1975–1976," Norges Offisielle Statistikk XII, p. 294.
    Fiskeridirektøren, Bergen.
Anonymous. 1980a. "Investigation of the Distribution of Seabirds at Sea," First annual
    report. Nature Conservancy Council, Edinburgh. 88 pp.
Anonymous. 1980b. International Commission for the Northwest Atlantic Fisheries. "Sta-
    tistical Bulletin," Vol. 28 (1978). Dartmouth, Canada.
Anonymous. 1982. Astand nytjastofna á Íslandsmidun og aflahorfur 1982. (The status of
    commercial fish stocks in Icelandic waters and prospects for 1982.) *Hafrannsóknir* **24.**
    (English summary.)
Asbirk, S. 1978. Tejsten *Cepphus grylle* som ynglefugl i Danmark. *Dansk Ornithologisk
    Forenings Tidsskrift* **72**, 161–178. (English summary.)
Asbirk, S. 1979a. A description of Danish Black Guillemots *Cepphus grylle* with remarks on
    the validity of ssp. *atlantis*. *Dansk Ornithologisk Forenings Tidsskrift* **73**, 207–214.

Asbirk, S. 1979b. The adaptive significance of the reproductive pattern in the Black Guille-mot *Cepphus grylle*. *Videnskabelige Meddelelser Dansk Naturhistorisk Forening* **141**, 29–80.

Asbirk, S. 1979c. Some behaviour patterns of the Black Guillemots *Cepphus grylle*. *Dansk Ornithologisk Forenings Tidsskrift* **73**, 287–296.

Ashcroft, R. E. 1976. Breeding, biology and survival of puffins. Unpublished D.Phil. thesis, University of Oxford, Oxford. 246 pp.

Ashcroft, R. E. 1979. Survival rates and breeding biology of puffins on Skomer Island, Wales. *Ornis Scandinavica* **10**, 100–110.

Ashmole, N. P. 1971. Sea bird ecology and the marine environment. *In* D. S. Farner and J. R. King (eds.), "Avian Biology," Vol. 1, pp. 223–286. Academic Press, New York and London.

Audubon, J. J. 1840–1844. The birds of America. First Octavo Ed, 7 vols. New York and Philadelphia.

Austin, O. L., Jr. 1932. The birds of Newfoundland–Labrador. *Memoirs of the Nuttall Ornithological Club* No. 7, 1–229.

Bagg, A. M. and R. P. Emery (eds.). 1961. Regional Reports, Northeastern Maritime Re-gion. *Audubon Field-Notes* **15**(5), 450–453.

Bailey, E. P. and G. H. Davenport. 1972. Die-off of Common Murres on the Alaska penin-sula and Unimak Island. *Condor* **74**, 213–219.

Bailey, R. S. and J. R. G. Hislop. 1978. The effects of fisheries on seabirds in the northeast Atlantic. *Ibis* **120**, 104–105.

Bailey, W. B., W. Templeman and R. P. Hunt. 1954. The horizontal distribution of tempera-tures and salinities off the Canadian Atlantic Coast. *Atlantic Oceanographic Group Manuscript Report Biological Station* No. 518, 1–28.

Baillie, S. R. 1982. Guillemot ringing recoveries: a European perspective. *In* P. Hope Jones (ed.), "Proceedings of the Seabird Group Conference," pp. 17–18. British Seabird Group, Uttoxeter.

Baillie, S. R. and C. J. Mead. 1982. The effect of severe oil pollution during the winter of 1980–81 on British and Irish auks. *Ringing and Migration* **4**, 33–44.

Bang, J. 1968. Tejsterne på Sejerø. *Danske Fugle* **20**, 13–14.

Bannerman, D. A. 1963. "The Birds of the British Isles," Vol. 12. Oliver and Boyd, London. 443 pp.

Bárcena, F., A. M. Teixeira and A. Bermejo. 1984. Breeding seabird populations in the Atlantic sector of the Iberian Peninsula. *In* J. P. Croxall, P. G. H. Evans and R. Schreiber (eds.), "Seabirds of the World: Their Status and Conservation," pp. 335–345. International Council for Bird Preservation, Cambridge, England.

Barnes, L. G., H. Howard, J. H. Hutchison and B. J. Welton. 1981. The vertebrate fossils of the marine Cenozoic San Mateo formation at Oceanside, California. *In* P. L. Abbott and S. Dunn (eds.), "Geologic Investigations of the Coastal Plain, San Diego County, California," pp. 53–70. San Diego Association of Geologists, San Diego, California.

Barrett, R. T. 1979. Small oil spill kills 10–20,000 seabirds in North Norway. *Marine Pollu-tion Bulletin* **10**, 253–255.

Barrett, R. T. 1981. Reported breeding failures in some Norwegian seabird colonies. *Seabird Group Newsletter* No. 31, 6–7.

Barrett, R. and W. Vader. 1984. The status and conservation of breeding seabirds in Nor-way. *In* J. Croxall, P. G. H. Evans and R. Schreiber (eds.), "Seabirds of the World: Their Status and Conservation," pp. 323–333. International Council for Bird Preserva-tion, Cambridge, England.

Baxter, E. V. and L. J. Rintoul. 1953. "The Birds of Scotland, their History, Distribution and Migration," Vol. 2. Oliver and Boyd, Edinburgh and London. 743 pp.

Beaman, M. A. S. 1978. The feeding and population ecology of the Great Black-backed Gull in northern Scotland. *Ibis* **120,** 126–127.

Beamish, F. W. O. 1978. Swimming capacity. *In* W. S. Hoar and W. J. Randall (eds.), "Fish Physiology," Vol. 7, pp. 101–187. Academic Press, London.

Bédard, J. 1966. New records of alcids from St. Lawrence Island, Alaska. *Condor* **68,** 503–506.

Bédard, J. 1969a. Adaptive radiation in Alcidae. *Ibis* **111,** 189–198.

Bédard, J. 1969b. Feeding of the Least, Crested and Parakeet auklets around St. Lawrence Island, Alaska. *Canadian Journal of Zoology* **47,** 1025–1050.

Bédard, J. 1969c. Nesting of the Least, Crested and Parakeet auklets on St. Lawrence Island, Alaska. *Condor* **71,** 386–398.

Bédard, J. 1969d. Histoire naturelle du Gode, *Alca torda* L., dans le golfe Saint-Laurent, province de Québec, Canada. *Etude du Service Canadien de la Faune* No. 7, 1–79.

Bédard, J. 1976. Coexistence, coevolution and convergent evolution in seabird communities; a comment. *Ecology* **57,** 177–184.

Bédard, J. and S. G. Sealy. 1984. Moults and feather generations in the Least, Crested and Parakeet auklets. *Journal of Zoology* **202,** 461–488.

Beddard, F. E. 1898. "The Structure and Classification of Birds." Longmans, Green, London. 548 pp.

Beddington, J. R. and R. M. May. 1982. The harvesting of interacting species in a natural ecosystem. *Scientific American* **247,** 62–69.

Belopol'skii, L. O. 1957. "Ecology of Sea Colony Birds of the Barents Sea." Israel Program for Scientific Translations, Jerusalem. 346 pp. (Translated from Russian, 1961.)

Bent, A. C. 1919. Life histories of North American diving birds. *U.S. National Museum Bulletin* **107,** 1–239.

Bergman, G. 1971. Gryllteisten *Cepphus grylle* in einen Randgebiet: Nahrung, Brutresultat, Tagesrhythmus und Ansiedlung. *Commentationes Biologicae* **42,** 1–26.

Bergman, G. 1978. Av naringsbrist fovorsakade stormingar i tejsterns (tobisgrisslans) *Cepphus grylle* hackning. *Memoranda Societatis pro Fauna et Flora Fennica* **54,** 31–32.

Berland, B. 1971. Piggha og lundefugl med gumestrik. *Fauna (Oslo)* **24,** 35–37.

Bertram, B. C. 1978. Living in groups: predators and prey. *In* J. R. Krebs and N. B. Davies (eds.), "Behavioural Ecology: An Evolutionary Approach," pp. 64–96. Blackwell, Oxford.

Bertram, G. C. L. and D. Lack. 1933. Notes on the birds of Bear Island. *Ibis* **3,** 283–301.

Beverton, R. J. H. and A. J. Lee. 1965. Hydrographic fluctuations in the North Atlantic Ocean and some biological consequences. *In* C. G. Johnson and L. P. Smith (eds.), "The Biological Significance of Climatic Changes in Britain," pp. 79–108. Institute of Biology Symposia No. 14. Academic Press, London and New York.

Bianki, V. V. 1967. "Gulls, Shorebirds and Alcids of Kandalaksha Bay." Israel Program for Scientific Translations, Jerusalem. 250 pp. (Translated from Russian, 1977.)

Bibby, C. J. 1972. Auks drowned in fish-nets. *Seabird Report* **2,** 48–49.

Bibby, C. J. 1981. An experiment on the recovery of dead birds from the North Sea. *Ornis Scandinavica* **12,** 261–265.

Bibby, C. J. and W. R. P. Bourne. 1974. Pollution still kills. *Birds (London)* **5,** 30–31.

Bibby, C. J. and C. S. Lloyd. 1977. Experiments to determine the fate of dead birds at sea. *Biological Conservation* **12,** 295–309.

Bigelow, H. B. and W. C. Schroeder. 1953. Fishes of the Gulf of Maine. *Fishery Bulletin* **53,** 1–577.

Biggar, H. P. 1924. The voyages of Jacques Cartier. *Publications of the Public Archives of Canada* No. 11, 330 pp.

Bird, C. G. and E. G. Bird. 1935. The birds of Jan Mayen Island. *Ibis* **5**, 837–855.

Birkhead, T. R. 1974. The movement and mortality rates of British Guillemots. *Bird Study* **21**, 245–254.

Birkhead, T. R. 1976a. Breeding biology and survival of Guillemots *Uria aalge*. Unpublished D.Phil. thesis, University of Oxford, Oxford. 204 pp.

Birkhead, T. R. 1976b. Effects of sea conditions on rates at which guillemots feed chicks. *British Birds* **69**, 490–492.

Birkhead, T. R. 1977a. The effect of habitat and density on breeding success in the Common Guillemot *Uria aalge*. *Journal of Animal Ecology* **46**, 751–764.

Birkhead, T. R. 1977b. The adaptive significance of the nestling period of guillemots *Uria aalge*. *Ibis* **119**, 544–549.

Birkhead, T. R. 1978a. Attendance patterns of guillemots *Uria aalge* at breeding colonies on Skomer. *Ibis* **120**, 219–229.

Birkhead, T. R. 1978b. Behavioural adaptations to high density nesting in the Common Guillemot *Uria aalge*. *Animal Behaviour* **26**, 321–331.

Birkhead, T. R. 1979. Mate guarding in the magpie *Pica pica*. *Animal Behaviour* **27**, 866–874.

Birkhead, T. R. 1980. Timing of breeding of Common Guillemots *Uria aalge* on Skomer Island, Wales. *Ornis Scandinavica* **11**, 142–145.

Birkhead, T. R. and R. E. Ashcroft. 1975. Auk numbers on Skomer Island. *Nature in Wales* **14**, 222–233.

Birkhead, T. R. and P. J. Hudson. 1977. Population parameters for the Common Guillemot *Uria aalge*. *Ornis Scandinavica* **8**, 145–154.

Birkhead, T. R. and D. N. Nettleship. 1980. Census methods for murres *Uria* species—a unified approach. *Canadian Wildlife Service Occasional Paper* No. 43, 1–25.

Birkhead, T. R. and D. N. Nettleship. 1981. Reproductive biology of Thick-billed Murres *Uria lomvia:* an inter-colony comparison. *Auk* **98**, 258–269.

Birkhead, T. R. and D. N. Nettleship. 1982a. Studies of alcids breeding at the Gannet Clusters, Labrador, 1981. *Canadian Wildlife Service "Studies on Northern Seabirds" Manuscript Report* No. 125, 1–144.

Birkhead, T. R. and D. N. Nettleship. 1982b. The adaptive significance of egg size and laying date in Thick-billed Murres *Uria lomvia*. *Ecology* **63**, 300–306.

Birkhead, T. R. and D. N. Nettleship. 1983. Studies of alcids breeding at the Gannet Clusters, Labrador, 1982. *Canadian Wildlife Service "Studies on Northern Seabirds" Manuscript Report* No. 149, 1–107.

Birkhead, T. R. and D. N. Nettleship. 1984a. Egg size, composition and offspring quality in some Alcidae (Aves: Charadriiformes). *Journal of Zoology* **202**, 177–194.

Birkhead, T. R. and D. N. Nettleship. 1984b. Food intake and weight increments of Common Murre *Uria aalge* chicks: A comment. *Ibis* **126**, 421–422.

Birkhead, T. R. and A. M. Taylor. 1977. Moult of the Guillemot *Uria aalge*. *Ibis* **119**, 80–85.

Birkhead, T. R., J. D. Biggins and D. N. Nettleship. 1980. Non-random, intra-colony distribution of bridled guillemots *Uria aalge*. *Journal of Zoology* **192**, 9–16.

Birkhead, T. R., S. D. Johnson and D. N. Nettleship. 1985a. Extra-pair matings and mate guarding in the Common Murre *Uria aalge*. *Animal Behaviour* **33**, 608–619.

Birkhead, T. R., R. Kay and D. N. Nettleship. 1985b. A new method for estimating the survival rates of the Common Murre *Uria aalge*. *Journal of Wildlife Management* **49**, 498–504.

Bjerknes, J. 1963. Climatic change as an ocean–atmosphere problem. *In* "Changes of Climate with Special Reference to Arid Zones," pp. 297–321. Proceedings Rome Symposium 1961. UNESCO, Paris.

Bjerknes, J. 1964. Atlantic air–sea interaction. *Advances in Geophysics* **10**, 1–82.

Björnsson, M. 1940. "Fuglemerkingar V–VIII Ár." Nátturingripasafuidi Reykjavik Reykjavik. 43 pp.

Björnsson, M. 1941. "Fuglemerkingar IX Ár." Nátturingripasafuidi Reykjavik, Reykjavik. 16 pp.

Blake, B. F., M. L. Tasker, P. H. Jones and T. J. Dixon. 1983. "Distribution of Seabirds in the North Sea." Final report of the Nature Conservancy Council's Seabirds at Sea Team, November 1979–November 1982. Nature Conservancy Council, Edinburgh. 443 pp.

Boertmann, D. 1979. Ornithjologiske observationer i Vestgrønland i somrene 1972–77. *Dansk Ornithologisk Forenings Tidsskrift* **73**, 171–176.

Bogan, J. A. and W. R. P. Bourne. 1972. Organochlorine levels in Atlantic seabirds. *Nature (London)* **240**, 358–359.

Bogorov, B. G. 1946. Pecularities of diurnal vertical migrations of zooplankton in polar seas. *Journal of Marine Research* **1**, 25–32.

Bonner, W. N. 1981. The Krill problem in Antarctica. *Oryx* **16**, 31–37.

Bonnycastle, R. 1842. "Newfoundland in 1842." Colburn, London.

Borg, K., H. Wanntorp, K. Evne and E. Hanko. 1969. Alkyl mercury poisoning in terrestrial Swedish wildlife. *Vitrery* **6**, 301–379.

Bourne, W. R. P. 1963. A review of oceanic studies of the biology of seabirds. *Proceedings of the International Ornithological Congress* **13**, 831–854.

Bourne, W. R. P. 1968. Oil pollution and bird populations. *Field Studies* 2, Supplement 1968, 99–121.

Bourne, W. R. P. 1969. Chronological list of ornithological oil pollution incidents. *Seabird Bulletin* **7**, 3–9.

Bourne, W. R. P. 1971. Influenza virus reappears. *British Trust for Ornithology News* **44**, 4.

Bourne, W. R. P. 1972. Threats to seabirds. *International Council for Bird Preservation Bulletin* **11**, 200–218.

Bourne, W. R. P. 1974. Guillemots with damaged primary feathers. *Marine Pollution Bulletin* **5**, 88–90.

Bourne, W. R. P. 1976. Seabirds and pollution. *In* R. Johnson (ed.), "Marine Pollution," pp. 403–502. Academic Press, London.

Bourne, W. R. P. 1983. Birds, fish and offal in the North Sea. *Marine Pollution Bulletin* **14**, 294–296.

Bourne, W. R. P., and C. J. Bibby. 1975. Temperature and the seasonal and geographical occurrence of oiled birds on west European beaches. *Marine Pollution Bulletin* **6**, 77–80.

Bourne, W. R. P. and J. A. Bogan. 1972. Polychlorinated biphenyls in North Atlantic seabirds. *Marine Pollution Bulletin* **3**, 171–175.

Bourne, W. R. P. and T. J. Dixon. 1973. Observations of seabirds 1967–1969. *Sea Swallow* **22**, 29–60.

Bourne, W. R. P. and T. J. Dixon. 1975. Observations of seabirds 1970–72. *Sea Swallow* **24**, 65–88.

Bourne, W. R. P., J. D. Parrack and G. R. Potts. 1967. Birds killed in the "Torrey Canyon" disaster. *Nature (London)* **215**, 1123–1125.

Bourne, W. R. P., T. J. Dixon and R. Yule. 1970. Note on the occurrence of avian pox in auks, with an appeal for the collection of sick birds and their parasites. *Seabird Report* pp. 52–53.

Bowers, A. B. 1980. The Manx herring stock, 1948–1976. *In* A. Savile (ed.), "The Assessment and Management of Pelagic Fish Stocks," Vol. 177, pp. 166–174. Rapports et Procès-Verbaux des Réunions Conseil International pour l'Exploration de la Mer, Copenhagen.

Boyd, J. M. 1958. The birds of Tiree and Coll. *British Birds* **51,** 41–56, 103–118.

Bradstreet, M. S. W. 1976. "Summer Feeding Ecology of Seabirds in Eastern Lancaster Sound, 1976." LGL Ltd., Toronto, environmental research associates. Report for Norlands Petroleums, Calgary. 187 pp.

Bradstreet, M. S. W. 1977. "Feeding Ecology of Seabirds along Fast-Ice Edges in Wellington Channel and Resolute Passage, N. W. T." LGL Ltd., Toronto, environmental research associates. Report for Polar Gas Project, Toronto. 149 pp.

Bradstreet, M. S. W. 1979a. Thick-billed murres and Black Guillemots in the Barrow Strait area, N. W. T., during spring: distribution and habitat use. *Canadian Journal of Zoology* **57,** 1789–1802.

Bradstreet, M. S. W. 1979b. Feeding ecology of seabirds in northwest Baffin Bay, 1978. Unpublished report by LGL Ltd., Toronto, for Petro-Canada Exploration, Calgary. 65 pp.

Bradstreet, M. S. W. 1980. Thick-billed Murres and Black Guillemots in the Barrow Strait area, N. W. T., during spring: diets and food availability along ice edges. *Canadian Journal of Zoology* **58,** 2120–2140.

Bradstreet, M. S. W. 1982a. Pelagic feeding ecology of dovekies *Alle alle* in Lancaster Sound and western Baffin Bay. *Arctic* **35,** 126–140.

Bradstreet, M. S. W. 1982b. Occurrence, habitat use and behavior of seabirds, marine mammals and arctic cod at the Pond Inlet ice edge. *Arctic* **35,** 28–40.

Bradstreet, M. S. W. 1983. The feeding ecology of alcids near the Gannet Islands, Labrador. Unpublished Report by LGL Ltd., Toronto, for Petro-Canada Exploration, Calgary, 117 pp.

Bradstreet, M. S. W. and W. E. Cross. 1982. Trophic relationships at high arctic ice edges. *Arctic* **35,** 1–12.

Bradstreet, M. S. W., D. N. Nettleship, D. D. Roby and K. L. Brink. 1981. Diet of dovekie *Alle alle* chicks in northwest Greenland. *Canadian Wildlife Service "Studies on Northern Seabirds" Manuscript Report* No. 98, 1–31.

Bray, J. R. 1971. Vegetational distribution, tree growth and crop success in relation to recent climatic change. *Advances in Ecological Research* **7,** 177–233.

Breckenridge, W. J. 1966. Dovekie on Little Diomede Island, Alaska. *Auk* **83,** 680.

Brien, Y. 1970. Statut actuel des oiseaux marins nicheurs en Bretagne 8. Mise au point en 1970: visites récentes et état actuel des effectifs par localité. *Ar Vran* **3,** 168–275.

Briggs, J. C. 1970. A faunal history of the North Atlantic ocean. *Systematic Zoology* **19,** 19–34.

Briggs, J. C. 1974. "Marine Zoogeography." McGraw-Hill, New York.

Briggs, K. T., K. F. Dettmen, D. B. Lewis and W. B. Tyler. 1984. Phalarope feeding in relation to autumn upwelling off California. *In* D. N. Nettleship, G. A. Sanger and P. F. Springer (eds.), "Marine Birds: Their Feeding Ecology and Commercial Fisheries Relationships," pp. 51–62. Canadian Wildlife Service Special Publication, Ottawa.

British Ornithologists' Union. 1956. Taxonomic sub-committee 1956. First Report. *Ibis* **98,** 157–168.

Brockelman, W. Y. 1975. Competition, the fitness of offspring and optimal clutch size. *American Naturalist* **109,** 677–699.

Brodkorb, P. 1967. Catalogue of fossil birds, Part 3. (Ralliformes, Ichthyornithiformes, Charadriiformes). *Bulletin Florida State Museum Biological Sciences* **11,** 99–220.

Brody, S. 1945. "Bioenergetics and Growth." Reinhold, New York. 1023 pp.

Brooke, M. de L. 1972. The puffin populations of the Shiant Islands. *Bird Study* **19**, 1–6.

Brooke, M. de L. 1977. The breeding biology of the Manx Shearwater. Unpublished D.Phil. thesis, University of Oxford, Oxford. 246 pp.

Brooke, M. de L. 1978. The dispersal of female Manx Shearwaters *Puffinus puffinus*. *Ibis* **120**, 545–551.

Brown, J. L. 1964. The evolution of diversity in avian territorial systems. *Wilson Bulletin* **76**, 160–169.

Brown, J. L. 1969. The buffer effect and productivity in tit populations. *American Naturalist* **103**, 347–354.

Brown, R. G. B. 1967a. Courtship behaviour in the Lesser Black-backed Gull *Larus fuscus*. *Behaviour* **29**, 122–153.

Brown, R. G. B. 1967b. Breeding success and population growth in a colony of Herring and Lesser Black-backed Gulls *Larus argentatus* and *L. fuscus*. *Ibis* **109**, 502–515.

Brown, R. G. B. 1968. Sea birds in Newfoundland and Greenland waters, April–May 1966. *Canadian Field-Naturalist* **82**, 88–102.

Brown, R. G. B. 1976. The foraging range of breeding Dovekies *Alle alle*. *Canadian Field-Naturalist* **90**, 166–168.

Brown, R. G. B. 1979. Seabirds of the Senegal upwelling and adjacent waters. *Ibis* **121**, 283–292.

Brown, R. G. B. 1980a. Seabirds as marine animals. *In* J. Burger, B. L. Olla and H. E. Winn (eds.), "Behavior of Marine Animals. Vol. 4: Marine Birds," pp. 1–39. Plenum Press, New York.

Brown, R. G. B. 1980b. The pelagic ecology of seabirds. *Transactions of the Linnaean Society of New York* **9**, 15–22.

Brown, R. G. B. 1982. Birds, oil and the Canadian environment. *In* J. B. Sprague, J. H. Vandermeulen and P. G. Wells (eds.), "Oil and Dispersants in Canadian Seas—Research Appraisals and Recommendations," pp. 105–112. Economic and Technical Review Report EPS 3-EC-82-2. Environmental Protection Service, Ottawa.

Brown, R. G. B. 1984. Seabirds in the Greenland, Barents and Norwegian Seas, February–April 1982. *Polar Research* **2**, 1–18.

Brown, R. G. B. and B. C. Johnson. 1980. The effects of "Kurdistan" oil on seabirds. *In* J. Vandermeulen (ed.), "Scientific Studies during the "Kurdistan" Tanker Incident: Proceedings of a Workshop," pp. 203–211. Bedford Institute of Oceanography Report Series BI-R-80-3. Dartmouth, Nova Scotia.

Brown, R. G. B. and D. N. Nettleship. 1981. The biological significance of polynyas to arctic colonial seabirds. *In* I. Stirling and H. Cleator (eds.), "Polynyas in the Canadian Arctic," pp. 59–65. Canadian Wildlife Service Occasional Paper No. 45. Ottawa.

Brown, R. G. B. and D. N. Nettleship. 1984a. Capelin and seabirds in the Northwest Atlantic. *In* D. N. Nettleship, G. A. Sanger and P. F. Springer (eds.), "Marine Birds: Their Feeding Ecology and Commercial Fisheries Relationships," pp. 184–194. Canadian Wildlife Service Special Publication, Ottawa.

Brown, R. G. B. and D. N. Nettleship. 1984b. The seabirds of northeastern North America; their present status and conservation requirements. *In* J. Croxall, P. G. H. Evans and R. Schreiber (eds.), "Seabirds of the World: Their Status and Conservation." pp. 85–100. International Council for Bird Preservation, Cambridge, England.

Brown, R. G. B., D. I. Gillespie, A. R. Lock, P. A. Pearce and G. H. Watson. 1973. Bird mortality from oil slicks off eastern Canada, February–April 1970. *Canadian Field-Naturalist* **87**, 225–234.

Brown, R. G. B., D. N. Nettleship, P. Germain, C. E. Tull and T. Davis. 1975. "Atlas of Eastern Candian Seabirds." Canadian Wildlife Service, Ottawa. 220 pp.

Brown, R. G. B., S. P. Barker, D. E. Gaskin and M. R. Sandeman. 1981. The foods of Great and Sooty Shearwaters *Puffinis gravis* and *Puffinus griseus* in eastern Canadian waters. *Ibis* **123**, 19–30.

Bruemmer, F. 1978. Hardship, hunger and happiness. *International Wildlife* **8**, 44–49.

Brun, E. 1969. Utbredelse og hekkebestand av Lomvi (*Uria aalge*) i Norge. (The breeding distribution and population of guillemots *Uria aalge* in Norway.) *Sterna (Stavanger)* **8**, 209–224. (English summary.)

Brun, E. 1971. Breeding distribution and population of cliff-breeding seabirds in Sør-Varanger, north Norway. *Astarte* **4**, 53–60.

Brun, E. 1979. Present status and trends in population of seabirds in Norway. *In* J. C. Bartonek and D. N. Nettleship (eds.), "Conservation of Marine Birds of Northern North America," pp. 289–301. U.S. Department of the Interior, Fish and Wildlife Service, Wildlife Research Report No. 11. Washington D.C.

Buckley, F. G. and P. A. Buckley. 1980. Habitat selection and marine birds. *In* J. Burger, B. L. Olla and H. E. Winn (eds.), "Behavior in Marine Animals. Vol. 4: Marine Birds," pp. 69–112. Plenum Press, New York.

Bull, K. R., R. K. Murton, D. Osborn, P. Ward and L. Cheng. 1977. High levels of cadmium in Atlantic seabirds and sea-skaters. *Nature (London)* **269**, 507–509.

Bureau, L. 1877. De la mue du bec et des ornements palpébraux du macareux arctique, *Fratercula arctica* (Lin.) Steph. après la saison des amours. *Bulletin Société Zoologique de France* **2**, 377–399.

Bureau, L. 1879. Récherches sur la mue du bec des oiseaux de la famille des Mermonides. *Bulletin Société Zoologique de France* **4**, 1–68.

Burger, J. 1981. A model for the evolution of mixed-species colonies of ciconiiformes. *Quarterly Review of Biology* **56**, 143–167.

Burton, R. W. 1982. Seabirds. *In* S. R. Williams (ed.), "Joint Services Expedition to Princess Marie Bay, Ellesmere Island, 1980," pp. 4.c.1–8. Directorate of Naval Physical Training and Sport-Joint Services Expedition Trust, Portland, England.

Butler, R. G. and P. Lukasiewicz. 1979. A field study of the effect of crude oil on Herring Gull (*Larus argentatus*) chick growth. *Auk* **96**, 809–812.

Cairns, D. K. 1978. Some aspects of the biology of the Black Guillemot *Cepphus grylle* in the estuary and the Gulf of St. Lawrence. Unpublished M.Sc. thesis, Université de Laval, Quebec. 89 pp.

Cairns, D. K. 1979. Censusing hole-nesting auks by visual counts. *Bird-Banding* **50**, 358–364.

Cairns, D. K. 1980. Nesting density, habitat structure and human disturbance as factors in Black Guillemot reproduction. *Wilson Bulletin* **92**, 352–361.

Cairns, D. K. 1981. Breeding, feeding and chick growth of the Black Guillemot (*Cepphus grylle*) in southern Quebec. *Canadian Field-Naturalist* **95**, 312–318.

Cairns, D. K. 1982. Black Guillemot investigations near the Nuvuk Islands. N. W. T. in 1981. *Canadian Wildlife Service Manuscript Report* No. 147, 1–59.

Carey, C., H. Rahn and P. Parisi. 1980. Calories, water, lipid and yolk in avian eggs. *Condor* **82**, 335–343.

Carnduff, D. 1981. Black Guillemots breeding in the inner Clyde estuary. *Scottish Birds* **11**, 195–196.

Carrick, R. and S. E. Ingham. 1970. Ecology and population dynamics of Antarctic sea birds. **In** M. W. Holdgate (ed.), "Antarctic Ecology," Vol. 1, pp. 505–525. Academic Press, London.

Carruthers, J. N. 1938. Fluctuations in the Herrings of the East Anglian autumn fishery, the yield of the Ostend spent Herring fishery, and the Haddock of the North Sea—in the light of relevant wind conditions. *Rapports et Procès-Verbaux des Réunions, Conseil Permanent International pour l'Exploration de la Mer* **107**, 1–15.

Carscadden, J. 1984. Capelin (*Mallotus villosus*) in the Northwest Atlantic. *In* D. N. Nettleship, G. A. Sanger and P. F. Springer (eds.)," Marine Birds: Their Feeding Ecology and Commercial Fisheries Relationships," pp. 170–183. Canadian Wildlife Service Special Publication, Ottawa.

Carscadden, J., G. H. Winters and D. S. Miller. 1981. Assessment of the division 3L capelin stock, 1967–1980, using SCAM. *Northwest Atlantic Fisheries Organization Scr Document* **81/11/3**, 13 pp.

Cartwright, G. 1792. "Journal of Transactions and Events, during a Residence of Nearly Sixteen Years on the Coast of Labrador; Containing Many Interesting Particulars, both of the Country and its Inhabitants not Hitherto Known." Volumes I, II and III, Allin and Ridge, Newark, England.

Cattley, J. G. 1950. Southern North Sea. Plankton. *Annales Biologiques, Conseil Permanent International pour l'Exploration de la Mer* **6**, 121–123.

Cattley, J. G. 1954. Zoo- and phytoplankton of the Flamborough Line, 1950–53. *Annales Biologiques, Conseil Permanent International pour l'Exploration de la Mer* **10**, 101–103.

Chabrzyk, G. and J. C. Coulson. 1976. Survival and recruitment in the Herring gull *Larus argentatus*. *Journal of Animal Ecology* **45**, 187–204.

Chandler, A. C. 1916. A study of the structure of feathers with reference to their taxonomic significance. *University of California Publications in Zoology* **13**, 243–446.

Chaney, R. W. 1924. Breeding conditions of the murres on the Farallones, June 1923. *Condor* **26**, 30.

Chapdelaine, G. 1980. Onzième inventaire et analyse des populations d'oiseaux marins dans les refuges de la Côte Nord du Golfe Saint-Laurent. (Eleventh census and analysis of seabird populations in the migratory bird sanctuaries of the north shore of the Gulf of St. Lawrence, Quebec.) *Canadian Field-Naturalist* **94**, 34–42.

Chapdelaine, G. and P. Brousseau. 1984. Douzième inventaire des populations d'oiseaux marins dans les refuges de la Côte-Nord du golfe du Saint-Laurent. *Canadian Field-Naturalist* **98**, 178–183.

Chapdelaine, G. and P. Laporte. 1982. Population, reproductive success, and analysis of contaminants in Razorbills *Alca torda* in the estuary and Gulf of St. Lawrence, Quebec. *Canadian Wildlife Service Progress Notes* **129**, 1–10.

Charnov, E. L. and J. R. Krebs. 1974. On clutch size and fitness. *Ibis* **116**, 217–219.

Christensen, O. and W. H. Lear. 1977. Bycatches in salmon drift-nets at West Greenland in 1972. *Meddelelser om Grønland* **205**,(5), 6–38.

Clark, B. D. and W. Bemis. 1979. Kinematics of swimming of penguins at the Detroit Zoo. *Journal of Zoology* **188**, 411–428.

Clark, C. W. 1975. "Mathematical Bioeconomics: The Optimal Management of Renewable Resources. Wiley, New York.

Clark, G. 1948. Fowling in prehistoric Europe. *Antiquity* **22**, 116–130.

Clark, R. B. and R. J. Kennedy. 1968. "Rehabilitation of Oiled Seabirds." Department of Zoology, University of Newcastle upon Tyne, Newcastle upon Tyne. 58 pp.

Clausager, J. 1979. Olieudslippet fra THUN TANK III i januar 1979. *Game Biology Station Manuscript Report*, Rønde, Denmark. 19 pp.

Clutton-Brock, T. H. and P. H. Harvey. 1979. Comparison and adaptation. *Proceedings of the Royal Society of London, Series B* **205**, 547–565.

Cody, M. L. 1966. A general theory of clutch size. *Evolution* **20**, 174–184.

Cody, M. L. 1971. Ecological aspects of reproduction. *In* D. S. Farner and J. R. King (eds.), "Avian Biology," Vol. 1, pp. 461–512. Academic Press, New York.

Cody, M. L. 1973. Coexistence, coevolution and convergent evolution in seabird communities. *Ecology* **54**, 31–44.

Collett, R. and F. Nansen. 1900. An account of the birds. *In* F. Nansen (ed.), "The Norwegian North Polar Expedition 1893–1896. Scientific Results," Vol. 1, pp. 1–53. Christiania.

Collin, A. E. and M. J. Dunbar. 1964. Physical oceanography in Arctic Canada. *Oceanography and Marine Biology* **2**, 45–75.

Conder, P. J. 1950. On the courtship and social displays of three species of Auk. *British Birds* **43**, 65–69.

Conroy, J. W. H. and E. L. Twelves. 1972. Diving depths of the Gentoo Penguin *Pygoscelis papua* and Blue-eyed Shag *Phalacrocorax atriceps* from the South Orkney Islands. *British Antarctic Survey Bulletin* **30**, 106–108.

Cooke, A. S. 1973. Shell thinning in avian eggs by environmental pollutants. *Environmental Pollution* **4**, 85–152.

Corkhill, P. 1971. Factors affecting auk attendance in the pre-egg stage. *Nature in Wales* **12**, 258–262.

Corkhill, P. 1972. Measurements of puffins as criteria of sex and age. *Bird Study* **19**, 193–201.

Corkhill, P. 1973. Food and feeding ecology of puffins. *Bird Study* **20**, 207–220.

Cottam, C. and H. C. Hanson. 1938. Food habits of some arctic birds and mammals. *Field Museum of Natural History Publications, Zoological Series* **20**, 405–426.

Coues, E. 1861. Notes on the ornithology of Labrador. *Proceedings of the Academy of Natural Sciences of Philadelphia* **13**, 215–257.

Coues, E. 1868. A monograph of the Alcidae. *Proceedings of the Academy of Natural Sciences of Philadelphia* **20**, 3–81.

Coulson, J. C. 1968. Differences in the quality of birds nesting in the centre and on the edges of the colony. *Nature (London)* **217**, 478–479.

Coulson, J. C. and J. Horobin. 1976. The influence of age on the breeding biology and survival of the Arctic Tern *Sterna paradisaea. Journal of Zoology* **178**, 247–260.

Coulson, J. C. and E. White. 1955. Abrasion and loss of rings among seabirds. *Bird Study* **2**, 41–44.

Coulson, J. C. and E. White. 1960. The effect of age and density of breeding birds on the time of breeding of Kittiwake *Rissa tridactyla. Ibis* **102**, 71–86.

Coulson, J. C. and E. White. 1961. An analysis of the factors influencing the clutch size of Kittiwakes. *Proceedings of the Zoological Society of London* **136**, 207–217.

Coulson, J. C. and R. D. Wooler. 1976. Differential survival rates among breeding Kittiwake Gulls *Rissa tridactyla* (L.). *Journal of Animal Ecology* **45**, 205–213.

Coulson, J. C., C. R. Potts and J. Horobin. 1969. Variation in the eggs of the Shag (*Phalacrocorax aristotelis*). *Auk* **86**, 232–245.

Craig, P. C., W. B. Griffiths, L. Haldorson and H. McElderry. 1982. Ecological studies of arctic cod (*Boreogadus saida*) in Beaufort Sea coastal waters, Alaska. *Canadian Journal of Fisheries and Aquatic Sciences* **39**, 395–406.

Cramp, S., W. R. P. Bourne and D. Saunders. 1974. "The Seabirds of Britain and Ireland." Collins, London. 287 pp.

Cross, W. E. 1982. Under-ice biota at the Pond Inlet ice edge and in adjacent fast ice areas during spring. *Arctic* **35**, 13–27.

Croxall, J. P. and P. A. Prince. 1980. Food, feeding and ecological segregation of seabirds at South Georgia. *Biological Journal of the Linnaean Society* **14**, 103–131.

Croxall, J. P. and P. A. Prince. 1982. Calorific content of squid (Mollusca: Cephalopoda). *British Antarctic Survey Bulletin* **55**, 27–31.

Cullen, J. P. and D. J. Slinn. 1975. ''The Birds of the Isle of Man.'' Manx Museum National Trust, Douglas. 40 pp.

Cushing, D. H. 1961. On the failure of the Plymouth herring fishery. *Journal of the Marine Biological Association* U.K. **41**, 799–816.

Cushing, D. H. 1966. Biological and hydrographic changes in British seas during the last thirty years. *Biological Reviews of the Cambridge Philosophical Society* **41**, 221–258.

Cushing, D. H. 1971. Upwelling and the production of fish. *Advances in Marine Biology* **9**, 255–334.

Cushing, D. H. 1975. ''Marine Ecology and Fisheries.'' Cambridge University Press, London and New York. 278 pp.

Cushing, D. H. 1976. The impact of climatic change on fish stocks in the North Atlantic. *Geographical Journal* **142**, 216–227.

Cushing, D. H. 1982. ''Climate and Fisheries.'' Academic Press, London and New York. 373 pp.

Daan, S. and J. Tinbergen. 1979. Young guillemots (*Uria lomvia*) leaving their arctic breeding cliffs: a daily rhythm in numbers and risk. *Ardea* **67**, 96–100.

Dale, I. M., M. S. Baxter, J. A. Bogan and W. R. P. Bourne. 1973. Mercury in seabirds. *Marine Pollution Bulletin* **4**, 77–79.

Davies, N. B. and A. I. Houston. 1981. Owners and satellites: the economics of territory defense in the Pied Wagtail, *Motacilla alba*. *Journal of Animal Ecology* **50**, 157–180.

Dawson, W. L. 1920. An oological revision of the Alciformes. *Journal of the Museum of Comparative Zoology* (*Santa Barbara, California*) **1**, 7–14.

Degerbøl, M. and U. Møhl-Hansen. 1935. Birds (Aves) of the Scoresby Sound Committee's 2nd East Greenland expedition in 1932 to King Christian IX's land. *Meddelelser om Grønland* **104**, 1–30.

De Groot, P. 1980. A study of the acquisition of information concerning resources by individuals in small groups of Red-billed Weaver birds *Quelea quelea*. Unpublished Ph.D. thesis, University of Bristol, Bristol.

de Korte, J. 1972. Birds observed and collected by 'De Niederlandse Spitsbergen Expeditie' in west and east Spitsbergen, 1967 and 1968–69; third and last part. *Beaufortia* **20**, 23–58.

de Korte, J. 1973. Nederlandse Groenland Expeditie Scoresbysund—1973, Preliminary Avifaunistical Report. Manuscript report, Zoological Museum, University of Amsterdam, Amsterdam. 10 pp.

de Korte, J. 1974. Nederlandse Groenland Expeditie Scoresbysund—1974, Preliminary Report on Fieldwork. Manuscript report, Zoological Museum, University of Amsterdam, Amsterdam. 8 pp.

de Korte, J. and C. Bosman. 1975. Nederlandse Groenland Expeditie 1975, Preliminary Report on Fieldwork. Verslagen en Technische Gegevens No. 6, Institute voor Taxonomische Zoologie, University of Amsterdam, Amsterdam. 10 pp.

Dement'ev, G. P., R. N. Meklenburtsev, A. M. Sudilovskaya and E. P. Spangeberg. 1951. ''Birds of the Soviet Union'' (G. P. Dement'ev and N. A. Gladkov, series eds.), Vol. II. Israel Program for Scientific Translations, Jerusalem. 533 pp. (Translated from Russian, 1968.)

Demme, N. P. 1934. Ptitchii bazar na skale Rubini (Ostrov Gukera, Zemlya Frantsa Iosifa). *Trudy Arkticheskogo Instituta* (*Leningrad*) **11**, 55–86.

Denys, N. 1672. "The Description and Natural History of the Coasts of North America (Acadia)." (Translated from French by W. F. Ganong, 1908.) The Champlain Society, Toronto. 625 pp.

De Steven, D. 1978. The influence of age on the breeding biology of the Tree Swallow *Iridoprocne bicolor*. *Ibis* **120**, 516–523.

Devold, F., N. Devold and T. Westergaard. 1972. Capelin investigations east of Labrador and Newfoundland in July–August 1971. *Fiskets Gang* **58**, 49–55. (Translated from Norwegian by Fisheries Research Board of Canada Translation Service, No. 2124, 1973.)

Dewar, J. M. 1924. "The Bird as a Diver." W. H. Witherby, London. 169 pp.

Diamond, A. W. 1978. Feeding strategies and population size in tropical seabirds. *American Naturalist* **112**, 215–223.

Dickson, R. R. 1971. A recurrent and persistent pressure-anomaly pattern as the principle cause of intermediate-scale hydrographic variation in the European Shelf seas. *Deutsche Hydrographische Zeitschrift* **24**, 97–119.

Dickson, R. R., M. J. Holden and J. G. Pope. 1974. Environmental influences on the survival of North Sea Cod. *In* J. H. S. Blaxter (ed.), "The Early Life History of Fish," pp. 69–80. Springer-Verlag, Berlin and New York.

Dietrich, G. 1954. Ozeanographisch meteorologische einflusse auf Wasserstand sunderungen des Meeres am Beispiel der Agelbeobachtungenvon Esbjerg. *Küste* **2**(2), 130–156.

Dietrich, G. 1969. "Atlas of the Hydrography of the Northern North Atlantic Ocean." Conseil International pour l'Exploration de la Mer, Service Hydrographique, Copenhagen. 140 pp.

Dietz, R. S. and J. C. Holden. 1970. The breakup of Pangaea. *Scientific American* **223**, 30–41.

Digby, P. S. B. 1961. The vertical migration and movements of marine plankton under midnight-sun conditions in Spitsbergen. *Journal of Animal Ecology* **30**, 9–25.

Divoky, G. J., G. W. Watson and J. C. Bartonek. 1974. Breeding of the Black Guillemot in northern Alaska. *Condor* **76**, 339–343.

Dixon, T. J. 1970. The extent of mortality from shooting in southern Norway. *Seabird Report* pp. 50–51.

Dobson, R. 1952. "The Birds of the Channel Islands." Staples, London. 252 pp.

Dobson, S. D., B. Dobson, R. K. Murton and N. J. Westwood. 1977. Physiological effects of organochlorine pollutants. *Annual Report of the Institute of Terrestrial Ecology, Cambridge, 1976* pp. 62–63.

Dooley, H. D. and D. W. McKay. 1979. The drift of herring larvae from the west coast to the North Sea. *Scottish Fisheries Bulletin* **45**, 10–12.

Dragesund, O., J. Hamre and O. Ulltang. 1980. Biology and population dynamics of the Norwegian spring-spawning herring. *In* A. Savile (ed.), "The Assessment and Management of Pelagic Fish Stocks," Vol. 177, pp. 43–71. Rapports et Procès-verbaux des Réunions, Conseil International pour l'Exploration de la Mer, Copenhagen.

Drent, R. H. 1965. Breeding biology of the Pigeon Guillemot *Cepphus columba*. *Ardea* **53**, 99–160.

Drent, R. H. and S. Daan. 1980. The prudent parent: energetic adjustments in avian breeding. *Ardea* **68**, 225–252.

Drury, W. H. 1973–1974. Population changes in New England seabirds. *Bird-Banding* **44**, 267–313; **45**, 1–15.

Drury, W. H. and J. A. Kadlec. 1974. The current status of the Herring Gull population in the northeastern United States. *Bird-Banding* **45**, 297–306.

Drury, W. H., C. Ramsdell and J. B. French, Jr. 1980. "Ecological Studies in the Bering Strait Region," Final Report, Research Unit 237. U.S. Department of Commerce, National Oceanic and Atmospheric Administration, Outer Continental Shelf Environmental Assessment Program (OCSEAP). Boulder, Colorado. 308 pp.

Duffey, E. and D. E. Sergeant. 1950. Field notes on the birds of Bear Island. *Ibis* **92,** 554–563.

Duffy, D. C. 1983. The ecology of tick parasitism on densely nesting Peruvian seabirds. *Ecology* **64,** 110–119.

Dunbar, M. J. 1942. Marine macroplankton from the Canadian eastern Arctic. I. Amphipoda and Schizopoda. *Canadian Journal of Research, Section D,* **20,** 33–46.

Dunbar, M. J. 1946. On *Themisto libellula* in Baffin Island coastal waters. *Journal of the Fisheries Research Board of Canada* **6,** 419–434.

Dunbar, M. J. 1957. The determinants of production in northern seas: a study of the biology of *Themisto libellula* Mandt. *Canadian Journal of Zoology* **35,** 797–819.

Dunbar, M. J. 1968. "Ecological Developments in Polar Regions: A Study in Evolution." Prentice-Hall, Englewood Cliffs, New Jersey. 119 pp.

Dunbar, M. J. 1972. The nature and definition of the marine subarctic, with a note on the sea-life area of the Atlantic Salmon. *Transactions of the Royal Society of Canada* **10,** 250–257.

Dunbar, M. J. 1981. Physical causes and biological significance of polynyas and other open water in sea ice. *In* I. Stirling and H. Cleator (eds.), "Polynyas in the Canadian Arctic," pp. 29–43. Canadian Wildlife Service Occasional Paper No. 45. Ottawa.

Duncan, N. 1978. The effects of culling on breeding Herring Gulls. *Ibis* **120,** 113–114.

Dunn, E. H. 1975a. Caloric intake of nestling Double-crested Cormorants. *Auk* **92,** 553–565.

Dunn, E. H. 1975b. Growth, body components and energy content of nestling Double-crested Cormorants. *Condor* **77,** 431–438.

Dunn, E. H. 1979. Time-energy use and life history strategies of northern seabirds. *In* J. C. Bartonek and D. N. Nettleship (eds.), "Conservation of Marine Birds of Northern North America," pp.141–166. U.S. Department of the Interior, Fish and Wildlife Service, Wildlife Research Report No. 11. Washington, D.C.

Dunnet, G. M. 1974. Impact of the oil industry on Scotland's coast and birds. *Scottish Birds* **8,** 3–16.

Dunnet, G. M. 1977. Observations on the effects of low flying aircraft at seabird colonies on the coast of Aberdeenshire, Scotland. *Biological Conservation* **12,** 55–63.

Dunnet, G. M. 1980. Seabirds and oil pollution. Energy in the balance. Some papers from the British Association Meeting, Westbury House, Guildford, 1979, pp. 51–64.

Dunnet, G. M. and J. C. Ollason. 1978a. Survival and longevity in the Fulmar. *Ibis* **120,** 124–125.

Dunnet, G. M. and J. C. Ollason. 1978b. The estimation of survival rate in the Fulmar, *Fulmaris glacialis. Journal of Animal Ecology* **47,** 507–520.

Durant, M. and M. Harwood. 1980. "On the Road with John James Audubon." Dodd, Mead, New York. 638 pp.

Durham, J. W. 1952. Early Tertiary marine faunas and continental drift. *American Journal of Science* **250,** 321–343.

Dutcher, W. 1904. Report of the A. O. U. Committee on the protection of North American birds, for the year 1903. *Auk* **21,** 97–208.

Dyck, J. and H. Meltofte. 1973. "Lomvieoptaellingen på Faerøerne 1972." Udgivet vad et samarbejde mellem Dansk Ornithologisk Forening, Fiskerilaboratoriet og Institut for sammenlignende Anatomi, Københavns Universitet, København et Tórshavn. 97 pp.

Dyck, J. and H. Meltofte. 1975. The guillemot *Uria aalge* population of the Faeroes 1972. *Dansk Ornithologisk Forenings Tidsskrift* **69,** 55–64.

Edinburgh Oceanographic Laboratory. 1973. Continuous plankton records: a plankton atlas of the North Atlantic and North Sea. *Bulletins of Marine Ecology* **7**, 1–174.

Einarsson, T. 1979. Fjöldi langvíu og stuttnefju í fuglabjörgum vid Island. (Numbers of Brunnich's and Common Guillemots at Icelandic breeding stations.) *Náttúrufraedingurinn* **49**, 221–228. (English summary.)

Ekman, S. 1953. "Zoogeography of the Sea." Sidgwick and Jackson, London. 417 pp.

Elliot, R., T. R. Birkhead and R. Odense. 1978. The Gannet Clusters, Groswater Bay, Labrador, 1978. *Canadian Wildlife Service "Studies on Northern Seabirds" Manuscript Report* No. 74, 1–42.

Ellis, D. V. and J. Evans. 1960. Comments on the distribution and migration of birds in Foxe Basin, Northwest Territories. *Canadian Field-Naturalist* **74**, 59–70.

Emlen, S. T. and N. J. Demong. 1975. Adaptive significance of synchronized breeding in a colonial bird: a new hypothesis. *Science (Washington, D.C.)* **188**, 1029–1031.

Evans, P. G. H. 1973. Report on Kerry Islands Expedition, 1973. Unpublished manuscript report, University of Aberdeen, Aberdeen. 10 pp.

Evans, P. G. H. (ed.). 1974a. Report on Aberdeen University expedition to Northwest Greenland, summer 1974. Unpublished manuscript report, University of Aberdeen, Aberdeen. 120 pp.

Evans, P. G. H. 1974b. Effects upon seabirds of helicopter flights to light-stations, S. W. Ireland. Unpublished report, Irish Wildbird Conservancy, Dublin. 5 pp.

Evans, P. G. H. 1975. Gulls and puffins on North Rona. *Bird Study* **22**, 239–248.

Evans, P. G. H. 1978. The birds of North Rona and Sula Sgeir. *Hebridean Naturalist* pp. 21–36.

Evans, P. G. H. (ed.) 1980. "Auk Censusing Manual." Unpublished guide, British Seabird Group, Sandy, Bedfordshire. 17 pp.

Evans, P. G. H. 1981a. Ecology and behaviour of the Little Auk *Alle alle* in west Greenland. *Ibis* **123**, 1–18.

Evans, P. G. H. 1981b. Report on N. E. Atlantic Whale and Seabird cruise, summer 1980. Unpublished manuscript report, University of Oxford, Oxford. 40 pp.

Evans, P. G. H. 1984. Seabirds of Greenland: their status and conservation. *In* J. P. Croxall, P. G. H. Evans and R. Schreiber (eds.), "Seabirds of the World: Their Status and Conservation," pp. 49–84. International Council for Bird Preservation, Cambridge, England.

Evans, P. G. H. and R. R. Lovegrove. 1974. The birds of the south-west Irish Islands. *Irish Bird Report* 1973, 33–64.

Evans, P. G. H. and G. Waterston. 1976. The decline of the Thick-billed Murre in Greenland. *Polar Record* **18**, 283–293.

Evans, P. G. H. and G. Waterston. 1977. Recent salmon netting restrictions in south-west Greenland. *Polar Record* **18**, 507–508.

Everett, M. J. 1982. Breeding Great and Arctic Skuas in Scotland in 1974–75. *Seabird Report* **6**, 50–58.

Farren, G. P. and W. Verwourt. 1951a. "Copepoda. Sub-order: Calanoida. Family: Calanidae." Conseil International pour l'Exploration de la Mer, Fiches d'identification No. 32. Høst, Copenhagen.

Farren, G. P. and W. Verwourt. 1951b. "Copepoda. Sub-order: Calanoida. Family: Pseudocalanus, Genera: Pseudocalanus, Microcalanus." Conseil International pour l'Exploration de la Mer, Fiches d'identification No. 37. Høst, Copenhagen.

Feduccia, A. 1980. "The Age of Birds." Harvard University Press, Cambridge, Massachusetts. 196 pp.

Feduccia, A. and P. O. McGrew. 1974. A flamingo-like wader from the Eocene of Wyoming. *Contributions to Geology, University of Wyoming* **13**, 49–62.

Ferdinand, L. 1969. Some observations on the behaviour of the Little Auk *Plautus alle* on the breeding ground, with special reference to voice production. *Dansk Ornithologisk Forenings Tidsskrift* **63**, 19–45.

Finley, K. J. and C. R. Evans. 1984. First Canadian breeding record of the Dovekie (*Alle alle*). *Arctic* **37**, 288–289.

Finney, G. and F. Cooke. 1978. Reproductive habits in the Snow Goose: the influence of female age. *Condor* **80**, 147–158.

Fisher, J. and R. M. Lockley. 1954. "Sea-birds." Collins, London. 320 pp.

Fisher, R. A. 1958. "The Genetical Theory of Natural Selection." Dover, New York. 291 pp.

Fjeldså, J. 1977. "Guide to the young of European precocial birds." Skarv Nature Publications, Tisvildeleje. 285 pp.

Flegg, J. J. M. 1972. The puffin on St. Kilda, 1969–71. *Bird Study* **19**, 7–17.

Flegg, J. J. M. and C. J. Cox. 1975. Mortality in the Black-headed gull. *British Birds* **68**, 437–449.

Folkestad, A. O. 1982. The effect of mink predation on some seabird species. *Viltrapport* **21**, 42–49.

Ford, R. G., J. A. Wiens, D. Heinemann and G. L. Hunt. 1982. Modelling the sensitivity of colonially breeding marine birds to oil spills: guillemot and kittiwake populations on the Pribilof Islands, Bering Sea. *Journal of Applied Ecology* **19**, 1–31.

Forrest, H. E. 1907. "The Vertebrate Fauna of North Wales." London. 523 pp.

Foster, R. J., R. L. Baxter and P. A. J. Ball. 1951. A visit to Grímsey (Iceland), July–August 1949. *Ibis* **93**, 53–59.

Fournier, R. O., M. van Det, J. S. Wilson and N. B. Hargreaves. 1979. Influence of the shelf-break front off Nova Scotia on phytoplankton standing stock in winter. *Journal of the Fisheries Research Board of Canada* **36**, 1228–1237.

Frakes, L. A. 1979. "Climates Throughout Geologic Time." Elsevier, Amsterdam and New York. 310 pp.

Frankel, O. H. and M. H. Soulé. 1981. "Conservation and Evolution." Cambridge University Press, London and New York. 327 pp.

Franzmann, N. E. 1974. Graesholm—en status på skaeret. *Feltornithologen* **16**, 58–59.

Fraser, J. H. 1965. "Zooplankton Indicator Species in the North Sea. Serial Atlas of the Marine Environment," Folio 8, pp. 1–2. American Geographical Society, New York.

Frazar, M. A. 1887. An ornithologist's summer in Labrador. *Ornithologist and Oologist* **12**, 1–3, 17–20, 34–35.

Freeman, M. M. R. 1970. The birds of the Belcher Islands, N. W. T., Canada. *Canadian Field-Naturalist* **84**, 277–290.

Fretwell, S. 1968. Habitat distribution and survival in the Field Sparrow *Spizella pusilla*. *Bird-Banding* **39**, 293–306.

Fretwell, S. 1969. On territorial behaviour and other factors influencing habitat distribution in birds. III Breeding success in a local population of Field Sparrows *Spizella pusilla*. *Acta Biotheoretica* **19**, 45–52.

Freuchen, P. and F. Salomonsen. 1958. "The Arctic Year." G. P. Putnam's Sons, New York. 438 pp.

Furness, R. W. 1977. Studies on the breeding biology and population dynamics of the Great Skua *Catharacta skua* Brunnich. Unpublished Ph.D. thesis, University of Durham, Durham.

Furness, R. W. 1978a. Ornithological studies on Foula 1975/6. *Brathay Field Studies Report* **30**, 1–38.

Furness, R. W. 1978b. Energy requirements of seabird communities: a bioenergetics model. *Journal of Animal Ecology* **47**, 39–53.

Furness, R. W. 1978c. Movements and mortality rates of Great Skuas ringed in Scotland. *Bird Study* **25**, 229–238.

Furness, R. W. 1981. Seabird populations of Foula. *Scottish Birds* **11**, 237–253.

Furness, R. W. 1982. Competition between fisheries and seabird communities. *Advances in Marine Biology* **20**, 225–307.

Furness, R. W. 1984. Seabird–fisheries relationships in the northeast Atlantic and North Sea. *In* D. N. Nettleship, G. A. Sanger and P. F. Springer (eds.), "Marine Birds: Their Feeding Ecology and Commercial Fisheries Relationships," pp. 162–169. Canadian Wildlife Service Special Publication, Ottawa.

Gadgil, M. and W. H. Bossert. 1970. Life historical consequences of natural selection. *American Naturalist* **104**, 1–24.

Gadow, H. 1889. On the taxonomic value of the intestinal convolutions in birds. *Proceedings of the Zoological Society of London* pp. 303–316.

Gardarsson, A. 1982. Status of Icelandic seabird populations. *Viltrapport* **21**, 23.

Garnett, M. 1984. Status and conservation of seabirds in the South Pacific. *In* J. Croxall, P. G. H. Evans and R. Schreiber (eds.), "Seabirds of the World: Their Status and Conservation," pp. 547–558. International Council for Bird Preservation, Cambridge, England.

Gaston, A. J. 1980. Population, movements and wintering areas of Thick-billed Murres *(Uria lomvia)* in eastern Canada. *Canadian Wildlife Service Progress Note* No. 110, 1–10.

Gaston, A. J. 1982. Migration of juvenile Thick-billed Murres through Hudson Strait in 1980. *Canadian Field-Naturalist* **96**, 30–34.

Gaston, A. J. and M. Malone. 1980. Range extension of Atlantic Puffin and Razorbill in Hudson Strait. *Canadian Field-Naturalist* **94**, 328–329.

Gaston, A. J. and D. N. Nettleship. 1981. The Thick-billed Murres of Prince Leopold Island—a study of the breeding ecology of a colonial high arctic seabird. *Canadian Wildlife Service Monograph Series* No. 6, 350 pp.

Gaston, A. J. and D. N. Nettleship. 1982. Factors determining seasonal changes in attendance at colonies of the Thick-billed Murre *Uria lomvia. Auk* **99**, 468–473.

Gaston, A. J., D. Cairns, D. Noble and M. Purdy. 1981. Seabird investigations in Hudson Strait: report on research in 1981. *Canadian Wildlife Service "Studies on Northern Seabirds" Manuscript Report* No. 130, 1–60.

Gaston, A. J., G. Chapdelaine and D. G. Noble. 1983a. The growth of Thick-billed Murre chicks at colonies in Hudson Strait: inter- and intra-colony variation. *Canadian Journal of Zoology* **61**, 2465–2475.

Gaston, A. J., R. I. Goudie, D. G. Noble and A. Macfarlane. 1983b. Observations on "Turr" hunting in Newfoundland: age, body condition, and diet of Thick-billed Murres *(Uria lomvia)*, and proportions of other seabirds, killed off Newfoundland in winter. *Canadian Wildlife Service Progress Note* No. 141, 1–7.

Gätke, H. 1895. "Heligoland as an ornithological observatory: the result of fifty years' experience." David Douglas, Edinburgh. 599 pp.

George, J. L. and D. E. H. Frear. 1966. Pesticides in the Antarctic. *In* N. W. Moore (ed.), "Pesticides in the Environment and Their Effects on Wildlife," pp. 155–167. Supplement to Journal of Applied Ecology, Vol. 3. Blackwell, Oxford. 311 pp.

Gerasimova, T. D. 1961. Rezul'taty ucheta morskikh kolonial'nykh ptits i gagi na Murmanskom poberezh'e. Voprosy organizatsii i metody ucheta resursov fauny nazemnykh pozvonochnykh. Unpublished thesis, Moskovskogo Universiteta, Moskva.

Gerasimova, T. D. 1962. Sostoyanie ptic'ikh bazarov Murmanskogo poberezh'ya. *Ornitologiya* **4**, 11–14.

Gerlach, S. A. 1981. "Marine Pollution—Diagnosis and Therapy." Springer-Verlag, Berlin and New York. 278 pp.

GESAMP. 1977. Impact of oil in the marine environment. *Reports and Studies—GESAMP* No. 6, 1–250.

Gibson, J. A. 1951. The breeding, distribution, population and history of the birds of Ailsa Craig. *Scottish Naturalist* **63**, 73–100, 159–177.

Gill, C., F. Booker and T. Soper. 1967. "The Wreck of the Torrey Canyon." David & Charles, Newton Abbot. 128 pp.

Gill, R. and L. R. Mewaldt. 1983. Pacific coast Caspian Terns: dynamics of an expanding population. *Auk* **100**, 369–381.

Gilliard, T. E. 1937. The gannets of Funk Island. *Auk* **54**, 379–381.

Glover, R. S. 1957. An ecological survey of the drift-net Herring fishery off the North-East coast of Scotland. *Bulletins of Marine Ecology* **5**, 1–43.

Glutz von Blotzheim, U. N. and K. M. Bauer (eds.). 1982. "Handbuch der Vögel Mitteleuropas. Band 8: Charadriiformes (1. Teil)." Akademische Verlagsgesellschaft, Frankfurt am Main. 1270 pp.

Gochfeld, M. 1980. Mechanisms and adaptive value of reproductive synchrony in colonial seabirds. *In* J. Burger, B. L. Olla and H. E. Winn (eds.), "Behavior of Marine Animals. Vol. 4: Marine Birds," pp. 207–270. Plenum Press, New York.

Godfrey, W. E. 1959. Notes on the Great Auk in Nova Scotia. *Canadian Field-Naturalist* **73**, 75.

Godfrey, W. E. 1966. The birds of Canada. *National Museum of Canada Bulletin* No. 203, 1–428.

Golovkin, A. N. 1963. Murre (*Uria* species) and Black-legged Kittiwake (*Rissa tridactyla*) fish consumption during the nesting period in the Barents Sea. *Zoologicheskii Zhurnal* **42**(3) 408–416. (Translated from Russian, 1983: Doenv Tr-2287, Environment Canada, Ottawa.)

Golovkin, A. N. 1967. The effect of colonial seabirds on development of the phytoplankton. *Oceanology* **7**(4), 521–529.

Golovkin, A. N. 1984. Sea birds nesting in the U.S.S.R.: status and protection of populations. *In* J. P. Croxall, P. G. H. Evans and R. Schreiber (eds.), "Seabirds of the World: Their Status and Conservation," pp. 473–486. International Council for Bird Preservation, Cambridge, England.

Golovkin, A. N., E. A. Zelickman and A. A. Georgiev. 1972a. Biology and feeding connections of Little Auks *Plautus alle* with the pelagic community in the north of Novaya Zemlya. *In* A. N. Golovkin (ed.), "Peculiarities of Biological Productivity of Waters Near Bird Bazaars in the North of Novaya Zemlya," pp. 74–84. Nauka, Leningrad. (Translated from Russian, 1979: C. Welling, University of Alaska, Fairbanks.)

Golovkin, A. N., V. N. Shirokolobov and G. P. Garkavaya. 1972b. Peculiarities of distribution of biogenic elements near bird bazaars in the north of Novaya Zemlya. *In* A. N. Golovkin (ed.), "Pecularities of Biological Productivity of Waters Near Bird Bazaars in the North of Novaya Zemlya," pp. 33–46. Nauka, Leningrad. (Translated from Russian.)

Goodman, D. 1974. Natural selection and a cost ceiling on reproductive effort. *American Naturalist* **108**, 247–268.

Gorbunov, G. P. 1932. Pticy Zemli Franca-Iosifa. (Die Vögel von Franz-Joseph Land.) *Trudy Arkticheskogo Instituta (Leningrad)* **4**, 188–244.

Gorman, M. L. and H. H. Milne. 1971. Seasonal changes in the adrenal steroid tissue of the Common Eider *Somateria mollissima* and its relation to organic metabolism in normal and oil-polluted birds. *Ibis* **113**, 218–228.

Gosling, W. G. 1910. "Labrador: Its Discovery, Exploration, and Development." Alston Rivers, London. 574 pp.

Goss-Custard, J. D., R. A. Jenyon, R. E. Jones, P. E. Newbery and R. Le B. Williams. 1977. The ecology of the Wash. *Journal of Applied Ecology* **14**, 701–719.

Graham, H. D. 1890. "The Birds of Iona and Mull." Edinburgh. 279 pp.

Graham, M. (ed.). 1956. "Sea Fisheries. Their Investigation in the United Kingdom." Edward Arnold, London. 487 pp.

Grainger, E. H. 1961. The copepods *Calanus glacialis* (Jaschnov) and *Calanus finmarchicus* (Gunnerus) in Canadian arctic-subarctic waters. *Journal of the Fisheries Research Board of Canada* **18**, 663–678.

Grainger, E. H. 1965. Zooplankton from the Arctic Ocean and adjacent Canadian waters. *Journal of the Fisheries Research Board of Canada* **22**, 543–564.

Grant, P. R. and D. N. Nettleship. 1971. Nesting habitat selection by puffins *Fratercula arctica* L. in Iceland. *Ornis Scandinavica* **2**, 81–87.

Greenwalt, C. H. 1962. Dimensional relationships for flying animals. *Smithsonian Miscellaneous Collections* No. 144, 1–46.

Greenwood, J. J. D. 1969. Oil pollution off the east coast of Britain February and March 1969. *Marine Pollution Bulletin* **17**, 12–14.

Greenwood, J. J. D., R. J. Donally, C. J. Feare, N. J. Gordon and G. Waterston. 1971. A massive wreck of oiled birds: northeast Britain, winter 1970. *Scottish Birds* **6**, 235–250.

Grenmyr, U. and J. A. Sundin. 1981. Fågelfaunan vid Vasterbottenskusten—forandringer sedan 1930–talet. *Vår Fågelvarld* **40**, 91–104.

Grenquist, P. 1965. Changes in abundance of some duck and sea-bird populations off the coast of Finland 1949–1963. *Finnish Game Research* **27**, 1–114.

Grieve, S. 1885. "The Greak Auk, or Garefowl *Alca impennis*, its History, Archaeology and Remains." Thomas C. Jack, London. 142 pp.

Gross, A. O. 1951. The Herring Gull–Cormorant control project. *Proceedings of the International Ornithological Congress* **10**, 533–536.

Groundwater, W. 1974. "Birds and Mammals of Orkney." Kirkwall Press, Kirkwall. 299 pp.

Gudmundsson, F. 1951. The effects of the recent climatic changes on the bird life of Iceland. *Proceedings of the International Ornithological Congress* **10**, 502–514.

Gudmundsson, F. 1953a. Islenzkir fuglar VI Teista *Cepphus grylle* (L). *Náttúrufraedingurinn* **23**, 129–132. (English summary.)

Guermeur, Y. and J. Y. Monnat. 1980. "Histoire et geographie des oiseaux nicheurs de Bretagne." Ministère de l'environnement et du cadre de vie, Direction de la protection de la nature, Clermont-Ferrand. 240 pp.

Gustafsson, L. and S. Hogstrom. 1981. Hur många fåglar hackar på Gotland? (How many birds breed in Gotland?) *Blacku* **7**, 81–138.

Gysels, H. and M. Rabaey. 1964. Taxonomic relationships of *Alca torda*, *Fratercula arctica* and *Uria aalge* as revealed by biochemical methods. *Ibis* **106**, 536–540.

Hachey, H. B. 1961. Oceanography and Canadian Atlantic waters. *Fisheries Research Board of Canada Bulletin* No. 134, 1–120.

Hailman, J. P. 1975. Review of J. R. Krebs' "Colonial nesting and social feeding as strategies for exploiting food resources in the Great Blue Heron *(Ardea herodias)*." *Bird-Banding* **46**, 256–257.

Hakluyt, R. 1904. "The Principal Navigations Voyages Traffiques and Discoveries of the English Nation made by Sea or Over-land to the Remote and Farthest Distant Quarters of the Earth at Any Time with the Compasse of these 1600 Yeeres," Vol. VIII. James MacLehose and Sons, Glasgow. 486 pp.

Haldane, J. B. S. 1955. The calculation of mortality rates from ringing data. *Proceedings of the International Ornithological Congress* **11**, 454–510.

Hallam, A. 1973. "A Revolution in the Earth Sciences: From Continental Drift to Plate Tectonics." Clarendon Press, Oxford.

Hantzsch, B. 1905. "Beitrag zur Kenntnis der Vogelwelt Islands." (Contribution to the knowledge of the Avifauna of Iceland.) Friedlander & Sohn, Berlin. 341 pp.

Hardy, A. C. 1936. The continuous plankton recorder. *Discovery Reports* **11**, 457–510.

Hardy, A. C. 1939. Ecological investigations with the continuous plankton recorder. *Hull Bulletins of Marine Ecology* **1**, 1–57.

Hardy, A. C. 1956. "The Open Sea: Its Natural History. Part I: The World of Plankton." Collins, London. 335 pp.

Hardy, A. C. 1959. "The Open Sea: Its Natural History. Part II: Fish and Fisheries." Collins, London. 322 pp.

Harris, M. P. 1970a. Breeding ecology of the Swallow-tailed Gull *Creagrus furcatus*. *Auk* **87**, 215–243.

Harris, M. P. 1970b. Differences in the diet of British auks. *Ibis* **112**, 540–541.

Harris, M. P. 1970c. Rates and causes of increases of some British gull populations. *Bird Study* **17**, 325–335.

Harris, M. P. 1976a. The present status of the puffin in Britain and Ireland. *British Birds* **69**, 239–264.

Harris, M. P. 1976b. The seabirds of Shetland in 1974. *Scottish Birds* **9**, 37–68.

Harris, M. P. 1976c. Lack of a 'desertion period' in the nestling life of the puffin *Fratercula arctica*. *Ibis* **118**, 115–118.

Harris, M. P. 1976d. Inter-colony movements of Farne Islands puffins. *Transactions of the Natural History Society of Northumbria* **42**, 115–118.

Harris, M. P. 1977. Puffins on the Isle of May. *Scottish Birds* **9**, 285–290.

Harris, M. P. 1978. Supplementary feeding of young puffins *Fratercula arctica*. *Journal of Animal Ecology* **47**, 15–23.

Harris, M. P. 1979. Measurements and weights of British puffins. *Bird Study* **26**, 179–186.

Harris, M. P. 1980. Breeding performance of puffins *Fratercula arctica* in relation to nest density, laying date and year. *Ibis* **122**, 193–209.

Harris, M. P. 1981. Age determination and first breeding of British puffins. *British Birds* **74**, 246–256.

Harris, M. P. 1982a. The breeding seasons of British puffins. *Scottish Birds* **12**, 11–17.

Harris, M. P. 1982b. Seasonal variation in fledging weight of the puffin *Fratercula arctica*. *Ibis* **124**, 100–103.

Harris, M. P. 1983a. Biology and survival of the immature puffin *Fratercula arctica*. *Ibis* **125**, 56–73.

Harris, M. P. 1983b. Parent-young communication in the puffin *Fratercula arctica*. *Ibis* **125**, 109–114.

Harris, M. P. 1984. "The Puffin." T. and A. D. Poyser, Calton. 224 pp.

Harris, M. P. and H. Galbraith. 1983. Seabird populations of the Isle of May. *Scottish Birds* **12**, 174–180.

Harris, M. P. and J. R. G. Hislop. 1978. The food of young puffins. *Journal of Zoology* **185**, 213–236.

Harris, M. P. and S. Murray. 1977. Puffins on St. Kilda. *British Birds* **70**, 50–65.

Harris, M. P. and S. Murray. 1978. "Birds of St. Kilda." Institute of Terrestrial Ecology, Natural Environment Research Council, Banchory. 42 pp.

Harris, M. P. and S. Murray. 1981. Monitoring of puffin numbers at Scottish colonies. *Bird Study* **28**, 15–20.

Harris, M. P. and D. Osborn. 1981. Effects of a polychlorinated biphenyl on the survival and breeding of puffins. *Journal of Applied Ecology* **18**, 471–479.

Harris, M. P. and S. Wanless. 1984. The effect of disturbance on weights and survival of young guillemots *Uria aalge*. *Seabird* **7**, 42–46.

Harris, M. P. and R. F. Yule. 1977. The moult of the puffin *Fratercula arctica*. *Ibis* **119**, 535–541.

Harris, M. P., S. Wanless and P. Rothery. 1983. Assessing changes in the numbers of Guillemots *Uria aalge* at breeding colonies. *Bird Study* **30**, 57–66.

Hartley, C. H. and J. Fisher. 1936. The marine foods of birds in an inland fjord region in west Spitsbergen. Part 2. Birds. *Journal of Animal Ecology* **5**, 370–389.

Hartung, R. 1967. Energy metabolism in oil-covered ducks. *Journal of Wildlife Management* **31**, 798–804.

Hartung, R. and G. S. Hunt. 1966. Toxicity of some oils to waterfowl. *Journal of Wildlife Management* **30**, 564–570.

Harvie-Brown, J. A. and H. A. Macpherson. 1904. "A Vertebrate Fauna of the North-West Highlands and Skye." Douglas, Edinburgh. 378 pp.

Hawkes, A. L. 1961. A review of the nature and extent of damage caused by oil pollution at sea. *Transactions of the North American Wildlife and Natural Resources Conference* **26**, 343–355.

Hayes, I. I. 1872. "The Land of Desolation: Being a Personal Narrative of Observation and Adventure in Greenland." Harper & Brothers, New York. 357 pp.

Hays, H. and R. W. Risebrough. 1972. Pollutant concentrations in abnormal young terns from Long Island Sound. *Auk* **89**, 19–35.

Hedgren. S. 1975. Det Häckande beståndet av sillgrissla *Uria aalge* i Östersjön. (The breeding population of guillemot *Uria aalge* in the Baltic Sea.) *Vår Fågelvårld* **34**, 43–52.

Hedgren, S. 1976. Om sillgrisslans *Uria aalge* foda vid Stora Karlsö. *Vår Fågelvårld* **35**, 287–290.

Hedgren, S. 1979. Seasonal variation in fledging weight of guillemots, *Uria aalge*. *Ibis* **121**, 356–361.

Hedgren, S. 1980. Reproductive success of guillemots *Uria aalge* on the island of Stora Karlsö. *Ornis Fennica* **57**, 49–57.

Hedgren, S. 1981. Effect of fledging weight and time of fledging on survival of guillemot *Uria aalge* chicks. *Ornis Scandinavica* **12**, 51–54.

Hedgren, S. and A. Linnman. 1979. Growth of guillemot *Uria aalge* chicks in relation to time of hatching. *Ornis Scandinavica* **10**, 29–36.

Helms, O. 1926. The birds of Angmagssalik. *Meddelelser om Grønland* **55**, 207–274.

Henry, J. and J. Y. Monnat. 1981. "Oiseaux marins de la façade Atlantique Française." Société pour l'Etude et la Protection de la Nature en Bretagne et Ministère de l'Environnement et du Cadre de Vie, Brest-Neuilly sur Seine. 338 pp.

Hermann, F. and P. M. Hansen. 1965. Possible influence of water temperature on the growth of the West Greenland Cod. *International Commission Northwest Atlantic Fisheries Special Publication* No. 6, 557–563.

Heubeck, M. and M. G. Richardson. 1980. Bird mortality following the "Esso *Bernica*" oil spill, Shetland, December 1978. *Scottish Birds* **11**, 97–108.

Hewitt, O. H. 1950. Fifth census of non-passerine birds in the sanctuaries of the north shore of the Gulf of St. Lawrence. *Canadian Field-Naturalist* **64**, 73–76.

Hickey, J. J. (ed.). 1969. "Peregrine Falcon Populations: Their Biology and Decline." University of Wisconsin Press, Madison. 596 pp.

Hilden, O. 1965. Habitat selection in birds. *Annales Zoologici Fennici* **2**, 53–75.

Hilden, O. 1966. Changes in the bird fauna of Valassaaret, Gulf of Bothnia, during recent decades. *Annales Zoologici Fennici* **3**, 249–269.

Hilden. O. 1978. Merenkurkun mokkikannan kehityksestia viime aikona. *Ornis Fennica* **55**, 42–44.

Hirschfeld, E., O. Holst, P. E. Jonsson, N. Kjellen, O. Persson and M. Ullman. 1982. Fåglar i Skane 1981. *Anser, Suppl.* **11**, 1–84.

Holdgate, M. W. (ed.). 1971. The seabird wreck in the Irish Sea autumn 1969. *Publications—Natural Environment Research Council, Series C (U.K.)* No. 4, 17 pp.

Holgersen, H. 1961. Norske lomviers vandringer. (On the movements of Norwegian guillemots.) *Sterna (Stavanger)* **6**, 229–240.

Holgersen, H. 1969. Stavanger Museums gjenfunn, 1967–1968. *Sterna (Stavanger)* **8**, 390–424.

Holgersen, H. 1974. Stavanger Museums gjenfunn 1971–73. Del. 1. Non-passeriformes. *Sterna (Stavanger)* **13**, 217–251.

Holgersen, H. 1980. Bird-ringing report 1976–78, Stavanger Museum. *Sterna (Stavanger)* **17**, 37–82.

Holm, G. 1918. Gunbjørns-Skaer og Korsøer. *Meddelelser om Grøland* **56**, 289–308.

Holmes, R.T. 1968. A Dovekie on the Pribilof Islands, Alaska (*Plautus alle* record). *Condor* **70**, 86.

Holmes, W. N. and J. Cronshaw. 1977. Biological effects of petroleum on marine birds *In* D. C. Milne (ed.), "Effects of Petroleum on Arctic and Subarctic Marine Environments and Organisms. Vol. II: Biological Effects," pp. 359–398. Academic Press, New York.

Homer, S. 1982. The quiet famine. *Equinox* **1**, 42–57.

Hoogland, J. L. 1979. Aggression, ectoparasitism and other possible costs of prairie dog (Scioridae *Cynomys* spp.) coloniality. *Behaviour* **69**, 1–35.

Hoogland, J. L. and P. W. Sherman. 1976. Advantages and disadvantages of Bank Swallow *Riparia riparia* coloniality. *Ecological Monographs* **46**, 33–58.

Hope Jones, P. 1978. Surveillance of cliff-nesting seabirds at their breeding sites in Orkney, 1976–1978. Unpublished report by Royal Society for Protection of Birds for Nature Conservancy Council, Aberdeen. 85 pp.

Hope Jones, P. 1980. Beached birds at selected Orkney beaches 1976–1978. *Scottish Birds* **11**, 1–12.

Hope Jones, P. 1982. The work of the seabirds at sea team off British coasts. *In* P. Hope Jones (ed.), "Proceedings of the Seabird Group Conference," pp. 21–22. British Seabird Group, Uttoxeter.

Hope Jones, P., G. Howells, E. I. S. Rees and J. Wilson. 1970. Effect of 'Hamilton Trader' oil on birds in the Irish Sea in May 1969. *British Birds* **63**, 97–110.

Hope Jones, P., J. Y. Monnat, C. J. Cadbury and T. J. Stowe. 1978. Birds oiled during the Amoco Cadiz incident—an interim report. *Marine Pollution Bulletin* **9**, 307–310.

Hopkins, D. M. 1959. Cenozoic history of the Bering Land Bridge. *Science (Washington, D.C.)* **129**, 1519–1528.

Hopkins, D. M. 1967. The Cenozoic history of Beringia. A synthesis. *In* D. M. Hopkins (ed.), "The Bering Land Bridge," pp. 451–484. Stanford University Press, Stanford, California.

Horn, H. S. 1968. The adaptive significance of colonial nesting in the Brewer's Blackbird *Euphagus cyanocephalus*. *Ecology* **49**, 682–694.

Hornung, M. and M. P. Harris. 1976. Soil water-levels and delayed egg-laying of puffins. *British Birds* **69**, 402–408.

Hørring, R. 1937. Birds collected on the Fifth Thule Expedition. "Report of the Fifth Thule Expedition 1921–1924." Vol. II, No. 6, pp. 1–134. Copenhagen.

Houghton, R. W., P. C. Smith and R. O. Fournier. 1978. A simple model for cross-shelf mixing on the Scotian Shelf. *Journal of the Fisheries Research Board of Canada* **35**, 414–421.

Howard, H. 1949. New avian records for the Pliocene of California. *Carnegie Institution of Washington Publications* No. 584, 177–199.

Howard, H. 1950. Fossil evidence of avian evolution. *Ibis* **92**, 1–21.

Howard, H. 1966. A possible ancestor of the Lucas auk (Family Mancallidae) from the Tertiary of Orange County, California. *Los Angeles County Museum of Natural History Contributions in Science* **101**, 1–8.

Howard, H. 1968. Tertiary birds from Laguna Hills, Orange County, California. *Los Angeles County Museum of Natural History Contributions in Science* **142**, 1–21.

Howard, H. 1971. Pliocene avian remains from Baja, California. *Los Angeles County Museum of Natural History Contributions in Science* **217**, 1–17.

Howard, H. 1976. A new species of flightless auk from the Miocene of California (Alcidae: Mancallinae) *In* S. L. Olsen (ed.), "Collected Papers in Avian Paleontology Honoring the 90th Birthday of Alexander Wetmore," pp. 141–146. Smithsonian Contributions to Paleobiology No. 27. Washington, D.C.

Howard, H. 1978. Late Miocene marine birds from Orange County, California. *Los Angeles County Museum of Natural History Contributions in Science* **290**, 1–26.

Howard, H. 1981. A new species of murre, genus *Uria* from the late Miocene of California (Aves: Alcidae). *Bulletin of the Southern California Academy of Sciences* **80**, 1–12.

Howard, H. 1982. Fossil birds from Tertiary marine beds at Oceanside, San Diego County, California, with descriptions of two new species of the genera *Uria* and *Cepphus* (Aves: Alcidae). *Los Angeles County Museum of Natural History Contributions in Science* **341**, 1–15.

Howarth, B., Jr. 1974. Sperm storage as a function of the female reproductive tract. *In* A. D. Johnson and C. W. Foley (eds.), "The Oviduct and its Functions," pp. 237–270. Academic Press, New York.

Hoyt, D. F. 1980. Adaptations of avian eggs to incubation period: variability around allometric regressions is correlated with time. *American Zoologist* **20**, 417–425.

Hudson, G. E., K. M. Hoff, J. V. Berge and E. C. Trivette. 1969. A numerical study of the wing and leg muscle of Lari and Alcae. *Ibis* **111**, 459–524.

Hudson, P. J. 1979a. The behaviour and survival of auks. Unpublished D. Phil. thesis, University of Oxford, Oxford. 110 pp.

Hudson, P. J. 1979b. The parent–chick fledging relationship of the puffin, *Fratercula arctica*. *Journal of Animal Ecology* **48**, 889–898.

Hudson, P. J. 1982. Nest site characteristics and breeding success in the Razorbill *Alca torda*. *Ibis* **124**, 355–359.

Humphrey, P. S. and K. C. Parkes. 1959. An approach to the study of molts and plumages. *Auk* **76**, 1–31.

Hunt, G. L., Jr. 1980. Mate selection and mating systems in seabirds. *In* J. Burger, B. L. Olla and H. E. Winn (eds.), "Behavior of Marine Animals. Vol. 4: Marine Birds," pp. 113–151. Plenum Press, New York.

Hunt, G. L., Jr., Z. Eppley, B. Burgeson and R. Squibb. 1980. "Reproductive Ecology, Foods and Foraging Areas of Seabirds Nesting on the Pribilof Islands, 1975–1979. Environmental Assessment of the Alaskan Continental Shelf," Final Report of Principal Investigators, Research Unit 83. U.S. Department of Commerce, National Oceanic and Atmospheric Administration, Outer Continental Shelf Environmental Assessment Program (OCSEAP), Boulder, Colorado. 244 pp.

Hunt, G. L., Jr., B. Burgeson and G. A. Sanger. 1981. Feeding ecology of seabirds of the eastern Bering Sea. *In* D. W. Hood and J. A. Calder (eds.), "The Eastern Bering Sea

Shelf: Oceanography and Resources," Vol. 2, pp. 629–648. University of Washington Press, Seattle.

Huntington, C. E. and E. H. Burtt. 1972. Breeding age and longevity in Leach's Storm-petrel. *Proceedings of the International Ornithological Congress* 15, 653.

Hussell, D. J. T. 1972. Factors regulating clutch size in arctic passerines. *Ecological Monographs* 42, 317–364.

Huxley, J. S. 1923–1924. On the relation between egg weight and body weight in birds. *Journal of the Linnean Society of London* 36, 457–466.

Idyll, C. P. 1973. The anchovy crisis. *Scientific American* 228, 22–29.

Ingold, P. 1973. Zur lautlichen Beziehung des Elters zu seinem küken bei Tordalken *(Alca torda)*. *Behaviour* 45, 154–190.

Ingold, P. 1974. Brutverhaeltnisse bei Tordalken *(Alca torda)* auf der Vogelinsel Vedøy (Lofoten). *Sterna (Stavanger)* 13, 205–210.

Ingold, P. 1980. Anpassungen der Eier und des Brutverhaltens von Trottellummen an das Brüten auf Felssimsen. *Zeitschrift für Tierpsychologie* 53, 341–388.

Ingolfsson, A. 1961. The taxonomy of Black Guillemots *(Cepphus grylle* (L.)) from Iceland and the Faroes. Unpublished B.Sc. thesis, University of Aberdeen, Aberdeen. 37 pp.

Innis, H. A. 1940. "The Cod Fisheries—the History of an International Economy." University of Toronto Press, Toronto. 522 pp.

Jangaard, P. M. 1974. The capelin *(Mallotus villosus)*. Biology, distribution, exploitation, utilization and composition. *Fisheries Research Board of Canada Bulletin* No. 186, 1–70.

Jarvis, M. J. F. 1974. The ecological significance of chick size in the South African Gannet *Sula capensis* (Lichtenstein). *Journal of Animal Ecology* 43, 1–17.

Jefferies, D. J. 1973. The effects of organochlorine insecticides and their metabolites on breeding birds. *Journal of Reproduction and Fertility, Supplement* 19, 337–352.

Jefferies, D. J. and J. L. F. Parslow. 1976. The genetics of bridling in guillemots from a study of hand-reared birds. *Journal of Zoology* 179, 411–420.

Jeffers, J. N. R. 1979. Conservation of the biological environment. *In* J. Lenihan and W. W. Fletcher (eds.), "Environment and Man. Vol. 9: The Biological Environment," pp. 122–160. Academic Press, New York. 164 pp.

Jehl, J. R. and S. I. Bond. 1975. Morphological variation and species limits in murrelets of the genus *Endomychura. Transactions of the San Diego Society of Natural History* 18, 9–23.

Jensen, S., A. G. Johnels, M. Olsson and G. Otterlind. 1969. DDT and PCB in marine animals from Swedish water. *Nature (London)* 224, 247–250.

Jespersen, P. 1934. The Godthaab Expedition, 1928. Copepoda. *Meddelelser om Grønland* 79, 1–66.

Joensen, A. H. 1966. "Fuglene på Faerøerne." Rhodos, Copenhagen. 185 pp.

Joensen, A. H. 1972a. Studies on oil pollution and seabirds in Denmark 1968–71. *Danish Review of Game Biology* 6(9), 1–32.

Joensen, A. H. 1972b. Oil pollution and seabirds in Denmark 1935–1968. *Danish Review of Game Biology* 6(8), 1–24.

Joensen, A. H. 1982. Seabird populations and negative factors in Denmark. *Viltrapport* 21, 17–22.

Joensen, A. H. and E. B. Hansen. 1977. Oil pollution and seabirds in Denmark 1971–1976. *Danish Review of Game Biology* 10(5), 1–31.

Joensen, A. H. and N. O. Preuss. 1972. Report on the ornithological expedition to northwest Greenland 1965. *Meddelelser om Grønland* 191, 1–58.

Johansen, H. 1958. Revision und Entstchung der Arktischen Vogelfauna. *Acta Arctica* 9, 5–131.

Johnsen, S. J., W. Dansgaard, H. B. Clausen and C. C. Langway. 1970. Climatic oscillations 1200–2000 AD. *Nature (London)* **227**, 482–483.

Johnson, R. A. 1938. Predation of gulls in murre colonies. *Wilson Bulletin* **50**, 161–170.

Johnson, R. A. 1940. Present range, migration and abundance of the Atlantic murre in North America. *Bird-Banding* **11**, 1–17.

Johnson, R. A. 1941. Nesting behaviour of the Atlantic murre. *Auk* **58**, 153–163.

Johnson, R. A. 1944. Weight records for Atlantic Alcidae. Wilson Bulletin **56**, 161–168.

Johnson, S. R. and G. C. West. 1975. Growth and development of heat regulation in nestlings, and metabolism of adult Common and Thick-billed Murres. *Ornis Scandinavica* **6**, 109–115.

Johnson, S. R., W. E. Renaud, W. J. Richardson, R. A. Davis, C. Holdsworth and P. D. Hollingdale. 1976. Aerial surveys of birds in eastern Lancaster Sound, 1976. Unpublished report by LGL Ltd., Toronto, for Norlands Petroleums, Calgary. 365 pp.

Johnston, R. (ed.). 1976. "Marine Pollution." Academic Press, London. 729 pp.

Joiris, C. 1978. Seabirds recorded in the northern North Sea in July: the ecological implications of their distribution. *Gerfaut* **68**, 419–440.

Joiris, C. 1983. Winter distribution of seabirds in the North Sea: an oceanological interpretation. *Gerfaut* **73**, 107–123.

Jones, A. M., Y. Jones, and W. D. P. Stewart. 1972. Mercury in marine organisms of the Tay region. *Nature (London)* **238**, 164–165.

Jones, P. J. and P. Ward, 1976. The level of reserve protein as the proximate factor controlling the timing of breeding and clutch size in the Red-billed Quelea *Quelea quelea*. *Ibis* **118**, 547–574.

Jourdain, F. C. R. 1922. The birds of Spitsbergen and Bear Island. *Ibis* **64**, 159–179.

Judin, K. A. 1965. Phylogeny and classification of Charadriiforme birds. *In* "Fauna of the U.S.S.R., Birds. Vol. II: Section 1, Part 1," pp. 1–261. Academy of Science USSR Science Publications New Series No. 91. Moscow and Leningrad.

Kadlec, J. A. 1976. A re-evaluation of mortality rates in adult Herring Gulls. *Bird-Banding* **47**, 8–12.

Kadlec, J. A. and W. H. Drury. 1968. Structure of the New England Herring Gull population. *Ecology* **49**, 644–676.

Kaftanovskii, Y. M. 1938. Kolonial'noe gnezdov'e kair i faktory vyzyvayushcie gibel' yaits i ptentsov. (Colony nesting of the murre and factors causing the death of eggs and nestlings.) *Zoologicheskii Zhurnal* **17**(4), 695–705.

Kaftanovskii, Y. M. 1941. Opyt sravnitel'noi kharakteristiki biologii razmnozheniya nekotorykh chistikovykh. (Studies on comparative characteristics of the reproduction of some murre species.) *Trudy Gosudarstvennogo Zapovednika "Sem'Ostrovov". Glavnoe Upravlenie po Zapovednikam pri SNK RSFSR* (Works by the "Seven Islands" Sanctuary. Main Board of Reserves attached to Council of Commissars of the RSFSR) **1**, 53–72.

Kaftanovskii, Y. M. 1951. Chistikovye ptitsy vostochnoi Atlantiki. Materialy k poznaniyu fauny i flory SSSR. (Birds of the murre group of the Eastern Atlantic. Studies of the fauna and flora of the USSR.) *Izdatel'stvo Moskovskogo Obshchestva Ispytatelei, Novaya Seriya, Otdelenie Zoologii* (Published by the Moscow Society of Naturalists, New Series, Zoology Section) **28**(13), 1–170.

Kampp, K. 1982. "Den Kortnaebbede lomvie *Uria lombia* i Grønland—vandringer, mortalitet og beskydning: en analyse af 35 års ringmaerkninger." Specialerapport til Naturvidenskabelig Kandidateksamen ved Københavns Universitet, Københavns. 148 pp.

Karpowicz, V. N. 1970. Bird colonies as habitat of *Ixodes persulcatus*. *Trudy Kandalakshskogo Gosudarstvennogo Zapovednika* **8**, 356–368.

Kartaschew, N. N. 1960. "Die Alkenvögel des Nordatlantiks." A. Ziemsen Verlag, Wittenberg. 154 pp.

Kaufmann, K. W. 1981. Fitting and using growth curves. *Oecologia* **49**, 293–299.

Keats, D. 1981. Marine natural history notes: II: Dovekies. *Osprey (St. John's, Newfoundland)* **12**, 10.

Keith, J. A. 1969. Some results and implications of pesticide research by the Canadian Wildlife Service. *Transactions of the 33rd Federal Provincial Wildlife Conference*, pp. 27–30. Canadian Wildlife Service, Ottawa.

Kellogg, T. B. 1980. Paleoclimatology and paleo-oceanography of the Norwegian and Greenland Seas: glacial–interglacial contrasts. *Boreas (Oslo)* **9**, 115–137.

Kendeigh, S. C. 1970. Energy requirements for existence in relation to size of bird. *Condor* **72**, 60–65.

Kennedy, P. G., R. F. Rutledge and C. F. Scroope. 1954. "The Birds of Ireland." Oliver and Boyd, London. 432 pp.

King, W. B., R. G. B. Brown and G. A. Sanger. 1979. Mortality to marine birds through commercial fishing. *In* J. C. Bartonek and D. N. Nettleship (eds.), "Conservation of Marine Birds of Northern North America," pp. 195–199. U.S. Department of the Interior, Fish and Wildlife Service, Wildlife Research Report No. 11. Washington, D.C. 319 pp.

Kinnear, P. K. 1975. Surveillance of seabird colonies in Shetland, summer 1975. Unpublished report, Nature Conservancy Council, Huntingdon. 58 pp.

Kinnear, P. K. 1977. Shetland seabird surveillance 1977. Unpublished report, Nature Conservancy Council, Lerwick and Huntingdon. 178 pp.

Klomp. H. 1970. The determination of clutch-size in birds. *Ardea* **58**, 1–124.

Knight, O. W. 1908. "The Birds of Maine." Charles H. Glass and Company, Bangor, Maine. 693 pp.

Knowlton, N. 1979. Reproductive synchrony, parental investment and the evolutionary dynamics of sexual selection. *Animal Behaviour* **27**, 1022–1033.

Koelink, A. F. 1972. Bioenergetics of growth in the Pigeon Guillemot. M.Sc. thesis, University of British Columbia, Vancouver. 71 pp.

Kohler, A. C. 1964. Variations in the growth of Atlantic cod (*Gadus morhua* L.). *Journal of the Fisheries Research Board of Canada* **21**, 57–100.

Kokhanov, V. D. and N. N. Skokova. 1967. Fauna ptits Ainovykh ostrovov. (Bird fauna of the Ainov Islands.) *Trudy Kandalakshskogo Gosudarstvennogo Zapovednika* No. 5.

Kolthoff, G. 1903. Bidrag till Kännedom om Norra Polartrakternas Däggdjur och Foglar. *Kungliga Svenska Vetenskapsakademiens Handlingar* **36**. 103 pp.

Kooyman, G. L. 1975. Behaviour and physiology of diving. *In* B. Stonehouse (ed.), "The Biology of Penguins," pp. 115–137. Macmillan, London.

Kooyman, G. L., C. M. Drabek, R. Elsner and M. B. Campbell. 1971. Diving behavior of the emperor penguin *Aptenodytes forsteri. Auk* **88**: 775–795.

Korschgen, C. E. 1979. Coastal waterbird colonies: Maine. *U.S. Fish and Wildlife Service, Office of Biological Services [Technical Report]* **FWS/OBS/79-09**. 84 pp.

Kortlandt, A. 1942. Leversloop, samenstelling en structuur der Nederlandse aalschulverbevolking. *Ardea* **31**, 175–280.

Koski, W. R. and W. J. Richardson. 1976. "Review of Waterbird Deterrent and Dispersal Systems for Oil Spills, PACE Report No. 76-6. Petroleum Association for the Conservation of the Canadian Environment, Ottawa. 122 pp.

Kozlova, E. V. 1957. "Fauna of USSR, Birds, Charadriiformes, Suborder Alcae." Zoological Institute of the Academy of Sciences USSR, New Series No. 65. Israel Program for Scientific Translations, Jerusalem. 143 pp. (Translation from Russian, 1961.)

Krasovski, S. K. 1937. Biologičeskie osnovy promyslovogo ispol'zovaniya ptič'ich bazarov. Etyudy po biologii tolstoklyuvoi kairy. *Trudy Arkticheskogo Instituta, Biologiya* **77**, 32–92. (Biological foundations for the economical exploitation of bird colonies. Studies on the biology of the Thick-billed Murres. *Transactions of the Arctic Institute, Biology* **77**, 32–92.)

Krebs, J. R. 1974. Colonial nesting and social feeding as strategies for exploiting food resources in the Great Blue Heron *Ardea herodias. Behaviour* **51**, 99–134.

Krebs, J. R. 1978. Colonial nesting in birds with special reference to the Ciconiiformes. *In* A. Sprunt, J. C. Ogden and S. Winckler (eds.), "Wading Birds," pp. 299–313. National Audubon Society Research Report No. 7. New York.

Kruuk, H. 1964. Predators and anti-predator behaviour of the Black-headed Gull *(Larus ridibundus L.). Behaviour, Supplement* No. 11, 1–130.

Kukla, G. J., J. K. Angell, J. Korshover, H. Dronia, M. Hoshiai, J. Namias, M. Rodewald, R. Yamamoto and T. Iwashima. 1977. New data on climatic trends. *Nature (London)* **270**, 573–580.

Kuroda, N. 1954. On some osteological and antomical characters of Japanese Alcidae *(Aves). Japanese Journal of Zoology* **11**, 311–327.

Kuroda, N. 1955. Additional notes on the osteology of the Alcidae *(Aves). Annotationes Zoologicae Japonenses* **28**, 110–113.

Kuyken, E. 1978. Beached bird surveys in Belgium. *Ibis* **120**, 122–123.

Kuyken, E. and P. M. Zegers. 1968. De Stookolieslach buffertelling van Februari 1968 largs de Nederlandse kust. *Amoeba* **44**, 153–158.

Kuyt, E., B. E. Johnson, P. S. Taylor and T. W. Barry. 1976. Black Guillemots' breeding range extended into the western Canadian arctic. *Canadian Field-Naturalist* **90**, 75–76.

Lack, D. 1950. The breeding seasons of European birds. *Ibis* **92**, 288–316.

Lack, D. 1954. "The Natural Regulation of Animal Numbers." Oxford University Press, London. 343 pp.

Lack, D. 1966. "Population Studies of Birds." Oxford University Press, London. 341 pp.

Lack, D. 1968. "Ecological Adaptations for Breeding in Birds." Methuen, London. 409 pp.

Lack, D. 1971. "Ecological Isolation in Birds." Blackwell, Oxford. 404 pp.

Lake, P. E. 1975. Gamete production and the fertile period with particular reference to domesticated birds. *Symposium of the Zoological Society of London* No. 35, 225–244.

Lamb, H. H. 1966. "The Changing Climate." Methuen, London.

Lamb, H. H. 1972. "Climate: Present, Past and Future. Vol. I: Fundamentals and Climate Now." Methuen, London. 613 pp.

Lamb, H. H. 1975. Remarks on the current climatic trend and its perspective. *Proceedings WMO/IAMAP Symposium on Long-term Climatic Fluctuations, Norwich* pp. 473–477. WMO, Geneva.

Lamb, H. H. 1982. "Climate, History and the Modern World." Methuen, London. 387 pp.

Lambrecht, K. 1933. "Handbuch der Palaeornithologie." Borntraeger, Berlin. 1024 pp.

Lasiewski, R. C. and W. R. Dawson. 1967. A re-examination of the relation between standard metabolic rate and body weight in birds. *Condor* **69**, 13–23.

Lea, D. and W. R. P. Bourne. 1975. The birds of Orkney. *In* R. Goodier (ed.), "The Natural Environment of Orkney," pp. 98–121. Nature Conservancy Council, Edinburgh.

Lear, W. H. 1980. Food of Atlantic Salmon in the West Greenland-Labrador Sea area. *Rapports et Procès-Verbaux des Réunions Counseil International pour l'Exploration de la Mer* **176**, 55–59.

Lebreton, J. D. and P. Isenmann. 1976. Dynamique de la population Carmarguaise de mouettes rieuses *Larus ridibundus* L.: Un modèle mathematique. *Terre et la Vie* **30**, 529–549.

Lee, A. J. and J. W. Ramster. 1981. "Atlas of the Seas around the British Isles." Ministry of Agriculture, Fisheries and Food, London. 98 pp.

Lee, D. S. and J. Booth. 1980. Seasonal distribution of offshore and pelagic birds in North Carolina waters. *American Birds* **33**, 715–721.

Lehn, W. H. and I. I. Schroeder. 1979. Polar mirages as aids to Norse navigation. *Polarforschung* **49**, 173–187.

Leim, A. H. and W. B. Scott. 1966. Fishes of the Atlantic coast of Canada. *Fisheries Research Board of Canada Bulletin* No. 155, 1–485.

Le Messurier, S. L. 1980. "The Fishery of Newfoundland and Labrador." Extension Service, Memorial University of Newfoundland, St. John's. 151 pp.

Lemieux, L. 1956. Seventh census of non-passerine birds in the bird sanctuaries of the north shore of the Gulf of St. Lawrence. *Canadian Field-Naturalist* **70**, 183–185.

Leslie, P. H. 1966. The intrinsic rate of increase and the overlap of successive generations in a population of guillemots *Uria aalge*. *Journal of Animal Ecology* **35**, 291–301.

Lewis, H. F. 1925. The new bird sanctuaries in the Gulf of St. Lawrence. *Canadian Field-Naturalist* **39**, 177–179.

Lewis, H. F. 1931. Five years' progress in the bird sanctuaries of the north shore of the Gulf of St. Lawrence. *Canadian Field-Naturalist* **45**, 73–78.

Lewis, H. F. 1937. A decade of progress in the bird sanctuaries of the north shore of the Gulf of St. Lawrence. *Canadian Field-Naturalist* **51**, 51–55.

Lewis, H. F. 1942. Fourth census of the non-passerine birds in the bird sanctuaries of the north shore of the Gulf of St. Lawrence. *Canadian Field-Naturalist* **56**, 5–8.

Lid, G. 1981. Reproduction of the puffin on Røst in the Lofoten Islands in 1964–1980. *Fauna Norvegica Ser. C, Cinclus* **4**, 30–39.

Lippens, L. and H. Willie. 1972. "Atlas des oiseaux de Belgique et d'Europe Occidentale. Tielt. 847 pp.

Lisitzin, A. P. 1972. Sedimentation in the world ocean—with emphasis on the nature, distribution and behavior of marine suspensions. *Society of Economic Paleontologists and Mineralogists Special Publication* No. 17, 1–218.

Lloyd, C. S. 1973. Attendance at auk colonies during the breeding season. *Skokholm Bird Observatory Annual Report 1972*, 15–23.

Lloyd, C. S. 1974. Movement and survival of British Razorbills. *Bird Study* **21**, 102–116.

Lloyd, C. S. 1975. Timing and frequency of census counts of cliff-nesting auks. *British Birds* **68**, 507–513.

Lloyd, C. S. 1976a. The breeding biology and survival of the Razorbill *Alca torda* L. Unpublished D.Phil. thesis, University of Oxford, Oxford. 150 pp.

Lloyd, C. S. 1976b. An estimate of the world breeding population of the Razorbill. *British Birds* **69**, 298–304.

Lloyd, C. S. 1977. The ability of the Razorbill *Alca torda* to raise an additional chick to fledging. *Ornis Scandinavica* **8**, 155–159.

Lloyd, C. S. 1979. Factors affecting breeding of Razorbills *Alca torda* on Skokholm. *Ibis* **121**, 165–176.

Lloyd, C. S. 1982. The seabirds of Great Saltee. *Irish Birds* **2**, 1–37.

Lloyd, C. S. and C. M. Perrins. 1977. Survival and age of first breeding in the Razorbill *Alca torda*. *Bird-Banding* **48**, 239–252.

Lock, A. R. 1971. Census of seabirds nesting in Nova Scotia, 18 May to 30 June 1971. Unpublished manuscript report, Canadian Wildlife Service, Ottawa. 46 pp.

Lock, A. R. 1979. Offshore Labrador Biological Studies (OLABS)—Part 2: Report on the 1978 survey of breeding seabirds in Labrador. *Canadian Wildlife Service "Studies on Northern Seabirds" Manuscript Report* No. 75b, 1–87.

Lockley, R. M. 1934. On the breeding habits of the puffin: with special reference to the incubation- and fledging-period. *British Birds* **27**, 214–223.

Lockley, R. M. 1953a. "Puffins." Devin-Adair, New York. 186 pp.

Lockley, R. M. 1953b. On the movements of the Manx Shearwater at sea during the breeding season. *British Birds* **46**, Supplement, 1–48.

Longstaff, T. G. 1924. Notes from Spitsbergen 1923. *Ibis* **66**, 480–495.

Løppenthin, B. 1963a. Immigration and distribution of the Alcidae in the Baltic area. *Proceedings of the International Ornithological Congress* **13**, 1128–1133.

Løppenthin, B. 1963b. Betragtninger over de dansk-baltiske alkfuglebestande. Modsigelse af reliktteorien. *Dansk Ornithologisk Forenings Tidsskrift* **57**, 85–93.

Lounsbury, R. G. 1934. "The British Fishery at Newfoundland 1634–1763." Yale University Press, New Haven, Connecticut. 398 pp.

Løvenskiold, H. L. 1964. Avifauna Svalbardensis with a discussion on the geographical distribution of the birds in Spitsbergen and adjacent islands. *Norsk Polarinstitutt Skrifter* No. 129, 1–460.

Lucas, F. A. 1890. The expedition to the Funk Island, with observations upon the history and anatomy of the Greak Auk. *Report of the U.S. National Museum 1887–88* pp. 493–529.

Lütken, E. 1969. Bird life on Bjørnøya 1965. *Norsk Polarinstitutt Årbok* 1967, 151–165.

Lysaght, A. (ed.). 1971. "Joseph Banks in Newfoundland and Labrador, 1766: His Diary, Manuscript and Collections." University of California Press, Berkeley and Los Angeles.

MacArthur, R. H. and E. O. Wilson, 1967. "The Theory of Island Biogeography. Princeton University Press, Princeton, New Jersey. 203 pp.

Mackay, D. and W. Harrison (eds.). 1973. "Oil and the Canadian Environment," Proceedings of Conference. Institute of Environmental Sciences and Engineering, University of Toronto, Toronto. 142 pp.

Macoun, J. and J. M. Macoun. 1909. Catalogue of Canadian birds. *Canada Department of Mines, Geological Survey Branch* No. 973, 1–761.

Macpherson, A. H. and I. A. McLaren. 1959. Notes on the birds of southern Foxe Peninsula, Baffin Island, Northwest Territories. *Canadian Field-Naturalist* **73**, 63–81.

Madsen. E. J. 1957. On the food habits of some fish-eating birds in Denmark. *Danish Review of Game Biology* **3**, 19–83.

Mahoney, S. P. 1979. Breeding biology and behaviour of the Common Murre *Uria aalge* (Pont.) on Gull Island, Newfoundland. M.Sc. thesis, Memorial University, St. John's, Newfoundland. 155 pp.

Mahoney, S. P. and W. Threlfall. 1981. Notes on the eggs, embryos and chick growth of Common Guillemots *Uria aalge* in Newfoundland. *Ibis* **123**, 211–218.

Manniche, A. L. V. 1910. The terrestrial mammals and birds of north-east Greenland. Biological observations. *Meddelelser om Grønland* **45**(1), 1–200.

Manning, T. H. 1946. Bird and mammal notes from the east side of Hudson Bay. *Canadian Field-Naturalist* **60**, 71–85.

Manning, T. H. 1949. The birds of north-western Ungava. *In* Mrs. T. Manning, "A Summer on Hudson Bay," pp. 153–224. Hodder and Stoughton, London.

Manning, T. H. 1952. Birds of the west James Bay and southern Hudson Bay coasts. *National Museum of Canada Bulletin* No. 125, 1–108.

Manning, T. H. 1981. Birds of the Twin Islands, James Bay, N.W.T., Canada. *National Museums of Canada Syllogeus Series* No. 30, 1–50.

Manning, T. H. and D. F. Coates. 1952. Notes on the birds of some James Bay islands. *Annual Report of the National Museum of Canada, 1950–1951, Bulletin* No. 126, 195–207.

Manning, T. H. and A. H. Macpherson. 1952. Birds of the east James Bay coast between Long Point and Cape Jones. *Canadian Field-Naturalist* **66**, 1–35.

Manuwal, D. A. 1972. The population ecology of Cassin's Auklet on southeast Farallon Island, California. Unpublished Ph.D. thesis, University of California, Los Angeles. 298 pp.

Manuwal, D. 1974a. The natural history of Cassin's Auklet *(Ptychoramphus aleuticus)*. *Condor* **76**, 421–431.

Manuwal, D. A. 1974b. Effects of territoriality on breeding in a population of Cassin's Auklet. *Ecology* **55**, 1399–1406.

Marsault, B. M. 1975. Auks breeding in captivity. *Bird Study* **22**, 44–46.

Marsh, D. C. 1870. Notice of some fossil birds from the Cretaceous and Tertiary formations of the United States. *American Journal of Science and Arts* **49**, 205–217.

Marshall, A. J. 1952. Non-breeding among arctic birds. *Ibis* **94**, 310–333.

Martin, M. 1698. "A Late Voyage to St. Kilda, the Remotest of All the Hebrides, or Western Isles of Scotland." Gent, London. 159 pp.

Martin, W. R. and A. C. Kohler. 1965. Variation in recruitment of cod *(Gadus morhua* L.) in southern ICNAF waters, as related to environmental change. *Special Publication International Commission for the Northwest Atlantic Fisheries* **6**, 833–846.

Marzocchi, J. F. 1982. Sur une observation du Pigouin torda *Alca torda* en Corse. *Oiseau et la Revue Française d'Ornithologie* **52**(3), 289.

Mathiassen, S. 1962. "Femtio års Fågelmärkningar vid Göteborgs Naturhistoriska Museum: en Tillbackablick. " Särtryck ur Göteborgs Naturhistoriska Museum Årstryck, Göteborg. 63 pp.

Mauchline, J. 1980. The biology of mysids and euphausiids. *Advances in Marine Biology* **18**, 1–681.

Mauchline, J. and L. R. Fisher. 1969. The biology of euphausiids. *Advances in Marine Biology* **7**, 1–454.

Mayr, E. 1969. "Principles of Systematic Zoology." McGraw-Hill, New York. 439 pp.

McEwan, E. H. and A. F. C. Koelink. 1973. The heat production of oiled mallards and scaup. *Canadian Journal of Zoology* **51**, 27–31.

McIntosh, W. C. 1903. Notes from the Gatty Marine Laboratory, St. Andrews—No. 14. 2. The effects of marine piscatorial birds on the food-fishes. *Annals and Magazine of Natural History* **11**, 551–553.

McKay, C., C. Prentice and K. Shepherd. 1981. Survey of breeding sea-birds in Yell-Sound, summer 1981. Unpublished report to Shetland Oil Terminal Environmental Advisory Group, Aberdeen. 59 pp.

McLaren, P. L. 1982. Spring Migration and Habitat use by seabirds in eastern Lancaster Sound and western Baffin Bay. *Arctic* **35**, 88–111.

McLaren, P. L. and W. E. Renaud. 1979. Distribution of sea-associated birds in northwest Baffin Bay and adjacent waters, May–October 1978. Unpublished report by LGL Ltd., for Petro-Canada Exploration, Calgary. 323 pp.

McWilliam, J. M. 1936. "The Birds of the Firth of Clyde Including Ayrshire, Renfrewshire, Buteshire, Dunbartonshire and South Argyllshire." Witherby, London. 164 pp.

Mead, C. J. 1974. The results of ringing auks in Britain and Ireland. *Bird Study* **21**, 45–86.

Mead, C. J. 1981. The black death. *British Trust for Ornithology News* No. 112, 1.

Mead, C. J. and A. Cawthorne. 1983. Massive auk wreck. *British Trust for Ornithology News* No. 125, 1.

Meinertzhagen, R. 1938. Winter in arctic Lapland. *Ibis 2*, 754–759.

Meinertzhagen, R. 1955. Flight spread and altitude of bird flight (with notes on other animals). *Ibis* **97**, 81–117.

Meltofte, H. 1975. Ornithological observations in northeast Greenland between 76°00' and 78°00'N. latitude, 1969–71. *Meddelelser om Grønland* **191**(9), 1–72.

Meltofte, H. 1976. Ornithologiske observationer i Scoresbysundområdet, Østgrønland, 1974. *Dansk Ornithologisk Forenings Tidsskrift* **70**, 107–122.

Meltofte, H., M. Elander and C. Hjort. 1981. Ornithological observations in northeast Greenland between 74°30' and 76°00'N latitude, 1976. *Meddelelser om Grønland, Bioscience* **3**, 1–53.

Melville, D. S. 1973. Birds and salmon nets. *Seabird Report* **3**, 47–50.

Menzies, R. G. 1965. Bird notes from a submarine at the arctic ice edge. *Sea Swallow* **17**, 80.

Merikallio, E. 1958. Finnish birds: their distribution and numbers. *Fauna och Flora Fennica* **5**, 1–181.

Meserve, J. M. 1974. "U.S. Navy Marine Climatic Atlas of the World. Vol. 1: North Atlantic Ocean," Navair 50-1C-528. U.S. National Climatic Center, Department of Commerce, Government Printing Office, Washington, D.C.

Mileykowskiy, S. A. 1979. Extent of the oil pollution of the World Ocean (literature review). *Oceanology* **19**, 547–551.

Miller, D. S., D. B. Peakall and W. B. Kinter. 1978. Ingestion of crude oil: sublethel effects in Herring Gull chicks. *Science (Washington, D.C.)* **199**, 315–317.

Miller, L. H. 1925. Avian remains from the Miocene of Lompoc, California. *Carnegie Institution of Washington Publications* No. 349, 107–117.

Miller, L. H. and R. I. Bowman. 1958. Further bird remains from the San Diego Pliocene. *Los Angeles County Museum Contributions to Science* **20**, 1–15.

Milne, J. 1875. Relics of the Great Auk on Funk Island. *The Field* March 27, April 3 and 10.

Mitchell, E. D. and R. R. Reeves. 1982. Factors affecting abundance of Bowhead Whales *Balaena mysticetus* in the eastern arctic of North America, 1915–1980. *Biological Conservation* **22**, 59–78.

Mitchell, P. C. 1896. On the intestinal tract of birds. *Proceedings of the Zoological Society of London* pp. 136–159.

Mitchell, P. C. 1901. On the intestinal tract of birds; with remarks on the valuation and nomenclature of zoological characters. *Transactions of the Linnaean Society of London, Zoology* **8**, 173–275.

Moisan, G. 1962. Eighth census of non-passerine birds in the bird sanctuaries of the north shore of the Gulf of St. Lawrence. *Canadian Field-Naturalist* **76**, 78–82.

Moisan, G. and R. Fyfe. 1967. Ninth census of non-passerine birds in the sanctuaries of the north shore of the Gulf of St. Lawrence. *Canadian Field-Naturalist* **81**, 67–70.

Monnat, J. Y. 1969. Statut actuel des oiseaux marins nicheurs en Bretagne VI. Haut-Tregor et Goelo (de Trébeurden à Paimpol). *Ar Vran* **2**, 1–24.

Montaque, F. 1926. Further notes from Spitsbergen. *Ibis* 2, 136–151.

Montevecchi, W. A. and J. M. Porter. 1980. Parental investments by seabirds at the breeding area with emphasis on northern gannets *Morus bassanus*. *In* J. Burger, B. L. Olla and H. E. Winn (eds.), "Behavior of Marine Animals. Vol. 4: Marine Birds," pp. 323–365. Plenum Press, New York.

Moore, N. W. and J. O'G. Tatton. 1965. Organochlorine insecticide residues in the eggs of seabirds. *Nature (London)* **207**, 42–43.

Moors, P. J. and J. A. E. Atkinson. 1984. Predation on seabirds by introduced animals, and Factors affecting its severity. *In* J. Croxall, P. G. H. Evans and R. Schreiber (eds.), "Seabirds of the World: Their Status and Conservation." pp. 667–690. International Council for Bird Preservation, Cambridge, England.

Morejohn, G. V., J. T. Harvey and L. T. Krasnow. 1978. The importance of *Loligo opalescens* in the food web of marine vertebrates in Monterey Bay, California. *In* C. W.

Recksiek and H. W. Frey (eds.), "Biological, Oceanographic and Acoustic Aspects of the Market Squid, *Loligo opalescens* Berry," pp. 67–98. California Department of Fish and Game, Fish Bulletin No. 169. Sacramento.

Moriarty, F. 1972. The effects of pesticides on wildlife: exposure and residues. *Science of the Total Environment* **1**, 267–288.

Moriarty, F. 1975. "Pollutants and Animals." Allen and Unwin, London. 140 pp.

Morison, S. E. 1971. "The European Discovery of America—the Northern Voyages, A.D. 500–1600." Oxford University Press, New York. 712 pp.

Mörzer Bruyns, M. F. 1958. The Herring Gull problem in the Netherlands. *International Committee for Bird Preservation Bulletin* **7**, 103–107.

Mosby, H. 1960. Havet. *In* G. Rollefsen (ed.), "Havet og våre fisker," pp. 13–42. J. W. Eides, Bergen.

Mothersole, J. 1910. "The Isles of Scilly, Their Story, Their Folk, and Their Flowers." Religious Tract Society, London.

Mudge, G. P. 1979. The cliff-breeding seabirds of East Caithness in 1977. *Scottish Birds* **10**, 247–61.

Murphy, R. C. 1936. "The Oceanic Birds of South America." American Museum of Natural History, New York. 1245 pp.

Murphy, R. C. and W. Vogt. 1933. The Dovekie influx of 1932. *Auk* **50**, 325–349.

Murray, K. G., K. Winnet-Murray, Z. A. Eppley, G. L. Hunt, Jr. and D. B. Schwartz. 1983. Breeding biology of the Xantus' Murrelet. *Condor* **85**, 12–21.

Murton, R. K. and N. J. Westwood. 1977. "Avian Breeding Cycles." Clarendon Press, Oxford, 594 pp.

Murton, R. K., D. Osborn and P. Ward. 1978. Are heavy metals pollutants in Atlantic seabirds? *Ibis* **120**, 106–107.

Musters, J. L. C. 1930. Fuglefaunaen på Jan Mayen. *Norsk Ornithologisk Tidsskrift* **3**, 216–219.

Myrberget, S. 1959a. Vekslinger i Antall lundefugl inner ved Kolonien. *Sterna (Stavanger)* **3**, 239–248. (English summary.)

Myrberget, S. 1959b. Lundrnua på Lovunden, og lundebastanden der. *Fauna (Oslo)* **12**(4), 143–156. (English summary.)

Myrberget, S. 1962. Undersøkelser over forplantnings biologien til lunde *[Fratercula arctica* (L.)]. Egg, ruging og under. *Meddelelser fra Statens Viltundersøkelser* **2**(11), 1–51. (English summary).

Myrberget, S. 1963. Systematic position of *Fratercula arctica* from a North Norwegian colony. *Nytt Magasin for Zoologi (Oslo)* **11**, 74–84.

Myrberget, S. 1973a. Ringmerking av Teiste langs den Skandinaviske vestkyst. *Sterna (Stavanger)* **12**, 33–40.

Myrberget, S. 1973b. Merking av toppskarv og lunde på Røst. *Sterna (Stavanger)* **12**, 307–315.

Myrberget, S. 1978. Bestandsutvikling hos norske sjøfugl. *Naturen* **102**, 123–128.

Namais, J. 1959. Recent seasonal interaction between North Pacific waters and the overlying atmospheric circulation. *Journal of Geophysical Research* **64**, 631–646.

Namais, J. 1964. Seasonal persistence and recurrence of European blocking during 1958-1960. *Tellus* **16**(3), 394–407.

Nansen, F. 1897. "Farthest North," Vol I and II. Archibald Constable, Westminster. 510 pp. and 671 pp.

Nansen, F. 1911. "In Northern Mists: Arctic Exploration in Early Times," Vol. I and II. Frederick A. Stokes Co., New York. 384 pp. and 420 pp.

Nash, A. 1975. A speculation on puffin fishing. *Bird Study* **22**, 238.

Nelson, C. H., D. M. Hopkins and D. W. Scholl. 1974. Cenozoic sedimentary and tectonic history of the Bering Sea. *In* D. W. Hood and E. J. Kelly (eds.), "Oceanography of the Bering Sea," pp. 485–516. Institute of Marine Science, University of Alaska, Fairbanks.

Nelson, J. B. 1964. Factors influencing clutch size and chick growth in the north Atlantic Gannet *Sula bassana*. *Ibis* **106**, 63–77.

Nelson, J. B. 1966. The breeding biology of the Gannet *(Sula bassana)* on the Bass Rock, Scotland. *Ibis* **108**, 584–626.

Nelson, J. B. 1978a. "The Gannet." T. and A. D. Poyser, Berkhampstead. 336 pp.

Nelson, J. B. 1978b. "The Sulidae: Gannets and Boobies." Oxford University Press, London. 1012 pp.

Nelson, T. H. 1907. "The Birds of Yorkshire." London. 843 pp.

N.E.R.C. 1983. Contaminants in marine top predators. *Natural Environment Research Council Publications Series C* No. 23, 1–30.

Nettleship, D. N. 1970. Breeding success of the Common Puffin [*Fratercula arctica* (L.)] on different habitats at Great Island, Newfoundland. Unpublished Ph.D. thesis, McGill University, Montreal. 122 pp.

Nettleship, D. N. 1972. Breeding success of the Common Puffin [*Fratercula arctica* (L.)] on different habitats at Great Island, Newfoundland. *Ecological Monographs* **42**, 239–268.

Nettleship, D. N. 1973a. Census of seabirds in the sanctuaries of the north shore of the Gulf of St. Lawrence, summer 1972. *Canadian Wildlife Service "Studies on Northern Seabirds" Manuscript Report* No. 20, 1–160.

Nettleship, D. N. 1973b. Canadian seabird research. *Marine Pollution Bulletin* **4**, 62–64.

Nettleship, D. N. 1974. Seabird colonies and distributions around Devon Island and vicinity. *Arctic* **27**, 95–103.

Nettleship, D. N. 1975a. A recent decline in gannets at Bonaventure Island, Quebec. *Canadian Field-Naturalist* **89**, 125–133.

Nettleship, D. N. 1975b. Effects of Larus gulls on breeding performance and nest distribution in Atlantic Puffins. *Proceedings of Gull Seminar, Sackville, New Brunswick* pp. 47–69. Canadian Wildlife Service, Sackville, New Brunswick.

Nettleship, D. N. 1976a. Census techniques for seabirds of arctic and eastern Canada. *Canadian Wildlife Service Occasional Paper* No. 25, 1–33.

Nettleship, D. N. 1976b. Gannets in North America: present numbers and recent changes. *Wilson Bulletin* **88**, 300–313.

Nettleship, D. N. 1977a. Seabird resources of eastern Canada: status, problems and prospects. *In* T. Mosquin and C. Suchal (eds.), "Proceedings of Symposium Canada's Endangered Species and Habitats," pp. 96–108. Canadian Nature Federation Special Publication No. 6. Ottawa.

Nettleship, D. N. 1977b. Studies of seabirds at Prince Leopold Island and vicinity, Northwest Territories. Preliminary report of biological investigations. *Canadian Wildlife Service Progress Note* No. 73, 1–11.

Nettleship, D. N. 1980. A guide to the major seabird colonies of eastern Canada: identity, distribution and abundance. *Canadian Wildlife Service "Studies on Northern Seabirds" Manuscript Report* No. 97, 1–133.

Nettleship, D. N. and A. J. Gaston. 1978. Patterns of pelagic distribution of seabirds in western Lancaster Sound and Barrow Strait, Northwest Territories, in August and September 1976. *Canadian Wildlife Service Occasional Paper* No. 39, 1–40.

Nettleship, D. N., and A. R. Lock. 1973. Tenth census of seabirds in the sanctuaries of the north shore of the Gulf of St. Lawrence. *Canadian Field-Naturalist* **87**, 395–402.

Nettleship, D. N. and P. A. Smith. 1975. "Ecological Sites in Northern Canada." Canadian

Committee for the International Biological Programme, Conservation Terrestrial, Panel 9. Ottawa. 330 pp.

Nettleship, D. N., T. R. Birkhead and A. J. Gaston. 1980. Reproductive failure among Thick-billed Murres associated with unusual ice conditions in Lancaster Sound, 1978. *Canadian Wildlife Service "Studies on Northern Seabirds" Manuscript Report* No. 77, 1–31.

Nettleship, D. N., G. A. Sanger and P. F. Springer. (eds.). 1984. "Marine Birds: Their Feeding Ecology and Commercial Fisheries Relationships," Canadian Wildlife Service Special Publication. Ottawa. 220 pp.

Newton, A. 1861. Abstract of Mr. J. Wolley's researches in Iceland respecting the Garefowl or Great Auk (*Alca impennis* Linn.). *Ibis* **3**, 374–399.

Newton, I., M. B. Hass and A. A. Bell. 1982. Pollutants in guillemot eggs. *Annual Report of the Institute of Terrestrial Ecology, Cambridge* 1981, 57–59.

Nicholson, J. K. and D. Osborn. 1983. Kidney lesions in pelagic seabirds with high tissue levels of cadmium and mercury. *Journal of Zoology* **200**, 99–118.

Nikolaev, V. M. (ed.). 1979 "Bulletin Statistique des Pêches Maritimes," No. 61, 1976. Conseil International pour l'Exploration de la Mer, Charlottenlund Slot. 303 pp.

Nikolaev, V. M. (ed.). 1980. "Bulletin Statistique des Pêches Maritimes," No. 62, 1977. Conseil International pour l'Exploration de la Mer, Copenhagen. 329 pp.

Nikolaev, V. M. 1982. "Bulletin Statistique des Pêches Maritimes," Conseil International pour l'Exploration de la mer, Vol. 64, 1979. Copenhagen. 103 pp.

Nisbet, I. C. T. 1973. Terns in Massachusetts: present numbers and historical changes. *Bird-Banding* **44**, 27–55.

Nisbet, I. C. T. 1975. Selective effects of predation in a tern colony. *Condor* **77**, 221–226.

Nisbet, I. C. T. 1978a. Recent changes in gull populations in the western North Atlantic. *Ibis* **120**, 129–130.

Nisbet, I. C. T. 1978b. Population models for Common Terns in Massachusetts. *Bird-Banding* **49**, 50–58.

Nisbet, I. C. T. 1979. Conservation of marine birds of northern North America—a summary. *In* J. C. Bartonek and D. N. Nettleship (eds.), "Conservation of Marine Birds of Northern North America," pp. 305–315. U.S. Department of the Interior, Fish and Wildlife Service, Wildlife Research Report No. 11. Washington, D.C. 319 pp.

Nord, I. 1977. Antalet hackande fåglar i Sormland. (Number of breeding birds in Sodermanland.) *Faglar i Sormland* **10**, 1–22.

Nordberg, S. 1950. Researches on the bird fauna of the marine zone in the Åland archipelago. *Acta Zoologica Fennica* **63**, 1–62.

Norderhaug, M. 1966. Ringmerking avi fugul på Svalbard 1962–1965. (Bird banding in Svalbard 1962–1965.) *Norsk Polarinstitutt Årbok* 1965, 181–183.

Norderhaug, M. 1967. Trekkforhold, stedstrohet og pardannelse hos alkekonge på Svalbard. *Fauna (Oslo)* **20**, 236–244.

Norderhaug, M. 1970. The role of the Little Auk *Plautus alle* (L.) in arctic ecosystems. *In* M. W. Holdgate (ed.), "Antarctic Ecology," Vol. 1, pp. 558–560. Academic Press, London and New York.

Norderhaug, M. 1974. Studier av sjøfuglkoloniene på Fuglehuken, Prins Karls Forland nasjonalpark. (Studies of the seabird colonies on Fuglehuken, Prins Karls Forland National Park.) *Norsk Polarinstitutt Årbok* 1972, 99–106.

Norderhaug, M. 1980. Breeding biology of the Little Auk (*Plautus alle*) in Svalbard. *Norsk Polarinstitutt Skrifter* No. 173, 1–45.

Norderhaug, M., E. Brun and G. U. Møllen. 1977. Barentshavets sjøfuglressurser. (Seabird resources of the Barents Sea.) *Norsk Polarinstitutt Meddelelser* **104**, 1–119. (Translated from Norwegian, 1981 by R. G. B. Brown, Canadian Wildlife Service, Dartmouth.)

Nordström, G. 1963. Die Vogelberingung in Finnland im Jahre 1962. *Memoranda Societatas pro Fauna et Flora Fennica* **40**, 5–173.

Nørrevang, A. 1958. On the breeding biology of the Guillemot *Uria aalge* (Pont.). *Dansk Ornithologisk Forenings Tidsskrift* **52**, 48–74.

Nørrevang, A. 1960. Søfuglenes udvaelogelse af ynglebiotop på Mykines, Faerøerne. (Habitat selection of sea birds in Mykines, Faeroes.) *Dansk Ornithologisk Forenings Tidsskrift* **54**, 9–35.

Nørrevang, A. 1977. "Fuglefungsten på Faeråerne." Rhodos, København.

Norris, C. A. 1953. The birds of Bardsey Island in 1952. *British Birds* **46**, 131–137.

Oberholzer, A. and B. Tschanz. 1969. Zum Jagen der Trottellumme *(Uria aalge aalge)* nach Fisch. *Journal für Ornithologie* **110**, 465–470.

O'Connor, R. J. 1967. A review of auk censusing problems. *Seabird Bulletin* **5**, 19–26.

O'Connor, R. J. 1975. Initial size and subsequent growth in passerine nestlings. *Bird Banding* **46**, 329–340.

O'Connor, R. J. 1977. Growth strategies in nestling passerines. *Living Bird* **16**, 209–238.

O'Connor, R. J. 1978. Brood reduction in birds: selection for fratricide, infanticide and suicide. *Animal Behaviour* **26**, 79–96.

O'Donald, P. 1983. "The Arctic Skua." Cambridge University Press, London. 324 pp.

Ogi, H. 1980. The pelagic feeding ecology of Thick-billed Murres in the North Pacific, March–June. *Bulletin of the Faculty of Fisheries, Hokkaido University* **31**, 50–72.

Ogi, H. and T. Tsujita. 1973. Preliminary examination of stomach contents of Murres (*Uria* spp.) from the eastern Bering Sea and Bristol Bay, June–August 1970 and 1971. *Japanese Journal of Ecology* **23**, 201–209.

Ogi, H. and T. Tsujita. 1977. Food and feeding habits of Common Murre and Thick-billed Murre in the Okhotsk Sea in summer, 1972 and 1973. *Research Institute of North Pacific Fisheries, Hokkaido University, Special Volume* pp. 459–517.

Ohlendorf, H. M., R. W. Risebrough and K. Vermeer. 1978. "Exposure of Marine Birds to Environmental Pollutants." U.S. Department of the Interior, Fish and Wildlife Service, Wildlife Research Report No. 9. Washington, D.C. 40 pp.

Olsen, B. 1980. "Lomvigateljingin á Høvdanum á Skúvoy frá 1973 til 1979." Delrapport til Faerøernes Løgting. Torshavn, Faroes.

Olsen, B. 1982. Nogle årsager til nedgangen i den Faerøske Lomviebestand vurderet ud fra Mønsteret i tilbagegangen og ringmaerkningsresultater. *Viltrapport* **21**, 24–30.

Olson, S. L. 1977. A Great Auk, *Pinguinus*, from the Pliocene of North Carolina (Aves: Alcidae). *Proceedings of the Biological Society of Washington* **90**, 690–697.

Olson, S. L. 1985. A selective synopsis of the fossil record of birds. *In* D. S. Farner, J. R. King and K. C. Parkes (eds.), "Avian Biology," Vol. 8, pp. 79–238. Academic Press, Orlando, Florida.

Olson, S. L. and A. Feduccia. 1980. *Presbyornis* and the origin of the Anseriformes (Aves: Charadriomorphae). *Smithsonian Contributions to Zoology* No. 323, 1–24.

Olson, S. L. and D. D. Gillette. 1978. Catalogue of type specimens of fossil vertebrates. Academy of Natural Sciences Philadelphia, Part III, Birds. *Proceedings of the Academy of Natural Sciences Philadelphia* **129**, 99–100.

Olson, S. L. and Y. Hasegawa. 1979. Fossil counterparts of giant penguins from the North Pacific. *Science (Washington, D.C.)* **206**, 688–689.

Olson, S. L., C. C. Swift and C. Mokhiber. 1979. An attempt to determine the prey of the Great Auk *Pinguinus impennis*. *Auk* **96**, 790–792.

Olsson, V. 1974. Forandringar inom en population av tordmule *Alca torda* och tobisgrissla

Cepphus grylle i Ostergotlands skargard 1954–1973. (Razorbill *Alca torda* and Black Guillemot *Cepphus grylle* on the Swedish east coast 1954–1973—changes in a population.) *Vår Fågelvarld* **33**, 3–14. (English summary.)

Onno, S. 1968. Ornithological research in Matsalu Bay. *In* E. Kumari (ed.), "Bird Life in Matsalu Bay," pp. 39–48. "Valgus" Publishing House, Tallinn. 59 pp.

Orr, C. D. and R. M. P. Ward. 1982. The fall migration of Thick-billed Murres near Southern Baffin Island and Northern Labrador. *Arctic* **35**, 531–536.

Osborn, D. 1978. A naturally occurring cadmium and zinc binding protein from the liver and kidney of *Fulmarus glacialis,* a pelagic North Atlantic seabird. *Biochemical Pharmacology* **27**, 822–824.

Osborn, D. 1979. Toxic and essential heavy metals. *Annual Report of the Institute of Terrestrial Ecology, Cambridge* 1978, 53–56.

Osborn, D. 1980. Toxic metals in puffins *Fratercula arctica* from the Isle of May and St. Kilda. *Annual Report of the Institute of Terrestrial Ecology, Cambridge* 1979, 72.

Osborn, D. 1982. Organochlorine pollutants in seabirds from St. Kilda. *Annual Report of the Institute of Terrestrial Ecology, Cambridge* 1981, 55–57.

Osborn, D., M. P. Harris and J. K. Nicholson. 1979. Comparative tissue distribution of mercury, cadmium and zinc in three species of seabirds. *Comparative Biochemistry Physiology* **64C**, 61–67.

Palmer, R. S. 1949. Maine birds. *Bulletin of the Museum of Comparative Zoology* **102**, 1–656.

Paludan, K. 1947. "Alken. Dens ynglebiologi og dens forekomst i Denmerk." Ejnar Munksgaard, København. 106 pp.

Paludan, K. 1960. Alkefugle. *Nordens Fugle i Farver* **3**, 207–251.

Parslow, J. L. F. 1973a. "Breeding Birds of Britain and Ireland—A Historical Survey." T. and A. D. Poyser Ltd., Berkhamsted. 272 pp.

Parslow, J. L. F. 1973b. Mercury in waders from The Wash. *Environmental Pollution* **5**, 295–300.

Parslow, J. L. F. and W. R. P. Bourne. 1973. Great Black-backed Gulls and other birds on Am Balg, West Sutherland. *Seabird Report* **3**, 15–24.

Parslow, J. L. F. and D. J. Jefferies. 1972. Elastic thread pollution of puffins. *Marine Pollution Bulletin* **3**, 43–45.

Parslow, J. L. F. and D. J. Jefferies. 1973. Relationships between organochlorine residues in livers and whole bodies of guillemots. *Environmental Pollution* **5**, 87–101.

Parslow, J. L. F. and D. J. Jefferies. 1975. Geographical variation in guillemot eggs. *Annual Report of the Institute of Terrestrial Ecology, Cambridge* 1974, 28–31.

Parslow, J. L. F., D. J. Jefferies and M. C. French. 1972. Ingested pollutants in puffins and their eggs. *Bird Study* **19**, 18–33.

Parsons, J. 1975. Seasonal variation in breeding success of the Herring Gull: an experimental approach to pre-fledging success. *Journal of Animal Ecology* **44**, 553–573.

Partridge, L. 1978. Habitat selection. *In* J. R. Krebs and N. B. Davies (eds.), "Behavioural Ecology," pp. 351–376. Sinauer Associates, Sunderland, Massachusetts.

Patterson, I. J. 1965. Timing and spacing of broods in the Black-headed Gull *Larus ridibundus. Ibis* **107**, 433–459.

Pavshtiks, E. A. 1968. The influence of currents upon seasonal fluctuations in the plankton of Davis Strait. *Sarsia* **34**, 383–392.

Pavshtiks, E. A., T. N. Semjonova and S. S. Drobisheva. 1962. Plankton investigations carried out by the PINRO in the ICNAF area during 1960–1961. *International Commission for the Northwest Atlantic Fishery Redbook* Part III, pp. 56–61.

Payne, R. B. 1965. The molt in breeding Cassin auklets. *Condor* **67**, 220–228.

Payne, R. B. 1972. Mechanisms and control of molt. *In* D. S. Farner and J. R. King (eds.), "Avian Biology," Vol. 2, pp. 103–155. Academic Press, New York and London.

Peakall, D. B. 1975. Physiological effects of chlorinated hydrocarbons on avian species. *In* R. Haque and V. H. Freed (eds.), "Environmental Dynamics of Pesticides," pp. 343–360. Plenum Press, New York.

Peakall, D. B., J. L. Linger, R. W. Risebrough, J. B. Pritchard and W. B. Kinter. 1973. DDE-induced egg-shell thinning: structural and physiological effects in three species. *Comparative and General Pharmacology* **4**, 305–313.

Peakall, D. B., D. N. Nettleship and P. A. Pearce. 1978. Chemical pollution: western Atlantic. *Ibis* **120**, 106.

Peakall, D. B., J. Tremblay, W. B. Kinter and D. S. Miller. 1981. Endocrine dysfunction in seabirds caused by oil. *Environmental Research* **24**, 6–14.

Pearce, P. A., I. M. Grunchy and J. A. Keith. 1973. Toxic chemicals in living things in the Gulf of St. Lawrence. *Canadian Wildlife Service, Pesticide Section, Manuscript Report* No. 25, 28 pp.

Pearce, P. A., D. B. Peakall and L. M. Reynolds. 1979. Shell thinning and residues of organochlorines and mercury in seabird eggs, eastern Canada 1970–76. *Pesticides Monitoring Journal* **13**, 61–68.

Pearson, T. H. 1968. The feeding ecology of seabird species breeding on the Farne Islands, Northumberland. *Journal of Animal Ecology* **37**, 521–552.

Peck, G. K. 1972. Birds of the Cape Henrietta Maria region, Ontario. *Canadian Field-Naturalist* **86**, 333–348.

Pedersen, A. 1930. Fortgesetzte Beiträge zur Kenntnis der Säugestier—und Vogelfauna der Ostküste Grönlands. *Meddelelser om Grønland* **77**(5), 341–508.

Pedersen, A. 1934. Die ornis des mittleren teiles der nordostküste Grönlands. *Meddelelser om Grønland* **100**(11), 1–35.

Penhallurich, R. D. 1969. "Birds of the Cornish Coast, Including the Isles of Scilly." Bradford Barton, Truro. 200 pp.

Penhallurich, R. D. 1978. "The Birds of Cornwall and the Isles of Scilly." Headland Publications, Penzance. 477 pp.

Pennant, T. 1778. "A Tour in Wales." John Murray, London.

Pennycuick, C. J. 1956. Observations on a colony of Brünnich's Guillemot *Uria lomvia* in Spitsbergen. *Ibis* **98**, 80–99.

Pennycuick, C. J. 1969. The mechanics of bird migration. *Ibis* **111**, 525–556.

Pennycuick, C. J. 1975. Mechanics of flight. *In* D. S. Farner and J. R. King (eds.), "Avian Biology," Vol. 5, pp. 1–76. Academic Press, New York.

Percy, J. A. and F. J. Fife. 1981. The biochemical composition and energy content of arctic marine macrozooplankton. *Arctic* **34**, 307–313.

Perrins, C. M. 1965. Population fluctuations and clutch size in the Great Tit *Parus major* L. *Journal of Animal Ecology* **34**, 601–647.

Perrins, C. M. 1970. The timing of birds' breeding seasons. *Ibis* **112**, 242–255.

Perrins, C. M. 1977. The role of predation in the evolution of clutch size. *In* B. Stonehouse and C. M. Perrins (eds.), "Evolutionary Ecology," pp. 182–192. Methuen, London.

Perrins, C. M. 1979. "British Tits." Collins, London. 304 pp.

Perrins, C. M., M. P. Harris and C. K. Britton. 1973. Survival of Manx Shearwaters *Puffinus puffinus*. *Ibis* **115**, 535–548.

Perry, R. 1940. "Lundy, Isle of Puffins." Lindsay Drummond, London. 267 pp.

Perry, R. 1948. "Shetland Sanctuary." Faber and Faber, London. 298 pp.

Peters, H. S. and T. D. Burleigh. 1951. "The Birds of Newfoundland." Newfoundland Department of Natural Resources, St. John's. 431 pp.

Peters, J. L. 1934. "Check-list of Birds of the World," Vol. 2. Harvard University Press, Cambridge, Massachussets. 401 pp.

Petersen, A. 1976a. Size variables in puffins *Fratercula arctica* from Iceland and bill features as criteria of age. *Ornis Scandinavica* **7**, 185–192.

Petersen, A. 1976b. Age of first breeding in puffin *Fratercula arctica* L. *Astarte* **9**, 43–50.

Petersen, A. 1977. Íslenskar Teistur endurheimtar vid Graenland og erlend Teista vid Ísland. *Náttúrufraedingurinn* **47**, 149–153.

Petersen, A. 1979. Varpfuglar Flateyjar á Breidafirdi og nokkurra naerliggjandi eyja. (The breeding birds of Flatey and some adjoining islets in Breidafjördur, N.W. Iceland.) *Náttúrufraedingurinn* **49**, 229–256. (English summary.)

Petersen, A. 1981. Breeding biology and feeding ecology of Black Guillemots. Unpublished D.Phil. thesis, Oxford University, Oxford. 378 pp.

Petersen, A. 1982. Sjófuglar. *In* A. Gardarsson (ed.), "Fuglar," pp. 15–60. Rit Landverndar 8, Reykjavik. 216 pp.

Pethon, P. 1967. The systematic position of the Norwegian Common Murre *Uria aalge* and puffin *Fratercula arctica*. *Nytt Magasin for Zoologi (Oslo)* **14**, 84–95.

Pettingill, O. S., Jr. 1939. The bird life of the Grand Manan Archipelago. *Proceedings of the Nova Scotian Institute of Science* **19**, 293–372.

Pettingill, O. S., Jr. 1959. Puffins and eiders in Iceland. *Maine Field Naturalist* **15**, 58–71.

Pfister, K. (ed.). 1980. "The 1979 Baltic Oil Spill." Department for Environmental Protection, Helsinki. 83 pp.

Phillips, G. C. 1962. Survival value of the white coloration of gulls and other sea birds. Unpublished D.Phil. thesis, University of Oxford, Oxford. 221 pp.

Phillips, G. C. 1964. The colouration of sea birds. *Triton Magazine* (November/December).

Pianka, E. R. 1970. On *r* and *K* selection. *American Naturalist* **104**, 592–597.

Piatt, J. F. and D. N. Nettleship. 1985. Diving depths of four alcids. *Auk* **102**, 293–297.

Piatt, J. F. and D. G. Reddin. 1984. Recent trends and implications for Thick-billed Murres of the West Greenland salmon fishery. *In* D. N. Nettleship, G. A. Sanger and P. F. Springer (eds.), "Marine Birds: Their Feeding Ecology and Commercial Fisheries Relationships," pp. 208–210. Canadian Wildlife Service Special Publication. Ottawa.

Piatt, J. F., D. N. Nettleship and W. Threlfall. 1984. Net mortality of Common Murres *Uria aalge* and Atlantic Puffins *Fratercula arctica* in Newfoundland, 1951–1981. *In* D. N. Nettleship, G. A. Sanger and P. F. Springer (eds.), "Marine Birds: Their Feeding Ecology and Commercial Fisheries Relationships," pp. 196–206. Canadian Wildlife Service Special Publication. Ottawa.

Pingree, R. D., G. R. Forster and G. K. Morrison. 1974. Turbulent convergent tidal fronts. *Journal of the Marine Biological Association U.K.* **54**, 469–479.

Pinhorn, A. T. (ed.). 1976. Living marine resources of Newfoundland–Labrador: Status and potential. *Bulletin Fisheries Research Board of Canada* No. 194, 1–64.

Plumb, W. J. 1965. Observations on the breeding biology of the Razorbill. *British Birds* **58**, 449–456.

Portenko, L. A. 1931. Proizvoditel'nye sily ornitofauny Novoi Zemli. (Productive capacity of the avifauna of Novaya Zemlya.) *"Tr. Biogeokhim. Lab., Akad. Nauk SSSR* **2**, Supplement.

Portenko, L. A. 1972. "Birds of the Chukchi Peninsula and Wrangel Island." Smithsonian Institution and the National Science Foundation, Washington, D.C. 446 pp. (Translated from Russian, 1981.)

Portier, P. and A. Raffy. 1934. Mecanisme de la mort des oiseaux dont le plumage est impregne de couburer d'hydrogine. *Comptes Rendus Hebdomadaires des Séances de l'Académie des Sciences* **198**, 851–853.

Potter, B. C. 1971. A visit to Burhou, Channel Islands. *Seabird Report* 1970, 33–34.

Potts, G. R. 1969. The influence of eruptive movements, age, population size and other factors on the survival of the Shag *[Phalacrocorax aristotelis (L.)]*. *Journal of Animal Ecology* **38**, 53–102.

Potts, G. R., J. C. Coulson and I. R. Deans. 1980. Population dynamics and breeding success of the shag *Phalacrocorax aristotelis* on the Farne Islands, Northumberland. *Journal of Animal Ecology* **49**, 465–484.

Powers, K. D. and W. T. Rumage. 1978. Effect of the 'Argo Merchant' oil spill on bird populations off the New England coast, 15 December 1976–January 1977. *In* "In the Wake of the 'Argo Merchant'," Proceedings of a Conference and Workshop, pp. 142–148. Center for Oceanographic Management Studies, University of Rhode Island, Kingston.

Prange, H. D. and K. Schmidt-Nielsen. 1970. The metabolic cost of swimming in ducks. *Journal of Experimental Biology* **53**, 763–777.

Preston, W. C. 1968. Breeding ecology and social behaviour of the Black Guillemot *Cepphus grylle*. Unpublished Ph.D. thesis, University of Michigan, Ann Arbor. 138 pp.

Preuss, N. O. 1981. Danske lomvier holder sig til Østersøen. *Fugle* **1**, 26–27, 47.

Rae, K. M. 1957. A relationship between wind, plankton distribution and haddock brood strength. *Bulletins of Marine Ecology* **4**, 247–269.

Rahn, H. and A. Ar. 1974. The avian egg: incubation time, water loss and nest humidity. *Condor* **76**, 147–152.

Rahn, H., C. V. Paganelli and A. Ar. 1975. Relation of avian egg weight to body weight. *Auk* **92**, 750–765.

Rankin, M. N. and E. A. G. Duffey. 1948. A study of the bird life of the North Atlantic. *British Birds* **41**, Supplement, 1–42.

Ratcliffe, D. A. 1970. Changes attributable to pesticides in egg breakage frequency and eggshell thickness in some British birds. *Journal of Applied Ecology* **7**, 67–115.

Reinert, A. 1976. Lomvigin I–VI. Dimmalaetting **99**(97)4, (98)5, (100)3, (102)5, (107)3,8, (114)4–5.

Reinsch, H. H. 1976. Zur ökologie der seevögel. *Beitraege zur Vogelkunde* **22**, 236–258.

Renaud, W. E. and M. S. W. Bradstreet. 1980. Late winter distribution of Black Guillemots in northern Baffin Bay and the Canadian high arctic. *Canadian Field-Naturalist* **94**, 421–425.

Renaud, W. E., P. L. McLaren and S. R. Johnson. 1982. The Dovekie *Alle alle* as a spring migrant in eastern Lancaster Sound and western Baffin Bay. *Arctic* **35**, 118–125.

Rheinwald, G. 1982. "Brutvogelatlas der Bundesrepublik Deutschland," Schriftenreihe des Dachverbandes Deutscher Avifaunisten No. 6. Bonn. 128 pp.

Richardson, M. G., G. M. Dunnet and P. K. Kinnear. 1981. Monitoring seabirds in Shetland. *Proceedings—Royal Society of Edinburgh, Section B* **80B**, 157–179.

Richdale, L. E. 1957. "A Population Study of Penguins." Oxford University Press, Oxford. 195 pp.

Ricketts, C. and P. A. Prince. 1981. Comparison of growth in albatrosses. *Ornis Scandinavica* **12**, 120–124.

Ricklefs, R. E. 1967. A graphical method of fitting equations to growth curves. *Ecology* **48**, 978–983.

Ricklefs, R. E. 1968. Patterns of growth in birds. *Ibis* **110**, 419–451.

Ricklefs, R. E. 1969. Preliminary models for growth rates in altricial birds. *Ecology* **50**, 1031–1039.

Ricklefs, R. E. 1974. Energetics of reproduction in birds. *In* R. A. Paynter (ed.), "Avian Energetics," pp. 152–297. Nuttal Ornithological Club No. 15. Cambridge, Mass.

Ricklefs, R. E. 1977a. On the evolution of reproductive strategies in birds: reproductive effort. *American Naturalist* **111,** 453–478.

Ricklefs, R. E. 1977b. A note on the evolution of clutch size in altricial birds. *In* B. Stonehouse and C. M. Perrins (eds.), "Evolutionary Ecology," pp. 193–214. Methuen, London.

Ricklefs, R. E. 1979. Adaptation, constraint and compromise in avian postnatal development. *Biological Reviews of the Cambridge Philosophical Society* **54,** 269–290.

Ricklefs, R. E. and W. A. Montevecchi. 1979. Size, organic composition and energy content of North Atlantic Gannet *Morus bassanus* eggs. *Comparative Biochemistry and Physiology A* **64A,** 161–165.

Ricklefs, R. E. and S. C. White. 1975. A method for constructing nestling growth curves from brief visits to seabird colonies. *Bird-Banding* **46,** 135–140.

Ridgway, R. 1919. The birds of North and Middle America, Part VIII. *United States National Museum Bulletin* No. 50, 1–852.

Risebrough, R. W. 1969. Chlorinated hydrocarbons in marine ecosystems. *In* M. W. Miller and G. G. Bery (eds.), "Chemical Fallout—Current Research on Persistent Pesticides," pp. 5–23. Charles C Thomas, Springfield, Illinois.

Risebrough, R. W. and G. M. Carmignani. 1972. Chlorinated hydrocarbons in Antarctic birds. *In* B. C. Parker (ed.), "Proceedings of the Colloquium on Conservation Problems in Antarctica," pp. 63–80. Allen Press, Lawrence, Kansas.

Roby, D. D., K. L. Brink and D. N. Nettleship. 1981. Measurements, chick meals and breeding distribution of Dovekies *Alle alle* in northwest Greenland. *Arctic* **34,** 241–248.

Rodebrand, S. 1979. Fåglar på on Jungfrun, national park i Kalmarsund. *Calidris* **8,** 3–18.

Rodewald, M. 1975. Unser schwankendes Klima. *Materia Medica Nordmark* **27,** 177–194.

Roelke, M. and G. Hunt. 1978. Cliff attendance, foraging patterns and post-fledging behaviour of known-sex adult Thick-billed Murres *Uria lomvia. Pacific Seabird Group Bulletin* **5,** 81.

Rosenthal, R. 1978. Combining results of independent studies. *Psychological Bulletin* **85,** 185–193.

Røv, N. 1982. Olje og sjøfugl på Helgelandskysten 1982. *Vår Fuglefauna* **5,** 91–95.

Royal Commission on Environmental Pollution. 1981. "Oil Pollution and the Sea." 8th Report of the Royal Commission on Environmental Pollution, Her Majesty's Stationery Office, London.

R.S.P.B. 1962. "Deaths of Birds and Mammals from Toxic Chemicals: January–June 1961." Royal Society for the Protection of Birds, Sandy.

R.S.P.B. 1981. Oil pollution in N.W. Europe and seabirds. *Advisory Committee on Oil Pollution of the Sea, Annual Report* 1980, 1–45.

Ruddiman, W. F. 1977. Late Quaternary deposition of ice-rafted sand in the subpolar North Atlantic (latitude 40° to 65° N). *Geological Society of America Bulletin* **88,** 1813–1827.

Ruddiman, W. F. and A. McIntyre. 1977. Late Quaternary surface ocean kinematics and climatic change in the high-latitude North Atlantic. *Journal of Geophysical Research* **82,** 3877–3887.

Russell, F. S. and N. Demir. 1971. On the seasonal abundance of young fish. XII. The years 1967, 1968, 1969 and 1970. *Journal of the Marine Biological Association U.K.* **51,** 127–130.

Russell, F. S., A. J. Southward, G. T. Boalch and E. I. Butler. 1971. Changes in biological conditions in the English Channel off Plymouth during the last half century. *Nature (London)* **234,** 468–470.

Ruttledge, R. F. 1966. "Ireland's Birds." Witherby, London. 207 pp.

Safriel, U. N. 1975. On the significance of clutch size in nidifugous birds. *Ecology* **56**, 703–708.

Salomonsen, F. 1935. Aves. *In* R. Spärck (ed.), "Zoology of the Faroes," Vol. 3, Part 2, No. 64, pp. 1–269. Andr. Fred. Høst and Son, Copenhagen. (Also supplement, 1942, 6 pp.)

Salomonsen, F. 1936. Report on the natural history expedition to northwest Greenland 1936. *Meddelelser om Grønland* **124**(1), 1–38.

Salomonsen, F. 1944. The Atlantic Alcidae. The seasonal and geographical variation of the auks inhabiting the Atlantic Ocean and adjacent waters. *Göteborgs Kungliga Vetenskaps- och Vitterhets-Samhälles Handlingar, Serie B* **3**(5), 1–138.

Salomonsen, F. 1945. Gejrfuglen et hundredaars minde. *Aarbog for Universitet Zoologiske Museum* 1944–1945, 99–100.

Salomonsen, F. 1950. "Grønlands Fugle." Munksgaard, Copenhagen. 604 pp.

Salomonsen, F. 1965. The geographical variation of the fulmar (*Fulmarus glacialis*) and the zones of marine environment in the North Atlantic. *Auk* **82**, 327–355.

Salomonsen, F. 1967. "Fuglene på Grønland." Rhodos, Copenhagen. 340 pp.

Salomonsen, F. 1970. Birds useful to man in Greenland. *In* W. A. Fuller and P. G. Kevan (eds.), "Productivity and Conservation in Northern Circumpolar Lands," pp. 169–175. International Union for Conservation of Nature (IUCN) Publications New Series No. 16. Morges.

Salomonsen, F. 1971a. Tolvte foreløbige liste over genfundne grønlandske ringfugle. *Dansk Ornithologisk Forenings Tidsskrift* **65**, 11–19.

Salomonsen, F. 1971b. Recoveries in Greenland of birds ringed abroad. *Middelelser om Grønland* **191**, 1–52.

Salomonsen, F. 1972a. Zoogeographical and ecological problems in arctic birds. *Proceedings of the International Ornithological Congress* **15**, 25–77.

Salomonsen, F. 1972b. "Fugletraekket og dets gåder." Munksgaard, Copenhagen. 362 pp.

Salomonsen, F. 1974a. "Fuglene i Menneskenes land—Tingmíssat, Kalâtdlit, Nunâne." Det Grølandske Forlag, Godthåb. 127 pp.

Salomonsen, F. 1974b. Forslag til vedtaegt om jagt på fuglene i Grønland. Diskussionsoplaeg til kommunalbestyrelserne udarbejdet på opfordring af Det grønlandske Landsråd. *Tidsskrift et Grønland* No. 5, 155–173.

Salomonsen, F. 1979a. Ornithological and ecological studies in southwest Greenland (59°46′-62°27′N. latitude). *Meddelelser om Grønland* **204**, 1–214.

Salomonsen, F. 1979b. Trettende førelobige liste over genfundne grønlandske ringfugle. *Dansk Ornithologisk Forenings Tidsskrift* **73**, 191–206.

Salomonsen, F. 1979c. Marine birds in the Danish Monarchy and their conservation. *In* J. C. Bartonek and D. N. Nettleship (eds.), "Conservation of Marine Birds of Northern North America," pp. 267–287. U.S. Department of the Interior, Fish and Wildlife Service, Wildlife Research Report No. 11. Washington, D.C. 319 pp.

Salomonsen, F. 1981. Fugle (Aves). *In* F. Salomonsen (ed.), "Grønlands Fauna," pp. 159–361. Gyldendal, Copenhagen. 464 pp.

Sanford, R. C. and S. W. Harris. 1967. Feeding behaviour and food consumption rates of a captive California murre. *Condor* **69**, 298–302.

Saville, A. and R. S. Bailey. 1980. The assessment and management of the Herring stocks in the North Sea and to the west of Scotland. *Rapports et Procés-Verbaux des Réunions Conseil International pour l'Exploration de la Mer* **177**, 112–142.

Savin, S. M. 1977. The history of the earth's surface temperature during the past 100 million years. *Annual Review of Earth and Planetary Sciences* **5**, 319–355.

Schloss, W. 1969. Funde Helgoländer Trottellummen (*Uria aalge*). *Auspicium* **3**, 139–152.

Schultz, H. 1947. "Die Welt der Seevögel." Verlag A. Lettenbauer, Hamburg. 260 pp.

Scott, D. A. 1970. The breeding biology of the Storm Petrel. Unpublished D.Phil. thesis, University of Oxford, Oxford. 193 pp.

Scott, J. M. 1973. Resource allocation in four syntopic species of marine diving birds. Unpublished Ph.D. thesis, Oregon State University, Corvallis. 97 pp.

Scott, J. M., J. A. Wiens and R. R. Claeys. 1975. Organochlorine levels associated with a Common Murre die-off in Oregon. *Journal of Wildlife Management* **39,** 310–320.

Scott, J. S. 1972. Morphological and meristic variation in northwest Atlantic Sand-lances. *Journal of the Fisheries Research Board of Canada* **29,** 1673–1678.

Sealy, S. G. 1972. Adaptive differences in breeding biology in the marine bird family Alcidae. Unpublished Ph.D. thesis, University of Michigan, Ann Arbor. 283 pp.

Sealy, S. G. 1973a. Adaptive significance of post-hatching developmental patterns and growth rates in the Alcidae. *Ornis Scandinavica* **4,** 113–121.

Sealy, S. G. 1973b. Breeding biology of the Horned Puffin on St. Lawrence Island, Bering Sea with zoogeographical notes on the north Pacific puffins. *Pacific Science* **27,** 99–119.

Sealy, S. G. 1974. Breeding phenology and clutch size of the Marbled Murrelet. *Auk* **91,** 10–23.

Sealy, S. G. 1975a. Feeding ecology of the Ancient and Marbled Murrelets near Langara Island, British Columbia. *Canadian Journal of Zoology* **53,** 418–433.

Sealy, S. G. 1975b. Egg size of murrelets. *Condor* **77,** 500–501.

Sealy, S. G. 1975c. Influence of snow on egg-laying in auklets. *Auk* **92,** 528–538.

Sealy, S. G. 1976. Biology of nesting Ancient Murrelets. *Condor* **78,** 294–306.

Sealy, S. G. and J. Bédard. 1973. Breeding biology of the Parakeet Auklet *(Cyclorrhynchus psittacula)* on St. Lawrence Island, Alaska. *Astarte* **6,** 59–68.

Sealy, S. G., J. Bédard, M. D. F. Udvardy and F. H. Fay. 1971. Records and zoogeographical notes on the birds of St. Lawrence Island, Bering Sea. *Condor* **73,** 322–336.

Seccion de Ornitoloxia. 1979. Informe sobre las aves marinas afectadas por el "Andros Patria", en las Costas Gallegas, del 3 al 21 de Enero de 1979. *Braña* **3,** 15–31.

Seligman, O. R. and J. M. Willcox. 1940. Some observations on the birds of Jan Mayen. *Ibis* **14**(4), 464–479.

Selous, E. 1901. "Bird Watching." J. M. Dent, London. 347 pp.

Selous, E. 1905. "The Bird-watcher in the Shetlands." J. M. Dent, London. 388 pp.

Sergeant, D. E. 1951. Ecological relationships of the guillemots *Uria aalge* and *Uria lomvia*. *Proceedings of the International Ornithological Congress* **10,** 578–587.

Sergeant, D. E. 1952. Little auks in Britain 1948–1951. *British Birds* **45,** 122–133.

Serventy, D. L. 1960. Geographical distribution of living birds. *In* A. J. Marshall (ed.), "Biology and Comparative Physiology of Birds," Vol. I, pp. 95–126. Academic Press, New York.

Sharp, M. 1980. Timing of breeding and census counts of Brünnich's Guillemots *Uria lomvia,* Hornstrandir Peninsula, north west Iceland. Unpublished report, Department of Geography, University of Aberdeen, Aberdeen. 25 pp.

Sherman, K., C. Jones, L. Sullivan, W. Smith, P. Berrien and L. Ejsymont. 1981. Congruent shifts in sand eel abundance in western and eastern North Atlantic ecosystems. *Nature (London)* **291,** 486–489.

Shkliarewicz, F. N. 1977. About changes in numbers of the kittiwake and murres in the Harlov Island colonies (Seven Islands, East Murmansk Coast). *All-Union Ornithological Conference, 7th, Kiev* Part 2, 344–345.

Shufeldt, R. W. 1903. Osteology of the Limicolae. *Carnegie Museum of Natural History Annual Report* **2,** 15–70.

Sibley, C. G. and J. E. Alquist. 1972. A comparative study of the egg white proteins of non-Passerine birds. *Peabody Museum of Natural History Yale University Bulletin* No. 39, 1–276.

Simmons, K. E. L. 1967. Ecological adaptations in the life history of the Brown Booby of Ascension Island. *Living Bird* **6**, 187–212.

Simpson, G. G. 1975. Fossil penguins. *In* B. Stonehouse (ed.), "The Biology of Penguins," pp. 19–41. University Park Press, Baltimore.

Simpson, G. G. 1976. "Penguins: Past, Present, Here and There." Yale University Press, New Haven. 176 pp.

Skira, I. 1979. Underwater feeding by Short-tailed Shearwaters. *Emu* **79**, 43.

Skokova, N. N. 1962. Tupik na Ainovych ostrovach. (The puffin on the Ainov Islands.) *Ornitologiya* **5**, 7–12.

Skokova, N. N. 1967. "On the Factors which Determine the State of the Population of Puffins during the Nesting Period." Kandalakshii State Reserve, Issue 5, Publication "Forest Industry" (Moscow), pp. 155–177. (Translated from Russian, 1968: Canadian Wildlife Service, Ottawa.)

Skutch, A. F. 1967. Adaptive limitation of the reproductive rate of birds. *Ibis* **109**, 579–599.

Sladen, W. J. L., C. M. Menzie and W. L. Reichel. 1966. DDT residues in Adelie Penguins and a Crabeater Seal from Antarctica. *Nature (London)* **210**, 670–673.

Slater, P. J. B. 1976. Factors influencing the number of guillemots present on cliffs during the breeding season. Manuscript report, University of Sussex, Sussex.

Slater, P. J. B. 1977. Tidal rhythm in a seabird. *Nature (London)* **264**, 636–638.

Slater, P. J. B. 1980. Factors affecting the numbers of guillemots *Uria aalge* present on cliffs. *Ornis Scandinavica* **11**, 155–163.

Slater, P. J. B. and E. P. Slater. 1972. Behaviour of the tystie during feeding of the young. *Bird Study* **19**, 105–113.

Smed, J. 1965. Variation of the temperatures of the surface water in areas of the northern North Atlantic. *International Commission Northwest Atlantic Fisheries Special Publication* No. 6, 821–826.

Smith, C. 1879. "The Birds of Guernsey and the Neighbouring Islands." Porter, London. 223 pp.

Smith, N. 1938. "Fifty-two Years at the Labrador Fishery." Arthur H. Stockwell Ltd., London. 199 pp.

Smith, T. G. and M. O. Hammill. 1980. Distribution and food habits of the birds along the southeastern Baffin Island coast. *Canadian Manuscript Report, Fisheries and Aquatic Sciences* No. 1573, 1–27.

Smith, W. J. 1977. "The Behavior of Communicating." Harvard University Press, Cambridge, Massachusetts. 545 pp.

Snapp, B. D. 1976. Colonial breeding in the Barn Swallow *Hirundo rustica* and its adaptive significance. *Condor* **78**, 471–480.

Snow, D. W. 1971. "The Status of Birds in Britain and Ireland," Blackwell, Oxford. 333 pp.

S. O. F. 1978. "Sveriges Fåglar." Stockholm. 131 pp.

Soikkeli, M. 1970. Mortality rate of Finnish Caspian Terns *Hydroprogne caspia*. *Ornis Fennica* **47**, 177–179.

Sømme, A. (ed.). 1960. "A Geography of Norden: Denmark, Finland, Iceland, Norway, Sweden." J. W. Cappelens Forlag, Oslo. 363 pp.

Sørenson, L. H. 1977. An analysis of Common Gull *(Larus canus)* recoveries recorded from 1931 to 1972 by the Zoological Museum in Copenhagen. *Gerfaut* **67**, 133–160.

Soulé, M. E. and B. A. Wilcox (eds.). 1980. "Conservation Biology." Sinauer Associates, Sunderland, Massachusetts, 395 pp.

Southern, H. N. 1962. Survey of bridled guillemots 1959–60. *Proceedings of the Zoological Society of London* **138**, 455–472.

Southern, H. N. 1966. Distribution of bridled guillemots in east Scotland over eight years. *Journal of Animal Ecology* **35**, 1–11.

Southern, H. N., R. Carrick and W. G. Potter. 1965. The natural history of a population of guillemots *Uria aalge. Journal of Animal Ecology* **35**, 1–11.

Southward, A. J. 1963. The distribution of some plankton animals in the English Channel and approaches. III. Theories about long-term biological changes, including fish. *Journal of the Marine Biological Association U.K.* **43**, 1–29.

Southward, A. J. 1980. The Western English Channel—an inconstant ecosystem? *Nature (London)* **285**, 361–366.

Southward, A. J., E. I. Butler and L. Pennycuick. 1975. Recent cyclic changes in climate and in abundance of marine life. *Nature (London)* **253**, 714–717.

Southwood, T. R. E. 1977. Habitat, the templet for ecological strategies? *Journal of Animal Ecology* **46**, 337–366.

Sowls, A. L., S. A. Hatch and C. J. Lensink. 1978. Catalog of Alaskan seabird colonies. *U.S. Fish and Wildlife Service, Office of Biological Services [Technical Report]* **FWS/OBS/78-78**. 252 pp.

Spaans, A. L. 1971. On the feeding ecology of the Herring Gull *Larus argentatus* Pont. in the northern part of the Netherlands. *Ardea* **59**, 73–188.

Sprague, J. B., J. H. Vandermeulen and P. G. Wells (eds.). 1982. "Oil and Dispersants in Canadian Seas—Research Appraisal and Recommendations." Environmental Protection Service Report Series, Environment Canada. Ottawa. 185 pp.

Spring, L. 1968. A comparison of functional and morphological adaptations in the Common Murre *(Uria aalge)* and Thick-billed Murre *(Uria lomvia)*. Unpublished Ph.D. thesis, University of Washington, Seattle.

Spring, L. 1971. A comparison of functional and morphological adaptations in the Common Murre *(Uria aalge)* and the Thick-billed Murre *(Uria lomvia)*. *Condor* **73**, 1–27.

Sprunt, A. 1938. The southern dovekie flight of 1936. *Auk* **55**, 85–88.

Squires, W. A. 1976. The birds of New Brunswick. *New Brunswick Museum Monographic Series* No. 7, 1–221. (Second edition.)

Stanley, S. M. 1979. "Macroevolution: Pattern and Process." W. H. Freeman Co., San Francisco. 332 pp.

Stearns, S. C. 1976. Life-history tactics: a review of the ideas. *Quarterly Review of Biology* **51**, 3–47.

Stearns, S. C. 1977. The evolution of life history traits: A critique of the theory and a review of the data. *Annual Review of Ecology and Systematics* **8**, 145–171.

Stechow, J. 1938. Ueber die jahreszeitliche Verbreitung der europaischen Lummen [*Uria aalge* (Pont.)]. *Vogelzug* **9**, 125–138.

Steenstrup, J. 1868. Matériaux pour servir a l'histoire de l'Alca impennis (Linn.) et recherches sur les pays qu'il habitait. *Bulletin de la Société Ornithologique Suisse* **2**, Part 1, 5–70.

Stemp, R. 1980. Davis Strait wildlife observation program in the vicinity of Aquitaine's Hekja drill site, July 25–October 4, 1980. Unpublished report, Aquitaine Company of Canada Ltd., Calgary. 53 pp.

Stempniewicz, L. 1980. Factors influencing the growth of Little Auk *Plautus alle* (L.) nestlings on Spitsbergen. *Ekologia Polska* **28**, 557–581.

Stempniewicz, L. 1981. Breeding biology of the Little Auk *Plautus alle* in the Hornsund region, Spitsbergen. *Acta Ornithologica* **18**, 1–26.

Stenhouse, J. H. 1930. The Little Auk *Alle alle (polaris* sub-species nov.) of Franz Joseph Land. *Scottish Naturalist* pp. 47–49.

Stephensen, K. 1933a. The Godthaab expedition, 1928. Schizopoda. *Meddelelser om Grønland* **79**(9), 1–20.

Stephensen, K. 1933b. The Godthaab expedition, 1928. Amphipoda. *Meddelelser om Grønland* **79**(7), 1–88.

Stettenheim, P. R. 1959. Adaptations for underwater swimming in the Common Murre *(Uria aalge).* Unpublished Ph. D. thesis, University of Michigan, Ann Arbor. 295 pp.

Steventon, D. J. 1979. Razorbill survival and population estimates. *Ringing and Migration* **2**, 105–112.

Stickel, L. F. 1973. Pesticide residues in birds and mammals. *In* C. A. Edwards (ed.), "Environmental Pollution by Pesticides," pp. 254–312. Plenum Press, New York.

Stonehouse, B. 1968. "Penguins." Barker, London. 96 pp.

Stonehouse, B. 1975. Introduction: the Spheniscidae. *In* B. Stonehouse (ed.), "The Biology of Penguins," pp. 1–15. Macmillan, London.

Storer, R. W. 1945. Structural modifications in the hind limb in the Alcidae. *Ibis* **87**, 433–456.

Storer, R. W. 1952. A comparison of variation, behaviour and evolution in the seabird genera *Uria* and *Cepphus. University of California Publications in Zoology* **52**, 121–222.

Storer, R. W. 1960. Evolution in the diving birds. *Proceedings of the International Ornithological Congress* **12**, 694–707.

Storer, R. W. 1964. Auk. *In* Sir A. Landsborough Thomson (ed.), "A New Dictionary of Birds," pp. 67–69. Nelson, London.

Stowe, T. J. 1982a. Recent population trends in cliff-breeding seabirds in Britain and Ireland. *Ibis* **124**, 502–510.

Stowe, T. J. 1982b. "Beached Bird Surveys and Surveillance of Cliff-breeding Seabirds." Royal Society for the Protection of Birds, Sandy, Bedfordshire. 207 pp.

Stowe, T. J. and M. P. Harris 1984. Status of guillemots and Razorbills in Britain and Ireland. *Seabird* **7**, 5–18.

Stowe, T. J. and L. A. Underwood. 1984. Oil spillages affecting seabirds in the United Kingdom 1966–1983. *Marine Pollution Bulletin* **15**, 147–152.

Strauch, J. G., Jr. 1978. The phylogeny of the Charadriiformes (Aves): a new estimate using the method of character compatibility analysis. *Transactions of the Zoological Society of London* **34**, 263–345.

Stresemann, E. and V. Stresemann. 1966. Die Mauser der Vögel. *Journal für Ornithologie* **107**, 1–447.

Summers, K. R. 1970. Growth and survival of the Rhinoceros Auklet on Cleland Island. Unpublished B.Sc. thesis, University of British Columbia, Vancouver. 34 pp.

Summers, K. R. and R. H. Drent. 1979. Breeding biology and twinning experiments of Rhinoceros Auklets on Cleland Island, British Columbia. *Murrelet* **60**, 16–27.

Sutton, G. M. 1932. The birds of Southampton Island. *Memoirs of the Carnegie Museum* **12**, Part 2, Section 2, 1–275.

Sverdrup, H. U., M. W. Johnson and R. H. Fleming. 1942. "The Oceans: Their Physics, Chemistry and General Biology." Prentice-Hall, Englewood Cliffs. 1087 pp.

Swartz, L. G. 1966. Sea-cliff Birds. *In* N. J. Willimovsky and J. N. Wolfe (eds.), "Environment of the Cape Thompson Region, Alaska," pp. 611–678. U.S. Atomic Energy Commission, Oak Ridge, Tennessee. 1250 pp.

Swartz, L. G. 1967. Distribution and movements of birds in the Bering and Chukchi Seas. *Pacific Science* **21**, 332–347.

Swennen, C. 1977. "Laboratory Research on Sea-birds. Report on a Practical Investigation into the Possibility of Keeping Sea-birds for Research Purposes." Netherlands Institute for Sea Research, Texel. 43 pp.

Swennen, C. and P. Duiven. 1977. Size of food objects of three fish-eating seabird species: *Uria aalge, Alca torda* and *Fratercula arctica* (Aves, Alcidae). *Netherlands Journal of Sea Research* **11**, 92–98.

Swennen, C. and A. L. Spaans. 1970. Der sterfte van zeevogels door olie in februari 1969 in het Waddengebied. *Vogeljaar* **18**, 233–245.

Szaro, R. C. and P. H. Albers. 1977. Effects of external applications of No. 2 fuel oil on Common Eider eggs. *In* D. A. Wolfe (ed.), "Fate and Effects of Petroleum Hydrocarbons in Marine Ecosystems and Organisms," pp. 164–167. Pergamon Press, New York.

Tanis, J. J. C. and M. F. Mörzer-Bruyns. 1968. The impact of oil pollution on seabirds in Europe. *International Conference on Oil Pollution of the Sea, Rome* Paper No. 4, 67–74.

Tatton, J. O'G and J. H. A. Ruzicka. 1967. Organochlorine pesticides in Antarctica. *Nature (London)* **215**, 346–348.

Taverner, P. A. 1922. Birds of eastern Canada. *Canada Department of Mines, Geological Survey Memoir, Biological Series* **104**(3), 1–290.

Taylor, G. K. 1982. Predator-prey interactions between Great Black-backed Gulls and puffins and the evolutionary significance of grouping behaviour. Unpublished Ph.D. thesis, University of St. Andrews, St. Andrews.

Taylor, G. K. and J. B. Reid. 1981. Earlier colony attendance by guillemots and Razorbills. *Scottish Birds* **11**, 173–180.

Teixeira, A. M. 1983. Seabirds breeding at the Berlengas, forty-two years after Lockley's visit. *Ibis* **125**, 417–420.

Templeman, W. 1945. Observations on some Newfoundland sea-birds. *Canadian Field-Naturalist* **59**, 136–147.

Templeman, W. 1965. Relation of periods of successful year-classes of Haddock on the Grand Bank to periods of success of year-classes for Cod, Haddock and Herring in areas to the north and east. *International Commission Northwest Atlantic Fisheries Special Publication* **6**, 523–534.

Tener, J. 1951. Sixth census of non-passerine birds in the bird sanctuaries of the north shore of the Gulf of St. Lawrence. *Canadian Field-Naturalist* **65**, 65–68.

Thoreson, A. C. and E. S. Booth. 1958. Breeding activities of the Pigeon Guillemot *Cepphus columba columba* (Pallas). *Walla Walla College Publications Department of Biological Science* No. 23, 1–36.

Threlfall, W. 1971. Helminth parasites of alcids in the north-western North Atlantic. *Canadian Journal of Zoology* **49**, 461–466.

Timmermann, W. G. 1949. Die Vögel Islands. Vísindafélag. *Íslendinga Rit* **28**, 239–524.

Tinbergen, N. 1959. Comparative studies of the behaviour of gulls (Laridae); a progress report. *Behaviour* **15**, 1–70.

Todd, W. E. C. 1963. "Birds of the Labrador Peninsula and Adjacent Areas." University of Toronto Press, Toronto. 819 pp.

Tompkinson, P. M. L. and J. W. Tompkinson. 1966. Eggs of the Great Auk. *Bulletin of the British Museum (Natural History) Historical Series* **3**(4), 97–128 (75 plates).

Townsend, C. W. 1918. "In Audubon's Labrador." Houghton-Mifflin, Boston and New York. 354 pp.

Townsend, C. W. and G. M. Allen. 1907. Birds of Labrador. *Proceedings of the Boston Society of Natural History* **33**(7), 1–277.

Trivers, R. L. 1971. The evolution of reciprocal altruism. *Quarterly Review of Biology* **46**, 35–57.

Trivers, R. L. 1972. Parental investment and sexual selection. *In* B. Campbell (ed.), "Sexual Selection and the Descent of Man," pp. 136–179. Aldine, Chicago.

Trivers, R. L. 1974. Parent-offspring conflict. *American Zoologist* **14**, 249–264.

Tschanz, B. 1959. Zur brutbiologie der Trottellumme (*Uria aalge aalge* Pont.). *Behaviour* **14**(1/2), 1–108.

Tschanz, B. 1968. Trottellummen (*Uria aalge aalge* Pont.). *Zeitschrift für Tierpsychologie* **4**, Beiheft, 1–103.

Tschanz, B. 1979a. Zur Entwicklung von Papageitaucherkuken *Fratercula arctica* in Frieland und Labor bei unzulänglichem und ausreichendem Futerangebot. (Development of puffin *Fratercula arctica* chicks in the field and laboratory with insufficient and sufficient food supply.) *Fauna Norvegica Series C, Cinclus* **2**, 70–94. (English summary.)

Tschanz, B. 1979b. Helfer-Beziehungen bei Trottellummen. *Zeitschrift für Tierpsychologie* **49**, 10–34.

Tschanz, B. and E. K. Barth. 1978. Svingninger i lomvibestandem på Vedøy på Røst. *Fauna (Oslo)* **31**, 205–219.

Tschanz, B. and M. Hirsbrunner-Scharf. 1975. Adaptations to colony life on cliff ledges: a comparative study of guillemot and Razorbill chicks. *In* G. C. Baerends and A. Manning (eds.), "Function and Evolution in Behaviour," pp. 358–380. Clarendon Press, Oxford.

Tuck, G. S. 1967. Sea and land bird observations from British ocean weather ships in the North Atlantic. *Sea Swallow* **19**, 11–14.

Tuck, G. S. 1970. Sea and land bird observations from ocean weather ships in the North Atlantic. *Sea Swallow* **20**, 7–17.

Tuck, J. A. 1975. "The Archaeology of Saglek Bay, Labrador. "National Museums of Canada, Museum of Man, Mercury Series No. 32. Ottawa.

Tuck, J. A. 1976. "Ancient People of Port au Choix: The Excavation of an Archaic Indian Cemetery in Newfoundland." Newfoundland Social and Economic Studies No. 17, Memorial University of Newfoundland, St. John's. 262 pp.

Tuck, L. M. 1953. History and present populations of murre colonies in Newfoundland and Labrador. *Canadian Wildlife Service Manuscript Report* No. CWSC-665. 51 pp.

Tuck, L. M. 1957. Wildlife investigations in the Cape Hay region, Lancaster Sound, 1957. *Canadian Wildlife Service Manuscript Report* No. 760, 74 pp.

Tuck, L. M. 1961. The Murres: their distribution, populations and biology—a study of the genus *Uria*. *Canadian Wildlife Monograph Series* No. 1, 260 pp.

Tuck, L. M. 1967. The birds of Newfoundland. *In* J. Smallwood (ed.), "The Book of Newfoundland," Vol. 3, pp. 265–316. Newfoundland Book Publishers, St. John's.

Tuck, L. M. 1971. The occurrence of Greenland and European birds in Newfoundland. *Bird-Banding* **42**, 184–209.

Tuck, L. M. and L. Lemieux. 1959. The avifauna of Bylot Island. *Dansk Ornithologisk Forenings Tidsskrift* **53**, 137–154.

Tuck, L. M. and H. J. Squires. 1955. Food and feeding habits of Brünnich's Murre (*Uria lomvia lomvia*) on Akpatok Island. *Journal of the Fisheries Research Board of Canada* **12**, 781–792.

Tufts, R. W. 1961. "The Birds of Nova Scotia." Nova Scotia Museum, Halifax. 481 pp.

Tull, C. E., P. Germain and A. W. May. 1972. Mortality of Thick-billed Murres in the west Greenland salmon fishery. *Nature (London)* **237**, 42–44.

Udvardy, M. D. F. 1963. Zoogeographical study of the Pacific Alcidae. *In* J. L. Gressit (ed.),

"Pacific Basin Biogeography: A Symposium," pp. 85–111. Bishop Museum Press, Honolulu.

Uspenski, S. M. 1951. Present status of the bird bazaars of Novaya Zemlya. *Nature Protection* **13**.

Uspenski, S. M. 1956. "The Bird Bazaars of Novaya Zemlya." Canadian Wildlife Service Translations of Russian Game Reports, Vol. 4. Ottawa. 159 pp. (Translated from Russian, 1958.)

Uspenski, S. M. 1959. Colonial seabirds breeding in the northern and far eastern seas of the U.S.S.R.: their distribution, number and role as consumers of the plankton and benthos. *Bulletin of the Moscow Society of Naturalists, Biology Section* **64**(2), 39–52.

Uspenski, S. M., R. L. Beme and A. J. Velizhanin. 1963. Avifauna ostrova Wrangelya (Avifauna of Wrangel Island). *Ornitologiya* **6**, 58–67.

Ussher, R. J. and R. Warren. 1900. "The Birds of Ireland." Gurney and Jackson, London. 419 pp.

Vader, W. 1980. The Great Skua *Stercorarius skua* in Norway and the Spitsbergen area. *Fauna Norvegica Series C, Cinclus* **3**, 49–55.

Vandermeulen, J. (ed.). 1980. "Scientific Studies during the *Kurdistan* Tanker Incident: Proceedings of a Workshop." Bedford Institute of Oceanography Report Series BI-R-80-3. Dartmouth. 227 pp.

van Franeker, J. A. and C. J. Camphuijsen. 1984. Report on *Fulmarus glacialis* Expedition II, Jan Mayen, June–August 1983. Verslagen en Technische Gegevens No. 39, Instituut voor Taxonomische Zoölogie, Plantage Middenlaan 53, Amsterdam. 34 pp.

van Franeker, J. A. and R. Luttik. 1981. Report on the *Fulmarus glacialis*-expedition Bear Island, July–August 1980. Verslagen en Technische Gegevens No. 32, Instituut voor Taxonomische Zoölogie, Plantage Middenlaan 53, Amsterdam. 21 pp.

Van Tets, G. F. 1965. A comparative study of some social communication patterns in the Pelicaniformes. *Ornithological Monographs* No. 2, 1–38.

Varoujean, D. H., S. D. Sanders, M. R. Graybill and L. Spear. 1979. Aspects of Common Murre breeding biology. *Pacific Seabird Group Bulletin* **6**, 28.

Vaughan, H. R. H. 1937. Flight speed of guillemots, Razorbills and puffins. *British Birds* **31**, 123.

Vauk, G. 1982. Bestandsentwicklung der Silbermöwe *Larus argentatus* und die Regulierung ihres Bestandes durch jagdlich Maßnahmen auf der Insel Helgoland. *Seevögel* **3**, 71–84.

Vaurie, C. 1965. "The Birds of the Palaearctic Fauna. A Systematic Reference. Non-Passeriformes." H. F. and G. Witherby, London. 763 pp.

Veen, J. 1977. Functional and causal aspects of nest distribution in colonies of the Sandwich Tern (*Sterna s.sandvicensis* Lath.). *Behaviour, Supplement* **20**, 1–193.

Ventura, C. and J. Wintz. 1971. Natural oil seeps: historical background. *In* D. Straughan (ed.), "Biological and Oceanographical Survey of the Santa Barbara Channel Oil Spill 1969–1970. Vol. 1: Biology and Bacteriology," pp. 11–16. Allan Hancock Foundation, University of Southern California, Los Angeles. 426 pp.

Verheyen, R. 1958. contribution à la systématique des Alciformes. *Bulletin de l'Institut Royal des Sciences Naturalles de Belgique* **34**, 1–15.

Vermeer, K. 1980. The importance of timing and type of prey to reproductive success of Rhinoceros Auklets *Cerorhinca monocerata*. *Ibis* **122**, 343–350.

Vermeer, K. and L. Cullen. 1979. Growth of Rhinoceros Auklets and Tufted Puffins, Triangle Island, British Colombia. *Ardea* **67**, 22–27.

Vermeer, K., L. Cullen and M. Porter. 1979. A provisional explanation of the reproductive failure of Tufted Puffins *Lunda cirrhata* on Triangle Island, British Columbia. *Ibis* **121**, 348–354.

Verwey, J. 1922. The moult of *Uria troille* (L.) and *Alca torda* (L.) *Ardea* **11**, 99–116.

Verwey, J. 1924. Results of a study of the moult of the guillemot, Razorbill and native species of divers. *Tijdschrift Nederlandsche Dierkundige Vereeniging* **19**, vii–viii.

Vladimirskaya, E. V. 1965. Quantitative distribution and seasonal dynamics of zooplankton in the Newfoundland area. *International Commission for the Northwest Atlantic Fisheries, Research Bulletin* **2**, 53–58.

von Fischer, F. and A. Polzeln. 1886. The birds of Jan Mayen. (Translated from German by W. E. Clarke, 1890.) *Zoologist* **48**(1890), 1–16, 41–51.

von Haartman, L. 1947. Tordmulekatastrofen och populationes decimering i Finland. (The catastrophic decrease in the population of the Razorbill in Finland.) *Dansk Ornithologisk Forenings Tidsskrift* **41**, 168–171.

von Haartman, L. 1971. Population dynamics. *In* D. S. Farner and J. R. King (eds.), "Avian Biology," Vol. 1, pp. 391–459. Academic Press, New York and London.

Voous, K. H. 1960. "Atlas of European Birds." Nelson, London. 284 pp.

Vowinckel, E. and S. Orvig. 1970. The climate of the north polar basin. *In* S. Orvig (ed.), "World Survey of Climatology. Vol. 14: Climates of the Polar Regions," pp. 129–252. Elsevier, Amsterdam and New York. 370 pp.

Walker, C. H. 1980. Species variations in some hepatic microsomal enzymes that metabolise xerobiotics. *In* J. W. Bridges and L. F. Chasseaud (eds.), "Progress in Drug Metabolism 5," pp. 113–162. Wiley, New York.

Walter, A. 1890. Ornithologische Ergernisse der von der Bremer Geographischen Gesellschaft in Jahre 1889 veranstalteten Reise nach Ostspitsbergen. *Journal für Ornithologie* **38**, 233–255.

Walter, M. 1979. "Eleonora's Falcon. Adaptations to Prey and Habitat in a Social Raptor." University of Chicago Press, Chicago.

Waltz, E. C. 1982. Resource characteristics and the evolution of information centers. *American Naturalist* **119**, 73–90.

Wanless, S., D. D. French, M. P. Harris and D. R. Langslow. 1982. Detection of annual changes in the numbers of cliff-nesting seabirds in Orkney 1976–80. *Journal of Animal Ecology* **51**, 785–795.

Ward, P. and A. Zahavi. 1973. The importance of certain assemblages of birds as "Information-Centres" for food-finding. *Ibis* **115**, 517–534.

Warham, J. 1975. The Crested Penguins. *In* B. Stonehouse (ed.), "The Biology of Penguins," pp. 189–269. Macmillan, London.

Warham, J. 1977. Wing loadings, wing shapes, and flight capabilities of Procellariiformes. *New Zealand Journal of Zoology* **4**, 73–83.

Warren, D. C. and L. Kilpatrick. 1929. Fertilization in the Domestic Fowl. *Poultry Science* **8**, 237–256.

Watson, G. E. 1968. Synchronous wing and tail moult in diving petrels. *Condor* **70**, 182–183.

Watson, P. S. and D. J. Radford. 1982. Census of seabirds at Horn Head, County Donegal, in June 1980. *Seabird Report* **6**, 26–34.

Wehle, D. H. S. 1976. Summer foods and feeding ecology of Tufted and Horned Puffins on Buldir Island, Alaska—1975. Unpublished M.Sc. thesis, University of Alaska, Fairbanks.

Wehle, D. H. S. 1980. The breeding biology of the puffins: Tufted Puffin *Lunda cirrhata*, Horned Puffin *Fratercula corniculata*, Common Puffin *Fratercula arctica* and Rhinoceros Auklet *Cerorhinca monocerata*. Unpublished Ph.D. thesis, University of Alaska, Fairbanks.

Wehrlin, J. 1977. Verhaltensanpassungen junger Trottellummen [*Uria aalge aalge* (Pont.)] ans Felsklippen—und Koloniebruten. *Zeitschrift für Tierpsychologie* **44**, 45–79.

Wendt, S. and F. G. Cooch. 1984. The kill of murres in Newfoundland in the 1977–78, 1978–79 and 1979–80 hunting seasons. *Canadian Wildlife Service Progress Note* 146, 1–10.

Werschkul, D. F. and J. A. Jackson. 1979. Sibling competition and avian growth rates. *Ibis* **121**, 97–102.

Wetmore, A. 1926. Fossil birds from the Green River deposits of eastern Utah. *Annals of the Carnegie Museum* **16**, 391–402.

Wetmore, A. 1940. Fossil bird remains from Tertiary deposits in the United States. *Journal of Morphology* **66**, 25–37.

W. G. A. S. (Working Group on Atlantic Seabirds) 1982. Capelin and the marine environment of Atlantic Canada. *Pacific Seabird Group Bulletin* **9**, 41–45.

Wheeler, A. 1969. "The Fishes of the British Isles and North-west Europe." Macmillan, London. 613 pp.

Whilde, A. 1979. Auks trapped in salmon drift-nets. *Irish Birds* **1**, 370–376.

Whitbourne, R. 1622. "A Discourse and Discovery of Newfoundland." Felix Kinston, London.

Wiens, J. A. and J. M. Scott. 1975. Model estimation of energy flow in Oregon coastal seabird populations. *Condor* **77**, 439–452.

Wiens, J. A., R. G. Ford and D. Heinemann. 1984. Information needs and priorities for assessing the sensitivity of marine birds to oil spills. *Biological Conservation* **28**, 21–49.

Wijs, W. J. R. 1978. De geografiese variatie van de Zeekoet [*Uria aalge* (Pontoppidan)] en de Mogelijke relatie Hiervan met de Laat-Pleistocene Geschiedenis van de Noordelijke Atlantiese oceaan. Unpublished D.Phil. thesis, University of Amsterdam, Amsterdam.

Wiley, R. H. 1974. Effects of delayed reproduction on survival, fecundity, and the rate of population increase. *American Naturalist* **108**, 705–709.

Williams, A. J. 1971. Ornithological observations on Bear Island 1970. *Astarte* **4**, 31–36.

Williams, A. J. 1972. The social behaviour of guillemots. Unpublished M.Sc. thesis, University of Sheffield, Sheffield. 94 pp.

Williams, A. J. 1974. Site preferences and interspecific competition among guillemots [*Uria aalge* (L.)] and [*Uria lomvia* (L.)] on Bear Island. *Ornis Scandinavica* **5**, 113–121.

Williams, A. J. 1975. Guillemot fledging and predation on Bear Island. *Ornis Scandinavica* **6**, 117–124.

Williams, G. C. 1966. Natural selection, the costs of reproduction, and a refinement of Lack's principle. *American Naturalist* **100**, 687–690.

Williams, L. E. and T. Joanen. 1974. Age of first nesting in the Brown Pelican. *Wilson Bulletin* **86**, 279–280.

Williamson, K. 1948. "The Atlantic Islands—a Study of the Faeroe Life and Scene." Collins, London. 385 pp.

Wilson, E. O. 1975. "Sociobiology: The New Synthesis." Belknap Press, Cambridge, Massachusetts. 697 pp.

Wimpenny, R. S. 1944. Plankton production between the Yorkshire coast and the Dogger Bank, 1933–1939. *Journal of the Marine Biological Association U.K.* **26**(1), 1–6.

Winn, H. E. 1950. The Black Guillemots of Kent Island, Bay of Fundy. *Auk* **67**, 477–485.

Witherby, H. F., F. C. R. Jourdain, N. F. Ticehurst and B. W. Tucker. 1941. "The Handbook of British Birds," Vol. 5. H. F. and G. Witherby, London. 365 pp.

Wittenberger, J. F. 1981. "Animal Social Behavior." Duxbury Press, Boston. 736 pp.

Wittenberger, J. F. and G. L. Hunt. 1985. The adaptive significance of coloniality in birds.

In D. S. Farner, J. R. King and K. C. Parkes (eds.), "Avian Biology," Vol. 8, pp. 1-78. Academic Press, Orlando, Florida.

Wittenberger, J. F. and R. L. Tilson. 1980. The evolution of monogamy: hypotheses and evidence. *Annual Review of Ecology and Systematics* **11,** 197–232.

Wolfe, J. A. 1971. Tertiary climatic fluctuations and methods of analysis of Tertiary floras. *Palaeogeography, Palaeoclimatology, Palaeoecology* **9,** 27–57.

Wood, R. C. 1971. Population dynamics of breeding South Polar Skuas of unknown age. *Auk* **88,** 805–814.

Woodhead, P. M. J. 1966. The behaviour of fish in relation to light in the sea. *Oceanography and Marine Biology* **4,** 337–403.

Wooler, R. A. and J. C. Coulson. 1977. Factors affecting the age of first breeding of the Kittiwake *Rissa tridactyla. Ibis* **119,** 339–349.

Wynne-Edwards, V. C. 1935. On the habits and distribution of birds on the North Atlantic. *Proceedings of the Boston Society of Natural History* **40,** 233–346.

Wynne-Edwards, V. C. 1952. The fulmars of Cape Searle. *Arctic* **5,** 105–117.

Yeatman, L. 1976 "Atlas des oiseaux nicheurs de France de 1970 a 1975." Société ornithologique de France, Ministère de la qualité de la vie et environnement, Environnement et Direction de la Protection de la Nature, Paris. 282 pp.

Yentsch, C. S. 1974. The influence of geostrophy on primary production. *Tethys* **6,** 111–118.

Yom-Tov, Y. 1980. Intraspecific nest parasitism in birds. *Biological Reviews of the Cambridge Philosophical Society* **55,** 93–108.

Zelickman, E. A. and A. N. Golovkin. 1972. Composition, structure and productivity of neritic plankton communities near the bird colonies on the northern shore of Novaya Zemlya. *Marine Biology (Berlin)* **17,** 265–274.

Zelickman, E. A., I. P. Lukashevich and S. S. Drobysheva. 1979. Year-round diurnal vertical migrations of the euphausiids *Thysanoessa inermis* and *T. raschii* in the Barents Sea. *Oceanology* **19,** 82–85.

Zusi, R. L. 1975. An interpretation of skull structure in penguins. *In* B. Stonehouse (ed.), "The Biology of Penguins," pp. 59–84. Macmillan, London.

Localities and Subject Index

The Index is divided into two parts: localities and subject. The Localities Index aims to be complete, serving both as a gazetteer to individual geographic locations and to indicate where in the text these appear and give important information. An attempt has been made to standardize place-names and locations. The major sources consulted to find spellings and geographic coordinates of localities mentioned in the text were the Gazeteers of Official Standard Names published by the Geographic Names Division, Board on Geographic Names, United States Office of Geography, Washington, D.C. When necessary, these were supplemented by the Pilots published by the Hydrographic Department of the British Ministry of Defense, the Time Atlas of the World (Comprehensive Edition), and regional, national and international atlases, gazetteers, and maps. Name preferences vary between nomenclature sources, and transliterations for Russian names presented a particularly tricky problem, though the U.S. Board on Geographic Names eased the decision-making process considerably. Overall, the name approved by the Board has been used for all locations presented, except in a small number of cases where another name is already deeply entrenched in the ornithological literature or where no clear name preference is evident.

The Subject Index coverage is selective without any aim to be all encompassing or comprehensive. Subjects not indexed are usually those which nearly always can be found by referring to chapter headings and subheadings directly.

LOCALITIES INDEX

542

Selected Locations

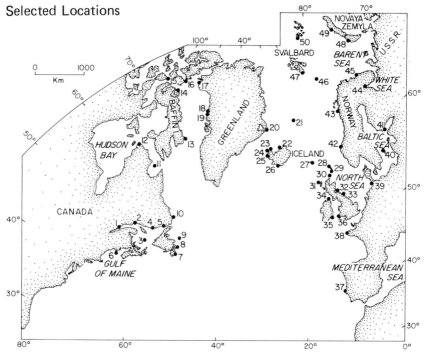

Selected locations of breeding alcids in the North Atlantic and adjacent seas. *Numbered points refer to the following colonies:* 1, Brandypot Is.; 2, Sept-Iles; 3, Bird Rocks; 4, St. Mary Is.; 5, Perroquet I.; 6, Machias Seal I.; 7, Great, Green, and Gull Is.; 8, Baccalieu I.; 9, Funk I.; 10, Gannet Is.; 11, Akpatok I.; 12, Digges I. and Cape Wolstenholme; 13, Reid Bay; 14, Cape Hay, Bylot I.; 15, Prince Leopold I.; 16, Coburg I.; 17, Thule region; 18, Kap Skackleton; 19, Horse Head; 20, Raffles Ø, Kap Brewster, and Steward Ø; 21, Jan Mayen; 22, Grimsey; 23, Hornbjarg; 24, Látrabjarg and Haelavíkurbjarg; 25, Flatey; 26, Vestmannaeyjar; 27, Faeroe Is.; 28, Hermaness; 29, Fair Isle; 30, Orkney Is.; 31, St. Kilda; 32, Isle of May; 33, Farne Is.; 34, Rathlin I.; 35, Saltee Is.; 36, Skomer and Skokholm Is.; 37, Berlengas Is.; 38, Les Sept Iles; 39, Helgoland; 40, Stora Karlsö; 41, Mickelskaren; 42, Rundøy; 43, Lovunden; 44, Kandalakshsk'aya Guba; 45, Murmansk Coast; 46, Bjørnøya; 47, Hornsund; 48, Guba Bezymyannaya; 49, Guba Arkhangel'skaya and Zaliv Vil'kitskogo; 50, Mys Flora.

---

* Spitsbergen refers to the archipelago made up of five large islands and many smaller ones; for clarity, the largest island of the group is called by its original name Vestspitsbergen, as opposed to Spitsbergen, its current name. The four other main islands comprising Spitsbergen are Nordaustlandet, Edgeøya, Barentsøya and Prins Karls Forland. Svalbard encompasses Spitsbergen (see above), Kvitøya, Kong Karls Land and Hopen (the latter three less than 100 km east or southeast of Spitsbergen) and Bjørnøya which is more than 200 km south of Spitsbergen.

Subject Index

Great Auk, 61–66
Razorbill, 69–70, 150
Thick-billed Murre, 103–106, 149
Breeding failure, Atlantic Puffin, 188,
451
Breeding habitat, 220–225
Atlantic Puffin, 181–182
Black Guillemot, 191–192
Common Murre, 165
Dovekie, 200–201
nitrogen–tolerant vegetation, 201
Great Auk, 178
Razorbill, 158
Thick-billed Murre, 172
Breeding range, defined, 57
Breeding-site fidelity, *see* Site tenacity
Breeding-site quality, 220–225
Breeding station, defined, 57
Breeding success, 162–163, 220–227
Atlantic Puffin, 188, 189, 258
Black Guillemot, 197–199, 258
Common Murre, 171, 258
Dovekie, 204
and habitat selection, 220–225
Razorbill, 161, 162, 164, 258
Thick-billed Murre, 177, 258
and timing of breeding, 227
Bridled murres, genetically determined,
369
Brisling, *see* Sprat
Brooding, of chicks, 333, 335
Brown rat (*Rattus norvegicus*), 123, 139,
see also Rats
Burrow digging, 18, 21

C

Caeca, 3
Calanoids (Calanidae), 266
Calanus spp. (Calanidae), 275, 295, 439,
see also Copepods
Calanus finmarchicus (Calanidae), 265,
266, 268, 270, 274, *see also* Copepods
Calanus glacialis (Calanidae), 266, 268,
see also Copepods
Calanus hyperboreus (Calanidae), 266,
268, 274, *see also* Copepods
Calorific value of prey, 266, 274–275, 276,
283, 289, 291, 295–296, 311, 316

Capelin (*Mallotus villosus*), 91, 93, 136,
138, 275, 277, 281, 282, 283, 286, 287,
289, 290, 291, 293, 300, 301, 302, 395,
396, 404, 409, 419, 440, 447, 449, 450,
451, 453, 476, 486
Cartwright, George (lived on the Labrador
coast (ca. 54° N) from 1770 to 1786),
reports of Great Auks, 62, 68, 409
Cassin's Auklet (*Ptychoramphus
aleuticus*), 217, 220, 229, 230, 320,
356, 365, 459
Cats (feral and domestic) (*Felis catus*),
456, 458, 459, 460
Census, aims, procedures and limitations,
234, 432, 480–484, 487
Cephalopods (Cephalopoda), 275, 277, 281,
294, 309, *see also* Short-finned squid
and Squid
Chaetognaths (Chaetognatha), 275
Charadriiformes (shorebirds, gulls, auks
and allies), 19, 20, 21
Charadriiformes, relations to auks, 19–21
Chick diet
all species, 314–315
Atlantic Puffin, 279, 294–299
Black Guillemot, 280, 309–311
Common Murre, 279, 288–291
Dovekie, 266, 268–270
Great Auk, 304–306
Razorbill, 279–280, 302–303
Thick-billed Murre, 277–279, 281–
283
Chick-rearing period and duration
Atlantic Puffin, 185–186, 187
Black Guillemot, 195–196
Common Murre, 168–169
Dovekie, 202–203
Razorbill, 160–161
Thick-billed Murre, 175–176
Chick, recognition, 367–368
Chlorinated hydrocarbon insecticides, *see*
Pollution, toxic chemicals
Ciconiiformes (Herons, storks, ibises,
flamingos and allies), 357
Classification, 19–21
Climate, changes, 10, 14, 435–441
effects of changes and severity, 76, 77,
82, 93, 144, 438–441, 474–477
and evolution of auks, 10–14
North Atlantic, 435–438

R

Rabbits (Leporidae: rabbits and hare), 182
Rape, 380
Raptors (Falconiformes: vultures, hawks and falcons), 470
Rats (*Rattus* spp.), 181, 456, 458, 459, 460, *see also* Brown rat
Raven, *see* Common Raven
Razorbill (*Alca torda;* species portrait, 23)
  adult diet, 301–302
  band recoveries, 405–407
  breeding distribution and abundance, 69–70, 150
  breeding habitat, 158
  breeding success, 161–162, 164, 258
  chick diet, 279–280, 302–303
  chick-rearing period and duration, 160–161
  clinal variation, 22–24
  colony attendance, 158
  departure of young, 161
  dispersal, 407
  egg size, 159–160
  fledging weights, 161
  foraging, 303–304
  geographic variation, 22–24
  incubation period and duration, 159
  mate fidelity, 160
  moult, 44
  pelagic distribution and movements, 404–407
  pelagic ecology, 407
  plumage, juvenal, 160–161
  populations, size and status changes, 70–78
  pre-laying period, 158
  replacement eggs, 160
  site tenacity, 159
  thermoregulation, chicks, 160
  timing of breeding, 159
Recruitment, *see* Immature auks
Rectrices, number, 4
Red-billed Weaver (*Quelea quelea*), 360
Red fox (*Vulpes vulpes*), 458, 459
Red-throated Loon (*Gavia stellata*), 465
Repertoire, social signals, 371, 379, 380
Replacement eggs, 217–218
  Atlantic Puffin, 185
  Black Guillemot, 195

Common Murre, 168, 171
Dovekie, 202
Great Auk, 179
Razorbill, 160
Thick-billed Murre, 175
Reproductive strategies, 228–231
Reproductive success, lifetime, 381
Rhinoceros Auklet (*Cerorhinca monocerata*), 215, 217, 229, 230, 320, 323, 330, 356, 459
Ribs, 4
Risk, to welfare of auks, 88, *see also* Threats, to auks
Ritualized walking, 377, 378
Rockfish (Scorpaenidae), 278–280, 308, 309
Rockhopper Penguin (*Eudyptes crestatus*), 206
Rockling (Gadidae)
  Ciliata sp., 297
  Gaidropsarus sp., 297
Role of seabirds in marine communities, 293, 318, 452 *see also* Predator-prey relationships
"r" strategy, 325
Rubber thread ingestion, 235, 239
Ruddy Duck (*Oxyura jamaicensis*), 15

S

Saithe (*Pollachius virens*), 295, 297, 440
Sampling procedure, chick growth, 326–327
Sandlance (*Ammodytes* spp.), 147, 169, 186, 267, 278–280, 282, 283, 287, 288, 289, 290, 293, 295, 296, 297, 301, 302, 303, 308, 309, 311, 313, 315, 395, 402, 419, 440, 450, 451, 452, 453, 468, 486
Sandwich Tern (*Sterna scandvicensis*), 376
Sardines, *see* Herring
Satellite imagery, use of in pelagic studies, 317
Sauries (*Scomberesox saurus*), 419, 420
Scapulars, 5
Sculpin (Cottidae), 267, 275, 276, 277, 278, 280, 281, 283, 286, 287, 302, 308, 309, 311, 313, 315, 395, 396, 419
Seabird conservation, *see* Conservation
Seaducks (Anatidae), 461

Seals (Phocidae), 91, 429, 443, 448, 488,
    see also individual species
Seals, relations to auks, 13
Sea otter (*Enhydra lutris*), 443
Sea robins (Pisces: Triglidae), 279, 295
Sea-snails (Pisces: Cyclopteridae), 278,
    280, 308, 309
Secondaries, number of, 4
Sexual behaviour, 371, 373–375
Sexual dimorphism, 3
Sexual relationships, 370–371
Shad (*Alosa* spp.), 304, 305, 307
Shag (*Phalacrocorax aristotelis*), 225,
    326
Shearwaters (*Puffinus* spp.), 306, *see also*
    individual species
Shorthorn sculpin (*Myxocephalus
    scorpius*), 304
Short-finned squid (*Illex illrebrosus*),
    289
Short-tailed Shearwater (*Puffinus
    tenuirostris*), 286
Site-ownership displays, 377–378,
    380
Site tenacity, 243
    Atlantic Puffin, 182
    Black Guillemot, 192
    Common Murre, 166
    Dovekie, 201
    Razorbill, 159
    Thick-billed Murre, 173
Smelt (Osmeridae: osmerids), 169, 267,
    278, 279, 288, 293, 309
Social relationships, 370
Social signals, 370–380
    defined, 370–371
    summary of, 372
Social stimulation, 184
Sonar imagery, use of in pelagic studies,
    317
Spectacled Guillemot (*Cepphus carbo*),
    116, 214, 356
Spheinsciformes (Penguins), 16, 19, *see
    also* Penguins
Spirontocaris spp. (Decapoda), 268
Sprat (*Sprattus sprattus*), 147, 186, 287,
    289, 290, 291, 294–297, 302, 395, 403,
    404, 419, 440, 450–453, 468, 486
Squid
    Aeloteuthis subulata (Loligonidae), 295

Gonatus fabricii (Gonatidae), 309
    See also Short-finned squid
Starling (*Sturnus vulgaris*), 220
Starvation, 238, 239, 241–242, 295
    in Atlantic Puffin, 186, 295
Steller's sea lion (*Eumetopias jubata*),
    443
Stercorarids (jaegers and skuas), 430,
    453, 456, *see also* individual species
Stercorariidae, *see* Stercorarids
Sterninae, *see* Terns
Sternum, 4
Sticklebacks (Gasterosteidae), 279, 295,
    301, 305
Striped bass (*Morone saxatilis*), 304,
    305, 307
Sublingual pouch, in Dovekie, 6, 266,
    274
Sulidae, *see* Sulids
Sulids (Sulidae: gannets and boobies),
    371, 374, 377, 430, *see also*
    individual species and Meeting
    ceremony
Surveys, population size and status
    aims, 234
    limitations, 55, 56–57, 150–151
    monitoring schemes, 480–486
    requirements, 94, 138, 139–140, 145,
        147, 151
    techniques, 151, 154
    See also Census and Monitoring systems
Survival, rates
    adults, 216, 242, 243–245
    biases, 242–243
    chicks, 227
    immatures, 252–254, 256–258
    relation to weight at fledging, 351–
        352
Swimming
    adaptations for, 4, 337
    compared to penguins, 2, 4
    efficiency, 50
    speed underwater, 16, 273, 293, 301
    See also Diving
Synchrony, breeding, 176, 187, 202,
    212–213, 363–365, 366, 381
Synthliboramphus spp. (Alcidae), 336, *see
    also* Ancient Murrelet and Japanese
    Murrelet
Syrinx, 3